Foundations of Social Work Practice

A Graduate Text

3rd Edition

Mark A. Mattaini
Christine T. Lowery
Carol H. Meyer
Editors

NASW PRESS

National Association of Social Workers
Washington, DC

Terry Mizrahi, MSW, PhD, *President*
Elizabeth J. Clark, PhD, ACSW, MPH, *Executive Director*

Cheryl Y. Bradley, *Publisher*
Paula L. Delo, *Executive Editor*
Susan Fisher, *Editor*
January Layman-Wood, *Acquisitions Editor*
Christina Bromley, *Editorial Assistant*
Jodi Bergeman Glasscock, *Copy Editor*
Robin Bourjaily, *Proofreader*
Bernice Eisen, *Indexer*

Cover design by Barry Cohen, Cohen Design, Rockville, MD
Typesetting by Cindy Stock, Electronic Quill Publishing Svcs.,
Silver Spring, MD

Library of Congress Cataloging-in-Publication Data

Foundations of social work practice : a graduate text / Mark A. Mattaini, Christine
T. Lowery, Carol H. Meyer, editors.— 3rd ed.
    p. cm.
  Includes bibliographical references and index.
  ISBN 0-87101-349-5
    1. Social service. I. Mattaini, Mark A. II. Lowery, Christine T. III. Meyer,
    Carol H., 1924–1996.

HV40 .F683 2002
361.3—dc21   2002020037

*In memory of **Roselyn Mike**, former Chair of the Moapa Paiutes,*
a social worker who contributed to her people;
*and of **Carol H. Meyer**, whose vision inspired this text*
and who reminded social workers to
"Think before they act."

Contents

Preface   vii

Introduction   ix
Mark A. Mattaini, Christine T. Lowery,
and Carol H. Meyer

SECTION I: FOUNDATION KNOWLEDGE

Chapter 1: The Ecosystems Perspective:
Implications for Practice   3
Mark A. Mattaini and Carol H. Meyer

Chapter 2: Social Justice and International
Human Rights   25
Christine T. Lowery

Chapter 3: Professional Values and Ethics   48
Brenda G. McGowan and Marian Mattison

Chapter 4: Diversity, Ethnic Competence,
and Social Justice   73
Christine T. Lowery

Chapter 5: Knowledge for Practice   95
Mark A. Mattaini

Chapter 6: Monitoring Social Work Practice   132
Mark A. Mattaini

SECTION II: THE FOUNDATIONS OF PRACTICE

Chapter 7: Practice with Individuals   151
Mark A. Mattaini

Chapter 8: Social Work with Families   184
Christine T. Lowery

Chapter 9: Practice with Groups   208
Randy H. Magen

Chapter 10: Practice with Communities   230
Susan P. Kemp and Edward Scanlon

Chapter 11: Practice with Organizations   263
Meredith Hanson

Chapter 12: Generalist Practice:
People and Programs   291
Mark A. Mattaini

SECTION III: THE CONTEXTS OF PRACTICE

Chapter 13: Fields of Practice   319
Sheila B. Kamerman

Chapter 14: The Profession in Historical
Context   340
Jerry R. Cates

Appendix A: NASW Code of Ethics   381

Appendix B: Universal Declaration
of Human Rights   400

Appendix C: Sample Classroom Exercises   405

Index   417

About the Editors   429

About the Contributors   431

Preface

Mark A. Mattaini

Entering its second century, this is an exciting time for social work. Community-centered practice, the strengths perspective, evidence-based practice, ethnoconscious services, and the richness offered by multiple cultures and groups are potent forces driving advances in knowledge and in the work we do. The challenges of changing political and economic forces continue to shape practice in profound ways. Curriculum guidelines of the Council on Social Work Education are also changing (but continue to recognize that there is certain foundational knowledge that all graduate social workers should have). This third edition of *The Foundations of Social Work Practice: A Graduate Text* builds on, and in some cases struggles with, these developments while maintaining the central emphasis on social justice, the sharing of power in practice, and the human rights core of our work. This edition also includes a completely new chapter on the profession of social work in historical context, authored by Jerry R. Cates.

The table of contents outlines the chapters in the book, and the introduction explains the book's rationale and organization. Because each school has its own programmatic approach to ordering and teaching the foundation course, this book is designed to facilitate easy "mixing and matching," in which the chapters may be assigned and used in essentially any order, consistent with an instructor's syllabus. The NASW *Code of Ethics* and the *Universal Declaration of Human Rights* are included as appendices, as is a collection of group and skills-building class exercises linked to the chapters, which may be useful for teaching to different modalities and learning styles. As in previous editions, the editors are eager for feedback from those using the book that may inform the next edition; a textbook like this is always, thankfully, a collective endeavor.

Introduction

Mark A. Mattaini
Christine T. Lowery
Carol H. Meyer

Social work practice can be thought of as a continuous rope
of practice events stretching through time. This rope is made up of many strands, all
of which work together to achieve the "purpose" of the rope. The strands include
knowledge, skills, values and ethics, and commitment—all of which inform every
practice event and decision. Each strand, in turn, consists of multiple threads. All
graduate-level social workers need certain core knowledge from each strand but will
pursue specific threads differentially, depending on the situation. It is not possible to
say everything that must be said in any one book or course or at any point in time.
Rather, readers are encouraged to explore and test those areas that are significant to
them and their clients in an ongoing, self-directed process of professional education.
Those inquiries should be grounded in the recognition that the threads and strands of
the profession are always intertwined and interdependent; none can be forgotten.

Not only can a rope be stretched out linearly, it can curve and loop back on itself.
This nonlinearity also characterizes practice; thus, it is not surprising to find that
the chapters that follow include transactional mixes of knowledge, skills, and practice examples. Although the chapters can be read in any order, ultimately, all of the
content is part of the core of professional practice and is organically and indivisibly
connected.

Experienced teachers of graduate-level social work students recognize that although
entering students are naturally preoccupied with learning skills that are immediately
applicable in fieldwork practice, only by integrating the teaching of skills with the
underlying knowledge base can students move beyond the role of technicians to that
of autonomous professionals. There is some professional knowledge that all graduate
social workers should share, and the chapter authors have tried to present or at least
sketch that essential core in this book. The approach on which this text is based involves an explicit mix of knowledge and skills, in which ideally a skills lab is interwoven with classroom content. We have therefore included a beginning set of
skills-building exercises as Appendix C; those exercises are conceptually linked to the
content of the book.

We began the first edition of this book because in our teaching we found that
existing texts, in an effort to be useful (and marketable) to a mixed undergraduate

and graduate audience, generally were not pitched at an adequately challenging level to meet the needs of master's students. As outlined by Meyer (1995), there are several differences between graduate- and undergraduate-level social work education. Graduate students, with a pre-existing base in the liberal arts, enter with a certain level of common language, having mastered basic concepts from the social, behavioral, and biological sciences and having a familiarity with history and literature. They are ready to go far beyond the basics. The graduate instructor, therefore, can build from this base and challenge each student to diversify his or her search for specialized knowledge. Finally, given that undergraduate education should have prepared the student to be a critical thinker, the entering graduate student comes with more questions than answers and often finds that rather than providing answers, graduate social work education may be of most help in refining the questions.

Our approach to the learning of social work practice knowledge and skills is rooted in "web teaching" (Patterson & Jaffe, 1994), an approach to adult learning in which the basic map or outline of a subject is presented initially. At later stages, knowledge of different areas and connections on the map is refined and deepened, with the final result a richly elaborated and interconnected understanding. That is how we view professional social work education. In this introductory chapter, we sketch the broad contours of the dimensions and factors that come to a nexus in each practice event, within a wider contextual field. The basic map for this work is shown in Figure I-1; note that this image can be thought of as a cross-section, at any one point, of the metaphoric rope described above.

Subsequent chapters gradually refine segments of this diagram in more detail. In fact, the rest of one's professional education, both in graduate school and in continuing education, throughout a social worker's career should continue to deepen knowledge and skills within this conceptual map. Some segments of the map are foreground in each chapter, but all others are implicitly present as well. In a chapter on work with families, for example, the reader might find reference to referring some family members for group services. Or, if the chapter on group work emphasizes work in health and family services settings, this does not mean that much of the content does not also apply in agencies serving primarily aging clients. Deciding what segments can or must be de-emphasized—although they are present—is often as important as deciding on what to focus on at each moment.

Social Work Purpose

The purpose of social work is to enhance adaptations among clients ("clients" may include individuals, families, communities, or other cultural entities) and the systems within which those clients are embedded, consistent with social justice. Both private troubles and public issues (Mills, 1959) reflect difficulties in these adaptations. Although professionals of other disciplines are often interested in some of the same problems, their core professional purposes are different (Meyer, 1993). Medicine—including psychiatry—is concerned with curing illness and enhancing health, essentially an individually focused mission. Psychology is primarily a science (sometimes applied) of individuals, with special emphasis on mental phenomena and individual behavior. In contrast, social work is—at its very core—concerned with the person-in-situation. This is substantively different from the purposes of allied professions, although some skills and knowledge are clearly shared. In early developmental stages of the profession, caseworkers looked at both the person and his or her environment, maintaining a dual focus in which each was alternately the foreground and the background. It was difficult to find ways of conceptualizing the interactions, seeing the interconnections between client and environment as the foreground, but early social workers tried to do so. This effort often was operationalized as lists of personal and environmental factors to be examined in the course of a social study (Richmond, 1917).

Given this professional purpose, it is clear that social workers must understand individuals and environments and how they interrelate; this is perhaps the most complex assignment of any profession. Issues with which contemporary social workers grapple every day (for example, the AIDS crisis in the U.S. and around the world, or family breakdown and violence associated with intergenerational, sometimes hopeless-appearing poverty) clearly demonstrate this complexity, but it has also been present historically. One has only to read the work of Charles Loring Brace (1872/1973) or Mary Richmond (1917) to see that solutions have never been easy.

Although many social work practice functions can be performed effectively by paraprofessional and bachelor's-level staff, the primary function of the graduate-level social worker is not so much to simply act as to think—to understand the perplexing intricacies of each client's unique dilemma and to develop interventive strategies that are based on that understanding. Therefore, professional practice cannot be based on simple formulas or step-by-step prescriptions. One never knows enough, and as the social worker faces the full complexities of social problems, comprehensive understanding is elusive. The professional social worker recognizes these facts and still must decide with the client what is to be done, even when the limits of the possible are so evident.

It is important to recognize that differences in theoretical and interventive approaches that characterize the practice world are not just academic. Social workers make decisions that occasionally mean the difference between life and death and that often contribute to the difference between a life of active empowerment and one of pain and unfulfilled promise. For any case, all interventions are not equivalent and interchangeable. For example, in child protective settings, Peile (1993) suggested the adoption of a "creative worldview" in which the worker "no longer seek[s] to control and predict her effects on [the client] and his parenting behavior" (p. 132). (In the case example provided, the client has seriously injured his six-year-old child.) From an alternate perspective, the worker, as a representative of society, takes as her primary responsibility the safety of the child, making use of existing empirical knowledge about ameliorating child maltreatment (Mattaini, McGowan, & Williams, 1996). Particularly in cases involving cross-cultural work or involuntary clients, both common in social work, discovering ways to share power and responsibility (Lowery & Mattaini, 2000), without abdicating the responsibilities and obligations that we carry, requires a sophisticated depth of understanding of practice theory as well as an appreciation of differing worldviews. Values must also guide such decisions. For example, in the child protection case mentioned earlier, professional and social values suggest that minimizing short- and long-term risk to the child should be the overriding consideration.

The Complexity of Social Work

The social work practitioner needs to see—and to the extent possible, know—everything at once. It is not possible to look at and deal separately with a client's emotional state, then the possible effects of family dynamics, and then the effects of racial and cultural factors. Adequate assessment in social work requires "thinking big"—seeing the full transactional situation all at once (Meyer, 1993). The practice setting, realities of the social problems being addressed, behavioral roots of those problems, larger sociocultural factors, and many other factors are facets of every case.

Social work encompasses a wide range of interests, and its multidimensional focus requires a broad base of knowledge and an equally broad repertoire of methods and skills. The scope of social work reaches from attention to the individual, family, group, and community to the arena of social policy, even at an international level. Social workers work with adults and children of different economic classes, racial and ethnic groups, cultures, gender identifications, and sexual orientations in hospitals, clinics, social agencies, schools, institutions, and community centers as well as on the street and at home. Their interventions span the realms of prevention and protection, support, and rehabilitation. Among the many social problems in which social workers intervene in the matrix just described are family dysfunction, child neglect and abuse, coping with disaster and trauma, marital conflict, separation and divorce, adolescent adjustment, challenges of aging, adaptation to physical and mental illness, homelessness, substance abuse, unemployment and job training, and child care. The post-industrial, technological society has engendered a new level of social isolation, value systems that more than ever privilege the individual over the collective, and heightened tensions and misunderstanding among cultures and generations that sometimes reach a fevered pitch. People (and groups) have responded differentially with depression, violence, or withdrawal. These responses are reflected in the caseloads of all social workers. At the same time, these changes also bring new opportunities, both for society and for practice, ranging from increased access to information and tools important to empowerment, to new possibilities to forge social connections via communications media.

This is the bare outline of the context in which social workers practice, and given the complexity of the tasks, the practice of social work is equally complex. The typical professional social worker must be skillful in multiple roles as an advocate, therapist, counselor, mentor, case manager, group leader, community organizer, agent of change, program developer, and evaluator. The ability to assume these roles flexibly, as particular cases demand, and to achieve an integration among them as "social worker" is not inborn. None of us is prepared to assume this level of responsibility for human welfare without concentrated learning, which includes mastery of an essential base of knowledge that is relevant to the domain of social work. This knowledge is usually conceptualized broadly as human growth and behavior, social science, social policy, and social work history and philosophy. Such knowledge can then be brought to bear on the varied kinds of problems and conditions reflected in social work cases. The intellectual and experiential demands on social workers notwithstanding, an additional dimension surrounds professional practice: the framework of ethics and values that must be internalized as a permanent guide to professional action.

Social work is a social institution and, as such, it carries certain mandates in the fields or arenas of health, welfare, and education. Except in the case of family and child welfare, where social work traditionally has been the primary service, social workers practice in "host agencies" such as hospitals, clinics, schools, the Red Cross, and, increasingly, in the workplace; in institutions for elderly people, children, and people with disabilities; and in correctional institutions. These fields and social institutions represent the concerns of the U.S. public and are supported by statutes and ordinances that provide legal sanction and funding by all levels of government. They are also supported in the voluntary sector by philanthropy and the leadership of boards of directors. The social welfare, health, and educational institutions of this country are its largest social and economic investment, and social work is deeply embedded in these arenas.

Historically, the social work profession has been organizationally based, partially because of the early social assignment and commitment of social workers to work with the poor and dispossessed, and partially because the breadth and complexity of necessary social services require organizational support. Because poor people's private resources are severely limited, publicly supported and organizationally based services are often the only route to the assistance they need. Bureaucracies can be cumbersome, but they became a permanent fact of life with the rise of industrialism and the urban world. For example, although few people would choose to be patients in hospitals, this is often—but not always—the most effective and efficient site to provide state-of-the-art care. Schools are in serious trouble (Greer, 1996), but some form of institutionalized education system available to all is clearly important for society's survival. Likewise, social agencies that offer multiple services could not function in any other way but to pool their resources within organizational boundaries. Since the 1970s, much has been learned by social workers and others about humanizing bureaucracies, both for employees and for consumers of services, and the development of electronic communications and information technology, if well handled, has enormous potential for enhancing service delivery as well.

Organizations can only truly "work for people" (Meyer, 1979), however, if they are deeply grounded in a dynamic of shared power, which is as yet very uncommon. In an interlocking organizational culture of shared power, all participants—clients, practitioners, administrators, and other stakeholders—have strong voices, all make contributions from their strengths and gifts, and all share responsibility for outcomes (Lowery & Mattaini, 1999). Bureaucracies grounded in competitive, coercive, and exploitive adversarial power can never facilitate the co-construction of better realities. Unfortunately, most contemporary social institutions rely to a greater or lesser extent on adversarial power; social workers often need to challenge that reliance and construct alternatives.

According to Abbott, a sociologist of professions, "the essence of a profession is its work, not its organization" (1988, p. 112). Historically there has been a recognition by all professions that they work they do is somehow "sacred," carrying obligations to other individuals and the human collective that go beyond self-interest. Social work is not a job, not a career, and not even a profession in the loose sense that the term is often used today. Social workers, to a significant degree, carry the responsibilities of society for social and economic justice. Social work is not about self, image, or ego. It is mission-driven work with the deep fabric of humanity. Practice that recognizes this mission is not an ideal, it is an ethical responsibility.

Social work, like all other professions, is not an academic pursuit but an applied practice, and thus its knowledge and professional roles and values are expressed in action. In social work, this action, or methodology, is loosely defined as practice with individuals, families, groups, and communities. All the many approaches that are in use incorporate the components of gathering or exploring the data of a "case," assessing and evaluating the case, and applying interventions differentially. This is the common framework for action in all professional practices. Professional skills are differentially applied based on one's understanding of the case one is working with; the actions taken are also deeply responsive to the complex context within

Figure I-1. The Dimensions of Social Work Practice in Context

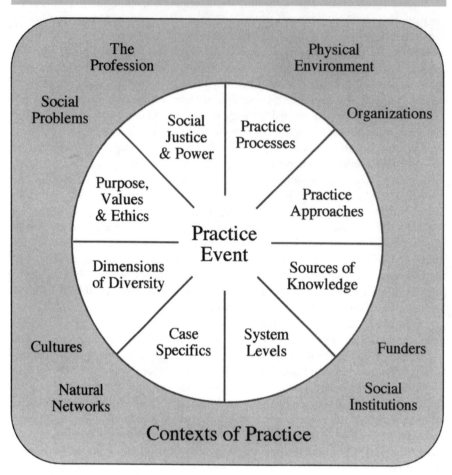

which the case is embedded. For this reason, a course on the foundations of social work practice needs to encompass the entire conceptual map, as sketched in Figure I-1 and presented in further detail in the next section.

The Conceptual Map

Imagine you are working with a neglected girl. It probably makes sense to you that your purpose relates to doing something about the fit between the child and her environment; that factors related to culture and social class, as well as to her mother's mental illness, may be relevant; and that it is important to understand the girl's emotional functioning, the mother's behavior, and the lack of positive exchanges between them. It is also necessary to apply what is known about neglect from research and practice experience to select the best practice model and to examine agency- and policy-level structures that may affect the case. While you think about all these factors, you must build genuine, empathic, respectful relationships with the child, the parent, and perhaps a "kinship" foster parent (a relative serving as a foster parent) within a matrix of shared power.

The challenge is clear: you certainly cannot sequentially step through each related factor until an effective and efficient case plan falls into place. These factors and their interconnections must be considered "all at once," as a transactional conceptual network. As the social worker carrying the case, you must filter data through this sort of richly interconnected net until the "event shape" (the complex configuration of what is happening in the client's life) (Auerswald, 1987) of the case emerges. Visual depictions and simulations of the case can function as helpful tools in this process (Mattaini, 1993; Meyer, 1993). Graphic images have a broad bandwidth; they can be seen "all at once." Figure I-2, for example, is a sequential ecomap (Hartman, 1978; Mattaini, 1993) portraying changes over time in the case of a depressed, single man.

At the beginning of the case (the upper left panel) you can look not only at the particular positive and negative interactions that the client experienced, but also at the

Figure I-2. Sequential Ecomaps

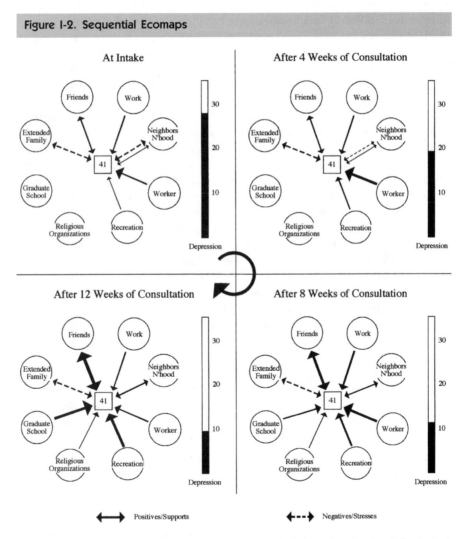

NOTE: These ecomaps portray the changing life situation and level of depression of a client (using the Beck Depression Inventory) over 12 sessions of interpersonal therapy.
SOURCE: Reprinted from M. A. Mattaini (1993). *More than a Thousand Words: Graphics for Clinical Practice* (p. 159). Washington, DC: NASW Press.

configuration of the case holistically: overall, the client is isolated, with few meaningful connections anywhere. Moving clockwise, you can observe changes in both the specifics as well as the broad overall pattern over time and how they relate to the presenting problem.

Every practice event involves each dimension of the conceptual network shown in Figure I-1. Note that this image is only one way to somewhat artificially divide what is in reality an indivisible whole; there are many other valid ways that the professional knowledge base could be partitioned. Each of the major areas is introduced in the sections that follow; subsequent chapters discuss them in greater detail and begin to integrate them into a holistic view of practice.

Social Justice and Power

Although social workers perform many different tasks and take on many different roles in many different social institutions, fulfilling social work's historic purpose requires a commitment to social justice and human rights that emerges from an authentic recognition of the connections among all people and their world. Social workers carry a heavy responsibility here, not to do charity for others or treat others' disorders, but rather to contribute from their personal gifts and professional training to the human web of which they and their clients are part. (This is why it is called "social work.") Historically "justice" and "social justice" have been defined in many ways, some of which have systematically included whole groups (see Chapter 2). A contemporary view of social justice can be defined by transactions that genuinely value people and peoples, foster inclusion while deeply respecting diversity of values and cultures, support the human rights of individuals and the collective rights of groups, and reduce reliance on coercion, threats, and violence. Justice is not a static state; it can only be realized in action.

As the profession has evolved, so has our recognition of the crucial importance of practicing within a framework of shared power, in which clients, social workers, and others involved (for example, family members or foster parents) all have crucial roles to play, roles that carry obligations and responsibilities (Lowery & Mattaini, 2000). There is no place in this model for paternalism or ego, as the social worker gives up the role of "expert" for something more genuine. Shared power minimizes the need to rely on adversarial processes and ensures recognition of the voice and value of each person and group and of the organic connections among us all. The resulting practice is a constructive process of co-creation, rather than the treatment of pathology. It is for this reason that conceptualizing social work practice as merely "therapy" is far too limited to capture the potential and meaning of the work. The recent explicit focus on strengths (Saleebey, 2002) has been an important advance beyond pathology-rooted practice, and an emphasis on shared power and collective healing may move the profession even further toward actualizing the power of "social work."

Professional Purpose, Values, and Ethics

Meyer (1993) indicated that "social work claims as its central purpose the enhancement of adaptations among individuals, families, groups, communities—and their particular environments" (p. 18), referring to a definition of clinical social work developed in 1979 (Ewalt, 1979). She noted that this central focus on the person-in-environment construct is unique to social work, despite interdisciplinary overlaps in skills and selected knowledge. This definition is broad enough to include both cause and function (Lee, 1929) but narrow enough to discriminate social work from other professions. The distinction and balance between function (a set of direct practice activities carried out with the sanction of the larger society) and cause (the organized effort to advocate for oppressed populations) has been an ongoing debate in the profession. Both personal troubles and public issues (Malagodi & Jackson, 1989; Mills, 1959) have always concerned social workers, even as the level of relative interest in each has ebbed and flowed.

Although the purpose of the profession as a whole may be as was just described, every person begins graduate social work education for his or her own reasons. Thinking these reasons through explicitly and discussing them with peers can help a student clarify his or her personal priorities in ways that are valuable for the conscious development of a professional identity (see Exercise 14 in Appendix C).

In addition to purpose, common values and professional ethics are characteristic of social work. Neither values nor ethics are easy to apply in practice, although they may sound straightforward. For example, although the importance of "client self-determination" may seem evident, if the worker recognizes that not all human behavior is under the unconstrained, conscious control of the person, limitations in the potential for self-determination are evident. When one individual's right to self-determination conflicts with his or her own or another person's right to safety (as when a frail, elderly patient in a hospital insists, against the wishes of family members, on returning to live alone in an apartment where no one is immediately available for emergencies), the worker must make difficult decisions. These decisions may be further complicated by organizational factors; for example, a high-status physician may forcefully insist on nursing home placement, resulting in potential conflict between the medical and social work departments. In addition, individuality is not regarded by some cultures as being as important as is the collective good, and only ethnocentrism would suggest that the individualistic alternative is somehow better—in fact, a strong argument can be made in the other direction. Social workers must find ways to be responsive to the dilemmas that such cultural differences may produce in practice. Practice consistent with professional values, therefore, requires continuous learning and questioning.

Client Diversity

The clients whom social workers see are deeply diverse on many dimensions. Recognizing and learning about this diversity is not a matter of political correctness but rather a crucial area of professional knowledge with enormous implications for practice. Clients differ in age, gender identification, health and physical ability, race, education, occupation, sexual orientation, physical attractiveness, intellectual and verbal abilities, behavior, and many other ways. In addition, individuals play out their lives as members of multiple cultural entities of all sizes, from families to social classes to ethnic and religious groups. Social workers commonly need to learn to be effective not only within their own group, but also across deep rifts of credibility and trust. If our multicultural society is to work, differences need to be understood and valued as sources of potentially useful variations for enriching the lives of members of all cultures. Unfortunately, as a result of various groups' long histories of oppression and disrespect in the United States, these divisions are often bitter; thus, bridging these gaps is a critical professional—and cultural—challenge. Oppression is a serious issue in all of social work. In contemporary U.S. culture, and many of the European cultures from which it emerged, major institutions and those receiving primary benefit from them have consistently relied on the exercise of coercive and adversarial power (threats, punishment, exploitation, and individualistic competition). This has usually been true (though often not recognized) of the "justice" system, the education system, major economic institutions, government agencies, international relations, and even the family (Sidman, 2001). While these coercive and adversarial arrangements are maintained by the results they produce for those in power, they ultimately have profoundly negative results for the collective (Sidman, 2001). That collective is the province of social work.

A good deal is known about sensitivity to differences and even, to some extent, about specific approaches that tend to be valuable in practice with members of particular groups (Castillo, 1998; Congress, 1997; McGoldrick, Pearce, & Giordano, 1996). However, every client is an individual, not just an accumulation of various descriptive categories, and levels of biculturalism and acculturation differ widely, as do personal life experiences. Hence, almost paradoxically, although deep awareness of difference sensitizes the worker, the essence of culturally sensitive practice is to be able to then individualize a case without being blinded by categorical labels.

Case Specifics

Consistent with the need to particularize each case is the shaping of interventive strategies to fit case events, conditions, and actors. (Sharing power among those involved facilitates this process.) Given the sometimes subtle, sometimes dramatic differences among cases, it is not possible to prescribe a course of action for, say, all cases of child abuse or all involving drug abuse. Data-based "practice guidelines" for particular issues or practice goals can be quite useful (Proctor & Rosen, in press), but need to be flexibly adapted to fit case realities. It is not uncommon and is often necessary for social workers and clients to design quite unique plans drawing from the clients' needs, values, and resources; other sources of professional knowledge like research and practice wisdom; and the worker's personal and professional experience, all as guided by the individualizing assessment.

System Levels

Social workers are professionally concerned with individuals, groups, couples, families, neighborhoods, formal and informal organizations, communities, and societies. Each of these systems is made up of subsystems and itself constitutes a subsystem of higher-order systems. System levels are organized hierarchically, so a particular system (for example, an individual) may at one moment be viewed as the focal system and at the next moment as a subsystem of another system (a family). General Systems Theory and recent advances in systems thinking (see Chapter 1) have proven helpful in identifying what these disparate systems have in common (for example, exchange of resources and energy with their environments across boundaries). At the same time, each level (individuals as systems, family systems, community systems, and so forth) has its own coherence. What happens in families is the aggregate of what individuals do but often is best understood at its own level: families establish and maintain regular patterns, their own "cultural practices." Those practices tend to continue over time, even when they may be costly (emotionally, physically, or otherwise) to some or all individuals involved (Mattaini, 1999). Even a simple parent–child dyad, for example, can fall into a repetitive coercive spiral, unpleasant for both, which can be understood only if one looks at the pattern of exchanges through a transactional lens (Patterson, 1976).

To be effective, the advanced generalist (see Chapter 12) needs specific knowledge about each system level and how all the levels fit together, but even social workers who specialize in work with one or two system levels must know something about each. If the social worker knows only about individuals, he or she is likely to view every case situation through an individual lens. If, however, he or she has learned to concurrently observe and, when indicated, work with multiple system levels, the available options expand dramatically (Nelsen, 1975).

Sources of Knowledge

An organized knowledge base is crucial to any profession. Bartlett (1970) emphasized the centrality of knowledge for practice, explicitly identifying values and knowledge as the "essential elements" in professional social work practice, as opposed to "method," which had traditionally been seen as the core of practice. Anyone can simply act; the professional is expected to act deliberately, taking the steps that are most likely to be helpful, parsimonious, and consistent with a client's welfare. Deciding on those steps requires an extensive knowledge base.

Among the sources of knowledge relevant to practice are the worker's personal and professional experiences, "practice wisdom" (often only partially systematized) gleaned from colleagues and supervisors, reports of quantitative and qualitative research, and information obtained by listening to and observing clients. Theory—coherent systems for understanding behavioral and social phenomena—and practice approaches ("models") also provide guidance for practice at a somewhat different level. Different sources sometimes suggest conflicting actions. The social worker then must act on the basis of the information that he or she has evaluated as being most relevant and rigorous. Rigor involves accuracy and objectivity, but even these, as seen in Chapter 5, are difficult concepts to capture. Nevertheless, practice that is based entirely on intuition or "common sense" is not only by definition not professional, but—what is far more important—is likely to be ineffective. Effectiveness, when it can be achieved, is an ethical mandate, and the need to monitor practice has become correspondingly clear.

In recent years, social workers have increasingly recognized the importance of what has come to be called *evidence-based practice*—practice that relies on neither intuition nor authority, but rather on critical examination of the best currently available evidence, particularly evidence that has been tested in rigorous, scientific ways (Gambrill, 1999). Certainly practice involves much more than this, as indicated in the Figure I-1, but the importance of testing what one does, and of seeking the best-validated information on which to base decisions can hardly be overemphasized.

Practice Approaches

It is essential to be forthright in representing social work to graduate students. The profession is fragmented on several dimensions; one of the most potentially divisive has to do with practice approaches, or "practice models," that reflect different and often conflicting worldviews. Although individual cases, and therefore specific interventions for each, are unique, the social worker seldom must, or should, develop overall interventive strategies de novo. Practice approaches are organized systems of intervention designed to be applied in relatively consistent ways across multiple cases (including groups and communities). Not only do practice approaches permit social workers to apply what has been learned from other cases to the current one, they are valuable in making explicit how the worker understands the case situation and what is to be done about it. In other words, when using a practice approach, the worker does not depend exclusively on amorphous, unarticulated intuition—which is no doubt always present—but also engages in critical analysis consistent with a coherent conceptual framework.

Some practice approaches are rooted in specific behavioral science theories; others are not. The psychosocial model of practice has traditionally been rooted in psychodynamic thought (including contemporary ego psychology, self-psychology, and object relations; Goldstein, 2001), for example, whereas behavioral and cognitive–behavioral approaches emerge from operant, respondent, and social-learning theories (Mattaini, 1997). The task-centered model (Reid, 1992) was designed to be applied regardless of the underlying theoretical base. The life model (Germain & Gitterman, 1996) applies ecological theory, focusing on mutuality in adaptation between the person and his or her environment. As discussed in Chapter 5, there have been important convergences among some of these approaches in recent years.

The existence of multiple practice approaches does not mean, however, that social workers have nothing in common. In addition to common core purposes, values, and knowledge, social workers share the person-in-situation construct, which suggests that all social workers need common ways to look broadly at cases that capture their interconnectedness. The ecosystems perspective (Chapter 1) is a conceptual framework for doing so that has achieved nearly universal acceptance in the profession. A perspective provides guidance about how to look at cases but not what to do about what one sees. The strengths perspective (Saleebey, 2002) similarly reminds the practitioner to look at and not neglect certain factors. Most practice approaches have been reexamined in recent years with an eye toward recognizing and supporting client strengths, helping to operationalize this emphasis in explicit ways. Practice models, considered in further depth in Chapter 5, are designed to provide guidance about what to do based on what one sees. Practice approaches, therefore, are applied within practice perspectives; the two are not interchangeable.

Practice Processes

Practice is nonlinear, but it is not random or chaotic. Certain processes must occur if social workers are to be helpful. These processes often tend to occur in a rough order, although they are recursive, and social workers will often find themselves cycling back to move ahead.

First, the social worker must be able to engage the client in a genuine human relationship of shared power, not as a separate process, but organically throughout the work. A good deal of research supports what every skilled worker knows: The facilitating conditions of empathic communication, warmth and respect, and authenticity are crucial. These principles were first elaborated by Carl Rogers and subsequently explicitly adopted and adapted by social workers (for example, Hepworth, Rooney, & Larsen, 1997), who had for many years recognized the centrality of the helping relationship (Perlman, 1979). The worker who cannot achieve these necessary—but not sufficient—conditions will fail with most clients. A complication is that we are often not the best judges of our own interpersonal skills, so that supervised practice, including feedback, is essential to ensuring competence in these skills.

Assuming that a social worker has these basic skills, he or she must then know how to intervene to help. Intervention is always rooted in data about a particular case that are uncovered during exploration and organized in a coherent way in an individualizing assessment. These processes, central to effective practice, are emphasized in subsequent chapters.

Contexts of Practice

All practice occurs in a context. That context shapes the practice. "Context" refers to the systems and conditions that constitute the environment of the case, sometimes at a substantial distance. The results of welfare reform and the changing economy, for example, have had major impacts on the way workers work with clients and communities. In health, managed care networks have become the norm, and there is much less emphasis on a private, entrepreneurial model of care. Therefore, the importance of focused, short-term work—which has been growing for some time—continues to grow.

Clients, workers, agencies, and service systems are always embedded in contexts. In work with an individual, for example, family or informal natural networks often are resources for the work but can also be sources of the problem and obstacles to intervention (Reid, 1992). Contextual factors that influence practice include (but are not limited to) policy and funding mechanisms, the physical environment, natural networks, institutions, cultures, and the profession itself. In every "case," the potential positive and negative effects of contextual factors must inform the social worker's thought. Obviously, those that are particularly salient in a case are likely to occupy the foreground, but it is important not to ignore others that may have less obvious, but still meaningful, effects on the case. It can also be valuable to think through contextual factors that affect cases within organizational and community networks, to take a fresh look now and then, and to think about implications of these forces for achieving the organizational mission. For example, family service agencies have recently moved toward a substantially strengthened recognition of the potential of "community-centered" practice, as opposed to more traditional approaches that tend conceptually and sometimes actually to amputate families from neighborhoods and community networks.

Social work's mission relates primarily to the severe social problems with which people, families, and communities grapple, with ameliorating (or preventing) difficulties, and intervening in crises. Issues such as violence (domestic and nondomestic), the maltreatment of children, substance abuse, homelessness, poverty, racism, effects of war and terrorism (and their complex roots), isolation, and mental and physical illnesses constitute both the content and context of social work practice. Social workers know a good deal about many of these problems, about their epidemiology and etiology, and about what may be helpful when a client system is faced with them. For example, there is a substantial existing knowledge base about what practice strategies are effective, under what circumstances, for work with clients struggling with substance abuse (Hester & Miller, 1995; Higgins & Katz, 1998). For instance, one treatment approach, the Community Reinforcement Approach (CRA), has been demonstrated in multiple studies to be substantially superior to traditional treatment for both inpatients and outpatients with serious alcohol (Meyers & Smith, 1995; Sisson & Azrin, 1989) and drug problems (Budney et al., 1991; Higgins, Budney, & Bickel,

1994). Although social workers need not apply this approach with every client with a substance abuse problem, if they will be working with such clients, they probably have an ethical mandate to know about it. They and their clients can then reach an informed, collaborative decision about whether to use some variation of the CRA, or whether there may be reasons to take a different route.

Most social work practice—even private practice—occurs as part of service systems within "fields of practice," organizations, and social institutions. Contemporary fields include families and children, health care, aging, mental health, school-based services, industrial social work, and others. Conceptual difficulties in finding the "bright lines" (Ainslie, 1993) that separate fields are many; note, for example, that the partial list just provided includes fields discriminated by setting, developmental stage, and type of problem. Despite this conceptual inelegance, each field has a certain ad hoc coherence because institutional structures, funding streams, and social policies tend to be organized along these lines, and each provides access to clients at important "crossroads of life" (Meyer, 1976). Fields are also continually evolving, with some fading and others emerging at any point in time.

A Final Word

Recognizing that social work is a complex (perhaps the most complex) professional field, this book deals with that complexity and thus is not an "easy read." However, the authors have made every effort to write as teachers engaged in a collaborative, progressive learning endeavor with the reader. The central purpose of this book is to support courses focused on the foundations of practice, by (a) introducing graduate students to the core knowledge and values of professional practice, (b) encouraging the development of practical skills consistent with that knowledge and those values, and (c) viewing the work of social work as supporting social justice in the web of human (and wider environmental) connectedness. Knowledge and experience accumulated beyond this course will then strike a familiar note because the broad contours of practice have been sketched here.

References

Abbott, A. (1988). *The system of professions: An essay on the division of expert labor.* Chicago: University of Chicago Press.

Ainslie, G. (1993). A picoeconomic rationale for social constructionism. *Behavior and Philosophy, 21*(2), 63–75.

Auerswald, E. H. (1987). Epistemological confusion in family therapy and research. *Family Process, 26,* 317–330.

Bartlett, H. M. (1970). *The common base of social work practice.* Silver Spring, MD: National Association of Social Workers.

Brace, C. L. (1973). *The dangerous classes of New York, and twenty years' work among them.* Silver Spring, MD: National Association of Social Workers. (Originally published in 1892).

Budney, A. J., Higgins, S. T., Delaney, D. D., Kent, L., & Bickel, W. K. (1991). Contingent reinforcement of abstinence with individuals abusing cocaine and marijuana. *Journal of Applied Behavior Analysis, 24,* 657–665.

Castillo, R. J. (Ed.). (1998). *Meanings of madness.* Pacific Grove: CA: Brooks/Cole.

Congress, E. P. (Ed.). (1997). *Multicultural perspectives in working with families.* New York: Springer.

Ewalt, P. (Ed.). (1979). *Toward a definition of clinical social work*. Washington, DC: National Association of Social Workers.

Gambrill, E. (1999). Evidence-based practice: An alternative to authority-based practice. *Families in Society, 80*, 341–350.

Germain, C. B., & Gitterman, A. (1996). *The life model of social work practice* (2nd ed.). New York: Columbia University Press.

Goldstein, E. G. (2001). *Object relations theory and self psychology in social work practice*. New York: Free Press.

Greer, R. D. (1996). The education crisis. In M. A. Mattaini & B. A. Thyer (Eds.), *Finding solutions to social problems: Behavioral strategies for change* (pp. 113–146). Washington, DC: American Psychological Association.

Hartman, A. (1978). Diagrammatic assessment of family relationships. *Social Casework, 59*, 465–476.

Hepworth, D. H., Rooney, R., & Larsen, J. (1997). *Direct social work practice* (5th ed.). Pacific Grove, CA: Brooks/Cole.

Hester, R. K., & Miller, W. R. (Eds.). (1995). *Handbook of alcoholism treatment approaches: Effective alternatives* (2nd ed.). Boston: Allyn & Bacon.

Higgins, S. T., Budney, A. J., & Bickel, W. K. (1994). Applying behavioral concepts and principles to the treatment of cocaine dependence. *Drug & Alcohol Dependence, 34*, 87–97.

Higgins, S. T., & Katz, J. L. (Eds.). (1998). *Cocaine abuse: Behavior, pharmacology, and clinical applications*. San Diego, CA: Academic Press.

Lee, P. R. (1929). Social work: Cause and function. In *Proceedings of the National Conference of Social Work*.

Lowery, C. T., & Mattaini, M. A. (1999). The science of sharing power: Native American thought and behavior analysis. *Behavior and Social Issues, 9*, 3–23.

Lowery, C. T., & Mattaini, M. A. (2000). Shared power in social work: A Native American perspective. In H. Briggs & K. Corcoran (Eds.), *Foundations of change: Effective social work practice*. Chicago: Lyceum.

Malagodi, E. F., & Jackson, K. (1989). Behavior analysts and cultural analysis: Troubles and issues. *Behavior Analyst, 12*, 17–33.

Mattaini, M. A. (1993). *More than a thousand words: Graphics for clinical practice*. Washington, DC: NASW Press.

Mattaini, M. A. (1997). *Clinical practice with individuals*. Washington, DC: NASW Press.

Mattaini, M. A. (1999). *Clinical intervention with families*. Washington, DC: NASW Press.

Mattaini, M. A., McGowan, B. G., & Williams, G. (1996). Child maltreatment. In M. A. Mattaini & B. A. Thyer (Eds.), *Finding solutions to social problems: Behavioral strategies for change* (pp. 223–266). Washington, DC: American Psychological Association.

McGoldrick, M., Pearce, J. K., & Giordano, J. (Eds.). (1996). *Ethnicity and family therapy* (2nd ed.). New York: Guilford Press.

Meyer, C. H. (1976). *Social work practice: The changing landscape* (2nd ed.). New York: Free Press.

Meyer, C. H. (1979). Introduction: Making organizations work for people. In C. H. Meyer (Ed.), *Making organizations work for people* (pp. 1–12). Washington, DC: National Association of Social Workers.

Meyer, C. H. (1993). *Assessment in social work practice*. New York: Columbia University Press.

Meyer, C. H. (1995). Introduction. In C. H. Meyer & M. A. Mattaini (Eds.). *The foundations of social work practice: A graduate text* (pp. vii–xv). Washington, DC: NASW Press.

Meyers, R. J., & Smith, J. E. (1995). *Clinical guide to alcohol treatment: The community reinforcement approach*. New York: Guilford Press.

Mills, C. W. (1959). *The sociological imagination*. New York: Oxford University Press.

Nelsen, J. C. (1975). Social work's fields of practice, methods, and models: The choice to act. *Social Service Review, 49*, 264–270.

Patterson, D. A., & Jaffe, J. (1994). Hypermedia computer-based education in social work education. *Journal of Social Work Education, 30*, 267–277.

Patterson, G. R. (1976). The aggressive child: Victim and architect of a coercive system. In E. J. Mash, L. A. Hamerlynck, & L. C. Handy (Eds.), *Behavior modification and families* (pp. 267–316). New York: Brunner/Mazel.

Peile, C. (1993). Determinism versus creativity: Which way for social work? *Social Work, 38*, 127–134.

Perlman, H. H. (1979). *Relationship, the heart of helping people*. Chicago: University of Chicago Press.

Proctor, E., & Rosen, A. (Eds.). (in press). *Target-based practice guidelines in social work*. New York: Columbia University Press.

Reid, W. J. (1992). *Task strategies*. New York: Columbia University Press.

Richmond, M. (1917). *Social diagnosis*. New York: Russell Sage Foundation.

Saleebey, D. (Ed.). (2002). *The strengths perspective in social work practice* (3rd ed.). New York: Longman.

Sidman, M. (2001). *Coercion and its fallout* (rev. ed.). Boston: Authors Cooperative.

Sisson, R., & Azrin, N. (1989). The community reinforcement approach. In R. K. Hester & W. R. Miller (Eds.), *Handbook of alcoholism treatment approaches* (pp. 242–258). New York: Pergamon Press.

Foundation Knowledge

CHAPTER 1

The Ecosystems Perspective: Implications for Practice

Mark A. Mattaini
Carol H. Meyer

Social work involves, at its core, work with interconnected transactional networks. The ecosystems perspective has been almost universally accepted in social work because it provides a framework
for thinking about and understanding those networks in their complexity.
This strategy for viewing the world can at first seem rather abstract, so it
may be useful to explore why it was developed and has been so widely
adopted. Since the beginning of the profession, practice has been focused
on the person and the environment. This "psychosocial" focus is so important as a distinguishing feature of social work that it has become its identified purpose: to address the psychosocial matrix of which individuals,
families, groups, and communities are constituents.

Although the person-in-environment concept has governed practice since
the work of Mary Richmond (1917) nearly a century ago and has been
defined and redefined (Hamilton, 1951; Hollis, 1972) over the years, its
hyphenated structure has contributed to a continuing imbalance in emphasis on the person or the environment. As a result, practitioners have
often attended primarily to one or the other, missing key dimensions of the
case. For example, a child who refused to attend school might have been
treated for depression, with limited or no attention paid to the role of his or
her school or his or her family (his or her environment) in his or her
behavior. Conversely, attention only to serious dysfunction in a school or a
family might have led to ignoring the plight of the child's response. Often,
practitioners have selected a focus that was compatible with their preferences, assigning peripheral status to either the person or environment.

Another consequence of the perceived separation of the person-in-
environment construct has been the tendency of practitioners to avoid

environmental interventions in favor of changing people in isolation from their life situations—because the environment is often seen as so intractable and so difficult to affect (Kemp, Whittaker, & Tracy, 1997). This emphasis has been encouraged by the development of extensive knowledge regarding human behavior and development, as contrasted with a less-well-developed, cohesive knowledge of the environment. Clinical social workers' choice to focus on the person to the exclusion of the environment may also have had something to do with the view that their professional status was dependent on their engaging in practice similar to psychiatrists and psychotherapists. Thus, the psychosocial purposes of social work were being eroded, and the person-in-environment construct did not appear to be helping. The problem was real and profoundly affected work with clients.

Beyond these consequences for direct practice, the severe social upheaval of the 1960s and 1970s brought awakened populations calling for social services. Previously noticed mainly in public services, poor people, members of ethnic and racial minority groups, women, people with severe social problems, and those with new (or newly acknowledged) lifestyles demanded help from social workers in the voluntary sector. Problems such as child abuse, family violence, AIDS, and homelessness caused all professions to redefine their approaches to account for the evident psychosocial features of these problems. By 1970 it became clear that it was essential to review and rethink the person-in-environment construct so that social workers would find it more possible to intervene in a more transactional fashion in cases that were clearly (nonhyphenated) psychosocial events. The "invented" construct was called "the ecosystems perspective."

The Ecosystems Perspective

The ecosystems perspective is a way of seeing case phenomena (the person and the environment) in their interconnected and multilayered reality, to order and comprehend complexity and avoid oversimplification and reductionism. It is a way of placing conceptual boundaries around cases to provide limits and define the parameters of practice with individuals, families, groups, and communities. It can be pictorialized as an ecomap (Hartman, 1978; Meyer, 1970), a graphic device for viewing the relevant, connected case elements together, within a boundary that clarifies for the practitioner the case system as the focus of work. A typical ecomap of a case in social work practice may look like Figure 1-1.

A fundamental purpose of all professional practice, including social work, is to individualize the case. (If all cases are to be treated in the same way, there is no need for professional judgment.) In the case of social work, this individualizing process applies to individual persons, families, groups, and

Figure 1-1. An Ecomap

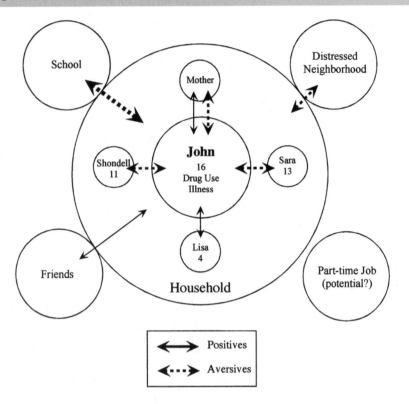

communities. Because no person can be understood apart from his or her defining social context, the ecomap presents the *field* of elements in which the person is embedded. The use of the ecomap makes it virtually impossible to separate the person and his or her environment in one's perception of the case phenomena. It guides one to see connectedness and to eliminate the hyphen between the person and his or her environment. This is important because the way one presents and works with case data depends on one's habits of thought. Research by Rosen and Livne (1992) demonstrated that social workers tend to focus particularly on intrapersonal issues at the expense of transactional problems with significant environmental roots. Lindsey (1998) found that social workers often do not recognize shortages of financial resources, housing assistance, social support, or substance abuse services as significant barriers to restabilizing homeless families and may also underestimate the importance of battering. Preliminary research by Mattaini (1993), however, indicated that social work students are more likely to view a case in its transactional complexity if they prepare an ecomap like John's, shown above in Figure 1-1.

The Roots of the Ecosystems Perspective

The ecosystems perspective (Auerswald, 1968; Meyer, 1976) emerged from two sets of ideas: ecology (DuBos, 1972) and general systems theory (GST) (von Bertalanffy, 1967), both of which originated in biology. Ecology is the science concerned with the adaptive fit of organisms and their environments and the means by which they achieve a dynamic equilibrium and maturity. Drawn from biology, ecological ideas denote the transactional processes that exist in nature and thus serve as a metaphor for human relatedness through mutual adaptation. GST is a general science of wholeness that describes sets of elements standing in interaction, or the systemic interconnectedness of variables, such as people and their environments. It is an organizing conceptual framework in which otherwise unconnected elements are integrated into a synthetic view and fall into place.

As GST explains, when the variables of a case construct a boundary and exhibit certain systemic properties (the "emergence" of a higher-order system from subsystem components, like a family from individuals), they demonstrate reciprocal responses. That is, if one factor in the case is touched by an action or an event, another factor is likely to respond because the two factors are systemically connected. For example, in John's ecomap, if he cannot withdraw from drugs, then his schoolwork will be affected, as will all of the other components of his life described within the circle of the case. If an intervention in another part of John's life is successful, it is theoretically possible that his drug use will be affected. When one intervenes in an interconnected system, such as in John's case, an intervention can take place directly or indirectly and target something that is distant from the objective of intervention, yet result in the desired outcome. For example, one may intervene in the school so that a teacher pays special attention to John, which will affect his self-esteem and lessen his interest in pursuing the drug culture. In GST this process is called "equifinality," which means that one might enter a case through multiple avenues, more than one of which will lead to comparable results. Notice also what does not appear on this ecomap, for example, any significant involvement with churches, extended family, or other possible supports for John or his family. Such missing transactions may also be the focus of intervention.

Recent Advances in Systems Thinking

As in other sciences, knowledge in ecological systems thinking continues to advance. Several principles with direct application to social work emerge from recent systemic research and theory. Capra (1996) provides a readable summary, although some of the material in his treatment remains quite controversial; Hudson (2000), reviews material on emergence and self-organization, key constructs in modern systems thinking, very well. Among important emerging concepts in systems thinking are the following:

- a shift to viewing networks of transactional relationships, rather than objects, as the basic elements of reality;
- the central importance of self-organization in those networks; and
- the crucial place of diversity in those self-organizing systems.

Brief summaries of work in each of these areas may be useful for deepening understanding of the value of systems thinking.

The primacy of relationships. Contemporary biology and physics recognize that reality does not consist of a collection of objects, but rather an "inseparable web of relationships" (Capra, 1996, p. 37). The primary components of this web are *patterns of transactional events*; objects (including organisms) are secondary and have reality only in networks of relationships. Cells, organisms, and ecosystems are all organized in this network pattern. "Hierarchies" in systems thinking of this kind consist of levels of networks rather than dominance hierarchies. For example, a community may be seen as a network of families, which in turn are themselves networks of people, which in turn are organic networks of biological organs and so forth. "Members of an ecological community are interconnected in a vast and intricate network of relationships, the web of life. They derive their essential properties and, in fact, their very existence from their relationships to other things" (Capra, 1996, p. 298).

This level of organic interdependence is core to contemporary systems thinking. The work of social work is action directed toward these transactional webs of relationship. The social worker is part of the web, the client is part of the web, and the work they do together will be supported, opposed, or both, by transactions elsewhere in the web.

Self-organizing networks. Recent systems work has also expanded our understanding of the structure and boundaries of such transactional networks (Hudson, 2000). These networks (technically termed *autopoietic*) are self-organizing and "self-making." The dynamic patterns of transactions that constitute the network are organized by the network itself and establish their own self-constructed boundaries. The boundary of such a network occurs as a natural result of its organization. These natural boundaries, for example, that of a family or a network of fictive kin constructed among a group of gay persons, need to be attended to in practice, with recognition that work inside of those boundaries is likely to take a different approach than work outside of them. Transactional entities exist only as long as the transactions continue. The patterns that constitute them are termed "dissipative structures" because, like a whirlpool, they exist only as long as the transactional processes continue. All living systems are dissipative in this sense.

Such networks "couple" with their contextual environments, with transactions across the boundary. How a network responds to an influence from outside is determined by the state and structure of the network, however. For example, two families may both be coupled to a dangerous neighborhood. One may respond by collapsing, with its boundaries diffusing and members lost to the street. Another may respond with great resilience, taking collective steps to couple with healthier networks (churches and youth organizations, for example). The response of each family cannot be predicted from knowledge of the impinging environment, because the enduring patterns of transactions within each family are key determinants. At the same time, increasing environmental stresses will gradually overwhelm the resilience of more and more families.

The role of diversity. Diversity is regarded as key to ecological stability and balance in ecology. "A diverse ecosystem will also be resilient. . . . The more complex the network is, the more complex its pattern of interconnections, the more resilient it will be" (Capra, 1996, p. 303). In human society, many regard respect and appreciation for diversity as primarily a matter of "political correctness," but systems thinking tells us diversity is key to cultural and spiritual survival. Consider the criminal "justice" system in the U.S. Traditional European American practice has produced an enormous and growing prison population, ultimately constituting an economic drain on society, although in the short run producing economic advantages for some. Incarceration produces profound damage (emotional, social, spiritual) for those enmeshed in the system, but note that not only prisoners are so enmeshed. So are those who work in the system—and ultimately, so are we all, for we really are all connected. The damage is serious and continuous, but there is no apparent way out of this cycle within the dominant culture's practices. Indigenous groups, however, have developed entirely different responses from their very different worldviews, responses that are much less expensive, more effective, and more humane. Tragically, cultural diversity is disappearing as rapidly as is biodiversity, with profound implications for human society.

The transactional focus, in which all processes are addressed to the person in the environment, distinguishes social work from other professional disciplines such as psychiatry or psychology. It implies that individuals and their environments are always actually or potentially adaptive to each other, and that interventions can be carried out in either sphere of the case or directly in the transactions and can be expected to affect other spheres. The ecosystems perspective has enabled social workers to enhance this psychosocial focus through the use of a systemic lens that does not separate the person from the environment but requires that they be seen in their transactional reality. The use of the ecomap as a graphic depiction of the case allows both the practitioner and the client literally to see things concretely. The reader will note that terms such as "see" and "lens" have been used to indicate that the ecosystems idea is a perspective, or a way of looking. It directs the vision of client and social worker toward the complex transactions in cases, helping connect them and recognizing their interactions.

It is crucial that those transactional layers be recognized, regardless of the practice approach preferred by the worker. It is possible to operate from any of several practice approaches while taking an ecosystems perspective, as long as that approach recognizes the multiple levels present. Although a few authors have suggested that the ecosystems perspective is a way of "integrating" practice theories, this is neither realistic nor desirable, as will be seen below. The ecosystems perspective, rather, is at a higher level of abstraction than a practice approach (or "practice model") and suggests that whether one is operating from an ecobehavioral (Mattaini, 1997), ecological (Germain & Gitterman, 1996), "psychosocial" in the psychodynamic sense (Goldstein, 2001), or other practice approach, the heart of professional social work practice requires examining the entire transactional field. A purely cognitive approach, for example, that focused only on patterns in the client's thinking would by definition not be ecosystemic, nor would an approach that focused only on the client's psychosexual development, without recognition of the social and physical environment within which the client is embedded.

Systemic Thinking versus Linear Thinking

Systemic thinking (used in the ecosystems perspective) allows the practitioner to recognize the interconnections present in a case, and thus to consider interventions anywhere in the case. Linear thinking, on the other hand, results in oversimplified understanding, creating a narrow view precluding attention to events and patterns significant to the case. Recent shifts from linear to systemic thinking in many disciplines are connected to the findings of modern physics, which recognize phenomena as "explosive," spontaneous, and sometimes ultimately unpredictable, as well as to the science of self-organizing networks just discussed. Contrast these ideas with linear Newtonian physics, where an apple falling from a tree had only one direction to go—straight down. This is an epistemological change in that the way of seeing or knowing has changed. We are not concerned here so much with the nature of things, but rather with the construction of reality, with what processes binding people and events together become the focus or attention.

Modern views of reality are more diverse and open to individual interpretation than ever before. For example, a child in an inner-city school and a child in a suburban school are likely to have very different views of educational institutions, although family culture will also affect their visions; a lesbian feminist and a fundamentalist will probably perceive differing biases in political processes; and a welfare commissioner will evaluate the worth of public services from a perspective that is foreign to a welfare client. Therefore, it is always useful to reflect on how one views phenomena, because one's standpoint makes an enormous difference in the reality one observes. (This is a good reason to have clients draw their own ecomaps.)

Linear thinking suggests greater certainty, even to asserting simplistic causal connections, such as "If x occurs, y will inevitably follow." In John's case, assuming that John had turned to drugs because his father rejected him would reflect linear thinking. In systems thinking, consequences (such as "y") are ascribed to, and contingent upon, multiple causes and their interactions. In John's case, systems thinking would note that as one consequence of his father's rejection, John relied more heavily on his peers, particularly an older boy who was a drug dealer. This new social environment influenced John to begin to skip school—in which his educational needs were being poorly addressed anyway—which brought him to the attention of the social worker. One can already see several possible entry points to this case through the use of systems thinking (including intervening with John, with the family, with peer networks, with the drug dealer, or with the school). Linear thinking can generate greater apparent certainty and predictability. Because this may result in missing crucial dimensions of the case, however, such practice often proves ineffective. Systems thinking is intended to recognize and accommodate multiplicity, complexity, and uncertainty.

In exchange for a certain lack of certainty and predictability, by thinking systemically the social worker and client gain a much broader palette of options to think about and from which to choose interventions. The transactional field (constituted of multiple transactional systems) affects clients in multiple ways; systems thinking therefore also brings one closer to clients' realities.

The Structure of Systems: Implications for Practice

Systems, as understood by GST and more recent perspectives, have a number of distinguishing properties that will be briefly considered here, for they can illuminate the usefulness of the ecosystems perspective for social work practice. John's ecomap, taken as a whole, is a case system that can illustrate basic principles of the structure and processes of systems in general. The following are some of its salient features:

1. Systems have boundaries; in fact, systems create their own boundaries as part of the self-organizing process. These boundaries can be reflected in physical space, as in a classroom in which the class is a system. Or they can be "drawn" conceptually, as in John's case, when one locates the salient transactional patterns and operationally defines a boundary (a circle) around them. (Systems have patterned relationships—students meet regularly in classrooms, for example. In contrast, if an accident happens on the street, the people who gather to watch it are not a system but a random aggregate.) A physical boundary is usually self-evident; a classroom or a school building, for example, has walls. When it comes to conceptual boundaries, however, the social worker's judgment is involved in discovering the boundaries used in creating the ecomap. Do John's family members belong inside the ecomap if they do not live in the same city as John? Should John's friend in prison be included because John considers him a role model?

There is some power in establishing the boundary of a system, because the picture that is finally drawn will shape the understanding of the case. This power should be shared with the client and often others involved as well. Therefore, the very definition of the case becomes a co-creative act. At the same time, system boundaries are not arbitrary. Social work usually involves work within existing systemic boundaries or in the transactional networks among systems. In some cases, however, the social worker and clients may envision new networks of transactions, new systemic entities to be constructed and elaborated.

2. All living systems are open: their boundaries are permeable, and they exchange energy (interact) with their environments. This exchange enables the system to grow and permits its elements to differentiate and develop. Closed (self-contained) systems, in contrast, cannot thrive because they use energy without accessing additional energy from their environments. In John's case, if he were to become isolated and afraid to leave home, he would sooner or later wind down like an unattended clock. In GST, this phenomenon is called entropy—a universal law of nature that all systems move toward disorganization or death without the importation of energy. When systems are open, they may import more energy from the environment than they expend (a condition labeled negative entropy—note that the word "negative" does not have negative connotations here). They then tend toward greater complexity through elaboration and differentiation. John's isolation implies that he is "closing down," and any number of social work interventions could help him maintain and extend his

connections with people and places in his environment, importing energy, information, and life.

3. Systems tend to preserve their transactional patterns (structure), even as the elements of the system may shift in their relatedness. For example, in family therapy, the members of the parental subsystem usually do not change, but the parents may behave differently. Systemic survival requires substantial structural stability. Because of this need to preserve their structure, systems tend to resist change as they seek to maintain a steady state. At the same time, because living systems are dissipative structures, that steady state is a dynamic balance, not a static equilibrium. If everything simply stopped, the system would collapse. Some transactions with environmental forces can also overwhelm the resilience of the system. A functioning system maintains its balance through rich but manageable transactions with the environment.

In viewing John's case as a (systemic) ecomap, one sees that his equilibrium might be "tipped" if most of his transactions were with the drug culture, or that he could "run down" if he continues to isolate from other environmental forces. Yet, we can recognize multiple sources of energy— relationships, events, programs, ideas—that might be tapped for John's replenishment. Helping him find his way back to school or to a new job, bringing his family members back into his life, or meaningful problem-solving dialogue are all possible, non-exclusive, options within a shared power relationship. Systems can also be overwhelmed if too much energy is introduced precipitously, as for example, if John does not have the time or tools to cope with these new inputs and still maintain his equilibrium. If John were slowly emerging from his isolation, the social worker should be sensitive about pushing him too quickly to join a group or find a girlfriend. If John felt overwhelmed, his self-balancing mechanisms would take over, and he might, out of self-preservation, pull back from the onrush of interventions.

4. The elements of systems are potentially reciprocal, in that they act on each other. Thus, if John's family members were brought back into his life, they would have an effect on him, just as he would have an effect on them. However, John and his family are not all that is reciprocal in this case. John's drug use, school, friends, and illness are reciprocally connected within the boundary of the case. Thus, as noted earlier, change in one part of the system generates effects in other parts; interventions in one or another aspect of the case always reverberate through other elements of the case in some way. These reverberating (and in some cases amplifying) effects have great practical implications because a social worker can sometimes influence "distant" parts of the case by intervening in more available or accessible areas. So, helping John distance himself from the drug culture may

have a reciprocal effect on the way John's mother responds to him, even if the social worker never has direct contact with her. Moves away from drug-using peers and toward family may also tip John back toward healthy peer connections, which in turn may produce additional effects.

5. In closed systems, the final state is determined by the initial conditions. For instance, the planetary system follows its course largely on the basis of its original structure. In personality theory, an example of a final state's dependence on its initial conditions might be the idea that after suffering an emotional trauma, a child is fixated at a certain age and his personality is forever determined by the original trauma. In contrast, in viewing the child on his or her developmental trajectory as an open system, one would factor in broadening experiences as the child matures, so that good teachers, friends, parents, and successful life experiences could counteract the effect of the original trauma and increase resilience. Changes introduced at any of multiple "locations" contribute to the end state, and there are multiple routes for arriving at a satisfactory conclusion (this is, in systems terms, *equifinality*). Thus, the child's life course can be viewed as contingent and not determined by his or her initial condition. Because of the rich transactional connectedness among elements, a single event occurring in a case, such as the birth of a baby or a carefully constructed intervention, will also have multiple effects. Awareness that the initial state does not determine the outcome offers an optimistic view of systemically oriented practice, while reminding social workers also to pay careful attention to unintended effects.

Ecological theory, GST, and recent advances in systems thinking have contributed to the ecosystems perspective and the ecomap, which represents a case system. Theoretical understandings of living systems offer a perspective for understanding the functions of case boundaries, the properties of open systems, and the ways in which case variables are related and transactional. After one begins to view cases systemically, as fields of connected events, institutions, and people, it is difficult to return to linear views of isolated case variables and not to notice the transactional potential among adjacent parts of the field, or to ignore the reverberating effects taking place in more remote parts of the field.

A few of the structures and processes that are characteristic of ecosystems thinking have been illustrated using John's individual case as an example. Imagine now that a community is "the case," for systems thinking applies to systems of all sizes. In the community under consideration (which is a real case), there is a neighborhood social services center used by young people and their families. The immediate neighborhood is bordered by a commercial area that includes three small stores, a restaurant, and a movie theater. A nearby park, a primary school, a police station, a health care

Figure 1-2. A Community Ecomap

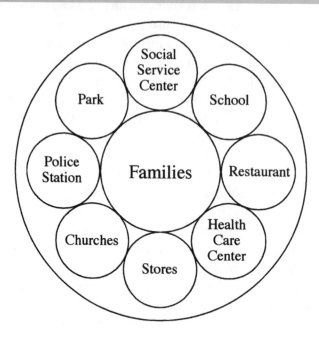

center, and two churches constitute the community within the boundary of the case. Figure 1-2 is a simplified ecomap of the community.

The problem brought to the attention of the neighborhood social services center was that a group of about a dozen 11-year-old boys had been harassing the storekeepers by menacing customers and drawing graffiti. The police could not catch them, their parents felt helpless to stop them, they resisted the pleas of their pastor and priest, they would not attend group sessions at the neighborhood center, and there were no after-school programs. Thinking systemically, the social worker at the neighborhood center assessed the situation of the aggressive boys and the lack of neighborhood resources and developed a plan. She approached the store owners and, after a heated exchange with them, helped them consider alternative ways of dealing with the boys. Chasing and scolding them were not working. The store owners (facilitated by the social worker) called the boys together for lunch at the neighborhood restaurant and created a neighborhood baseball team, bought the boys uniforms (with the names of the stores on them) and equipment, and took turns managing the team when it played other teams in the park. Needless to say, all of the people in the neighborhood who had felt the effect of the boys' destructive behavior were relieved.

As in John's case, there were many options for intervention, including clinical treatment with the boys and their families. The social worker chose what appeared to be both a parsimonious and a powerful intervention. One can only speculate about the later well-being of the neighborhood: the increase in the boys' sense of competence and the relief of the parents, the police, the pastor and priest, and the store owners and their customers. Developmentally, it was crucial that something be done immediately, before the emerging group of youths began to move more deeply into gang culture. Systemic principles illustrated in this case example include identification of meaningful boundaries, connectedness and reciprocity, equifinality, and the shifting of dynamic balances.

The Ecomap and Choices in Practice

Drawing an ecomap that clarifies the significant elements of a case and the transactions among them offers the practitioner and client(s) opportunities to explore and assess the dynamic relationships among case variables. Furthermore, although neither systems thinking nor the ecomap prescribes actions, laying out the case as a field of forces enables the practitioner to select interventive approaches likely to influence the primary transactional issues that emerge. Instead of a predefined template that is too often determined by preexisting expectations, an ecomap opens options and ensures that the most critical factors in the case receive attention. Its use can recast traditional modes of helping, so that the practitioner might use any or all of the social work modalities (individual, family, group, community) and one or several methodological approaches selected for their relevance to the case (Meyer, 1983). This flexibility is possible because the power of transactional networks is harnessed for the work. Thus, the social work practice repertoire, as well as the ecomap, remains an open system.

In addition, recognition of the full field of events and transactions present in a case moves the focus away from a narrow view of cases grounded primarily in individual pathology and problems ("What is wrong with this client?") toward a view that recognizes both challenges and resources, acknowledging not only issues, but also strengths and resources of the client in transaction with the environment. A second important emerging "perspective" in social work is the *strengths perspective*, which suggests that the vision one has of people and systems should focus extensively on their strengths. At root, strengths are not "things" that one carries; rather, systems thinking suggests that strengths are realized (made real) in transactions in which a person has the skills to engage. If personal strengths are seen as consisting of what people can do in transaction with other persons and other systems, the strengths perspective and the ecosystems perspective become deeply intertwined. The strengths perspective reminds us to attend not only to current transactions, and not only to problems, but to transactional patterns that may possible in the process of reshaping a client's reality. In addition, the strengths perspective directs attention to the many resources available in the transactional field that may support positive actions.

The following are some examples of the ways in which systemic principles can contribute to the recasting of case situations. The foregoing example of the neighborhood boys turning from a gang into a baseball team reflects the systemic thinking of the practitioner, who chose the simplest intervention that would have the broadest effect (equifinality).

Another example is a case of a boy with "school phobia," classically treated through either psychodynamic or behavior therapy. An ecomap of a boy's situation of being afraid to go to school might depict his mother who has just had a baby, a teacher who is excessively demanding, and a tough neighborhood through which the child must walk to school. Interventions in any or all of these arenas have the potential of improving the mutual adaptations of the child and his family, his school, and his neighborhood. Such interventions are likely to rely on actual or potential strengths and resources already present in the situation, if only they can be identified in a process of shared power. What could the family contribute? What could the teacher contribute? What can the social worker contribute? And, critically, what power does the child bring to the situation? Again, one notes the opening of interventive options, because the ecomap has displayed the transactional field from which options can be chosen or constructed. This approach allows the practitioner to enter cases at the points at which there appear to be real capacity for change.

The ecomap enables people's environments to be depicted as the matrix of their lives, not only as background. As a result, one can better understand the emergence of family therapy. Once, the family was considered the background in a person's life. Today, family members are recognized as parts of a self-organizing system. Thinking systemically, a practitioner would not treat a young child without directly engaging the child's parents. Practice with families is becoming increasingly community-centered as well (Sviridoff & Ryan, 1997), recognizing the deep transactional connectedness between the family and other elements of community networks, which can support or sabotage the collaborative efforts of the family and social worker.

In the case of a group of tenants who are dissatisfied with their housing manager, a systems-oriented practitioner might mediate a meeting between tenants and manager rather than assuming the total responsibility for advocating on the tenants' behalf. Even better, a shared power perspective might also suggest working with the tenants as a collective, which could creatively elaborate and implement strategies impossible for an individual, drawing on the differential power and gifts each member carries.

Systems thinking has also affected the way organizational processes are viewed. In health settings, although medical authority still prevails, practitioners of other related disciplines are no longer viewed as secondary; rather, the approach to patients is multidisciplinary, in which members of several disciplines share responsibility for cases in holistic ways. In systems terms, a health setting is constituted of interrelated elements in transaction; multidisciplinary teams are more reflective of that reality than is a traditional hierarchical model. In each example, note the connections between thinking ecosystemically and working within a shared power framework (Lowery & Mattaini, 1999). Everyone within the boundary of the case potentially has something to contribute, and responsibility for outcomes is also shared.

The ecomap lays out multiple transactional dimensions of a case and allows the social worker to view the elements of the case in different ways, offering newer and deeper insights into the dynamics present. The ecomap depicts an open system in which the social worker and client can contemplate multiple points of entry into the case. In keeping with the range of roles that social workers enact, the ecosystems perspective helps the practitioner envision many possibilities for professional action, which may be combined and phased in an ever-changing mix. In John's case, one might see the potential for advocacy with the school, therapy with his family, group work with John and others in his situation, a drug program, or community action in the neighborhood.

The use of the ecomap also allows the social worker and client to evaluate progress by (figuratively or literally) placing a transparency of an ecomap at Time 2 over an ecomap at Time 1, to note changes in the overall configuration over time. By generating the presentation of case phenomena in such a way that attention is drawn to the possibilities of what might be done, an ecomap is a tool for assessment, the process by which cases are individualized. It is also a tool for operationalizing the ecosystems perspective, providing the broadest possible canvas on which the social work practitioner and client can sketch a plan for intervention. Note that it is also a tool for building hope, because power and resources that may contribute to a successful outcome are found throughout the transactional field being mapped.

Advantages and Limitations of the Ecosystems Perspective for Practice

Although the ecosystems perspective has been almost universally accepted over the past three decades in social work, some critiques (for example, Wakefield, 1996a, 1996b) draw the profession's attention to the perspective's inevitable limitations and have also been helpful in sharpening ecosystemic thought. Other perspectives, like that of strengths, clearly are also useful in social work. Perspectives (and practice theories) are valuable to the extent that they contribute to positive outcomes. No single perspective, theory, or worldview is universally best; remember the importance of diversity for survival of any living system, including that of the social work profession. Nonetheless, the ecosystems perspective has demonstrated its usefulness in a number of ways, outlined below.

As described previously, the ecosystems perspective is not a practice model, and as such it does not provide direct guidance regarding what to do in a case. This is not its purpose. Rather, the ecosystems perspective provides guidance regarding what to look at in the case. The purpose of the ecosystems perspective is to ensure that the practitioner pays attention to the multiple interacting elements that are always present in a case, particularly in assessment. Wakefield's insistence on the need for substantive theory to guide intervention is surely accurate, but identification of transactional factors important to the case is a prior step, important regardless of theoretical approach.

The importance of expanding social workers' view of cases is more than rhetorical, given research indicating that practitioners tend to focus on some areas at the expense of others. Social workers, like everyone else, pay attention to those questions they ask themselves or are asked about (Williams, 1981). As discussed above, there is considerable research indicating that social work practitioners and students tend not to look at multiple transactional levels of their cases unless they rely on a structure for ensuring that they do so. The function of the ecosystems perspective is to ensure that questions about the broad case field are asked.

Many practice approaches can be encompassed within an ecosystems perspective, as long as they honor the transactional realities of life. For example, an ecobehavioral model that attends to the behavioral events (public and cognitive) and transactions among all actors in a case (client, family, workmates) within an environmental setting (physical environment, neighborhood) can be ecosystemic. By contrast, some narrower behavioral models (still occasionally found in the literature), which focus only on diagnosing and treating the dysfunctional behavior of the client, by definition are not ecosystemic. Similarly, a psychosocial model with roots in psychodynamic thought can be ecosystemic (for example, Meyer, 1988) or can narrowly focus on psychotherapy for clients' intrapsychic dysfunctions. In these examples, the first is consistent with social work purpose, while the second is not. Note that no claim is made here that ecosystems theory somehow enables social workers to "integrate" incompatible practice approaches or models, although some authors (Greif & Lynch, 1983;

Vickery, 1974) have on occasion made such a suggestion. This is clearly neither possible nor desirable.

Assessment

Wakefield (1996a), in his critique of the ecosystems perspective, suggested that it is not very useful for assessment. Several arguments can be made for its utility for just that purpose, however. First, the perspective has stimulated the development of tools for assessment, including the ecomap and many others (Jordan & Franklin, 1995), which direct the practitioner's attention to potentially critical areas that are otherwise often missed.

Second, the perspective draws attention to factors that have a major effect on cases, even if they cannot be addressed directly. For example, the experiences of a person of color with personal and institutional racism need to be recognized—and often directly addressed—in practice, even when there is little that can be done about them directly. The client or worker may find it empowering to become involved in advocacy and social action related to these issues, and the client may develop new strategies for dealing with new incidents that arise, but only if the reality is acknowledged. Despite claims to the contrary, many social workers who do not ask the core ecosystems question, "What are the principal positive and aversive transactions the client experiences or could experience, and how can they be addressed?" simply miss such factors. As one of the first author's clients replied in response to his question about a problem with a potential landlord, "Race is always part of the issue!" So are gender, socioeconomic status, the physical and social environments, and other variables toward which the ecosystems perspective points.

Third, practitioners operating without an ecosystems framework may agree with Wakefield's (1996a) assertion that, "Assessment is, to a large extent, a matter of defining the client's problem. . . . A framework that does not help with problem definition cannot be said in any significant sense to help in assessment" (p. 14). Social work assessment, however, is not primarily about diagnosing a client's problem but rather about determining what new reality should be constructed, how this differs from the present reality, and what resources will be required to move from the latter to the former. A medical model suggests that finding a simple diagnosis of client pathology and treating it is the essence of the work, but social work practice is far broader than this (Mattaini & Kirk, 1991). Assessment in social work consists of the co-construction with the client of a vision of an improved life configuration and the development of a plan to get there (see Chapter 7). Problem definition is only one, sometimes minor, dimension of such assessment.

Connectedness

The ecosystems perspective emphasizes the connectedness among case elements, consistent with contemporary physical, behavioral, and ecological science as well as many important philosophic traditions. This emphasis has been criticized, however. For example, Wakefield (1996a) suggested that more linear "domain-specific clinical theories" are required to decide which of the possible or actual connections are relevant to a case and doubted the "general existence of the proposed circular transactions in social work cases" (p. 11). The first observation is in one sense true; one needs both a coherent theoretical model and a broad ecosystemic view of cases to practice social work.

The examples given to support Wakefield's second observation, however, are problematic. For example, Wakefield (1996a) indicated that the notion of connectedness and transactional causation might suggest false circular causes, for example, that "institutionalized mental patients' symptoms are due to feedback from the asylum's social structure. . ." (p. 12), and indicated that "almost all instances of abuse of children seem to be best explained by linear causal processes originating entirely in the environment" (p. 13). These illustrations are actually excellent examples of complexity and reciprocal transaction. Although the underlying causes of schizophrenia appear to be primarily biological, for example, the form and severity of symptoms are in fact extensively shaped by the institutional or family environment within which the patient is embedded (Wong, 1996), and the course of the illness is profoundly affected by cultural factors (Castillo, 1997). The child maltreatment research indicates that children with more difficult temperaments (generally viewed as present from birth) are at higher risk for abuse (Rutter, 1987), and that many transactional factors within and outside the family appear to be involved in the etiology of abuse (National Research Council, 1993).

Note that this says nothing about blame or responsibility, only that psychosocial phenomena are at root deeply interconnected. A child born with a difficult temperament is not responsible for being abused, for example. However, helping children learn to get what they need in less challenging ways does in fact reduce the chances that they will be abused and increase the chances that they will receive affection and attention from parents, teachers, and peers; we do them no favor by ignoring that fact. Of course, the primary intervention in cases of child maltreatment involves work with the parent, but the outcome of that work is also profoundly affected by other social transactions experienced by the parent (Dumas & Wahler, 1983). Similarly, perhaps the most widely accepted approach to reducing domestic violence is to ensure that the batterer does not have access to his or her victim (who certainly bears no responsibility for the abuse) by helping the victim make a "safety plan" (Reiss & Roth, 1993). Although robbery victims are not to blame for the crime perpetrated against them, their availability is an important occasion for the crime, as is a lack of observing witnesses. In many cases, the most effective preventive and interventive programming for human problems focuses on recognizing and manipulating such indirect variables rather than on simple unicausal or linear approaches (Mattaini & Thyer, 1996). Connectedness is real.

A shared power perspective on practice rooted in "web thinking" (Lowery & Mattaini, 1999, 2001) requires the connectedness principle of ecosystems. From this view (grounded in Native American thought), all actions on the part of the social worker (and the client and other actors in the case) either contribute to or damage the interconnected reality within which people (worker, clients, and others) are embedded. The focus of practice is on working toward a point at which all actors with a stake in the case (for example, biological parents, foster parents, foster child, social worker, and other professionals) have strong voices in planning, make contributions from their respective strengths (note the link to the strengths perspective here) and share responsibility for the outcome. This is not to say all bear "equal" responsibility, because each carries different responsibilities, but all participate in overall responsibility for the child's welfare. This approach is possible only if the essential interconnections among case elements are recognized.

Summary

This chapter introduced the ecosystems perspective, a conceptual framework that allows the social work practitioner to organize the complexity that exists in clients' worlds. The ecological metaphor of mutual adaptation between person and environment is the context for the principles of GST and more recent work in systems theory. These principles explain the way case variables interrelate and reverberate and the way the structures and functions of open systems can serve as a model for social work cases. The transactional ecomap provides a concrete depiction of the elements in a case, enabling the practitioner and the client literally to draw its components.

The ecomap has many uses in social work practice. It can help draw order out of apparent chaos, illustrate the ways in which the case system functions, serve as a communication tool between practitioner and client and among professionals, and chart the progress in a case. One of its most important functions is its use as a tool in assessment, for the ecomap can show assets and liabilities present in the case configuration, and the patterns of positive and negative transactions within which the client is embedded. Finally, the ecomap can expand the perspective of the practitioner seeking points of intervention, opening consideration of the use of multiple modalities, methods, and roles with any or all of the actors and conditions in the case.

The open view of social work practice supported by the ecosystems perspective characterizes every chapter in this volume. Although reading a book is a linear experience, the reader will discover that each chapter contributes to a holistic, systemic perspective on practice. The concepts of connectedness, of attention to self-organizing systems, and of attending to transactional elements in assessment and intervention are elaborated and reverberate throughout.

References

Auerswald, E. H. (1968). Interdisciplinary versus ecological approach. *Family Process, 7,* 202–215.

Capra, F. (1996). *The web of life.* New York: Anchor Books.

Castillo, R. J. (1997). *Culture and mental illness: A client-centered approach.* Pacific Grove, CA: Brooks/Cole.

DuBos, R. (1972). *The God within.* New York: Charles Scribner's Sons.

Dumas, J. E., & Wahler, R. G. (1983). Predictors of treatment outcome in parent training: Mother insularity and socioeconomic disadvantage. *Behavioral Assessment, 5,* 301–313.

Germain, C. B., & Gitterman, A. (1996). *The life model of social work practice* (2nd ed.). New York: Columbia University Press.

Goldstein, E. G. (2001). *Object relations theory and self psychology in social work practice.* New York: Free Press.

Greif, G. L., & Lynch, A. A. (1983). The eco-systems perspective. In C. H. Meyer (Ed.), *Clinical social work in the eco-systems perspective* (pp. 35–71). New York: Columbia University Press.

Hamilton, G. (1951). *Theory and practice of social casework.* New York: Columbia University Press.

Hartman, A. (1978). Diagrammatic assessment of family relationships. *Social Casework, 59,* 465–476.

Hollis, F. H. (1972). *Casework: A psychosocial therapy* (2nd ed.). New York: Random House.

Hudson, C. G. (2000). From Social Darwinism to self-organization: Implications for social change theory. *Social Service Review, 74,* 533–559.

Jordan, C. & Franklin, C. (1995). *Clinical assessment for social workers.* Chicago: Lyceum.

Kemp, S. P., Whittaker, J. K., & Tracy, E. M. (1997). *Person-environment practice.* New York: Aldine de Gruyter.

Lindsey, E. W. (1998). Service providers' perception of factors that help or hinder homeless families. *Families in Society, 79,* 160–172.

Lowery, C. T., & Mattaini, M. A. (1999). The science of sharing power: Native American thought and behavior analysis. *Behavior and Social Issues, 9,* 3–23.

Lowery, C. T., & Mattaini, M. A. (2001). Shared power in social work: A Native American perspective of change. In H. Briggs & K. Corcoran (Eds.), *Social work practice: Treating common client problems* (pp. 109–124). Chicago: Lyceum.

Mattaini, M. A. (1993). *More than a thousand words: Graphics for clinical practice.* Washington, DC: NASW Press.

Mattaini, M. A. (1997). *Clinical practice with individuals.* Washington, DC: NASW Press.

Mattaini, M., & Kirk, S. A. (1991). Assessing assessment in social work. *Social Work, 36,* 260–266.

Mattaini, M. A., & Thyer, B. A. (Eds.). (1996). *Finding solutions to social problems: Behavioral strategies for change.* Washington, DC: American Psychological Association.

Meyer, C. H. (1970). *Social work practice: A response to the urban crisis.* New York: Free Press.

Meyer, C. H. (1976). *Social work practice: The changing landscape* (2nd ed.). New York: Free Press.

Meyer, C. H. (Ed.). (1983). *Clinical social work practice in an ecosystems perspective.* New York: Columbia University Press.

Meyer, C. H. (1988). The eco-systems perspective. In R. A. Dorfman (Ed.), *Paradigms of clinical social work* (pp. 275–294). New York: Brunner/Mazel.

National Research Council. (1993). *Understanding child abuse and neglect.* Washington, DC: National Academy Press.

Reiss, A. J., Jr., & Roth, J. A. (Eds.). (1993). *Understanding and preventing violence.* Washington, DC: National Academy Press.

Richmond, M. E. (1917). *Social diagnosis.* New York: Russell Sage Foundation.

Rosen, A., & Livne, S. (1992). Personal versus environmental emphases in formulation of client problems. *Social Work Research & Abstracts, 29*(4), 12–17.

Rutter, M. (1987). Psychosocial resilience and protective mechanisms. *American Journal of Orthopsychiatry, 57,* 316–331.

Sviridoff, M., & Ryan, W. (1997). Community-centered family service. *Families in Society, 78,* 128–139.

Vickery, A. (1974). A systems approach to social work intervention: Its uses for work with individuals and families. *British Journal of Social Work, 4,* 389–404.

von Bertalanffy, L. (1967). General systems theory. In N. Demerath & R. A. Peterson (Eds.), *Systems change and conflict* (pp. 119–129). New York: Free Press.

Wakefield, J. C. (1996a). Does social work need the eco-systems perspective? Part 1: Is the perspective clinically useful? *Social Service Review, 70,* 1–32.

Wakefield, J. C. (1996b). Does social work need the eco-systems perspective? Part 2: Does the perspective save social work from incoherence? *Social Service Review, 70,* 183–213.

Williams, J. B. W. (1981). DSM-III: A comprehensive approach to diagnosis. *Social Work, 26,* 101–106.

Wong, S. E. (1996). Psychosis. In M. A. Mattaini & B. A. Thyer (Eds.), *Finding solutions to social problems: Behavioral strategies for change* (pp. 319–343). Washington, DC: American Psychological Association.

CHAPTER 2

Social Justice and International Human Rights

Christine T. Lowery

Women must be included in any satisfactory theory
of justice. (Okin, 1989, p. 14).

During the "16 Days of Activism against Gender Violence" in 1991, a petition was faxed around the world that advocated "women's rights as human rights" across the globe. The petition called for the 1993 UN World Conference in Vienna to "comprehensively address women's human rights at every level of its proceedings" and to recognize gender-based violence "as a violation of human rights requiring immediate action" (Friedman, 1995, p. 28). Originally distributed in Spanish, French, and English, and ultimately translated into 23 languages, the petition cited the Universal Declaration of Human Rights. The International Women's Tribune Centre (IWTC) and the Center for Women's Global Leadership shared original sponsorship (Bunch & Reilly, 1994).

> Copies were returned to IWTC in languages staff could not recognize and signed with fingerprints. . . . Batches [of faxes] were received from U.S.-based organizations that had received the petition from overseas. The petition drive lasted until the World Conference with batches of 75,000 periodically sent to the UN to urge conference organizers to include women's issues on their agenda. (Friedman, 1995, p. 28)

When the World Conference convened in Vienna in 1993, more than 1,000 groups had signed up to cosponsor the petition, and almost 500,000 signatures had been gathered from 124 countries (Bunch & Reilly, 1994). People around the world could relate to the simple and broad meaning the petition carried; the petition informed and involved them; people "translated it into whatever issue was most pressing for the group of people they were working with" (Carillo cited in Friedman, 1995, p. 28). Timing for the petition tapped into organizing efforts on behalf of women all over the world that had gained international momentum in the past 20 years. Two years later, the 1991 petition led to a global tribunal that presented violence against women as human rights violations.

Why are women's issues so important? Half the world's population is female, and before equality can be discussed, people must understand how gender is enacted through labor and economics, social upheavals and war, immigration, race, class, religion, and ethnicity, and how gender is marginalized and violated in societies around the world. The time for human rights and the contributions of women all over the world to world policy is now.

Introduction

Why should social workers understand a human rights perspective? Research findings have revealed that "verbal support for civil liberties and human rights is weak and limited" (Devall, 1976, p. 346). The rights of whole groups of people are lost "overnight" with no outcry from the general population. "Opinion leadership sometimes emerges to counter human rights violations" (p. 346), but political strength and timing are limiting factors.

The power behind human rights and a human rights ethic is information and an educated public opinion. International tribunals, "courts, ombudsmen, study commissions, private groups, educational institutions" (Devall, p. 347), and responsible media serve to educate. Social workers are part of a professional body that educates through practice, education, research, and advocacy. A basic tenet of the social work profession is the dignity and worth of human beings, and social workers have advocated for the rights of others in health, mental health, education, and social services, even while less engaged in the political and social policy arena (Midgley, 1997). Knowledge of human rights encourages the support and enforcement of human rights through supporting institutions. The goal of human rights and enforcement is not punishment; it is prevention (Devall, 1976).

How people treat each other as human beings reflects their morality. How social workers treat others shapes their ethics in a professional relationship. If social workers hope to shape their future as human beings in a global village, they must place human rights at the nexus of social justice. The goal of this chapter is to help the student think about social justice principles centered on human rights with a focus on global women's rights. Principles of justice and human rights must be reflected in social policy, acted out in everyday morality, and implemented through relationships in social work practice and advocacy.

An international perspective exposes the realities of living in a world where a global economy, consumption patterns of rich countries, exploitation of human and environmental resources in poor countries, and the desperate poverty of a billion people worldwide alter gender, ethnic groups, cultures, philosophies, worldviews, and lifeways (Rasmussen, 1994). From these perspectives, issues of diversity—gender, ethnicity, race, age, sexual orientation, and physical and mental challenges—are woven into international justice issues, and oppression and domination are subsumed in the continuum of violence that is poverty, injustice, and corruption.

This chapter has two intersecting components: (1) foundational knowledge, including history and policy, and (2) social justice concepts and examples. First, the reader is exposed to a short review of moral philosophy followed by a discussion of rights and relationships, including legal, moral, and human rights. Building on this base, the five instruments of the International Bill of Human Rights are described as an example of social policy. The Declaration of Human Rights for Indigenous Peoples is briefly discussed as an example of those voices that have not been heard, despite the universalistic nature of the International Bill of Human Rights. Second, justice as social empowerment and violence as social disempowerment are explored. Violence against women as a human rights violation is the primary example, including war crimes, trafficking in prostitution, and human rights abuses within the family. This section also includes international advocacy strategies on behalf of women.

A Philosophical Base: Rights and Relationships

Social justice theories or moral rules and principles emerged from moral philosophy, and the reader must understand whose moral philosophy and purposes these rules and principles served. The concepts of liberty, justice, and contract have seeds in the writings of St. Thomas Aquinas (1224–1274), descended through feudal systems of the Middle Ages, and later were shaped by Locke (1632–1704), Hume (1711–1776), Rousseau (1712–1778), and others (Barker, 1962). These politically liberal ideas were built on doctrines concerning the relationship of society and government in the Bible (God ordained powers and made covenants), Roman law (authority), and Aristotelian principles (king-tyrant; accountability to the masses) (Barker, 1962). Benhabib (1992) argued that the modern universalist moral theorists from Hobbes (1588–1679) to Rawls (1921–) are substitutionalist and depend on the experiences of one group—white, male, propertied professionals—to substitute for all, essentially the cultural imperialism of colonialism.

Ancient and medieval moral systems considered man-as-he-ought-to-be, man-as-he-is, and rules for "just relations in his human community" and included man's place in relationship to natural forces. Indigenous peoples worldwide still claim moralities based on a Mother Earth relationship or one's relationship to natural forces. Benhabib (1992) continues, "the attack of medieval nominalism and modern science, the emergence of capitalist exchange relations and the subsequent division of the social structure into the economy, the polity, civil associations and the domestic-intimate sphere, radically alter[ed] moral theory" (p. 154). Modern theorists claimed a disconnection from the limitations of nature, and morality was no longer bound by this relationship.

Autonomy and the Public–Private Sphere

The early contract theorists of the 18th century defended privacy and the autonomy of the self, distinguished justice from the good life, and founded the split between public and private domains (Benhabib, 1992). The public–private divide denotes the spheres of home and family separated from paid work and the ensuing power of men over women in the public domain. This experience is characteristic of Western industrialized nations during the past two centuries (Boyd, 1997). Autonomy of the self was privatized in this process, and women and the domestic-familial sphere were swallowed up in this privacy. This privacy set the context that has hampered the exposure of violence in the home and has made gender equality and childcare needs difficult to achieve in the workplace. An entire domain of human activity, namely, nurture, reproduction, love and care, which becomes the woman's lot in the course of the development of modern bourgeois society, is excluded from moral and political considerations, and relegated to the realm of "nature." (Benhabib, 1992, p. 155)

Currently, the transition from subsistence economies in developing countries to money economies ripples through cultures and affects gender roles worldwide. Women's status in traditional cultures is enhanced by their contributions to food gathering, childbearing, and care for families. What has happened to women in the West is now happening to women in developing countries moving from agricultural phases to industrial phases to technological phases, sometimes all at once. As a woman's work of household production and maintenance is devalued, she is excluded from social and economic power and resources (Pietilä & Vickers, 1996). As at the turn of the last century, the role of gender in the shaping of economic and political realities is crucial. Jean-Bertrand Aristide, returned head-of-state in Haiti, recognized the role of women in world affairs:

Studies around the world have shown that when household budgets are in the hands of women, they are more likely to be spent for primary needs (food, education, and health care). I predict that when the budgets of nations are in the hands of women we will see the same result (Aristide, 2000, p. 41)

Rights and Relationships

The concept of "rights" stands at the intersection of morality, justice, and relationships, as a triangulated base of social justice. Smith (1994) described rights as "the obligations embedded in some social or institutional context where expectation has moral force" (p. 25). From a feminist perspective, Young (1990) considers rights in terms of relationships:

> Rights are not fruitfully conceived as possessions. Rights are relationships, not things; they are institutionally defined rules specifying what people can do in relation to one another. Rights refer to doing more than having, to social relationships that enable or constrain action. (p. 25)

Rights differ from wants or needs in that they are specific entitlements. "Rights emphasize morality in the *relational and reciprocal nature* of the concept, in the obligation or duty required, and in the contribution to well-being, an inherent quality of morality" [emphasis added] (Smith, 1994, p. 23).

Legal and moral rights. Rights may protect people from the power of the state (right to a fair trial) or delineate entitlements from the state (Smith, 1994). Legal rights can be defended in the courts, whereas moral rights appeal to general principles, such as democracy and the right to have a voice, for example. Legal and moral rights can be further divided into liberty-oriented rights and security-oriented rights or claim rights that protect people's physical and material status. Civil or political rights in freedom of action are liberty-oriented. Property rights, unemployment, and social security are examples of security-oriented rights.

Relationship is emphasized when the interests of one group must be negotiated in some way with the interests of another group in light of a "more important moral or political ideal" (Smith, 1994, p. 38). "Struggles are frequently engaged to make moral rights legal, the vote for black South Africans being an obvious case" (p. 38). Human beings are treated differently from place to place, and the justification for such treatment also varies. Hence, rights are relative in their importance, interpretation, and practice from society to society. Smith gave a broad example of how the nature of different societies is reflected in struggles for rights:

> Capitalist societies tend to prioritize individual liberty and property rights, while socialist societies place more emphasis on collective entitlements from

the state. Basic civil liberties are more of an issue in South Africa than in Britain, where social security is a major concern. (p. 38)

Human Rights. Human rights are moral rights supported by the belief in the moral worth and dignity of human beings. Ideally, people have entitlement to these rights as human beings, regardless of age, race, class, gender, religion, national origin, or language. For the social work student, human rights serves as one foundation for framing a personal perspective on social justice and social policy, woven into the ethics of the profession and translated concretely into social work practice, day to day.

Economic, social, and cultural rights were linked with civil and political rights, as a body of rights at the First International Conference on Human Rights in Teheran, Iran, in 1968. Twenty-five years later, the World Conference on Human Rights in Vienna (1993) recognized the universal nature of human rights to address racism, discrimination, xenophobia (fear of foreigners), and intolerance with an emphasis on the rights of women; children; members of ethnic, religious, and linguistic minority groups; and indigenous peoples.

How are human rights related to social justice? Peffer (cited in Smith, 1994) provided the following criteria. Both are concerned with fundamental human needs. Both present obligations that the state or other individuals can legitimately force people to meet. Both provide a basis for justifying actions and seeking protection of others and provide grounds for justifying or criticizing social institutions, programs, or policies. The work of the United Nations on human rights and the struggle of indigenous peoples to save their lands, cultures, and resources will be used as examples.

The International Bill of Human Rights as Social Policy

Social policy requires at least three elements: moral authority (rights), legal force (implementation and review), and commitment of partnerships (ratification). The UN International Bill of Human Rights provides one example of social policy in process. Five major United Nations legal instruments exist to define and to guarantee the protection of human rights: 1) The Universal Declaration of Human Rights (1948); 2) the International Covenant on Economic, Social and Cultural Rights (1966); 3) the International Covenant on Civil and Political Rights (1966); and 4) and 5) the two Operational Protocols to the latter Covenant. The Declaration is a manifesto with primarily moral authority. The Covenants are treaties binding on the States that ratify them. Together they constitute the document known as the International Bill of Human Rights.

The Universal Declaration of Human Rights (reprinted in Appendix B), adopted in 1948, serves as a standard against which member states can measure their progress, but the declaration requires enforcement procedures. The two comprehensive categories of rights (economic, social, and cultural, and civil and political) make up the legal force required for implementation and include protocols for review of implementation and commitment to relationship among the partners who have ratified the document. Most importantly, social justice ideals are actualized through legal means (procedural justice) through the incorporation of human rights standards into policies of member states. If the system is working, policies are sanctioned; ensuing practices examined; information is fed back into the process; and policies are refined, changed, updated, or eliminated.

Among the rights in the 30 articles of the Declaration is a right to a free, elementary education. "Men and women of full age" have the right to marry and have a family with equal rights in the marriage and at its dissolution (International Bill of Human Rights, 1993, p. 6). People have a right to a nationality, freedom of movement, the right to seek asylum, the right to social and international order, and the right to participate in the cultural life of the community. The equal rights of men and women, right to work, fair wages, the right to form and join unions, and the right to adequate standards of living are among the rights recognized under the Covenant on Economic, Social, and Cultural Rights. Life, liberty, and safety, the right to privacy, and the right to a fair trial are recognized by the Covenant on Civil and Political Rights (International Bill of Human Rights, 1993).

A Declaration of Human Rights for Indigenous Peoples

Despite the noble and far-reaching language of the UN Declaration, there are peoples (pre-invasion, pre-colonial societies) who have not been heard in this process, and an analysis of social justice must question, Who is being excluded from this list of human rights? Who has not been heard? Who is not here? "Julian Burger, of the UN Center for Human Rights, calculates that in half of the 161 states in the UN, the rights of indigenous peoples to self-determination are being denied or restricted" (cited in Davidson, 1994, p. 67). Davidson contended that the UN declaration becomes "empty sentiment" as member governments try to eradicate small, scattered groups of indigenous peoples for their land and resources. For example, Brazil is one of the states most resistant to the Indigenous Declaration. Brazil is one of several countries in which Amazonian rain forests are burned to open grazing land to feed cattle for the world beef market and to build roads for mining operations, which displaces indigenous peoples who have lived there for centuries.

The power behind human rights and environmental justice is an educated public opinion. Global communication helps us to enter the international dialogue to organize education and resistance across the world, while working locally. While global communication separates us in the digital divide, global comparisons and patterns help us to recognize who is absent in the global dialogue.

Since 1982, leaders of the 200–250 million indigenous peoples have worked on the UN Draft Declaration on the Rights of Indigenous Peoples. In 1995, the draft was approved by a UN subcommission and since then has faced a stalemate at the Commission on Human Rights level. Continued refusal to acknowledge indigenous peoples as partners is as central to the struggle as is the language of the document. The Declaration includes a statement that because of colonization and dispossessed lands, territories, and resources, indigenous peoples are prevented from exercising the right to development based on their own needs and interests. Indigenous peoples ask for "control of their lands and territories and restitution of that which is traditionally owned or has been confiscated, occupied, used or damaged without . . . their consent" (United Nations Working Group on Indigenous Peoples, 1998).

There is hope. "Indigenous rights are on the radar screen and the language is showing up in documents which contain references to indigenous rights and the special status of indigenous peoples," reports Elizabeth Homer, former director of the Office of American Indian Trust (Oct. 5, 2000). The Organization of American States has an American Declaration for Rights of Indigenous Peoples, although "paralyzed" by lack of funds for working groups to function. The new president of the working group is a former human rights activist, Ronalth Ocheaeta Argueta, now the ambassador from Guatemala. Argueta wants real indigenous participation and expert consultation in the process at the regional level, according to Andrew Wiggin, a Mesquito Indian and head of the Latin American Division at the American Indian Law Center in Washington D.C. (Oct. 5, 2000). In 2000, the UN approved the establishment of a Permanent Forum for Indigenous Peoples. The structure and function of the Permanent Forum are still unclear, and there is much work to be done.

Indigenous peoples worldwide carry an ancient understanding of their ecological environments, now being scientifically "discovered." This knowledge base has not been consulted as dams are erected, migration sites are eradicated in favor of land development, and rivers are polluted as millions of acres are cleared in the rain forests. However, this knowledge may prove useful in any future attempts to reconcile the destruction to physical and social environments.

Justice and Violence: Social Empowerment and Social Disempowerment

Social justice and human rights are empowering for societies if commitments to relationships through just policies are honored. On the other end of the continuum, social disempowerment is experienced when there is violence in the form of poverty, corruption, and injustice. Violence affects quality of life and opportunity through fear and poverty, including educational, social, economic, and political deprivation. Violence takes the lives of women and children through physical and sexual abuse; erodes social justice through graft, crime, and political corruption; exploits and destroys the physical environment; and savagely plows through nations, their peoples, and cultures in acts of war, territorial disputes, and terrorism. Injustice is evident through domination and what Young (1990) called the five faces of oppression: cultural imperialism, marginalization, exploitation, powerlessness, and violence.

To understand the disempowering role of violence and injustice as a continuum engulfing private and public spheres in society, the definition of violence must be expanded. The Panel on Understanding and Control of Violent Behavior formed by the National Academy of Sciences defined violence as "behaviors by individuals that intentionally threaten, attempt, or inflict physical harm on others" (Reiss & Roth, 1993, p. 2). Admittedly, this definition masks the diversity of violence that causes death or is hidden in "statistical classifications of nonfatal crimes" (Reiss & Roth, 1993, p. 2). The UN Declaration on the Elimination of Violence against Women expands gender-based violence to include "physical, sexual or psychological harm or suffering to women including threats of such acts, coercion or arbitrary deprivation of liberty, whether occurring in public or private life" (Pietilä & Vickers, 1996, p. 143). Famine of the mind (educational deprivation), body (starvation), and spirit (poverty) must also be included in a continuum of violence. From indigenous worldviews, violence is not only physical, but also contains emotional, environmental, spiritual, spatial, and geographical components, as well as generational time—past, present, and future.

Who perpetrates violence on whom? What type of violence (poverty, injustice, and corruption) is being perpetrated, and for what purpose? Whose rights are acknowledged, protected, or violated? If one looks closely enough, control of resources, social control, and coercion are at the heart of violence. For the interested reader, Noam Chomsky (1999) documented U.S. policies which contradict human rights, including sanctions, in *The Umbrella of U. S. Power*. The political nature of both culture and religion must also be questioned, and practitioners must "listen with skepticism and care" (Rao, 1995, p. 174). Rao used women within culture as an example when she cautioned:

> Without questioning the political uses of culture, without questioning whose culture this is and who its primary beneficiaries are, without placing the very notion of culture in historical context and investigating the status of the interpreter, we cannot understand the ease with which women become instrumentalized in larger battles of political, economic, military, and discursive competition in the international arena. (p. 174)

The continuum from social justice and human rights to violence or social empowerment to social disempowerment forces social work students to redefine how they conceptualize social problems and to acknowledge how social power is used, on whose behalf, and for what purposes.

Social Power: Force, Wealth, and Knowledge

Toffler (1990) included violence as part of the triad of social power: force, wealth, and knowledge. Violence or force is seen as a low-quality power because one can use it only to punish. Wealth has greater flexibility and is a medium-quality power. Knowledge, "the most democratic form of power" (Toffler, 1990, p. 20), has the greatest flexibility and efficiency: "to punish, reward, persuade . . . transform" (p. 16). Wealth is the least "maldistributed" source of power; Toffler argued that "an even greater chasm separates the armed from the unarmed and the ignorant from the educated" (p. 20). In the analysis of social justice (morality, justice, and relationship) or violence (poverty, injustice, and corruption), social work students must examine the quality and relationship among the elements of social power in social policies and the implementation, and interventions in an era of global change. For example, countries with technological power rely less on agricultural or industrial countries and use technologies (knowledge) to make wealth with each other by creating multinational organizations and further separating rich and poor countries (Toffler & Toffler, 1995). Susan George, of the Transnational Institute (the Netherlands), described economic apartheid. At the apex of this pyramid are the transnationals and beneath this, a middle class. At the ever-widening base, is "an underclass of people who are unimportant both as producers and as consumers, for which the system has absolutely no plans" (cited in Pietilä & Vickers, 1996, p. 154). The limited gains in global health and global economics of recent decades (in South Korea and Indonesia, for example) are being swallowed in the gap between rich and poor, swept away as the movement from rural to urban areas and immigration from south to north overloads social structures (Barten, 1994). Changing social priorities and funding have moved away from the basic tenets of disease prevention, for example, which require continuity and vigilance (Nakajima, 1997).

In contrast, knowledge is becoming available to more people in countries worldwide, and shifts in power can occur. For example, alliances among small and medium states from both the north and south have forged bans on antipersonnel land mines, and are collectively working to get 60 states to ratify a treaty to establish an International Criminal Court (Human Rights Watch, 1997). Globally, southern states with fresh experiences in fighting repression bring new and bold leadership to these coalitions by upholding the principle of universality and defending human rights in the face of waning commitment of the major powers (China, the United States, and Russia) (Human Rights Watch, 1997). Multinational corporations, with power to influence governments around the world, can be held accountable for their own human rights practices through the collective power of nongovernmental organizations (NGOs) using moral force (Human Rights Watch, 1997).

Next, the continuum of gender-based violence from an international perspective and within the context of women's human rights will be examined. In the past 30 years, incremental, painstaking organization and the work of many women, in many organizations around the world, have laid groundwork for interrelated issues—violence against women, women's rights, and the role of women in economic development and the environment—to be acknowledged on the international agenda.

Human Rights Abuses against Women and Advocacy for the World's Women

"How have women been affected by limited forms of democracy? What has been the impact on women of narrow definitions of human rights? Why have so many degrading life experiences of women not been understood as human rights issues?" (Bunch, 1995, p. 11). Integrating women's issues into the human rights agenda is process building on an international scale. How did women's rights become a critical issue in the 1990s? Three strategies are briefly discussed here: (1) making relationships through worldwide women's conferences and networks, (2) mainstreaming agendas into human rights agendas with moral force, (3) dealing with the grassroots of women's everyday lives, and preparing for the future through the "girl-child" developmental perspective.

Worldwide Conferences and Agendas. Although women had organized worldwide against injustices in their own political contexts, Friedman (1995) acknowledges the UN Decade for Women (1975–1985) as "the watershed both for placing women on the international intergovernmental agenda and for facilitating women's cooperation" (p. 23). The role of non-governmental organizations (NGOs) at the World Conferences for Women in Mexico (1975), Copenhagen (1980), Nairobi (1985), and Beijing (1995) was critical. NGO forums provided environments for women from all over the world to talk, to make relationships, and to construct strategies for making their governments accountable (Friedman, 1995).

In 2000, the UN hosted Beijing+5, in New York City. Human Rights Watch reported that while there is greater attention to the abuses of women's human rights and use of human rights rhetoric, the legal and moral force required to change policies and practices in many countries are still culturally bound.

The South African government, for example, could proudly declare its commitment to women's rights at Beijing+5, yet thousands of South African women farmworkers had no ability to establish work contracts independently of their husbands. Similarly, the government of Peru condemned violence against women, while obliging domestic violence victims to undergo mandatory conciliation sessions with their abusers. The Uzbekistan government maintained constitutional guarantees of women's equality but women wishing to divorce their husbands faced major, gender-specific obstacles. The Taliban in Afghanistan shrouded its denial of women's rights in the rhetoric of protection but its forces raped ethnic Hazara and Tajik women with impunity. Japan's government treated trafficked women not as victims of abuse but as criminals (http://www.hrw.org/wr2k1/women/index.html).

Growing out of the Decade for Women, the Convention on the Elimination of All Forms of Discrimination Against Women (CEDAW), which came into force 20 years ago, was a powerful tool for women's equality—"from family to workplace to government" (Friedman, 1995, p. 23). A network of international organizations to ensure education and compliance with CEDAW followed: the International Women's Rights Action Watch; Latin American Committee for the Defense of Women's Rights; the Asia-Pacific Forum on Women, Law, and Development; and Women in Law and Development in Africa. National and international women's organizations facilitate information sharing in England, Canada, the Philippines, France, and the United States. As of December 2000, the Committee on the Elimination of Discrimination against Women can now consider petitions from individual women or groups of women who have exhausted all national remedies. The Optional Protocol proposed in 1999, which allows this, was ratified by 13 states and has now come into force, giving governments time to incorporate this into their national policies.

Mainstreaming Agendas. The rights of marginalized social groups are typically treated as special issues without full integration into the political agenda. Not until the 1970s did the UN agenda specifically address women's issues and recognize women as resources (Pietilä & Vickers, 1996). Women's rights were still viewed as a sub-issue of human rights, the public sphere of the state-sanctioned oppression, without considering the private sphere where most violations of women's rights occur (Peters & Wolper, 1995). Historically, women's oppression was not seen as a political issue by the United Nations, and thus sex discrimination and violence were also excluded from the human rights agenda (Stamatopoulou, 1995). The creation of specialized bodies to address women's rights allowed major UN human rights bodies to "absolve themselves of this responsibility" (p. 45) and relegated women's rights to add-ons (a common political tactic with minority concerns) rather than politically integrated issues.

However, focusing attention on violence against women was a powerful tool for reshaping human rights through women's experience. An international human rights framework already existed with political power and protocols supported by governments. Violence was already "a gripping issue that paralleled an existing human rights paradigm" (Friedman, 1995, p. 20). Slavery, torture, and terrorism represented everything the human rights community was combating, but did not include women's experiences. Women's human rights advocates used the continuum of violence in the public and private spheres to educate and hold governments accountable (Friedman, 1995). "The process of including women transforms agendas" and challenges "the hierarchy of rights, with civil and political rights at the pinnacle" (p. 20) with the notion that all human rights—political, civil, social, economic, cultural—are indivisible. What frameworks exist for mainstreaming social work issues? How were women's experiences used to "transform agendas"? The Global Tribunal on Violations of Women's Human Rights in Vienna in 1993 (discussed later in this chapter) is one example of mainstreaming agendas.

Grassroots and Women's Everyday Lives. How can women influence the international agenda on a local level? Suarez Toro (1995) focused on the everyday lives of women in Central America, where "equality before the law is not equality in life for women" (p. 190). Using their own life experiences as starting points, the women popularize women's issues and educate. In groups, the women identify the first time their human rights were violated because they were women and the first time they reclaimed their rights. They analyze international human rights instruments to see what protects them and what does not, and they determine what needs to be changed. Next, the women concretely name strategies that can help change their daily lives and construct strategies for influencing policy at the local, national, and international levels. The women process their own resistance, fears, excitement, and support each other as they act. This methodology broadens the "facts of their lives, as part of larger social, political, and cultural constructs as well—as part of a global problem" (p. 193).

To acknowledge violence and discrimination against women as lifelong patterns of abuse, the strategic objectives of the Global Platform for Action for Beijing (1995) are formally extended to the "girl-child," nurturing her education, her safety, and her health care, and encouraging the development of her social, economic, and political power.

The Global Campaign and Vienna Tribunal for Women's Human Rights. New women's coalitions made old divisions—along north-south lines and among women working in non-governmental, governmental, and UN agencies—obsolete in the active lobbying to get women and human rights on the agenda for the World Conference in Vienna (Bunch & Reilly, 1994). Starting in November 1992, grassroots hearings on violations of women's human rights were taking place from India to Costa Rica, from the United States to Argentina, and this evidence was sent to the UN Centre for Human Rights (Bunch & Reilly, 1994). These hearings culminated at The Global Tribunal on Violations of Women's Human Rights in Vienna, which coincided with the World Conference in June 1993. In one day, 33 women testified to the "failure of existing human rights mechanisms to protect and promote women's human rights" (Friedman, 1995, p. 30). Four judges documented joint recommendations at the end of the hearings:

> We affirm the principle of universality that protects all of humanity, including women. Universal human rights standards are rooted in all cultures, religions, and traditions, but those cultural, religious and traditional practices that undermine universality and prove harmful to women cannot be tolerated. (Bunch & Reilly, 1994, p. 32)

War Crimes. The UN Declaration of Human Rights (1948) states that "No one shall be subject to torture or to cruel, inhuman or degrading treatment or punishment." The Fourth Geneva Convention states "in case of conflict or occupation" and in non-international conflicts, women are protected against "attack on their honour. . . rape, enforced prostitution and any form of indecent assault" (Bunch & Reilly, 1994, p. 33).

In the 1930s, the Japanese established army brothels, sexually enslaving and serially raping some 200,000 women daily, mostly girls under age 20. The women were from Korea (80 to 90 percent), China, Taiwan, the

Philippines, Indonesia, and some European countries (Bunch & Reilly, 1994). In 1992, the University of Zagreb School of Medicine reported 10,000 rapes in Bosnian Serbian army camps; estimates from other reports are as high as 60,000 (Bunch & Reilly, 1994). Systematic ethnic cleansing by Serbians using rape and forced pregnancy is but one side of the corruption of war. Governments use statistics on rape to incense hatred of the enemy (Bunch & Reilly, 1994). Male violence against women, aggressively supported by governments, is anesthetized in terms such as "Japanese comfort women" and "ethnic cleansing," as women's lives are smothered.

Trafficking in Prostitution. From the Nairobi Forward-Looking Strategies for the Advancement of Women come the following:

> Forced prostitution is a form of slavery imposed on women by procurers. It is . . . . the result of economic degradation that alienates women's labor through processes of rapid urbanization and migration resulting from underemployment and unemployment. It also stems from women's dependence on men. . . . Sex tourism [and] forced prostitution . . . reduce women to mere sex objects and marketable commodities. (paragraph 290)

In 1993, the Foundation against Trafficking in Women in the Netherlands reported assisting women from Asia and Central and Eastern European countries—Poland, Bulgaria, the Ukraine, Russia—where economic changes had not stabilized. Women paid low wages in other countries are lured to the Netherlands with promises of legitimate work and better pay; once there these women are trafficked into prostitution (Bunch and Reilly, 1994). U.S. newspaper reports continue to document stories of unsuspecting women who have experienced being bought and sold in trafficking rings.

The Medium Term Philippine Development Plan, or Philippines 2000, transitions an economy based on U.S. military bases to U.S. "rest and relaxation preserves" and multinationals, propped up by Filipino women as cheap labor and sexual commodities (Largoza-Maza, 1995). Where farmlands are being displaced by industrial estates fueled by foreign investment and increasing sex tourism, women are easily exploited in an economic environment where a daily wage averages $4.20 and daily cost of living for an average family of six is $10.20 (Largoza-Maza, 1995). GABRIELA is a coalition of Filipino women's organizations that emerged from the anti-Marcos struggle (1983–1986). GABRIELA addresses issues ranging from

> U.S. military bases to nuclear power plants to rape, domestic violence and prostitution; from U.S. imperialism to the stranglehold of multinational companies to militarization to Filipino "comfort women" through organizing, research, and education; legislative action, campaigns, mobilization;

welfare and crisis intervention; and local and international networking. (Largoza-Maza, 1995, p. 65)

In 2000, the Coalition Against Trafficking in Women (CATW), with the International Human Rights Network, gained ground in a strong and in-clusive definition of trafficking, a definition central to the new UN Proto-col to Prevent, Suppress and Punish Trafficking in Persons, especially Women and Children. This protocol supplements the United Nations Con-vention against Transnational Organized Crime, which took two years of negotiations and drafting. The Convention and three Protocols on the Traf-ficking in Persons, the Smuggling of Migrants, and the Trafficking in Arms, are currently open for signatures by states (http://www.uri.edu/artsci/wms/ hughes/catw/tocv.htm).

Violations of the Body. Female genital mutilation (FGM) is the excision of genitalia in the name of cultural and social constructions of femininity and wifely obedience. FGM "affects 100 million women who live in 26 African countries, a few minorities in some Asian countries, and immi-grants in Europe, Canada, Australia, and the United States" (Bunch & Reilly, 1994, p. 53). Nahid Toubia, a medical doctor from the Sudan, asserted that "As women, we too have the right to decide what parts of our culture we want to preserve and what we want to abandon. . . . These women [who have been mutilated] are holding back a silent scream so strong it could shake the earth" (cited in Bunch & Reilly, 1994, p. 53). Asma Abedel Haleem, a human rights lawyer and Islamic scholar from the Sudan reports, "It is not sufficient for religion to shun the practice. Religion should be used as a tool for condemning and preventing its occurrence. The participation of women in the reinterpretation of religion will be crucial" (cited in Bunch & Reilly, 1994, p. 54).

Sexuality. Rebeca Sevilla from Peru, co-chair of the International Les-bian and Gay Association, reported that 2,000 murders of gay people have been documented in the media from 1983–1993 in Brazil. "Social cleansing claims lesbians, gay men, prostitutes, and street kids (Bunch & Reilly, 1994).

Currently, the Minnesota Gay Homicide Study, a three-year research project (2000–2003), seeks to measure the incidence of gay, lesbian, bi-sexual, and transgender homicides in Minnesota and its border cities. The lives of the victims will be explored through interviews with family and friends. Sentence and release patterns for gay homicide offenders will be studied. Education and consultation on gay homicide issues is to be devel-oped (http://www.mngayhomicide.org/timeline.html).

Disability, Reproduction, and Population Control. Nicaraguan Petrona Sandoval recounted her experience of becoming paralyzed from epidural anesthesia during childbirth, one of 600 to 2,000 estimated cases in 10 years, according to a study by a Swedish group. There has not been a thorough investigation, and the cause is uncertain, but is "most likely" expired medications (Bunch & Reilly, 1994). Uniformed consent, "coerced abortions and sterilization, unsafe contraceptive devices, unnecessary hysterectomies, and the incompetent use of epidural anesthesia and episiotomies" are some of the reproduction and population control violations of women's rights in health (Bunch & Reilly, 1994, p. 57).

Human Rights Abuses within the Family. An advocacy group in Kenya, Women Rights Awareness Program, reported that 70 percent of the men and women interviewed knew their neighbors beat their wives; almost 60 percent blamed the women. Agnes Siyiankoi, age 30, was beaten by her husband with a cattle club and carried to the hospital. Hospitalization requires an official complaint, and this often deters victims from speaking out. With support from her brother, who is a lawyer, she filed assault charges after 13 years of abuse. She formally challenged the traditional power structure among the Masai tribal peoples in Kenya and now suffers the anger of other women, for "it is unheard of in Masailand to put your husband in jail" (Kenyan Tradition Confronted, 1997, p. A5).

Gayla Thompson, an African American woman living in New York, testified before the Global Tribunal on Violations of Women's Human Rights:

> [My husband] beat me bad enough to cause an abortion. . . . . I was able to get away at one point and call the police and when they arrived—because my husband was in his police uniform and had me on the floor kicking me and beating me and punching me—the other officers thought I was fair game and so they joined in. (cited in Bunch & Reilly, 1994, p. 26)

Political persecution is narrowly defined, but when combined with citizenship and discrimination, these complex realities are not addressed in inadequate institutions and systems. Maria Olea, an immigrant to the United States from Chile, escaped domestic violence in a "dictatorial political system" that supports men who can legally abuse women and sought refugee status with her two children. Domestic violence is not considered grounds for obtaining refugee status in the United States, and she faces death if returned to Chile. Maria Olea's invisibility as an undocumented women subjects her to another set of laws that further diminish her chances and the lives of her undocumented children in the United States (Bunch & Reilly, 1994).

Migration to cities in Morocco and countries around the Mediterranean has encouraged more couples to live alone rather than within a Muslim family network. Urban living has contributed more education for women. However, it has also removed them from protection by their fathers and brothers and exposed them to more abuse, repudiation of the marriage, and divorce, according to Fatima Zahra Tamouth, a professor of African history at the University of Rabat (cited in Simons, 1998). In 1993, women's groups collected one million signatures to move divorce and child custody rules from the Mudawana, the Muslim family law, into the civil code (Simons, 1998). Reforms, made without the input of women, have had little impact, and women now want a part in abolishing repudiation and making rules for child custody and divorce, which now affects 50 percent of couples. Activists cite the UN International Women's Conference in Beijing (1995) as a catalyst for women "among the more emancipated of the Arab world" in Morocco, Tunisia, and Algeria (Simons, 1998, p. A6).

Social Justice and Economic Development

Those who are marginalized are easily exploited; the labor of one social group (class, gender) is used to benefit another social group in pursuit of profit and power (Young, 1990). The global search for cheap labor, exploitation of Hispanic garment workers in California, trafficking in prostitution, and child labor in Pakistan are examples. The resulting powerlessness is a function of position in a hierarchical structure and inhibits the realization of one's capacity, one's decision making in working life, and exposure to disrespectful treatment because of status (Young, 1990).

In 1992, equity, social justice, and eliminating poverty were linked to sustainable development at the Earth Summit in Rio de Janeiro, Brazil (Rasmussen, 1994). Questions, interventions, and policies framed in social justice and social empowerment must include the diversities of philosophies, cultures, realities, environmental limits, and also must include a promise of a quality future for the coming generations. Women are already collectively asking "What kind of economic development is best suited to the promotion of human development?" rather than "What kind of human development would promote competition and growth?" (Pietilä & Vickers, 1996). In 1984, Devaki Jain from India assessed development in an essay:

> Economic development, that magic formula, devised sincerely to move poor nations out of poverty, has become women's worst enemy. Roads bring machine-made ersatz goods, take away young girls and food and traditional art and culture; technologies replace women, leaving families even further impoverished. Manufacturing cuts into natural resources (especially trees),

pushing fuel and fodder sources further away, bring home-destroying floods or life-destroying drought, and adding all the time to women's work burdens. (cited in Pietilä & Vickers, 1996, p. 35)

And where does the road go? Kunstler (1993) wrote about the modern American landscape and reflected similar pessimism about economic development.

The [American] road is now like television, violent and tawdry. The landscape it runs through is littered with cartoon buildings and commercial messages. We whiz by them at fifty-five miles an hour and forget them, because one convenience store looks like the next. They do not celebrate anything beyond their mechanistic ability to sell merchandise. We don't want to remember them. We did not savor the approach and we were not rewarded upon reaching the destination, and it will be the same next time, and every time. There is little sense of having arrived anywhere, because everyplace looks like no place in particular. (p. 131)

Summary and Conclusion

This discussion has centered on two continua: social justice (social empowerment) and violence (social disempowerment), and violence as a continuum bridging both public and private spheres. Four triads demonstrate relationships among concepts. (1) Morality, justice, and relationship support social justice. (2) Social power is contained in force, wealth, and knowledge. (3) Social policy is treated as a subset of social justice including moral authority, legal force, and commitment to relationship. (4) Violence embedded in poverty, corruption and injustice—including cultural imperialism, exploitation, marginalization, and powerlessness—is acknowledged.

International human rights, including women's rights as human rights, were examined as the central focus of social justice. The International Bill of Rights, the proposed Declaration of Indigenous Rights, and violence against women and violations of human rights from war crimes (public sphere) to domestic violence (private sphere) have served as the primary examples. Finally, advocacy strategies from the international to the local were reviewed. The act of writing this chapter is another strategy, for its placement in a textbook for social work students serves to educate, to inform, and to move to action.

Indigenous peoples understand that spiritually, and in reality, justice is shaped every day through attitudes and reinforced through interactions with others and with the environment. These attitudes and actions can nurture or contaminate future generations. To help shape social justice, social work students must understand that social work must be more than a paycheck, more than a career. Social justice requires the understanding that diversity fuels life, that the Earth and its populations are vulnerable to violence, the misuse of power, and oppression. Social workers who respond to social justice understand that this requires continual study and vigilance, self-reflection, the courage to change as new information comes to light, and the responsibility to act, both individually and collectively, as new understandings are formed. Above all, social justice requires the recognition of that which is dead and temporary, that which is living, that which must be respected, and that which must be preserved.

References

Aristide, Jean-Beltran, (2000). *Eyes of the Heart: Seeking a path for the poor in the age of globalization.* Common Courage.

Barker, F. (1962). *Social contract.* New York: Oxford University Press.

Barten, F. (1994). Health in a city environment. *World Health, 47* (3), 24–25.

Benhabib, S. (1992). *Situating the self: Gender, community and postmodernism in contemporary ethics.* New York: Routledge.

Boyd, S. (1997). Challenging the public/private divide: An overview. In S. Boyd (Ed.), *Challenging the public/private divide: Feminism, law, and public policy.* Toronto: University of Toronto Press.

Bunch, C. (1995). Transforming human rights from a feminist perspective. In J. Peters & A. Wolper (Eds.), *Women's rights, human rights: International feminist perspectives* (pp. 11–17). New York: Routledge.

Bunch, C., & Reilly, N. (1994). *Demanding accountability: The global campaign and Vienna Tribunal for Women's Human Rights.* New Brunswick, NJ: Rutgers University, Center for Women's Global Leadership.

Davidson, A. (1994). *Endangered peoples.* San Francisco: Sierra Club Books.

Devall, W. B. (1976). Social science research on support of human rights. In R. P. Claude (Ed.), *Comparative human rights* (pp. 326–352). Baltimore: Johns Hopkins University Press.

Friedman, E. (1995). Women's human rights: The emergence of a movement. In J. Peters & A. Wolper (Eds.), *Women's rights, human rights: International feminist perspectives* (pp. 18–35). New York: Routledge.

Human Rights Watch (1997). Available online at http://www.hrw.org; (2000b) http://www.hrw.org/wr2k1/women/index.html

International Bill of Human Rights (1993). New York: United Nations.

Kenyan tradition confronted: A beaten wife goes to court. (1997, October 31). *New York Times,* p. A5.

Kunstler, J. H. (1993). *The geography of nowhere.* New York: Simon & Schuster.

Largoza-Maza, L. (1995). The Medium Term Philippine Development Plan toward the year 2000: Filipino women's issues and perspectives. In J. Peters & A. Wolper (Eds.), *Women's rights, human rights: International feminist perspectives* (pp. 62–65). New York: Routledge.

Midgley, J. (1997). *Social welfare in a global context.* Thousand Oaks, CA: Sage Publications.

Nakajima, H. (1997). Let's work together to control infectious diseases. *World Health, 50* (1), p. 3.

Minnesota Gay Homicide Study. Available online at http://www.mngayhomicide. org/timeline.html.

Okin, S. M. (1989). *Justice, gender, and the family.* New York: Basic Books.

Peters, J., & Wolper, A. (1995). *Women's rights, human rights: International feminist perspectives.* New York: Routledge.

Pietilä, H. & Vickers, J. (1996). Making women matter: The role of the United Nations (3rd ed.). Atlantic Highlands, NJ: Zed Books.

Rao, A. (1995). The politics of gender and culture in international human rights discourse. In J. Peters & A. Wolper (Eds.), *Women's rights, human rights: International feminist perspectives* (pp. 167–175). New York: Routledge.

Rasmussen. L. L. (1994). And earth ethic for survival. In *Ethics & Agenda 21: Moral implications of a global consensus* (pp. 54–57). New York: United Nations.

Reiss, A., & Roth, J. A. (Eds.). (1993). *Understanding and preventing violence* (Vol. 1). Washington, DC: National Academy Press.

Simons, M. (1998, March 9). Cry of Muslim women for equal rights is rising. *New York Times*, pp. A1, A6.

Smith, D. M. (1994). *Geography and social justice.* Oxford: Blackwell.

Stamatopoulou, E. (1995). Women's rights and the United Nations. In J. Peters & A. Wolper (Eds.), *Women's rights, human rights: International feminist perspectives* (pp. 36–48). New York: Routledge.

Suarez Toro, M. (1995). Popularizing women's human rights at the local level: A grassroots methodology for setting an international agenda. In J. Peters & A. Wolper (Eds.), *Women's rights, human rights: International feminist perspectives* (pp. 1189–1194). New York: Routledge.

Toffler, A. (1990). *Powershift: Knowledge, wealth, and violence at the edge of the 21st century.* New York: Bantam Books.

Toffler A., & Toffler, H. (1995). *Creating a new civilization: The politics of the third wave.* Atlanta: Turner.

United Nations Working Group on Indigenous Peoples. (1998). *Draft of the Declaration of Human Rights for Indigenous Peoples.* Available online at http:// www.hawaiination.org/iitc/decltext.html.

Young, I. M. (1990). *Justice and politics of difference.* Princeton, NJ: Princeton University Press.

Additional Resources

Web Sites

http://www.un.org/rights   International Bill of Human Rights
http://www.hrw.org   Human Rights Watch
http://www.un.org/rights   U. N. Commission on Human Rights
http://www.un.org/womenwatch/un   Womenwatch

The UN Human Rights Umbrella

UN Children's Fund
Office of the UN High Commissioner for Refugees—legal and humanitarian
    protection
UN Commission on the Status of Women—women's rights
International Labor Organization—worker's rights
UN Educational, Scientific, and Cultural Organization—human rights
UN Development Program—economic and social development respectful of
    human rights
World Health Organization—right to health
UN High Commission for Human Rights—human rights complaints; human
    rights database

Human Rights Laws

Convention on the Prevention and Punishment of the Crime of Genocide (1948)
Convention Relating to the Status of Refugees (1961)
International Convention on the Elimination of All Forms of Racial Discrimina-
    tion (1965)
Convention on the Elimination of All Forms of Discrimination against Women
    (1979)
Convention against Torture and Other Cruel, Inhuman or Degrading Treatment
    or Punishment (1984)
Convention on the Rights of the Child (1989)
International Convention on the Protection of the Rights of All Migrant Workers
    and Members of their Families (1990; ratified by 9 countries, requires 20)

Who monitors compliance? Six committees (listed below) monitor the compliance of states and parties to specific treaties and laws listed above. Committees
may call on governments to respond to allegations and may adopt decisions and
punish governments without criticisms or recommendations. *Rapporteurs* (representatives) or experts gather facts, visit prisons, interview victims, and make

recommendations on how to increase respect for human rights in specific areas: torture, religious intolerance, racism, sale of children, and violence against women. Reports of the rapporteurs help mobilize international attention.

Committee on the Elimination of Racial Discrimination
Committee on the Rights of the Child
Committee on Education, Social and Cultural Rights
Committee against Torture
Committee on the Elimination of Discrimination against Women
Human Rights Committee

CHAPTER 3

Professional Values and Ethics

Brenda G. McGowan
Marian Mattison

Professional social work education has tended to emphasize the acquisition of knowledge and skills required for effective practice while somewhat neglecting understanding of the values that affect practice decisions. Yet social workers' values, both professional and personal, are the primary determinant of their service decisions and actions on behalf of clients. Thus, it seems essential that a text on foundations of social work practice present an overview of social work values and ethical issues before addressing the specifics of different modalities and methods of practice.

This chapter examines the ways in which values shape professional decision making; reviews historical shifts in professional ethical concerns; identifies core social work values, ethics, and legal responsibilities; examines the ways social workers address ethical issues; explores alternative frameworks for analyzing ethical dilemmas; and presents an applied case example of systematic ethical decision making.

Role of Values in Social Workers' Decision Making

The primacy of professional values in practitioners' decision making and action derives from four sources. First, the social services programs and other institutions in which social workers are employed have all been established to serve specific populations and to accomplish definite purposes. Decisions about whom to serve and to what end always reflect choices among values. Beginning students need only review the mission statements of different field placement settings to realize how these choices differ from one organization to another and how value-laden the settings are. Even apparently neutral goals such as "promoting independence," "preventing delinquency," or "enhancing family life" reflect decisions about which social issues should be given priority.

Second, as Reamer (1990) has demonstrated, decisions made by individual practitioners about service objectives and priorities in different cases reflect value choices about which are most important. These value choices are shaped by professional training and agency imperatives (Billingsley, 1964; Congress, 1986), professional roles (Holland & Kilpatrick, 1991), and the individual preferences of the decision maker (Abramson, 1996). Take, for example, the case of a substance-abusing single mother who had been in recovery but has started drinking again. Her case is under supervision from child protective services for neglectful behavior toward her children, ages eight and 10. The social worker learns that she has not shown up for work for three days, spending much of her time in an alcoholic stupor and neglecting the children's needs.

The children plead with the social worker to "give Mom one more chance." The mother acknowledges her mistake and promises to stop drinking immediately. In a show of resolution, she pours all the remaining alcohol in the house down the drain as the social worker looks on. Knowing that if she reports the substance abuse the children will be removed from the household, the social worker must decide what course of action to take. Should she report the drinking? Is the priority to help the mother re-enroll in an alcohol treatment program? Is it in the best interests of the children to remove them from the home to prevent further neglect? Should the social worker advocate for the mother at her workplace, knowing that employment is the lifeline that will keep this family together? The ultimate selection of a preferred choice of action lies in the case circumstances and the value system or preferences of the social worker (Keith-Lucas, 1977).

Third, because time and resources are chronically scarce in human services agencies, social workers must frequently make choices about the amount of time they will devote to different activities with different clients and which clients will be granted access to supplementary benefits such as summer camp opportunities for children, food vouchers, or psychiatric consultation. When a social worker must cancel two scheduled appointments because he or she is called to appear in court, should the clients' ability to pay be a consideration? If the worker has time to see only one of these clients later in the day, should the alternative time slot be given to the client with full insurance reimbursement in preference to the one who can make only a modest payment? Lewis (1972) convincingly argued that such decisions reflect value choices about which clients are most worthy or deserving of help and which types of problems deserve the greatest attention.

Finally, as Loewenberg (1984) discussed, because of limitations in empirically based social work knowledge and a relative absence of the middle-range theories required to guide practice, social workers often resort to personal value preferences when deciding which theoretical approach or modality to employ in a specific case. For example, in cases of wife abuse, practitioners have no hard evidence available to help them decide what they should try to accomplish and whether they should rely on feminist, family systems, or behavioral theory to help these families. Consequently, they are likely to choose the approach that fits best with their agencies' or their own values regarding marital and family relationships and the primacy of different family members' interests.

Shifts in Professional Ethical Concerns

Despite the primacy of values in professional decision making, social workers value priorities and concerns have shifted dramatically over the years. In the late 19th century, the friendly visitors who volunteered in such agencies as the Charity Organization Society and the Association for Improving the Condition of the Poor focused their concerns primarily on the morality of their clients. The writings of this period referred frequently to the shortcomings of the destitute and distinguished repeatedly between the "worthy" and "unworthy" poor. The consistent emphasis of these early workers was on helping poor people reform themselves by overcoming their alleged "character defects" of thriftlessness, laziness, intemperance, and immorality.

This attitude began to shift around the turn of the century with the development of the settlement house movement. Some of the leading figures in this movement raised persistent questions about the morality of social and economic institutions that denied poor people the opportunity to care properly for themselves and their children. Although these early social reformers advocated vigorously for changed societal values, they gave little explicit attention to the task of defining their own professional values.

It was only in the 1920s that social workers began to examine the morality of the profession itself and to discuss how best to define professional ethics. Despite several efforts to draft a professional code of ethics during that decade, no formal code of social work ethics was established until the American Association of Social Workers adopted one in 1951. The National Association of Social Workers (NASW), established in 1955 in a merger of seven professional social work organizations, adopted its first code of professional ethics in 1960 (Loewenberg & Dolgoff, 1996).

One reason for the delay in promulgating a code of professional ethics is that the efforts to do so in the 1920s were initiated in the context of a broader movement to obtain full professional status for the field of social work.

Consequently, primacy was given to the tasks of identifying common professional knowledge and skills rather than values, and this emphasis continued throughout the next few decades. Reamer (1983) suggested that another reason for the relative inattention to professional ethics from the 1930s to the 1950s was that "the early years of the profession also happened to coincide with an era in which science and the scientific method were in the academic limelight" (p. 31). (Muriel Pumphrey's classic 1959 text was a clear exception to this characterization of the period.) As a result, during this period social work, like other professions, focused on issues that could be addressed empirically, not on ethical and value concerns.

Until the 1970s, professional education emphasized basic knowledge of the social work values that underscore professional identity and practice. As resources became scarce, malpractice suits increased, and technology advanced far beyond abilities to distinguish clearly between right and wrong, social workers increasingly found themselves confronted with the task of making difficult judgments about the correctness of their actions with clients. Since that time, social workers, like many other professional groups, have given increased attention to ethical and value dilemmas and ways to reduce subjectivity in decision making. This shift in orientation has been demonstrated by the introduction of many graduate and undergraduate courses on ethics and by the publication of multiple articles and texts on the topic of social work ethics (see, for example, Levy, 1976; Lewis, 1972; Loewenberg & Dolgoff, 1996; Reamer, 1983, 1990; Reamer & Abramson, 1982; Rhodes, 1991). Among the many reasons for this renewed interest in ethical issues are the following:

- rapid social and technological changes that have posed new value dilemmas for the profession
- increased attention to ethical issues by other human services professionals as evidenced, for example, by the development of bioethics committees in hospitals and required courses on ethics for medical students
- consumers' challenges to the assumed authority of all professionals
- more stringent regulation of social work and other human services professions by public funding agencies and the courts
- more widespread publicity in the media about egregious violations of client rights by members of different professions
- greater political sophistication about the inherent conflict of interests between human services bureaucracies and the people they are designed to serve
- growing recognition of the ways in which even the development and use of different types of knowledge reflect professional value choices.

Distinguishing Values, Ethics, and Legal Responsibilities

Values and Ethics

Although the terms "values" and "ethics" are often used interchangeably, they refer to different concepts. As Loewenberg and Dolgoff (1996) noted, "values are concerned with what is *good* and *desirable*, while ethics deal with what is *right* and *correct*" (p. 21). Although professional values are often defined as one of the core distinguishing characteristics of the social work profession, these values reflect larger societal values and express general preferences rather than specific directives for action.

Professional ethics, in contrast, provide guidelines about how members of the profession can translate their values into action. In other words, they provide direction about how people *ought to act*. They are, therefore, more specific, demanding, and potentially controversial. Although professional values offer social workers directives and "conceptions of the desirable" (Kluckhohn, 1951, p. 403), they are frequently stated at a general level and thus cannot provide social workers with sufficient behavioral directives (Perlman, 1976).

Although there have been repeated debates throughout the history of the profession about how social work values are best implemented, there is relative agreement about the values themselves and which should be emphasized in the training of new social workers. Discussions of social work values frequently highlight such concepts as upholding the dignity and worth of each individual, facilitating client self-determination, respecting diversity, providing the opportunities and resources that people need to achieve self-actualization, fostering the empowerment of clients, promoting social justice, safeguarding clients' confidentiality, respecting colleagues, and accepting responsibility for one's own professional conduct. The manner in which one operationalizes these values into behavioral acts is less certain (Perlman, 1976). What are the boundaries and limits to client self-determination? At what point should self-determination be sacrificed if the client engages in behavior that the social worker views as self-destructive? Should client confidentiality be sacrificed when it may result in harm to others?

The importance attached to values and ethics in social work education is demonstrated in the requirements of the Council on Social Work Education (CSWE), the accrediting body for all schools of social work in the United States. The recently revised *Educational Policy and Accreditation Standards* of CSWE (2001) highlights the requirements as follows:

> Social work education programs integrate content about values and principles of ethical decision making as presented in the National Association

of Social Workers Code of Ethics. The educational experience provides students with the opportunity to be aware of personal values; develop, demonstrate, and promote the values of the profession; and analyze ethical dilemmas and the ways in which these affect practice, services, and clients. (Section IV.A)

The potential value of specific ethics courses has been argued in the professional literature (Reamer & Abramson, 1982) and documented by research. Social workers who have taken a separate or discrete course in ethics demonstrate broader analytic and decision-making skills as these relate to ethical decisions (Joseph & Conrad, 1983).

Ethics refers to those rules of conduct that direct people to act in a manner consistent with the values they profess (Lewis, 1982). For social workers, these rules are embodied in the NASW *Code of Ethics* (presented in Appendix A), which was adopted in 1979 and revised in 1990, 1994, 1996, and 1999. This code is designed "to serve as a guide to the everyday conduct of professional social workers" (NASW, 1999) by articulating the profession's basic values, ethical principles, and ethical standards. Based on the fundamental values of the profession, the code specifies standards of behavior regarding social workers ethical responsibilities to clients, to colleagues, in practice settings, as professionals, to the profession, and to the broader society. The code is also recognized as the source of professional standards against which social workers' behavior will be measured in cases of alleged ethical misconduct.

Although technically only NASW members can be held responsible for abiding by the provisions of the code, many schools of social work mandate that their students follow this code, and state regulatory agencies and courts often rely on provisions of the code to determine whether social workers who are charged with violations have acted in accordance with accepted professional principles. Therefore, it is important for all professional social workers and social work students to be informed about the ethical provisions of this code and to behave accordingly. Unfortunately, recent research confirms that, all too often, social workers are unfamiliar with the basic provisions of the code (Mattison, 1994). Social workers do not consistently meet their obligations to "take into consideration all the values, principles, and standards in this *Code* that are relevant to any situation in which ethical judgment is warranted" (NASW, 1999, p. 3).

Legal Responsibilities

Interestingly, although social work values and ethics reflect collective voluntary preferences and decisions about what professionals should believe and how they should act, many of these values and ethical standards are embodied in state laws and regulations and court decisions promulgated to regulate the behavior of social workers. In the early days of social work, there were few, if any, laws governing professional performance. Since the 1970s, however, there has been a rapid expansion of regulatory mechanisms designed to govern the behavior of social workers and other human services professionals. Social workers must now be knowledgeable about their legal duties as well as their ethical responsibilities and the ways in which the two may converge and diverge.

Social work is a socially mandated profession that has been given authority to perform certain functions for the community and prohibited from performing other activities that are delegated to different professions. With the authority to perform certain social functions comes legal responsibility to perform these tasks in an acceptable manner and a set of legal obligations to the clients one is serving. These legal duties are perhaps best understood as an essential component of the fiduciary relationship that social workers develop with clients.

As Kutchins (1991) discussed in his seminal article on this topic, the fiduciary relationship with clients derives from the fact that social workers, like other professionals, have specialized knowledge and skills that their clients do not possess. Therefore, when clients consult with a social worker—or a physician or a lawyer—they essentially grant the professional the authority to influence them in unforeseen ways and trust that the professional will act in their best interests. This arrangement is different from a business contract in which it is assumed that the two parties are equal and that they each must protect their own interests.

The concept of fiduciary responsibility is usually applied to relationships in which the professional or trustee assumes some financial obligation in relation to a client and makes economic decisions on behalf of this person. However, a number of recent court cases have used this concept to describe the obligations that human services professionals have to their clients. Although legal theory and case law in this area is still evolving, Kutchins (1991) identified three key areas in which the fiduciary responsibilities of the social worker seem clear: (1) confidentiality, (2) duty to tell the truth, and (3) loyalty to clients.

Right to Confidentiality. The right to confidentiality is protected legally as a result of a series of case decisions as well as by the statutes of many states granting clients of licensed or certified social workers privileged information status. This means that the information clients divulge to their social workers cannot be revealed without their consent unless there is a significant, legally recognized reason such as a mandated report of suspected child maltreatment or the threat of imminent danger to the client or another person.

Duty to Tell the Truth. The duty to tell the truth encompasses not only the social worker's responsibility to deal honestly with clients and to report honestly on his or her practice, but also the fiduciary obligation to ensure that clients give informed consent to any proposed social work intervention and to the release of any information about them. This means that clients must be fully informed about the nature and intent of any proposed service or release of information, possible risks and benefits, potential effects on them and their significant others, available alternatives, and projected costs (Reamer, 1987). The potential ramifications of this obligation are enormous and have not been fully examined by the profession. For example, social workers are often encouraged to exaggerate or modify diagnoses to make clients eligible for specific services or insurance reimbursements. Yet, as Kutchins (1991) pointed out, "Deliberate misdiagnoses place practitioners in great jeopardy of being sued by clients, insurance companies, and others. Practitioners also risk loss of their licenses and criminal prosecution" (p. 111).

Concept of Loyalty. The concept of loyalty to clients means that the professional has a fiduciary responsibility to place client interests first when there is any conflict of duty to the client, the employer, or another interested party. Unfortunately, this concept can sound deceptively simple. Because the NASW *Code of Ethics* also spells out social workers' responsibilities to colleagues, their practice settings, the profession, and society at large, social workers often feel torn between these potentially competing loyalties. The profession has provided relatively little guidance to social workers in the past about how best to resolve such conflicts. However, recent malpractice suits have led to "growing recognition of the fiduciary relationship and legal obligations that result from the trust that clients place in professionals" (Kutchins, 1991, p. 112). Thus, one may expect clearer standards for professional performance in the future.

Ethical Dilemmas in Social Work Practice

Ethical dilemmas arise when social workers are confronted by situations that pose two conflicting values and they find that they are unable to serve each obligation with equal justice. Hospital social workers, for example, are often torn between trying to arrange safe discharge plans for frail, elderly patients who cannot care for themselves safely at home alone and respecting the patients' right to decide where they want to live and whether they want any support from family members or providers of home health care. In such cases, the social workers face an ethical dilemma, a situation in which the choice is between two or more courses of action that cannot be attained simultaneously, each of which may be potentially good or bad. They must decide whether they want to promote client self-determination or protect the well-being of their patients. Which value should be served foremost?

Often, in practice, when a social worker conforms to one principle set forth by the NASW *Code of Ethics*, another must be abandoned (Aroskar, 1980). Although the principles espoused in the *Code* "help to create a normative system which should provide guidelines in a variety of practice situations" (Goldmeir, 1984, p. 47), by its very nature, the *Code* is not designed to be prescriptive.

> The NASW *Code of Ethics* does not specify which values, principles, and standards are most important and ought to outweigh others in instances when they conflict. Reasonable differences of opinion can and do exist among social workers with respect to the ways in which values, ethical principles, and ethical standards should be rank ordered when they conflict. Ethical decision making in a given situation must apply the informed judgment of the individual social worker and should also consider how the issues would be judged in a peer review process where the ethical standards of the profession would be applied. (NASW, 1999, p. 3)

Consider the case of Anna, a divorced 23-year-old mother of two. Anna has been in treatment for seven months following a suicide attempt and repeated episodes of depression. She has established a warm and trusting relationship with the social worker, saying "She's the only one I can talk to." While her children are visiting their father, Anna's depression worsens. She calls the social worker, threatening suicide, and pleads with the worker to come to her home to "help me." Anna cannot be convinced to leave her home and come to the clinic. Agency policy prohibits home visits under any circumstances because the agency has been unable to secure liability insurance to cover meetings with clients outside the clinic. Should the social worker visit the client in her home, acting on the professional obligation "to help people in need" (NASW, 1999, p. 5)? Can violating agency policy be justified based on the potential greater good that may result for the client? To what extent is the social worker obligated to uphold the policy of the agency when, in the social worker's judgment, this conflicts with the best interests of the client?

Social workers must consider the entire range of principles in the NASW *Code of Ethics* that may be applicable in situations such as this. Determining which standards have relevance is by no means absolute. Practitioners bring to the process their proclivities toward interpreting relevance through their personal preferences, professional roles, obligations to follow specific laws and policies, practice experiences, motivations, attitudes, and other individualized perspectives. Because the code specifies responsibilities at many different levels (client, colleagues, practice setting, society, and profession), "different principles apply to different responsibilities" (Levy, 1993, p. 38). In the face of competing obligations and loyalties, social workers often find that professional obligations, as described in the *Code*, contradict one another when applied to concrete situations.

It is not uncommon for social workers to find that professional values conflict with the policies of their practice settings (Vigilante, 1983), creating additional ethical tensions. In Anna's case, a review of the standards of the NASW *Code of Ethics* indicates that the "Social workers' primary responsibility is to promote the well-being of clients" (NASW, 1999, Standard 1.01, p. 7). At the same time, Standard 3.09a states that "Social workers generally should adhere to commitments made to employers and employing organizations," and Standard 3.09d stipulates that "Social workers should not allow an employing organization's policies, procedures, regulations, or administrative orders to interfere with their ethical practice of social work" (NASW, 1999, p. 21). This identification of applicable ethical standards is a necessary step in the resolution of ethical dilemmas such as the one faced by Anna's social worker. However, given some of the tensions inherent in the *Code*, the social worker must also engage in a systematic decision-making process to resolve the conflict in a manner that is "consistent with the spirit as well as the letter of this *Code*" (NASW, 1999, p. 3).

Professional values may conflict with one another, as well as with agency policy. To illustrate, in a study of ethical dilemmas facing hospital social workers in St. Louis, Proctor, Morrow-Howell, and Lott (1993) discovered that 85 percent of the conflicts cited by the social workers reflected a conflict in the NASW *Code of Ethics*. Unlike attorneys, who define their responsibilities to clients as absolute, social workers are expected to consider the effect of their actions on others in their clients' environment and to remember their responsibilities to their practice settings and to society at large. Consequently, they are often forced to choose between doing what may best for their clients and what is best for other members of clients' families as, for instance, when they must decide whether to report a suspicion of child abuse against parents who have made real progress in marital treatment. Equally difficult questions arise when a member of a client family is too young or too impaired to act responsibly on his or her own behalf. For example, should a 14-year-old's right to confidentiality take precedence over the social worker's obligation to disclose information about the teenager's pregnancy to her parents when this information was shared in confidence? In a situation such as this, it may be impossible for the social worker to both "protect the confidentiality of all information obtained in the course of professional service" (NASW, 1999, Standard 1.07c, p. 10) and to "take reasonable steps to safeguard the interests and rights of those clients" who lack the capacity to make informed decisions (NASW, 1999, Standard 1.14, p. 14).

Increasingly, greater attention is being drawn to the conflicts that arise when the social worker feels obligated to represent professional values that he or she feels reluctant or unwilling to espouse. Strain develops when professional values are not compatible with the practitioner's personal values (Levy, 1976). For example, personal biases in areas such as sexual orientation can potentially prejudice the social worker's interventions with lesbian and gay clients. Yet, as Hess and Hess (1998) pointed out, "the profession's commitment to prepare practitioners who demonstrate respect for the inherent dignity and worth of all persons and actively pursue social justice and social change on behalf of vulnerable and oppressed individuals and groups explicitly includes persons of differing sexual orientations" (p. 32).

Unfortunately, there have been very few systematic studies of the ethical dilemmas social workers confront or how these dilemmas are resolved. As Holland and Kilpatrick (1991) noted, "Little is known about how practitioners respond to moral and ethical issues, how they understand and cope with these aspects of their work, or what resources are used or needed for improving performance in this area" (p. 138). The few research findings that are available raise troubling questions about social workers' apparent ignorance of and inattention to ethical standards (see, for example, Billingsley, 1964; Congress, 1986; Holland & Kilpatrick, 1991; Mattison, 1994).

These research findings are perhaps not surprising when one considers the complexity and intensity of historical debates regarding the proper criteria for resolving moral dilemmas. As Reamer (1983) noted, "The challenge of resolving difficult ethical dilemmas is an ancient one involving many schools of philosophical thought and principles of ethics regarding what constitutes right and wrong conduct and action" (p. 34). Such abstract debates are often of little interest to the doers and activists who tend to become social workers. However, all social workers have a responsibility to assess the ethical implications of their decisions and to develop a framework for addressing the value dilemmas that inevitably arise in practice. Furthermore, some may wish to assume a more active role in professional ethical debates by serving as members of hospital bioethics committees, agency ethics committees, or NASW's local and national committees on inquiry.

Ethical Relativism and Ethical Absolutism

In an attempt to resolve ethical dilemmas, social workers typically rely on two primary modes of reasoning that are rooted in moral philosophy. Although social workers may be unfamiliar with formal theories of contemporary philosophy, they often rely implicitly on the two major theories that underscore most approaches to ethical decision making: ethical relativism and ethical absolutism (Loewenberg & Dolgoff, 1996).

For ethical relativists, or Utilitarians, the ultimate criterion for what is to be considered morally right or wrong or obligatory is the amount of good produced as a result of the practice decision or action. Actions in themselves are not defined as inherently good or bad, but they may be viewed as good or bad by virtue of their consequences. Traditionally, social workers have been grounded in this utilitarian approach, making choices that they think will result in the greatest good for the greatest number. From this perspective, the client's right to self-determination can be limited if the exercise of this right would threaten the well-being of others. Believing that different and changing situations call for different ethical decisions, social workers are trained to pay careful attention to situational circumstances and to weigh the possible consequences of each proposed action.

In contrast, the ethical absolutists, or Deontologists, argue that certain actions are inherently good or right and emphasize the importance of fixed moral rules such as the client's right to self-determination. They believe that once formulated, ethical rules should be applied universally to all circumstances, regardless of the consequences they produce (Lewis, 1984).

Although these philosophical arguments are often used to justify different types of professional action, social work ethicists generally agree that neither approach provides sufficient guidance for ethical decision making in practice. Consequently, several alternative frameworks for the ethical analysis of dilemmas in social work practice have been proposed. Although no simple formula can ever be applied to the resolution of ethical dilemmas, these systematic frameworks are an attempt to move ethical decision making away from the intuitive and toward a cognitive approach grounded in reason and supported by an intellectual base (Emmet, 1962).

Frameworks for Analyzing Ethical Dilemmas

Reamer (1990), perhaps the leading ethicist in social work currently, proposed a systematic decision-making framework based on the principle of generic consistency proposed by moral philosopher Alan Gewirth (1978). This principle assumes that any responsible person will hold that he or she has a right to freedom and well-being; hence, to be consistent, the ethical person must refrain from interfering with the freedom and well-being of others. Gewirth also argued that conflicting duties can be rank ordered in hierarchical fashion based on the goods involved.

Based on the principle of generic consistency, Reamer formulated six rules or guidelines that can be used to analyze and resolve ethical dilemmas in social work (Figure 3-1). These guidelines are presented in lexical order so that each principle is stated in order of priority, with the higher-order principles taking precedence over the lower ones. Although the application of these guidelines will not result in clear solutions to all individual case dilemmas, this approach helps practitioners to make their value assumptions more explicit and to think more systematically about the ethical conflicts they confront. Guidelines such as these "require considerable interpretation, speculation, and inference, all of which invite and ordinarily result in some measure of disagreement" (Reamer, 1995, p. 63).

Figure 3-1. Ethical Guidelines Proposed by Frederic Reamer

1. Rules against basic harms to the necessary preconditions of action (such as life, health, food, shelter, mental equilibrium) take precedence over rules against harms such as lying or revealing confidential information, or threats to additive goods, such as recreation, education, and wealth.

2. An individual's right to basic well-being (including goods that are essential for human action) takes precedence over another individual's right to self-determination.

3. An individual's right to self-determination takes precedence over his or her own right to basic well-being.

4. The obligation to obey laws, rules, and regulations to which one has voluntarily and freely consented ordinarily overrides one's right to engage voluntarily and freely in a manner that conflicts with these laws, rules, and regulations.

5. Individuals' rights to well-being may override laws, rules, regulations, and arrangements of voluntary associations in cases of conflict.

6. The obligation to prevent basic harms such as starvation and to promote public goods such as housing, education, and public assistance overrides the right to complete control over one's property.

SOURCE: From *Ethical Dilemmas in Practice*, by F. G. Reamer © 1989 Columbia University Press, and most recently in *Social Work Values and Ethics*, by F. G. Reamer © 1995 Columbia University Press. Reprinted with the permission of the publisher.

Figure 3-2. Ethical Principles Screen

Ethical Principle 1: Principle of the protection of life

Ethical Principle 2: Principle of equality and inequality

Ethical Principle 3: Principle of autonomy and freedom

Ethical Principle 4: Principle of least harm

Ethical Principle 5: Principle of quality of life

Ethical Principle 6: Principle of privacy and confidentiality

Ethical Principle 7: Principle of truthfulness and full disclosure

SOURCE: Reprinted with permission from Loewenberg, F. M., & Dolgoff, R. (1996). *Ethical Decisions for Social Work Practice* (5th ed., p. 39). Itasca, IL: F. E. Peacock.

In the fifth edition of their now classic text on social work ethics, *Ethical Decisions for Social Work Practice*, Loewenberg and Dolgoff (1996) presented their approach to ethical decision making, which is based on a lexical ordering of principles (Figure 3-2). In this respect, it is similar to Reamer's style of analyzing ethical dilemmas. Although there is no evidence that resolving ethical dilemmas according to a hierarchy of principles results in preferred ethical behaviors, both of these models organize ethical criteria logically and encourage practitioners to engage in systematic, deliberate decision-making processes.

A more recent model proposed by Mattison (1997) detailed a step-by-step process that social workers can readily adapt and use to resolve ethical dilemmas. The hallmarks of this approach are a pragmatic framework to guide the analysis and resolution of ethical dilemmas and a continuous awareness that the process of ethical decision making is highly sensitive to the values and preferences of the decision maker. At each progressive stage of decision making, the social worker is encouraged to be alert to the mutual interdependence of the analytic tool and the individual exercising the decision-making process. A case example will serve to illustrate the use of this framework.

Case Example

Martin (age 68) has diabetes and is hospitalized for an infection related to his recent surgery to remove his lower left leg. He is soon to be discharged from the local hospital. Martin has emphysema and has had recurrent hospitalizations over the past six months. Martin's other medical conditions include chronic arthritis and psoriasis.

Martin's wife Elizabeth (age 65) is in good health. She has become increasingly frustrated with the chronicity of Martin's deteriorating health. She is angered by his constant demands, physical needs, and the fact that he "won't do" for himself. Elizabeth reports she is "housebound" caring for Martin "day in and day out."

Martin is eligible for a number of community services but refuses to cooperate with the providers. He wants only his wife to tend to his daily care. He has been verbally abusive toward the nurses and home health providers; as a result, these providers visit at the bare minimum, adding to the burden on Elizabeth to change dressings, administer medication, and maintain daily personal grooming. Slowly, Elizabeth has withdrawn from outside social contacts and activities as Martin's demands for her attention have increased. In confidence, Elizabeth shares with the social worker that she has, on occasion, been physically abusive toward Martin. She has denied him meals, refused to bathe him, and once struck him in anger. She is embarrassed and ashamed of these behaviors.

At a meeting with the social worker to finalize discharge plans, Elizabeth shares that the pressure has become so great that prior to Martin's release from the hospital she plans to move out of their home. She feels that her husband "will learn" to accept the help of other providers if she is not there to "coddle him." She says, "I've reached the end of my rope. Now with the added pressure of the amputation, I can't take it anymore." Elizabeth confides that her son has been providing her with a monthly allowance that she has secretly set aside over the past six years. A friend has a room to rent, and Elizabeth plans to use these savings to pay the costs of renting the room. Elizabeth intends to apply for public assistance by declaring that she is without income. She pleads with the social worker not to tell anyone of her plans.

Martin's discharge assessment indicates that he is capable of providing self-care, yet the social worker strongly suspects that Martin will not assume responsibility for his daily care. Although there is no conclusive evidence to suggest that Martin should not be discharged, with the new information regarding Elizabeth's plans, the social worker is hesitant to discharge immediately. Although the social worker believes that with a little more time and some "convincing" Elizabeth could be coaxed to reconsider her plans to move out, there is the pressure to empty the bed.

Model for Analyzing Ethical Dilemmas

Phase 1: Gather and Assess Case Background Information and Case Details. The process of ethical decision making begins with the clear understanding of case details and background information. The social worker must gather and assess the particular case circumstances as they relate to the client and the client system. Information gathering and assessment is by no means a value-free process. The inclusion or omission of certain information, the decision about who is the primary client to whom the social worker is obligated, and the presentation of the facts in any given order are each influenced and shaped by the decision maker.

Phase 2: Separating the Practice Considerations and Ethical Components. How well social workers respond to ethical dilemmas depends, in part, on whether the ethical issues are distinguished from the practice issues and how the worker has learned to think about the ethical issues. Without distinguishing the practice considerations from the value issues, the worker runs the risk of selecting a course of action based on practice principles. Both practice considerations and ethical considerations must be assessed for the decision maker to ultimately justify the choice of action. For example, from a practice perspective, in the case of Martin, the worker needs to know what legal obligation she has to report the suspected abuse and must be clear on policies regarding client confidentiality. These are both elements of sound practice. The ethical considerations include questions such as the following:

- Is the legal obligation to report the suspected abuse absolute?
- Based on possible consequences of reporting, is it possible that a greater good may be served by not reporting?
- At what point is the disclosure of confidential information justifiable or warranted based on the possible consequences of such actions?
- Is it justifiable for the social worker to "convince" Elizabeth to remain in the home?

Table 3-1 illustrates how social workers might distinguish practice and ethical elements of this case. The listing is by no means all inclusive; the value perspective of the decision maker will shape how one differentiates the practice and ethical components.

Phase 3: Identifying Value Tensions. Identifying the competing responsibilities to which one is obliged aids the decision maker in determining which priority to favor. The ultimate resolution of the ethical dilemma involves selecting one obligation over others, knowing that meeting one obligation may come at the expense of others.

The following are value tensions:

- self-determination versus professional paternalism
- confidentiality versus disclosure based on "compelling professional reasons"

Table 3-1. Practice Considerations versus Ethical Considerations in the Case Study	
Practice Considerations	Ethical Considerations
Securing the best possible care and medical attention	Client's right to self-determination
Facilitating discharge planning in a timely manner	Professional paternalism
	To whom does the social worker owe primary loyalty, service, and consideration?
Well-being of the client and client system	
Legal obligations: Suspected abuse	Protecting client confidentiality; are there compelling professional reasons for disclosure?
Financial deception	
Client confidentiality	
Agency policies relevant to case circumstances	Discretionary judgment based on practice wisdom, personal biases, and preference influences
Theoretical knowledge of the aging process	
Understanding of caregiver burdens and consequences	
Knowledge of community resources	
Familiarity with adult protective services	

- legal obligation versus perceived "greater good"
- commitment to agency policy versus discretionary judgment
- the client's right to self-determination versus judgments shaped by personal values
- the rights of the individual versus the well-being of the family system.

Phase 4: Identifying Principles in the Code of Ethics That Bear on the Case. Social workers should consult the NASW *Code of Ethics* (1996) to understand the ethical standards to which they are obligated and by which standards their actions will be judged. Social workers are cautioned to remember that identifying which principles in the *Code* are applicable to a particular case is conditioned by the judgment of the decision maker. Among the standards social workers might consider in the case of Martin and Elizabeth are the following:

1. Social workers' ethical responsibilities to clients
    1.01 Commitment to clients
    1.02 Self-determination
    1.03 Informed consent
    1.06 Conflicts of interest (a) and (d)
    1.07 Privacy and confidentiality (a), (c), (d), (e), (f), and (g)
2. Social workers' ethical responsibilities to colleagues
    2.03 Interdisciplinary collaboration (a)
    2.05 Consultation (a)

3. Social workers' ethical responsibilities in practice settings
   3.09 Commitments to employers (a) and (d)
4. Social workers' ethical responsibilities as professionals
   4.04 Dishonesty, fraud, and deception.

Phase 5: Identifying Possible Courses of Action. As discussed, social workers judge possible courses of action based on consideration of the potential risks and benefits of each or a commitment to a law, rule, or policy that relates to the given case. As a part of this analysis, the decision maker is encouraged to identify the possible courses of action available and the extent to which the needs of different members of the client system might be served or not served by each option. An ethical dilemma is such that any possible course of action will result in both benefits and harms simultaneously. The decision maker is encouraged to consider the benefits and harms to the client system, to the social worker, and to the broader society. (A preferred treatment option is usually one in which there is no ethical dilemma present.)

The four potential courses of action listed in Table 3-2 are not listed in rank order fashion nor are they exclusive of one another. They are not meant to represent all possible courses of action for this case.

Phase 6: Assessing Which Obligation Deserves Priority and Justifying the Choice of Action. This stage in the process involves the weighing and measuring of information gathered in the previous stages. The decision maker has been engaged in considering the obligations on all levels and now must determine which priority, obligation, or value to honor above the others. It is here that explicit consideration be given to why a particular choice of action seems most appropriate. This consideration not only requires a review of all the facts and information, but also self-reflection on the part of the social worker:

- Should the decision be based on an absolute ethical principle?
- Does the social worker feel an obligation to adhere to a rule or principle independent of the consequences?
- Upon which ethical principle can the decision be justified?
- Should a choice of action be selected based on the possible consequences that might follow?
- Is the social worker relying on a list of principles or obligations and satisfying higher-order obligations over lower obligations?

Ultimately, the priority for action may be based on practice principles; legal imperatives; the social worker's experiences with cases of a similar

Table 3-2. Evaluating Possible Courses of Action in the Case Study

Possible Courses of Action

Preferred treatment option: Reconcile tensions between Martin and Elizabeth and develop a strategy that serves the compromised interests of both.

1. Maintain Elizabeth's confidence; discharge Martin to his home.
2. Maintain Elizabeth's confidence; "convince" Elizabeth to remain at home.
3. Disclose Elizabeth's plan to move, and respect her decision; discharge Martin to his home.
4. Report suspected abuse.

POSSIBLE BENEFITS/HARMS TO PROPOSED COURSES OF ACTION

Plan 1: Maintain Elizabeth's confidence; discharge Martin to his home.

Client focus: Elizabeth

Possible Benefits	Possible Harms
Elizabeth's right to self-determination is fostered.	Martin is without or refuses needed care.
Elizabeth is afforded the opportunity to regain personal and social strength.	Elizabeth experiences guilt over abandonment.
Elizabeth feels relieved of Martin's care.	Martin's health deteriorates.
Martin is pressed to accept outside care.	

Client focus: Martin

Possible Benefits	Possible Harms
Martin learns to accept outside care.	Martin is overwhelmed by the discovery that his wife has moved away.
Martin becomes more self-sufficient.	Martin is without or refuses needed care.
Martin is no longer the victim of abuse.	Martin experiences health declines.
	Martin loses his will to live.

Focus: Social Worker

Possible Benefits	Possible Harms
Plan fosters client self-determination.	Client is readmitted to the hospital in the near future; additional planning is required.
Plan adheres to legal and professional responsibility.	Martin feels deceived by lack of disclosure.
Client confidentiality is protected.	
Social worker executes a timely discharge.	

Focus: Societal Resources

Possible Benefits	Possible Harms
Elizabeth returns to being a productive and contributing member of society.	Fraudulent financial reporting occurs.
Protective services is not burdened with the costs of an unfounded investigation.	Limits resources needed by others.
	Martin's rights to protection are thwarted if report of suspected abuse is not made.

Plan 2: Maintain Elizabeth's confidence; "convince" Elizabeth to remain in the home.

Client focus: Elizabeth

Possible Benefits	Possible Harms
Elizabeth fulfills her marital responsibility. Family system remains intact.	Old patterns are perpetuated. Elizabeth's right to self-determination is compromised. Elizabeth remains at home and experiences frustration and anger. Elizabeth conforms under pressure from the social worker.

Client focus: Martin

Possible Benefits	Possible Harms
Martin receives daily medical and social care. Stability of familiar patterns favor Martin's recovery.	Martin is the victim of abuse and neglect. Elizabeth's resentment builds.

Focus: Social Worker

Possible Benefits	Possible Harms
Timely discharge is executed. Perceived "best interests" of client are served. Martin receives adequate health care. Social worker abides by legal and agency policy. Social worker maintains Elizabeth's confidentiality.	Elizabeth is denied the right to self-determination. Elizabeth denies Martin care; readmission is necessary. Elizabeth experiences anger and depression.

Focus: Societal Resources

Possible Benefits	Possible Harms
Costs of skilled care are avoided. Family system remains intact.	Adequate protection of a citizen is denied.

Plan 3: Disclose Elizabeth's plans to move, and respect her decision; discharge Martin to his home.

Client focus: Elizabeth

Possible Benefits	Possible Harms
Elizabeth no longer bears the "secret." Martin recognizes the serious nature of the caregiver burden. Elizabeth is free to engage in her chosen lifestyle.	Client confidentiality and trust are disrupted. Client is exposed to Martin's anger. Client is worried about Martin's well-being.

Continued

Table 3-2. Continued

Client focus: Martin

Possible Benefits	Possible Harms
Self-determination is supported.	Daily care is unmet.
Martin begins to accept outside services.	Depression occurs.
Martin's relationship with his wife grows.	Physical and mental deterioration occurs.
	Only limited contact with his wife occurs.

Focus: Social Worker

Possible Benefits	Possible Harms
Plan respects client's self-determination.	Social worker fails to protect Martin's health and well-being.
Plan facilitates a timely discharge.	Social worker fails to protect Elizabeth's confidence.
Social worker relates to Martin in an honest fashion.	Social worker violates legal and professional obligation to protect confidence.

Focus: Societal Resources

Possible Benefits	Possible Harms
Client remains in his own home.	Unmet medical and social needs lead to more costly hospitalization.
Client maintains control over his destiny.	Martin is isolated.
Less costly home care is used.	Physical and emotional crises result.

Plan 4: Report suspected abuse.

Client focus: Elizabeth

Possible Benefits	Possible Harms
Client's "cry" for help is addressed	Client experiences shame and humiliation.
Client is free of "secret."	Relationship with Martin further deteriorates.
Client receives supportive counseling and advocacy.	Client experiences an invasion of privacy.
Protective services oversees case.	

Client focus: Martin

Possible Benefits	Possible Harms
Abusive and neglectful behavior ceases.	Elizabeth's anger is heightened.
Resulting services relieve tensions.	Client experiences an invasion of privacy.
Monitoring prevents future episodes.	Elizabeth blames or threatens Martin.
	Elizabeth acts on plan to move out.

Focus: Social Worker

Possible Benefits	Possible Harms
Social worker fulfills legal obligation to report suspected abuse.	Clients lose faith in the social worker.
Agency obligations are met.	Clients feel violated.
Elderly client receives protection.	Clients lose faith in the helping process.
Central record is established with protective services.	
Social worker is protected if further harm occurs.	

Focus: Societal Resources

Possible Benefits	Possible Harms
Elderly citizen receives protection from harm.	Costs of investigation outweigh resulting benefits.
Intervention results in improved marital relationship.	Investigation of unfounded cases exhausts limited resources.
	Invasion of privacy destroys marital relationship.

nature; a commitment to agency rules and obligations; professional paternalism; the assumptions, biases, or preferences of the decision maker; the social worker's role within the agency; or other considerations. The decision maker must justify the choice of action by indicating on what basis it was predicated.

Phase 7: Resolution and Reflection. Once the choice of action has been selected, justified, and implemented, there is benefit to the social worker in reflecting on the value preferences selected in the particular case. Understanding which values or ethical principles were given priority from among the competing alternatives can inform the social worker about his or her value patterning. Questions such as the following should be considered:

- To what extent did legal obligation influence my decision in this case?
- Was I willing to act outside of my legal obligations if doing so meant serving the client's best interests?
- Did the case involve a conflict between different clients' best interests?
- If the case involved a conflict between client self-determination andpaternalism, which value did I judge to be essential to honor foremost?
- To what extent did my personal values or philosophies influence the preferred choice of action?

As social workers evaluate their ethical decision making across cases, comparing past cases with present ethical decisions, they are likely to identify their patterns of response. This feedback can inform social workers about their individualized approaches to ethical dilemmas and inform future decision making. As social workers recognize their individual decision-making styles or patterns, they can strive to account for biases that may unknowingly influence their practice decisions.

Conclusion

The goal of this chapter is to heighten social workers' awareness of the value and ethical components of decision making in practice. Although decisions in practice are grounded in theoretical and technical knowledge, there is growing recognition that there are aspects of social work that require thinking beyond scientific proficiency. In any given case situation, numerous interests are involved and competing obligations exist. What the social worker is supposed to do is not always precise or clear. Social workers are encouraged to make reflective moral judgments by uncovering hidden assumptions and unexamined values that influence ethical decision making in practice. The goal is to move ethical decision making away from the intuitive and to treat moral decisions with the rigor afforded "practice decisions."

How social workers respond to ethical dilemmas depends in large measure on how they have learned to think about the value components of practice situations. The use of guides for ethical decision making does not ultimately resolve such conflicts, but guides do offer a structured approach to analyzing ethical dilemmas. The resolution of value conflicts inevitably involves the use of discretionary latitude. As stated in the NASW *Code of Ethics*, a code "cannot resolve all ethical issues or disputes or capture the richness and complexity involved in striving to make responsible choices within a moral community" (NASW, 1999, p. 4). The ultimate resolution of any ethical dilemma relies heavily on the choices made by the decision maker. Social workers are challenged to make their personal criteria for ethical decision making explicit and to recognize the ways in which their individual preferences factor into the ethical decision-making equation.

References

Abramson, M. (1996). Reflections on knowing oneself ethically: Toward a working framework for social work practice. *Families in Society, 77,* 195–202.

Aroskar, M. (1980). Anatomy of an ethical dilemma: The theory and practice. *American Journal of Nursing, 80,* 658–663.

Billingsley, A. (1964). Bureaucratic and professional orientation patterns in social casework. *Social Service Review, 38,* 400–407.

Congress, E. P. (1986). *Analysis of ethical practice among field instructors in social work.* Unpublished doctoral dissertation, City University of New York Graduate Center, New York.

Council on Social Work Education. (2001). *Educational Policy and Accreditation Standards.* Alexandria, VA: Author.

Emmet, D. (1962). Ethics and the social worker. *British Journal of Psychiatric Social Work, 6,* 165–172.

Gewirth, A. (1978). *Reason and morality.* Chicago: University of Chicago Press.

Goldmeir, J. (1984). Ethical styles and ethical decisions in health settings. *Social Work in Health Care, 10*(1), 46–60.

Hess, P. M., & Hess, H. J. (1998). Values and ethics in social work practice with lesbian and gay persons. In G. P. Mallon (Ed.), *Foundations of social work practice with lesbians and gay persons* (pp. 31–46). New York: Haworth Press.

Holland, T., & Kilpatrick, A. (1991). Ethical issues in social work: Toward a grounded theory of professional ethics. *Social Work, 36,* 138–144.

Joseph, M. V., & Conrad, A. P. (1983). Teaching social work ethics for contemporary practice: An effectiveness evaluation. *Journal of Education for Social Work, 19*(3), 59–68.

Keith-Lucas, A. (1977). Ethics in social work. In *Encyclopedia of social work* (17th ed., pp. 350–355). Washington, DC: National Association of Social Workers.

Kluckhohn, C. (1951). Values and value-orientations in the theory of action: An explanation in definition and clarification. In T. Parsons & E. A. Shils (Eds.), *Toward a general theory of action* (pp. 388–433). Cambridge, MA: Harvard University Press.

Kutchins, H. (1991). The fiduciary relationship: The legal basis for social workers' responsibilities to clients. *Social Work, 36,* 106–113.

Levy, C. S. (1976). *Social work ethics.* New York: Human Sciences Press.

Levy, C. S.(1993). *Social work ethics on the line.* New York: Haworth Press.

Lewis, H. (1972). Morality and the politics of practice. *Social Casework, 5,* 404–417.

Lewis, H. (1982). *The intellectual base of social work practice.* New York: Haworth Press.

Lewis, H. (1984). Ethical assessment. *Social Casework, 65,* 203–211.

Loewenberg, F. M. (1984). Professional ideology, middle range theories and knowledge building for social work practice. *British Journal of Social Work, 14,* 309–322.

Loewenberg, F. M., & Dolgoff, R. (1996). *Ethical decisions for social work practice* (5th ed.). Itasca, IL: F. E. Peacock.

Mattison, M. (1994). *Ethical decision making in social work practice.* Unpublished doctoral dissertation, Columbia University, New York.

Mattison, M. (1997, October). *Ethical decision making in social work practice.* Paper presented at the 15th Annual Baccalaureate Program Directors Conference, Philadelphia.

National Association of Social Workers. (1999). *Code of Ethics.* Washington, DC.

Perlman, H. H. (1976). Believing and doing: Values in social work education. *Social Casework, 57,* 381–390.

Proctor, E., Morrow-Howell, N., & Lott, C. (1993). Classification and correlates of ethical dilemmas in hospital social work. *Social Work, 38,* 166–177.

Pumphrey, M. (1959). *The teaching of values and ethics in social work education.* New York: Council on Social Work Education.

Reamer, F. G. (1983). Ethical dilemmas in social work practice. *Social Work, 28,* 31–35.

Reamer, F. G. (1987). Informed consent in social work. *Social Work, 32,* 425–429.

Reamer, F. G. (1990). *Ethical dilemmas in social service* (2nd ed.). New York: Columbia University Press.

Reamer, F. G. (1995). *Social work values and ethics.* New York: Columbia University Press.

Reamer, F. G., & Abramson, M. (1982). *The teaching of social work ethics.* New York: Hastings Center.

Rhodes, M. L. (1991). *Ethical dilemmas in social work practice.* Milwaukee, WI: Family Service America.

Vigilante, J. L. (1983). Professional values. In A. Rosenblatt & D. Waldfogel (Eds.), *Handbook of clinical social work* (pp. 58–69). San Francisco: Jossey-Bass.

CHAPTER 4

Diversity, Ethnic Competence, and Social Justice

Christine T. Lowery

The problem is we're not seeing or hearing the same
things. Even church bells mean something different to us.
She hears them and sets her watch. I hear them and
remember the endless funerals in the villages outside the
capital. But what right do I have to be angry with her? It
is not her fault that her culture has made her who she is.

—Demetria Martìnez (1994, p. 128)

Illana Harlow, a folklorist, highlights the exchange of
cultural symbols in her photographic exhibition. The subject is Cypress
Hills, a nonsectarian cemetery in the "graveyard belt along the Brooklyn–
Queens border" where Jackie Robinson, "the Brooklyn Dodger who integrated baseball" is buried (Dugger, 1997, p. B1). In the photos of these
"neighborhoods of the dead," a crucifix coincides with the Jewish custom
of placing small rocks on a gravestone and a food offering of shrimp dump-
lings, soy chicken, and sticky rice is accompanied by White Castle
miniburgers. A Puerto Rican woman leaves a yellow napkin topped by a
stone, "a visual echo" of the prayers for the dead left on the Chinese tombstones nearby. Older Greek and Lithuanian tombstones coexist with newer
forms. Now popular with black and Hispanic people, "black granite markers, etched with photographic likenesses of the dead, are common and
were brought by Jewish refugees who began pouring into New York following the collapse of the Soviet Union" (p. B3). Among the living, Italian
bands, remnants of the Little Italy-to-Chinatown immigrant transition, still
play Christian hymns for Buddhist services at Chinese funeral parlors on
Mulberry Street.

How do Buddhists view the transition from life to death? How have these views been integrated into a multicultural setting? How do Christian influences manifest for these groups? How has the expression of grief and remembrances changed from immigrant generations through first, second, third, and fourth American-born generations? How have language, education, new occupations, geographical mobility, interracial marriage, and interracial children influenced the social life and the cultural practices and rituals of families in their multiple communities?

Social work focuses on people in their cultural environments, whether these families were new immigrants in the tenements of ethnic communities of the 1930s or constructed families in the gay community (including people of color) facing AIDS in the 1980s and through the present. The movement of social services from monocultural and ethnocentric perspectives to ethnic-sensitive perspectives and culturally competent approaches holds limited promise because inequalities in societal power are not addressed (Gutierrez & Nagda, 1996). An ethnoconscious or empowerment approach not only includes, but also incorporates, the power of communities of color in advocacy, partnership, and social transformation (Gutierrez & Nagda, 1996). As the global age of the 21st century unfolds, a multicultural perspective coupled with a sense of social justice becomes imperative, not just for social workers, but for anyone who must negotiate power differentials, multiple cultures, multiple environments—all in unsynchronized transformation—from birth to the grave.

This chapter examines the complexities of diversity in social work, including the political, historical, and sociological factors. Students are encouraged to think of issues in social work at the intersections of diversity (including time, both present and historical) and contexts, rather than in lists (race, gender, and ethnicity). Anthropologist James W. Green (1995) has done thoughtful work in multiethnic approaches, and his work is used for general concepts, including ethnicity and culture.

Multiculturalism, Pluralism, and Ethnic Competence

Multiculturalism and pluralism, celebrated and debated as they are (D'Souza, 1992), evoke a range of responses from tolerance to appreciation for differences, but often without enthusiastic intercultural learning or transcultural understanding (Gould, 1996). A *New York Times* review of Wolfe's (1998) book, *One Nation, After All* (note the claim in the title), reported the outcomes of in-depth interviews with 200 people living in the suburbs of Tulsa, Oklahoma; Atlanta; San Diego; and Boston. American middle-class morality promotes nonjudgmentalism—from racial integration to working mothers to multiculturalism—while holding firm to a strict moral code for one's own behavior. Wolfe predicted no culture wars with this brand of pluralism, but he did predict battles for gay rights because homosexuality lies outside the circle of middle-class nonjudgmentalism. This is one difference that cannot be reconciled when viewed as a moral issue, or a choice, as those most hostile frame homosexuality.

For gay activists, the shift from marginality to the "heartland" was symbolized by a short-lived victory on the basis of discrimination in public accommodations in New Jersey (Bruni, 1998). James Dale, the son of a military man, was dismissed as assistant scoutmaster in 1990 and "[thrown] out of the Boy Scouts" (Wadler, 1998, p. B2) when it was discovered that he was gay. The New Jersey court ruled "against excluding openly gay young men from the Boy Scouts of America" and shifted from "fundamental legal protections in employment and housing to the inclusion of homosexuals in some of the most traditional, conservative institutions in American society" (Bruni, 1998, p. 36). In California, the state supreme court "ruled that the Boy Scouts could exclude homosexuals, agnostics and atheists from its ranks because it is a private membership group not covered by the state's civil rights laws" (Purdum, 1998, p. A1). In a 5–4 decision in June, 2000, the U.S. Supreme Court upheld the policy of excluding gays and lesbians by the Boy Scouts of America on the basis that the law cannot compel an organization to accept members in opposition to its purpose. The New York school system, the largest in the country, will sever ties with the Boy Scouts when contracts run out in 2002. Facilities will no longer be used for meetings, and educators cannot sponsor or recruit scouts through school programs. School systems in Chicago, Minneapolis, and San Francisco also severed ties with the Boys Scouts because school policies prohibit discrimination on the basis of sexual orientation. Social work students should keep abreast of developments in this area, including the work of alternative organizations, such as Scouting for All at www.scoutingforall.org.

Many issues stand outside the circle of middle-class nonjudgmentalism, a position inured by suburban isolation and monoculturalism. Cultural homogeniety—"underneath, we are all the same"—is far less threatening than cultural dissimilarity, particularly when that dissimilarity is associated with redistribution of resources, status, power, or "special privileges" (Green, 1995): affirmative action, bilingual programs, recognition of Native American fishing and land claims, and acknowledgment of the rights of transgendered people. Dissimilarity engenders a range of reactions from discomfort, to aversion, to fear of loss, to guarding one's terrain "like threatened lands one wants to conquer" (Agar, 1994, p. 234).

Green (1995) credited James Leigh, a social worker and former instructor at the University of Washington, with coining the term "ethnic competence," denoting one "who can provide professional services in a way that is congruent with behavior and expectations that are normative for a given community" (p. 89). The ethnically competent social worker may be uncomfortable until he or she becomes familiar with the cultural terrain. However, he or she understands three realities: (1) social workers must be lifelong learners; (2) culture is augmentative, complex, and changing; and (3) attention to social justice is a necessary component in unraveling ignorance, biases, prejudices, and racism.

Most schools of social work have an ecological and systemic orientation (micro- and macro-level factors). Still, social work directors surveyed in 89 homeless shelters in North Carolina and Georgia who worked with homeless families "were no less likely to attribute successful restabilization to client's attitude and motivation" (Lindsey, 1998, p. 170) than were non–social workers. How does worker perception of the causes of homelessness influence services to people with children trying to stabilize their lives when macro-level factors such as affordable housing or employment opportunities are lacking? Johnson, Renaud, Schmidt, and Stanek (1998) suggested that clinical social workers (N = 302) may overlook the environmental contexts (neighborhood violence, economic distress, drugs, and the stress of caring for a child with mental and emotional disabilities) of parental behaviors. Two-thirds of the clinical social workers in this study agreed with blaming statements such as, "Family dynamics are usually the major cause of children's emotional disorders" (p. 181).

Lifelong Learning

Social workers must understand that to develop cultural understanding, they must become lifelong learners, listeners, and participant observers. They become practitioner–scientists when their learning is systematic and, at times, experimental. Significantly, meaningful learning requires feedback loops of self-reflection and community feedback, both formal and informal, to enrich social workers' self-knowledge and their practice.

Social workers must be authentic about their own discomfort in cross-cultural situations and examine their value base, biases, prejudices, and racism as part of their own self-assessment. They must be critical thinkers and recognize that there are multiple perspectives and interpretations of events and experiences. They must recognize that resources are not always formal, but informal as well.

It is not our role to speak to people about our own view of the world, nor to attempt to impose that view on them, but rather to dialogue with the people about their view and ours. We must realize that their view of the world, manifested variously in their action, reflects their situation in the world. (Freire, 1994, p. 77)

Dialogue is co-creation, transforming, and requires humility (Freire, 1994). Critical thinking contributes to dialogue, and only dialogue contributes to critical thinking (Freire, 1994):

> Critical thinking contrasts with naive thinking, which sees "historical time as a weight, a stratification of the acquisitions and experiences of the past," from which the present should emerge normalized and "well-behaved." For the naive thinker, the important thing is accommodation to this normalized "today." For the critic, the important thing is the continuing transformation of reality, in behalf of the continuing humanization of men. (p. 73)

Social workers must be open to lessons that present themselves through clients who teach us how they survive under difficult circumstances and through people who share histories and understand the experiences of their communities. Practitioners must recognize that they bring a certain expertise to their work, but that there are many forms of knowledge, and that people with whom they work bring their own expertise. It is the ethnically competent social worker who can help facilitate work that makes room for others to contribute to advocacy and the work of solving social problems. "The oppressors are the ones who act upon the people to indoctrinate them and adjust them to a reality which must remain untouched" (Freire, 1994, p. 75). It is the ethnically competent social worker who recognizes that he or she is not the only one with power, but one of many with power, and that social work is an opportunity where powerful work can take place.

Attention to power begins with an acknowledgement of privilege, conferred power, and the potential to abuse power on an individual, professional, group, and national level. On September 11, 2001, the U.S. experienced a serious challenge to a set of privileges most American citizens and immigrants to America took for granted—a sense of security and safety, air travel, and financial and military power. Threats of war from the country's leadership were immediate, asserting these privileges as protection of freedom and the protection of future generations from terrorism. Little attention was focused on the imperialistic use of power by the American government and multinational corporate systems to expand financial markets and economic power at the expense of devalued populations—and their cultures and values—around the world. The roots of terrorism—on an individual, group, and national level—begin with invisibility, marginalization, devaluation,

Sidebar 4-1. Hmong Veterans, Their Families, and Welfare.

Social workers must be aware of the socio-political-cultural position of refugees and their collective histories with the United States, amid changing sentiments, forgotten promises, and newly constructed policies. One such example are the Hmongs, tribal peoples from the mountains of Laos who aided the Central Intelligence Agency (CIA) during the Vietnam War (1961–1974) for at least 13 years. After the war, their homelands had been lost. Acting on promises made by the United States, the Hmongs made their way to refugee camps in Thailand in the late 1970s where they stayed, sometimes for years, while refugee status was reviewed and granted. In the United States, they were settled primarily in California, Wisconsin, and Minnesota.

Weiner (1997) reports Hmongs faced the loss of food stamps and welfare benefits as one group (170,000) among 1.8 million legal immigrants in the U.S. (p. A-1, A-5). The Hmongs who fought with the CIA are now in their mid-40s to mid-50s, suffer age and racial discrimination, a lack of education, and the physical and mental wounds of war. Their families are large, eight–10 members, and minimum wage jobs cannot support families this size. A formal statement in the budget act acknowledged the wartime contributions of the Hmongs, categorized them as Vietnam veterans, and asserted that their families deserved assistance, but the statement "lacked the force of law" (Weiner, 1997, p. A-5). The cutbacks to the Hmongs, which constituted "1/30th of one percent of the annual Federal food stamp budget" (about $9 million), has had an impact on about "16,000 veterans and tens of thousands of their family members" (Weiner, 1997, p. A-5). Despite cultural taboos, the despair and believed betrayal by the government has been demonstrated in the suicides of three women (one an elder), two in California and one in Wisconsin (Weiner, 1997, p. A-5).

In 1999, the Institute for Wisconsin's Future (IWF) reported that there were more than 39,000 Hmong residents in Wisconsin. That year, more than 1,000 Hmong faced termination of cash assistance under the 1997 welfare-to-work program (W-2). In a survey of 137 Hmong, IWF found that work assignments did not provide Hmong families with the training or education needed for unsubsidized employment. More than 50% of the respondents wanted technical training or apprenticeships; only 11% could communicate with W-2 workers in English; and 80% reported that W-2 made their family's life worse (Moore & Selkowe, 1999).

and exclusion. Finally, those with power use vilification and dehumanization to justify extermination.

On an individual and system level, social workers must continually examine the relationship of White privilege, unearned advantage, and permission to dominate, discussed by McIntosh (1988) in her classic article on White privilege. Conferred dominance and White privilege grant cultural turf, belongingness, and obliviousness to anything outside the dominant cultural circle. She poses the question, "Once I am conscious of [W]hite privilege and power, what will I do to end it?"

Culture Is Augmentative, Complex, and Changing

Cultural contacts made under conditions of choice (as opposed to colonization or domination) can be expansive, but not without engendering complexities and stresses that must be processed. Buriel (1984) analyzed generational patterns in Mexican American families. He reported that *integration* in Mexican American culture "represents a highly adaptive strategy" for adjusting to Anglo American society and a freedom and fluidity in choice of "skills, roles and standards of behavior that are necessary to translate their native ability into conventional forms of success" (Buriel, 1984, p. 126). In his award-winning sociological study, *Streetwise*, Anderson (1990) explained that the young Black man is caught in a "cultural catch-22," negotiating symbols and action in the borderlands between Black neighborhoods and White gentrification. The young Black man dresses the part to "act right"—by tough "ghetto standards" (p. 181)—to avert victimization by strangers in his peer group or ridicule by his own peers. Whether he is law abiding or crime prone, law-abiding White and Black people may interpret his "pose" as threatening or "predatory."

> As a culture comes into contact with other cultures, new traits do not simply replace old ones. Rather, old traits are modified and new ones appear. … To recognize new forms of social complexity as they emerge in the behavior of individuals or families, and to value the creativity of people's responses to social change, is to acknowledge the integrity and capability inherent in their traditions and values. This view of culture, as a source of creative complexity rather than substitutive replacement, is the philosophical essence of ethnic competence. (Green, 1995, p. 96)

Social Justice

The ethnically competent social worker understands that ethnicity is significant in self-identity, but broadens regarding access to social and economic privileges and social justice issues. Devore and Schlesinger (1996) approached this reality with the term "ethclass," which is the intersection of social class (occupation and education) with ethnicity (race, religion, and national origin).

Sidebar 4-2. Black Nationalism and Islam

The pairing of Black nationalism and Al-Islam, Mahmoud (1996) gives a strong example of how the intersection of cultures—political-religious-ethnic—creates new forms through time, shapes leaders, and draws followers, practitioners, and dissidents, and shapes communities. Cultural influences between Noble Drew Ali who founded the Moorish American Science Temples (1913) and Marcus Garvey and the United Negro Improvement Association, influenced the Honorable Elijah Muhammad who consolidated principles from Garvey and Ali for his organization. Al-Hajj Malik al-Shabazz (Malcolm X) was the son of a Garveyite who followed Muhammad, pulled away, and was later killed. In the late 1970s, Muhammad's son "led a massive demonstration of his father's followers into the orthodox practice of Islam. . . ." Minister Louis Farrakhan and his followers now maintain the pairing of Black nationalism and Islam in the tradition of Muhammad.

International contacts between African Muslims and African American Muslims, Sunni Muslims and Saudi Arabia, and contacts among African, Arabic countries, and the United States will continue to shape the cultures of African American Muslims, and social workers who work with these populations must be aware of the cultural changes through time and the challenges of being Muslim in a non-Islamic society.

The intellectually curious reader who doesn't have this information would ask, "What are the principles of Islam? How are these principles interpreted from group to group?" The ethnically competent worker preparing to work with this population relishes the challenge of long-term study (participation in the community, observation, reading, processing experiences) and self-reflection and gradually incorporating this study as one matures personally and professionally.

Separate and unequal, issues of injustice, are glaring enough for all to see. Different and unequal are tightly braided into the social and economic fabric of North America. Different and feared remain a volatile xenophobic combination. For example, it was assumed that Middle Eastern terrorists were involved in the bombing of a federal building in 1995 in Oklahoma City before two White American males were described. When the first television pictures of the destruction caused in the bombing were transmitted, many Arab American, Iranian American, and Iraqi American people and international students from the Middle East bore the reactions of suspicion and rejection by those nearby. This scenario was repeated following the 2001 destruction of the World Trade Center, when mosques and Islamic schools were closed because of threats of destruction. American citizens in Muslim communities, who were just as horrified and saddened by the event, were threatened, harassed, beaten, or killed in incidents across the country. The hate crimes following the Oklahoma bombing were not well-publicized. Within two days of the attack on the World Trade Center, Arab American activists, civil rights workers, and the FBI were sitting at the table in the Justice Department asking what needed to be done (Richards, 2001). Christians stood side-by-side with Muslims to protect mosques. The balance of identity, citizenship, security, and rights will continue to be strained.

Separate and Unequal: "Calculated Unfairness"

For many children outside the circle, there is a lack of opportunity to engage in a democratic society at all. Kozol (1991) wrote about the school systems of East St. Louis, Missouri; Chicago; New York; Detroit, Michigan; San Antonio, Texas; and Camden, New Jersey, in the book *Savage Inequalities*. School systems are primarily funded by property taxes supplemented by state and federal funds. States should provide enough funds to equalize poor and rich districts at a "foundation" level. The reality "guarantees that every child has an equal minimum," (p. 209) but not the same education. A 14-year-old girl describes these injustices succinctly:

> Every year in February we are told to read the same old speech of Martin Luther King. . . . "'I have a dream." . . . We have a school in East St. Louis named for Dr. King.. . . The school is full of sewer water and the doors are locked with chains. Every student in that school is black. It's like a terrible joke on history. (Kozol, 1991, p. 35)

"Children reach the heart of these hypocrisies much quicker than the grown-ups and the experts do" (Kozol, 1991, p. 35). "About injustice, most poor children in America cannot be fooled" (p. 57). One teacher in Camden, New Jersey, commented that what impresses her is that kids get up and come to school at all. "They're old enough to know what they are coming to." There are too few textbooks, no laboratory equipment, few computers per student—where computers are found—and toxic waste dumps nearby. Students enter buildings that are falling apart, teachers are poorly paid, and rote learning for standardized tests compare Black students unfavorably with White students who have access to so much more in school districts just minutes away. Roughly half of the freshman that start junior high never make it to high school in some of the poorest school districts in these cities, systems that "bear the appearance of calculated unfairness" (p. 57).

There exists no more powerful force for rigidity of social class and the frustration of natural potential . . . . than a differential magnitude between the education of two children, the sole justification for which is an imaginary school district line. (Coons, Clune, & Sugarman, 1970, cited in Kozol, 1991, pp. 206–207)

Culture and Ethnicity

Culture and ethnicity are not essential or innate properties of persons; they are the meanings that two people act on in a specific relationship. This emphasis on relational rather than essentialist aspects of culture may, in fact, be the only useful way to think about cultural differences in a complex, heterogeneous society such as our own. (Hannerz, 1986, cited in Green, 1995, p. 15)

Behavior and meanings in relationship with one another (family), and in subgroups with others (work), within even larger systems of other people (geographic region), form a culture. This concept of culture is broad and made more adaptable, moving from the association primarily with ethnicity and race to systems and communities while still encompassing generational transmission of practices and beliefs. Consider social work as a professional culture. We have academic cultures and organizational cultures in hospitals, nursing homes, and child welfare. There are different cultures in addiction treatment (Alcoholics Anonymous as a culture), in mental health, in schools for people who are deaf or blind, and in homeless shelters. We have family cultures; neighborhood cultures; regional cultures; and national cultures and subcultures.

Consider the Farm Belt and the generational transformation to a culture of aging. Nebraska, Iowa, the Dakotas, and Kansas lead the nation with the highest proportion of those age 85 years and older, "the oldest old" (Rimer, 1998, p. A1). Red Cloud, Nebraska, where almost half the residents are over 65 years, is being reshaped by the generational erosion of young families looking for jobs and leaving behind their grandparents and great-grandparents (Rimer, 1998). Raymond T. Coward, dean of the School of Health and Human Services at the University of New Hampshire, compared retirement communities of the Sunbelt and the Plains states. Demographically, they are similar; environmentally, they are "distinct cultural and social environments in which to grow old" (Rimer, 1998, p. A1). In rural communities, "when everyone else leaves, somebody has to be mayor, head of the cemetery committee, and the school board. Older people step up, and do those jobs very well" (p. A14). Some rural communities offer meaningful community roles that help maintain a vigorous older community whose members help sustain the economy and psychologically support one another.

Ultimately, however, it is a balance of old and young that ensures Red Cloud's future as a community. As the elderly gradually die, communities struggle with the question of who will fill these positions. Some Iowa communities have sought Hispanic immigrant families to help their communities, but transitions for these immigrants are still bounded by differentness, "American" expectations, and discrimination.

Cultures become more complex as ethnicity is added to the context of behaviors in relationship. Ethnicity encompasses a sense of peoplehood. The essential elements of peoplehood are kinship, the biological nature of unity over generations; commensuality (eating together); social intimacy despite distance—geography, genealogy; and core beliefs that explain the world in the collective present and history (Nash, 1989). Normally, surface features of ethnicity are observed: family rituals and physical characteristics (kinship); food preferences and sharing patterns; and behaviors, values, norms, ethnohistory, and celebrations (beliefs) (Nash, 1989). Two different examples that express how ethnicity is interpreted follow.

Interpreting Barbie

Within-ethnicity perceptions are diverse and complex, and in this example intersect with popular culture, marketing and sales, and geography. In 1997, when Mattel introduced the Puerto Rican Barbie doll, Puerto Rican people on the island were delighted. However, Americans of Puerto-Rican descent saw the doll as Anglo-looking (Puerto Ricans are racially mixed) and the inscription on the box, "The U.S. lets us govern ourselves," as "condescending." Puerto Rico was ceded to the United States by Spain at the end of the Spanish-American War a century ago (Navarro, 1997). As a commonwealth of the United States, Puerto Rico has options for statehood, independence, or the status quo. Currently, residents are U.S. citizens who can be drafted and to whom federal laws apply. They do not pay federal income taxes, vote for president, or elect members of Congress ("Choice for Puerto Rico," 1998).

Navarro's (1997) analysis focused on the sociopolitical positions of the 2.8 million Puerto Ricans in the United States, who struggle with stereotypes in a multiethnic society, and the 4 million Puerto Rican people, who constitute a majority in Puerto Rico, to whom the doll represents recognition of the island's culture. The two perspectives on boundaries and boundedness reflect the relationship of each group in its respective societal context.

Who Is a Jew?

The timeless struggle of old and new, the reshaping of ideologies in the context of religion and politics, engendered by cross-continental perspectives, experiences, history, and tradition, intersect in the question, "Who is a Jew?" The question centers on who can carry out conversions to Judaism. In the United States religious leaders of conservative, reform, and orthodox Judaism movements may carry out conversions; in Israel, only conversions by orthodox rabbis are legally valid and "confer eligibility for citizenship" (Schmemann, 1998, p. A7). Underlying the issues of conversion and citizenship is the challenge to orthodox rabbis in Israel from the reform and conservative branches of Judaism, stronger in the United States than in Israel. The reform movement gives women equality and sanctions mixed marriages and "is anathema to the stern, black-garbed keepers of the faith in Israel" (p. A7), who resist any acknowledgment of these branches.

In 2002, the Israeli Supreme Court ruled that "Israelis converted by the Conservative or Reform movements" will be listed in the official population registry as Jews (Bennet, 2002). Evidence of one Jewish grandparent provides Israeli citizenship under Israel's "law of return" (Bennet, 2002).

Categorical and Transactional Ethnicity, Politics, and Race

Categorical Ethnicity

Green (1995) interpreted the work of Bennett (1975) in *The New Ethnicity: Perspectives from Ethnology* and Barth (1969) in *Ethnic Groups and Boundaries*. Greene (1995) distinguished between categorical and transactional concepts of ethnicity; one is rigid, the other evolving; one is simple, the other complex; one expects assimilation as an intervention, the other looks to indigenous models for intervention and "anticipates resistance to politics and cultural dominance" (p. 28).

Categorical ethnicity has permeated North American thinking and beliefs; specific cultural traits, usually stereotypical, are assumed. Seductively, strengths that ethnicity contributes are recognized; however, acculturation into a homogenous whole is tacitly expected. *Cultural pluralism*, the "separate-but-equal harmony" or "tossed salad" model of ethnic celebration, falls into categorical ethnicity (Green, 1995). Green contended that White people define ethnicity for themselves in "surface features"—food, clothing, rituals and celebrations, geography, and national labels. Politically, this perspective "locates ethnicity exclusively in others and excuses [White people] from having to consider their own participation in the management and enforcement of *separateness*" (p. 21).

Pluralism and politics. The dark side of pluralism is political; the dominant group defines the categories and controls resources, and differences
become a threat (Green, 1995). Pluralistic social services are satisfied with
semi-inclusive agency policies and abound with empowerment terminol-
ogy but focus more on territorial funding issues with no intention of confronting social injustice and inequalities. Indeed, national policy in the
1970s reflected such an ideology in the guise of pluralism and called for
"nonintervention in human issues as though that were a benevolent respect for cultural differences" (Green, 1995, p. 26). Payne (1997) cautioned against embracing political empowerment ideology, whose goal is to
limit state services while placing responsibility on individuals for providing their own needs.

Federal welfare law work rules provide an example. Such work rules not
only strike hard in geographically isolated regions, but also create barriers
to implementation. Native American tribal governments saw an opportunity to exercise their tribal sovereignty and to develop realistic welfare-to-
work requirements for tribal members within their own economic and
cultural contexts (Belluck, 1997). Under the federal law, tribal governments
have the right, as states do, "to set rules on who can receive welfare and for
how long" (p. A1). Although states pay up to one-third of the costs of
welfare-to-work programs, the law does not require them to contribute a
share for welfare services delivered by tribes within the states. Tribes have
the federal share, but tribes without money are essentially denied participation; only 11 of 557 federally recognized tribes have applied to run their
own programs. Only Oregon and Arizona (each state has two tribes that
have applied) have agreed to transfer funds that would have been spent
had tribal members remained on state welfare rolls. States are mandated to
coordinate Medicaid and food stamp programs with tribal welfare programs
(Belluck, 1997).

Tribes in South Dakota make up 7.4 percent of the population but contribute 53 percent of the welfare recipients (Belluck, 1997). The Sisseton–
Wahpeton Sioux is the only tribe in South Dakota that can supplement the
federal share with $200,000 a year from tribal funds. Among other innova-
tions, they will combine welfare and training at the tribal college, supporting those on welfare for two years and allowing time for completion of an
associate's degree, unlike one year of support for students on welfare under
the state plan. Of a population of 5,500, the Sisseton–Wahpeton Sioux
have 80 welfare families on their rolls (as of October 1, 1997) (Belluck,
1997). Recently, the economy and employment picture on the reservation
has benefited from a plastic bag factory and three casinos that pull in gam-
blers from North Dakota and Canada.

The Rosebud reservation to the south borders Nebraska and presents a more common scenario. Rosebud has a population of 20,000, with 11 percent of the eligible adults working (Belluck, 1997). Rosebud, too, has a casino that is the only major employer. Profits help to pay water and electricity bills for destitute families and provide $75 clothing vouchers for school children. If Rosebud could afford its own welfare program, even more flexibility would be built in for its people. For example, suggested work activities would include hunting, fishing, and making quilts, all part of tribal life and normal work activity.

Transactional Ethnicity and Race

The *transactional model* of ethnicity presents a pattern of evolving values within "boundaries. . . using cultural traits as markers for inclusion and exclusion as situations require," (Green, 1995, p. 27). The model suggests that maintaining "boundedness" with those like us and maintaining boundaries to distinguish ourselves from others in multiethnic milieus are what motivates ethnic distinctions to be "continuously defined, redefined, and reinforced" (p. 27). Within this framework, changing ethnic group names (Black, African American, Chicano, Hispanic, Latino, Native American, American Indian, First Nations, and indigenous peoples) reflect changing perceptions of ethnic boundaries in relationship to others, including dominant society. Within this framework, can a different dialogue about race take place?

Current State of Race

Kotlowitz (1998) documented the racial stasis, symbolized by the St. Joseph River, between Benton Harbor and St. Joseph, in southwestern Michigan. As he moved between Black and White communities, he found he could more easily talk with Black people about race in the 1990s. Former President Clinton called for a national conversation on race in the 1990s. Still, for White people in the United States, race "poses no urgency. . . does not impose on their daily routines. . . . Among [W]hites, there's a reluctance—or lack of opportunity—to engage" (p. 23).

The hope that anonymous experience of the Internet would provide the opportunity to "engage" in frank discussions about race (Marriott, 1998) has not been supported. Once a hopeful example, America Online's ethnicity channel, which premiered for Black History Month in 1998, is now spared any race-related discussion. Chat rooms are segregated by ethnicity—Hispanic, African American, Asian, and European—and the goal is social.

On the other hand, *boundedness* with those like us, may be influenced by information on the Internet. Web sites for different countries, groups,

Sidebar 4-3. Reconstructing the World. . .

Essayist Nancy Mairs (1996) writes of her life and the effects of multiple sclerosis on her body in *Waist-High in the World*, indicating a view from her wheelchair.

As one of my idiosyncrasies, I prefer to call myself a cripple. . . .For one thing, because it is a word many people with disabilities find deeply offensive, I apply it only to myself, and so it reminds me that I am not speaking for others. For another, it lets you know what my condition is: I can't use my limbs as I once could. Blindness, deafness, intellectual impairment all qualify as "disabilities" (or "differing abilities" to people with mealy mouths), but the circumstances they impose are nothing like mine. "Mobility impaired," the euphemizers would call me, as though a surfeit of syllables could soften my reality. No such luck, I still can't sit up in bed, can't take an unaided step, can't dress myself, can't open doors (and I get damned sick of waiting in the loo until some other woman needs to pee and opens the door for me.)

My choice may reflect a desire for accuracy more than anything else. In truth, although I am severely crippled, I am hardly disabled at all, since, thanks to technology and my relatively advantaged circumstances, I'm not prevented from engaging in the meaningful activities and relationships the human spirit craves. . . .But I think it is very, very important to distinguish "disability". . . from some of the circumstances associated with it, often by people who have little direct knowledge of physical and mental limitations and their consequences. Like all negative terms, "disability" is part of a binary, existing in relation to a privileged opposite: that is, one is "disabled" only from the point of view of another defined by common social values as "able". . . ."I" am disabled, then, only from "your" point of view. . . .When I have occasion to refer to a class with a broader spectrum of impairments, I use the more conventional "people with disabilities," or the "disabled" for short; and people who lack them I call "the nondisabled," since in relation to me, they are the deficient ones. Already, in this way, I begin to reconstruct the world (pp. 12–14).

and political issues from genocide in Armenia to the biodiversity of Zaire abound. On an individual level, finding one's ethnic place may start at www.knowyourheritage.org.

The Internet did not spawn an increase in membership for hate groups or what was touted as the "digital White rebellion." Instead, parents became aware of the racism of hate groups and made their concerns known. HateWatch (www.hatewatch.org), a civil rights organization, was developed in 1995 to combat this concern and posted a good-bye in 2001. Instead, they recommended several sites: a civil rights site on bigotry and tolerance worldwide at www.paragraph175.org; a watchdog on the political right and activities to undermine diversity at www.publiceye.org; a bigotry/terrorism watch at www.hatemonitor.org; and the media watch for the Gay and Lesbian Alliance against Defamation (GLAAD) at www.glaad.org. The American Jewish Committee is concerned with strengthening the basic principle of pluralism as the best defense against anti-Semitism and other forms of bigotry at www.ajc.org. The Next Movement explores multiple perspectives on civil rights in a weekly one-hour live web-interview show at www.img2.com.

Boundedness, race, ethnicity, and power. In an international example of boundedness, White people in South Africa have a fervent dedication to race. Religion, the Afrikaans language, color (White, colored, Black), and political power have served to ensure the ethnic boundedness of the Afrikaners—the descendants of Dutch, German, and French settlers who make up seven percent of the current population. The Afrikaner supremacy ended in 1999 when the coalition government between the African National Congress and the National Party ended (Goodwin & Schiff, 1995). The post-apartheid transitions for Afrikaners provide a stark example of the struggle of "identity work" on many levels: individual, national, ethnic, political, and ideological. Their culture "blended Europe and Africa in ways seen nowhere else" (Daley, 1998, p. 11). Their culture also established rigid boundaries under apartheid and—as the will of God—denied Black people a decent education, the right to vote, the right to own land where they wanted, the right to live where they wanted, and the right to move about in freedom. What does an 11th-generation Afrikaner teach his children about their heritage in the transition from apartheid to Black majority leadership? (Daley, 1998).

Generational, geographical, and emotional responses to a new era in South Africa vary. Some still control segregation when and where they can; some are angered by the loss of Afrikaans television; others avoid the "moral debate about their culpability" or participate in "the new martyrdom" (Daley, 1998, p. 11)—the backlash against being blamed. New-order Afrikaners question the culpability of their institutions, create new opportunities for investment that use a Black empowerment model, and create opportunities for university students to work in poor areas (Daley, 1998). Goodwin and Schiff (1995) contended that there is no moral transformation; for most Afrikaners the shift is political with a motivation to hold on to as much power as possible. Separatist messianism—"bringing Christianity to Africa while remaining separate" (Goodwin & Schiff, 1995, p. 13)—is still the "volk's true calling" for some Afrikaners.

Elna Trautmann, an Afrikaner who has spent time in intercultural learning, took an introspective look at post-apartheid South Africa. Couched in anxiety, uncertainty, and hope, she suggested that "the only way the Afrikaners can guarantee their continued existence" is to acknowledge "the great reservoirs of compassion among South Africa's [B]lacks":

> One thing about the [B]lack man is that in essence he's not aggressive. I don't believe at all that Africa hasn't got compassion. Here they call it ubuntu (a belief that a person exists through other people). I don't believe that any [B]lack wants to do to the Afrikaner what the Afrikaner has done to him. I have never in a discussion with anyone found any [B]lack who said he wanted to do that. (cited in Goodwin & Schiff, 1995, p. 375)

Can the volk change? Trautmann despaired as she considered those who are not educating their children for the political change or for changing their inherited racism. Change will come only when those who do not know how to renegotiate status and power die out.

In December 2000, an apology for apartheid was published by a group of 450 White, prominent intellectual and civic leaders. The brief Declaration of Commitment unexpectedly laid bare wounds and opened bitter debate among South Africa's Whites about their place in South Africa (Salopek, 2001a). Under the African National Congress (ANC), President Thabo Mbeki has kept the South African economy stable. The huge disparities in Black and White incomes, the racialized politics, and privileged lifestyles of Whites also remain constant. Antjie Krog, a poet and writer, who led the declaration, sees the White angst and public debate as useful. In spite of their history, this public debate among Whites has not honestly occurred. She summarized, "Acknowledging the past actually opens some political space for [W]hites to criticize the present" (Salopek, 2001a, p. 1-12).

When 46 years of apartheid was lifted in South Africa, "the rest of Africa literally came pouring in" (Salopeck, 2001b, p. 1-12). As in the United States, immigration and border control are volatile issues. Unlike the United States, with more than 200 years of immigration, South Africa's experience with immigration is new. The isolation of apartheid insulated both Whites and Blacks in South Africa from the rest of the continent. Current estimates range from 500,000 to 4 million illegal immigrants from Zimbabwe, Angola, Senegal, Congo, Botswana, and Mozambique. The competition for jobs and housing has produced a Black backlash against strangers (Salopeck, 2001b) and hate crimes against *makwerekwere* or outsiders are rising. Human Rights Watch has criticized South Africa's lack of due process in expelling thousands of legal and illegal immigrants and human rights investigations of anti-immigrant abuses continue (Salopeck, 2001b).

Race, Gender, Sexual Orientation, and the Political Context: An Analysis

> In [W]hite America, cultural conservatism takes the form of a chronic racism, sexism, and homophobia. Hence, only certain kinds of [B]lack people deserve high positions, that is, those who accept the rules of the game played by [W]hite America. In [B]lack America, cultural conservatism takes the form of an inchoate xenophobia (e.g., against [W]hites, Jews, and Asians), systemic sexism, and homophobia.
>
> —*Cornel West (1993, p. 27)*

In 1991, Clarence Thomas sat for televised confirmation hearings on his nomination for the U.S. Supreme Court. In a real-life drama, Anita Hill, then a law professor in Oklahoma, came forward and challenged the confirmation on the basis of sexual harassment. The response was tumultuous. Thomas charged his detractors with a racially motivated, "high-tech lynching." No sexual harassment claim was ever brought against Thomas (Hill, 1998), and Thomas was subsequently placed on the Supreme Court.

Cornel West (1993), theologian, activist, Harvard professor, and African American, analyzed the 1991 confirmation hearings. In the Thomas–Hill stalemate, West (1993) accused Black leadership of resorting to a "vulgar form of racial reasoning" (p. 24) by rendering an opportunity to critically discuss race and gender in the Black community to a "crude discourse" that "bespeaks a failure of nerve of [B]lack leadership" (p. 23). Racial reasoning presumes a racial consensus while simultaneously "invoking an undeniable history of racial abuse and racial struggle" (p. 26). Racial reasoning has three elements: (1) Black authenticity, (2) Black closing-ranks mentality, and (3) "[B]lack male subordination of [B]lack women in the interests of the [B]lack community in. . . a racist country" (p. 24).

West (1993) suggested that "all people with [B]lack skin and African phenotype are subject to [W]hite supremacist abuse" (p. 25). Thus, all Black Americans have an interest in resisting racism on an individual or community level, and there are various methods, which are politically defined and ethnically enacted, for resisting racism. Calls to Black authenticity belie the complexity of political and ethical differences within Black America, according to West. Black closing-ranks mentality ignores gender, class differences, and sexual orientation, primarily at the expense of Black women (West, 1993). West cautioned that any claims to Black authenticity by Black nationalists or Black male centrists that exclude women or gay men and lesbians are suspicious, for these claims not only feed Black closing-ranks mentality, but also feed "Black patriarchal and homophobic power" (p. 24), the core of Black cultural conservatism. West concluded that Thomas claimed Black authenticity for self-promotion and successfully "played the racial card of [B]lack victimization and [B]lack solidarity at the expense of Anita Hill. . . . [who like his sister Emma Mae] could be used and abused for his own self-interested conception of [B]lack authenticity and racial solidarity" (p. 27).

To dismantle racial reasoning, West (1993) proposed a framework of moral reasoning based on mature Black identity, coalition strategy, and Black cultural democracy. The underlying premises support freedom based on ethical principles, "wise politics" (p. 25), and egalitarian relations in and outside the Black community. Rather than questioning, "Is Thomas [B]lack enough to be defended?" (p. 25), all Black responses to the undeniable racism in America must be morally and ethically assessed. Black closing-ranks mentality is replaced by "a coalition strategy that solicits genuine solidarity with those deeply committed to antiracist struggle" (pp. 28–29). Black cultural democracy supplants Black conservatism, rejects the "pervasive patriarchy and homophobia in [B]lack American life" (p. 29), and promotes the equality of Black women and Black gay men and lesbians.

In a framework of moral reasoning, Black leaders would not have felt pressured to choose between Thomas, a Black man, and Hill, a Black woman, both lawyers and right-wing supporters. Thomas would have been opposed on his lack of qualifications, and his "high-tech lynching" appeal to racial victimization would not have been allowed to mask his moral principles (West, 1993). Finally, West summarized his opinion of the Black leadership in America and the collusion with White racist stereotypes:

> The very fact that no [B]lack leader could utter publicly that a [B]lack appointee for the Supreme Court was unqualified shows how captive they are to [W]hite racist stereotypes about [B]lack intellectual talent. The point here is not simply that if Thomas were [W]hite they would have no trouble shouting this fact from the rooftops. The point is also that their silence reveals that [B]lack leaders may entertain the possibility that the racist stereotype may be true. Hence their attempt to cover Thomas's mediocrity with silence. (p. 23)

The costs of racial reasoning are divisive and foment suspicion. Social workers, including social workers of color, must test the principles of moral reasoning. Do these principles strengthen ethnic boundaries within and build useful relationships outside communities of color? Do these principles achieve social justice? What are the benefits and costs of moral reasoning?

Conclusion

We can legitimately say that in the process of oppression someone oppresses someone else; we cannot say that in the process of revolution someone liberates someone else, nor yet that someone liberates himself, but rather that human beings in communion liberate each other.

—*Paulo Freire (1994, p. 114)*

As learners sitting next to each other in class, with all our differences, we must recognize that there is someplace that we can go together. As social workers, we must be aware that in the absence of dialogue and understanding, self-reflection and the opportunity for self-knowledge are also absent. In this void is the absence of shared reason, collective action, and the danger for a misuse of professional privilege and power.

References

Agar, M. (1994). *Language shock: Understanding the culture of conversation.* New York: William Morrow.

Anderson, E. (1990). *Streetwise: Race, class, and change in an urban community.* Chicago: University of Chicago Press.

Barth, F. (1969). *Ethnic groups and boundaries.* Boston: Little, Brown.

Belluck, P. (1997, September 9). Tribe's new power over welfare may come at too high a price. *New York Times,* pp. A1, A20.

Bennet, J. (February 24, 2002). Soldier's burial as non-Jew adds to list of Israel's pain. www.nytimes.com/2002/02/24/international/mideast/24SOLD.html.

Bennett, J. W. (1975). *The new ethnicity: Perspectives from ethnology.* St. Paul: West.

Bruni, F. (1998, March 8). A battlefield shifts: Gay scout's court victory shows how far movement has progressed. *New York Times,* p. 36.

Buriel, R. (1984). Integration with traditional Mexican-American culture and sociocultural adjustment. In J. L. Martinez, Jr., & R. H. Mendoza (Eds.), *Chicano psychology* (pp. 95–130). Orlando, Florida: Academic Press.

"Choice for Puerto Rico." (1998, March 9). *New York Times,* p. A18.

Coons, J. E., Clune III, W. H., & Sugarman, S. D. (1970). *Private wealth and public education.* Cambridge, MA: Harvard University Press.

Daley, S. (1998, February 22). Africa's "White Tribe" fears dark past is prologue. *New York Times,* pp. A1, A11.

Devore, W., & Schlesinger, E. G. (1996). *Ethnic-sensitive social work practice* (4th ed.). Boston: Allyn & Bacon.

D'Souza, D. (1992). *Illiberal education: The politics of race and sex on campus.* New York: Vintage Books.

Dugger, C. W. (1997, October 28). Outward bound from the mosaic: Where dead are mourned, many traditions mingle. *New York Times,* pp. B1, B3.

Freire, P. (1994). *Pedagogy of the oppressed* (rev. ed.). New York: Continuum.

Goodwin, J., & Schiff, B. (1995). *Heart of whiteness: Afrikaners face Black rule in the new South Africa.* New York: Scribner.

Gould, K. H. (1996). The misconstruing of multiculturalism: The Stanford debate and social work. In P. L. Ewalt, E. M. Freeman, S. A. Kirk, & D. L. Poole (Eds.), *Multicultural issues in social work* (pp. 29–42). Washington, DC: NASW Press.

Green, J. W. (1995). *Cultural awareness in the human services: A multi-ethnic approach* (2nd ed.). Boston: Allyn & Bacon.

Gutierrez, L., & Nagda, B. A. (1996). The multicultural imperative in human services organizations: Issues for the twenty-first century. In P. R. Raffoul & C. A. McNeece (Eds.), *Future issues for social work practice* (pp. 203–213). Needham Heights, MA: Allyn & Bacon.

Hill, A. (1998, March 19). A matter of definition. *New York Times,* p. A21.

Johnson, H. C., Renaud, E. F., Schmidt, D. T., & Stanek, E. J. (1998). Social workers' views of parents of children with mental and emotional disabilities. *Families in Society, 79,* 173–187.

Kotlowitz, A. (1998, January 11). Colorblind: How can you have a dialogue on race when Blacks and Whites can see no gray? *New York Times Magazine,* pp. 22–23.

Kozol, J. (1991). *Savage inequalities: Children in America's schools.* New York: HarperPerennial.

Lindsey, E. W. (1998). Service providers' perceptions of factors that help or hinder homeless families. *Families in Society, 79,* 160–172.

Mairs, N. (1996). *Waist-high in the world.* Boston: Beacon Press.

Marriott, M. (1998, March 8). Frank racial dialogue thrives on the web. *New York Times,* National Section, pp. 1, 26.

Martìnez, D. (1994). *Mother tongue.* New York: Ballantine Books.

McIntosh, P. (1988). White privilege: Unpacking the invisible knapsack. Excerpted from P. McIntosh, *White privilege and male privilege.* Wellesley, MA: SEED Project, Wellesley College.

Moore, T., & Selkowe, V. (1999). *The impact of welfare reform on Wisconsin's Hmong aid recipients.* Milwaukee, WI: The Institute for Wisconsin's Future.

Nash, M. (1989). *The cauldron of ethnicity in the modern world.* Chicago: University of Chicago Press.

Navarro, M. (1997, December 27). A new Barbie in Puerto Rico divides island and mainland. *New York Times,* pp. A1, A9.

Payne, M. (1997). Empowerment and advocacy. In *Modern social work theory* (2nd ed., pp. 266–285). Chicago: Lyceum Books.

Purdum, T. S. (1998, March 23). California justices allow Scouts to bar gay and atheist members. *New York Times,* pp. A1, A19.

Richards, S. E. (2001, September 30). Arab-American victims: Venom finds easy target in land of the free. *Chicago Tribune Perspective*, pp. 2-1, 2-5.

Rimer, S. (1998, February 2). Rural elderly create vital communities as young leave void. *New York Times*, pp. A1, A14.

Salopek, P. (2001a, January 8). Apology exposes anger, angst of S. Africa whites. *Chicago Tribune*, pp. 1-1, 1-12.

Salopek, P. (2001b, January 16). Intolerance in "rainbow nation." *Chicago Tribune*, pp. 1-1, 1-12.

Schmemann, S. (1998, January 27). "Who's a Jew" puzzle gets more tangled. *New York Times*, p. A7.

Wadler, J. (1998, March 10). A matter of scout's honor, gay victor says. *New York Times*, p. B2.

Weiner, T. (1997, December 27). Many Laotians in U.S. find their hopes betrayed. *New York Times*, pp. A1, A5.

West, C. (1993). The pitfalls of racial reasoning. In *Race matters* (pp. 21–32). Boston: Beacon Press.

CHAPTER 5

Knowledge for Practice

Mark A. Mattaini

$\mathbf{A}$s noted by Bartlett, "mature professions rest on strong bodies of knowledge and values" (1970, p. 63). A case can be made that professionals and nonprofessionals may share similar values (discussed in Chapter 3), although holding them *in common* is crucial for a profession, and therefore that knowledge is the most distinctive characteristic of professional practice. This chapter discusses the difficulties in defining and sharing knowledge and explores a variety of strategies for discovering and testing knowledge valuable to social workers.

Knowledge

The nature of knowledge is not straightforward. Among the definitions of knowledge listed in *The New Shorter Oxford English Dictionary* (1993) are the following:

a) the fact of knowing a thing, state, person, etc.; acquaintance, familiarity gained by experience;

b) intellectual perception of fact or truth; clear and certain understanding or awareness, esp. as opposed to opinion, and

c) theoretical or practical understanding of an art, science, industry, etc. (p. 1503)

"Knowledge propositions," Bartlett (1970) suggested, "refer to verifiable experience and appear in the form of rigorous statements that are made as objective as possible" (p. 63). Even without becoming enmeshed in the contemporary "crisis in philosophy"(Smith, 1988, p. 51), one can see the potential difficulties here: What counts as "practical understanding," "intellectual perception," "fact or truth," or "clear and certain awareness," for example?

Theoreticians of social work also engage in conflicts regarding the nature of evidence; the possibility of objectivity; and appropriate strategies for observing, making sense of, and transforming reality (see, for example, Pieper & Pieper, 1993; Wakefield, 1993). Scientists and philosophers long ago recognized people's almost limitless potential for self-deception, especially when beliefs are differentially rewarded by those who surround a person. The scientific method (to the extent there is a single "scientific method"), in fact, is a system of rules for controlling impulses to believe whatever one wishes to believe, a self-correcting process for testing belief against reality (Ainslie, 1993).

Misperceptions of causal relationships are another danger. Actions that are followed by something positive tend to be repeated, because they seem to "pay off." Note, however, that the relationship is at base temporal—whatever comes before a positive outcome is likely to be repeated, *whether or not there is a genuine causal connection*. Even pigeons readily develop superstitions: If a pigeon happens to be scratching or turning when it receives a food pellet delivered randomly, scratching or turning increases (Skinner, 1948). Similar processes occur with people and even cultures. When a client improves after a social worker provides an emotionally supportive environment for several sessions, a connection between the two is possible but by no means certain. The cause of the change may be something else, such as an increase in hours of daylight that ameliorates seasonal affective disorder or concurrent resolution of an ongoing interpersonal conflict.

Rules to limit such misperceptions are clearly important. At the same time, recent contributions by social constructionists remind us that "belief is . . . a form of behavior and subject to the needs and wishes of the individual, with or without the mediation of culture" (Ainslie, 1993, p. 72). In other words, it is difficult to see clearly through lenses clouded by experiences, theoretical stances, and incentives to believe one among several possible alternatives. In the method used to understand this subjective reality ("deconstruction"), one attempts to discern the meaning for the speaker or author of a narrative or text.

It is possible to "marry" empiricism and constructionism, as long as the possibility of connecting—to some extent—with reality is acknowledged. Radical constructionists, however, suggest that reality is altogether unknowable, that no attempt at developing knowledge corresponding to objective fact is possible, and that the scientific method is just another set of beliefs with no special claim to validity. This radical stance, which now appears to be waning, has been taken seriously in some areas of the humanities, social sciences, and philosophy of science—although generally not in the natural sciences themselves (Searle, 1993).

Radical constructionism is not a serious alternative for social work practice any more than it is in engineering or other professions. Bridges stand or fall, and a hungry child, a battered spouse, or an alcoholic person racked by despair is real enough to be accepted as genuine by most practitioners, even though they recognize that their observations may include some distortion. Most people accept that external reality exists and that they can observe and affect it to some extent. At the same time, there are multiple ways to examine and understand that reality, each of which has limitations. These approaches are the subject of this chapter.

Although the distinctions are somewhat artificial, sources of knowledge that will be considered here include practice wisdom gleaned from narrated experience of the profession and professional colleagues, the personal experience of the practitioner, art and literature, history and current events, cultural perspectives, descriptive research (qualitative and quantitative), experimental research, information provided by the case itself, and theoretical and conceptual frameworks. With regard to the last source, there is substantial variation in theoretical and practice approaches within the profession, and it will be necessary to examine that area in some depth. The social worker may draw on some of these sources of knowledge explicitly in making a specific practice decision (which may be as apparently simple as whether to say "I wonder how that affected you?" or "What happened next?"—to go deeper or to move on). Other sources may remain unarticulated background, but still shape practice in crucial ways. For example, the social worker may talk with the client about the history of oppression experienced by the client's ethnic group. The specific questions asked in this discussion depend in part on a practice approach, which structures the practitioner's thought process even when it is not mentioned (a behaviorist, for example, would consider probable emotional effects of coercive processes, whereas a Bowenian family therapist might look for intergenerational patterns).

Sources of Knowledge

Practice Wisdom

Although it is often mentioned in discussions of social work practice, "practice wisdom" is seldom defined or explored in-depth in textbooks on practice. Practice wisdom is a slippery concept, yet there can be little doubt that much of what happens in practice is based on something like it. In this chapter, "practice wisdom" is used to refer to two separate but related phenomena: (1) explicit rules, handed down to others by experienced practitioners, that appear to "work"—heuristic rules viewed as "good enough" to guide much of practice—and (2) patterns of professional behavior, which may or may not be articulated, that have been shaped and refined during years of practice and often serve as models for other workers. These two forms of knowledge are passed on from generation to generation of social workers, sometimes as a form of oral tradition.

Examples of the first type of practice wisdom include general maxims such as, "Start where the client is." Also, there are more specific rules such as, "With this client population, it is important to meet concrete needs before trying to explore emotional issues." Although such suggestions could be examined empirically, social workers do not have time to test everything, and a common core of generally accepted knowledge of this kind probably guides much of practice. Experienced social workers often have learned a tremendous amount that can be of value to others, and the importance of this type of knowledge should not be minimized.

There are risks associated with a reliance on such rules, however. First and most important, the rules may be inaccurate (having been passed on persuasively by those who strongly believe them to be true) and therefore result in less-than-adequate services to clients. For example, social workers in the field of substance abuse often rely on codependency theory, which "assert[s] that a woman married to an alcoholic contribute[s] to her husband's addiction because of her own disturbed personality needs" (Collins, 1993, p. 471). Although this concept is commonly presented as a fact and many social workers now operate according to this framework, there is no evidence of a universal "codependent personality," and in fact there is enormous variation among those partnered with persons struggling with substance abuse (Collins, 1993). "Codependency" is perhaps a useful narrative for some, but carries clear risks; in some of its common forms, codependency theory defines most or all families as dysfunctional and shared responsibility for collective outcomes as bad, and it suggests that attention should be directed primarily to dysfunction rather than strengths and power.

Another risk is that accepted rules sometimes grow more from what works for the practitioner than what works for the client. For example, it is common to hear practitioners say that some clients, or even whole classes of clients, are "not ready," "not motivated," or "resistant" to intervention, and therefore the clinician concentrates on other less-troublesome clients. There are reasons for resistance, however; sometimes resistance is the result of actions by those whose goal is to help (Miller & Rosnick, 1991) or of the structure and procedures of service systems. In fact, it is often possible to work effectively with clients who initially seem resistant, if the worker understands the dynamics of the situation (Gitterman, 1983).

The second type of practice wisdom, patterns of professional behavior shaped by practice experience, is also essential, although it is more difficult to capture. Sometimes workers know what they are doing, and why, and can accurately describe this verbally. At other times, effective practitioners cannot explain exactly what they do or why, but by observing their timing or the inflection of their voices during clinical sessions, for example, others can learn to do much the same thing. This is one reason why videotaped or audiotaped sample sessions and real or simulated clinical presentations are valuable. Not only can those observing notice the principles that are the particular focus of a session or demonstration, but they may be able to observe and learn, consciously or not, from the many subtle behavioral events that occur simultaneously.

These behaviors sometimes are described as part of the "art" of practice, which has been shaped, often outside the social worker's awareness, by practice events during years of experience. Some researchers have tried to develop methods to extract principles from such unarticulated practice (for example, Schön, 1983) with some success. "Knowledge engineering" in the development of computerized expert systems is a related approach, in which an expert is interviewed in a structured way in an attempt to extract the rules on which the expert bases his or her professional decisions. The expert does not always recognize the factors that shape his or her behavior, however, and there is some risk that the explanation presented may be plausible but inaccurate. This kind of knowledge engineering has proven quite difficult in social work, and such research, active a decade ago, has now largely faded. It is apparently more difficult than some had hoped to extract meaningful rules from the complexities of social work practice in this way.

Despite its essential role, practice wisdom should be applied cautiously. Because of the possibility of distortion, it is important for the social worker to monitor whether approaches rooted in this body of knowledge (or any other) contribute to meeting a client's goals. If they do not, other options should be examined. Knowledge that has been hardened by support from multiple sources (practice wisdom and empirical testing, for example, or common rules suggested by multiple experienced practitioners) should ordinarily be preferred to inferences and hypotheses that lack such support. Interventive strategies that are experimental should be presented as such to the client and should be monitored closely to avoid iatrogenic outcomes (negative outcomes resulting from the intervention itself).

Because of the risks associated with relying on authority or consensus (often the case with practice wisdom), a movement toward *evidence-based practice* (or EBP; Gambrill, 1999) has recently emerged in social work. As described by Gambrill:

In EBP a sharp distinction is made between claims that rely on authority or consensus and those that have survived critical tests of their accuracy. 'Evidence-based practice is the conscientious, explicit, and judicious use of current best evidence in making decisions. . . ' (Sackett, Richardson, Rosenberg, & Haynes, 1997, p. 2). . . It involves integrating individual practice expertise with the best available external evidence from systematic research as well as considering the values and expectations of clients. Hallmarks of evidence-based practice (EBP) include: 1) an individualized assessment; 2) a search for the best available external evidence related to the client's concerns and an estimate of the extent to which this applies to a particular client; and 3) a consideration of the values and expectations of clients (Sackett et al., 1997). (1999, p. 346)

Note that, as Gambrill describes it, EBP does not take the place of individualizing assessment, and honors the practitioner's expertise and the client's voice. There is also no claim that currently available research can guide all of practice. This *is*, however, a recognition of the obligation to locate, critically evaluate, and rely on the best currently available evidence in intervention planning and on the importance of research for doing so.

Biological, Behavioral, and Cultural Sciences

Social workers work with people (who are biological, emotional, behavioral, and social beings); with families, groups, communities, and organizations (which are sociocultural entities); and with the relationships among and between people, social entities, and the physical world. Because these are the "raw materials" of practice, it is important to understand as much as possible about them. Thus, social workers must know not only about practice and social issues, but also about the basic sciences that underlie them, including biology and genetics, ecological science, behavioral science, and the disciplines that examine larger systems, including sociology, anthropology, and cultural analysis.

Biology, Genetics, and Behavior. Much of the behavior of many animals is genetically determined. Sociobiologists suggest that the same is true for human beings, but critical examination of the data suggests that only very limited areas of human behavior (primarily some of what is common among people but not how they differ) can be understood in this way (Harris, 2000). For example, behavior such as facial expressions and the specifics of some forms of sexual behavior appear to have substantial biological roots (Fisher, 1992), but many of them can be overridden by learning. Some conditions that social workers deal with also have clear physiological dimensions; for instance, although the effects of the environment appear to be important determinants of the course and severity of schizophrenia, the evidence is now quite strong that the illness has a biological basis (Kaplan & Sadock, 1996). Similarly, severe depression is associated with changes in the levels and actions of neurotransmitters in the brain (Bentley & Walsh, 1996).

Feelings and behavior are physiological phenomena. That "psychological" interventions are valuable for many cases of depression (Nathan & Gorman, 1998) again demonstrates the essential unity of the organism. Appropriate medication is often essential for stabilizing or ameliorating certain psychotic and affective disorders. It is also known that children of people with severe addictions to alcohol are at substantially increased risk for alcohol problems themselves, and there are many psycho-physiological connections in substance abuse (Kaplan & Sadock, 1996; Vaillant, 1995). Therefore, knowledge of biological and medical information in whatever area the social worker is practicing is essential.

Ecological Science. E. O. Wilson (1992) noted that

> Humanity is part of nature, a species that evolved among other species. The more closely we identify ourselves with the rest of life, the more quickly we will be able to discover the sources of human sensibility and acquire the knowledge on which an enduring ethic, a sense of preferred direction, can be built. (p. 348)

Since the 1960s, social workers have recognized that ecological science has much to offer them for understanding practice in a complex, interconnected world. First of all, human beings are literally part of the natural world and, like other animals, need to be able to obtain certain resources, including food, shelter, and social interaction, from their environments to survive effectively. (Even these basic needs are missing, tragically, for many homeless and poor people.) The connectedness among people and other parts of the natural world is an essential underpinning of shared power in social work practice, which requires recognizing that service is not about doing something for someone else, but rather about contributing to the interconnected web within which each of us is simply a nexus (Goodenough, 1998; Lowery & Mattaini, 2001). This epistemological stance changes the definition of practice in potentially profound ways and clarifies the importance of exploring the interlocking environmental events, human actions, and cultural practices within which client struggles occur.

Ecological science is therefore one of the theoretical roots of the ecosystems perspective (see Chapter 1). It is also the defining metaphor in the life model (Germain & Gitterman, 1996) of social work practice. The ecological concepts of niche, habitat, and pollution, for example, are applied in a relatively direct way to human and social phenomena in the life model. Ecologists have also elaborated an interactive, tripartite approach to knowledge development (intertwining organized observations, the development of explanatory models, and experiments in the natural environment [Bates, 1950/1990]) that may be particularly useful in developing approaches to social problems (Mattaini, 1996b). There is much for the practitioner to learn and apply, directly or indirectly, from ecological science and natural history.

Behavioral and Social Sciences. There is no way to summarize, or even suggest, the tremendous wealth of information that social workers draw on from the behavioral and social sciences; most graduate programs include several courses focused on human behavior in the social environment. Knowledge from psychology, social psychology, sociology, anthropology, economics, demography, epidemiology, and political science, as well as from professions such as medicine, psychiatry, and family therapy, is critical for effective practice. For example, recent work in the analysis of cultural practices (Biglan, 1995; Mattaini, 1996a) can be useful for determining what needs to change in an overall ecological field to reduce the incidence of social problems such as violence and to increase the rates of pro-social acts like effective parenting.

At the same time, social workers do not practice social psychology, anthropology, or medicine; information from these sources greatly informs practice but must be incorporated into practice models and approaches. Thus, both knowing the information and determining how it can usefully be applied in the messy world of practice are important challenges. A few thoughts about evaluating such knowledge may be useful. Much of behavioral science is based on—and involves testing of—theory. To a significant extent, this situation also applies to social sciences at higher system levels. Theory is discussed in a later section of this chapter, but it is important to note here that adequate science depends on adequate theory, and vice versa. One way of evaluating the extent to which findings from the sciences are applicable to practice is to determine whether the findings fit coherently within or conflict with an overall conceptual framework for looking at cases. In the first case, they may provide guidance for practice; in the second, they may suggest that the practice approach being used is inadequate.

Practice-Relevant Research

In some cases social workers and professionals from related practice disciplines have done their own research precisely because the questions for which they needed answers had not been asked in ways applicable to practice; in other cases work from other disciplines could be immediately useful. The two primary forms of research critical to social work practice are naturalistic research, which examines social phenomena as they lie, and experimental research, in which the researcher makes changes in the situation and studies the outcomes.

Naturalistic Research. Naturalistic research is the rigorous observation of phenomena that are important to social work practice. Just as many natural events can be studied only through observation (as in astronomy or some branches of ecology), many social phenomena with which social workers are concerned can be understood best when examined in their natural state.

There are a wide variety of approaches to naturalistic research. For example, the social worker may use existing epidemiological or agency data, or may gather new data by interviews or questionnaire, and may use quantitative methods, qualitative methods, or a combination of the two. Gerontological research often relies on the use of large national data sets, and information about large-scale demographic shifts is often highly relevant to understanding social phenomena (Foot, 1996). By contrast, intensive qualitative interviews with a small number of clients can produce the kind of rich data required to conceptualize entirely new, culturally specific intervention models (see, for example, Lowery, 1998). The research questions may relate to who clients (or potential clients) are; the extent and patterns of problems experienced; the identification of other factors that may cause, result, or otherwise be associated with the problem; or the way practice itself is conducted and the evaluation of its outcomes. If knowledge is the basis of professional practice, workers need to know a great deal about such questions.

For example, the 2000 volume of the journal *Social Work Research* included reports of naturalistic studies of work after welfare, difference in resources between elderly Whites and elderly Blacks, the effects of poverty on the mental health of children, and other areas of concern to social work practice on various levels—from work with individuals to community and policy practice.

Knowing what is happening and to whom, as well as when, where, and why, is obviously essential. Why, then, is the importance of such research sometimes controversial in the profession? There seem to be several reasons. The least defensible reason is that research is not always easy to understand. For example, in his article "Ideological Influences on Public Support for Assistance to Poor Families," Groskind (1994) reported the results of techniques such as factor analysis and multiple regression, including statistics, significance levels, and other information that is important in quantitative research. For those who understand these things, the results are meaningful, but for those who do not, they may seem like an unknown language. The phenomena with which social workers deal are, by their very nature, complex. Therefore, analytic techniques adequate to capture the issues will also be complex, and social workers must rise to the challenge of learning to understand those techniques. Although research of this kind is not always informative for practice, some of it is, and the only way for a professional to know the difference is to be able to judge for oneself.

Another issue that complicates the use of research is the controversy in some professional circles over the relative values of quantitative and qualitative research. *Quantitative research*, which uses methods that have been developed during the past century (and in some cases much earlier) in the natural and social sciences, emphasizes objectivity (measures that remain constant over time and often across studies) and efforts to quantify a phenomenon (to determine "how much" of a phenomenon exists) by counting frequencies of events (such as how many children died from child abuse in the past year) or using standardized ratings and scales (to determine, for instance, how depressed a client is, using the Beck Depression Inventory). (Quantitative research also often places particular value on experimental results.)

Qualitative research, in contrast, emphasizes efforts to understand phenomena holistically, including their subjective aspects. Qualitative researchers often use their data as a guide for developing their categories and concepts inductively, and sometimes view themselves as the "instruments" of the research (Lincoln & Guba, 1985). The methodology tends to focus on techniques such as participant observation, semi-structured interviews, and hermeneutic analysis of "texts." Qualitative studies such as Floersch (2000), which used narrative methods to determine the extent to which what was written in the case record reflected the realities of practice, can produce findings that are rich in detail and accessible in ways that other approaches cannot equal.

Resolution of the split between quantitative and qualitative methods is difficult (for more details, see Fortune and Reid, 1999), although some researchers have been able to combine the two approaches coherently (Miles & Huberman, 1994). To the extent that the epistemologies within which the approaches are based are incommensurate, the issue cannot be resolved by logical argument. However, one principle that may help the practitioner through this philosophical minefield is that rigor is important. If research is to guide practice with people facing difficult or painful problems, there should be persuasive evidence that the data presented reflect more than the researcher's personal biases. The literature is littered with case studies that describe the amazing effectiveness of every imaginable technique (Wakefield,

1993), including many that have ultimately been found to be dangerous, so there is reason to maintain a healthy skepticism about all results that do not present persuasive evidence.

In quantitative studies, "controls," statistics, and measures of reliability and validity provide such evidence. In qualitative studies, techniques such as presenting extensive direct quotations so the reader can make his or her own judgments and having several other researchers examine the raw data to ensure that the findings do not reflect a single researcher's own biases are critical. The increasing use of matrices and networks that explicitly indicate and model connections extracted from qualitative data is an important development in qualitative analysis (Miles & Huberman, 1994). Of course, no one study can be regarded as definitive; it is essential that important findings be replicated by other researchers.

There is much to learn from a variety of types of naturalistic research. The rich detail provided by qualitative methods can be especially valuable for suggesting hypotheses (structured observation has proven crucial, especially in the discovery stage, in many sciences), and patterns that seem to be present can later be tested in other ways. For example, a network of causal connections among variables discovered by qualitative methods could be tested for accuracy and the magnitude of direct and indirect effects using path analysis, a quantitative method rooted in multiple regression. At the same time, the precision and generality offered by quantitative approaches can be critical for understanding large-scale social problems, as well as for testing the results of interventive strategies. Qualitative research may identify important factors and relationships in a single case or in examination of a service system that would otherwise be missed. Quantitative research can be helpful in specifying patterns among the data to determine how important and reliable those factors and relationships are.

Experimental Research. "To experiment, to try it, seems to me the natural impulse, inhibited and replaced in our education by subservience to authority, acceptance of dogma, from our parents or our leaders" (Bates, 1950/1990, p. 274). Experimentation is valuable precisely because it allows social workers to test accepted wisdom and to try new approaches that may result in better outcomes for clients.

There are two major subtypes of experimental research and many variations of each. One general approach is the *group design*, in which (in its standard form), one group of clients receives an intervention, and the other group—the control group—does not, with each measured before and after the intervention. (In the purest designs, clients are randomly assigned to these groups.) The researcher then looks to see whether a statistically— and socially—significant difference in the outcome for the two groups is present. Because there are ethical problems in withholding treatment from one group in many cases, common variations include giving one group the "standard intervention" and giving the other group the proposed innovative treatment or comparing the efficacy of two different interventive packages. An example of a group experimental study with immediate practice implications is that by Brunk, Henggeler, and Whelan (1987), in which the outcomes of a structured parent training program were compared with multisystemic family therapy for abusive and neglectful parents. By using a creative design and a variety of measures, the authors found that different approaches seemed to be best for different types of families. Some of the findings might at first glance seem surprising; the parent training group proved to be particularly helpful with system problems, probably, according to the authors, because of the level of sharing that occurred among group members regarding available resources. An important aspect of this success may be that a group such as this can offer opportunities for shared power.

Although such group designs clearly have many benefits, they also have their limitations (Johnston, 1988), some of which are particularly significant. A major limitation is that the results of group designs are averages and usually reflect some people who did very well, some who did marginally well or for whom the intervention had no effect, and some who actually did worse. Group designs do not allow one to disaggregate these results or to trace the possible causes of the differences. It is not possible to vary the intervention in response to individual client differences in a group experiment without losing rigor, although different factors and interventions may be relevant to each. Practically speaking, an individual social worker also usually cannot muster the level of financial and human resources necessary to implement a group design. For these and other reasons, a number of researchers in social work and other helping fields have increasingly turned to single-case experimental designs (also called "single-subject" or "single-system" designs).

Single-case designs reflect an effort to test the value of interventions with individual client systems (which may be individuals, families, groups, communities, or other systems) in as rigorous a way as possible (Bloom, Fischer, & Orme, 1999; Mattaini, 1993b; Fortune & Reid, 1999). Simple descriptive case studies have been a staple of social work literature since the earliest days of the profession and were a first approximation to single-case designs. Unfortunately, all of the issues discussed earlier with regard to subjective bias can come into play in such descriptions. As Wakefield (1993) noted, "Every one of the therapeutic theories . . . is supported by case evidence . . . including dramatic cures" (p. 675), so a substantial measure of caution is required in using such descriptions. Much more rigorous single-case designs that provide controls for "threats to internal validity"—alternate explanations for observed change—have therefore been developed during the past 40 years (see Chapter 6).

Single-case designs also have limitations. Measuring complex clinical issues is always challenging. In addition, demonstrating that an intervention works with one client does not mean that it will work with others, so multiple replications with different clients in different contextual situations, by different workers, and in different settings are necessary to begin to establish the generalizability of such findings. This is not as serious an issue as it may appear, because if every case is routinely monitored, the social worker and client will be able to determine whether the client's situation is or is not responsive to a particular intervention plan, as well as to examine the effects of multiple variables unique to the case. Single-case designs are, therefore, particularly useful for practice monitoring (see Chapter 6 for more details).

Another advantage of single-case designs is that they do not necessarily require extensive resources to complete, and it is therefore possible for a practitioner who is trained in their use to make contributions to the knowledge base of the profession as a "practitioner–researcher." Many of the most useful single-case studies have, in fact, been conducted by practitioners because of their deep familiarity with the realities of day-to-day practice and the constraints that affect it. The next generation of practitioners will have many opportunities to contribute in this way, probably even as members of organized practice research networks. Practitioners do not have time to do rigorous research on every case, but when they discover particularly effective approaches, they may have an ethical obligation to study the processes involved and share them with the profession.

Most of the naturalistic observations and experiments that inform practice have been done by others, and the social worker learns about them by becoming immersed in the professional literature. The social worker also compiles a collection of more or less rigorous observations and experimental data from the cases—on whatever systemic level—that he or she works with. In other words, some of the knowledge that informs practice comes directly from the case itself.

Knowledge from the Case

The client (an individual, family, or other system) and the environmental context within which the client is embedded provide a good deal of particularized information that is specific to the case, is more or less objective, and can guide collaborative assessment and intervention. Because many things that the client experiences and knows must be part of the shared worker–client knowledge base for intervention to be maximally effective, a social worker usually asks a number of questions, both during the initial engagement and throughout the intervention process. The client may not know or understand everything that is relevant, but it is a mistake to dismiss information—even partial, distorted, and relatively subjective information—that the client provides; the social worker's own view is likely to include just as much distortion, and, except when there is a clear reason not to, it is far better to begin by believing the client (Cowger & Snively, 2002). Clients often can describe their situations, behavior, and feelings relatively accurately. A sophisticated understanding of human behavior can be helpful in sorting out the circumstances under which such descriptions may not be accurate. These circumstances tend to be of two types: (1) when clients have a reason for not providing an accurate description (for example, when there are legal factors encouraging falsification), and (2) when clients lack the capacity for accurate description because of impaired reality testing (e.g., in severe mental illness) or because the person has simply never learned to recognize and describe feelings accurately.

It is always important to hear and understand the client's own perceptions as important case data. How information is collected can also affect the quality of information provided. Opportunities for clients to tell their stories in their own way, in their own voices, rather than being asked to respond to a barrage of interrogation-like questions, are likely to produce deeper, more meaningful information. Offering such an opportunity is a crucial aspect of sharing power. This approach leads to empowerment and enriched outcomes consistent with client values and cultural realities, outcomes that are not possible if the social worker tries to maintain an "expert" stance in a hierarchical arrangement.

Observation of clients and client systems can also provide valuable knowledge. For example, the combination of observations of repetitive patterns of exchange—positive or negative—in a couple or a family with research about the importance of such patterns (see, for example, Burman, John, & Margolin, 1992) can provide a great deal of direction to the family clinician. When such observations are also viewed in the context of environmental transactions (Mattaini, Grellong, & Abramovitz, 1992)—information about which often comes from the family and segments of their social networks—the potential for broadly based family-centered practice that transcends the limitations of family therapy alone is enhanced.

Frequently, there are substantial advantages to rigorous observation of clients, family members, and group or community members. Depending on the circumstances, such observation can be done by clients themselves or by the worker. For example, with regard to parenting issues, actually counting and charting a child's behavior is valuable not only for case-monitoring purposes, but also for motivational ones (Mattaini, 1999). Gradual improvements in such cases can be graphically evident when parents chart them but may not otherwise be noticed. Self-observation and self-monitoring may also be empowering for clients because they are involved directly in the assessment, and self-monitoring increases their involvement and control throughout the intervention process (Kopp, 1993). The data presented are also extremely useful to the worker because they lend precision in what may otherwise be a rather unstructured and subjective process.

Finally, every case is in some measure a single-case experiment. Although the worker may be confident of the efficacy of the interventive strategy and tactics that he or she and the client have agreed to adopt, the final test lies in how the case evolves over time. Thus, monitoring cases is important, not primarily because it is increasingly required by funders and bureaucratic structures, but because it is crucial for social workers to know what they are trying to accomplish with their cases and whether they are succeeding. Any intervention should be regarded as experimental and therefore should be monitored until its efficacy for a particular case has been established. One way to do so is using a "clinical analytic" single-case design, which permits the intervention to evolve over time as guided by the case (see Figure 5-1).

Luckily, the social worker does not need to start from scratch with each case, however. To make sense of information from the case in the context of knowledge from the other sources discussed thus far, the graduate social worker needs a conceptual framework to organize all of this. That is the function of theoretical analyses and practice approaches. Such analyses, however, always occur in the context of other factors, including one's own life experiences, historical and current events, and cultural perspectives, each of which requires attention.

Personal Experience

In addition to learning from research and the experiences of other practitioners as captured in practice wisdom, social workers base their work on their own life experiences (personal and professional). It is crucial for them to do so (in effect, to develop their own personal practice wisdom) so they do not need to begin again with every client. The basic interpersonal and problem-solving skills that social workers have developed throughout their lives also inform their practice.

It is important to recognize explicitly the influence of personal history because one may over-generalize from one's experiences, transforming a potential resource into an obstacle. For example, a success or failure with

Figure 5-1. An Example of a Clinical Analytic Design

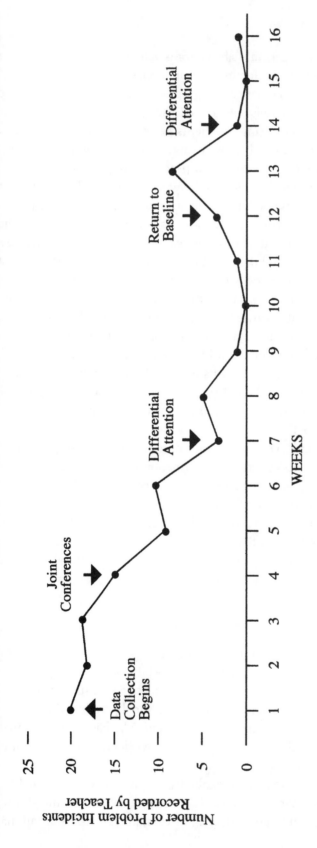

NOTE: In this hypothetical case of a child displaying behavior problems in a classroom, the social worker begins by gathering baseline data. After three weeks, she might begin twice-weekly conferences among the student, the teacher, and herself to improve student and teacher communication and to help clarify expectations and needs. In this figure, note that although the problems abated somewhat with this intervention, they continued at a distressing level. As a result, the worker might introduce an additional procedure (designing a program to ensure high levels of peer attention to appropriate behavior and extinction of inappropriate behavior; Ervin, Miller, & Friman, 1996). If this program resolved the problem, as seems to be the case here, the social worker and the teacher might try to withdraw this somewhat demanding procedure to see whether it is still required. Note that on the graph, withdrawal led to a resurgence of the classroom problems, which again remitted after the differential reinforcement procedure was reinstated. (Naturally in cases where inappropriate behavior has resulted in attention for years, it may take some time to eliminate that behavior.) The graph suggests both that the problems have been brought under control and that the intervention was responsible for the improvement.

one client may lead the worker to select or avoid particular intervention strategies again, and that is as it should be. Nevertheless, an intervention that works or does not work in one case may produce different results in other cases in which a different configuration is present. Therefore, the ability to individualize a case and be open to learning new state-of-the-art approaches is crucial for effectiveness and is also an ethical responsibility.

Personal life experience can inform or impede practice in other ways. Personal values that are learned early in life often guide a practitioner's professional activities. These values can be beneficial when they are congruent with professional values, as is the case with acceptance and caring. However, when personal values conflict with professional values, they create a dilemma for practitioners—witness the struggle of some social workers who believe that abortion is wrong but are required by professional values to support a client's right to choose (self-determination).

There is no simple answer to these dilemmas, but the profession holds that conduct that is consistent with professional values is ordinarily required. Self-determination is among those professional values, but even it is not as simple as it may appear to be. In many cultures, the good of the group rather than self-interest is seen as primary, suggesting the need for sophisticated re-examination of this concept within a multicultural context (Ewalt, 1994). The extent to which clients can freely choose among courses of action—either because of limited personal capacity or because many theories of behavior suggest that much of human action is determined by factors outside the awareness or control of the individual—also requires careful thought. Of course, when self-determination and safety conflict, social workers must make difficult decisions.

A situation in which a client is struggling with issues that the social worker herself or himself has dealt with in the past presents both advantages and challenges. Although such common experiences may increase the practitioner's empathy for the client, they may also lead the practitioner to push the client toward particular alternatives (those that worked for the practitioner), and away from others that may be a better fit for the client. For example, a worker who has benefited (as many have) from a 12-step program for substance abuse may consider those programs to be the most effective available (although the research indicates that the situation is far more complex) and refer clients to those programs to the exclusion of others that may be a better fit for the client (see Marlatt, 1998; and Meyers & Smith, 1996, for discussions of other possibilities). Each case is different; each person is different and may have different needs.

Likewise, issues of self-disclosure become significant when the social worker has had personal experiences similar to the client's. For example, a practitioner who has been treated for cancer may sometimes find it helpful to share that fact with clients who have been diagnosed with cancer, but in other cases, this disclosure of personal information may inhibit the practice process. The client may be concerned that if the social worker has handled this issue so well, for instance, that worker may judge the client harshly if he or she appears weak. In such cases, clients may avoid expressing honest emotions. The research on self-disclosure has not yet clarified specifically how and in what situations it should be used, so social workers must decide what information to disclose and when to disclose it on a case-by-case basis. A moderate level of self-disclosure, consciously used to benefit the client (rather than to meet the needs of the social worker) can often be valuable for communicating empathy and demonstrating authenticity. Practitioners now use self-disclosure more than they did in the past (Anderson & Mandell, 1989), which suggests that the value of appropriate self-disclosure has become part of the profession's body of practice wisdom and may also reflect cohort and social-class effects—practitioners may be more like clients, and vice versa, than was true a generation ago.

A potential dilemma occurs when a client is struggling with an issue that the worker is also currently facing. This situation usually poses a serious problem; although self-disclosure is generally not appropriate under those circumstances, the issues go well beyond that. For example, a practitioner who is going through a divorce may find it difficult to work effectively with couples (because of "countertransference"—a form of overgeneralization). Similarly, a worker with a substance abuse problem may minimize, deny, or project such problems onto clients. Also, a practitioner who continues to be deeply disturbed by images of abuse in her childhood is unlikely to be able to deal effectively with either a victim or a perpetrator of abuse.

In such circumstances, social workers need, at a minimum, close supervision and consultation, but because the welfare of the clients is the primary consideration, such cases may have to be transferred to other practitioners. In addition, a social worker who is significantly impaired (emotionally or by substance abuse, for example) has an ethical responsibility to get help, and his or her colleagues who are aware of the problem have an ethical responsibility to assist the practitioner to get help and to protect his or her clients.

Clearly, such situations illustrate the need for personal self-awareness by practitioners. Social workers must be in touch with their own constantly shifting thoughts and emotions in practice, recognize that their needs and experiences may color what they see and do, and recognize that possible distortions introduced by such thoughts and emotions may interfere with the quality of service given to clients. When social workers notice strong emotions in themselves, they should reflect on the roots of these feelings and be willing to talk with a supervisor, a respected colleague, or a thera-pist who can help them make sense of what is happening. Putting these struggles into words and sharing them is a primary way of clarifying and sorting them out. The client, however, is not an appropriate audience for such reflections. Practitioners should also take time to think about how their life experiences and values may affect their work in the future and prepare to deal with the probable conflicts that may arise from them.

History and Current Events

Because all of practice is embedded in the broader social context, knowl-edge of social policy (both current policy and its historical roots) and of shifting social forces is important for workers at all levels. Although this domain is treated primarily in social policy courses, its integral intercon-nections with practice need to be recognized. For example, the realities of clients and cultures who have faced and survived forces of exploitation, oppression, and extermination (such as the genocidal experiences of the Jewish and Native American peoples or the effect of centuries of enslave-ment and dehumanization of African American people) are profoundly shaped by those experiences and must be recognized and respected by prac-titioners. Shifting events, like those that began with the terrorist attacks on New York City and the Pentagon in 2001—and all that followed (for ex-ample, the widespread attacks on persons of Middle Eastern and South Asian descent)—shape the realities and perceptions of many clients simul-taneously, and therefore social work practice at many levels. Issues involv-ing human rights are ubiquitous in social work practice not only at the policy level, but also moment by moment in direct work with individuals and families. Extensive familiarity with the human rights literature pro-vides a critical perspective for understanding and helping clients to see the larger forces affecting their lives. Battered women, for example, are not just depressed individuals, they are often the survivors of torture whose hu-man rights have been violated by their batterers and whose societies have tacitly accepted and in fact often actively encouraged the violation. This view changes the meaning of, and approaches for working with, such ex-periences in profound ways.

Historical documents, the technical policy literature, the mass media, and, increasingly, the Internet provide sources of historical and policy in-formation that can inform practice at all levels. Social workers must view data from any source critically in the context of their full knowledge base because each source observes and reports events according to its own value base and political position. Given careful analysis, however, there is a tre-mendous amount of information now available, and access to very current data regarding events relevant to social issues and practice is increasingly easy (see, for example, http://www.bfsr.org for links to a number of useful sites for social workers and others committed to social, economic, and ecological justice).

It is common for stories in the mass media to be reported in less than fully objective ways—and with some inaccuracies—but the same is true even of the more technical literature. Even relatively objective "facts," such as the number of persons living below the poverty line, tend to be reported and interpreted differently by those of varying political bents. The differences are even more profound in discussions of the causes of and potential solutions to social problems. Perhaps because of their entertainment value, and consistent with a society that often relies on coercion and conflict in all institutions, many such discussions are structured as debates in which each side tries to defeat the other—even if this means relying on partial truth and distortion. Genuine critical dialogue, in which different voices are respected and participants recognize their obligation to work toward collective outcomes is very uncommon, at least in dominant U.S. culture. Although this situation can be frustrating, and one may be tempted to simply avoid the issues, subjects such as these must be engaged because they are important to the well-being of clients. The only defensible solutions are to read widely to avoid slipping blindly into one's own selective bias, to think critically in the context of professional values, and to consider alternative perspectives that may be more informative, including those of other cultural groups.

Cultural Perspectives

We suggested in Chapter 1 that diversity in cultural perspectives is critical to societal functioning and even survival. Familiarity with and respect for multiple cultural perspectives are critical for social work practice for at least two reasons. One is that social workers must recognize that those they work with—clients, program participants, community collaborators—genuinely see the world in different ways, depending on their cultural experiences. People who are deeply grounded in traditional African values, for example, are likely to see issues and evaluate solutions in ways that are dramatically different from dominant European American society. Individuals who appear for services have been deeply shaped by the many cultural networks to which they belong, and need to be understood and helped in terms that make sense within such multicultural matrices.

In addition, ethnoconscious social services that emerge from deep cultural roots may offer possibilities that would never occur to practitioners otherwise. Agencies guided by the *Ma'at* (Seven Cardinal Virtues: order, balance, harmony, compassion, reciprocity, justice, and truth) and the *Nguzo Saba* (Seven Pillars of Strength: unity, self-determination, collective work and responsibility, cooperative economics, purpose, creativity, and faith) (O'Donnell & Karanja, 2000) are likely to deal with funders, communities, and clients in quite different ways than do agencies who see their operations as part of consumer society—what John Lame Deer called "the Green Frog Skin [money] World" in which "each blade of grass or spring of water has a price tag on it" (Lame Deer & Erdoes, 1972, p. 32). Culturally rooted services may be particularly helpful to persons who identify with those cultures, of course, but the potential goes beyond this. Cultures survive because their practices have—at least in some environmental contexts—worked, and social work often finds new possibilities in diverse cultural perspectives that prove useful for everyone.

While social work has come to rely heavily on ecological metaphors, it is also literally true that human beings and human society are rooted in the physical world, the natural environment, which includes the web of human connections. Modern western society has done tremendous damage to that environment, damage that in fact has produced serious health and social justice issues with the most immediate impact on the poor, but ultimately on everyone. Indigenous cultures carry knowledge about how to do so that has often been lost by other groups; they know some important things about how to live collectively in the world. This includes knowledge essential to physical and spiritual survival (LaDuke, 1999), as well as knowledge of how to heal the terrible damage that modern society sometimes creates in the human web (Ross, 1996), and live "the way of the human being" (Martin, 1999). There is an enormous amount that social work can learn from Native cultures, which can have an immediate impact on how social work is practiced and how social agencies are organized (Lowery & Mattaini, 1999, 2001). The emphasis on shared power found throughout this book is one key example. When Vine Deloria (1994) wrote, "for this land, God is red" (p. 292), one of the things he was suggesting is that Native peoples know how to live successfully in this environment.

One key dimension of the cultural is the spiritual (and social work practice done in a good way is spiritual work). Religious and spiritual practices and experiences are core to many people's lives, and cannot be ignored in work with the human web. Many Latino people, for example, rely on both traditional healers and organized religions; traditional and Western practices are often amalgamated and integrated in contemporary Latino celebrations, rituals, and other practices. It is important to wonder about and honor this dimension of people's lives. Clients appreciate respect for their worldviews, values, and practices including the religious and spiritual, and only by appreciating these does the social worker see the whole person.

Social workers themselves need to examine how their own religious and spiritual beliefs and practices may influence the work, for better (by enriching recognition for human connection, for example), or for worse (by imposing one's own beliefs on others, for instance).

Defining Art and Literature

Professional social work practice is grounded in a broad knowledge of the liberal arts, including art and literature, which capture and define cultural values and wisdom differently than does anything else. Art and literature provide both context and content for decision-making and action in practice. For example, the "ash-can" school of painting in the early 20th century captured and emphasized the realities of urban life in new ways, providing a clear vision of emerging social phenomena. Japanese sumi-e ink paintings and Zen art, by contrast, use symbols and simplicity to express enduring truths. Art that is meaningful for clients, of course, can also be important. For example, when an Alaska Native health corporation took over a clinic formerly run by the federal Indian Health Service, they decorated the entire clinic with historical photographs of village life and Native art, reminding both patients and staff for whom the clinic existed and grounding modern services in tradition. Much more than this is required, of course, to achieve ethnoconscious services (Gutierrez, 1997); in this case, however, the art was integral to a Native-administered strategy of service provision in which indigenous voices were primary.

Although for European American cultures in recent centuries artistic products have been produced primarily to produce emotional or cognitive effects, in indigenous cultures the connections between art and everyday life are often much closer. For example, Dockstader (n.d.) indicated, "Indian art was made to do work. In later years there came into existence a body of articles meant simply to beautify, but earlier 'art' objects had to perform a service, and only secondarily were intended to beautify" (p. 20). In addition, however, a beautiful elaboration of functional objects often speaks to the organic cultural meanings associated with everyday activity as opposed to the "alienation" commonly found in modern society between worker and work (Skinner, 1987).

Literature, narrative, and poetry open a different set of windows for viewing reality. How better to remind oneself of the dignity and value of every person, of genuine acceptance and respect, than with the words of Walt Whitman (1892/1992):

> None has understood you, but I understand you,
> None has done justice to you, you have not done justice to yourself,

None but has found you imperfect, I only find no imperfection in you,
   None but would subordinate you, I only am he who will never consent to
subordinate you,
   I only am he who places over you no master, owner, better, God, beyond
what waits intrinsically in yourself. (p. 177)

Drama, novels, other classical and contemporary literature, as well as films help define the cultural worlds within which client and worker live out their lives and can immeasurably enrich practice. From authors such as William Shakespeare, Toni Morrison, Herman Melville, and Adrian Louis come many of the words and shared experiences that inspire and guide practice, whether explicitly or implicitly.

Theoretical and Conceptual Frameworks

"There is nothing so practical as a good theory" (Lewin, 1951/1976, p. 169). Observations and facts are valuable but, by themselves, provide only limited guidance for practice; theory explicates the connections among them, leading to the identification of meaningful patterns. In any complex case, one needs a theoretical framework to make sense of the particularized patterns found. Information from biological, behavioral, and social sciences does not simply map on to the case; the worker requires a theoretical base to make sense of case events. Theory, then, is not so much a discrete source of knowledge as much as an essential way of organizing and integrating knowledge from all of the sources discussed thus far.

   Theories are available at all practice levels, although their breadth and the extent to which they are well explicated and tested vary considerably. There is a tremendous range of theories that attempt to explain individual behavior; there is substantial theory at the family and group levels and some explaining organizational phenomena, but only quite limited theory has emerged to guide community practice. Although each of the behavioral and social sciences has theoretical frameworks, only some of these theories have been rigorously tested against reality. Hence, it is important for social workers to know how solidly established and well supported the various theoretical approaches and models are. Selecting theory based on personal comfort or uninformed preference, of course, would be deeply unfair to clients.

   Selection of theories. The philosophy of science provides some guidance about how to select theoretical frameworks. Along with the extent to which a theory has been supported by experiment and observation, other important considerations include breadth and simplicity. All else being equal, a

higher-level theory that explains a broader range of phenomena is prefer-
able to a lower-level theory that explains only a few events. For example,
a theory of human behavior that partially explains why people become
anxious about particular situations or events is useful, a theory that explains the connections between anxiety and relationship issues is better,
and a theory that explains the connections among a wide range of emotional and behavioral issues and external events over the life course is
more valuable still.

Simple explanations generally are preferred to more complicated ones,
as well. The Copernican revolution occurred when it became clear that if
one assumed that the Earth (and other planets) revolved around the sun,
rather than the other way around, it was much easier to trace the path that
each planet takes. Science generally relies on Occam's razor, a rule that
suggests that parsimonious theory is to be preferred. If, for example, it is
possible to explain and predict the rate of a particular behavior (for example, a child's tantrums) on the basis of social and environmental events,
little is gained by hypothesizing that an unobservable and untestable cognitive "tantrum schema" becomes activated and is filtered through an unobservable and untestable mental representation of the external world, which
then causes the tantrum. (Note that this is not to say that intervening variables should not be included in theoretical models when they are observed
to make a difference, improving prediction or intervention.) Simpler theoretical elaborations also allow the field to codify what has been learned and
move on to new issues and questions that the model suggests.

Adequate theory predicts events and connections among them that can
be tested. If a theory suggests that the primary reason for depression is
anger produced by inadequate parenting in childhood but also indicated
that such (unconscious) anger can be inferred only from the level of depression, the explanation risks becoming circular. Testing theory of this
type requires either some other evidence for the hypothesized unobservable factors (anger in this case) or theoretically rooted predictions (for example, one might assist the client to express anger and see whether the
level of depression changed). Things that cannot be seen are sometimes
real but, of course, they can be useful for practice only if they can be con-
tacted in some way.

For the purposes of practice, theory must be able to guide intervention
with the types of situations and issues the practitioner is working with. For
example, it is clear that cognitive–behavioral theories (Beck et al., 1978;
Ellis & Dryden, 1997) provide guidance for effective intervention in many
cases of serious depression (Nathan & Gorman, 1998). (Note that interpersonal therapy, direct behavioral intervention, and certain pharmacothera-
pies also often produce excellent outcomes, with some variations depending

on the case.) There are limitations to the use of exclusively cognitive approaches for some client–situation configurations, however (Poppen, 1989). Some environments in which clients are embedded are extremely aversive, and helping clients to accept these circumstances cognitively may not be a responsible, or effective, approach. Theory-based approaches also shift over time based on new empirical findings and conceptual advances; recent information suggests that the active ingredient in cognitive–behavior therapy for depression may be behavioral activation, which leads to greater exposure to positive experiences (Jacobson et al., 1996) Changes in self-talk (cognition) may in some case remove barriers to behavioral activation (Mattaini, 1997), but may not be necessary at all in many cases.

It may already be clear from this discussion that "theory" actually refers to several types of integrated understanding. In particular, there are underlying theories that help explain why people and larger systems function as they do (generally emerging from basic research in the behavioral and social sciences, although social workers have made substantial contributions as well) and practice theories (usually developed by social workers) that explain and predict what will happen when particular interventive strategies and techniques are used with particular types of cases in social work practice. Psychodynamic theories (including contributions from modern ego psychology, self-psychology, and object relations theory) may help the worker to understand case events, but one does not "do" object relations, for example. The practitioner who operates from this basic framework is likely to apply a psychosocial (or psychodynamic) practice approach, using one of the multiple theoretical paradigms or practice approaches in current use (see, for example, Goldstein, 2001).

Some practice approaches are deeply grounded in one or more relatively well-developed theoretical or conceptual frameworks, while others are more shallowly rooted conceptually and rely primarily on aggregations of practice wisdom and specific research. For example, contemporary psychosocial practice (Goldstein, 2001, Woods & Hollis, 1999) is based in traditional psychodynamic and ego psychological thought, but also object relations, self psychology, to some extent ecosystems, and in some cases family systems theory. Ecobehavioral practice (Mattaini, 1997, 1999) emerges from behavioral, cultural analytic, and cognitive theory, a shared power paradigm, and ecosystems, with significant influence from the strengths perspective and family systems. The life model relies on ecosystems, ecological theory, and ego psychology in particular, but also has links to several other bodies of theory. Models based deeply in coherent, broad theory can provide direction in even novel situations, which can be an important advantage if the theoretical base is well established. By contrast, there are a number of approaches in current use that rely primarily on less comprehensive theory, but offer rich guidance based on principles that have been selected eclectically, but at least somewhat rigorously. Structural practice (Wood & Middleman, 1989), and Poulin's collaborative strengths-based generalist practice (2000) are examples that many practitioners find very useful. Contemporary expressions of some of these approaches often incorporate feminist and post-modernist thought in comprehensive ways.

Although it is possible to use nearly any practice approach within an ecosystems perspective, published accounts and actual practice vary in the extent to which this occurs. Contemporary psychosocial, ecological (for example, life model), task-centered, and ecobehavioral models usually explicitly identify their ecosystemic nature, and descriptions of practice based on them tend to include interventions focused on environmental, family, and personal issues and their interconnections. Some other models, such as Wright's (1988) elaboration of cognitive therapy or solution-focused work, do not emphasize those links, and to some extent this probably reflects the realities of day-to-day practice. Those models with more extensive links on the figure may be applicable to a broader range of practice situations.

Practice approaches. Social work practice, similar to other "helping" professions, is grounded in the practitioner's understanding of the phenomena involved, including individual experiences and action, social phenomena, and the environmental context within which these occur. In the roughly 100 years during which the profession has evolved, many different practice "models" or approaches have emerged. There are, however, a few key clusters that encompass most of those practice approaches. Each has contributed something to professional practice, and the graduate social worker certainly should have some exposure to each, if for no other reason than to be able to communicate with colleagues. At the same time, it is critical to avoid an "eclectic stew," in which concepts from multiple approaches are randomly mixed. Different approaches see the multiple causes of human action in different, and to some extent, incompatible ways. A "moral" model for understanding substance abuse, for example, would indicate the need for an act of will on the part of an alcoholic person while denying much of what has been learned about substance abuse in recent decades, whereas a disease model would suggest the need to acknowledge powerlessness as an early step toward treatment. A social worker's core understandings of human action are unlikely to change from moment to moment and person to person, although there is much to be said for looking from a fresh perspective at times. Because different theoretical frameworks often understand human behavior and other social forces in incompatible ways, practice approaches grounded in the most adequate and well-established underlying conceptual understandings should clearly be privileged.

The oldest professional practice framework in social work is the psychosocial approach, which has continuously evolved since Richmond's (1917) *Social Diagnosis*. This approach, for at least six decades, relied primarily on psychodynamic theory (including modern developments in ego psychology and object relations). The key to understanding human behavior and emotion in this approach is the developmental process over the life course, much of which is seen as not in the client's conscious awareness. Because development occurs primarily through experience, there is a place for the social and physical environment in this approach, but this place may primarily be historical. Current environmental forces are certainly recognized by psychosocial social workers but are somewhat difficult to work into a single conceptual framework. Perhaps the best contemporary statement of this approach is outlined by Goldstein (1995; 2001), who attempted to address historical limitations of the model.

Partly in response to the bias often found in psychosocial work toward identifying individual dysfunction as opposed to transactional issues, the ecological approach (in particular the life model [Germain & Gitterman, 1996]) emphasizes mutual adaptation between person and environment. The life model applies ecological constructs such as habitat, niche, parasitism, and stress and coping very directly to the social world. (Note the overlap with the ecosystems perspective. It is possible, however, to practice ecosystemically from any practice approach; see Chapter 1.) This approach also is grounded in process, including human development over the life course and the processes of helping over time. The model focuses particularly on certain classes of problems, including life transitions, traumas, dysfunctional relationship patterns, and coping with environmental stressors. Related approaches include person-environment practice (Kemp et al., 1997), which placed particularly heavy emphasis on assessing and enriching social support networks, based on both well-explicated theory and emerging research.

The third major cluster of practice approaches is the behavioral–cognitive (or cognitive–behavioral) approach. Similar to other early approaches, behavioral models were initially somewhat narrow, but were from the beginning deeply grounded in both theory and research. Modern ecobehavioral practice encompasses both overt action and private experiences (cognitive and emotional), and recognizes the environmental origins (as the psychosocial model does) and current environmental influences (as the ecological model does) that shape human experience (Mattaini, 1997, 1999). In its contemporary manifestations, ecobehavioral practice places a heavy focus on shared power in the practice relationship and on the co-construction of an improved personal reality (as contrasted with treating problems). There is also an explicit focus on applications of behavioral, cognitive, and cultural analytic science in these approaches.

In addition to these broad, theory-grounded practice approaches, a number of other contemporary and emerging approaches deserve special note. Particularly important are culturally specific models of practice, for example, Afrocentric models that structure practice according to traditional African values and cultural practices (Schiele, 1996), and models that in some cases may be very specific to a single indigenous nation (e.g., a Lakota-specific approach, Voss et al., 1999). Many such approaches, not surprisingly, incorporate heavy focus on family and community context, and de-emphasize individual, pathology-focused diagnosis. Such models can be implemented independently, or components of the models can be integrated with other approaches to practice. This is also true of feminist practice, which has contributed a great deal to nearly every contemporary practice model.

All practice approaches that survive evolve and change over time. For example, the task-centered approach originally was explicitly atheoretical and certainly was designed to work for practitioners with psychodynamic backgrounds as well as others. More recent statements of the model (for example, Reid, 1992, 2000) can probably best be described as fitting within the behavioral–cognitive cluster (Gambrill, 1994), and are heavily evidence-based. Most contemporary models evolved from earlier approaches; for an extensive consideration of this history and figures tracing it, see Germain (1983). Germain also predicted in 1983 that the major practice approaches in the field would converge in important ways, and this has in fact happened during the past two decades. A psychosocial theorist like Eda Goldstein, for example, now includes a significant amount of ecological content in her work (1995), and the ecobehavioral approach integrates ecological and cognitive-behavioral content. There also appears to be considerable mutual respect among those developing differing approaches at this point, which is certainly a healthy development for the field.

Two other recent shifts are particularly important. One is the movement toward *evidence-based practice* (Gambrill, 1999), which guides the social work practitioner, all else being equal, to rely on interventive strategies that have withstood rigorous, critical evaluation. If "what works" is at least to some extent known, there is often an ethical imperative to use that knowledge. Some authors involved in the movement toward evidence-based practice believe that it will eventually replace concern with models and approaches, and social workers will simply do what has been shown to be most effective. The field is not yet there, but there clearly are areas in which progress toward that point is occurring. A second recent shift is also important. This is what has been called the "strengths perspective" (Saleebey, 2002). The strengths perspective is usually not seen as complete enough to constitute a full practice model, although in some fields of practice this may no longer be true. The strengths approach, however, has been quite important in helping social workers view clients as competent human beings who bring their own strengths to the social work consultation. Clients are not, in this view, seen as bundles of pathology or as problems to be solved, but rather as partners in a collaborative process of shared power. The shift is much more profound than may at first be apparent, because much of social work in recent decades has relied heavily on diagnosing "what is wrong"—in part due to an over-reliance on psychiatric models of understanding human beings. Most contemporary statements of social work practice models, at least to some extent, incorporate the strengths perspective.

There are other narrower approaches that have valuable insights to offer but are too limited to be applied exclusively in many social work settings. For example, the existential approach (Krill, 1988) can be useful for people whose difficulties primarily lie in the realm of acceptance (Hayes, Strosahl, & Wilson, 1999), but it is often not be adequate to deal with cases with major social justice dimensions. The cognitive approach has much to offer in terms of understanding how people's perceptions of the world influence their actions and in varying forms has been incorporated into several practice approaches, including the life and ecobehavioral models. An exclusive focus on changing what clients say to themselves, however, is not adequate for dealing with many case situations and can constitute a subtle form of blaming the victim when applied irresponsibly. In part for these reasons, but also because the research suggests that behavioral components are often critical to the effectiveness of cognitive intervention, recent cognitive practice in all helping disciplines has attended to behavioral and environmental factors more extensively than was true at some points in the past (Ellis & Dryden, 1997; Jacobson et al., 1996).

Some practice approaches have been developed for and applied in work with individuals, families, groups, communities, and organizations, whereas others focus on fewer system levels. The task-centered model, developed by Reid and his collaborators, has been elaborated primarily for work with individuals, families, and groups (Tolson, Reid, & Garvin, 1994), for example, whereas the life model focuses particularly on work with individuals and families but has close links with the mutual-aid model of group work (refer to Chapter 9) and some forms of organizational practice. Ecobehavioral approaches have been presented for each system level, but some (e.g., individuals and families) have been much more comprehensively developed than others (especially organizational and community work; see Chapter 12). Cognitive approaches are used primarily with individuals and in groups; even marital treatment is often conducted individually by those working cognitively (for example, Ellis et al., 1989). Some models are specific to particular system levels (especially certain group work and community practice approaches); these are explored further in subsequent chapters.

Use of Theory. Sophisticated practitioners must be familiar with each of the major theoretical frameworks and practice approaches that are commonly applied in practice for at least two reasons. First, they must be able to communicate with other professionals who may be operating from a different conceptual framework than their own. Second, because no theory is adequate to explain all phenomena at all levels of practice, social workers may sometimes need to turn to theories other than the ones from which they usually operate. For example, a social worker whose primary base is psychodynamic and ego psychological may find himself or herself dealing with severe child behavior problems in families. So far, *only* behavioral practice has demonstrated efficacy in work with such problems (Corcoran, 2000). It is not enough, however, to apply such techniques blindly; practitioners must understand the theoretical frameworks well enough to select which to use and to tailor the approach to the specifics of a case. Doing so requires understanding the underlying theory.

At the same time, each social worker must have a relatively coherent, integrated way of understanding client and community reality to structure his or her practice. Drawing techniques randomly from psychodynamic, behavioral, ecological, and humanistic–existential approaches when working with individuals without having reasons for doing so creates confusion, because each theory often suggests doing something different. Such random eclecticism will certainly confuse, and probably alienate, the client as well. Imagine a clinical social worker seeing a family and operating for a few sessions from a behaviorally oriented task-centered approach (emphasizing collaboration with the client in specifying goals and developing interventive tasks). If the worker then suddenly and inexplicably switched to a strategic approach that emphasized paradoxical assignments that clients are expected to defy, the family would certainly struggle with the process and may reasonably think that their collaborative contract had been violated.

A far better approach is to identify a basic theoretical paradigm, based on the criteria identified earlier (empirical support, breath, simplicity, and coherence), and to rely on that framework for understanding complex phenomena in a coherent way. The more difficult and confusing the cases they are dealing with, the more social workers need to turn to theoretical understanding of the issues for guidance. At the same time, a disciplined eclecticism in which techniques and strategies are drawn from multiple approaches, are selected based on their empirical support, and are applied and structured within a coherent conceptual framework can be very useful. Random eclecticism, however, in which practice is not shaped by any coherent understanding, but rather simply emerges from momentary preference, intuition, or whim is neither professional, nor likely to be effective—and therefore poses serious ethical problems. Such practice usually emerges from an inadequate knowledge base or a serious misunderstanding of the responsibilities of professionalism. When a social worker decides to use "rebirthing" techniques as a result of which a healthy child dies of asphyxiation (as happened recently in Colorado), simply because they somehow appeal to her, it becomes clear that selection of approaches involves more than personal preference.

An additional, crucial determinant of one's underlying practice approach must be the extent to which it can be applied with clients whose worldviews and experiences may be very different from the social worker's own. Many of the bodies of theory from which practice approaches have evolved had European and Anglo American roots, and some can be extended more comfortably than others. An approach that emphasizes individual autonomy as healthy may, for example, be damaging when working with clients whose cultural reality is more collective. Alternative approaches may, therefore, be more effective with such groups (see, for example, Ross, 1996).

The foregoing discussion also hints at the importance of recognizing that phenomena must be understood theoretically and conceptually at the appropriate systemic levels. Although everything that occurs in a family interaction could be described in terms of biological processes that occur within the individuals in combination with biological and physical events in the environment, this reductionistic description would not help the worker (or the family) understand the processes that are occurring. Family dynamics are not organized at those levels. Family systems theories, in contrast, may be much more helpful because they attempt to explain what happens within families at a more appropriate systemic level.

Not all social workers see practice at any system level through the same theoretical lenses. The ecosystems perspective, if properly applied, can provide some assurance that all social workers are seeing the basic facts and events in cases—one crucial link among different theoretical approaches. Although different theories occasionally suggest similar interventions, they often suggest very different ones. In many cases, one strategy will produce better outcomes for clients than another will. A good deal is already known about "what works," and certainly the social worker needs to stay very current with the literature to know such things. Because there is not yet general agreement in the field about which approaches generally produce the best outcomes for which kinds of cases, however, the need to monitor practice, to find ways to track whether a particular case is moving in the desired direction, is an ethical responsibility. Blind faith in any theory cannot be justified.

Finally, because social work cases are complex, social workers must achieve a high level of theoretical sophistication in their chosen areas. If, for example, one adopts ecological theory as the core of his or her practice, and perhaps the life model (Germain & Gitterman, 1996) as the primary practice approach, it is not enough simply to know that from this perspective client issues are seen as problems related to traumatic events, stressful life transitions, environmental problems, or dysfunctional patterns of interpersonal relationships and communication. Responsible professionals must also strive to stay current with emerging findings in ecological science (Hudson, 2000; Wilson, 1992), in the evolutionary biology and natural history in which ecology is itself based, and in the social sciences that are closely tied to these (see Harris, 2000). Because the life model also relies on scientific findings related to the life course and stress and coping, these are additional areas in which social workers practicing from this model should be immersed. Not only should they be familiar with popular treatments of these areas, but they should also achieve the sophistication needed to understand the primary sources.

Integrating Sources of Knowledge in the Case

It may seem overwhelming to think about integrating science, theory, practice wisdom, information specific to the case, and all of the other material discussed here when dealing with a case, and it can be. For students, important resources include field instructors, who can draw out areas as appropriate and therefore ensure that all areas are considered. Other professionals, instructors, required and recommended readings assigned in courses, and other literature are also valuable sources. Ultimately, students and social work professionals are responsible for ensuring that they expose themselves to the necessary sources of knowledge; however, courses, supervision, and peer consultation can be helpful in making the links among sources of knowledge that result in excellence in practice. Staying current with the state-of-the-art by reading, attending continuing education programs, and interacting with colleagues is an ethical imperative because it can substantively affect the well-being of clients.

Approaching cases analytically (that is, thoughtfully and with an eye to understanding the dynamics of what is happening) is central to professional practice. During the course of this work, practitioners will often face questions for which they have no good answers. This is a clear signal that it is time to stop and think about the case theoretically or conceptually, to pull a book off the shelf, to do a literature review, to consult with others, or to engage with the client in collaborative experimentation. All of these steps are consistent with, and required by, evidence-based practice. Given the complexity of the phenomena with which social workers practice, this effort is never-ending.

References

Ainslie, G. (1993). A picoeconomic rationale for social constructionism. *Behavior and Philosophy, 21*(2), 63–75.

Anderson, S., & Mandell, D. (1989). The use of self-disclosure by professional social workers. *Social Casework, 70,* 259–267.

Bartlett, H. M. (1970). *The common base of social work practice.* Silver Spring, MD: National Association of Social Workers.

Bates, M. (1990). *The nature of natural history.* Princeton, NJ: Princeton University Press. (Originally published in 1950).

Beck, A. T., Rush, A. J., Shaw, B. F., & Emery, G. (1978). *Cognitive therapy of depression.* New York: Guilford Press.

Bentley, K. J., & Walsh, J. (1996). *The social worker and psychotropic medication.* Pacific Grove, CA: Brooks/Cole.

Biglan, A. (1995). *Changing cultural practices.* Reno, NV: Context Press.

Bloom, M., Fischer, J., & Orme, J. G. (1999). *Evaluating practice: Guidelines for the accountable professional* (3rd ed.). Boston: Allyn & Bacon.

Brunk, M., Henggeler, S. W., & Whelan, J. P. (1987). Comparison of multisystemic therapy and parent training in the brief treatment of child abuse and neglect. *Journal of Consulting and Clinical Psychology, 55,* 171–178.

Burman, B., John, R. S., & Margolin, G. (1992). Observed patterns of conflict in violent, nonviolent, and nondistressed couples. *Behavioral Assessment, 14,* 15–37.

Collins, B. G. (1993). Reconstruing codependency using self-in-relation theory: A feminist perspective. *Social Work, 38,* 470–476.

Corcoran, J. (2000). Family treatment of preschool behavior problems. *Research on Social Work Practice, 10,* 547–588.

Cowger, C., & Snively, C. A. (2002). Assessing client strengths: Individual, family, and community empowerment. In D. Saleebey (Ed.), *The strengths perspective in social work practice* (3rd ed.) (pp. 106–123). New York: Longman.

Deloria, V., Jr. (1994). *God is red: A Native view of religion.* Golden, CO: Fulcrum.

Dockstader, F. J. (n.d.). *Indian art in America.* New York: Promontory Press.

Ellis, A., & Dryden, W. (1997). *The practice of rational emotive behavior therapy* (2nd ed.). New York: Springer.

Ellis, A., Sichel, J. L., Yeager, R. J., DiMattia, D. J., & DiGiuseppe, R. (1989). *Rational-emotive couples therapy.* New York: Pergamon Press.

Ervin, R. A., Miller, P. M., & Friman, P. C. (1996). Feed the hungry bee: Using positive peer reports to improve the social interactions and acceptance of a socially rejected girl in residential care. *Journal of Applied Behavior Analysis, 29,* (251–253).

Ewalt, P. L. (1994). Visions of ourselves [Editorial]. *Social Work, 39,* 5–7.

Fisher, H. E. (1992). *Anatomy of love: The natural history of monogamy, adultery, and divorce.* New York: W. W. Norton.

Floersch, J. (2000). Reading the case record: The oral and written narratives of social workers. *Social Service Review, 74,* 169–192.

Foot, D. K. (1996). *Boom, bust and echo.* Toronto: Macfarlane, Walter & Ross.

Fortune, A. E., & Reid, W. J. (1999). *Research in social work* (3rd ed.). New York: Columbia University Press.

Frances, R. J., & Miller, S. I. (Eds.). (1998). *Clinical textbook of addictive disorders* (2nd ed.). New York: Guilford.

Gambrill, E. (1994). What's in a name? Task-centered, empirical, and behavioral practice. *Social Service Review, 68,* 578–599.

Gambrill, E. (1999). Evidence-based practice: An alternative to authority-based practice. *Families in Society, 80,* 341–350.

Germain, C. B. (1983). Technological advances. In A. Rosenblatt & D. Waldfogel (Eds.), *Handbook of clinical social work* (pp. 26–57). San Francisco: Jossey-Bass.

Germain, C. B., & Gitterman, A. (1996). *The life model of social work practice* (2nd ed.). New York: Columbia University Press.

Gitterman, A. (1983). Uses of resistance: A transactional view. *Social Work, 28,* 127–130.

Goldstein, E. G. (1995). *Ego psychology and social work practice* (2nd ed.). New York: Free Press.

Goldstein, E. G. (2001). *Object relations theory and self psychology in social work practice.* New York: Free Press.

Goodenough, U. (1998). *The sacred depths of nature.* New York: Oxford.

Gould, S. J. (1993). *Eight little piggies: Reflections in natural history.* New York: W.W. Norton.

Groskind, F. (1994). Ideological influences on public support for assistance to poor families. *Social Work, 39,* 81–89.

Gutierrez, L. (1997). Multicultural community organizing. In M. Reisch & E. Gambrill (Eds.), *Social work in the 21st Century* (pp. 249–259). Thousand Oaks, CA: Pine Forge.

Harris, M. (2000). *The rise of anthropological theory* (updated edition). Walnut Creek, CA: AltaMira Press.

Hayes, S. C., Strosahl, K. D., & Wilson, K. G. (1999). *Acceptance and commitment therapy: An experiential approach to behavior change.* New York: Guilford.

Hudson, C. G. (2000). From Social Darwinism to self-organization: Implications for social change theory. *Social Service Review, 74,* 533–559.

Jacobson, N. S., Dobson, K. S., Truax, P. A., Addis, M. E., Koerner, K., Gollan, J. K., Gortner, E., & Prince, S. E. (1996). A component analysis of cognitive-behavioral treatment for depression. *Journal of Consulting and Clinical Psychology, 64,* 295–304.

Johnston, J. M. (1988). Strategic and tactical limits of comparison studies. *The Behavior Analyst, 11,* 1–9.

Kaplan, H. I., & Sadock, B. J. (1996). *Concise textbook of clinical psychiatry.* Baltimore: Williams & Wilkins.

Kemp, S. P., Whittaker, J. K., & Tracy, E. M. (1997). *Person-environment practice: The social ecology of interpersonal helping.* New York: Aldine de Gruyter.

Kopp, J. (1993). Self-observation: An empowerment strategy in assessment. In J. B. Rauch (Ed.), *Assessment: A sourcebook for social work practice* (pp. 255–268). Milwaukee, WI: Families International.

Krill, D. F. (1988). Existential social work. In R. A. Dorfman (Ed.), *Paradigms of clinical social work* (pp. 295–316). New York: Brunner/Mazel.

LaDuke, W. (1999). *All our relations.* Cambridge, MA: South End Press.

Lame Deer, J. (F.), & Erdoes, R. (1972). *Lame Deer: Seeker of Visions.* New York: Washington Square Press.

Lewin, K. (1976). Problems of research in social psychology (1943–1944). In D. Cartwright (Ed.), *Field theory in social psychology: Selected theoretical papers* (pp. 155–169). Chicago: University of Chicago Press. (Originally published 1951.)

Lincoln, Y. S., & Guba, E. G. (1985). *Naturalistic inquiry.* Beverly Hills, CA: Sage Publications.

Lowery, C. T. (1998). American Indian perspectives on addiction and recovery. *Health & Social Work, 23,* 127–135.

Lowery, C. T., & Mattaini, M. A. (1999). The science of sharing power: Native American thought and behavior analysis. *Behavior and Social Issues, 9,* 3–23.

Lowery, C. T., & Mattaini, M. A. (2001). Shared power in social work: A Native American perspective of change. In H. Briggs & K. Corcoran (Eds.), *Social work practice: Treating common client problems* (pp. 109–124). Chicago: Lyceum.

Marlatt, G. A. (Ed.). (1998). *Harm reduction: Pragmatic strategies for managing high-risk behaviors.* New York: Guilford.

Martin, C. L. (1999). *The way of the human being.* New Haven: Yale University Press.

Mattaini, M. A. (1993b). *More than a thousand words: Graphics for clinical practice.* Washington, DC: NASW Press.

Mattaini, M. A. (1996a). Envisioning cultural practices. *Behavior Analyst, 19,* 257–272.

Mattaini, M. A. (1996b). Public issues, human behavior, and cultural design. In M. A. Mattaini & B. A. Thyer (Eds.), *Finding solutions to social problems: Behavioral strategies for change* (pp. 13–40). Washington, DC: American Psychological Association.

Mattaini, M. A. (1997). *Clinical practice with individuals.* Washington, DC: NASW Press.

Mattaini, M. A. (1999). *Clinical intervention with families.* Washington, DC: NASW Press.

Mattaini, M. A., Grellong, B. A., & Abramovitz, R. (1992). The clientele of a child and family mental health agency: Empirically derived household clusters and implications for practice. *Research on Social Work Practice, 2,* 380–404.

Meyers, R. J., & Smith, J. E. (1996). *Clinical guide to alcohol treatment: The community reinforcement approach.* New York: Guilford.

Miles, M. B., & Huberman, A. M. (1994). *Qualitative data analysis: An expanded sourcebook.* Thousand Oaks, CA: Sage Publications.

Miller, W. R., & Rosnick, S. (1991). *Motivational interviewing: Preparing people to change addictive behavior.* New York: Guilford.

Nathan, P. E., & Gorman, J. M. (Eds.). (1998). *A guide to treatments that work.* New York: Oxford.

The New Shorter Oxford English Dictionary. (1993). Oxford, England: Clarendon Press.

O'Donnell, S. M., & Karanja, S. T. (2000). Transformative community practice: Building a model for developing extremely low income African-American communities. *Journal of Community Practice, 7*(3), 67–84.

Pieper, M., & Pieper, W. J. (1993). Response to "Psychoanalytic fallacies: Reflections on Martha Heineman Pieper and William Joseph Pieper's Intrapsychic Humanism." *Social Service Review, 67,* 651–654.

Poppen, R. L. (1989). Some clinical implications of rule-governed behavior. In S. C. Hayes (Ed.), *Rule-governed behavior: Cognition, contingencies, and instructional control* (pp. 325–357). New York: Plenum Press.

Poulin, J. and contributors (2000). *Collaborative social work: Strengths-based generalist practice.* Itasca, IL: Peacock.

Reid, W. J. (1992). *Task strategies.* New York: Columbia University Press.

Reid, W. J. (2000). *The task planner: An intervention resource for human service professionals.* New York: Columbia University Press.

Ross, R. (1996). *Returning to the teachings.* Toronto: Penguin Books Canada.

Sackett, D. L., Richardson, W. S., Rosenberg, W., & Haynes, R. B. (1997). *Evidence-based medicine: How to practice and teach EBM.* New York: Churchill Livingstone.

Saleebey, D. (Ed.). (2002). *The strengths perspective in social work practice* (3rd ed.). New York: Longman.

Schiele, J. H. (1996). Afrocentricity: An emerging paradigm in social work practice. *Social Work, 41,* 284–294.

Schön, D. A. (1983). *The reflective practitioner: How professionals think in action.* London: Temple Smith.

Searle, J. R. (1993). Rationality and realism, what is at stake? *Daedalus, 122*(4), 55–83.

Skinner, B. F. (1948). "Superstition" in the pigeon. *Journal of Experimental Psychology, 38,* 168–172.

Skinner, B. F. (1987). What is wrong with daily life in the Western world? In B. F. Skinner, *Upon further reflection* (pp. 15–31). Englewood Cliffs, NJ: Prentice Hall.

Smith, H. (1988). The crisis in philosophy. *Behaviorism, 16,* 51–56.

Tolson, E. R., Reid, W. J., & Garvin, C. D. (1994). *Generalist practice: A task-centered approach.* New York: Columbia University Press.

Vaillant, G. E. (1995). *The natural history of alcoholism revisited.* Cambridge, MA: Harvard University Press.

Voss, R. W., Douville, V., Little Soldier, A., & Twiss, G. (1999). Tribal and shamanic-based social work practice: A Lakota perspective. *Social Work, 44,* 228–241.

Wakefield, J. C. (1993). Following the Piepers: Replies to Tyson, Steinberg, and Miller. *Social Service Review, 67,* 673–682.

Whitman, W. (1992). *Leaves of grass* (The deathbed edition). New York: Quality Paperback Book Club. (Originally published in 1892).

Wilson, E. O. (1992). *The diversity of life.* Cambridge, MA: Belknap/Harvard University Press.

Wood, G. G., & Middleman, R. R. (1989). *The structural approach to direct practice in social work.* New York: Columbia.

Woods, M. E., & Hollis, F. (1999). *Casework: A psychosocial therapy* (5th ed.). New York: McGraw-Hill.

Wright, F. D. (1988). Cognitive therapy. In R. A. Dorfman (Ed.), *Paradigms of clinical social work* (pp. 179–195). New York: Brunner/Mazel.

CHAPTER 6

Monitoring Social Work Practice

Mark A. Mattaini

In the chapters that follow, which outline practice with individuals, families, groups, communities, and organizations, the need to monitor and evaluate practice will be discussed repeatedly. Certain central questions about monitoring cross-cut practice at all system levels, questions with critical ethical and professional implications, including "How is the client doing?" and "Is my practice working (that is, helping)?" This chapter sketches a framework for addressing these questions at all system levels, and this framework will be further elaborated in subsequent chapters. It is not meant to provide a complete description of how to go about monitoring practice because this is a rich and complex area requiring book-length treatment (e.g., Bloom, Fischer, & Orme, 1999) to achieve adequate coverage. Rather, this chapter is meant as an introduction to essential concepts related to critical questions about what happens in practice.

All social workers want to believe that they are doing well, in addition to doing good, and need to communicate that message if they want financial support and community sanction. Still, believing they are effective is not the same as knowing that they are or being able to demonstrate it, both to themselves and to others. A serious debate about practice effectiveness emerged in the profession in the 1970s and 1980s (see Fischer, 1973, 1976; Gordon, 1983; Mullen & Dumpson, 1972; Reid & Hanrahan, 1982; Thomlison, 1984; Videka-Sherman, 1985; Wood, 1978). Without revisiting the details, it is now clear that some practice "works" well and some probably does not. And whether practice is effective matters.

Social workers are responsible to themselves, the community, and especially their clients for trying to determine how their cases are progressing in as objective a way as possible. At a minimum, they simply must know whether the client is or is not doing better (or, for clients for whom avoiding deterioration or relapse is the objective, whether they are maintaining a particular level of functioning). It clearly matters whether a parent is using alternatives to severe physical punishment, whether an overstressed family achieves a more satisfying balance with its environment, whether several depressed members of a treatment group are becoming less depressed, or whether a neighborhood is achieving an increased level of empowerment leading to economic development and family stability. Collaboratively determining how to track changes in cases is also critical to a shared power approach to practice, because involvement in self-monitoring can be empowering for clients (Kopp, 1993). Clarity about interventive goals also demystifies the social work consultation process; both client and worker can see whether change is occurring in the areas important to the client.

When possible, social workers naturally also want to know whether their practice is contributing to changes observed. There are, therefore, two essential questions to be addressed in monitoring practice: (1) Is the client system approaching its goals efficiently and satisfactorily? and (2) Is the joint work being done by client and social worker responsible for whatever change is being achieved? Determining the extent to which the intervention is responsible for the change requires a level of control that is often not easily available in practice settings, so compromises here are often necessary. However, it is always possible—although not always simple—to find some way to determine at least whether progress toward client goals is or is not being achieved. In some cases, monitoring the *process* of practice, what clients and workers are doing, is also important, although ultimately, of course, outcome matters most.

The basic principles of monitoring are the same regardless of the size or complexity of the client system involved. If focal issues (target problems and consultation goals) have been clearly specified and agreed on at any of these system levels, the creative, thoughtful practitioner can find a way to track whether they are being achieved in a manner that is organic to, rather than imposed on, the practice. The available evidence also suggests that clients prefer that some clear method of monitoring outcome be used as opposed to relying on practitioners' global opinions (Campbell, 1988).

Nevertheless, monitoring is often not straightforward. The behavior of individual clients is easier to measure, for example, than are environmental events or the actions of representatives of large bureaucratic systems, both because a wider range of measures exists at the level of the individuals, and because clients are easier to reach. If the issue is depression, for example, it may make sense to monitor the case using a standardized rapid assessment instrument such as the Beck Depression Inventory (Beck et al., 1978). However, if the depression is largely caused by situational factors over which the client has limited control (for example, severe and persistent battering), a lack of progress should not be attributed to the client's resistance, a personality disorder, or other factors that fail to take the full case situation into account. In this case, the client's depression is the focal issue and is appropriate to track, but intervention should be directed toward the causal factors in the social and physical environment (an assessment issue).

Granted that monitoring is important, there are at least two major bodies of knowledge with which social workers should be familiar before they can effectively monitor their practice. First, social workers need to know about approaches for measuring progress on focal issues (measurement). Secondly, they need to know how to apply these measures and structure treatment so as to track what is going on (design). Although "measurement" and "design" are research terms, no foreign, scientistic approach is being suggested here. Research is really nothing more than a rigorous way of seeking the answers to questions; in this case, the interest is in finding relatively rigorous ways to answer the practice questions "Is the client doing better?" and "Am I helping the client?" Monitoring is an indivisible aspect of practice, not something extraneous that is layered onto it.

Measurement

There are many ways to measure the progress of people or systems toward achieving their goals. Some ways are more reliable and valid than are others, some are narrow and some are broad, and some require more specific training than do others. Professional social workers who use any monitoring strategy must be familiar with technical details of measurement, such as reliability and validity (just as physicians must understand how to read laboratory tests). Although it is not possible to review all of the available approaches, and practitioners commonly must develop new ones to fit case situations, the discussion of a few approaches may help the reader think about possibilities that may fit a particular form of practice or a particular case.

The most accurate way to measure is usually through direct observation (especially, of course, if it is done by multiple observers). In many practice settings, such observation may be impractical, but this strategy is often dismissed too quickly. In working with parents to teach parenting skills, for example, social workers can often observe parents' and children's behavior directly, and such observations may provide extraordinarily useful data for ongoing interventive planning (see, for example, Mattaini, McGowan, & Williams, 1996). Such simple methods as a chart tracking an autistic child's successful efforts at toileting (see Figure 6-1) or the number of times partners in an intimate relationship perform simple actions that the other appreciates (as in the "caring days" procedure, Stuart, 1980), are often both helpful for planning, and motivating as well.

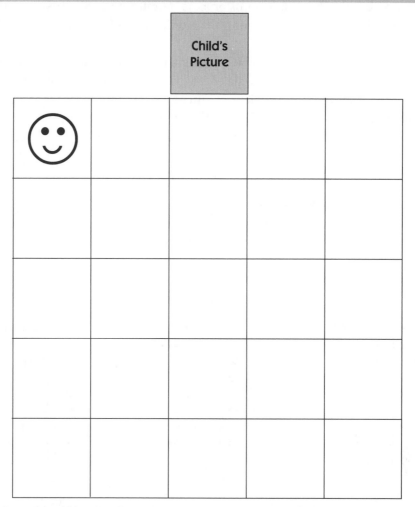

Figure 6-1. A Chart of Toileting Successes, To Be Kept by Parent and Child

A picture of the child on the toilet or potty chair is attached at the top, reminding the child of the desired behavior. Smiling faces, stars, or stickers, can be drawn or attached—preferably by the child—each time he or she uses the toilet. When a row is completed (5 correct toiletings), the child can be rewarded with something he or she enjoys, like having a story read.
SOURCE: *The Power of Positive Parenting,* by G. I. Latham, (North Logan, UT: P & T Ink. 1994).

Note, as in Figure 6-1, that observational monitoring forms can and should be developed in ways that are immediately accessible and comprehensible for clients.

Various types of rating scales can be useful when direct observation is not realistic. One is Task Attainment Scaling (Tolson, Reid, & Garvin, 1994), in which the level of achievement of agreed-on tasks is rated on a scale of 1 (minimally or not achieved), 2 (partially achieved), 3 (substantially achieved), to 4 (completely achieved)—or "no" for no opportunity to attempt. This technique can be applied in every session, in any form of practice in which client, worker, or joint tasks are relevant (as they are in most practice). This is a form of process monitoring and is based on the empirically supported assumption that completion of tasks contributes to outcome.

Self-anchored scales, on which a client is asked to rate, for example, how sad he or she feels on a scale of 1 to 10, are relatively straightforward and have been used in a variety of situations, ranging from pathological jealousy (Slomin-Nevo & Vosler, 1991) to depression (Nugent, 1992). They are usually easy for clients to relate to and can have excellent psychometric

Figure 6-2. Mood Thermometers

How I Feel Right Now

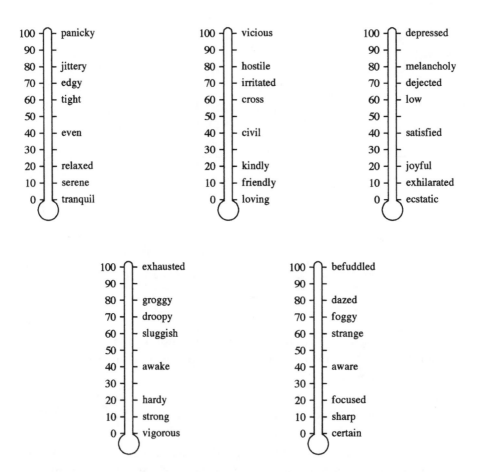

SOURCE: Reprinted with permission from B. W. Tuckman (1988). The Scaling of Mood. *Educational and Psychological Measurement, 48,* p. 421. Copyright 1988 by Sage Publications.

properties (Nugent, 1992). Several such scales can be used together, as in the Mood Thermometers (Tuckman, 1988) (see Figure 6-2).

Clinician rating scales, such as the Clinical Rating Scale for family assessment (on which the clinician rates family functioning on six dimensions as well as overall), also are easy to use and can have excellent measurement properties (Epstein, Baldwin, & Bishop, 1983; Miller et al., 1985).

Reliability and validity can be enhanced by adding behavioral descriptions to the points on a rating or self-anchored scale, to clarify what is meant by, for example, a 3 on a 5-point scale of conflict containment in a family. Figure 6-3 is an example of two such behaviorally anchored rating scales (Daniels, 2000) developed to monitor a clinical case (Seidenfeld & Mattaini, in press).

Figure 6-3. Behaviorally Anchored Rating Scales for Two Clinical Issues

Level of Goal Attainment	Decision-Making	Social Contacts
5	Client regularly seeks opportunities to make choices, tracks consequences effectively, and readily takes reasonable risks to obtain valued reinforcement	Client engages in a rich and varied social life in which he can identify the sources and nature of social reinforcers that he experiences; he readily engages with new people who may be potential friends
4	Client can independently identify available choices and possible outcomes for each and act on this data under most circumstances with only limited need for consultant support	Client can identify several people other than his regular contacts (consultant, girlfriend, colleagues at work) who provide a variety of social reinforcers on a regular basis and client can describe what he values in those contacts
3	Client is able to make and act on some decisions after his consultant assists him to elaborate possible choices and clarify possible consequences for each; client acts on choices only with substantial encouragement	Client can identify at least two other friends who provide social reinforcement that he values
2	Client avoids acting on decisions until he experiences significant aversives for failing to act	Client's primary social contacts are with consultant, girlfriend, and people at work
1	Client fails to make or act on decisions—even when lack of action results in significant aversives	Client's social contact is limited primarily to that required for survival

SOURCE: Reprinted with permission from Seidenfeld, M., & Mattaini, M. A. (in press). Personal and Family Consultation Services: An Alternative to Therapy. *Behavior and Social Issues*.

(Ratings on such scales can be graphed over time and can also be combined and quantified on standardized Goal Attainment Follow-Up Guides
for program evaluation purposes; see Bloom, Fischer, & Orme, 1999, and
Kiresuk, 1973, for more detail.)

Graphing progress on such instruments is useful because both the client
and the social worker may find it reinforcing to see progress or motivating
not to see it. Graphing is also usually an integral part of self-monitoring, an
empowering strategy for client systems of all sizes (Kopp, 1988, 1993). By
graphing multiple self-anchored or rating scales concurrently, clients and
social workers can examine connections among various aspects of client and
environmental functioning over time, which may help identify relationships
and, not incidentally, also protect them from oversimplifying complex cases.
For example, Figure 6-4 portrays three dimensions of the Marital Happiness
Scale (Azrin, Naster, & Jones, 1973), completed before each session by both
partners in a couples case seen by the author. Each dimension on this 10-
dimension scale is rated on a 1 (completely dissatisfied) to 10 (completely
satisfied) scale, so higher scores reflect higher satisfaction. (For each dimension, each partner is asked "If my partner continues to act in the future as he/
she is acting *today* with respect to this relationship area, how happy will I be
with this area of our relationship?" The scale can be used for all intimate
partnerships, including gay and straight, marital and cohabiting.)

The first five sessions occurred as a block. Subsequently, booster sessions
were available on an "as-needed" basis (when difficulties had arisen—note
the lower scores when the instrument was completed just before each booster).
A single follow-up data point (suggesting a high level of satisfaction) is also
shown. Note that the husband believed at intake that communication was
not a significant problem, whereas the wife saw it differently. During these
first few sessions, progress in this area was uneven, as is typical in early
stages of couples work. In other areas, however, initial progress is evident;
for example, although Jerry was always fairly satisfied with his own level of
independence, Linda's satisfaction with her own independence improved
considerably (as was also true of overall happiness with the relationship, not
shown). Some other areas, such as affection, show a much more uneven
pattern, requiring work throughout the phases. Data such as these, in which
multiple factors can be tracked together, can be enormously informative for
tracing ongoing client satisfaction with their lives, as well as with the intervention. Similar multivariable procedures can be used to examine concurrent changes among levels of support and aversives from environmental
systems and a client's mood or family functioning, which can be traced over
time using quantified sequential ecomaps (see Figure I-2).

Also available are a wide variety of rapid assessment instruments (RAIs),
brief paper-and-pencil instruments that are designed to be completed quickly

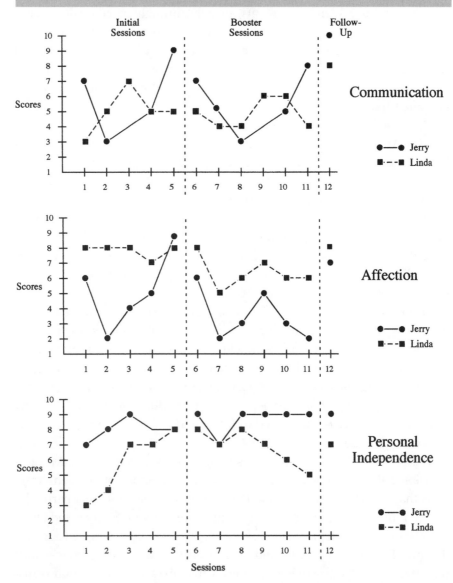

Figure 6-4. A Couple's Scores on Communication, Affection, and Personal Independence on the Marital Happiness Scale

Notes: These scores were for a five-session block of joint work and for six booster sessions scheduled when the couple requested them. Also included are scores for a single follow-up point several months after the last booster session. Refer to Exercise 6-1 in Appendix C for further analysis of these data.

and often by a client. Such instruments can be used to measure moods, self-talk, assertiveness, family functioning, peer relations and social interactions, magical thinking, and many other dimensions of human and social functioning (see Corcoran & Fischer for many examples of such measures). Hudson and his colleagues (1989) have done extensive work during two

decades to develop an integrated package of instruments that are specifically targeted for use with social work clients. It is important to learn how
to select and use such instruments, usually through specific course content, because it is essential to understand their psychometric properties,
how cultural differences that may affect responses and interpretation, and
how to integrate data from RAIs with other information to complete a comprehensive clinical assessment. RAIs offer tremendous flexibility, however,
and often have excellent reliability and validity.

Many such instruments can also be used with clients who are seen in
groups. Another strategy, useful at all systemic levels but demonstrated
here for use with a group, is the qualitative matrix (Miles & Huberman,
1994) used to track, for example, group members' progress in learning
social skills in a structured skills training group (see Figure 6-5).

Other qualitative strategies may also be useful in tracing the interventive
process with individuals, families, groups, and communities. Reid's (1988)
Case Process Chart is one approach to monitoring the progress of a case
that relies primarily on rich narrative data, rather than numbers, but allows the relationships among events to emerge using a matrix structure.

Although monitoring change at a community level may be more complicated, the same basic principles as are used with smaller systems apply
(Biglan, 1995). Changes can be tracked by interviews or questionnaires,
which may include many of the types of measures just described as well as
others; by direct observation (for example, of the number of people hang-
ing out on a street or the number of vacant buildings on a block); and by
examining incidence data related to focal issues (for example, juvenile ar-
rests or dropouts).

The list of tools discussed here is by no means exhaustive, and professional social workers will find that they often must adapt or even create
tools that will adequately capture the critical data elements in a particular
case or group of cases at whatever systemic level. Bloom, Fischer, and Orme
(1999) provide much more detail about such measurement (as well as about
design). The challenge is to find an approach that can capture the most
important complexities of a case in ways that are also practical and realistic. How often these measures are taken, and how, are design questions,
which are discussed next.

Design

Two general classes of design can be valuable for monitoring and evaluating practice: (1) single-system designs, and (2) group designs. Practice is
ultimately done with single systems (a person, a family, a community, or an
organization). Even in group work, the primary goal is often to improve or

Figure 6-5. Tracking Matrix for a Social Skills Group Showing Skills for Which Group Members Have Met the Established Criterion Level

SESSION 1

Member	Skill # 1	2	3	4	5	6	7	8	9	10
Jill	○	●	○	●	●	○	○	○	○	○
George	●	○	○	●	●	○	●	●	●	○
Mary Kay	○	●	○	○	●	○	○	○	●	○
Ernie	○	○	○	○	○	○	○	●	○	○
Sarah	○	○	○	○	○	○	○	○	○	○
Kate	○	●	○	●	○	○	○	○	○	○
Sharee	○	○	○	○	○	○	○	○	○	○
Maxine	○	○	○	○	○	○	○	○	○	○

SESSION 2

Member	Skill # 1	2	3	4	5	6	7	8	9	10
Jill	●	●	○	●	●	○	○	○	○	○
George	●	●	○	●	●	○	○	●	○	○
Mary Kay	●	●	○	○	●	○	○	○	○	○
Ernie	●	●	○	●	○	○	○	○	●	●
Sarah	○	○	○	○	○	○	○	○	○	○
Kate	●	●	○	●	●	○	○	○	○	○
Sharee	●	○	○	○	○	○	○	○	○	○
Maxine	●	○	○	○	○	○	○	○	○	○

SESSION 3

Member	Skill # 1	2	3	4	5	6	7	8	9	10
Jill	●	●	●	●	●	●	●	●	○	○
George	●	●	●	●	○	○	●	●	●	●
Mary Kay	●	●	●	●	●	●	●	●	●	●
Ernie	●	●	●	●	○	●	○	●	●	●
Sarah	○	○	●	●	●	●	●	●	○	○
Kate	●	●	●	●	●	●	●	●	●	○
Sharee	●	●	●	●	●	●	●	●	●	●
Maxine	●	●	●	●	○	○	○	○	○	○

SESSION 4

Member	Skill # 1	2	3	4	5	6	7	8	9	10
Jill	●	●	●	●	○	○	○	○	○	○
George	●	○	●	●	○	○	●	●	●	○
Mary Kay	●	●	●	●	○	○	○	○	○	○
Ernie	●	●	●	●	○	○	○	●	○	○
Sarah	○	○	●	●	○	○	○	○	○	○
Kate	●	●	○	●	○	○	○	○	○	○
Sharee	●	●	●	○	○	○	○	○	○	○
Maxine	●	●	●	●	○	○	○	○	○	○

SESSION 5

Member	Skill # 1	2	3	4	5	6	7	8	9	10
Jill	●	●	●	●	●	●	●	○	○	○
George	●	●	●	●	●	●	●	●	○	○
Mary Kay	●	●	●	●	○	○	●	○	○	○
Ernie	●	●	●	●	○	○	●	○	●	●
Sarah	○	●	●	○	○	○	○	○	○	○
Kate	●	●	○	●	●	●	●	○	○	○
Sharee	●	●	●	●	●	●	●	○	○	○
Maxine	●	●	●	●	●	●	●	○	○	○

SESSION 6

Member	Skill # 1	2	3	4	5	6	7	8	9	10
Jill	●	●	●	●	●	●	●	●	○	○
George	●	●	●	●	●	●	●	●	●	●
Mary Kay	●	●	●	●	●	●	●	●	●	●
Ernie	●	●	●	●	●	●	○	●	●	●
Sarah	○	●	●	●	●	●	●	○	○	○
Kate	○	●	○	●	●	●	●	●	●	○
Sharee	●	●	●	●	●	●	●	●	●	●
Maxine	●	●	●	●	●	●	●	●	○	○

Source: Reprinted from M. A. Mattaini (1993). *More than a Thousand Words: Graphics for Clinical Practice* (p. 163). Washington, DC: NASW Press.

maintain the level of functioning or quality of life of each member, and results for each may vary. (In some cases, however, the goal is change at the level of group culture, in which case the entire group should be regarded as the focal system.) For these reasons, the main emphasis here will be on what are called "single-case" or "single-system" designs. A brief consideration of group designs, which can be useful for some program evaluation purposes, especially when combined with single-system designs, is presented later in the chapter. (Technically, "design" refers to ways to structure data collection that help determine the extent to which an intervention is causally related to outcomes. Many of the designs that are practical for everyday practice monitoring can address this question only in limited ways, providing only limited control over what are called "alternative explanations" of change. For example, it is sometimes difficult to rule out seasonal changes that co-occur with intervention. Nonetheless, a certain amount of rigor—provided by design—is often possible in practice.)

Many research courses focus on group designs. Although some of the concepts learned in such courses (such as internal validity or generalizability) apply regardless of the type of design, group designs are generally inappropriate for the routine monitoring of practice. Group designs require a relatively large number of similar clients and the use of untreated control groups or comparison groups receiving different treatments, preferably with random assignment. Group studies also "wash out" differences among cases, which may not matter for research purposes but does matter a great deal for clinical purposes. For example, on average a group of cases may improve, but this aggregate may include some clients who do much better, some who do a bit better, and some who deteriorate greatly. In practice, intervention should be varied for each case to achieve the best possible outcome, but such variation fatally compromises rigorous group designs. For these and other reasons (conceptual and practical, Johnston, 1988), practitioners ordinarily use some form of single-case design instead of group designs. In single-case designs, whatever controls for alternative explanations are present are provided by the case itself, rather than an external control group.

Single-Case Designs

There are many types of single-case designs currently in use, but only a few are highlighted here to demonstrate the range of designs that are available. The reader should refer to the specialized literature for further detail (for example, Bloom, Fischer, & Orme, 1999; Tripodi, 1994). In some circumstances, particularly in emergencies, the social worker simply starts to intervene and at the same time tracks the level of problems experienced. For example, with a client with severe depression, one would ordinarily begin treatment immediately and monitor the level of depression over time, using perhaps an RAI or a self-anchored scale. This approach is called a "B design," because the accepted convention is to label the baseline phase (measurements of the problem taken before intervention begins) "A" and to label intervention phases "B" (and "C," "D," and so forth if multiple types of interventions are used). In the work noted with the depressed client, baseline data is not collected; thus, this is a B design. Note that a B design is adequate for showing that depression is declining during the course of treatment, but does not provide a stable picture of how depressed the client was at the beginning (which would require collecting baseline data at several points in time before initiating intervention—which would clearly be inappropriate here). Such B designs also cannot demonstrate that the intervention was responsible for the change because something else may be the cause of the improvement, including artifacts—clients tend to enter treatment when things are at their worst, so data often improve to some extent as a result of "regression toward the mean." Even if such alternative explanations cannot be ruled out, however, monitoring level of depression is clearly essential.

In other cases, social workers can collect some baseline data (in some cases retrospectively) and then continue to collect data during intervention and, ideally, also during follow-up. Figure 6-6 is an example of such an A–B design, with a single follow-up point.

(In single-case designs, data are usually graphed to simplify analysis, and visual analysis is characteristic of such designs.) The figure illustrates an interesting case, in which the client was disturbed by jealous thoughts about her husband's first wife, who had passed away before he and the client met (Slomin-Nevo & Vosler, 1991).

The extent of client change is clear here, and it is reasonable to suppose that the intervention may have contributed to the change, although this cannot be definitively proved. If the primary goal was scientific knowledge building, such uncertainty would be an issue, but for clinical purposes, these data are probably persuasive enough. In other cases, the first intervention does not have the desired effect, and the worker may use a clinical analytic design with multiple sequential interventive phases, some of which may include combinations of several interventions, until a satisfactory outcome is achieved (see Figure 5-1 for an example). Generally, the goal in social work practice is to achieve a very clear and obvious change that is immediately evident on the graph (a "slam-bang" effect). Clinically significant effects that are really meaningful ordinarily should emerge clearly and persuasively from the graph because client goals usually involve quite substantial change that is visually evident. It is also possible, however, and in some cases desirable, to supplement visual analysis of single-case data with

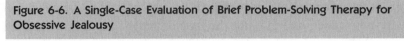

Figure 6-6. A Single-Case Evaluation of Brief Problem-Solving Therapy for Obsessive Jealousy

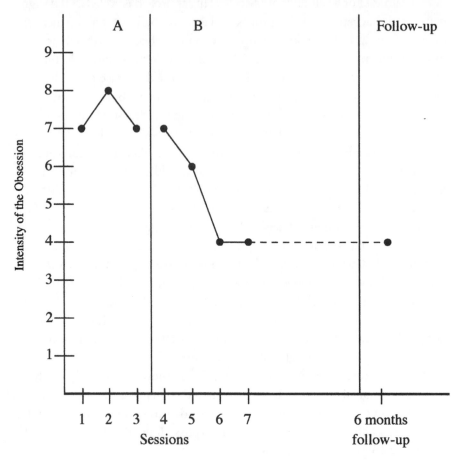

Source: Reprinted with permission from V. Slomin-Nevo & N. R. Vosler (1991). The use of single-system design with systemic brief problem-solving therapy. *Families in Society, 72,* p. 42.

simple or complex statistical tests that have been developed for time-series data (Tripodi, 1994, Nugent, Bruley, & Allen, 1998).

Other more involved designs enable social workers to better untangle causality (for example, multiple baseline, changing criterion, or withdrawal designs [Mattaini, 1993]), as well as to select the best of several possible interventive strategies to pursue with a particular case (for example, alternating treatment designs [McNight et al., 1984]). Refer to the specialized literature for more detail about such designs (e.g. Bloom, Fischer, & Orme, 1999). What is perhaps most important to clarify is that designs and measurements should be chosen because they fit the logic of a particular case and the treatment plan, rather than the other way around.

Single-system designs are applicable even when the system involved includes many people or groups. For example, if a neighborhood organization wished to reduce the rate of violent crimes on the street, it might test two different approaches, such as increased patrolling by the police (negotiated with the local precinct) and establishment of a youth anti-violence board, and determine the relative effectiveness of each approach. This strategy might involve establishing a baseline from data on violent crimes over the past year (A), followed by two months of increased patrolling (B), then two months of youth work (C), or two months of both (BC). Note that although the crime data involve multiple individuals, it is the aggregate data for the neighborhood that the neighborhood organization would trace— a single-system strategy. Other possibly confounding effects (seasonal patterns, for instance) should also be considered in such evaluations. Refer to Biglan (1995) for more information about the use of single-system time-series designs with larger systems like communities.

Group Designs

Although single-system designs have particular power for practice monitoring, there are times when group designs may be useful, particularly at programmatic or community levels. For example, if an agency decided to implement a new short-term treatment project, it might want to compare the effectiveness of that approach with the standard open-ended approach currently being used. No clients would go untreated—this would be a contrast group, rather than an untreated control group design. As long as the same measures (for example, a package of RAIs) were used with both groups, and reasonable decisions could be made about when to use them, such a design could be practical. Note, however, that there is no reason why single-case designs could not be incorporated within this group design, and they probably ought to be. It is really not enough to know that the average outcome is as good or better for the new program as it was for the old, although that information is important. It is still critical for clinical purposes to monitor how each client is doing. One interventive stream would last longer than the other in this example, but what happens during those periods, for each client, should be driven by the specifics of the case.

Comparison-group studies may also be useful if a social worker and a community group were working to prevent school dropouts, for example. They might establish a new tutoring and support program in one school and compare the dropout data for students in this school during a period of time with those in similar schools in which such a program is not in place. Although this is a weak design (other factors—alternative explanations again—may be responsible for differences found), it provides at least some basis for comparison. It is important to examine such data because some "prevention" programs may have a range of benefits but may not actually have any effect on the problem to be prevented. In a world of limited resources, it is essential to know this.

Monitoring at the programmatic level blends into program evaluation (see Chapter 12). Although evaluation is a specialized field and evaluation research can become extremely complex (Rossi, Freeman, & Lipsey, 1999), completing a simple evaluation that may include tracking clients' satisfaction and simple measures of goal attainment or task achievement need not require major effort, particularly given the current widespread availability of personal computers. Data that are routinely collected can often be used for simple evaluations that require few agency resources.

Conclusion

Practice monitoring need not be arcane and does not require advanced mathematical and research skills. There are risks if monitoring is poorly done, because, for example, a requirement for monitoring may lead social workers to focus on what is easiest to see—often the behavior of clients, rather than what is most important—which may include larger systemic factors (Kagle & Cowger, 1984). However, there is no choice. A professional cannot practice ethically without paying attention to whether clients are achieving their goals. Therefore, social workers must learn the skills of monitoring. This is a special challenge because awareness of the importance of, and the development of tools for, monitoring practice are recent advances in the profession. Some of the methods and instruments available are rough and need a good deal more elaboration. Many social workers, administrators, and supervisors in the field have limited knowledge in this area, so new graduates are increasingly looked to as the "experts" in this area. In many settings, the demands by funders to document effectiveness and measure outcomes have become intense, another reason to develop expertise in this area. However, the primary reason to struggle to find ways to track progress and outcome is that it is the only way in which one can know whether a client is reaching his or her goals, and whether one is helping the client to do so.

References

Azrin, N. H., Naster, B. J., & Jones, R. (1973). Reciprocity counseling: A rapid learning-based procedure for marital counseling. *Behaviour Research & Therapy, 11,* 365–382.

Beck, A. T., Rush, A. J., Shaw, B. F., & Emery, G. (1978). *Cognitive therapy of depression.* New York: Guilford Press.

Biglan, A. (1995). *Changing cultural practices: A contextualist framework for intervention research.* Reno, NV: Context Press.

Bloom, M., Fischer, J., & Orme, J. (1999). *Evaluating practice: Guidelines for the accountable professional* (3rd ed.). Boston: Allyn & Bacon.

Campbell, J. A. (1988). Client acceptance of single-system evaluation procedures. *Social Work Research & Abstracts, 24*(2), 21–22.

Corcoran, K., & Fischer, J. (1994). *Measures for clinical practice: A sourcebook* (3rd ed., Vols. 1 and 2). New York: Free Press.

Daniels, A. C. (2000). *Bringing out the best in people* (2nd ed.). New York: McGraw-Hill.

Epstein, N. B., Baldwin, L. M., & Bishop, D. S. (1983). The McMaster Family Assessment Device. *Journal of Marital and Family Therapy, 9,* 171–180.

Fischer, J. (1973). Is casework effective? A review. *Social Work, 18,* 5–20.

Fischer, J. (1976). *The effectiveness of social casework.* Springfield, IL: Charles C Thomas.

Gordon, W. E. (1983). Social work revolution or evolution? *Social Work, 28,* 181–185.

Hudson, W. W. (1989). *Computer assisted social services.* Tempe, AZ: Walmyr Publishing.

Johnston, J. M. (1988). Strategic and tactical limits of comparison studies. *Behavior Analyst, 11,* 1–9.

Kagle, J. D., & Cowger, C. D. (1984). Blaming the client: Implicit agenda in practice research. *Social Work, 29,* 347–351.

Kiresuk, T. J. (1973). Goal Attainment Scaling at a county mental health service. *Evaluation (Monograph 1),* pp. 12–18.

Kopp, J. (1988). Self-monitoring: A literature review of research and practice. *Social Work Research & Abstracts, 24*(4), 8–20.

Kopp, J. (1993). Self-observation: An empowerment strategy in assessment. In J. B. Rauch (Ed.), *Assessment: A sourcebook for social work practice* (pp. 255–268). Milwaukee, WI: Families International.

Latham, G. I. (1994). *The power of positive parenting.* North Logan, UT: P & T Ink.

Mattaini, M. A. (1993). *More than a thousand words: Graphics for clinical practice.* Washington, DC: NASW Press.

Mattaini, M. A., McGowan, B. G., & Williams, G. (1996). Child maltreatment. In M. A. Mattaini & B. A. Thyer (Eds.), *Finding solutions to social problems: Behavioral strategies for change* (pp. 223–266). Washington, DC: American Psychological Association.

McNight, D. L., Nelson, R. O., Hayes, S. C., & Jarrett, R. B. (1984). Importance of treating individually assessed response classes in the amelioration of depression. *Behavior Therapy, 15,* 315–335.

Miles, M. B., & Huberman, A. M. (1994). *Qualitative data analysis: An expanded sourcebook.* Thousand Oaks, CA: Sage Publications.

Miller, I. W., Epstein, N. B., Bishop, D. S., & Keitner, G. I. (1985). The McMaster Family Assessment Device: Reliability and validity. *Journal of Marital and Family Therapy, 11,* 345–356.

Mullen, E. J., & Dumpson, J. R. (1972). *Evaluation of social intervention.* San Francisco: Jossey-Bass.

Nugent, W. R. (1992). Psychometric characteristics of self-anchored scales in clinical application. *Journal of Social Service Research, 15*(3/4), 137–152.

Nugent, W. R., Bruley, C., & Allen, P. (1998). The effects of aggression replacement training on antisocial behavior in a runaway shelter. *Research on Social Work Practice, 8,* 637–656.

Reid, W. J. (1988). The metamodel, research, and empirical practice. In E. R. Tolson (Ed.), *The metamodel and clinical social work* (pp. 167–192). New York: Columbia University Press.

Reid, W. J., & Hanrahan, P. (1982). Recent evaluations of social work: Grounds for optimism. *Social Work, 27,* 328–340.

Rossi, P. H., Freeman, H. E., & Lipsey, M. W. (1999). *Evaluation: A systematic approach* (6th ed.). Thousand Oaks, CA: Sage Publications.

Seidenfeld, M., & Mattaini, M. A. (in press). Personal and family consultation services: An alternative to therapy. *Behavior and Social Issues.*

Slomin-Nevo, V., & Vosler, N. R. (1991). The use of single-system design with systemic brief problem-solving therapy. *Families in Society, 72,* 38–44.

Stuart, R. B. (1980). *Helping couples change.* New York: Guilford.

Thomlison, R. J. (1984). Something works: Evidence from practice effectiveness studies. *Social Work, 29,* 51–56.

Tolson, E. R., Reid, W. J., & Garvin, C. D. (1994). *Generalist practice.* New York: Columbia University Press.

Tripodi, T. (1994). *A primer on single-subject design.* Washington, DC: NASW Press.

Tuckman, B. W. (1988). The scaling of mood. *Educational and Psychological Measurement, 48,* 419–427.

Videka-Sherman, L. (1985). *Harriett M. Bartlett Practice Effectiveness Project: Report to NASW Board of Directors.* Silver Spring, MD: National Association of Social Workers.

Wood, K. M. (1978). Casework effectiveness: A new look at the research evidence. *Social Work, 23,* 437–459.

The Foundations of Practice

CHAPTER 7

Practice with Individuals

Mark A. Mattaini

In the Reform Era, when social workers practiced in settlement houses and as friendly visitors through the Charity Organization Societies, they offered their helping services to people as individuals, families, groups, and communities. This was long before the professionalization of social work, and the helpers of the late 19th and early 20th centuries simply did what seemed to be necessary in case situations using common sense. When Richmond (1917) codified a casework approach to helping people, she devised the first methodology in social work, making it possible to replicate and teach casework practice. . . . Thus, casework, or practice with individuals, was the first professionally defined modality in social work. Practices with families (1950s), groups (1940s), and communities (1960s) were similarly developed and, in turn, contributed to the diversified practice repertoire of social workers. . . . The ecosystems perspective has helped to conceptualize the social work practitioner's multiple roles (using the diverse modalities) by laying out the 'picture' of a case and enabling the practitioner to determine which modality is most appropriate to use—where and when—in the case. . . . The chief indicator of the progress that has been made from the earliest days of identification solely with a method is that modern social workers first attempt to assess what is needed and is possible to achieve in a case and then choose a modality that is appropriate to the circumstances.

(Meyer & Palleja, 1995, pp. 105–106)

This chapter is about what is probably still the most common modality in social work practice, that is, work with individuals. We have learned a good deal during the past century about "what works" in working with individual clients to help shape an improved reality, as reflected in the contemporary movement toward evidence-based practice. Practice with individuals is not always the best choice, however; family-centered practice, for example, is a powerful and important modality

(Hartman & Laird, 1983; Mattaini, 1999; see also Chapter 8). Given the experiences of oppression experienced by many people and groups, advocacy and work on behalf of communities is also clearly an ethical imperative; some believe such advocacy should preempt work with individuals. Bertha Capen Reynolds (1934/1982) struggled with this very question during the Great Depression. Her resolution, and that of this chapter, is that suffering members of the human web cannot be left alone in their plight, because all human beings are connected. Building healthy communities is one way to build healthy people (Specht & Courtney, 1994), in which every social worker should participate, but assisting individual people in achieving and maintaining health is also one way to build healthy communities.

This chapter will examine three basic areas: (1) the organizational and economic contexts within which practice occurs, (2) defining the boundaries of a "case" ecosystemically, and (3) core processes and skills of practice with individuals. There is much more that can and has been said about these areas than can be included in a single chapter, of course; the goal here is simply to sketch an outline that will be filled in and extended by further course work, reading, and practice experience. The emphasis in this chapter is on work with verbal clients who are of school age or older. Naturally, the process must be adapted depending on developmental considerations, cognitive capacities, and the nature of the issues to be addressed. In addition, specialized skills are required for certain populations with major developmental problems (e.g., autistic adolescents), as well as for work with young children (in which case some level of family work should usually be primary—see Chapter 8 and Mattaini, 1999). Considerable additional reading will always be required to be well prepared to work with the populations and issues seen in particular settings.

The Changing Contexts of Contemporary Practice

The Organizational Context of Services

Most social work occurs by necessity in organizational settings, because the complexities of client issues often require extensive and interdisciplinary assistance and because a great deal of social work occurs at the interface with critical cultural institutions (schools, the medical care system, the housing market, or employment settings, for example). Although some social workers have private practices, one of the results of managed care is that it is increasingly difficult to support oneself with private practice alone. In addition, the problems of the poor and dispossessed persons with whom social work has always been allied are often not amenable to private practice.

For both practical and service-related reasons, therefore, social work is primarily an organizationally based profession.

The organizational context within which practice is embedded (and the larger context within which the organization is, in turn, embedded) shapes practice in profound ways. An organization that effectively operationalizes an empowerment culture, for example, is an organization in which practitioners and clients interact on the basis of shared power. An organization rooted in competitive, adversarial power, in contrast, tends to support abusive power relations (among staff and between staff and clients), and to structure dominance hierarchies that stand in the way of sharing power. Given the reliance of the larger U.S. culture on adversarial power and coercion, however, explicit organizational attention to power dynamics is required to escape that paradigm; cultures of shared power need to be intentionally constructed, they do not just happen (Lowery & Mattaini, 1999).

Organizational factors often determine how client problems are defined (for example, as family issues or mental disorders) as well as how they are treated. For example, some agencies still require that parents and small children be treated separately, despite a great deal of evidence that attention to family dynamics, family culture, and the critical role of the parent in any work with the child must be emphasized to achieve significant change, particularly for children (Mattaini, 1999). If social work services are viewed only as "psychotherapy," all client issues and hopes are likely to be redefined as mental disorders, and interventive options may narrow excessively. (The movement toward "community-centered" services is one response to such narrowing.) Certainly, some social workers do "treatment," at some times, in some settings, but this is too constricted a definition to capture social work's professional purpose, or much of what social workers do (or can do), even in work with individuals. The professional social worker, then, faces at least two challenges in work that is organizationally based: first, to participate in the construction of an environment of shared power and, second, to ensure that evidence-based services responsive to client needs—and visions—are not overridden by outdated or unresponsive agency practices. Both of these objectives must somehow be achieved in ways that are organizationally realistic, which is a challenging but usually not impossible order. These issues are further explored in Chapters 11 and 12.

Changes in Funding for Services

Social work practice, like social work clients, is deeply grounded in the contemporary sociocultural situation, which in turn shapes practice in dramatic ways. When the first edition of this text was prepared, the chapter on practice with individuals discussed the effects of the coming of managed care on practice in health and mental health settings, a movement that has since intensified, of course, across the country. However, managed care and the movement to privatization had not yet begun to significantly influence other areas of practice such as family services and foster care—but this is no longer true. The drive for cheaper, shorter-term services is increasingly universal. Decisions about who will receive how much service are increasingly made by insurance company reviewers or funders, and specificity of objectives and ways to track them are increasingly essential. There is much to be said, perhaps paradoxically, for clarity of purpose and goals (and for time-limited work related to some, but not all, client issues), and social workers must be realistic about what is possible given reality constraints. At the same time, professional ethics require that practitioners advocate forcefully when issues of social justice are involved. Thus, they sometimes must refuse to participate in systems that only support and perpetuate oppression.

What is the Case?

One of the messages of the ecosystems perspective, a view of reality that recognizes the organic unity of life (Chapter 1), is that everything is connected. To avoid becoming immobilized by complexity, practitioners in concert with their clients must figuratively "draw a boundary" around the case to determine which factors to address directly and which to regard as background or context. This setting of boundaries includes a determination of which people to work with directly or indirectly, what other systems may require attention, and for what period of time to work with the case—issues of the social, physical, and temporal boundaries of the case. To the extent possible, such boundary drawing should reflect the actual systems present in the case, because, as discussed in Chapter 1, living systems construct their own boundaries, within which effective practice must work. Ignoring the family system in work with an individual, for example, often limits the potential of the work that can be done. In fact, there is reason to believe that contact with members of the social network reduces the need for professional contact while supporting positive outcomes in work with individuals, and should therefore always be seriously considered (Gottlieb & Coppard, 1987; Kemp, Whittaker, & Tracy, 1997).

Perhaps the most useful way to conceptualize the process of defining the case is using a transactional ecomap. Social work students (and probably graduates) tend to look more evenly at transactional factors in a case if they actually draw the case out for themselves (Mattaini, 1993; Meyer, 1976). Clients also usually respond very well to this approach, which communicates a genuine effort to understand their lives and can also usefully capture change over time (Hartman, 1978). There are situations, of course, in which clients would not find this useful, but the social worker in such cases should usually at least sketch the situation out for himself or herself. The case of Ms. Todd, a client of the author's seen for individual consultation, is an example of capturing a case in this way:

Ms. Todd is a 41-year-old African American woman raised in the South but who has lived in a large northern city for about a decade. She is being seen in a private, nonprofit agency specializing in individual and family consultation for a range of problems in living. Ms. Todd was referred by her caseworker at a transitional shelter for homeless women with mental illness because of a history of severe depression continuing to the present time and difficulties between shelter staff and Ms. Todd regarding compliance with shelter policies and procedures.

Ms. Todd had become homeless after leaving a psychiatric inpatient unit. She had moved in with her mother several years earlier but began sinking more and more deeply into depression; she was hospitalized, believing herself to be dying of physical causes, when she could no longer get out of bed. Neither she nor her mother was willing for her to return to her mother's home after leaving the hospital, and she stayed in several temporary arrangements before becoming homeless.

At the point Ms. Todd was referred for services, she had some minimal involvement with several agencies in what she called "the mental system" and was receiving social security. She was bright, well-educated with some college, and had strong social skills when she felt up to engaging. Her vision of her priorities at the time of intake included moving into her own apartment, ameliorating the depression, and moving toward school attendance and an ultimate return to work.

The ecomap shown in Figure 7-1 portrays the shared knowledge about this case between the social worker and the client after a telephone call from the shelter and an initial contact between the client and the practitioner (the case situation as it evolved over time is presented later in this chapter).

The strength of the transactional exchanges depicted by the arrows is represented by the thickness of the lines in the figure.

The case boundary clearly must be drawn to include the client herself (in all of her behavioral and emotional dimensions), the multiple agencies with which the client is involved, her extended family, and her physical world. Also potentially important, although somewhat minimal at this point, are other personal social contacts. Foreground in this case certainly includes the client's emotional state and housing situation and the overall limitations in positive transactions in Ms. Todd's life situation. It was not yet clear to what extent the client's extended family and some of the other

Figure 7-1. A Transactional Ecomap Clarifying a Client's Overall Situation at Intake

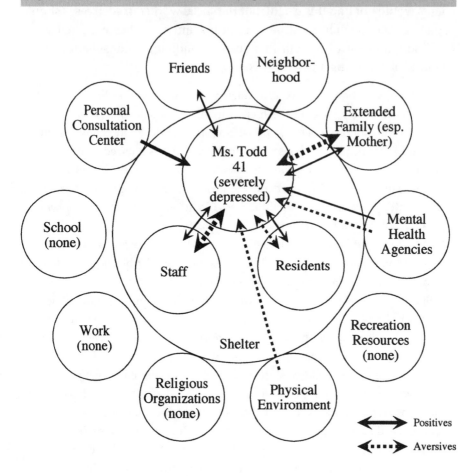

systems in the case configuration might become focuses for work and to what extent they would be primarily contextual factors, to be considered in terms of their effects on other areas but not directly addressed. An individual modality made sense at least at this point, although a shift to family work—or at least some contact with her mother—was kept open as a later possibility.

The next decision to be made related to duration of treatment. For many focused issues and goals, short-term, time-limited approaches are demonstrably effective and are increasingly supported by funders who wish to provide services to as many people as possible with limited resources. Open-ended services to people with limited difficulties may be counterproductive, developing dependence rather than supporting strength (as portrayed in movies, for example, where the "neurotic" patient needs to run every decision by his or her therapist before acting). For clients struggling with long-term issues such as severe substance dependence or serious mental illness, however, longer-term support is typically required. In some cases, episodic involvement during an extended or indefinite period is needed.

Decisions about length of service must be made based on the needs of the case and the available resources and may require painful decisions regarding prioritization and triage when the level of demand is high relative to available professional resources. In Ms. Todd's case, it was possible to offer services that could extend during perhaps a two-year period, which seemed reasonable given the enormous challenges involved in moving from homelessness to stability while coping with a serious affective illness. Goals in a case such as this often need to be reexamined at intervals as the case situation changes.

Core Practice Processes and Skills

A good deal of variation exists among practice approaches regarding the central processes, knowledge, and skills required for practice with individuals. There is also significant commonality; some of the differences are primarily matters of emphasis. The psychosocial approach, for example, focuses in particular on assessment but recognizes the importance of relationship, whereas the life model pays particular attention to processes of building relationships with clients but also acknowledges assessment as important. Within an ecobehavioral approach, the practice process can be viewed as organic and connected, but with four core functions, as shown in Figure 7-2: (1) *engagement* with the client in a relationship of shared power, (2) *envisioning* an improved case configuration to be constructed (or a positive configuration to be maintained), (3) collaborative *assessment* of the case, and (4) *intervention* to make or maintain change.

To some extent, all of these functions are present in every practice event, but typically there is a differential emphasis over time. In general, attention is first paid particularly to engagement, which blends (notice the overlap) into envisioning. That in turn blends into assessment, from which intervention emerges. The arrow in Figure 7-2 shows this general flow.

This order is neither rigid nor invariant, however; in some cases (in crisis situations in particular) the social worker may act immediately after a very minimal assessment and then shift into other functions as the crisis abates. A child protective services worker, for example, may quickly determine that a child may be at imminent risk and remove the child from the home, but far more assessment and engagement with the family will be required to develop a long-term plan. Clients who have been traumatized by natural or man-made disasters, or by individually traumatic experiences,

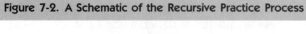

Figure 7-2. A Schematic of the Recursive Practice Process

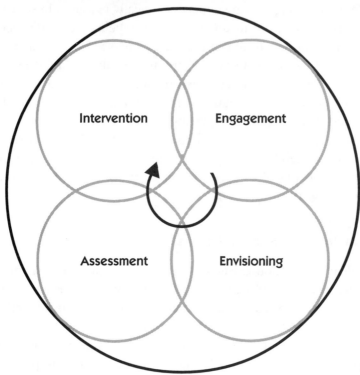

may require rapid cycling between support (active listening), active concrete problem solving, and construction or reinforcement of social support networks. However, determining which of these steps is appropriate at any moment requires ongoing assessment. Other changes may also dictate shifts among these core functions. For example, a homeless client who finally achieves a reasonably stable housing situation may then be interested in envisioning new directions that the collaboration with the social worker may take. These processes are interwoven and recursive over time, but conceptually there is a certain order among them.

Engagement

Some level of relationship is necessary to any useful or effective practice. At a minimum, the client must be willing to interact in some way with the social worker, and for some kinds of cases a very intense relationship may be required—for example, in many cases in which a client is trying to overcome the emotional damage caused by abuse or violence. Many cases seen by social workers are "involuntary," or at least not entirely voluntary. Even in these cases, before a social worker can be useful, some level of relationship is required. For example, if the client is a parent in a child protective case, the client at least must believe what the worker says, reaching some level of trust. To move very far, the client must also at some level contract with the worker to work together to achieve some abstract goal (for example, "getting my child back") or specific objective (for example, completing forms required to obtain assistance). Constructing a meaningful relationship is important in obtaining cooperation, in convincing clients to return for services and to trust the worker's statements. In cases where clients have had limited experiences with trusting relationships, achieving authentic engagement in such a relationship can be an important helping experience in itself, but may require significant time and commitment on the part of the social worker.

Several repertoires are helpful for constructing and strengthening the professional relationship. Perhaps most important, the social worker can really listen, in a respectful and nonjudgmental way. By doing so, the practitioner functions as a nonpunitive audience, which most people find enormously helpful as they sort out their experiences verbally. Many social work clients have seldom or never had such an audience; many, in fact, have been punished overtly or covertly for speaking honestly and from the heart. A nonpunitive audience can help the client to find his or her "voice," and over time the client will typically share more and more emotionally difficult material. Treating someone nonpunitively requires that the social worker somehow come to view the client's actions as natural responses (the best he or she knew how to make) to the client's subjective world, even if the behavior may not be something the practitioner could ever condone. For some clients, for example those who are struggling with serious loss, the opportunity to simply explore one's experiences and emotions can be a valuable step toward acceptance and, ultimately, moving on.

If the social worker can also communicate that he or she can to some extent see the client's reality and experience the client's responses (demonstrating empathy), the client's level of trust will increase, sometimes quickly, sometimes slowly and unevenly, depending on the client's previous experience with relationships. If the social worker communicates interest, empathy, and respect, treating the client as important, a demoralized client is also more likely to begin to view himself or herself as valuable through a cognitive process (the construction of an equivalence relation, such as "me ≈ worth listening to ≈ valuable").

There are as many ways to communicate these qualities and experiences of the worker to the client as there are social workers. The nonverbal channel is crucial; facial expression, tone of voice, body position, physical

distance and touch when appropriate, eye contact, and even arrangement
of the space where the exchange occurs are all important and will vary a
great deal based on factors such as age, gender, and cultural expectations.
It is particularly useful to role-play and discuss this area with classmates
and supervisors, to obtain objective feedback for oneself, and to test these
factors cross-culturally.

In addition, there is a wide range of verbal responses that can be useful
in building the relationship; generally, these involve expressions of empathy (particularly regarding emotions), recognition, and understanding of
the client's reality. Statements such as those shown in Figure 7-3 are particularly useful but of course should be used in ways that are natural to the
social worker and familiar to the client.

Direct expressions recognizing the strengths and value of the client, the
importance of the client's voice, the client's potential contributions to resolving whatever issues are present, and statements of shared responsibility

Figure 7-3. Worker Statements That May Prompt and Reinforce Client Sharing, Support Client Strengths, and Communicate Empathy in the Engagement Process

- I see. . .
- Can you tell me more about that. . .
- It looks like this is hard to talk about. . .
- It sounds like you felt really angry, and also maybe a bit hurt, when he didn't come home that night?
- I know this may be painful, but can you tell me what happened next?
- And that made you feel better? Did that last?
- Let me see if I have this right; what you are saying is that it was the deception that most disturbed you?
- What strengths do you bring to this situation?
- It's very impressive, given all that, that you are doing so well. . .
- I'm particularly impressed that. . .
- Hmm. . .
- What was going through your mind at that point?
- Imagine that things changed as you'd like . . . what would be different?
- That must have been pretty frightening. . .
- Wow. . .
- Sometimes when something like that happens people feel a certain satisfaction . . . was that true for you? Can you tell me a little about that. . . ?
- And then you felt. . . ?
- That's pretty normal. . .
- But. . .
- What about now? Do you still feel that way?

for the outcome of the work are critical. The ultimate goal is the co-construction, with the client, of a relationship of shared power (Lowery & Mattaini, 2001). In sharing power, each participant has a strong voice in the process, and all recognize and expect that each has his or her own power, own gifts, and own vision to contribute to the work. Every client has strengths, an intimate knowledge of his or her life experiences and reality, and often a wide range of other knowledge and skill; the potential power of these factors is critical to the outcome. From this perspective, a client is not an aggregation of pathologies, although we all have challenges and damage with which to contend. Constructing a better life reality can come only from power, not from weakness. Similarly, the social worker brings unique knowledge, gifts, and power to the process. Together, the two (and others if involved, which is often important) carry different but important obligations and responsibilities for the outcome of the work.

Note that a relationship of shared power in direct practice is one of the interfaces between social work and social justice. In a shared power relationship, the social worker gives up a hierarchical stance in which he or she acts as the "expert," instead taking on a role of one essential participant in a practice event in which each party has something valuable to contribute and shares responsibility for the outcome. The contrast with early social work, in which caseworkers saw themselves as facilitating moral uplift, or with a practice stance rooted in diagnosis of pathology, could hardly be more stark. A genuine shared power relationship requires that the social worker give up certain forms of "ego" gratification, not out of sacrifice but out of recognition that they are unjustified. Social workers also often are required to recognize that people from differing life experiences, social classes, and cultural identities have perspectives as valid as the worker's own and may know more than the worker in many areas.

The word "empowerment" is widely used in the social work literature. It is important to note, however, that the root of that word is "power," and there are real advantages to talking explicitly about power, both the constructive power the client, worker, and others bring to their work together, and also the coercive, oppressive power that clients often experience in their lives. There are some complications with the verb empowerment, as well, because it is a transitive verb, indicating that someone empowers someone (even if oneself). This may not communicate the transactional realities of a shared power relationship completely. The authors in this book, therefore, tend to write in terms of shared power, which underlies empowerment.

A relationship of shared power is constructed gradually and can be enriched and deepened during each phase of the work together. There is no single, "right" way to achieve shared power, of course, but there are many points in which the social worker can guide the relationship in that direction. For example, during early engagement, an explanation like the following can be incorporated into the conversation:

> I have been working with people to improve their lives for some time now, and what I've learned is this: We, together, probably have the power to make some real changes in your life. To do this, we need to act as a team; you may not be able to do it alone, given how hard things are right now, and I certainly can't do it by myself. But you know the saying, "Two heads are better than one?" Our work is like that. If I do what I can, and you do, too, sharing my power and yours, there's lots of hope. You have a voice, I have a voice, we do it together . . . how does that sound?

Of course, clients who are experiencing little power in their lives may find this difficult to believe; that is natural and should be accepted. The worker can, in such cases, empathize with the experience of powerlessness and ask the client to give "our team" a chance. In some cases, depending on the client, words like "partnership" or "collaboration" may be a better fit, but there is a good deal to be said for explicitly discussing power early on because this will often prove useful in later stages, can also build hope— and can be, frankly, powerful.

Enhancing shared power can occur continuously while engaging in the other core practice functions, and examples are provided throughout the material that follows, but a brief discussion of this point may be useful here. During the envisioning process, of course, the client's voice should be primary, and taken very seriously; the worker, however, brings skills and experience in clearly elaborating a vision, so both participants have critical roles. During assessment, some of the first questions (as outlined in the Interview Guide later in this chapter) involve what is going right for the client, what his or her strengths are, in what areas of life he or she does have power. Intervention usually explicitly involves tasks for both client and worker; these tasks can and usually should be framed in terms of moving toward enhancing the client's power to shape a life that works for him or her. In addition, there are many moments in work with individuals that offer opportunities to support client power (e.g., "I see that as a real strength of yours . . . tell me more about how you achieved that") and to deepen the extent of collaborative power sharing (e.g., "Here's a chance for us to really join forces and work this out together"). Many of the same basic strategies are required in work with others involved in the case: family members, agency representatives, and other stakeholders (e.g., teachers, foster and biological parents), because power sharing ought to involve all relevant actors in the case. There is no standard recipe for constructing a relationship of shared power, of course, but constant attention, retrospective evaluation of how well one is using opportunities to share power in work with clients, consultation, and reading the empowerment and shared power literature can all help to strengthen skills in building relationships of shared power with clients and others involved in the case.

The process of building a relationship overlaps substantially with the next function—envisioning—and continues throughout the practice process; discussions regarding those other processes often provide the content through which the relationship develops. Relationship construction begins with the first acknowledgments and thoughtful empathic observations the worker makes in the early minutes of contact and continues to evolve and shift throughout the work until the time of termination. (By that point, if the use of time has been clarified and honestly discussed throughout the work together, the client should be well prepared to leave without a major emotional or practical disruption. The bigger challenge is sometimes ensuring that the social worker is ready to let go; this should be dealt with through supervision, because it can be difficult to acknowledge to oneself.) A good deal is known about how to build and deepen practice relationships, even in particularly challenging situations. Students should pursue this material in depth (see, for example, Germain & Gitterman, 1996; Hepworth, Rooney, & Larsen, 1997).

Envisioning

The second of the major practice functions is working with the client to develop a preliminary vision of what a satisfactory outcome for the case would look like, jointly envisioning the construction (or maintenance) of a positive life configuration (including as relevant intrapersonal, interpersonal, and larger systemic conditions and transactions). In one way or another, some of the earliest questions to be asked include something like the following:

- "If we are successful, how will your life be different?"
- "Who will be doing what differently?"
- "What would an observer see or hear that would be different than it is now?"
- "What is your situation like now, and how would you like it to change?"
- or the "miracle question" often asked in solution-focused treatment (Furman & Ahola, 1992), "If you woke up tomorrow and all your problems were solved, what would be happening?"

Envisioning often occurs concurrently with efforts to deepen engagement and can be a useful way of moving the focus toward hope and away from focusing primarily on problems and pathology. Although empathic engagement requires authentic recognition of the client's pain or struggles, dwelling on the negative without building hope can be demoralizing. In addition, because of the dynamics of human behavior, it is more workable to construct new, positive repertoires and transactions (thus reducing problem behaviors indirectly) than to directly try to eliminate problems, which often requires more coercive strategies (Mattaini, 1997; Sidman, 2001).

One useful way to conceptualize envisioning is to think, literally or figuratively, about collaboratively developing a "goal ecomap"—an image of how the overall situation might change as a result of the work together. This approach reminds the worker to think about more than just a single issue; for example, the goal ecomap shown in Figure 7-4 for Ms. Todd (who was introduced earlier in the chapter) shows a shift in mood, but also portrays the kinds of social, environmental, and educational changes that will probably be necessary to stabilize the affective change.

Figure 7-4. Goal Ecomap Portraying the Contextual Situation To Be Constructed through Collaborative Consultation

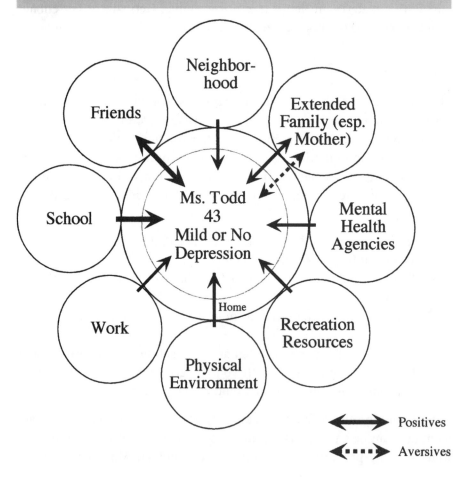

An image such as this ensures that the social worker will not only work toward, for example, cognitive change (assisting the client to learn new self-talk), but also will assist in planning and problem solving about moving toward stable housing, school attendance, and a restructuring of the relationship with the client's mother.

Some clients find it difficult, especially in the beginning, to focus on goals or the construction of positive alternatives because they are more used to thinking about the problems and struggles with which they are dealing. In such cases, the client and worker may begin at that point ("starting where the client is"—a classic "practice wisdom" phrase in social work), reaching at least a preliminary agreement about the issues to be resolved. Over time, however, it is important to move the process toward "constructional," positive change, even if this needs to happen gradually.

Assessment

The initial vision developed by the social worker and client is a first step, but in most cases more data are needed to clarify the realities of the client's life and often to further refine the joint vision developed. This refinement happens through the assessment process, a key to professional practice. Intuitively helpful, positive people may be able to engage others and help them to imagine goals, but professional assessment also requires an extensive knowledge base. This knowledge is one of the things that the social worker should bring to the shared power relationship. The assessment process itself, like the larger practice process, involves several subprocesses, which naturally tend to occur in a particular order but overlap and interweave and often happen in an interactive way. The reader might think about Figure 7-5, which portrays these processes, as a more detailed expansion of the "Assessment" bubble shown in Figure 7-2.

Examples of the kinds of questions that may be useful in completing these assessment functions are found in the Interview Guide shown in Figure 7-6.

It is important that this guide be seen only as a tool to help structure the process, with clear recognition that different types of questions will be required in every practice setting and for every case. Questions that are asked and observations and suggestions made should occur in the natural flow of an authentic conversation, communicating real concern, support, and interest in understanding, rather than being presented as a rigid, invariant interrogation. Assessment should be seen as a collaborative process between social worker and client, not something the social worker does "to" the client; it is not a process of diagnosing the client's pathology, rather, it is a process of coming to a joint understanding and plan for the case.

Figure 7-5. A Schematic of the Assessment Process

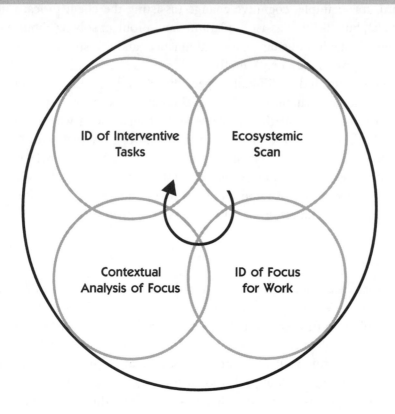

It is also essential to recognize that assessment occurs in every form of practice, including crisis work and very-short-term treatment. Even if a social worker in a busy emergency room has only 20 minutes with a person, a professional never acts without having a reason, and what is done is always based on assessment, rapid though it may be. The process may need to be accelerated dramatically from that occurring in some other practice settings, but it still must occur. It may be helpful to compare this with the emergency medical services paramedic, who must perform a quick evaluation before taking action. While an examination that occurs, say, at the Mayo clinic might be much more extended and detailed, some assessment is always required. The assessment conducted by the paramedic on the street is at least as critical as the more leisurely evaluations conducted at the medical center.

Ecosystemic scan. To develop a realistic plan, it is essential that the worker and client have a clear picture of the client's current life in its contextual complexity. Conducting an ecosystemic (ecobehavioral) scan

Figure 7-6. Sample Interview Guide

I. Ecosystemic scan.

I'd like to ask you a few questions so I can understand your situation. Let's try to develop a picture of what your life is like (you may wish to draw an ecomap during this stage or explore systemic transactions that may have relevance to the case, as suggested below).

- Let's start with what's right. . . what areas of your life are currently going best for you?
- What are your strengths? In what areas in your life do you have power?
- Who are the most important people in your life? (For first person identified:) How is that relationship? What's positive about it? How often do those positive things happen? On a scale of 0 (not at all) to 5 (a lot), how much satisfaction do you get from her? Are there also some struggles? How often do those come up? Same 0 to 5 scale, how much pain do those problems cause you?
- Who else (as above)?
- Does anyone else live in your home? How are your relationships with them? (For this and each of the following areas, inquire specifically about both positive and negative exchanges as necessary, and quantify.)
- What kind of contacts do you have with your extended family? Who else?
- Do you have many friends? How often do you see friends? How are those relationships? Anyone else?
- What about at work or school? What's going well there? So on our 0 to 5 scale . . . Are there things that are not going too well? About a __ on our scale?
- Tell me a little about where you live. How satisfied are you with your home and your neighborhood?
- Do you have any religious or church affiliation? Are you active?
- Are you a member of any other groups or organizations?
- Any legal involvement?
- How is your physical health?
- How much do you drink? Do you take any medications or use any drugs?
- What would you like to do more of? What would you like to do less? (Suggest self-monitoring or observational measures to expand data.)
- What about emotions? Do you feel sad, tense, or angry very often? When does that happen? How long have you felt that way? (Pursue further depending on responses, including use of self-anchored scales or rapid assessment instruments.)
- Are there any thoughts or images that disturb you? (Expand discussion as necessary.)

II. Identification of focus for work [contracting for change goals].

- So out of all of this, where do you think we should begin? What's most important to you?
- I notice that you seem to experience a fair amount of struggle with __. Is that something we should work on?
- What do you think would be a realistic goal here? Will that be satisfactory, or should we start somewhere else?
- Is there anything else we should work on at this point, do you think?
- So specifically, one of your goals is . . . (explicate in behavioral terms).

(continues)

Figure 7-6. Continued

III. Contextual analysis of focal behaviors and transactions

Now, let's see if we can reach a clear understanding of your first goal or focal issue, which is . . . . [General flow is from current undesirable situation to goal state; this kind of analysis should occur for each identified target behavior, whether it is a behavior of the client, like angry outbursts, or of someone else, like a teenage child who is getting into trouble or a landlord who has not made repairs.)

- As near as you can tell, how did this problem start?
- When was that?
- Does this problem behavior ever pay off in any way for anyone—does it ever produce any advantages?
- Who or what supports the current behavior?
- What are the costs? What other problems does it cause?
- What seems to trigger the problem? Are there times when it doesn't happen? (Identify occasions.)
- Are there some times when this is not a problem? Tell me about those times . . . When is the problem most likely to arise? (Search for motivating antecedents.)
- What do you think it would take to get from where you are to where you want to be? (Explore resources, including tangible, personal and social.)
- We each have contribution to make here, and we're both responsible for working toward the outcome. Let's talk about what we each could contribute to reaching this goal. Some of the power you bring to our work together is . . . . What other power and resources can you contribute? Some of the power I bring to our work is . . . . What else might I bring?
- Who else would be willing to help you achieve this goal, or resolve this problem? What could they contribute?
- Who or what might stand in the way?
- How important is this to you? Why? How will reaching this goal enrich your life? How quickly do you think that will happen? (Building motivation.)

IV. Identification of interventive tasks.

(This part of the interview needs to be highly individualized. It should include exploration of possible interventive options for mobilizing the resources discussed in the previous section and for addressing obstacles identified, emphasizing approaches with the best evidence-based support within the realities of the case situation. Tasks should explicitly involve contributions from everyone involved to achieve desired outcomes. Careful specification of the multiple steps required to work toward the goal is often required. Explore possible reinforcers to be used along the way as well.)

of the client's life situation begins with and overlaps with the envisioning process but moves deeper, ensuring that the multiple dimensions that may be relevant and important to intervention are considered. Depending on the issues and goals in the case, it may not be essential to examine all areas in depth, and in modern, fast-paced practice there is often limited time to do so. Still, using a tool such as the Quick Scan (see Figure 7-7) or other form of transactional ecomap, it is possible to sketch major

Figure 7-7. A Blank Quick Scan Form for Rapid Assessment

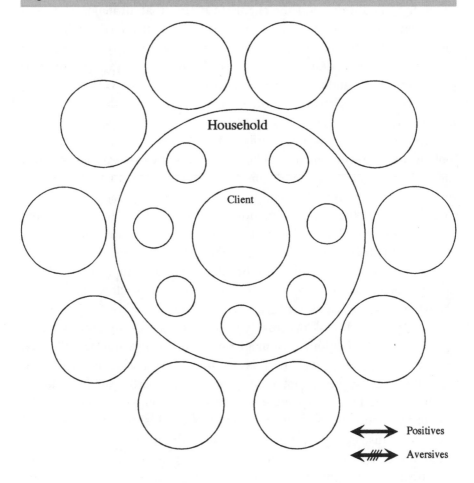

intrapersonal and transactional dimensions of a client's life in a few minutes, and it may be crucial to do so.

Intrapersonal issues—emotional, cognitive, and behavioral—can be noted in the inner circle representing the client. Client strengths and power, as well as current and potential environmental resources, should be noted, as should challenges and issues. The goal is to capture the entire situation, not only "what is wrong." Although using color is especially effective, if you have only one pen, arrows representing negative exchanges can be distinguished by cross-hatching, and those for positives can be plain.

It is important to note excesses and deficits of exchanges occurring between the client and other people and systems, as well as behavioral, emotional, and cognitive excesses and deficits with which the client is personally struggling. A small preliminary study (reported in Chapter 8 of Mattaini,

1993) indicates that it is important to actually sketch out such an ecomap (often but not always with the client) to ensure that all major areas and dimensions that may be relevant to the case are considered. In addition, most students discover that their clients find developing an ecomap to be an empowering experience, and one that communicates the student's empathic interest in understanding the client's life. This process is often recursive with envisioning, because new information that emerges is incorporated into the joint vision of where the case is going.

Although practice can occur only in the present, it is often of value to look also at ways in which the client's circumstances have changed over time. The roots of current problems can sometimes best be understood in this way, and it is often important to recognize the temporal trajectory of a case. Sometimes the current situation is not too bad but reflects ongoing deterioration that, should it continue, may result in more acute distress over time. In other cases, despite a high level of current stress, there may be a pattern of improvement that can be labeled to build hope and used as a resource. Sequential ecomaps, and other instruments such as timelines or genograms, can be useful for this process (Mattaini, 1993).

In the process of looking broadly at the client's life situation, issues of oppression and violations of human rights and their sequelae will often surface. It is essential that these issues be identified and openly voiced when they are discovered; not to do so would be to participate in "blaming the victim" and in the perpetuation of the oppression. For example, in the case of Ms. Todd, at one point in examining her history, the worker and client were discussing a problem she had had with a housing provider, where there seemed to be inequities in the way several potential clients were treated. A straightforward discussion of systematic racism in the network of mental health services opened an area that was very important for acknowledging the client's experiences. Gender dynamics were also involved in the case, because the client had experienced sexual harassment and unwanted advances in the "helping" systems.

Identification of a focus for work. As a result of the ecosystemic scan, the client and worker achieve at least a preliminary shared understanding of the case as it currently stands and, to the extent relevant, as it has developed over time. Many possible areas for focus—problems, challenges, and opportunities—may emerge from this work, more than can often be directly addressed (recognizing, however, that work focused in one area may affect others as well). It is usually necessary for the client and worker to select a small number of focuses for work (usually one to three at any one time, except in residential or day treatment programs where there is more contact time) on which to concentrate, at least at any particular time. Explicit contracting or verbal agreement must occur; if worker and client have different agendas, it is very unlikely that the case will move toward an outcome that will be satisfactory to those involved. It is particularly essential that there not be hidden, unspoken agendas. This is more difficult to do than it may sound because social workers naturally have their own opinions and values, which may not be consistent with those of the client. Still, genuine common ground must be found.

Reaching an agreement can be difficult, but it is essential even in involuntary situations. The client and the worker may not agree on everything, but they must at least have high-level agreement on goals, which may be as broad as, "We both want to keep you out of jail" or as narrow as, "We will work to help you find and keep more friends." The more specific the focus for work, the easier other practice processes may be, but the most critical factor is that both participants (and ultimately any others involved) leave the encounter with a clear and consensual understanding of what they are about in their work together.

To achieve the necessary specificity, the focus selected should involve a change or stabilization of someone's behavior—but "behavior" as used here is very broad, including everything from overt motor behavior (for example, battering) to covert verbal behavior (what one says to oneself—self-talk), and includes physiological processes involved in anxiety or depression, and cognitive phenomena such as memories (Poppen, 1989). The behavior to concentrate on may be that of the client (for example, to increase life satisfaction and social life), that of someone else (a child the client is concerned about), or, most often, transactions occurring among actors that could be tracked on a transactional ecomap (for example, to improve marital dynamics or eliminate battering). The focal behavior may also, however, be that of systems actors (for example, actions required to have a social security eligibility determination reversed). It is particularly common that the focus for work involves changes in transactional exchanges, rather than simply action on the part of one actor.

This level of specificity also greatly simplifies the process of monitoring the case. As discussed in Chapter 6, there are a variety of ways to monitor practice, many of which apply to work with individuals. Simple counting and graphing of problem or goal-related events, scores on rapid assessment instruments or behaviorally anchored rating scales, or tracking changes in transactional exchanges using sequential ecomaps are all useful approaches that flow directly from envisioning the desired case outcome and targeting specific focal behaviors and transactions for attention. Graphing changes on a behaviorally anchored rating scale developed with Ms. Todd (see Figure 7-8), for example, says a good deal about the trajectory of the case, as well as the possible need for adjustments in the work being done.

Figure 7-8. A Behaviorally Anchored Rating Scale for One Dimension Important in the Case Discussed in this Chapter

Level of Goal Attainment	Rewarding Activity
5	Engaged in rewarding activities for most of the day each day
4	Engaged in rewarding activities more than daily
3	Engaged in rewarding activities nearly every day
2	Engage in rewarding activities a few times a week
1	Engaged in rewarding activities less than a few times during the week

Contextual Analysis of Focal Behaviors and Transactions. Identifying the focus for work in a case is an important step but does not immediately indicate what must be done. Every client who is depressed will not benefit from the same intervention nor will every client who is lonely, battered, or a substance abuser. What is required is an analysis of those issues in their ecosystemic context, since even where the initial focus is on depression, intervention is likely to focus on shifts in transactions. Consistent with this recognition, Reid (1985) suggested that the *identification of causes of problems, obstacles to surmounting them, and resources available or required to deal with those causes and problems* are central factors in a contextual analysis. Of course, in a shared power relationship, the power carried by each person involved and others who are recruited are critical resources.

To complete this phase of practice adequately, the social worker's full professional knowledge base is required. Although not everything is analyzed, understanding the focuses for work, as well as factors that may have shaped and now maintain them, often requires both extensive practical and empirical knowledge as well as a clear theoretical framework for organizing this information. One individual who is homeless and demoralized may find substance abuse treatment useful, whereas another may require residential stability first, for example. One person with a couples problem may benefit from joint counseling, whereas another may require shelter services. Cultural-level knowledge can also be crucial. For example, one American Indian young man attending a boarding school was experiencing severe emotional distress as a result of dreams of a recently deceased relative. An American Indian social worker called in for a consultation suggested that he set aside a small portion of his meals to "feed" his relative, a traditional way of recognizing, remembering, and expressing respect for an ancestor (and thereby remaining connected with one's collective identity) in certain Native cultures. This intervention was successful. Cultural consultation was required to understand the problem; this intervention would never have been arrived at by chance. There are also many situations in which helping persons from a client's own culture may need to be intensely involved, using traditional rituals, for example; only cultural consultation will clarify such options.

Factual knowledge, theory, and the information gathered in early phases of the assessment must be integrated in a coherent way before the client and social worker can determine what needs to be done. Particularly important is an examination of antecedents and consequences of the focal behaviors and transactions. For example, many people do what they have seen others do (modeling). What one says to oneself, for instance, "No one cares about me," can be another critical antecedent to emotional experiences. Environmental events and conditions (severe deprivation, for example) can be important motivating antecedents that make even relatively low-quality payoffs, such as those associated with some substances or somewhat abusive relationships, more attractive.

Problematic interpersonal behavior such as tantrums or even depressive talk is often shaped by attention from others (a consequence), a process that can become cyclical. Attention to constructing more positive antecedents and consequences can be crucial to helping clients take the steps required. If the focus for work is the client's completing school, for example, it may be critical to identify the action steps (by the client and others) required to reach that distant goal, determine what kinds of contextual supports (antecedents and consequences) will be necessary to help the client or other target person take those steps, and determine who will provide those antecedents and consequences. All of those steps then may need to be included in the intervention plan.

In work with individuals, the two key players always available are the social worker and the client; identifying what steps each can take to support positive actions required to reach the goals established is a central task in contextual analysis. Consistent with principles of evidence-based practice, it is common that the social worker will need, in this process, to take a careful look at the literature, and particularly at approaches that have substantial evidence of effectiveness, as the client and worker move into the final step of the assessment, identifying specific action tasks that can be undertaken.

Identification of Interventive Tasks. After the focuses for work have been carefully analyzed in their contextual complexity, the worker, client, and in some cases others involved are ready to decide what active steps may be useful to work toward construction of the envisioned reality. It is quite useful to think of these steps as "tasks" (Reid, 1992), specific actions to be taken, remembering that actions (behaviors) may be overt or private and physical, cognitive, or emotional. Interventive tasks identified may include actions to be taken by the client, by the worker, by both jointly, or by others involved in the plan. Everyone involved should be expected to make some contribution, although what is done will often be quite different for each person depending on role, talents, knowledge, resources, and others. (Recall also that it is often important to involve others from the social network in the work in some way, which of course expands the base for shared power, so tasks may include making those contacts.)

In many cases, steps to be taken can usefully be framed as processes of self-monitoring and self-management, an empowering direction (Kopp, 1993); the monitoring strategies discussed in Chapter 6 can be very helpful in this work. The general self-monitoring strategy involves four steps (Mattaini, 1997):

- Clarifying the goal to be achieved and the reasons to do so (this involves envisioning, of course)
- Pinpointing specific actions to take to reach the goal, usually progressively, beginning at a level that can almost certainly be achieved (most people set initial goals too high)
- Tracking progress on the pinpointed actions (e.g., charting number of healthy meals or hours spent with one's child)
- Ensuring positive consequences for progress (often recognition from others, but sometimes small rewards for oneself for achieving a bit of progress).

Reporting regularly to someone else, like the social worker, is usually essential to self-management (most people, not just clients, tend not to keep challenging personal resolutions). Lack of progress can be used as a signal that more assessment is necessary, to identify obstacles standing in the way, reduce temporarily unrealistic levels of expectation, or increase the positive consequences for reaching target levels.

Although there are certain general types of interventive strategies that can commonly be employed, it is often necessary to creatively craft unique interventions that are responsive to case dynamics. Professional social work practice, therefore, cannot be reduced to a "cookbook" approach, although practice guidelines for particular case configurations can clearly be useful. For example, Reid's (2000) *Task Planner* identifies a wide range of possible interventive tasks that have some empirical support for working with particular client issues. Such resources can provide considerable guidance and point to critical literature that should be examined in the course of planning. Some issues call for very specific approaches; for instance, one student was assigned a case of nocturnal enuresis with a six year old child. Only very specific interventions, including bladder training, scheduled awakening, and urine alarms, are effective with this problem (Reid, 2000; Sloane, 1979/1988). Generic approaches like empathic listening and examination of family dynamics by themselves will not resolve the problem, but they may be part of the work, as contextual supports may need to be addressed to make implementation possible.

Decisions about what steps to take should naturally be part of the "contract" or working agreement constructed collaboratively between client and social worker. Such decisions are always tentative, and it is common to revisit this process as needed during intervention. Referring back to Figure 7-2, although identification of interventive tasks as part of assessment generally precedes active intervention, as for other processes discussed, the reality is often iterative, and multiple processes may overlap and interweave. For example, completing a coherent assessment often builds hope and in that sense is an intervention in itself.

Relative specificity about interventive tasks leads to collaborative clarity in contracting and can simplify the monitoring process as well. In general, in practice with individuals there are two levels of monitoring that are useful: the level of attainment of goals established and the extent to which interventive tasks are completed. (If tasks are being completed but goals are not being reached, this would suggest a breakdown in the analytic process, necessitating a return to the previous process—contextual analysis of focal issues.)

Before looking at the most common interventive strategies available, one final reminder: Given the time constraints present in much contemporary social work practice, assessments often must be completed very rapidly. If a practitioner is working with suicidal clients in an emergency department, for example, the time available may be very compressed. The general framework presented here, however, is still applicable; it simply needs to be done very quickly. It is still important to know something about the client's life situation to identify focal issues and goals, to understand them, and to plan what to do, but all of this may need to occur within a 30-minute interval. In other settings, the pace may be more relaxed, but the same kinds of questions are important.

Intervention

The practice process generally moves from assessment into intervention in a relatively seamless way, with the worker and client beginning to implement the tasks they have identified, some of which may happen in private sessions, some by working together in the client's natural environment, and others as "homework" to be completed by one or more of the participants. In general, there are three major strategic clusters of interventions that capture much of what social workers and clients do together: (1) facilitating exposure to new or different transactions and experiences, (2) working with cognitive and other private events, and (3) learning new skills (Mattaini, 1997). In many cases these interventions are mixed and phased, but it is useful to look at each separately for analytic purposes. The material here simply touches on each cluster; many books have been written and a great deal of research has been done about each, and social work students must read deeply and widely to be adequately informed about the state of the art (and science) in practice.

Exposure to Different Transactions and Experiences. The purpose of social work as operationalized in this chapter is related to constructing a life reality that is more reinforcing and less aversive for clients. Recalling that social work is ultimately about changing patterns of transactions in the human web, in a very real way all of social work practice is directed to helping clients achieve a new balance of transactions with their social and physical environments. In some cases this is done indirectly, for example, by working with the client to practice different self-talk that he or she can use later, which will then affect his or her experiences. The most immediate way to affect a client's reality, however, is to work with the client to change transactions between the client and environmental actors and systems directly.

Ways of increasing exposure to positive experiences and transactions include such disparate tactics as assisting the client to access benefits to which he or she is entitled, assisting the client to organize his or her family's living space (as many family preservation programs do), connecting the client to sources of social support (often using the social worker as a temporary bridge to other relationships), or working with family members to construct a more satisfying and less coercive family culture (see Chapter 8). In some cases, the social worker may participate in changing other aspects of the client's world, for example, by referring to a group (see Chapter 9); by working with neighborhoods, communities, or other larger aggregates (see Chapter 10); or by advocating for organizational change (Chapter 11). All of these approaches, from assisting in establishing eligibility for benefits, to network therapy (work with multiple actors in the client's life at the same time), fall into the "exposure to new or different transactions and experiences" cluster of interventions. Many of them also have social justice implications. For example, if one's client is a battered woman, referral to an empowering support group can be helpful in many ways (Tutty, Bidgood, & Rothery, 1993). The client may receive help in protecting her right to security of person and perhaps become an advocate for others to whom this basic human right is denied. Some of these approaches are sometimes seen as "merely" tangible services or case management, but if they are grounded in a professional assessment, they are every bit as professional and "clinical" as doing family therapy or cognitive restructuring. Many specific types of intervention fall into this general cluster, including network therapies, referrals, and efforts to coordinate the many agencies and systems that may be involved with an individual or family.

The kinds of connections and transactions that will be experienced as positive and aversive for a client greatly depend on his or her personal life experiences, especially family and larger cultural experiences. Some individuals find a rich network of kin and friends very satisfying, whereas others may find such a network too intense; these determinations should emerge from the individual assessment completed. Knowledge of commonly valued connections and experiences for members of different cultural groups can provide some guidance here (McGoldrick, Giordano, & Pearce, 1996), but individuals differ by biology, by social class, by age cohort, by immigrant generation, by membership in multiple augmentative and varied cultural networks, and by many other factors (see Chapter 2); therefore, such information can only suggest possibilities. Many clients find it helpful (if challenging) to "experiment with life," to try exposing themselves to a variety of new experiences, because without previous experience they may not know what will actually work for them.

Work with Verbal and Private Events. A second general cluster of interventive strategies involves work (both in the session and as "homework") with what clients say and with cognitions and other private events. (Private events are those that are not directly observable to someone else: memories, dreams, emotional conditions, and self-talk are examples.) Generally this is the realm of traditional "talk therapy," although the pathological connotations associated with the term "therapy" may not be consistent with much of contemporary social work practice in which empowerment and building on strengths as opposed to "curing" dysfunction underlie the work. (The challenge here, of course, is that "therapy" has a certain contemporary cachet and may be hard to give up for ego-related reasons, and because it may in some cases insulate and distance the social worker from the client, reinforcing a hierarchical arrangement in which the expert "cures" the disordered person. There is no doubt that healing breaches in the human web is social work's professional function, but in many cases other language, e.g., "healing," "social work consultation," or "our work together" may be more consistent with a genuine process of shared power.)

Many clients come to the attention of social workers when they are struggling with some sort of dilemma or are faced with a problem for which they have no ready solution. Assistance in sorting out and evaluating the available options is, under those circumstances, very useful. In fact, one major stream of social work practice theory for several decades was the problem-solving model (Perlman, 1957); that approach was also one of the major roots of the contemporary task-centered approach (Reid, 1992). Multiple problem-solving paradigms are found in the literature; a straight-forward first approach is "Choices and Consequences" (Mattaini, 1997), in which the heart of the work is identifying the available choices and identifying the usually multiple consequences associated with each. There are generally both short- and long-term positive and negative consequences (or possible consequences) associated with each choice; clients often find decision making much easier if they have carefully thought out, and in some cases written out, all of these consequences. Note that the concept of "choices and consequences" is consistent with a shared power perspective; the worker's role is emphatically not to tell the client what to do, but rather to facilitate the client's own evaluative process.

Work with self-talk (cognitive therapy) is another widely used approach in contemporary practice. The core notion underlying this work is that what one tells oneself is a major determinant of what one does and what one feels. For example, if one believes that failure is inevitable no matter what he or she does, it is very hard to take action. There are many possible cognitive distortions (see, for example, Beck et al., 1993; Ellis & Dryden, 1997; Mattaini, 1997), but some common ones are listed below:

- "I am and always will be a failure."
- "I must do everything perfectly."
- "I cannot influence my world."
- "The future looks very bleak."
- "My world (physical and social) is a terrible place."
- "Things I don't like must not happen to me, or it's awful."

It is easy to see how statements such as these, repeated over and over by others and oneself until they become automatic, would be associated with stress or demoralization. The current research also suggests that changing these verbal patterns by testing them against the real world can lead to behavioral activation, which leads in turn to better experiences and there-fore, ultimately, emotional changes.

An important cutting-edge variation of this approach is Acceptance and Commitment Therapy (ACT) (Hayes, Strosahl, & Wilson, 1999). This emerging approach emphasizes that how one feels currently is natural given one's experiences, and changing experiences will change how one feels; therefore, one must first commit to acting in new ways even while acknowl-edging the reality of current feelings. The first basic shift in ACT is from "I'd like to do something new, but I feel too depressed" to "I'd like to do something new, *and* I feel depressed"—accepting the feeling as real and understandable based on one's history and circumstances, but not viewing the emotion as an obstacle to taking action. As a result, the individual can commit to action, which later will produce change in affect.

There are many other valuable interventions for working with this cluster of issues. For example, exposure to the feared situation, event, condition, or object is a critical strategy for working with a person who may be struggling with a variety of anxiety-related issues. Even discussion of distressing memories, for example, is one form of such exposure. Relaxation skills can be very useful for managing physiological aspects of anxiety, either in conjunction with exposure or separately. Solution-focused work (Franklin et al, 2001; Walter & Peller, 1992) provides another route to building on clients' strengths, helping them to do more of what works for them and less of what does not work. There are many books and articles, by social workers and those of other disciplines, that are valuable reading to prepare for work with verbal and other private events with clients. Two critical keys for evaluating these approaches are (1) To what extent are they authentically congruent with shared power? and (2) To what extent have they been demonstrated to be useful with clients similar to one's own (evidence-based practice again)? The most interesting and intellectually fascinating approaches may not be those that work best for clients, and that matters enormously.

Skills training. One gift that the social worker can bring to clients is the knowledge of particular skills for living that clients may find give them new options, which can be empowering because by using those skills clients may come to have more voice and influence over their worlds. Although group modalities can be particularly useful for skills training because clients can act as models and respondents for each other as they experiment (shared power based in client strengths), skills training is also commonly used in work with individuals.

One simple skill with broad utility is self-monitoring. Self-monitoring is a straightforward process in which clients themselves track events in their lives, including their own actions and reactions to experiences. In addition to being useful for assessment purposes, self-monitoring can be a particularly empowering process, giving clients a sense of control over their lives (Kopp, 1993). Methods of self-monitoring range from the simple task of making a check mark on a chart on the refrigerator each time one exercises to keeping a detailed structured or unstructured journal that can be used to track cognitive self-talk. In some cases, clients' behavior changes as a result of monitoring alone (it is "reactive"); therefore, such monitoring can function independently as an intervention. In other cases, it is the first step in a more extended process of self-management (briefly discussed earlier) in which other interventions are included.

Perhaps the most common use of skills training is related to social skills. Many ways of relating to other people can be constructed and refined in this way, including assertiveness, expressing positive feelings to others, listening empathically, negotiating disagreements, and refusing demands and requests (Mattaini, 1997). Before beginning the social skills training process, it is important to decide collaboratively with the client what approaches are personally and culturally acceptable, recognizing that the purpose of this work is to expand the client's options but not to dictate what he or she should do. For some people, particularly those from certain cultural communities (some Latino and Asian groups, for instance), what is viewed by White Americans as appropriate assertion may be seen as offensive, particularly toward people who culturally should be respected (elders, for example). Particular sensitivity may be required in situations of bicultural or multicultural people who use different repertoires under different circumstances. In all cases, determination regarding what skills to work on must emerge from collaborative discussion, but this is particularly crucial in cross-cultural situations in which the worker may not know the issues that must be considered.

The general techniques used for social skills training include simple instructions, modeling by the social worker, rehearsal and testing by the client, and feedback in an effort to refine the approaches being used. For example, if a woman is trying to determine how to request what she wants more assertively and refuse her husband's unreasonable demands, the worker may first take the wife's role, and she her husband's; they would then switch as the client experimented with new alternatives; and both would work together to tailor even better alternatives for this particular family.

Certain caveats should be noted, however. If there is risk of violence, assertiveness training may not always be the most appropriate interventive strategy; safety planning and support groups may be indicated instead. Skills training that includes attention to such issues can be very powerful. There is considerable evidence, for example, that unilateral work with the concerned other (CO, usually the spouse) of a person who abuses substances can lead to successful engagement in treatment (Barber & Gilbertson, 1996; Meyers & Smith, 1996). Perhaps the most useful approach for this work was developed by Sisson and Azrin (1986), and includes modeling and rehearsal of skills for:

- reducing the risk of physical abuse to the CO,
- encouraging sobriety,
- encouraging engagement in treatment, and
- assisting in treatment after the substance abusing partner enters.

Those interested in this approach should carefully study the detailed practice manuals that are now available (e.g., Meyers, Dominguez, & Smith, 1996).

Clients are not always ready to use new skills in their real world, and their right to set their own pace should be respected. Furthermore, some clients have the necessary skills but do not use them under circumstances when they might. For example, most people can control their anger with their bosses but may not have learned to do so with family members. The issue then involves practicing using existing skills on different occasions.

A more extensive variation of skills training is inoculation, an approach commonly used with anger problems, some kinds of anxiety, stress, and even pain. The basic process involves breaking typical problem situations into stages (for example, before the provocation, during the provocation, and after the provocation) and learning and practicing particular behavioral, verbal, and cognitive skills that may apply to each (Mattaini, 1997).

In general, all practice approaches—those rooted in ego psychology (Goldstein, 1995), those emerging from ecological theory (Germain & Gitterman, 1996), and ecobehavioral and cognitive–behavioral approaches (Mattaini, 1997; Reid, 1992)—rely on some variations of the three clusters of interventive strategies outlined here. All major approaches in some way deal with working with the client toward exposure to different experiences— in fact, any practice approach that fails to address this directly is too narrow to capture much of what social work practice with individuals must address. All approaches deal with emotions and thoughts, and all deal with changes in the client's behavior, although sometimes in very different ways. Practice with individuals, in common with all social work practice at other system levels, has as its purpose changing or stabilizing transactions between the client and his or her ecosystemic field in ways that are more satisfying and produce better long-term outcomes for the client and the human web within which the client is indivisibly embedded. Success can happen only within a respectful relationship of shared power.

References

Beck, A. T., Wright, F. D., Newman, C. F., & Liese, B. S. (1993). *Cognitive therapy of substance abuse.* New York: Guilford Press.

Barber, J. G., & Gilbertson, R. (1996). An experimental investigation of a brief unilateral intervention for the partners of heavy drinkers. *Research on Social Work Practice, 6,* 325–336.

Dorfman, R. A. (Ed.). (1998). *Paradigms of clinical social work* (Vol. 2). New York: Brunner/Mazel.

Ellis, A., & Dryden, W. (1997). *The practice of rational emotive behavior therapy* (2nd ed.). New York: Springer.

Franklin, C., Biever, J., Moore, K., Clemons, D., & Scamardo, M. (2001). The effectiveness of solution-focused therapy with children in a school setting. *Research on Social Work Practice, 11,* 411–434.

Furman, B., & Ahola, T. (1992). *Solution talk: Hosting therapeutic conversations.* New York: W. W. Norton.

Germain, C. B., & Gitterman, A. (1996). *The life model of social work practice* (2nd ed.). New York: Columbia University Press.

Goldstein, E. G. (1995). *Ego psychology and social work practice* (2nd ed.). New York: Free Press.

Gottlieb, B. H., & Coppard, A. E. (1987). Using social network therapy to create support systems for the chronically mentally disabled. *Canadian Journal of Community Mental Health, 6,* 117–131.

Hartman, A. (1978). Diagrammatic assessment of family relationships. *Social Casework, 59,* 465–476.

Hartman, A., & Laird, J. (1983). *Family-centered social work practice.* New York: Free Press.

Hayes, S. C., Strosahl, K. D., & Wilson, K. G. (1999). *Acceptance and commitment therapy.* New York: Guilford.

Hepworth, D. H., Rooney, R. H., & Larsen, J A. (1997). *Direct social work practice: Theory and skills* (5th ed.). Pacific Grove, CA: Brooks/Cole.

Kemp, S. P., Whittaker, J. K., & Tracy, E. M. (1997). *Person-environment practice: The social ecology of interpersonal helping.* New York: Aldine de Gruyter.

Kopp, J. (1993). Self-observation: An empowerment strategy in assessment. In J. B. Rauch (Ed.), *Assessment: A sourcebook for social work assessment* (pp. 255–268). Milwaukee, WI: Families International.

Lowery, C. T., & Mattaini, M. A. (1999). The science of sharing power: Native American thought and behavior analysis. *Behavior and Social Issues, 9,* 3–23.

Lowery, C. T., & Mattaini, M. A. (2001). Shared power in social work: A Native American perspective of change. In H. Briggs & K. Corcoran (Eds.), *Foundations of change: Effective social work practice* (pp. 109–124). Chicago: Lyceum.

Mattaini, M. A. (1993). *More than a thousand words: Graphics for clinical practice.* Washington, DC: NASW Press.

Mattaini, M. A. (1997). *Clinical practice with individuals.* Washington, DC: NASW Press.

Mattaini, M. A. (1999). *Clinical intervention with families.* Washington, DC: NASW Press.

McGoldrick, M., Giordano, J., & Pearce, J. K. (1996). *Ethnicity and family therapy* (2nd ed.). New York: Guilford Press.

Meyer, C. H. (1976). *Social work practice: The changing landscape* (2nd ed.). New York: Free Press.

Meyer, C. H., & Palleja, J. (1995). Social work practice with individuals. In C. H. Meyer & M. A. Mattaini (Eds.), *The foundations of social work practice: A graduate text* (pp. 105–125). Washington, DC: NASW Press.

Meyers, Dominguez, T. P., & Smith, J. E. (1996). Community reinforcement training with concerned others. In V. B. Van Hasselt & M. Hersen (Eds.) *Sourcebook of psychological treatment manuals for adult disorders* (pp. 257–294). New York: Plenum Press.

Meyers, R. L., & Smith, J. E. (1996). *Clinical guide to alcohol treatment: The community reinforcement approach*. New York: Guilford Press.

Perlman, H. H. (1957). *Social casework: A problem-solving process*. Chicago: University of Chicago Press.

Poppen, R. L. (1989). Some clinical implications of rule-governed behavior. In S. C. Hayes (Ed.), *Rule-governed behavior: Cognition, contingencies, and instructional control* (pp. 325–357). New York: Plenum Press.

Reid, W. J. (1985). *Family problem-solving*. New York: Columbia University Press.

Reid, W. J. (1992). *Task strategies: An empirical approach to clinical social work*. New York: Columbia University Press.

Reid, W. J. (2000). *The task planner.* New York: Columbia University Press.

Reynolds, B. C. (1982). *Between client and community: A study in responsibility in social case work*. Washington, DC: National Association of Social Workers. (Originally published in 1934).

Richmond, M. (1917). *Social diagnosis*. New York: Russell Sage Foundation.

Sidman, M. (2001). *Coercion and its fallout* (2nd ed.). Boston: Authors Cooperative.

Sisson, R. W., & Azrin, N. H. (1986). Family member involvement in initiate and promote treatment of problem drinkers. *Journal of Behavior Therapy and Experimental Psychiatry, 17,* 15–21.

Sloane, H. N. (1988). *The good kid book*. Champaign, IL: Research Press. (Originally published in 1979).

Specht, H., & Courtney, M. (1994). *Unfaithful angels*. New York: Free Press.

Tutty, L. M., Bidgood, B. A., & Rothery, M. A. (1993). Support groups for battered women: Research on their efficacy. *Journal of Family Violence, 8,* 325–343.

Walter, J., & Peller, J. (1992). *Becoming solution-focused in brief therapy.* New York: Brunner/Mazel.

CHAPTER 8

Social Work with Families

Christine T. Lowery

Julia Loktev's *Moment of Impact*, a documentary of her family life, was a surprise winner in the director's category at the Sundance Film Festival in early 1998. The Loktevs, Jewish immigrants from Leningrad (now St. Petersburg), came to the United States in 1979 when Julia was nine years old. Her parents worked as computer programmer analysts in a suburb in Colorado, where Julia described herself as "the only brunette in a blond American town" (cited in Firestone, 1998, p. B2). In 1989, when Julia was 19, her father, Leonid Loktev, was struck by a car while crossing the street to a garage sale—the "moment of impact." A traumatic brain injury rendered him "neither paralyzed or speechless, but unable to initiate movement or speech on his own . . . stuck somewhere between life and death," Julia described (p. B2).

Loktev's film documented the daily rituals of her mother, Larisa, as she feeds, washes, and dresses the 50-year-old man who is her husband. Larisa sings, she speaks Russian to him, she rages; she talks about her felt invisibility, countered only by going to aerobics. Intermittently, she and her daughter lie next to each other, speaking Russian in "intimate and often humorous ways," discussing their reactions to an unpredictable situation, now more than 10 years old (Firestone, 1998, p. B2). The morning comes, and the rituals begin once more.

The documentary illustrates themes social workers and families may face together. For the Loktevs these include the aftermath of the accident, disability and aging, care giving and caregiver stress, "invisibility," and isolation (including cultural isolation); emerging careers and careers interrupted at midlife; daily rituals, medical interventions, managed care, long-term care, and finances; coping and planning over time; family support, the father–mother–daughter relationship, and their tandem development in the life span. These experiences are all sifted through a screen of meanings embedded in ethnicity, cultures, community, an immigration

experience and political transition, communication between two generations, and the passage of time. Hungry for resolution, social workers sometimes forget the tempo of life pronounced in the repetitive devices (rituals)
and themes—credited for the director's prize—in this visual story.

As a social worker, working with this family, what are the skills and
knowledge required? What assumptions have already been made? What
must be learned? What can this family teach about their experience? What
interventions can be constructed—combining the needs, strengths, values,
and the work of Larisa and Julia and Leonid, their ethnicity, history, U.S.
experience, and the overlay of multiple cultures in relationship with the
social worker-in-agency, other helping professionals, and community resources in a suburb in Colorado? What state, regional, or national resources
are available?

Introduction

Usually, when people have conflict or experience developmental transitions or life-threatening accidents that require additional understanding
and help, it is within the context of family life. As family configurations
and the multisystem challenges families face become more complex, models of helping families and family groups must prove flexible. Social workers, too, must be flexible. They must move away from labels such as "normal"
and "dysfunctional." Social workers must understand how biological family groups or constructed families in neighborhoods and communities work
to meet the needs of the group, take care of family members, and deal with
internal and external stressors, both positive and negative (Walsh, 1993).

Social workers must rethink boundaries and categories. All families are
not necessarily bound by marriage or blood kin, for example. Although
they are sometimes rejected by blood relations, gay men and lesbians create
chosen families, families of peer relationships and "fictive kin," bound by
love, pushing the edge in new traditions and rights: custodial parenting for
gay people and domestic partner rights (Weston, 1997). In another example, Boyd-Franklin (1993) indicated that particular values need not be
tied to socioeconomic status. Because of their values and expectations for
their children, poor and working-class African American families may be
seen as middle-class in their own communities (Boyd-Franklin, 1993).
Family roles do not consistently reflect Western stereotypes. Hamer (1997)
reported a qualitative study of 38 Black noncustodial fathers who shaped
their own roles and functions based on what they wished they had experienced with their own fathers. They responded to their own children by
first spending time with them, providing emotional support, providing

discipline, being role models, teaching gender roles, and as a final priority, providing economic support (Hamer, 1997).

The Ecological Perspective

How do families respond to predictable (births, adolescence, a planned move, a new job, blended families) and unpredictable (natural disasters, accidents, illnesses, sudden job loss) stressors, challenges, and events? What are the coping strategies and consequences used by individuals within the family culture and by family groups within larger cultures and environments? How do these strategies change over time, during the life course? What is the history of adversity and strength in this family group, the person-in-environment fit? What can we build on now?

Ecological concepts that characterize the life-model of social work practice are outlined by Germain and Gitterman (1996): transactions, person–environment fit, stress and coping, human relatedness, power and vulnerability, human habitats, and the life course. Social workers must see the whole picture when working with vulnerable populations and understand where advocacy is required to make structural changes in society. Transactions between people and their environment act to shape behaviors and consequences. How good is the fit—"needs, capacities, behavioral styles, goals of people and characteristics of the environment" (p. 9)—between the person and his or her environment? Is there a flourishing relationship (adaptedness)? Adaptation requires continuous change and action geared to benefit human potential and growth and to improve the person–environment fit. What are the life stressors (threats of harm and loss) in the external environment, and what internal stress do they produce? If a client has the personal and environmental resources to address the life stressors, these might be perceived more positively as challenges or be considered irrelevant or benign.

Reciprocity is evidence of human connectedness, including connectedness to the natural world; this relatedness enhances competence to support self-esteem; and competence and self-esteem give one self-direction. Coercive power is the "antithesis of growth-promoting, self-healing life forces" (Germain & Gitterman, 1996, p. 19). Disempowerment and technological pollution destroy life. Human habitats are located in the physical, social, and cultural structures of community and can be neutral, supportive, or disempowering. Within the social structure of the community, rights and protections should shape niches or status for groups and individuals; yet it is tolerance for abuse of power that maintains disempowering niches for segments of society. Within the intersections of human and cultural diversity and new forms of family groups, life cycles or life stages of development lose

Sidebar 8-1. Habitat, Neighborhood, and Social Justice:
Henry Street Settlement

Helen Hall, a social worker trained in the New York School of Philanthropy
(the precursor of Columbia University School of Social Work), discussed
the importance of settlement work or family-centered neighborhood work.
Her own commitment spanned over three decades (1933–1967) as a resident and director of the Henry Street Settlement in New York City. In 1933,
social and health services were centralized to save money, and specialization in social work practice and the influence of psychiatry on social work
took hold. City slums were reputed to be fading from American life, and the
settlement movement was deemed unnecessary. Hall's experience taught her
otherwise: "neighborhood work had an increasingly important role to play,
for the neighborhood is where vulnerability is highest, where observations
should be keenest, and services most ready" (p. xiii). "Anywhere that poverty degrades a neighborhood and surrounds its children with misery, we
are mortgaging our future as a country. It is not only cruel, but stupid"
(p. 107). To say settlement houses were no longer necessary, was tantamount
to warnings by the New York City health commissioner to tightly cover the
garbage cans to starve the rats, while tons of garbage remained uncollected
in the backyards of tenement buildings (Hall, 1971).

Hall divides her account, *Unfinished Business,* into the depression years
(1929–1939), the war years (1940–1944), and the postwar years (1945–1955)
when gang warfare was a major concern. Heroin addiction and individual
violence were the most disruptive elements in neighborhood life (1955–1965)
and overlapped with the nonviolent to violent rebellion of youths in the late
1960s when the fight for civil rights was paramount. The book *Addict in the
Street* (Larner & Tefferteller, 1965, cited in Hall, 1971) became the most "far-
reaching contribution made by Henry Street" (p. 249). As a social justice
contribution, *Addict* drew national attention to drug addiction and exposed
human suffering to those removed from life in the tenements.

consistency. Alternately, life course recognizes shifting norms, global and
local environments, and human behavior as "indeterminate" (p. 21).

Preparation, Engagement, Assessment, Planning,
Monitoring, and Termination

In quality work with a family, the processes of preparation, engagement,
assessment, planning, monitoring, and termination are intimately linked.
Each is reiterative; the practitioner should always prepare for the next phase,

negotiate relationships as events change them, and gather new data over time in assessment. If workers monitor or feed information back into the system, their planning should be evolving, and the family and the social worker should be able to see what they have or have not accomplished, and recognize when their work is done.

Preparing for Engagement and Assessment

As society becomes more complex, quality social work requires that practitioners update their knowledge in the field while they build more specialized knowledge. Preparation includes gathering background information to bridge gaps in knowledge. This preparation should not be limited to a review of the case record or consultation with the social workers in the last agency that worked with the family. It is important that where there are knowledge gaps, practitioners search the professional literature in health, psychology, social work, or related fields. In the Loktev example, ethnocultural factors intersected with health and social issues of a specific type of disability (brain injury), aging, and caregiving, predictably critical issues for 21st-century health and social work. Social workers cannot claim ignorance in an age of information and technology. National resources have web sites on the Internet with links to specific topics. Professional journals abound. For example, *Health & Social Work* alerted social workers to interrelated practice issues on disabilities and aging (Gilson & Netting, 1997). Life-long disability versus late-life disability and changing life circumstances were considered. The need for cross-training of aging and disability professionals was mentioned. Stereotypes of client incompetence and worker bias were discussed. The loss of independence and depression were addressed. The crisis of impending nursing home placement and ensuing anger and grief was covered. Alternative services, including home health care services and caregiving by family members, were reviewed. Ethical issues of self-determination, the multiple roles of a social worker, including partnering with the person with disabilities, were discussed. When and how could these issues become part of the intervention process for the Loktevs?

One need not go to a social work library for every case; however, investing in one's continuing education after graduate school is part of being a well-informed and responsible social worker. For example, subscribing to family services journals keeps recently published material within reach. If one works in a multiservice agency in a multiethnic neighborhood, a resource book (for example, McGoldrick, Giordano, & Pearce, 1996) on working with families from different ethnic backgrounds coupled with a resource book (for example, Rauch, 1993) in assessing families in different situations would prove useful. The NASW Policy Statements and Encyclopedia of Social Work (includes theory and practice) are updated periodically and cover the field of social work. These resources could be purchased as part of an agency's commitment to informed social work practice. A working knowledge of community resources and a current community resource directory are invaluable.

As social workers become more practiced, they must not assume that they know the terrain without the guidance of a family's unique experience and perspective. Resources only provide a place to begin. As practice deepens and journal reading reinforces what social work students learn in research classes, they can compare information clusters and note changes in the development of a social problem and the response of an agency over time. Documented and researched knowledge provides powerful material for advocacy on behalf of the families with whom social workers work. Such knowledge is also imperative for updating agency practices and policies; this, too, is a mandate of social work.

General Preparation for Work with the Loktev Family

As the social worker reviews selected book chapters and journal articles and forms questions, he or she is reminded that this process helps to become familiar with potential issues and to ground himself or herself, but not to construct the client's reality. The client will define that reality in the assessment, the plan, and the monitoring process.

Disabilities. The population is living longer; one in three people will experience some form—or combination—of disability. Disabilities can be physical (arthritis), sensory (loss of hearing, speech), emotional (depression), mental (schizophrenia), cognitive (Alzheimer's disease), intellectual (developmental delays), or health-related (diabetes and dialysis) (NASW, 2000). Rolland (1993) also considered other disabilities, including movement (stroke with paralysis), stamina (heart disease), disfigurement (mastectomy), and conditions associated with social stigma (AIDS). In the case of illness, disability, and death, the questions when, what type of condition, how serious, and for how long, rather than "if," are inevitable (Rolland, 1993). As part of end-of-life decisions, social workers may be present in cases of assisted suicide (Callahan, 1997; NASW, 2000), ruled out as a constitutional right by the Supreme Court in 1997 but within the jurisdiction of the states, such as Oregon, which passed legislation that permits assisted suicide.

An ecological perspective in assessing families is evident in Rolland's (1993) caution for "goodness of fit between family style and the psychosocial demands of different disorders over time" (p. 447). What is expected to happen in the course of an illness over time? What are the immediate demands on the family? How will demands change as the course of the illness changes through the life course?

Ethnicity and Immigration. After a brief review of two decades of work and study in ethnicity, Levine (1982) declared, "In all of these experiments, one fact stood out. Ethnocultural factors are more powerfully played out in family relations than in any other arena" (p. xi). In the context of immigration, Chazin (1997) outlined factors that could be relevant in an assessment of a family that has immigrated. These include phase of immigration, time of immigration, age at immigration, condition of families who have immigrated, condition of families who are left behind, policies of country of origin, policies of country of entry, and history of policies since immigration.

What are possible ethnic and cultural contexts for the Loktevs, who immigrated in 1979? Although they have been in the United States for more than 20 years, the immigration experience is not irrelevant, for people carry their ethnicity within them. The social worker must be aware of how experiences of the disability, aging, or caregiving are interpreted and what meaning these experiences have for different members of the Loktev family, including Mr. Loktev. Because he is without voice, health care and social services providers must not ignore his presence in the family.

In a climate of anti-Semitism after the 1917 Russian Revolution, many young Soviet Jews shed their Jewish ethnic identity and culture and entered the professional ranks in science, government, and industry to help build a new Russian industrial society (Feigin, 1996). What is the cultural history for the Loktevs? Those who come from the urban centers such as Moscow and St. Petersburg are primarily Russian in culture. Is this consistent for the Loktev family? What other cultural affiliations do they have? In contrast, immigrants from the Ukraine and Belorussia are more likely to be craftspeople with a strong Jewish culture and a history of the Holocaust (Feigin, 1996). Feigin noted that Jewish families from Russia "seek support and compassion through verbal expression of their emotional discomfort" (p. 633). Values suggest collectivity, mutual dependency, and group responsibility versus the U.S. ideals of individualism, self-reliance, and independence (Feigin, 1996). How might this orientation be reflected in Larisa's roles as a wife, mother, and caregiver, and her attention to her individual needs?

Health Care and Caregiving. Foot and Stoffman (1996) indicated that the baby boomers (those born between 1947 and 1966) will not be turning 65 until 2012 through 2031. However, the need for hospital care begins to increase in a person's mid-50s (1997 for early baby boomers). By the time someone reaches the late 70s, the rate of hospitalization increases to five times one's lifetime rate; by the late 80s, this increases to 12 times the life-time rate (Foot & Stoffman, 1996). Health care costs, high in the mid-1990s, will be even higher as boomer aging increases the demand for hospital care in an era in which hospital closures are prematurely planned. In preparing for the assessment, Larisa Loktev is developmentally at an age where her own health care, as well as the health care of her husband, will need more attention.

Family caregiving first gained attention when community-based resources were to supplant institutional care to address needs of patients with mental illnesses in the 1960s and 1970s (Hatfield, 1987). During the past decade, post-hospital care, including long-term care, has been transferred from publicly funded hospitals to the home, with increasing implications for families and caregivers capable of filling these service gaps (Foot & Stoffmann, 1996; Tebb, 1995). Caregiving is again more evident in the literature because of recent health trends, attention to people with disabilities, and the effects of AIDS (see Lynch & Wilson, 1996). The caregiver's well-being and perception of the burden of caregiving tasks are instrumental in deciding whether an older person (or a person with disabilities) is institutionalized (Zarit et al., 1986, cited in Tebb, 1995). Tebb proposed a caregiver well-being scale based on a strengths perspective, including resiliency and ability to use support to develop and expand strengths that reinforce positive experience in caregiving. This scale may be useful in the assessment process for Larisa Loktev, because it identifies both strengths and areas of change in which caregivers may need some help. The scale is not available in the article; however, the analysis provides categories of basic human needs and activities of daily living that would be important in the assessment, particularly if one knew little about caregiving. Students are encouraged to contact authors to request information about the availability of instruments or scales.

What are Julia's developmental needs? Her filmmaking career is beginning, demanding time far from home. What are her concerns? Are there potential conflicts in her roles as a daughter/career woman when seen through an ethnic-cultural lens? By scanning information for possible social work issues in the professional literature—including issues of cultural diversity—community resources, and information the practitioner may receive in a referral, the social worker is initially prepared to meet the Loktevs. The worker should also have identified possible elements of an ecological assessment. Recognizing that there is much to learn, practitioners must take stock of themselves.

- Where are worker apprehensions and strengths centered?
- Can the worker talk about disability, illness, loss, grief, and even death?
- Does the worker minimally understand the medical systems within which he or she may have to work?
- How can the worker get more information about the environment in which the Loktevs live and the systems on which they rely?

Assessment, Planning, and Monitoring

How does a family function? A family-centered focus treats the family as the unit of intervention; an ecological perspective understands the family as part of the environment within an even-larger configuration of institutional systems. The interaction of behaviors within the family and with their environment can sometimes be complex and difficult to understand. A good assessment with the family reflects the family's reality—their cultural interpretations of the situation—adds the perspectives of the professional helpers, outlines potential consequences of different interventions, and helps the family identify priorities for intervention. Ecomaps and envisioning improved life situations (see Chapter 7) help give structure and meaning to these interactions and at the same time demonstrate what stressors the family is responding to and how these interactions affect individual members and the family as a whole. If a recently divorced, single mother feels fragmented and tired all the time, the complexity of an ecomap may actually provide some relief. Additionally, a cultural assessment addresses the meaning of the life event, its causes, and cultural interventions for members of the family within a set of cultural explanations.

Meyer (1993) described assessment as twofold. First, relevant information is gathered with the purpose of enhancing adaptations between individuals and families and their environments. Practice models (psychosocial, behavioral) guide the process and inform intervention. Second, as a product, the assessment describes "what is the matter" and defines the case situation. The assessment explains the connections relevant in the plan and determines the roles the social worker will take and the levels at which the social worker will operate. Note how these processes are intertwined in the following family-in-tribal-environment example.

When Emily, a young Native American woman from a tribe in Arizona, came to the Indian child welfare agency, she initially requested adoption information. The social worker framed an initial response with information about the Indian Child Welfare Act of 1978, which lists placement preferences for the adoption of American Indian children: family members, tribal members, and other Indian families. In the assessment that followed, it was found that Emily had been pregnant at 16 and had an eight-year-old son whom her mother was raising and who was doing well in school. The young woman was now three months pregnant. Abortion was out of the question with the first pregnancy, as in the current situation, because of Emily's religious upbringing. Emily believed she had made the same mistake at 24, an age when she "should have known better," that she had at 16. Her sisters criticized her for allowing her mother, a widow, to bear the full responsibility of raising her son because of Emily's history of alcohol and marijuana abuse and irresponsible behavior. Currently, she was in a community college program that she would complete about the time the baby was due. Emily was aware of the effects of alcohol and drugs and smoking on the fetus; her drinking had lessened since she had started school a year ago. She had not had a drink since she found out she was pregnant a month previously, but she was still smoking.

In the assessment of the family context, it was found that family members were usually supportive when Emily showed responsible behavior. From a cultural perspective, the young woman acknowledged that she could not "give the baby away" without telling her family. The three-month pregnancy introduced a limited time factor and an intervention was constructed in the first session with Emily.

After assessing that there were no other reasons for wanting adoption, the social worker suggested a partnership in which both social worker and client could talk with interested family members in a family meeting. "If

Sidebar 8-2. Solution-Focused Brief Therapy

In *Becoming Solution-Focused in Brief Therapy*, Walter and Peller (1992) outlined working assumptions that inform their work and are focused on two questions: (1) What maintains the problem? (2) How, then, do we construct solutions?

Change is incremental and constant. Family members have their own interpretations and make meanings of events, and know what they want to change. To reinforce solutions, talk is solution-focused and feedback is positive. Exceptions to the problems are used as material upon which to build solutions: When are things going right? What can we affirm in these situations and what elements can we extend to other situations?

People may disagree about what the problem is and how to solve it, but those who acknowledge a problem and agree something has to be done become members of the treatment group (teachers, therapists, friends, etc.). Not every member of the family has to show up; work with those who are there.

you want to do this, I will come with you and talk to them." Although this suggestion produced anxiety for Emily, she was willing. The work of contacting members for a family meeting and disclosing the pregnancy was divided. The social worker visited and informed the mother, who used the news to explain her daughter's recent withdrawal.

At the family meeting the following week, the team of the social worker and the client fulfilled previously discussed roles as co-facilitators. The social worker, who was ten years older, opened the meeting and voiced the concerns of the client, her doubts, and her fears in bringing this to the family. Emily acknowledged her own history of multiple partners and irresponsible drinking. She introduced her dilemma of whether or not to give this child up for adoption. The baby's father had not been a responsible partner in the past, and the family distrusted him based on his history. Emily acknowledged that, if she were to keep this child, she would be parenting without his help or support.

Eleven family members, including Emily's mother, her son, a paternal aunt, and three sisters and a brother and their spouses, came to the meeting and took turns speaking. Each acknowledged Emily's chaotic history, but also acknowledged her growth in the past two years. Each person talked about how he or she personally supported Emily, about what he or she could do to help, and about making a place for the baby in the family. Even the client's eight-year-old son, comfortable beside his grandmother, spoke his welcome for the baby and was heard by the group. After each person spoke, the final decision was always returned to Emily.

Now that Emily could move past some of her guilt and fear, she spent the next week talking more personally with her mother and sisters. She decided to raise the child within the boundaries of her extended family. Had Emily decided to seek a formal adoption, she and the social worker had agreed to return to the family to discuss the options for keeping the child within the family. If needed, options for keeping the child in the tribe, according to the practices of her tribal group, and compatible with the protections of tribal groups under the Indian Child Welfare Act would be discussed. A legal advocate from the tribal law program would have been included as part of the planning team, if necessary.

The short-term case required the initial contact and assessment, one home visit and two telephone calls for coordinating the family meeting, two hours for the intervention meeting itself, and a brief follow-up meeting to monitor and terminate care. Emily already had a prenatal care plan in place. Although her family was supportive, Emily realistically recognized that there was much work to be done. It was agreed that nothing else was needed from the child welfare agency, and the relationship was ended with the client being encouraged to return if necessary.

Cultural and ethnic priorities will shape how a family responds, to what stressors a family will respond, and how they may use their support networks. In the Native American family example, values shaped by a specific tribal culture intersect with values from a Catholic religious perspective that, in this meeting, supported views of family, family interdependence, trust, and honesty. Having the social worker initially "speak" for the young woman, hearing the voices of the entire family group, including Emily's son, and coming to a decision among the women in the family supported tribal practices. Additionally, child welfare services, health care services, and legal services were all available on this particular reservation.

Elements of Healthy Family Functioning

The Native American family group example demonstrated elements in a balanced system that Walsh (1993) summarized as important for healthy family functioning. In an assessment of the family, these markers must be acknowledged and reinforced as part of the intervention and monitoring processes.

There was an essence of commitment and connectedness as a supportive family group at this point in the family's development. This element was balanced by a respect for individual differences and needs, which in this case was Emily's decision whether or not to seek adoption. Within this connectedness, intergenerational well-being from the youngest to the oldest is fostered (Walsh, 1993). Although the group was supportive, they were honest and accurate in their communication of Emily's past and present behavior (both negative and positive), and the young woman acknowledged this.

A range of emotions was acceptable in the family communication, and responses were empathetic in an atmosphere of mutual trust (Walsh, 1993). The sisters acknowledged their own past drinking behavior and how they valued their family life now. Emily cried when she expressed her shame about her own behavior in a "good family"; her mother expressed sorrow about any possibility of "not knowing the baby." Humor balanced the seriousness in the meeting, and the transitions were comfortable, well-paced, and affirmative. The family had a shared belief system in their religious background despite the differing levels of current religious activity. All supported Emily's choice not to seek an abortion and openly spoke of her son's contributions to the family since his birth. Her sisters and mother voiced their concern about Emily's commitment to being a full-time mother for this child. Emily acknowledged their concerns and expressed her own.

Parents who model effective problem-solving and conflict resolution strategies can teach skills that demonstrate ethical values and socialize their children to contribute to the larger community (Walsh, 1993). Although no decisions were made in the family meeting, groundwork for further discussion was laid. Emily took the responsibility to activate her renegotiated relationships with the women in the family to reach a decision and to initially plan for supporting the baby. Problem solving often presents a series of opportunities over time to discuss, act, and re-evaluate. Demonstrating, processing, and evaluating problem solving with the family is the essence of family work.

Predictability, comprehensibility, and flexibility of the family rules within a consistent organizational structure promote trust among members and enhance adaptability (Gravitz & Bowden, 1985; Walsh, 1993). Children are nurtured and protected, and authority is appropriately delegated (Gravitz & Bowden, 1985). For children raised in families in which violence and addiction impinge on their safety and ability to trust, reestablishing predictability and clarity of family rules is vital. Life course transitions or unpredictable stressors and challenges require that a family group have flexibility and adaptability to respond to internal and external stressors.

Walsh (1993) continued her list of elements with sharing of power and responsibilities recommended for couples. Recognizing that each member brings a different kind of power to the family group, shared power and responsibilities could be considered for all members of the family group and between the family and their community. Community-based family support programs demonstrate the sharing of power in learning collectives with families as learners and teachers, through mutual aid, multiple-family celebrations, and family mediation skills (Lightburn & Kemp, 1994).

Delgado-Gaitan (1994) reported on a case study of family socialization and cultural change in Mexican immigrant families and first-generation Mexican families in Carpinteria, California, schools. Because these families wanted their children to be successful, parents tried to "remake their roles as primary socializing agents and to rethink their goals in the face of historical and current community influences" (p. 80). Thus, the home culture became more congruent with the school culture and the community at large. At the same time, the parent and community organization provided structure for immigrant families and a way to participate without rejection of their language and culture. From this participation came a family-based empowerment process—"beyond that of school-mediated interventions" (p. 80)—that pushed the schools to improve their programs for Spanish speakers. Contact with other families empowered learning and provided an opportunity for these families to use their own cultural values to create learning environments for their children that met the school's expectations about "expressive language" (p. 80). Many first-generation parents had experienced cultural isolation and loss of their language. In one generation, they turned their own experiences in school into more positive experiences for their children.

Finally, to have a healthy society, the community within larger social systems must provide adequate economic security within which social networks (kin, friendship, coworkers, and social networks) provide psychosocial support for the family group (Walsh, 1993).

Working with Families: Empowerment Needed

Belsey, Backett, and Davies (1996) placed family functioning at three basic levels within an ecological and social justice framework.

1. There are families who function within the norms of their culture despite the stress of social development and change.
2. There are families who are vulnerable but who have not yet experienced serious breakdown.
3. There are families whose functions are seriously compromised or who can no longer meet the basic needs of their group (physical needs, emotional care, individual, and development). The family members may have experienced psychological or physical exploitation or abuse or suffered injustice in the distribution of rights and may be at risk for breakup because of economic, social, or political forces.

The survival of the family is ultimately threatened by "severe deprivation, inadequate economic resources, unemployment, hunger, isolation, forced displacement or serious disease" (Belsey, Backett, & Davies, 1996, p. 412). Under these circumstances, the biological family functions of care and protection are impaired, the economic and social support functions cannot operate, the educational and sociocultural and socialization functions of the family wither, and the psychological functions (intrafamily relationships and affection) are disrupted. Interventions with families in social work must address the valuable functions of the family and the societal injustices that perpetuate disruptions in family functioning from generation to generation.

Social work in the 21st century must incorporate social justice goals with and on behalf of families, emphasize an ecological perspective for intervention plans, and demand empowerment and social action in family work. In the examples presented here, three basic interventions with families are reviewed: multiple-family groups, family support, and family preservation.

Multiple-Family Groups

McFarlane (1991) described multiple-family therapy initiated in the 1960s with families of patients with schizophrenia in institutional settings.

Deinstitutionalization of mental health patients in the 1970s transferred the functions of state hospitals to families including "monitoring symptoms, managing medication compliance, instituting rehabilitation efforts, and controlling dangerous and bizarre behavior" (p. 365), all without training or support. Family psychoeducation was a trained effort to create an environment that compensated for a complex set of issues: a functional disability or impairment of the brain in a group member, the use of psychotropic drugs, and the difficult and complex burdens on the family group.

The multifamily therapy process was developmental. Initially, the patients and their families met to discuss ward management problems. Latent benefits included improvement in symptoms and sociability for patients and morale and communication with family members.

> Families were sufficiently joined to each other that messages of blame coming from therapists were usually neutralized, while direct emotional support and opportunities for trading successful techniques for managing illness-related behavior often dominated the discussions. (McFarlane, 1991, p. 365)

In later stages, families worked on balancing the needs of the patients with their own needs, resisting the clinician's need to categorize the families into "theoretical dysfunctional patterns" (McFarlane, 1991).

Boyd-Franklin (1993) recognized the power of multiple-family group therapy. Such work strengthens social systems and empowerment in African American communities and counters the isolation that violence and drugs bring to inner-city neighborhoods; it can also bring change to inner-city schools and other nonresponsive systems. These groups are closely related to what McKnight (1997) called associational communities from which care or "the consenting commitment of one person for another" (p. 120) is developed. Meezan and O'Keefe (1998) reported that variations of multiple-family therapy or group therapy (MFGT) have been used with battered women and their children (Rhodes & Zelman, 1986); inner-city and multiproblem families (Aponte et al., 1991; McKay et al., 1995); families with difficult parent–child relationships (Cassano, 1989); and adopted adolescents and their families (Lang, 1993).

One form of MFGT was described by O'Shea and Phelps (1985, cited in Meezan & O'Keefe, 1998). Trained therapists used psychosocial interventions when working simultaneously with two or more families. Work was primarily focused on a specific problem shared by two generations (parents and children) and at least two family members per family; for example, work on decreasing drinking or smoking behaviors of mothers and their pregnant teenage daughters living at home. Patterns of interfamily interaction and alliances among intrafamily members were incorporated.

Ideally, multiple-family group therapy relies on the strengths and experiences of families "who have been there" combined with the knowledge and skills of the therapist(s) in an environment of shared power. The power of modeling discussion and problem solving and practicing new behaviors should not be underestimated. The opportunity to learn from one's clients and gain new understanding should not be ignored by the therapists.

Meezan and O'Keefe (1998) evaluated MFGT as part of a package of services (including group therapy and case management services and outreach) to improve family functioning and child behavior with 42 abusive and neglectful caretakers in environmentally stressful living situations in Van Nuys, California. A comparison group of 39 other families, randomly assigned, participated in family therapy with case management services. The menu of approaches for MFGT was extensive: "family systems, stress and coping, structural family therapy, group therapy, behavior modification, cognitive–behavioral therapy, reality therapy, parent education, crisis intervention" (Meezan & O'Keefe, 1998, p. 33). Goals included increasing social support, fostering parent-to-child nurturing, improving children's behavior, and enhancing children's social competence. Six to eight families at a time worked with four therapists for eight months (34 sessions, 2.5 hours per week) between 1991 and 1995. Developmental issues (age-appropriate behavior), discipline, self-respect, feelings, multiple roles and concomitant behaviors, and communication were the underlying themes.

Outcomes measuring family functioning included parent–child interactions, supports to parents, financial management, developmental stimulation, and caregiver interactions. Parent–child interactions produced the only statistical difference (p = .03) between MFGT and family therapy groups at close of service, with caregivers in the MFGT reporting improvement. Child behavior differences showed that children in MFGT were more assertive than children in the traditional family therapy program (p = .02). Sixty-two percent of the families in the MFGT group had a planned termination, indicating greater program involvement, compared with 30 percent of the traditional family therapy group. MFGT caregivers were more likely to name a member of their group rather than a therapist when describing interpersonal help. Help in concrete need areas came from informal support systems outside the agency.

Family Support and Family Preservation

Family Support. Family support programs focus primarily on prevention and are family-centered and neighborhood-based, reminiscent of the settlement house approach. In some programs, an empowerment approach is used, and families work with human service workers to set goals and define activities. Comer and Fraser (1998) listed the goals of family support programs: to empower families as consumers and improve the health, safety, and well-being of children. Services range from informal counseling for stress and life skills training, to job searches, child health care, parent education, and organized sports or activities.

Social work, preoccupied with clinical practice, has not been a leading profession in this work, and contemporary programs are primarily multidisciplinary alliances among early childhood education, maternal and infant health, and family medicine (Lightburn & Kemp, 1994). Recent interest in strengthening communities has been spurred by "a conservative backlash against the War-on-Poverty social programs [and] academic and practitioner interest in theories of social capital and civil society. Social work, meanwhile, remains on the sidelines. Some observers even suggest the profession will have a hard time reclaiming its historic dual mission of changing people and systems" (Ryan et al., 2000, p. 8).

Because family support programs use multiple interventions, they are difficult to evaluate. Comer and Fraser (1998) analyzed outcome data from six family support units that had already undergone evaluation using an experimental or quasi-experimental design. They examined program description, intervention strategies (home visiting; child development screening; parent training; and social, emotional, and educational support for parents), target population (multiethnic), evaluation design, outcome measures, and observed outcomes across these six programs. All program evaluations used multiple measures, including client self-reports. Data for small samples of families that completed programs and little data on families that did not complete programs were limitations in these evaluations. These programs demonstrated positive outcomes with early intervention for young children and parents, but effectiveness for work with adolescents and their families was not demonstrated, which should suggest to the social worker that other approaches be explored for this group (see Mattaini, 1999). The question, "What are the characteristics of the families who complete programs and those who do not?" remains open. What are the environmental elements that enhance or impede growth for these families?

Students should be aware of disclaimers in program evaluations that note that their services cannot counter the effects of extreme poverty and racism. What would services to counter economic, social, and political ostracism look like? McKnight (1997) reviews de Toqueville's 1831 observations and descriptions of Americans acting as citizens in a democracy and working on local problems through relationships de Toqueville called "associations" (p. 119). The plan was simple: decide what the problem is, decide how to solve the problem, and organize to implement the solution. McKnight (1997) compared the citizen model to the system model where need, clients, and control are relevant. "In summary, systems provide control, mass production, consumption, and clienthood. Associational communities depend on consent and allow choice, care, and citizen power" (McKnight, 1997, p. 120).

Can these tools be integrated? Ernesto Cortès, Jr. (1997) described the collective work of the Communities Organized for Public Service (COPS), a federation of religious congregations in San Antonio, and how COPS has dealt with annual block grant negotiation, priority setting, and project selection. For more than 20 years, civics and philosophy intertwined as community people met in "house meetings concerned with one street or drainage issue, to neighborhood meetings proposing a package of projects, to meetings in each city council district to shape a proposal with the council member" (p. 198). With the support of one sister organization, COPS has brought $800 million in "streets, parks, housing, sidewalks, libraries, clinics, street lights, drainage, and other infrastructure to the poor neighborhoods of the inner city" (p. 198).

What is the current thinking in family service agencies? Client-centered interventions vs. community-centered interventions represent parallel worlds explored by Sviridoff & Ryan (1997) for the Alliance for Children and Families (formerly Family Service America) and its members. Among agencies surveyed, perspectives on community ranged from the place where clients' families live, to a strategic location for delivering services to families, to resource-rich networks to which families can contribute.

Family Preservation. Family preservation services or intensive family intervention programs target those families who are in danger of losing their children to foster care. The Family Preservation and Support Services Act (P. L. 103-6) includes funding to states for family preservation services and community-based family support services. Family preservation services are 24-hour, home-based, family-centered, intensively monitored, multilevel services to help families demonstrate planned objectives. Services can be as concrete as providing transportation and teaching housekeeping skills to building links between the socially isolated family and community resources, to crisis intervention.

Hoge (1998) contended that, "the price of admission into a program designed to foster competence is to accept the definition of oneself and one's family as socially incompetent in the extreme" (p. 18). Ironically, the focus of intervention is on the strengths of the family, and structural change must occur in about 90 days. Family preservation models that incorporate behavioral models for positive discipline or models that addressed family or social support have improved the effectiveness of parent training (Berry & Cash, 1998).

Campbell (1997) qualitatively compared three cases of child abuse and neglect and the level of success with intensive family intervention and demonstrated the complexity and depth of the issues social workers must confront. Intergenerational child abuse and neglect and unsuccessful "mainstream adult living including substance abuse, violence, and criminal activity" characterized the first case. Here, family preservation "may temporarily counter-balance personal despair and hostile forces; [however] rapid withdrawal of this support can give rise to anger, disappointment and rejection of further offers of help" (p. 288). Campbell characterized the second case of child neglect as a "reactive crisis of demoralization" (p. 288). In this case, disorganization was temporary, the family was usually stable, and parenting was basically effective. Family competence was reinforced, and empowerment strategies validated the family members' responses to a crisis. Intensive family intervention outcomes improved in this case. In the third case, the mother had a mild intellectual disability and was divorced from a husband who had sexually abused the children. One child had developmental delays. A "chronic deficit in the family structure" compounded by social isolation and disability "called for ways to augment family life . . . to fill the leadership gap and ensure continuity of core family functions" (p. 289). Intensive family intervention served as a "kickstart" but could not serve those who needed continued support.

Drisko (1998), in a qualitative–quantitative evaluation, compared one public and one private intensive family services program and raised questions about the characteristics of families requiring child abuse intervention, ancillary services, and the termination process. Psychological testing of 47 families referred from state social services programs indicated that almost one-third of the parents "appeared to be intellectually challenged, mainly with borderline intellectual functioning (WAIS [Wechsler Adult Intelligence Scale] 70–85) that could be either organic or secondary to environmental limitations. A few parents were possibly mildly retarded ([intelligence quotient] 55–70)" (p. 63). Mental health and mental retardation services were recommended as part of the planning for client needs. In comparison, one-half the families had substance abuse histories, including cocaine use; however, services here did not seem to be lacking. A lack of housing and jobs was noted by 25 percent of the parents as a reason for their children not being able to return home. Half the group commented that program length—three to five hours per week for eight weeks—was not enough time to reach their goals. Finally, consideration for the termination process was evident because parents worried about what would happen when services ended.

Sidebar 8-3. Genograms and Intergenerational Patterns

(See Appendix C, Exercise 8 for a description of a genogram).

Family genograms in the context of poverty, racism, alcoholism, historical trauma, murder, and loss can be powerful tools in helping new social workers understand how day-to-day realities are embedded in intergenerational patterns. Genograms may document patterns of immigration or cultural practices or strengths.

In a pregnancy prevention exercise, preteens might chart the patterns of teenage pregnancies and partnered and unpartnered women and men in their families, including other health and social issues their families have dealt with. In working with blended families, including lesbian and gay families in which children from previous unions are present, a genogram may open discussion of family memberships (kin and fictive kin), role changes, and decision-making processes while examining intergenerational connections. Genograms with an emphasis on cultural practices can help mixed-race families or families of different cultures explore contrasting or similar practices and beliefs and open doors for sharing cultural practices not recognized before. In parenting classes with Native American families who have experienced intergenerational boarding school placements, charting family members who have been placed and discussing parenting styles may be useful for discussion.

Hartman and Laird (1983) considered genograms in child welfare agencies as part of the adoptive home study in exploring how a child will fit into the existing family system and what issues of identity will be considered. A genogram with the natural parents can contribute a family history for the child. In working with foster parents and natural parents, family genograms can guide narratives about child-rearing practices or family rituals and support understanding of dissimilar or similar family backgrounds.

Where one or two family members have sexually abused groups of women or children, a genogram exploring intergenerational sexual abuse patterns may be useful in documenting a record of abuses. In such situations, a genogram may encourage those who were sexually abused to share their experiences in an effort to heal and understand. Intergenerational charts for family groups that have experienced mental illness (schizophrenia), physical illness (diabetes, heart ailments), alcoholism and drug addiction, family violence, or divorce and separations can help family groups put disruptive family patterns into perspective. Genograms may also reveal the strengths of family members who have made other choices in dealing with these issues.

Summary Questions

- What level of functioning does the family display?
- What are the social elements that impinge on their functioning?
- How long can resources realistically be provided?
- What types of services must social workers and clients advocate?
- What societal injustices must be challenged?

Conclusion: From the Literature—An Ecobehavioral Model

Lutzker (1997) suggested that it is only logical that treatment for families mirror everyday life. He described Project 12-Ways, a treatment and prevention model for child abuse and neglect, and reviewed several examples of behavioral antecedent procedures such as using simple prompts (large bright cards) to help mothers independently start stimulation activities with their babies that they had previously learned. Project 12-Ways services included parent–child training, stress reduction, basic skills training for children, home safety, home cleanliness, and abuse prevention strategies for mothers.

Lutzker (1997) described a specific example for how a mother, with mental retardation and inability to read, learned nutritious meal planning and shopping skills to have her child returned to the family. A match-to-sample procedure was described and evaluated with a pretest–post-test design assessing one food group at a time (Saber et al., 1983, cited in Lutzker, 1997). Pictures of food, representing the four basic food groups, were cut from magazines and placed on index cards of four colors: (1) meats on red cards, (2) fruits and vegetables on green cards, (3) dairy products on white cards, and (4) grains and carbohydrates on blue cards. A large planning board was divided horizontally to represent breakfast, lunch, and dinner and vertically to represent the four food groups; each row had a corresponding color-coded envelope. The mother's task was to match the color of the card (with food photograph) at the bottom of the row with the corresponding envelope for each meal she was planning. Seven of these boards were necessary to plan for a week's worth of meals. To shop for food items, the mother matched food photos and placed a second set of photos in a plastic page of a ringed binder, which served as a visual shopping list. When she went grocery shopping, she again matched pictures on her shopping list with items in the store. When her environment changed—a new supermarket was built near her home—learning was generalized from a small grocery store to the large supermarket.

What procedures are described in the research literature and are waiting to be explored and tested by social workers? What activities for social action have been documented? When looking for effective interventions and monitoring tools for social work with families, one does not have to reinvent the wheel: It already exists complete with technological advances. Social workers should be broad in their reading and specific in their research. One of the most powerful ways to learn is to contribute to the strength of families through teaching or sharing of information and sharing of power in social action. In a process of gaining health, families can then contribute to each other and, in this interconnected way, to society.

References

Aponte, H. J., Zarski, J., Bixenstine, C., & Cibik, P. (1991). Home/community based services: A two-tier approach. *American Journal of Orthopsychiatry, 61,* 403–408.

Belsey, M., Backett, M., & Davies, A. M. (1996). *The concept of family health. Family challenges for the future.* Geneva: United Nations Publications.

Berry, M. & Cash, S. J. (1998). Creating community through psychoeducation groups in family preservation work. *Families in Society, 79,* 15–24.

Boyd-Franklin, N. (1993). Race, class, and poverty. In F. Walsh (Ed.), *Normal family processes* (2nd ed., pp. 361–376). New York: Guilford Press.

Callahan, J. (1997). Assisted suicide, community, and the common good [Editorial]. *Health & Social Work, 22,* 243–245.

Campbell, L. (1997). Child neglect and intensive-family-preservation practice. *Families in Society, 28,* 280–290.

Cassano, D. R. (1989). The multi-family therapy group: Research on patterns of interaction—Part I. *Social Work with Groups, 12*(1), 3–14.

Chazin, R. (1997). Working with Soviet Jewish immigrants. In E. P. Congress (Ed.), *Multicultural perspectives in working with families* (pp. 142–166). New York: Springer.

Comer, E. W., & Fraser, M. W. (1998). Evaluation of six family-support programs: Are they effective? *Families in Society, 79,* 134–148.

Cortès, Jr., E. (1997). Reweaving the social fabric. *Families in Society, 78,* 196–200.

Delgado-Gaitan, C. (1994). Socializing young children in Mexican-American families: An intergenerational perspective. In P. M Greenfield & R. R. Cocking (Eds.), *Cross-cultural roots of minority child development* (pp. 55–86). Hillsdale, NJ: Lawrence Erlbaum.

de Toqueville, A. (1945). *Democracy in America.* New York: Alfred A. Knopf. (Originally published in 1831).

Drisko, J. W. (1998). Utilization-focused evaluation of two intensive-family-preservation programs. *Families in Society, 79,* 62–74.

Feigin, I. (1996). Soviet Jewish families. In M. McGoldrick, J. Giordano, & J. K. Pearce (Eds.), *Ethnicity and family therapy* (2nd ed., pp. 631–637). New York: Guilford Press.

Firestone, D. (1998, January 30). From a daughter, scenes of a life in limbo. *New York Times*, p. B2.

Foot, D. K., & Stoffman, D. (1996). *Boom, bust, and echo: How to profit from the coming demographic shift.* Toronto: Macfarlane Walter & Ross.

Germain, C. B., & Gitterman, A. (1996). *The life model of social work practice* (2nd ed.). New York: Columbia University Press.

Gilson, S. F., & Netting, F. E. (1997). When people with pre-existing disabilities age in place: Implications for social work practice. *Health & Social Work, 22,* 290–298.

Gravitz, H. L., & Bowden, J. D. (1985). *Recovery: A guide for adult children of alcoholics.* New York: Simon & Schuster.

Hall, H. (1971). *Unfinished business: In neighborhood and nation.* New York: Macmillan.

Hamer, J. F. (1997). The fathers of "fatherless" Black children. *Families in Society, 78,* 564–578.

Hartman, A., & Laird, J. (1983). *Family-centered social work practice.* New York: Free Press.

Hatfield, A. (1987). Families as caregivers: A historical perspective. In A. B. Hatfield & H. P. Lefley (Eds.), *Families of the mentally ill* (pp. 3–29). New York: Guilford Press.

Hoge, L. A. (1998). Another view. *Families in Society, 79,* 18.

Lang, R. (1993). *A multi-family group intervention to facilitate open communication between adopted adolescents and their adoptive parents.* Unpublished doctoral dissertation, Department of Psychology, Rutgers University, New Brunswick, NJ.

Levine, I. M. (1982). Introduction. In M. McGoldrick, J. K. Pearce, & J. Giordano (Eds.), *Ethnicity and family therapy* (pp. xi–xii). New York: Guilford Press.

Lightburn, A., & Kemp, S. P. (1994). Family-support programs: Opportunities for community-based practice. *Families in Society, 75,* 16–26.

Lutzker, J. R. (1997). Ecobehavioral approaches in child abuse and developmental disabilities mirroring life. In D. M. Baer & E. M. Pinkston (Eds.), *Environment and behavior* (pp. 243–248). Boulder, CO: Westview Press.

Lynch, V. J., & Wilson, P. A. (1996). *Caring for the HIV/AIDS caregiver.* Westport, CT: Auburn House.

Mattaini, M. (1999). *Clinical intervention with families.* Washington, D. C.: NASW Press.

McFarlane, W. R. (1991). Family psychoeducational treatment. In A. S. Gurman & D. P. Kniskem (Eds.), *Handbook of family therapy* (Vol. 2, pp. 363–395). New York: Brunner/Mazel.

McGoldrick, M., Giordano, J., & Pearce, J. K. (Eds.). (1996). *Ethnicity and family therapy* (2nd ed.). New York: Guilford Press.

McKay, M. M., Gonzalez, J. J., Stone, S., Ryland, D., & Kohner, K. (1995). Multiple family therapy groups: A responsive intervention model for inner city families. *Social Work with Groups, 18*(4), 41–56.

McKnight, J. L. (1997). A 21st-century map for healthy communities and families. *Families in Society, 78,* 117–127.

Meezan, W., & O'Keefe, M. (1998). Multifamily group therapy: Impact on family functioning and child behavior. *Families in Society, 79,* 32–44.

Meyer, C. H. (1993). Assessment: The idea and the process. In *Assessment in social work practice* (pp. 17–42). New York: Columbia University Press.

National Association of Social Workers. (2000). *Social work speaks: NASW policy statements* (5th ed.). Washington, DC: NASW Press.

Rauch, J. B. (Ed.). (1993). *Assessment: A sourcebook for social work practice.* Milwaukee, WI: Families International.

Rhodes, R. M., & Zelman, A. B. (1986). An ongoing group in a women's shelter. *American Journal of Orthopsychiatry, 56,* 120–130.

Rolland, J. S. (1993). Mastering family challenges in serious illness and disability. In F. Walsh (Ed.), *Normal family processes* (2nd ed., pp. 444–502). New York: Guilford Press.

Ryan, W. P., DeMasi, K., Heinz, P. A., Jacobson, W., & Ohmer, M. (2000). *Aligning education and practice: Challenges and opportunities in social work education for community-centered practice.* Milwaukee, WI: The Alliance for Children and Families.

Sviridoff, M. & Ryan, W. (1997). Community-centered family service. *Families in Society, 78,* 128–139.

Tebb, S. (1995). An aid to empowerment: A caregiver well-being scale. *Health & Social Work, 20,* 87–92.

Walsh, F. (1993). Conceptualization of normal family processes. In F. Walsh (Ed.), *Normal family processes* (2nd ed., pp. 3–72). New York: Guilford Press.

Walter, J. L., & Peller, J. E. (1992). *Becoming solution-focused in brief therapy.* New York: Brunner/Mazel.

Weston, K. (1997). *Families we choose: Lesbians, gays, kinship* (rev. ed.). New York: Columbia University Press.

CHAPTER 9

Practice with Groups

Randy H. Magen

The progressive era that spawned the early caseworkers also produced the first group workers. The ancestors of caseworkers and group workers were mindful of democratic values, critical of the political-economic system, concerned with the needs of individuals, and inspired by religiously based notions of humanity (Schwartz, 1986). Unlike casework, however, the roots of group work can also be found in the recreation movement and the progressive education movement (Germain, 1983).

At the beginning of the 20th century, groups were used for two purposes: (1) to instill democratic values, and (2) to socialize individuals. In settlement houses, groups were established for people to learn the skills necessary to participate in their neighborhoods and communities. John Dewey, one of the fathers of the progressive education movement, was influential in settlement houses' development of the democratic purpose of groups. For a short time, he lived and worked at Hull House under the leadership of Jane Addams. Dewey (1922) wrote that groups provided experience in democratic action through participation in activities in which there was shared decision making and a focus on common social problems. This is what Addams (1910/1960) referred to as groups serving as a ". . . building block of democracy" (p. 97). These groups were designed to promote social justice.

Addams, the founder of Hull House, was also one of the founding officers of what eventually became known as the National Recreation Association (Reid, 1991). From the recreation movement came the use of groups to socialize the individual. In organized associations such as the Young Men's and Young Women's Christian Associations and the Boy Scouts and the Girl Scouts and, to a lesser extent in the settlement houses, a variety of small groups were established in which children could play, develop friendships and participate in recreational activities (Reid, 1991; Schwartz, 1986). Children's participation in groups was believed to promote healthy

development through character building—what is now called "the acquisition of social skills."

In comparing early casework to early group work, Toseland and Rivas
(1998) listed five differences between the methods.

1) In casework, clients changed as a result of the development of insight
   and through concrete assistance, whereas in group work, their change
   was a function of participating in group activities.

2) Whereas casework focused primarily on problem-solving, group work
   focused on both recreation and problem-solving.

3) Caseworkers worked with clients, whereas group workers were involved with members. This was more than a difference in terminol-
   ogy; it also resulted in a difference in the quality of the relationship
   between the social worker and the person being helped.

4) As a result of the differences in their relationship with clients, group
   workers placed more emphasis than did caseworkers on shared decision making and shared power.

5) The interaction of multiple members in a group required a different
   set of skills than those developed by caseworkers.

Before World War II there were some limited attempts to use group work
in settings other than settlement houses and recreational organizations,
but it was not until World War II that group work moved solidly into
rehabilitation settings. Several factors propelled group work into the new
settings. The development of group work practice theory in social work
(see, for example, Coyle, 1937) as well as research on small groups by
social scientists (see Lewin, Lippet, & White, 1939; Sherif, 1936) helped
to "clarify the method" (Garvin, 1997, p. 28). At the same time, group work
was increasingly taught in the curricula of schools of social work. The influence of Freudian psychoanalysis and the increased collaboration between
psychiatrists, psychologists, and social workers as members of treatment
teams also led to the use of groups for psychotherapy. Finally, the push for
group work came from the thousands of soldiers and veterans who needed
assistance for physical and emotional problems. Thus, by the 1950s, groups
could be found in such settings as psychiatric institutions, veterans' hospitals, correctional facilities, and child guidance clinics. From the movement
of groups into these new settings a third purpose for groups developed,
namely, the diagnosis and treatment of the individual in the group.

In 1952, the Council of Social Work Education (CSWE) published its
first curriculum policy statement. This document, which was the basis for
accrediting professional social work education programs, defined social
work practice as casework, group work, and community organizing. These
three methods became the organizing structure for social work curricula

for many years. In 1969, CSWE changed its curriculum policy statement to promote the integration of methods and to encourage training for generalist social work practice. One of the effects of this change in policy has been the precipitous decline in the institutionalization of group work in social work curricula. In 1963, 76 percent of social work graduate programs had concentrations in the group work method. With the growth of generalist and advanced generalist curricula by 1974, only 22 percent of the programs had this concentration and by 1981 only nine schools did (Rubin, 1982). After 1982, the *Statistics on Social Work Education* no longer reported the number of schools with group work concentrations (Rubin, 1983). A survey conducted in 1991 (Birnbaum & Auerbach, 1992) of 89 of the 97 graduate schools of social work accredited by CSWE revealed that only 6 programs (7 percent) offered a concentration in group work.

At the same time, there appears to be a resurgence of interest in group work. In this era of cost containment and managed care, it is generally recognized that group services are more cost-efficient than individual interventions (Toseland & Siporin, 1986), and there has been an explosion of self-help and 12-step-style groups. If social workers are to continue to stay true to their professional roots and be responsive to clients' needs, they must have knowledge and skills in social work group work. This chapter provides a basic foundation in social work group work for the beginning social worker, but it is no substitute for the specialized knowledge and training that are necessary to be a competent social work group worker.

Approaches to Group Work Practice

Social work group work has been defined as, "goal-directed activity with small groups of people aimed at meeting socioemotional needs and accomplishing tasks. This activity is directed to individual members of a group and to the group as a whole" (Toseland & Rivas, 1998, p. 12). With this definition it is clear that throughout the life span, people belong to a variety of groups, starting with the family and progressing through, for example, play groups, educational groups, work groups, and task groups or committees (Northen, 1982). Although groups are a natural and constant force in people's lives, social workers need a system for organizing and understanding the various types of "goal-directed activities" that take place in small groups. Presumably, a differential application of professional knowledge and skills is required in distinct types of small groups.

In examining various types of groups, one may logically distinguish between natural and formed groups. A family is natural group, membership in which is gained through birth and adoption. In other natural groups— peer groups and social networks—membership may come about serendipitously. In formed groups, membership is dependent on the fit between the purpose of the group and the needs or skills of the potential members. This distinction may be logical, but the concept of a formed group is so inclusive that it provides little guidance. Furthermore, the unique history of natural groups requires a different approach by the social worker, as is evident by the voluminous literature on social work with families.

One of the first useful systems for distinguishing types of group work approaches was developed by Papell and Rothman (1966), who differentiated group work approaches by function. The differences in function, or group purpose, lead to differences in the focus of the group's activities and the role of the group worker. The three approaches to group work practice identified by Papell and Rothman were (1) the social goals model, (2) the reciprocal model, and (3) the remedial model. Although Papell and Rothman referred to these types of groups as "models," it is more accurate to adopt the nomenclature of Germain (1983) and hence to conceive of them as "approaches." According to Germain,

> the term *approach* is preferred over the more common *model*, because of the confusion between a theoretical model in science, useful for its predictive value, and a practice model—so called—that merely sets forth the several dimensions of a coherent consistent approach to social work practice but has no predictive value (p. 31).

The interaction among group function, role of the worker, and focus of the group for the four most common types of groups can be seen in Figure 9-1.

These four common models of groups are now examined in greater detail.

Social Goals Model

The core function of the social goals model is the translation of "private troubles into public issues" (Schwartz, 1969, p. 22). The target for this model of group work is the social order, often defined as a neighborhood or community. The group's work is directed toward action and primary prevention, with a focus on the future. The vision of the future, from the perspective of a social goals model group, is one based on ideals of social justice. To achieve its purpose, the social goals group requires its members as one of their first tasks, to increase their "social consciousness" and "social responsibility" (Papell & Rothman, 1966). The group worker in such a group may be a consultant or a convener, whose role is to promote the democratic functioning of the group. Manor (2000) discusses the need for the group worker to prevent the worker-member relationship from paralleling the oppressive relationships members experience outside the group.

Figure 9-1.

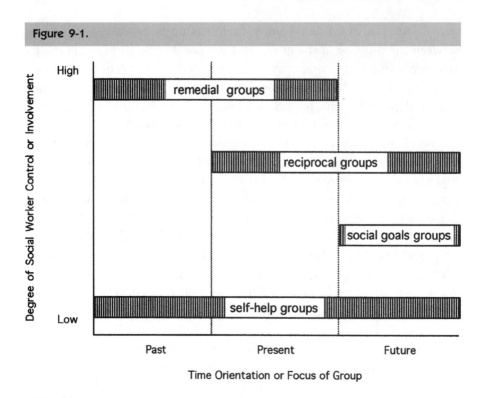

SOURCE: Middleman, R. R. (1981). The Pursuit of Competence through Involvement in Structured Groups. In A. N. Maluccio (Ed.), *Promoting Competence in Clients: A New/Old Approach to Social Work Practice* (p. 187). Copyright 1981 by the Free Press, a division of Simon and Schuster, Inc. Adapted with permission of the publisher.

In a social goals group the social worker may purposely refrain from exerting power or authority over the group. Clearly, the social goals model of group work has its roots in the group work of the settlement houses. Today, groups that function within this approach can be found in public housing complexes where tenants organize themselves to fight crime.

Reciprocal Model

What Papell and Rothman (1966) labeled the "reciprocal model" of group work has today become known as the "mutual aid model." The focus of activity in this model of group work is the reciprocal or "symbiotic" relationship between individual clients and the group. The social worker is an enabler or mediator who seeks to prevent imbalances in the relationship or boundaries between the individual and the group and to help the group release its power to change—to learn how to be a mutual aid system. Schwartz (1986) referred to the social worker's role as ". . . the two clients conception, in which the worker's function is to help both the individual and the group, the one to meet his needs within the system, the other to pursue its collective tasks" (pp. 17-18). The reciprocal or mutual aid model requires the social worker to share power and control over the group with its members. Gitterman and Shulman (1994) gave many examples of mutual aid groups, for example, a group of people with AIDS in which they receive support and reassurance and are mobilized to take control over their lives. Groups that are commonly referred to as support groups fall within this conceptualization of the reciprocal model. Schopler and Galinsky (1993) suggest that support groups "lie midway between" remedial groups and self-help groups in terms of their leader's behavior and the control that members have.

Remedial Model

The focus of the remedial model is on the treatment of the individual through the use of a group method. In this model the group is the means or context for achieving individual goals, and changes to group structure and group process are a means to an end, rather than an end in themselves. One of the characteristics of the remedial group is that the social worker exerts a great deal of power and influence over the formation and operation of the group. Group members are selected by the social worker, who is guided in composing the group by the purpose of the group; members are often selected because of similarities in presenting problems or target complaints. In fact, the most critical issue in the effectiveness of remedial model groups may be group composition. A group that fits the definition of a remedial model group would be a skills-training relapse-prevention group for people who are recovering from alcohol abuse.

Mainstream Model

The broadening of social work practice and knowledge in the 1970s and 1980s resulted in some types of group work falling outside Papell and Rothman's (1966) original typology. Several group work theorists (Lang, 1979; Middleman & Wood, 1990) recognized this fact when they suggested that the practice of group work could be conceptualized with one model—the mainstream model. Papell and Rothman (1980) distinguish the mainstream model from group psychotherapy by the latter's focus on changing the individual through the use of a group context. Group work approaches that fall within the mainstream model are all concerned with developing a mutual aid system within the group, an interest in moving the group through developmental phases, and members' shared goals. The leader role in the mainstream model gradually shifts from the social worker to the group members as the group develops over time.

Although the mainstream model is an eclectic approach to group work that is consistent with the movement within social work to identify a nucleus of practice concepts, this author agrees with Garvin (1997) who suggested that it is "premature" if not impossible to encompass all group work approaches in one model. For example, the mainstream model does not accurately conceptualize one of the most common types of groups that social workers are likely to encounter—the self-help group. Therefore, the mainstream model has not been included in Figure 9-1.

Self-Help Groups

The most famous and the oldest self-help group is Alcoholics Anonymous (AA). AA was founded in 1935, and there are now more than 58,000 groups in the United States and Canada (Kurtz, 1997). Furthermore, more than 250 different self-help groups exist that use the name "Anonymous" or a version of the twelve steps (Kurtz, 1997). Self-help groups, like AA, are typically sponsored by international, national, or regional organizations. These sponsoring organizations often prescribe the format and procedures used in group meetings. However, leadership and control of the self-help group lie with the group members. Studies of self-help groups indicate that members of these groups not only have clear goals about how they want to end up, but clear ideas of how they want to move toward their goals (what the process should be) (Lieberman & Borman, 1979). The primary difference between self-help groups and the reciprocal model of group work is that in self-help groups the social worker serves as a consultant, resource person, or referral source *outside* the group (Schopler & Galinsky, 1993). Self-help groups can also be distinguished from informal helping networks by the existence of a group structure and boundaries.

Other conceptualizations abound in the social work literature as a means for organizing knowledge and skills for group work (see for example, Garvin, 1997; Toseland & Rivas, 1998). The importance of any typology is in helping the social worker develop a schema for categorizing small groups that allows him or her not only to generalize from group to group, but to begin to understand how to work with specific types of groups.

Group Purpose and Structure

Purpose

Given the definition of a group presented earlier, in theory there should be no such thing as a group without a purpose. However, the failure of many groups can be attributed to the lack of a consensus on the purpose of the group. The purpose of any group should be a clear and specific statement pertaining to how the group will address an unmet client need. The statement of the group's purpose sets parameters for issues of structure (selection of members, group composition, and orientation), time (duration, frequency and length, and group development), and leadership (characteristics and number). Thus, in group work, "structure follows function." Of course, other systems and forces, such as an agency's policy, affect the composition and structure of a group, but the most important factor is the group's purpose.

Structure

Selection of members. A great deal has been written in the group work literature about the importance of the selection of members (Dies & Teleska, 1985; Ormont, 1969; Papell & Rothman, 1966). Members must feel that they fit in and belong to the group (Beck, 1983). The selection of members is the process that affects the goodness of fit between members and the group. Although Shulman (1994) argued that guidelines for the selection of group members are "myths" because leaders take what they can get, this statement does not mean that every applicant is appropriate to be a group member.

The guiding principal in the selection of members is that extremes are a problem. Obviously, when there are too many members, the group members lose the ability to interact with each other; when there are too few members, the advantages of conducting a group are lost. At the risk of being redundant, the size of the group depends on the purpose of the group. In general, the group work literature contains examples of groups that have four to 10 members. Social goals groups may be able to tolerate more clients, whereas in remedial groups with clients who are experiencing severe problems, the groups are usually kept small. As the size of the group gets larger, the ability of each member to participate fully in the group decreases.

Groups with extremely heterogeneous or homogeneous members are also problematic (this includes individual characteristics such as age as well as presenting problems). For example, in groups of parents who met for support and parent training, mixing parents of teenagers with parents of preschoolers resulted in the failure of the members to identify with each other's problems, whereas a group composed of parents with preschoolers successfully mixed single and married mothers (Magen & Rose, 1994). Similarly, one can imagine how slow and silent a group with all individuals suffering severe depression would be.

The best rule for avoiding extremes is to never have only one of anything in a group. Yalom (1985) referred to this rule as the "Noah's Ark principle." There is some evidence that clients from dominant groups (such as White people and men) prefer groups that mirror the racial and gender composition of society. For Black people, however, one study indicated a preference for groups that are composed of equal numbers of White people and Black people (Davis, 1979). The literature on women's membership in mixed-gender groups indicates that women prefer large groups, but also suggests that they are less expressive in these groups (Davis & Proctor, 1989).

Although groups that are homogenous in terms of race or gender are often discouraged, in some instances the purpose of the group dictates that the group be homogeneous. For example, a group to enhance racial, ethnic, or gender identity (often referred to as a "consciousness-raising group") would be most effective with a homogenous membership. At the other extreme, a group that is designed to decrease racial tensions and to promote social justice by fighting racism would be most effective with members of different racial groups.

The social worker must assess whether there is some common ground between the unmet needs of the client and the purpose of the group. This mutuality of interests is essential for the client to be able to connect with the work of others in the group. Clients must also have the interpersonal skills necessary to participate in a group of five to 10 other members (Rose, 1989), because it is only through interpersonal interaction that the work of the group takes place. Finally, clients must have the cognitive skills to participate in the group at a level similar to that of other group members. For some groups, such skills may be the ability to read and write, whereas for others, the skills may be the ability to help problem solve at a developmentally compatible level. Thus, group workers must examine and assess the fit of client's characteristics, needs, interpersonal skills, and cognitive abilities with other group members, as well as with the group's purpose.

Composition

Group composition refers to whether the group can continually accept members (an open group) or whether the membership is fixed at some point (a closed group). Burlingame and Fuhriman (1990) reported that 60 percent of the groups they examined were open, while the remaining 40 percent were closed. An agency's mission affects this aspect of the group as well; for example, an acute care psychiatric inpatient unit has a fairly high turnover rate of patient; thus, any group it operates must either be of short duration (such as one session) or maintain some form of open membership. A support group for survivors of child sexual abuse might maintain a fixed membership to minimize difficulties in relation to trust and self-disclosure.

Fixed membership and flexible membership can be thought of as two poles on a continuum. Some groups have a fixed membership but allow members to drop in and out according to their needs. Other groups may start as flexible membership groups but become fixed membership groups at a predetermined point. For example, a large agency in New York City that operates support groups for individuals with cancer has flexible membership in the first two group sessions. After the second session, though, the group has "formed," and the remaining 10 sessions are held with a fixed membership.

Orientation

Orientation to the group, or what some might call "socialization to the client role" is a crucial task of the group worker. Orientation is the shaping of members in their role as group members. It involves both the establishment of ground rules (Tuckman, 1965) as well as the differentiation of roles (Garvin, 1985). Brower (1988) argued that group members enter the group with their own perceptions—their unique cognitive schema of the group. The task of the group worker, then, is to help members develop a shared cognitive schema of the group, a capacity toward mutual aid and purpose (Glassman & Kates, 1990), and common perceptions and expectations.

Dies and Teleska (1985) cited evidence that one of the factors involved in negative group experience is unrealistically high expectations. Flowers (1987) reported that members who did not improve were the members who did not agree with others on a rank ordering of curative factors. He suggested that these group members may have come to the group with different expectations than did other group members; another explanation may be that the group did not initially induce the same expectations in these members as it did in the other members. Thus, one of the central tasks for the group worker and the group in the forming phase is to help members develop appropriate expectations for the group. Kaul and Bednar (1986) noted that structure, especially in early sessions, helped to induce appropriate expectations and to socialize members in their roles. Perhaps the most direct method for inducing expectations in a structured manner is through contracting. Shulman (1994) discussed three areas for which contracts can be made in group work: (1) the role of the worker, (2) the mutual needs of the members, and (3) the mutual obligations of the members and leaders.

Time

There are three ways to examine time in group work: (1) the duration of the group, (2) the frequency and length of group sessions, and (3) group development.

Duration

Descriptions of groups that have lasted a single session to several years can be found in the literature. Open-ended groups have no fixed ending point, whereas close-ended (or time-limited) groups have a set termination date. The duration of a group may be constrained by the clients' circumstances, by the agency environment, or by the group's purposes. For example, an inner-city hospital used single-session groups for prevention of HIV transmission in intravenous drug users who were patients in the emergency department.

Although there is little empirical evidence to guide the social worker when planning the duration of a group, one general rule could be stated: More is not necessarily better. At least, a close-ended group means that a termination date has been established a priori; the establishment of an end point facilitates movement toward goals.

Frequency and Length

Across models of group work, the most common frequency for group meetings is once a week, and the average length of a group session is one to three hours. Although there is little to no empirical evidence to support this widespread practice, there are many practical reasons for this type of scheduling including cost, the availability of a meeting space, and the coordination of the members' multiple schedules. Rose (1989) suggested that an optimal model for close-ended groups would involve fading the frequency and duration of group meetings. Thus, when the group was first forming there would be frequent meetings, but as the group moved closer to the final session, the time between group meetings would increase or the length of group sessions would decrease. This variability in the time schedule for a close-ended group may be particularly valuable in the remedial model of groups.

Group Development

A variety of group development sequences have been offered to help the social worker understand changes in groups over time. These typologies have ranged from three stages (Schwartz, 1986) to nine (Beck, 1983). There is a considerable overlap in the labels applied to the stages and, more significantly, in the conceptualization of the stages. Tuckman (1965) suggested four stages of group development that he summarized as forming, storming, norming, and performing. Tuckman's stages fail to include a termination phase; in keeping with Tuckman's rhyme this author proposes a fifth and final stage: adjourning. The crucial issue is not what the stages are, but the group worker's understanding of and skill in assisting the group to develop.

Although the concept of group development is of heuristic value, there are multiple problems with the current state of knowledge of group development. The problems identified in the group development literature include the failure to validate stages of group development empirically, the arbitrary division of the group into phases, the failure to realize that development is not *one* predetermined sequence, and the attribution of stages as group phenomena when in fact what is actually being described may be the development of an individual member (Beck, 1983; Brower, 1988; Burlingame, Fuhriman, & Drescher, 1984; Glassman & Kates, 1990; MacKenzie, 1987; Tuckman, 1965). For example, Galinsky and Schopler (1989) pointed out that developmental patterns in open-ended groups are affected by the frequency of turnover among members and the extent to which membership is modified. On one hand, open-ended groups with frequent and extensive turnover of members would not be expected to move beyond the forming stage of group development. On the other hand, groups with an infrequent and small turnover would develop in a manner similar to close-ended, fixed membership groups.

Leadership

It is axiomatic that group leaders should have the capacity, skills, values, and attitudes required of any social worker. It is also clear that group work necessitates a set of skills caseworkers do not need. Schwartz (1966) summed up the difference in the requisite social work skills as follows:

> The group leadership role demands that the worker give up much of the interview control to which she has, often unconsciously, become accustomed. Caseworkers have often told me that they had never realized how rigidly they controlled the client-worker interaction until they began to function as group workers, where changes of subject could be effected by anyone in the group, where people often turned to each other rather than to the worker for reinforcement and support, where clients could verify each other's "wrong" ideas, where mutually reinforced feelings could not be turned off when they became "dangerous," and where, in short, one's faith in the client's autonomy and basic strength were put to its severest test. (p. 575)

Recently, the Association for the Advancement of Social Work with Groups (AASWG) has published *Standards for Social Work Practice with Groups* (1999). These standards are similar to other standards of practice that have been published by the National Association of Social Workers (NASW).

The AASWG standards delineate both the essential knowledge and values that should guide group workers as well as the primary worker tasks in each phase of the group's development. While the AASWG standards are rather generic, given the need to be applicable to a wide range of groups, they do provide group workers with a guide for responsible leadership of groups.

Aside from the issue of the group worker's skills, another important issue in leadership is whether to use one or two leaders. There is no consistent evidence in the empirical literature that two heads are better than one. In fact, Kolodny (1980) summarized the literature on coleadership by writing that, "the requirement would seem to be that one's co-leader be someone whom one knows well and is compatible with, who agrees with one theoretically, possesses equal knowledge, and is similar to oneself in competence and professional stature, but is definitely not a friend" (p. 34). Having a coleader increases the financial cost to the agency or the clients. Another potential problem with coleadership is that the leaders may dominate the discussion or, to put it more strongly, that two leaders typically talk too much. In groups with coleaders, Rose (1989) recommended that the leaders develop a "no back-to-back talking" rule, so they do not dominate discussions within the group.

There are four situations in which coleadership is desirable: 1) during training when it is often helpful for social workers to colead their first group; 2) for groups that require specialized knowledge or skills, such as those for sexually abused children or people with AIDS; 3) when there are issues of physical or emotional safety, such as in groups of men who batter; and 4) in couples groups when it is useful to have both male and female leaders. The danger in coleadership, particularly in groups with male and female leaders, is that there may be real or imagined differences in leaders' status. Several studies have found that men are perceived as being of a higher status than are women when coleading. Similarly, when coleaders were members of different racial groups, clients have attributed more negative attributes to the group leader who was not from their racial group than to the same-race group leader (Davis & Proctor, 1989).

Group Processes

The term "group processes," rather than "group process," is used in this section because many variables have been identified in the literature as belonging to the phenomena of group process. Therefore, it is more accurate, linguistically as well as conceptually, to discuss group process as a composite of phenomena, rather than as a single phenomenon (Fuhriman, Drescher, & Burlingame, 1984).

Novice group workers are often admonished for not paying attention to group processes. However, the problem usually is not that they ignore group processes but that they do not know what is meant by group processes. Even when group workers are given an explanation of group processes, the definitions, such as "process is everything in the group that is not content" (Yalom, 1985, p. 137), are often useless.

Unfortunately, no one clear definition of group processes exists. The following three definitions have been suggested: (1) "the way of working as opposed to the substance of the work" (Gitterman & Shulman, 1986, p. 42); (2) "changes that take place in group conditions" (Garvin, 1997, p. 104); and (3) "an aspect or characteristic of group behavior, the ecological characteristics of the group" (Fuhriman, Drescher, & Burlingame, 1984, p. 431). This author prefers the third definition because it is specific to group work, includes interpersonal relationship behavior, and also encompass "characteristics" of the group that are more than individual transactions (Burlingame, Fuhriman, & Drescher, 1984). Whichever definition of group processes the reader chooses to adopt, it is clear that a constellation of factors are necessary for the functioning of an effective small group but are not sufficient for the group to achieve its goals. These "necessary but not sufficient" factors are collectively referred to as "group processes."

Cohesion is an important process variable in group work, but as is the case with group development and group processes, there is little agreement on how to define it. Kaul and Bednar (1986) remarked that "research on group cohesion . . . continues to be based on definitions and methods of measurement so impoverished [they] . . . can only produce a noncohesive body of literature" (p. 640). In spite of this criticism, whether one defines *cohesion* as attraction to the group (Lieberman, Yalom, & Miles, 1973), attraction to other members, or a common schema (Brower, 1988), it is clear that cohesive groups are more likely to achieve their purpose. High cohesiveness has been linked to change, whereas low cohesiveness has been shown to correlate highly with members dropping out of groups (Dies & Teleska, 1985; Lieberman, Yalom, & Miles, 1973). In group work, as in other methods of social work, dissatisfied clients drop out or terminate prematurely. Several suggestions have been made in the literature for maximizing group cohesion, including the use of a break with a snack, modeling, and reinforcing self-disclosure (Rose, 1977). In fact, intimacy in self-disclosure is associated with members' perceptions of group cohesion (Kaul & Bednar, 1986).

There is also general agreement that clients profit from self-disclosure (Kaul & Bednar, 1986). Wright and Ingraham (1985) concluded from their analysis of behavior in four interpersonal learning groups that self-disclosure is a function not only of individual differences, but of the relationship among group members. This finding suggests that the quality of inter-member relationships may affect the quantity of self-disclosure in a group.

Feedback, or what Yalom (1985) referred to as "interpersonal learning" is a group process which has been shown to contribute to therapeutic change (Dies & Teleska, 1985, p. 120). There is widespread agreement that clients benefit from constructive feedback under the right circumstances. The group leader then, should encourage, if not teach, members to give feedback to each other.

Although the evidence regarding the relative strength of group problem solving over individual problem solving is equivocal (see, for example, Davis & Toseland, 1987), it is clear that the mechanisms involved in group problem solving are central processes in group work. The components of group problem-solving have been defined differently by group theorists (see Gitterman & Shulman, 1994; Yalom, 1985) but all agree that problem solving is important in group work.

As Table 9-1 indicates, the nomenclature used to label group processes varies by theorist, as well as by model of group work. A definitive list of group processes is probably not possible, given that group processes are influenced by the group work approach, the stage of the group's development, forces outside the group, and individual differences within the group (Yalom, 1985).

Table 9-1. Common Group Processes in Remedial and Reciprocal Groups

Remedial Group Processes (Yalom, 1985)	Reciprocal Group Processes (Shulman, 1994)
Instillation of Hope Altruism Cohesiveness	Mutual Support Strength in Numbers
Universality	All-in-the-Same-Boat Phenomenon
Guidance	Sharing Data
Identification	Rehearsal
Interpersonal Learning Self-Understanding	Problem Solving Dialectical Processes Mutual Demand
Catharsis	Discussing a Taboo Area
Existential Factors	Developing a Universal Perspective
Collective Recapitualization of the Primary Family Group	(Note: no exact parallel in Reciprocal Model Groups)

SOURCES: Shulman, L. (1994). Group work method. In A. Gitterman & L. Shulman (Eds.), *Mutual Aid Groups, Vulnerable Populations, and the Life Cycle* (2nd, ed., pp. 29–58). New York: Columbia University Press; and Yalom, I.D. (1985). *The Theory and Practice of Group Psychotherapy.* New York: Basic Books.

The social worker who is able to identify group processes as they develop over the life of a group is in a position to harness their power in moving the group toward its goal or goals. A social worker who fixes his or her focus solely on the tasks or outcome of the group runs the risk that group processes will serve an inhibiting, rather than a facilitating, function.

Participation

A fundamental aspect of the first group meeting is participation by every group member. (Rose, 1977). One task of the group leader, unlike that of the caseworker, is to deemphasize his or her role and to stress the value of intermember relations within the group (Dies & Teleska, 1985). Coyle (1947) who wrote the first social work textbook on group work, addressed the issue of participation by writing that,

> a full orchestra can have no instruments that are silenced when they should be expected to come in. For that reason the . . . leader needs, first, . . . to have all participate and then to be aware of the extent of the existing participating. If his ear becomes trained to this he is then in a position to encourage participation where it is inadequate (p. 23).

The quality of participation is not the issue; the mere act of participating may be more crucial. Not only is participation, which is basically the development of socializing skills, one of the essential conditions of group membership, it can reduce the probability of members dropping out. For example in a survey of practitioners, one of the most common reasons given for members dropping out was that they felt socially isolated and were less well integrated into the groups than were other members (Dies & Teleska, 1985). In addition, initial participation predicts later, and deeper, self-disclosure. MacKenzie (1987) reported that his analysis of "critical incident reports" revealed that the initial stages of groups were characterized by superficial self-disclosure, whereas the later stages of the group were characterized by deeper self-disclosure.

Although the social worker has the responsibility for maximizing member's participation in the group, certain forms of participation can be a problem. One of the most common types of problems is scapegoating (Shulman, 1994). Whereas Garvin (1986) suggested that scapegoating in a group is parallel to families seeking change in an identified patient, others such as Tsui and Schultz (1988) consider it a reflection of larger societal tensions. Whatever the etiology of this form of communication, the group worker has the responsibility to provide help. The question then is, "what is most helpful when communication is a problem in the group?"

Although the group worker may be inclined to "protect" the scapegoat there is general agreement that this strategy only places him or her in conflict with the group (Gitterman & Shulman, 1994). One tactic is to empathize with the individual; another is to confront the group with its here and now behavior (Anstey, 1982). Another strategy is to find the common ground between the group and the scapegoat (Gitterman & Shulman, 1994); however, this approach has been criticized as taking too long to implement as well as being unrealistic (Anstey, 1982). Finally, Rose (1989) suggested treating scapegoating as a "group problem" and centering the intervention on defining the problem and engaging the group in a problem-solving process. Whichever strategy the worker uses, it should follow a careful assessment of the problem and be designed to promote the work of the group.

Efficacy

Although the use of a specific group method should follow and be linked to assessment, there are several general advantages of group work. First, groups can relieve real or imagined isolation—a characteristic that Shulman (1994) referred to as the "all in the same boat phenomenon" (p. 44) and Yalom (1985) labeled "universality." Whatever the exact process, the group offers multiple opportunities for validation and reinforcement. Second, the group is a natural laboratory for learning and discussion. Clients or members are forced to deal with each other's attitudes, behaviors, and feelings, which helps them develop social skills either explicitly as part of the group contract or implicitly in the group interaction.

Toseland and Siporin (1986) examined the literature comparing individual and group interventions and asked, "Which is more effective?" In 24 of 32 studies they found no statistical differences in the outcome of the modalities, but in the remaining eight studies, they found group treatment to be statistically more effective than individual treatment. Toseland and Siporin added that there was no clear pattern regarding the types of problems that are most effectively treated in a group setting. When this study is examined in terms of a "box score," it seems safe to conclude that the work done in groups is no worse than that conducted on an individual basis. However, the question to ask is not "Which is more effective?" but, "Which is more effective with these particular problems under these conditions?" (Paul, 1967). Toseland and Siporin's inability to ask this question is a reflection of the failure of group workers to systematically evaluate their practice (Galinsky & Schopler, 1993).

Monitoring and Evaluation

Although there is research to support the efficacy of group interventions, there is evidence that some clients have negative experiences in groups. Yalom and his colleagues (Lieberman, Yalom, & Miles, 1973) documented that almost 10 percent of encounter-group participants experienced psychological disturbances attributable to their group experience. Recent research by Smokowski, Rose, Todar & Reardon linked negative group experiences to group leader behavior. Social workers have an ethical responsibility to "do no harm." Given this mandate and the research on negative group experiences, social workers must monitor and evaluate group work practice.

All the methods that have been suggested for monitoring and evaluating social work practice (see Chapter 6) are applicable to group work. Rose (1984), for example, suggested the use of a post-session questionnaire. This consumer satisfaction instrument allows the social worker to monitor group member's satisfaction on a session-by-session basis. Other forms of monitoring have included using observers or coleaders to record the frequency of participation among group members. The participation data can then be provided to the group to encourage more participation from members who talk infrequently and to diminish the participation of members who talk frequently. Questionnaires have been developed to assess member's perceptions of group processes (see, for example, Yalom, 1985). These questionnaires can be used in their entirety or subscales (for example, cohesion) can be chosen to track the development of changes in group processes. Regardless of the type of group being implemented, social workers must systematically monitor the group's changing environment. Finally, there are several observational systems for monitoring group processes (for a comprehensive review of these systems see Beck & Lewis, 2000).

Monitoring the group over time is not enough, social workers must also evaluate progress toward the attainment of the group's goals. This requirement underscores the importance of a clear group purpose; without a clear purpose it becomes impossible to evaluate whether the group has achieved its goal or goals. In remedial groups, rapid assessment instruments can be used to evaluate changes in individual clients. Goal attainment scaling (see Chapter 6) has also been used in remedial groups to evaluate progress toward individual goals. In reciprocal model groups and social goals groups, goal attainment scaling can be used to assess progress toward the collective group's goals. Although self-help groups have been subjected to much less outcome research, there is evidence from a limited number of studies that changes in individual members can be evaluated. For example, Kurtz (1997) suggested that social workers look for evidence of a "conversion experience" or changes in self-perception as a result of self-help group participation. With curiosity, creativity, and tenacity a social worker will be able to monitor and evaluate group work interventions.

Social workers must move away from a focus on method or model and start where the client is. If group workers think of themselves as social workers first, they will not prematurely confine themselves to working with one client system or one particular method of helping (Nelsen, 1975).

References

Addams, J. (1960). *Twenty years at Hull House*. New York: Signet. (Originally published in 1910).

Anstey, M. (1982). Scapegoating in groups: Some theoretical perspectives and a case record of intervention. *Social work with groups, 5*(3), 51–63.

Association for the Advancement of Social Work With Groups. (1999). *Standards for social work practice with groups*. Akron, OH: Author.

Beck, A. P. (1983). A process analysis of group development. *Group, 7* (1), 19–28.

Beck, A. P., & Lewis, C. M. (2000). *The process of group psychotherapy: Systems for analyzing change*. Washington, DC: American Psychological Association.

Birnbaum, M. L., & Auerbach, C. (1992, February). *Group work in graduate social work education: The price of neglect*. Paper presented at the Annual Program Meeting, Council on Social Work Education, Kansas City.

Brower, A. M. (1988). Group development as constructed social reality: A social-cognitive understanding of group formation. *Social Work with Groups, 12*(2), 23–41.

Burlingame, G., Fuhriman, A., & Drescher, S. (1984). Scientific inquiry into small group process: A multidimensional approach. *Small Group Behavior, 15*(4), 441–470.

Burlingame, G. M., & Fuhriman, A. (1990). Time-limited group therapy. *The Counseling Psychologist, 18* (1), 93–118.

Council on Social Work Education. (1952). *Curriculum policy for the master's degree program in social work education*. New York: Author.

Council on Social Work Education. (1969). *Curriculum policy for the master's degree program in social work education*. New York: Author.

Coyle, G. L. (1937). *Studies in group behavior*. New York: Harper & Row.

Coyle, G. L. (1947). *Group experience and democratic values*. New York: The Women's Press.

Davis, L. (1979). Racial composition of groups. *Social Work, 24*, 208–213.

Davis, L. E., & Proctor, E. K. (1989). *Race, gender & class: Guidelines for practice with individuals, families, and groups*. Englewood Cliffs, NJ: Prentice Hall.

Davis, L., & Toseland, R. (1987). Group versus individual decision making. *Social Work with Groups, 10* (2), 95–105.

Dewey, J. (1922). *Human nature and conduct*. New York: Random House.

Dies, R. R., & Teleska, P.A. (1985). Negative outcome in group psychotherapy. In D. T. Mays & C. M. Franks (Eds.), *Negative outcome in psychotherapy and what to do about it* (pp. 141–181). New York: Springer.

Flowers, J. V. (1987). Client outcome as a function of agreement or disagreement with the modal group perception of curative factors in short-term, structured group psychotherapy. *International Journal of Group Psychotherapy, 37* (1), 113–118.

Fuhriman, A., Drescher, S., & Burlingame, G. (1984). Conceptualizing small group process. *Small Group Behavior, 15*(4), 427–440.

Galinsky, M. J., & Schopler, J. H. (1989). Developmental patterns in open-ended groups. *Social Work with Groups, 12*(2), 99–114.

Galinsky, M. J., & Schopler, J. H. (1993, October). *Social group work competence: Our strengths and challenges*. Plenary address at the 15th Annual Symposium of the Association for the Advancement of Social Work with Groups, New York City, NY.

Garvin, C. D. (1985). Group process: Usage and uses in social work practice. In M. Sundel, P. Galasser, R. Sarri, & R. Vinter (Eds.), *Individual change through small groups* (2nd ed.) (pp. 203–225). New York: Free Press.

Garvin, C. (1986). Family therapy and group work: "Kissing cousins or distant relatives" in social work practice. In M. Parnes (Ed.), *Innovations in social group work: Feedback from practice to theory* (pp. 1–15). New York: Haworth Press.

Garvin, C. D. (1997). *Contemporary group work* (3rd edition). Boston: Allyn & Bacon.

Germain, C. B. (1983). Technological advances. In A. Rosenblatt & D. Waldfogel (Eds.), *Handbook of clinical social work* (pp. 26–57). San Francisco: Jossey-Bass.

Gitterman, A., & Shulman, L. (Eds.). (1986). *Mutual aid groups and the life cycle.* Itasca, IL: F.E. Peacock.

Gitterman, A., & Shulman, L. (Eds.). (1994). *Mutual aid groups, vulnerable populations, and the life cycle.* New York: Columbia University Press.

Glassman, U., & Kates, L. (1990). *Group work: A humanistic approach.* Newbury Park, CA: Sage Publications.

Kaul, T. J., & Bednar, R. L. (1986). Experiential group research: Results, questions, and suggestions. In S. L. Garfield & A. E. Bergin (Eds.), *Handbook of psychotherapy and behavior change* (3rd edition) (pp. 671–714). New York: John Wiley & Sons.

Kolodny, R. (1980). The dilemma of co-leadership. *Social Work with Groups, 3*(4), 31–34.

Kurtz, L. F. (1997). *Self-help and support groups: A handbook for practitioners.* Thousand Oaks, CA: Sage.

Lang, N. (1979). A comparative examination of therapeutic uses of groups in social work and in adjacent human service professions: Part II—The literature from 1969–1978. *Social Work with Groups, 2*(3), 197–220.

Lewin, K., Lippitt, R., & White, R. (1939). Patterns of aggressive behavior in experimentally created "social climates." *Journal of Social Psychology, 10*, 271–299.

Lieberman, M., & Borman, L. (Eds.). (1979). *Self-help groups for coping with crisis.* San Francisco: Jossey-Bass.

Lieberman, M. A., Yalom, I. D., & Miles, M. B. (1973). *Encounter groups: First facts.* New York: Basic Books.

MacKenzie, K. R. (1987). Therapeutic factors in group psychotherapy: A contemporary view. *Group, 11*(1), 26–31.

Magen, R. H., & Rose, S. D. (1994). Parents in groups: Problem solving versus behavioral skill training. *Research on Social Work Practice, 4*(2), 172–19.

Manor, O. (2000). *Choosing a groupwork approach: An inclusive stance.* London: Jessica Kingsley Publishers.

Middleman, R. R. (1981). The pursuit of competence through involvement in structured groups. In A. N. Maluccio (Ed.), *Promoting Competence in Clients: A new/old approach to social work practice* (pp. 185–210). New York: Free Press.

Middleman, R., & Wood, G. (1990). Reviewing the past present of group work and the challenge of the future. *Social Work with Groups, 13*(3), 3–20.

Nelsen, J. C. (1975). Social work's fields of practice, methods, and models: The choice to act. *Social Service Review, 49*(2), 264–270.

Northen, H. (1982). *Clinical social work.* New York: Columbia University Press.

Ormont, L. R. (1969). Acting in and the therapeutic contract in group psychoanalysis. *International Journal of Group Psychotherapy, 11*, 420–432.

Papell, C. P., & Rothman, B. (1966). Social group work models: Possession and heritage. *Journal of Education for Social Work, 2*(2), 66–77.

Papell, C., & Rothman, B. (1980). Relating the mainstream model of social work with groups to group psychotherapy and the structured group approach. *Social Work with Groups, 3*(2), 5–23.

Paul, G. L. (1967). Outcome research in psychotherapy. *Journal of Consulting Psychology, 31*, 109–118.

Reid, K. E. (1991). *Social work practice with groups: A clinical perspective.* Pacific Grove, CA: Brooks/Cole.

Rose, S. D. (1977). *Group therapy: A behavioral approach.* Englewood Cliffs, NJ: Prentice Hall.

Rose, S. D. (1984). Use of data in identifying and resolving group problems in goal oriented treatment groups. *Social Work with Groups, 7*(2), 23–36.

Rose, S. D. (1989). *Working with adults in groups: Integrating cognitive-behavioral and small group strategies.* San Francisco: Jossey-Bass.

Rubin, A. (1982). *Statistics on social work education in the United States: 1981.* New York: Council on Social Work Education.

Rubin, A. (1983). *Statistics on social work education in the United States: 1982.* New York: Council on Social Work Education.

Schopler, J. H., & Galinsky, M. J. (1993). Support groups as open systems: A model for practice and research. *Health and Social Work, 18*(3), 195–207.

Schwartz, W. (1966). Discussion of three papers on the group method with clients, foster families, and adoptive families. *Child Welfare, 45*(10), 571–575.

Schwartz, W. (1969). Private troubles and public issues: One social work job or two? *The Social Welfare Forum.* New York: Columbia University Press.

Schwartz, W. (1986). The group work tradition and social work practice. *Social Work with Groups, 8*(4), 7–27.

Sherif, M. (1936). *The psychology of social norms.* New York: Harper.

Shulman, L. (1994). Group work method. In A. Gitterman & L. Shulman (Eds.), *Mutual aid groups, vulnerable populations, and the life cycle* (2nd ed.) (pp.29–58). New York: Columbia University Press.

Smokowski, P. R., Rose, S. D., Todar, K., & Reardon, K. (1998). Post-group casualty status, group events and leader behavior: An early look into the dynamics of damaging group experiences. *Research on Social Work Practice, 9*(5), 541–554.

Toseland, R. W., & Rivas, R. F. (1998). *An introduction to group work practice* (3rd ed). Boston, MA: Allyn and Bacon.

Toseland, R., & Siporin, M. (1986). When to recommend group treatment: A review of the clinical and research literature. *International Journal of Group Psychotherapy, 36*(2), 171–201.

Tsui, P., & Schultz, G. L. (1988). Ethnic factors in group process: Cultural dynamics in multi-ethnic therapy groups. *American Journal of Orthopsychiatry, 58*(1), 136–142.

Tuckman, B. W. (1965). Developmental sequence in small groups. *Psychological Bulletin, 63*(6), 384–399.

Wright, T. L., & Ingraham, L. J. (1985). Simultaneous study of individual differences and relationship effects in social behavior in groups. *Journal of Personality and Social Psychology, 48*(4), 1041–1047.

Yalom, I. D. (1985). *The theory and practice of group psychotherapy.* New York: Basic Books.

CHAPTER 10

Practice with
Communities

Susan P. Kemp
Edward Scanlon

Social workers have always been concerned with en-
hancing individual and social well-being through intervention in the community. Indeed, the community is a natural site for practice that reflects the
social work profession's historic commitment to empowering and contextual practice (Kemp, Whittaker, & Tracy, 1997). Endorsed in this chapter
is the belief, inherent in social work practice since its earliest beginnings,
that communities of all kinds provide singular opportunities for participation, democratic citizenship, and collective action for social justice. At the
same time, communities can be just as exclusionary, oppressive, and conservative as any other social structure. Empowering community practice is
located in the space between these two realities: supporting socially just
connections between people and communities and between communities
and larger social structures.

The approach outlined in this chapter calls for community involvement
by all social workers, to whatever degree and in whichever ways make
sense in a particular practice context. It neither privileges macro practice
nor denies the value of direct practice—skills from both domains are essential. Indeed, there is currently a resurgence of interest in the community
among social workers in direct practice. In 1997, Family Service America
proposed a renewed emphasis on community-centered family services,
defined by a focus on strengthening communities as a key resource for
families (Sviridoff & Ryan, 1997). Claudia Coulton (1995), a leading social work community researcher, has noted the need for "a modernized
vision of community social work practice" designed to "use the community to strengthen families, create economic opportunity, and protect vulnerable individuals" (p. 439). In health social work, Poole (1997) likewise

described an "urgent need for community capacity building" (p. 165). In the prevention arena, John McKnight's work, which focuses on harnessing community assets and strengths (Kretzmann & McKnight, 1993; McKnight, 1997), has been influential across a range of social work practice domains.

This renewed interest in community has multiple sources. Among practitioners, there is growing awareness of the impact of community conditions, for good or ill, on individual and family well-being. At the same time, a rich array of grassroots social movements and coalitions has emerged, providing new opportunities for community-based social work practice and partnerships. An increasingly robust body of empirical knowledge on neighborhoods and communities is also available as a foundation for effective community practice (see, for example, Brooks-Gunn, Duncan, & Aber, 1997; Chaskin, 1997; Coulton, Korbin, & Su, 1996; Korbin & Coulton, 1997). These various influences and intellectual foundations are reflected in the approach to community practice developed in this chapter.

The chapter has three main components: (1) the meaning of community is discussed, both in historical context and from a contemporary perspective; (2) the reader is introduced to the range of models in contemporary community practice; and (3) the core components of a generalist approach to empowering community practice, designed to bridge the gap that is often constructed between practice with individuals, families, and groups and practice with communities, is outlined. The chapter focuses primarily on theory and skills of immediate relevance to entry-level social workers in a variety of settings and fields of practice. Although social administration and social policy are both highly relevant to community practice, these fields have their own bodies of knowledge and skills and are not explored here. Nor are the more technical aspects of community practice, such as program development and social planning, discussed in depth.

The Meaning of Community

A desire for community is embedded deeply in U.S. life. In a society defined by individualism, the belief nonetheless persists that life was and is better when people are connected to one another in meaningful ways. However, "community" is one of the most complex of social ideas. Laden with the mythology of an idealized colonial past, it evokes nostalgic visions of small-town values and habits, of places where people know one another, look out for each other, and act together for the common good. The wish to recapture this mythic community has been a theme in U.S. society at least since the late 19th century, when industrialization, mass migration and immigration, the growth of cities, and increased social mobility transformed a social structure defined previously by ties to blood and soil (Rupp, 1991).

Although the desire for community continues to resonate in U.S. life (Chavis & Wandersman, 1990), recognition of the value of community ties competes with the even more compelling quest for individual fulfillment. In their landmark study of U.S. culture, *Habits of the Heart*, Bellah and colleagues (1985) found a yearning for "meaning and coherence" in the midst of the pursuit of individualism. They concluded, as has communitarian Amitai Etzioni (1993), that this meaning could be found through renewed commitment to community and civic responsibility. There is little evidence, however, that people in the United States readily put the common good ahead of individual advancement. Efforts to develop community as a vehicle for social integration and shared meaning must, therefore, confront the reality that the rhetoric of community cloaks deep ambivalence about the value of connection. As this ambivalence ebbs and flows, social workers find more or less opportunity for effective community practice.

Defining Community

The concept of community is inherently slippery. Each person has his or her own ideas about what community means and how it can be identified. Most commonly, however, community is defined either geographically (as connections between residents of a particular place) or socially (as relationships based in shared concerns and interests). To these definitions Heller (1989) added a third: community as collective political power. All three definitions assume that in a community people have something in common that brings them together—"some combination of shared beliefs, circumstances, priorities, relationships, concerns . . . that provides for the possibility of group identity and collective action" (Chaskin, 1995, p. 1). People typically belong to multiple communities, defined as much by shared interests and sense of identity as by geographic proximity. These communities differ depending on whether people are linked primarily by affect (the ties of kinship, land, religion, culture, ethnicity, or nationality) or by collective interest. Each presents different issues and challenges for the community practitioner.

Community as Place

Many commonly used definitions of community reflect the idea of community as place (see, for example, Barker, 1995; Warren, 1978)—a group of people who live in a particular geographic area or neighborhood. Chaskin (1995) defined the *neighborhood* as "a specific *context* of relationships, opportunities, and constraints that, to a large degree are spatially defined or delimited" (p. vi). In neighborhoods, common local concerns often are reinforced by social connections based on proximity, shared social circumstances, and the ties of ethnicity or culture.

A good deal of community social work practice is locally based, with the goal of improving the quality of life for people in a particular neighborhood. Practitioners should be cautious, however, in defining communities primarily in geographic terms. First, people who live near one another do not necessarily feel connected. Unless other areas of common ground exist, such as shared social class, ethnic background, or religious identity, territory may have little to do with sense of community. Second, several communities often coexist in one geographic space. Third, many people develop a sense of investment in their local community as much around specific issues as through profound and ongoing ties to particular people and places. Some are interested more in being free of community demands than in developing ties with their neighbors. Others, particularly those who live in neighborhoods that are perceived as dangerous or hostile, may very carefully screen their ties with the local community. In a study of "resilient" mothers in a low-income housing project, for example, Brodsky (1997) found that the ability to keep a distance from neighborhood influences was considered essential to the well-being of these women and their families. With little faith in their community as a resource, these mothers tended to keep their children close to home; to relate to the community only in very strategic ways; and, very often, to look to schools, churches, and personal networks outside the community for support and enrichment.

Within any neighborhood, therefore, "community" is a complex entity, existing in multiple ways and at multiple levels. In addition to seeking out traditional, place-based networks, social workers should also be aware of the existence of more transitory "limited liability" communities that form around particular local issues (Chaskin, 1995) and also, as noted later, of the many communities of interest that may or may not have a geographic base.

Community as Shared Social Ties

For many people, relational communities based on shared interests, concerns, and needs are as important as the communities in which they live. In solidarity communities, an important form of relational community, people share a common heritage (such as religion, ethnicity, culture, or nationality) that provides members with a strong sense of identity and a common system of values and beliefs (Rubin & Rubin, 1992). Ties to such communities tend to be deep-seated and long-lasting and are maintained in a variety of ways, including through common language, food, customs, traditions, and religious observances. In emergent ethnic communities, as Rivera and Erlich (1992) have noted, relationship-based social networks, informal exchange, and natural support systems are particularly important.

In some instances, social solidarity is imposed on a group by the tendency in the larger society to assume that people who share common demographic characteristics constitute a community (Rubin & Rubin, 1992). Thus, people speak of the Asian community, of the African American community, or of the urban poor as though each is a homogeneous group. Such monolithic classifications can obscure the rich diversity within such groups and the extent to which people vary in their identification with particular communities.

In earlier times, communities of interest and place were deeply interwoven. As society has become both more mobile and more technological, however, communities of interest (also called "functional communities") increasingly are uncoupled from locality. These "communities without propinquity" (Webber, 1963) may be organized around shared interests (such as environmental issues, professional concerns, or gay rights), common needs and problems (such as parents of children with rare diseases), or both. Non-local communities are even more prevalent now that the Internet has become the modern equivalent of the village square. In cyberspace, "virtual communities" provide opportunities for sociability, information exchange, social support, and mutual aid (Wellman & Gulia, 1995). At the same time, the mediated and essentially anonymous nature of computer-based networks dilutes what is commonly understood by "community" and fragments conventional social solidarities (Wellman et al., 1996). The new interactive technologies thus open up possibilities for social intervention but at the same time call for a rethinking and careful analysis of what social workers mean by and expect from community-oriented interventions.

Community as Collective Power Relationships

Despite the rhetoric that America is a classless society, U.S. communities are deeply defined by class divisions. Social class, based on income, education, and ownership of property, determines the degree to which individuals, families, and communities have access to opportunities and resources. Upper-class communities generally have ready access to and control over opportunities and services and a good deal of power over community boundaries and norms. The members of low-income communities, such as urban housing projects, in contrast, often have little access to, and even less control over, a wide range of opportunities, including employment, education, housing, health services, and public amenities. Additionally, members of disadvantaged communities may feel powerless in the face of their increased vulnerability to external surveillance and containment. The price of external services and supports is very often increased supervision and control: a mix that fuels feelings of frustration, dependency, and impotence in marginalized communities (Murray, 1995).

Although community practice has always been centrally concerned with the distribution of power in communities, the focus has traditionally been on locating, engaging, and influencing those in the community who already have power (Cox, 1987). An empowerment perspective highlights the need for a more critical and comprehensive analysis that addresses power relationships not only in political terms, but also with regard to the ways in which broader structural arrangements play out at the community level and influence personal and collective life chances (Dodd & Gutierrez, 1990).

Models of Community Practice

The past 30 years have been ones of continuing development, refinement, and specification in community social work practice. As knowledge has evolved and new issues have emerged, so community practice has progressively been shaped to fit the needs and concerns of the times.

Five major practice domains are typically included in community social work practice (Rothman, 1970; Taylor & Roberts, 1985): (1) community development, in which the focus is on enhancing community participation and competence through, for example, community service programs, self-help efforts such as the prevention of violence, and efforts to enhance social networks; (2) program development and service coordination; (3) social planning, which is a largely technical process of problem solving with regard to substantive social problems such as delinquency, inadequate housing, and mental illness; (4) political and social action, in which the focus is on organizing disadvantaged groups to change the policies and services of formal organizations; and (5) community liaison, which brings into community practice the many community-related activities undertaken by social workers in direct practice, including case management, with its central concern with accessing, coordinating, and monitoring community resources and relationships.

For many years the tendency was to group these approaches under the general rubric of macro-practice, defined as practice that "deals with aspects of human activity that are non-clinical in nature, but rather focus on broader social approaches to human betterment, emphasizing such things as developing enlightened social policy, organizing the effective delivery of services, strengthening community life, and preventing social ills" (Rothman

& Tropman, 1987, p. 3). From this perspective, community practice and clinical practice are distinct entities.

The 1990s, however, saw a distinct trend toward hybrid models of community practice (Bradshaw et al., 1994), characterized by flexible integration of macro-practice strategies and those focused on the individual and small-group processes that are the building blocks of community empowerment. Emergent perspectives on community practice with women and communities of color endorse the feminist credo that "the personal is political" and highlight the importance of links between individual and collective empowerment. These approaches challenge the construction of community practice in rational–technocratic, expert, and masculine terms and emphasize interventions that encourage process and participation, diminish power and status differentials, and empower vulnerable people and populations (Bradshaw et al., 1994; Hyde, 1996; Weil, 1986, 1994).

In response both to these emerging commitments and to a perceived need for greater clarity about the match between models of community practice and community needs, Weil and Gamble (1995) developed an eight-model framework for community practice. Their approach, which is set out in Table 10-1, organizes models of practice around four main dimensions of community practice: development, organizing, planning, and change. Community organizing is separated into two categories: (1) organizing in place-based communities, and (2) organizing in communities of interest (functional communities). The social change dimensions of community practice are also separated to distinguish among political and social action, community practice with coalitions, and community practice with social movements.

Empowering Community Practice: A Generalist Approach

Although knowledge and skills in community practice are used to different degrees in different contexts, they are an important component of the practice repertoire of all social workers. A generalist practitioner may intervene at any systemic level, drawing on a wide range of knowledge and skills and applying them flexibly as the situation demands. What remains constant is the intellectual structure that he or she applies to the tasks at hand.

This generalist approach fits well with the practical realities of everyday work with communities. In many communities, a prerequisite for change is to develop shared identity, connections, and the ability to work together among community members (a "sense of community"). Community members also must determine priorities among competing needs. In their ongoing work with individuals and small groups, social workers in direct practice have many opportunities to support the development of community

Table 10-1. Current Models of Community Practice for Social Work

Models

Comparative Characteristics	Neighborhood and Community Organizing	Organizing Functional Communities	Community Social and Economic Development	Social Planning	Program Development and Community Liaison	Political and Social Action	Coalitions	Social Movements
Desired outcome	Develop capacity of members to organize; change the impact of citywide planning and external development	Action for social justice focused on advocacy and on changing behaviors and attitudes; may also provide service	Initiate development plans from a grassroots perspective; prepare citizens to make use of social and economic investments	Citywide or regional proposals for action by elected body or human services planning councils	Expansion or redirection of agency program to improve community service effectiveness; organize new service	Action for social justice focused on changing policy or policy makers	Build a multi-organizational power base large enough to influence program direction or draw down resources	Action for social justice that provides a new paradigm for a particular population group or issue
System targeted for change	Municipal government; external developers; community members	General public; government institutions	Banks; foundations; external developers; community citizens	Perspectives of community leaders; perspectives of human service leaders	Funders of agency programs; beneficiaries of agency services	Voting public; elected officials; inactive/potential participants	Elected officials; foundations; government institutions	General public; political systems
Primary constituency	Residents of neighborhood, parish, or rural county	Like-minded people in a community, region, nation, or across the globe	Low-income marginalized, or oppressed population groups in a city or region	Elected officials; social agencies and interagency organizations	Agency board or administrators; community representatives	Citizens in a particular political jurisdiction	Organizations that have a stake in the particular issue	Leaders and organizations able to create new visions and images
Scope of concern	Quality of life in the geographic area	Advocacy for particular issue or population	Income, resource, and social support development; improved basic education and leadership skills	Integration of social needs into geographic planning in a public arena; human services network coordination	Service development for a specific population	Building political power; institutional change	Specified issue related to social need or concern	Social justice within society
Social work roles	Organizer Teacher Facilitator	Organizer Advocate Writer/ communicator Facilitator	Negotiator Promoter Teacher Planner Manager	Researcher Research writer Communicator Manager	Spokesperson Planner Manager Proposal writer	Advocate Organizer Researcher Candidate	Mediator Negotiator Spokesperson	Advocate Facilitator

Source: Reprinted from Weil, M., & Gamble, D. N. (1995). Community Practice Models. In R. L. Edwards (Ed.-in-Chief), *Encyclopedia of Social Work* (19th ed., Vol. 1, p. 581). Washington, DC: NASW Press.

consciousness and to encourage community participation. These community-building efforts provide a foundation for effective action by the community to address issues of concern. As the community moves toward action, the support, advocacy, brokerage, and negotiation skills of social workers become increasingly salient. Research, planning, and communication skills also come into play as social workers and communities collaborate to develop resources and services tailored to community needs. In ways large and small, as a major or minor part of their daily professional activities, on a continuum ranging from radical social action to a concern with enhancing the everyday contexts of individual clients, social workers are thus an important source of support for community change. As Germain (1985) pointed out:

> The community is an integral part of the life space of individuals and collectivities that we serve. . . . Reciprocally, when the client is the community, then the individuals and collectivities within the community must be in the foreground of attention throughout the processes of assessment, intervention, and prevention (p. 32).

Theoretical Foundations: Ecological Systems and Empowerment Theory

Core theoretical support for a generalist approach to community practice comes from ecological systems theory (Germain, 1985; Meyer, 1983), which directs attention to the interdependence of people and their environments at multiple and interlocking systems levels. Given the complex nature of the challenges facing communities and their residents, productive community intervention typically has multiple dimensions; develops structural connections among individuals, collectivities, and broader social structures; and, as in the following example, may well involve several social workers with different roles and perspectives:

> In a neighborhood struggling with high levels of violence, a community worker who is assisting a group of parents in developing a block patrol uses sophisticated interpersonal and group process skills to engage parents and to facilitate their planning process. At the local child and family agency, a clinical social worker with many of these same parents on her caseload lobbies her agency for the resources to develop an empowerment group in which parents can explore issues of parenting in this community environment. At a meeting convened to coordinate planning for an interagency grant application, the two workers discuss ways in which they might better collaborate. Both are committed to working in partnership with local residents and want to build links between direct services, community-level interventions, and larger policy initiatives.

The wide-angle lens of the ecosystems perspective ensures a multidimensional approach to the issues and challenges confronting communities, but it is largely silent on issues of power and social justice. To incorporate these into community practice, social workers must look to empowerment practice and to the literature on diversity. In community practice, as in other fields of practice, the emergence of new ethnic communities, transitions in established communities of color, the rise of the women's movement, and the increasing visibility of the gay and lesbian communities have contributed significantly to a growing emphasis on multiculturalism, pluralism, and empowerment (Weil, 1994).

An Empowerment Perspective

A concern with community is an essential element of empowerment practice:

> [Empowerment] suggests both individual determination over one's life and democratic participation in the life of one's community, often through mediating structures such as schools, neighborhoods, churches, and other voluntary organizations . . . .It is a multilevel construct applicable to individual citizens as well as to organizations and neighborhoods. (Rappaport, 1987, pp. 121–130)

A fundamental goal of empowerment practice is for individuals and communities to develop the capacity to resist and to change environmental conditions that negatively affect life chances and access to resources and services. As a *product*, community empowerment is defined by competence, connectedness, a concern for the common good, and a sense of commitment to and participation in the community (Zimmerman & Rappaport, 1988). The *process* of empowerment involves the development of the personal and collective beliefs, attitudes, and skills that will enable effective action (Parsons, 1991). To become empowered is both to perceive oneself and one's community as effective and potent and to develop the ability to act to change the conditions of daily life (Pecukonis & Wenocur, 1994; Simon, 1990). The relationship between competence and environmental action is reciprocal—each reinforces the other (Zimmerman & Rappaport, 1988). Empowering community practice thus has two primary and interlocking objectives: the empowerment of people and the redistribution of existing power and resources (Mondros & Berman-Rossi, 1991). Both strands are essential to the goal of an empowered community:

> An empowered community is a community in which individuals and organizations apply their skills and resources in collective efforts that lead to community competence. Through such participation and control, the community is able to meet the needs of its individuals and organizations. (Gerchick, 1990, cited in Schulz et al., 1995, p. 312)

Empowering Strategies in Community Practice

Effective community practice builds on and incorporates the knowledge and skills for interpersonal practice outlined in previous chapters. Working with people around community issues, social workers constantly use their relationship skills. Like empowering practice in general, however, empowering community practice differs from clinical practice as it is traditionally constructed. At the interpersonal level, this difference is demonstrated by an emphasis on mutuality and collaboration, a commitment to client participation, a focus on the development of critical consciousness, and the use of dialogue as a primary strategy for change.

Collaboration

Empowering community practice assumes an engaged worker who helps community members to understand their experience in political and personal terms. The social worker's ideological stance and external perspective "lend a vision" and serve as a catalyst for the development of alternative ways of understanding. Robust models for such engaged practice are readily available in feminist practice (Van Den Bergh & Cooper, 1986) and in the emerging literature on community practice with people of color (Rivera & Erlich, 1992).

In empowering practice, social workers replace paternalistic and elitist forms of intervention (those that assume that the worker knows best) with approaches that maximize people's rights, strengths, and capabilities through careful attention to issues of power, social distance, and control. As much as is possible, practitioners use their expertise in ways that do not perpetuate oppressive social conditions. The professional skills and institutional resources available to social workers are both real and valuable but must be offered within a relationship characterized by mutuality rather than professional distance. Collaboration and consultation are thus key aspects of community practice. Appropriate social work roles are those of enabler, facilitator, teacher, resource provider, consultant, compatriot, organizer, advocate, broker, negotiator, and activist (Gutierrez, 1990; Parsons, Jorgensen, & Hernandez, 1994). Clients are regarded as citizens and consumers, as members and partners, and, very often, as victims of oppressive social conditions.

Participation

In empowering community practice, attention shifts from personal and interpersonal deficits to the relationship between people and their sociopolitical environment and to the rights of a community to opportunities, resources, and services. Central to this shift in perspective is the assumption that people should participate actively in defining their concerns and any action to be taken to address them (Maluccio, 1981). Efforts to enhance participation thus constitute an important aspect of community practice (Mattaini, 1993a). Incentives for participation may be intrinsic (deriving from the activity itself) or extrinsic (such as the offer of food, child care, or other benefits in return for participation).

Studies of community participation have demonstrated that active involvement and perceptions of influence and control contribute significantly to the personal empowerment of community members (Rich et al., 1995; Zimmerman & Rappaport, 1988) and result in more positive and durable project outcomes (Itzhaky & York, 1991; Mattaini, 1993a). Participation can take many forms, such as involvement in committees and coalitions, the contribution of a consumer voice in service development and delivery, participation in program planning and management, and involvement in participatory action research.

It must be noted, however, that participation alone is not sufficient: To be correlated with empowerment, participation must be associated with the belief that one really can influence decisions being made and have an effect on actions taken (Schulz et al., 1995). Too often, the involvement of community residents (in community planning, for example) is little more than tokenism. Participation may also be empty if it is unlikely to result in meaningful change. Halpern (1993) has rightly pointed out, for example, that in "depleted" communities, real change in opportunity structures depends on external social and economic structures. In such communities, projects must be careful not to squander valuable (and scarce) human resources or to further victimize community members by promising more than they can deliver. Thoughtful work is thus required, with consumers and the institutions and services in which they participate, to ensure that participation is meaningful and effective (Briscoe, Hoffman, & Bailey, 1975; Keenan & Pinkerton, 1991).

Critical Consciousness

An essential foundation for empowerment is the development of what Freire (1973) called "critical consciousness," which is defined as the ability to reflect on one's experience not just in personal terms, but with awareness that the everyday lived experiences of individuals are profoundly shaped by events and conditions in the social and political environment (Parsons, 1991; Weick, 1993). Critical reflection contextualizes personal experience by connecting it to external realities, opens up new perspectives, and enables individuals and communities to visualize alternative ways of "being in the world."

The process of consciousness-raising necessarily involves praxis, a mixture of reflection and action, to ensure that social action is grounded in a critical analysis of the relationship between everyday experiences and wider social and structural issues (Longres & McLeod, 1980). Freire (1973) suggested that it is the development of critical consciousness—the ability to "think against" the status quo—that enables people to act together to change oppressive social conditions.

Dialogue as a Basis for Community Action

Consciousness-raising is most readily achieved through dialogue, whether between individuals, in small groups, or in larger collectives. The use of dialogue and narrative to facilitate empowerment and social justice has sturdy roots in the women's and other grassroots movements. More recently, narrative techniques have emerged as a central aspect of dialogic and constructivist approaches to intervention in family therapy and social work (Allen, 1993; Anderson & Goolishian, 1992; Holland & Kilpatrick, 1993; Laird, 1993; Saleebey, 1994; White & Epston, 1990).

Empowering dialogue differs from traditional therapeutic conversations in two ways. First, the social worker joins the conversation with the goal of helping people to express, understand, and redefine their daily experiences in social as well as personal terms. Second, empowering dialogue necessarily includes critical examination of the wider sociopolitical environment and issues of power and domination. Strategies for facilitating dialogue build on core social work skills: empathy, mutual respect, and active, nonjudgmental listening. The worker is an ethnographer or "ecological explorer" (Auerswald, 1968): a curious and respectful stranger who, through a process of joint exploration, seeks to be educated about how individuals and communities understand their social reality (Laird, 1993; Leigh, 1997).

Freire (1973) termed his dialogical strategy the "pedagogy of the question" (p. 35), a technique that encourages people both to find their own answers and to shape further questions (Simon, 1990). Using this strategy, the social worker asks community members to question why things are as they are, what patterns they can see in their shared experiences, and what social and environmental factors contribute to their circumstances. This process of questioning creates a space in which alternative views can emerge (Holland & Kilpatrick, 1993). Dominant cultural and social interpretations are challenged, and groups are encouraged to develop explanations that reflect their particular identity and history. In this way, multiple realities and perspectives have the opportunity to emerge and to be validated.

Thinking Contextually

Social workers in all settings know a great deal about the environmental and community experiences of their clients. They often fail, however, to make connections between one case and another or, as Wood and Middleman (1991) put it, to "look beyond the client" (p. 57) to collective experience. Faced with a series of clients with depression, for example, a social worker in direct practice may feel more pressure to "tool up" on treating depression than to consider whether there is a need for community-level analysis and intervention.

The ability to think flexibly from "case" to "cause" and back again is at the core of generalist community practice: It ensures that the needs of individuals are connected to broader efforts to link people with common experiences and to construct effective and equitable social structures. Attention to community issues is often constrained, however, by assumptions that are deeply embedded in the ecology of practice. Rosen and Livne (1992) have demonstrated, for example, that social workers in direct practice tend to attribute presenting problems more to psychological factors than to environmental factors, even when the client defines his or her problems in environmental terms. Similarly, a study of practice reasoning (Nurius, Kemp, & Gibson, 1999) found that workers tended not to include environmental variables unless they were explicitly prompted, suggesting that this lack of attention to context is not simply an artifact of the worker–client interaction.

To respond effectively to people in their community settings, social workers must develop "habits of mind" that direct attention to context as well as client. Because deliberate effort is needed to overcome bias (Nurius, Kemp, & Gibson, 1999), such habits of mind should also be reinforced by the routine use of methods that open up issues for attention. (Many assessment tools, such as clinical diagnostic systems, are designed to reduce complexity [see, for examples, Mattaini & Kirk, 1991].) Examples of reinforcers, or prompts, that encourage contextual mindfulness include the use of ecosystemic measures in assessment (such as ecomaps or social network maps [Mattaini, 1993b]); regular involvement in the daily life of the community; openness to consumer and community input; and efforts to ensure that consumers participate actively in the planning, delivery, and monitoring of services.

Community Assessment

Effective practice at the community level begins with a thorough understanding of a particular community and its needs. As Poole (1997) has noted, "There is little room for formula or 'cookie-cutter' thinking in community capacity-building. What works well in one community may not work in another" (p. 168). A comprehensive community assessment builds on the following general principles:

- an understanding of different kinds of communities and of the ways in which a particular community is similar to and different from these general models.
- the use of multiple methods to generate data, including both quantitative and participatory/ethnographic approaches.
- the willingness to approach the community as a "respectful outsider" who is willing to learn about it from its members, and who does not impose externally constructed definitions. Meaning should be understood as local and historically situated.
- a focus on identifying community strengths, competencies, and resources as well as needs and challenges (see Kretzmann & McKnight, 1993; Parsons, 1991; Saleebey, 1992; and Sullivan, 1992, for material on a strengths approach to assessment).
- a commitment to involving members of the community in the generation, analysis, and application of community knowledge.

A collaborative approach that involves community members in defining and assessing their community is an essential check against misplaced assumptions and external bias. Involvement in the assessment process educates community members (who often are not well-informed about the parameters of particular issues), enhances levels of participation and motivation, demystifies the planning process, and facilitates the development of collaborative relationships (Fagan, 1987). Collaboration increases the probability that both problem-posing and problem-solving will be meaningful and appropriate. As people become active subjects rather than just objects of assessment and intervention and develop capacities that can be used in other contexts, the likelihood of sustained change is also increased.

Mapping the Neighborhood Community

An accurate reading of what constitutes a particular neighborhood is often critical to the success of a community-level intervention. Comprehensive outlines for developing a profile of a geographic community can be found in Johnson (1992) and Sheafor, Horejsi, and Horejsi (1991). Major domains include:

- physical setting,
- history,
- demographics of the population,

- cultural factors,
- economic system,
- political system,
- sociocultural system,
- human services system,
- major problems and concerns of the community, and
- general aspects of community functioning (such as sense of identity and belonging, decision-making structures, and autonomy).

Mapping Communities using Quantitative Data

Community-based social workers regularly use quantitative data sources to identify key measures of neighborhood social and health functioning (Coulton, 1995). These "neighborhood indicators" are often chosen by interested stakeholders, who identify outcome areas that are of concern to a particular community (Kingsley, 1988). Examples might include such indicators as infant mortality rates, homicide rates, child poverty rates, child maltreatment rates, or neighborhood employment levels. Data are gathered that help policy makers and organizers to evaluate areas in which neighborhood functioning is improving or worsening. These data provide directions for policy decisions and guide the use of limited funds for neighborhood improvement. Much of the objective data for a community assessment is available from census data and other materials (for example, public health statistics, uniform crime reports, city planning data, and labor market statistics) compiled by state and local agencies that are involved in community planning (such as the United Way; local governments; and economic development, labor, and human services agencies). The U.S. Department of Housing and Urban Development has endorsed the use of neighborhood indicators and is currently making better neighborhood data available through the creation of the American Community Survey. In comparison with the decennial census, this survey will provide data that focus on smaller units of analyses and that is released on a more timely basis.

Specific methodologies and software applications are also being developed to make quantitative methods of community data analysis more accessible to those without technical training. Geographic Information Systems (GIS) are computer programs that allow the storage, manipulation, and analyses of data according to geographic location (Hoefer, Hoefer, & Tobias, 1994; Tompkins & Southward, 1998). While the use of many of these programs requires a high level of technological skill, recent user-friendly versions developed by the U.S. Department of Housing and Urban Development allow community practitioners to produce high-quality maps of city and neighborhood indicators with relatively little training (Kingsley, 1998). Other software programs, such as those that can analyze mortgage lending patterns in geographically focused areas, have also been developed for use by quantitatively untrained community practitioners.

Mapping Communities Using Qualitative Data

Quantitative data on community conditions provides essential information for supporting community change efforts, but does not provide a view of the community through the eyes of its members. For this, community workers and researchers turn to qualitative data, which provides information on the community from the inside out. Such data bring the community to life, allow for more nuanced and valid interpretations of quantitative data (when data gathered from within the community are set against data derived from external sources), and provide important opportunities for community members to be active participants in generating community information.

Strategies for gathering qualitative and experiential data include ethnomethodological approaches, such as participant observation, field observations, and informal interviews with key community figures and local residents. Participatory action research models, which integrate research and practice by involving community members in the creation and use of knowledge about the community, are particularly recommended (Curtis, 1989; Sarri & Sarri, 1992). Creative strategies for involving residents in community assessments include the use of documentary methods, such as photography, video, and interviews with other residents, that enable residents to construct a living and multidimensional picture of their community (Wang, Burris, & Ping, 1996). More conventional strategies include the use of focus groups, key informant interviews, and resident surveys. The Concerns Report Method developed by Fawcett and colleagues (1980) also offers a structured approach to generating consumer input.

The value of the social worker's local knowledge must also be emphasized. Regardless of their work setting, social workers should be physically acquainted with the community in which their clients live. They should walk and drive around the community, take the time to talk informally with local people, and generally explore. Often there is no substitute for the particular kind of environmental and community knowing that comes from direct personal experience.

Mapping Community Capacity

Too often, community inventories become a compilation of community deficits and problems. Communities that are the focus of social work attention are frequently defined in the language of risk and pathology—as high-risk, disorganized, socially isolated, or underclass. Such perspectives stigmatize, isolate, and immobilize. They also imply, as Delgado (1996) pointed out, that resources and skills for change mostly are not available within the community and must therefore be imported from outside.

In the 1990s scholarship from a strengths perspective and the growing literature on resilience stimulated renewed interest in the strengths, capacities, resources, and potentialities of individuals, families, groups, and communities. In community practice, the work of John McKnight and his colleagues has been particularly influential (Kretzmann & McKnight, 1993; McKnight, 1997). McKnight argued that all communities have untapped resources, skills, and capacities that can provide the building blocks of positive and empowering change. The process of "mapping" these assets is thus an important foundation for community-building efforts. Kretzmann and McKnight (1993) differentiated three major categories of assets: (1) individuals (including households and families), (2) citizens' associations, and (3) formal institutions. These range in turn from those that are located in the community and under community control to those that originate outside the community and are controlled largely by outsiders. Asset-based community development begins from the premise that "outside resources will be much more effectively used if the local community is itself fully mobilized and invested, and if it can define the agendas for which additional resources must be obtained" (Kretzmann & McKnight, 1993, p. 8). It is a bottom-up, relational, and deeply participatory approach to community development.

Mapping Power and Social Justice

None of the approaches to community assessment discussed so far focuses in a sustained and complex way on issues of power and social justice. However, a multidimensional power analysis, encompassing both power as influence (the view from the top) and power as it is experienced in everyday life (the view from below) is central to empowering community practice.

1. Power as Influence. From this perspective, a power analysis is focused on identifying those in the community who exert power and influence and who can "get things done." (For a comprehensive discussion of assessing community power structures, see Hardcastle, Wenocur, & Powers, 1997.) Strategies include surveys; interviews with key informants; and studies of newspapers, board lists, and other documentary sources. Knowing who the key players are in a community (and how to access them) is very often essential to the success of community projects, particularly in the early stages of a new initiative.

2. *Power in Everyday Life.* The analysis of power from the "bottom up," in contrast, focuses on understanding power relations from the perspective of community members (Gutierrez, 1990; Hagan & Smail, 1997). Such an analysis, which Hagan and Smail have termed "power-mapping," involves three key steps. First, it is necessary to map the distribution of power and resources in the community across key domains. Second, it is important to analyze how conditions of powerlessness are affecting residents. Third, it is essential to identify sources of actual or potential power at the community level. Such an analysis enhances critical consciousness of the distribution of power in the community and its consequences, provides important information on resources and strengths available to the community effort, and opens up perspectives on what needs to be done for community residents to obtain power in key life domains.

A Value Framework for Empowering Community Practice

Although the choice of strategies for community action varies from situation to situation, community-oriented social work practice is framed always by the values and ethics of the profession. In addition, Fawcett (1991) suggested that community practice should reflect the following principles:

- Workers should avoid "colonial" relationships with community members—relationships in which power, authority, and ownership of knowledge are vested in the worker. In collaborative and empowering relationships, both parties have "equal moral agency" (Simon, 1994): Their contributions may be different, but they are of equal value to the community effort.
- Project goals should reflect consumer concerns, needs, and perspectives. Criteria for success (outcomes) should also be constructed in terms that are meaningful to community members (Rapp, Shera, & Kisthart, 1993).
- Both selection of participants and choice of interventions should reflect the "multilevel and systemic nature of community problems" (Fawcett, 1991, p. 625). Change targets should include not only those individuals (and their proximate environments) who experience a problem directly, but also the institutional and social structures that create and sustain problems.
- Workers should plan for "small wins" at multiple system levels while maintaining a vision of larger-scale change. In community practice, where issues often seem overwhelming and intractable, it is particularly important to "think globally and act locally" and to accept that large system change is likely to be incremental. Fawcett (1991) defined small wins as "those concrete outcomes of modest significance that attract allies and deter opponents" (p. 627).

- Interventions should be replicable and sustainable with local resources. That is, interventions should build on and enhance existing capacity within the community. Fawcett et al. (1984) also recommended that strategies selected for community intervention should, where possible, be: inexpensive; demonstrably effective; decentralized (that is, local and small scale); flexible; sustainable with local resources; simple; and compatible with existing customs, beliefs, and values.

Strategies for Community Empowerment

Empowering community practice focuses on enhancing the capacity of the community to resolve its own problems and needs. Two concepts frequently used to conceptualize this process are community capacity (Poole, 1997) and community competence (Cottrell, 1977). Community capacity refers to characteristics of communities that affect their ability to identify, mobilize, and act to resolve community issues and concerns. Key dimensions include participation and leadership, access to and wise use of resources, social and inter-organizational networks, sense of community, a community history of collective action, community power, shared core values, and the capacity to engage in critical reflection (Poole, 1997).

Community competence, a very similar concept, has been defined as the ability of any kind of community to problem-solve effectively and thus to master social and environmental challenges (Eng, Salmon, & Mullan, 1992). Cottrell (1977) suggested that the process of enhancing community competence typically involves the following:

- activities that strengthen investment and commitment;
- clarification of issues and interests in the community;
- development of the ability of community members to articulate views, attitudes, needs, and intentions;
- enhancement of communication skills;
- the ability to negotiate differences and manage conflict; and
- membership participation.

Community groups can achieve their goals only if their members have the knowledge and skills to negotiate effectively with those who control access to needed resources and services. Where these core skills are not available by virtue of social class, education, or experience, they must be developed. Community members also need assistance to identify and strengthen existing skills and resources. Social workers make an important contribution, in small groups and community forums, when they model, teach, and support skill identification and development. The role of educator, although often overlooked in social work, is central to effective community practice (Lightburn & Black, in press).

Key areas for skills development include problem solving; assertive communication (public speaking, issue presentation, chairing meetings); conflict management (collaboration, negotiation, and bargaining); political skills (influence and advocacy); and the technical skills associated with identifying, obtaining, and using resources (Cottrell, 1977; Mattaini, 1993a). Strategies for skill development draw heavily on social learning theory and include didactic teaching, experiential approaches such as coaching and role playing, and modeling of effective behaviors.

Leadership development is also a critical need in many communities. Natural leaders may or may not be effective in negotiations with larger social systems. Supporting the development of informed and effective indigenous leadership, particularly through participation in decision-making, is thus an important aspect of community development efforts (Bradshaw, Soifer, & Gutierrez, 1994).

Community competence is predicated also on the ability of community members to work together on areas of common concern. Here the social worker is challenged to help community members find common ground while also recognizing that there is value and strength in diversity (Bradshaw, Soifer, & Gutierrez, 1994). Similarly, social workers play an important role in the development of coalitions between different interest groups and organizations in the community. At both these levels, there is a need to facilitate dialogue actively, "translate" different perspectives and expectations (a particularly important skill in cross-cultural practice), mediate power relationships to ensure equitable participation, and encourage an open approach to problem-solving.

Community Practice and Mediating Structures: Groups, Social Networks, and Community-Based Programs

Berger and Neuhaus (1977) envisioned the community as a mediating structure between people and the institutional and social structures of the wider society. In this sense the community provides a buffer, or cushion, between people and social conditions that are often alienating and oppressive. Four aspects of community practice are particularly relevant to the mediating function of community: (1) the use of small groups, (2) the development of social networks, (3) the construction of communities in social programs, and (4) asset-based social welfare programs.

Small Groups

Groups are the fundamental building blocks of neighborhood and community development (Mondros & Berman-Rossi, 1991; Ramey, 1992).

Community workers interact with and facilitate many different kinds of groups, including issues groups, community meetings, planning groups, task groups, self-help groups, coalitions, neighborhood associations, and social action groups. Groups are also critical to the process of empowerment (Brown & Ziefert, 1988; Gutierrez, 1990). Cox (1991) described, for example, the progressive empowerment of a group of welfare mothers as they worked together for change in the welfare system.

Mondros and Berman-Rossi (1991) suggested that group work skills are particularly important in the initial stages of a community project, when the worker brings community members together to explore and validate different perspectives, to develop shared understandings, to enhance commitment and motivation (and negotiate conflict), and to determine a plan of action. Noting that community organizers tend to focus more on the tasks to be accomplished than on the process of implementation, Mondros and Berman-Rossi argued that "organizers invite trouble for themselves if they don't attend to how and why people join groups, the meaning of group experience for individuals, and matters of group process during these beginning efforts" (p. 204). Knowledge of the stages of group development and skills in facilitating group process at different points in the life cycle of community projects are thus important aspects of community social work practice.

Social Networks

For at least the past decade, social workers have been increasingly interested in identifying, supporting, and creating social networks, both to enhance support for clients and to buttress other interventions (Tracy & Whittaker, 1990; Whittaker et al., 1983). Rubin and Rubin (1992) defined a social network as "a pattern of linked relationships across which help and information flow on a particular issue" (p. 86). Networks may consist of family and kin, friends, workmates, church members, or people who come together around a shared concern. There is growing recognition of the centrality of social networks to efforts to build community, particularly within emergent ethnic communities (Daley & Wong, 1994; Lewis & Ford, 1990). Robust social networks provide members with material assistance and services (caretaking), emotional nurturance and counseling, problem-solving advice and referral, and a forum for collective action and advocacy (Eng, Salmon, & Mullan, 1992).

The Social Network Map (Tracy & Whittaker, 1990) enables workers and clients to assess the nature and availability of social network supports. Developed primarily for use with individuals, it also has the potential to be used with groups to determine patterns of support and isolation in communities. Although natural networks constitute an important resource in community practice, social workers must be careful not to overburden or disempower natural helpers. Nor can it be assumed that all networks are supportive; some, such as those in drug-ridden communities, are toxic to their members, and others may not be perceived in positive terms (Brodsky, 1997). Nonetheless, interventions designed to strengthen the supportive functions of naturally occurring social networks and to encourage new connections between community members are an important element of community building.

Social Programs

It is not always possible or reasonable to rely on informal social networks as primary sources of community change. Some communities and their natural support systems, such as those in inner-city neighborhoods, are so depleted and overextended that little more can be asked of them (Garbarino, Kostelny, & Dubrow, 1991; Halpern, 1993). In such environments, it is important for social programs to offer opportunities for connection, safety, support, recovery, and action that in different circumstances would have been provided by networks of kin and friends. Provided they are culturally relevant, the social networks formed in community-based programs such as the Head Start Family Support Centers (Lightburn & Kemp, 1994) are an important link in the chain from individual empowerment to community transformation. Empowering program communities provide a safe haven in violent and isolated environments, enable the development of individual and collective skills and resources, and provide a springboard for action in the wider environment. A commitment to developing, supporting, and working in such programs is thus an important, although neglected, dimension of community practice.

Asset-Based Social Welfare Programs and Community Development

Asset-based social welfare is an approach to community development that focuses on increasing the assets of low-income individuals. Michael Sherraden (1990, 1991) argues that government social and tax policies increase the wealth of middle- and upper-income citizens, but cause lower-income populations to forego opportunities to accumulate assets. He proposes a shift to social welfare and tax policies that allow low-income citizens to have access to savings accounts, investments, owner-occupation of homes, and business opportunities. His asset-based welfare model is currently influencing neighborhood agencies, housing developers, and youth agencies to construct structured savings programs (Individual Development Accounts), small business development for the poor (micro-enterprise programs), and targeted low-income homeownership programs (Scanlon, 1998). All of these programs attempt to build the assets of low-income citizens, often in targeted geographic contexts. Evaluations of recent asset-accumulation efforts demonstrate that the poor do have the capacity to save, invest, and become homeowners, particularly when structured program supports are in place (Sherraden et al., 2000).

Sherraden's theory of asset-based social welfare is partially rooted in the tradition of community economic development (CED). This work has been described as "corrective capitalism" because it endeavors to extend market opportunities and economic resources to communities bypassed by capitalist development (Peirce & Steinbach, 1987). CED developed in the early 1970s as a response to spatially concentrated poverty, de-industrialization, and economic stagnation (Perry, 1987). CED activities often take place in community development corporations (CDCs), which have grown in strength and number since the early 1980s (Peirce & Steinbach, 1987). Other organizations, such as credit unions, nonprofit housing agencies, community action agencies, and youth job training programs also engage in community economic development practices. More specifically, these programs are designed to provide housing, jobs, human capital, job training, and access to banking services and business capital. In a similar vein, Midgley (1999) argues that social service programs should be tied to economic investment and positive economic outcomes. He contends that this sort of "productivist" framework offers an alternative paradigm for social work, which he sees as overly focused on service provision rather than on development of the capacities and resources of communities.

Challenging Social Systems

Although many community practice approaches emphasize the importance and value of consensus and collaboration, there will always be instances in which individual and community needs cannot be met by such an approach. In these situations, social workers often become involved in advocacy and social action on behalf of community members. It is at this point, also, that many social workers become uncomfortable with community interventions.

Advocacy at the community level is concerned with improving services and resources for people as a group (class advocacy) rather than for a specific client at a particular time (case advocacy). A helpful guideline for the use of confrontational tactics is provided by Middleman and Goldberg (1974), who suggested that social workers should apply the principle of "least contest" in their choice of interventive strategies. That is, less-confrontational tactics should be used before those that escalate conflict. Middleman and Goldberg suggested a hierarchy of interventive roles, ranging from mediation to advocacy. McGowan (1978), who also promoted a strategic approach to the use of advocacy, listed the following methods:

- intercession (request, plead, persist);
- persuasion (inform, instruct, clarify, explain, argue);
- negotiation (dialogue, sympathize, bargain, placate);
- pressure (threaten, challenge, disregard);
- coercion (deceive, disrupt, administrative redress, legal action); and
- indirect (client education, community organizing, system dodging, constructing alternatives).

Even when the decision has been made to challenge social and institutional structures, workers thus have recourse to a range of strategies and can select from among them those most appropriate given the developmental stage of the project, the level of comfort of community members with conflict, and the nature of the target system.

Monitoring and Evaluating Community Practice

An extensive body of literature is available on the formal evaluation of community-based programs and services. Although a review of this literature is beyond the scope of this chapter, social workers involved in program development and implementation at the community level should certainly become familiar with it (for examples of particular relevance to empowering community practice, see Fetterman, Kaftarian, & Wandersman, 1996).

Although little has been written to guide the community practitioner in ongoing monitoring of his or her practice in the community, empowering community practice necessarily incorporates systematic practice monitoring as workers and community residents in partnership learn about community needs, determine actions to be taken, and continuously monitor the efficacy and fit of community-building activities. This collaborative and ongoing process of monitoring and feedback is essential to the integrity of an empowerment approach, which relies at its core on the reflexive interplay between action and reflection (see, for example, Parsons, 1998; Ristock & Pennell, 1996; Sohng, 1998). In empowering community practice, social workers and community should together determine how progress and outcomes will be assessed and by what means data will be used as a base for reflection and further action. Preferably, data collection will include both qualitative and quantitative approaches to encompass the stories that people tell about the process of community change as well as progress on desired outcomes at the personal, interpersonal, and community levels. In the process of generating knowledge, community members become the owners as well as the providers of information on their community, participating as equals and full citizens in defining and redefining the relationships between knowledge and power in their community context.

References

Allen, J. A. (1993). The constructivist paradigm: Values and ethics. *Journal of Teaching in Social Work, 8*(1–2), 31–54.

Anderson, H., & Goolishian, H. (1992). The client is the expert: A not-knowing approach to therapy. In S. McNamee & K. J. Gergen (Eds.), *Therapy as social construction* (pp. 25–39). Newbury Park, CA: Sage Publications.

Auerswald, E. H. (1968). Interdisciplinary versus ecological approach. *Family Process, 7*, 202–215.

Barker, R. L. (1995). *The social work dictionary* (3rd ed.). Washington, DC: NASW Press.

Bellah, R. N., Madsen, R., Sullivan, W. M., Swidler, A., & Tipton, S. M. (1985). *Habits of the heart: Individualism and commitment in American life.* New York: Harper & Row.

Berger, P. L., & Neuhaus, R. J. (1977). *To empower people: The role of mediating structures in public policy.* Washington, DC: American Enterprise Institute for Public Policy Research.

Bradshaw, C., Soifer, S., & Gutierrez, L. (1994). Toward a hybrid model for effective organizing in communities of color. *Journal of Community Practice, 1*(1), 25–41.

Briscoe, R. V., Hoffman, D. B., & Bailey, J. S. (1975). Behavioral community psychology: Training a community board to problem solve. *Journal of Applied Behavior Analysis, 8*, 157–168.

Brodsky, A. E. (1997). Resilient single mothers in risky neighborhoods: Negative psychological sense of community. *Journal of Community Psychology, 24*, 347–363.

Brooks-Gunn, J., Duncan, G. J., & Aber, J. L. (Eds.). (1997). *Neighborhood poverty. Volume II: Policy implications in studying neighborhoods.* New York: Russell Sage Foundation.

Brown, K. S., & Ziefert, M. (1988). Crisis resolution, competence and empowerment: A service model for women. *Journal of Primary Prevention, 9*, 92–103.

Chaskin, R. J. (1995). *Defining neighborhood: History, theory, and practice.* Chicago: Chapin Hall Center for Children.

Chaskin, R. J. (1997). Perspectives on neighborhood and community: A review of the literature. *Social Service Review, 71*, 521–547.

Chavis, D. M., & Wandersman, A. (1990). Sense of community in the urban environment: A catalyst for participation and community development. *American Journal of Community Psychology, 18*, 55–81.

Cottrell, L. S., Jr. (1977). The competent community. In R. L. Warren (Ed.), *New perspectives on the American community: A book of readings* (3rd ed., pp. 546–560). Chicago: Rand McNally.

Coulton, C. J. (1995). Riding the pendulum of the 1990s: Building a community context for social work research. *Social Work, 40*, 437–439.

Coulton, C.J. (1995). Using community-level indicators of children's well-being in comprehensive community initiatives. In J. P. Connell, A. C. Kubisch, L. B. Schorr, & C. H. Weiss (Eds.), *New approaches to evaluating community initiatives: Concepts, methods and contexts.* Washington, DC: Aspen Institute.

Coulton, C. J., Korbin, J. E., & Su, M. (1996). Measuring neighborhood context for young children in an urban area. *American Journal of Community Psychology, 24*(1), 5–32.

Cox, E. O. (1991). The critical role of social action in empowerment oriented groups. *Social Work with Groups, 14*(2), 77–90.

Cox, F. M. (1987). Communities: Alternative conceptions of community: Implications for community organization practice. In F. M. Cox, J. L. Erlich, J. Rothman, & J. E. Tropman (Eds.), *Strategies of community organization: Macro practice* (4th ed., pp. 232–243). Itasca, IL: F. E. Peacock.

Curtis, K. A. (1989). Help from within: Participatory research in a low-income neighborhood. *Urban Anthropology, 18*, 203–217.

Daley, J. M., & Wong, P. (1994). Community development with emerging ethnic communities. *Journal of Community Practice, 1*(1), 9–24.

Delgado, M. (1996). Community assessment by Latino youths. *Social Work in Education, 18*, 169–178.

Dodd, P., & Gutierrez, L. (1990). Preparing students for the future: A power perspective on community practice. *Administration in Social Work, 14*(2), 63–78.

Eng, E., Salmon, M. E., & Mullan, F. (1992). Community empowerment: The critical base for primary health care. *Family and Community Health, 15*, 1–12.

Etzioni, A. (1993). *The spirit of community: The reinvention of American society.* New York: Touchstone.

Fagan, T. (1987). Neighborhood education, mobilization, and organization for juvenile crime prevention. *Annals of the American Academy of Political and Social Science, 494*, 54–70.

Fawcett, S. B. (1991). Some values guiding community research and action. *Journal of Applied Behavior Analysis, 24*, 621–636.

Fawcett, S. B., Seekins, T., Whang, P. L., Muiu, C., & Suarez de Balcazar, Y. (1980). Involving consumers in decision making. *Social Policy, 13*(2), 36–41.

Fawcett, S. B., Seekins, T., Whang, P. L., & Suarez de Balcazar, Y. (1984). Creating and using technologies for community empowerment. *Prevention in Human Services, 3*, 145–171.

Fetterman, D. M., Kaftarian, S. J., & Wandersman, A. (Eds.). (1996). *Empowerment evaluation: Knowledge and tools for self-assessment and accountability.* Thousand Oaks, CA: Sage Publications.

Freire, P. (1973). *Education for critical consciousness.* New York: Seabury Press.

Garbarino, T., Kostelny, K., & Dubrow, N. (1991). *No place to be a child: Growing up in a war zone.* Lexington, MA: Lexington Books.

Germain, C. B. (1985). The place of community work within an ecological approach to social work practice. In S. H. Taylor & R. W. Roberts (Eds.), *Theory and practice of community social work* (pp. 30–55). New York: Columbia University Press.

Gutierrez, L. M. (1990). Working with women of color: An empowerment perspective. *Social Work, 35,* 149–153.

Hagan, T., & Smail, D. (1997). Power-mapping—I. Background and basic methodology. *Journal of Community and Applied Social Psychology, 7,* 257–267.

Halpern, R. (1993). Neighborhood-based initiative to address poverty: Lessons from experience. *Journal of Sociology and Social Welfare, 20,* 111–135.

Hardcastle, D. A., Wenocur, S., & Powers, P. R. (1997). *Community practice: Theories and skills for social workers.* New York: Oxford University Press.

Heller, K. (1989). The return to community. *American Journal of Community Psychology, 17,* 1–15.

Hoefer, R. A., Hoefer, R., & Tobias, R.A. (1994). Geographic information systems and human services. *Journal of Community Practice, 1,* 3, 113–128.

Holland, T. P., & Kilpatrick, A. C. (1993). Using narrative techniques to enhance multicultural practice. *Journal of Social Work Education, 29,* 302–308.

Hyde, C. (1996). A feminist response to Rothman's "The interweaving of community intervention approaches." *Journal of Community Practice, 3*(3/4), 127–145.

Itzhaky, H., & York, A. S. (1991). Client participation and the effectiveness of community social work intervention. *Research on Social Work Practice, 1,* 387–398.

Johnson, L. C. (1992). *Social work practice: A generalist approach* (4th ed.). Boston: Allyn & Bacon.

Keenan, E., & Pinkerton, J. (1991). Some aspects of empowerment: A case study of work with disadvantaged youth. *Social Work with Groups, 14*(2), 109–124.

Kemp, S. P., Whittaker, J. K., & Tracy, E. M. (1997). *Person–environment practice: The social ecology of interpersonal helping.* New York: Aldine de Gruyter.

Korbin, J. E., & Coulton, C. J. (1997). Understanding the neighborhood context for children and families: Combining epidemiological and ethnographic approaches. In J. Brooks-Gunn, G. J. Duncan, & J. L. Aber (Eds.), *Neighborhood poverty. Volume II: Policy implications in studying neighborhoods* (pp. 65–79). New York: Russell Sage Foundation.

Kingsley, T. J. (1998). *Neighborhood indicators: Taking advantage of the new potential.* Working Paper. Chicago: American Planning Association.

Kretzmann, J. P., & McKnight, J. L. (1993). *Building communities from the inside out: A path toward finding and mobilizing a community's assets.* Chicago: ACTA Publications.

Laird, J. (1993). Family-centered practice: Cultural and constructionist reflections. *Journal of Teaching in Social Work, 8,* 77–109.

Leigh, J. W. (1997). *Communicating for cultural competence.* Boston: Allyn & Bacon.

Lewis, E. A., & Ford, B. (1990). The Network Utilization Project: Incorporating traditional strengths of African-American families in group work practice. *Social Work with Groups, 13*(4), 7–22.

Lightburn, A., & Black, R. (in press). *Social workers as educators.* New York: Columbia University Press.

Lightburn, A., & Kemp, S. P. (1994). Family-support programs: Opportunities for community-based practice. *Families in Society, 75*(1), 16–26.

Longres, J. F., & McLeod, E. (1980). Consciousness raising and social work practice. *Social Casework, 61,* 267–275.

Maluccio, A. (Ed.). (1981). *Promoting competence in clients.* London: Free Press.

Mattaini, M. A. (1993a). Behavior analysis and community practice: A review. *Research on Social Work Practice, 3,* 420–447.

Mattaini, M. A. (1993b). *More than a thousand words: Graphics for clinical practice.* Washington, DC: NASW Press.

Mattaini, M. A., & Kirk, S. A. (1991). Assessing assessment in social work. *Social Work, 36,* 260–266.

McGowan, B. G. (1978). The case advocacy function in child welfare practice. *Child Welfare, 57,* 275–284.

McKnight, J. L. (1997). A 21st-century map for healthy communities and families. *Families in Society, 78,* 117–127.

Meyer, C. H. (Ed.). (1983). *Clinical social work in the eco-systems perspective.* New York: Columbia University Press.

Middleman, R. R., & Goldberg, G. (1974). *Social service delivery: A structural approach to social work practice.* New York: Columbia University Press.

Midgley, J. (1999). Growth, redistribution, and welfare: Toward social investment. *Social Service Review, 73,* 1, 3–21.

Mondros, J. B., & Berman-Rossi, T. (1991). The relevance of stages of group development theory to community organization practice. *Social Work with Groups, 14*(3–4), 203–221.

Murray, M. (1995). Correction at Cabrini-Green. *Environment and Planning: Society and Space, 13,* 311–327.

Nurius, P. S., Kemp, S. P., & Gibson, J. W. (1999). Practitioners' perspectives on sound reasoning: Adding a worker-in-context component. *Administration in Social Work, 23,* 1–27.

Parsons, R. J. (1991). Empowerment: Purpose and practice principle in social work. *Social Work with Groups, 14*(2), 7–21.

Parsons, R. J. (1998). Evaluation of empowerment practice. In L. Gutierrez, R. J. Parsons, & E. O. Cox (Eds.), *Empowerment in social work practice: A sourcebook* (pp. 204–219). Pacific Grove, CA: Brooks/Cole.

Parsons, R J., Jorgensen, J. D., & Hernandez, S. H. (1994). *The integration of social work practice*. Pacific Grove, CA: Brooks/Cole.

Pecukonis, E. V., & Wenocur, S. (1994). Perceptions of self and collective efficacy in community organization theory and practice. *Journal of Community Practice, 1*(2), 5–21.

Peirce, N. & Steinbach, C. (1987). *Corrective capitalism: The rise of America's Community Development Corporations*. New York: Ford Foundation.

Perry, S. (1987). *Communities on the way: Rebuilding local communities in the United States and Canada*. Albany, NY: State University of New York Press.

Poole, D. L. (1997). Building community capacity to promote social and public health: Challenges for universities [Editorial]. *Health & Social Work, 22,* 165–170.

Ramey, J. H. (1992). Group work practice in neighborhood centers today. *Social Work with Groups, 15*(2–3), 193–206.

Rapp, C. A., Shera, W., & Kisthart, W. (1993). Research strategies for empowerment of people with severe mental illness. *Social Work, 38,* 727–735.

Rappaport, J. (1987). Terms of empowerment/exemplars of prevention: Toward a theory for community psychology. *American Journal of Community Psychology, 15,* 121–145.

Rich, R. C., Edelstein, M., Hallman, W. K., & Wandersman, A. H. (1995). Citizen participation and empowerment: The case of local environmental hazards. *American Journal of Community Psychology, 23,* 657–676.

Ristock, J. L., & Pennell, J. (1996). *Community research as empowerment: Feminist links, postmodern interruptions*. New York: Oxford University Press.

Rivera, F. G., & Erlich, J. L. (Eds.). (1992). *Community organizing in a diverse society*. Boston: Allyn & Bacon.

Rosen, A., & Livne, S. (1992). Personal versus environmental emphases in formulation of client problems. *Social Work Research & Abstracts, 29*(4), 12–17.

Rothman, J. (1970). Three models of community organization practice. In F. M. Cox, J. L. Erlich, J. Rothman, & J. E. Tropman (Eds.), *Strategies of community organization: A book of readings* (pp. 20–36). Itasca, IL: F. E. Peacock.

Rothman, J., & Tropman, J. E. (1987). Models of community organization and macro practice perspectives: Their mixing and phasing. In F. M. Cox, J. L. Erlich, J. Rothman, & J. E. Tropman (Eds.), *Strategies of community organization: Macro practice* (4th ed., pp. 3–26). Itasca, IL: F. E. Peacock.

Rubin, H. J., & Rubin, I. S. (1992). *Community organizing and development* (2nd ed.). New York: Maxwell.

Rupp, G. (1991). Communities of collaboration: Shared commitments/common tasks. In L. S. Rouner (Ed.), *On community* (pp. 192–208). Notre Dame, IN: University of Notre Dame Press.

Saleebey, D. (Ed.). (1992). *The strengths perspective in social work practice*. New York: Longman.

Saleebey, D. (1994). Culture, theory, and narrative: The intersection of meanings in practice. *Social Work, 39*, 351–359.

Sarri, R. C., & Sarri, C. M. (1992). Organizational and community change through participatory action research. *Administration in Social Work, 16*, 99–122.

Scanlon, E. (1998). Low-income homeownership policy as a community development strategy. *Journal of Community Practice, 5* (2), 137–154.

Schulz, A. J., Israel, B. A., Zimmerman, M. A., & Checkoway, B. N. (1995). Empowerment as a multi-level construct: Perceived control at the individual, organizational and community levels. *Health Education Research: Theory and Practice, 10* (3), 309–327.

Sheafor, B. W., Horejsi, C. R., & Horejsi, G. A. (1991). *Techniques and guidelines for social work practice* (2nd ed.). Boston: Allyn & Bacon.

Sherraden, M. (1990). Stakeholding: Notes on a theory of welfare based on assets. *Social Service Review, 64*, 4, 580–601.

Sherraden, M. (1991). *Assets and the poor: A new American welfare policy*. Armonk, NY: Sharpe.

Sherraden, M., Johnson, L., Clancy, M., Beverly, S., Schreiner, M., Zahn, M., & Curley, J. (2000). *Savings patterns in IDA programs*. St. Louis: Washington University.

Simon, B. L. (1990). Rethinking empowerment. *Journal of Progressive Human Services, 1*(1), 27–39.

Simon, B. L. (1994). *The empowerment tradition in American social work: A history*. New York: Columbia University Press.

Sohng, S. S. L. (1998). Research as an empowerment strategy. In L. M. Gutierrez, R. J. Parsons, & E. O. Cox (Eds.), *Empowerment in social work practice: A sourcebook* (pp. 187–203). Pacific Grove, CA: Brooks/Cole.

Sullivan, W. P. (1992). Reconsidering the environment as a helping resource. In D. Saleebey (Ed.), *The strengths perspective in social work practice* (pp. 148–157). New York: Longman.

Sviridoff, M., & Ryan, W. (1997). Community-centered family service. *Families in Society, 78*, 128–139.

Taylor, S. H., & Roberts, R. W. (1985). The fluidity of practice theory: An overview. In S. H. Taylor & R. W. Roberts (Eds.), *Theory and practice of community social work* (pp. 3–29). New York: Columbia University Press.

Tompkins, P. L., & Southward, L. H. (1998). Geographic information systems: Implications for promoting economic and social justice. *Computers in Human Services, 15*, 2/3, 209–226.

Tracy, E. M., & Whittaker, J. K. (1990). The social network map: Assessing social support in clinical social work practice. *Families in Society, 71*, 461–470.

Van Den Bergh, N., & Cooper, L. B. (Eds.). (1986). *Feminist visions for social work*. Silver Spring, MD: National Association of Social Workers.

Warren, R. L. (1978). *The community in America* (3rd ed.). Chicago: Rand McNally.

Webber, M. (1963). Order in diversity: Community without propinquity. In L. Wingo, Jr. (Ed.), *Cities and space: The future use of urban land* (pp. 23–54). Baltimore: Johns Hopkins University Press.

Weick, A. (1993). Reconstructing social work education. *Journal of Teaching in Social Work, 8*(1–2), 11–30.

Weil, M. (1986). Women, community, and organizing. In N. Van Den Bergh & L. B. Cooper (Eds.), *Feminist visions for social work* (pp. 187–210). Silver Spring, MD: National Association of Social Workers.

Weil, M. (1994). Editor's introduction to the journal. *Journal of Community Practice, 1*(1), xxi–xxii.

Weil, M., & Gamble, D. N. (1995). Community practice models. In R. L. Edwards (Ed.-in-Chief), *Encyclopedia of social work* (19th ed., Vol. 1, pp. 577–594). Washington, DC: NASW Press.

Wellman, B., & Gulia, M. (1995). When social networks meet computer networks: The policy implications of virtual communities. Paper presented to the American Sociological Association, Washington, DC.

Wellman, B., Salaff, J., Dimitrova, D., Garton, L., Gulia, M., & Haythornethwaite, C. (1996). Computer networks as social networks: Collaborative work, telework, and virtual community. *Annual Review of Sociology, 22,* 213–238.

White, M., & Epston, D. (1990). *Narrative means to therapeutic ends.* New York: W. W. Norton.

Whittaker, J. K., Garbarino, J., & Associates. (1983). *Social support networks: Informal helping in the human services.* New York: Aldine.

Wood, G. G., & Middleman, R. R. (1991). Advocacy and social action: Key elements in the structural approach to direct practice in social work. *Social Work with Groups, 14*(3–4), 53–63.

Zimmerman, M. A., & Rappaport, J. (1988). Citizen participation, perceived control and psychological empowerment. *American Journal of Community Psychology, 16,* 725–750.

CHAPTER 11

Practice with Organizations

Meredith Hanson

Humans always have been and always will be group people (Johnson & Johnson, 2000), and in modern society many of the groups in which we live take the form of complex, formal organizations. In 1964, Amitai Etzioni introduced his classic primer on modern organizations by writing ours "is an organizational society."

> We are born in organizations, educated by organizations, and most of us spend much of our lives working for organizations. We spend much of our leisure time paying, playing and praying in organizations. Most of us will die in an organization, and when the time comes for burial, the largest organization of all—the state—must grant official permission (p. 1).

Fifteen years later, Carol Meyer (1979) added that "functions once thought to be private and belonging to the family and the intimate community have been transferred to institutions or organizations that are, in sanction and function, 'public'" (p. 1).

In this organizational society, in which public institutions have taken over many private functions, social workers are the organizational professionals who aid many of our most vulnerable citizens as they travel through institutional and organizational mazes during times of personal crises. Most social workers carry out their functions as employees and affiliates of social and human services organizations.

The social agency is "the hidden reality of social work" (Weissman, Epstein, & Savage, 1983, p. 3). It is "the locus of practice and professional services" (Vinter, 1959, p. 242). From the earliest days of the charity organization societies and settlement houses, social work's existence has been tied firmly to social agencies. "Unlike other professions, social work was almost exclusively a corporate activity, with little opportunity for independent practice.

To carve out a niche, the social worker had to attain hegemony within the agency" (Lubove, 1965, p. 159).

Although most social work practice occurs in social and human service agencies (Hasenfeld, 1983) and host settings like the military and business corporations (Dane & Simon, 1991; Kurzman & Akabas, 1993), many professional social workers do not grasp the extent to which organizational context affects practice. Nor do they understand how they can influence their agencies. Consequently, they miss opportunities to intervene in agency policies and procedures to keep them responsive to clients' needs and congruent with social work values and ethics.

Social work practice settings shape social work practice (Hartman, 1993; Zald, 2001). Social agencies legitimize and sanction social services (Hasenfeld, 1983). They control many of the resources social workers need to assist clients (Hasenfeld, 1987; Toseland & Rivas, 1998). Agency function delimits the forms and goals of practice (Vinter, 1959). Ultimately, by vesting social workers with authority, the practice setting becomes a major source of power for social workers, who embody "the mission, function, structures, and policies of the organization" (Gitterman, 1989, p. 166). Conflicts between agencies and professionals may lead to a loss of benefits and services for clients, low morale among workers, and organizational dysfunction and decline (Lipsky, 1984; Marriott, Sexton, & Staley, 1994).

This chapter is about social work practice in and with organizations. It introduces readers to the work setting as a context, target, and means of professional influence. It defines social and human service agencies, discusses several organizational components that are central to understanding agency dynamics, and illustrates ways to assess, influence, and use organizational structures and processes to promote client autonomy and community well-being.

Definitions

Social and Human Service Agencies

Social and human service agencies are formal organizations with stated purposes to enhance "the social, emotional, physical, and/or intellectual well-being of some component of the population" (Brager & Holloway, 1978, p. 2). They include such diverse practice settings as hospitals, schools, family services agencies, nursing homes, settlement houses, employee assistance programs, domestic violence shelters, and prisons. They differ from other organizations with similar aims in at least two key ways. First, their "raw materials" are people who become clients and are transformed, processed, or assisted in some specified manner. Secondly, society mandates them to serve both client interests and societal interests (Hasenfeld, 1983, 1992a).

We (that is, society) create human service agencies to address personal and social problems and to promote equity and social justice. As such, they are products of ambivalent and contradictory societal ideologies (Brager & Holloway, 1978; Sarri & Hasenfeld, 1978). Services contain implicit and explicit meanings about the worth of clients, as well as societal expectations for how people ought to behave and be treated. Thus, human service agencies engage in "moral work" (Hasenfeld, 1992a).

Because their raw materials are people, and they owe their existence to societal mandates and political policies (for example, financing and sanction), human service agencies are highly dependent on their external environments. Consequently, environmental factors, such as a changing political climate and economic conditions, influence agency operations profoundly. In such circumstances, management can become preoccupied with organizational survival, and individual workers can become absorbed with their personal survival in the agency. In the process, the interests of the clients can be lost.

Agencies are accountable to multiple and shifting constituent groups with conflicting interests and agendas (Martin, 1987; Perrow, 1978; Taber, 1987). Attempts to be responsive to one group may interfere with an agency's ability to be accountable to another. For example, the current health care environment is economically driven. Reform efforts designed to contain rising health care costs have affected access to care (through insurance and reimbursement policies) and quality of care (e.g., by specifying which services are reimbursable and by favoring out-patient and shorter-term treatments). Competing mandates to control costs and to provide access to quality care create potential ethical and role conflicts for social workers who try to balance the cost containment interests of insurance groups and other funders with the treatment needs of clients. They often encounter these conflicts when agencies struggle with managed care providers over clinical decision making. The resolution of the conflicts affects not only the social worker's decision about what services to recommend but also clients' decisions about undergoing the treatment.

Although we establish social agencies to serve particular client groups, agency goals are not defined unilaterally. Goals evolve out of negotiations between human service organizations and their constituents, including funders, political groups, and community members. Although professional codes of ethics may prescribe service ideals that give primacy to client interests, human services agencies are not bound to place individual client interests above those of the agency (Gouldner, 1963; McGowan, 1978;

Rhodes, 1991; Vinter, 1959). It is in the context of these organizational arrangements and competing interests that ethical questions emerge and can be understood (Walsh-Bowers, Rossiter, & Prilleltensky, 1996). For example, because of funding constraints agencies may try to simplify technologies and routinize procedures. As complexity decreases, supervision and staff management costs decrease, thus saving the agency money (Savage, 1987). These changes, however, may limit and devalue the complexity of clinical practice, and they may actually impede the agency's capacity to meet client-related service goals effectively. Thus, social workers must resolve value dilemmas as they decide whether to comply with agency procedures or question and challenge them.

Formal Organizations

To fully understand the forces that affect social work practice settings, social workers must comprehend formal organizations. Writers have proposed literally hundreds of definitions for formal organizations. Some definitions overlap, others are contradictory, but all reflect particular theoretical perspectives (Bolman & Deal, 1997; Hasenfeld, 1992b; Katz & Kahn, 1978; Morgan, 1997; Perrow, 1986; Scott, 1992; Shafritz & Ott, 2001). At the most basic level, an organization is any social unit with identifiable boundaries that has evolved or been created to attain some purpose or purposes. *Formal organizations*, such as social and human services agencies, are social units that have been "consciously designed *a priori*" (Blau & Scott, 1962, p. 5). Written policies, rules, and procedures that guide routine interactions characterize formal organizations. Formal organizations usually are complex. That is, they employ personnel from several professional disciplines who perform intricate tasks that require specialized education or training (Hage & Aiken, 1970).

Traditionally, formal organizations have been depicted as goal-oriented, rationally designed, thinking machines. The word "organization," itself, is derived from the Greek word *organon,* which means tool or instrument (Morgan, 1997). Thus, it is not surprising that the first definitions of formal organizations emphasized their bureaucratic administrative structures and underscored such rational features as goals (purposes), hierarchical authority structures, divisions of labor, and specialized task arrangements (Gerth & Mills, 1958; Weber, 1924/1947). Classical theorists saw organizations as the means through which goals were achieved. They distinguished formal organizations from other social systems by their rational-legal nature and the priority they placed on goal attainment. Classical analyses focused on mechanisms and organizational arrangements that affected efficiency and effectiveness.

Sidebar 11-1. Diversity in Organizations

Organizational diversity has many sources including the professional disciplines of an agency's membership, demographic and personal characteristics, professional interests and job functions, and individual skills and capacities. Effective organizations and work groups accept, value, and promote diversity. A considerable amount of research demonstrates the positive impact of diversity on organizational climate and productivity. Job satisfaction and turnover, for example, are related to employees' perceptions that they fit into an agency and the agency values their contributions (Chernesky, 1998). Diversity among organizational members deters "group think" and helps ensure that multiple points of view are applied to work assignments. Work groups with members who have heterogeneous technical skills tend to perform better in production tasks (Jackson, 1992). Groups whose members have complementary and heterogeneous abilities out-perform more homogeneous groups in decision-making tasks (Johnson & Johnson, 1989). Homogeneous groups tend to avoid risks; they lack controversy and may become dull. The "clash of perspectives" and contention that are so important to high-quality performance and creative decision making often are missing in less diverse organizations (Johnson & Johnson, 2000).

While many benefits accrue from organizational diversity, diversity can lead to undesirable and harmful consequences. For example, the increased conflict associated with heterogeneity raises tensions in organizations. Turnover rates seem to be higher and cohesion may be lower in diverse work groups (e. g., Johnson & Johnson, 2000; O'Reilly, Caldwell, & Barnett, 1989; Terborg, Castore, & DeNinno, 1976). As a result, social agencies that do not attend to the potential negative consequences of diversity may experience divisiveness, excessive bias, stereotyping, and poorer performance.

Organizations that promote and value diversity act in proactive ways to recognize and appreciate the expertise diverse members offer. They strive to transform organizational culture and become multicultural (Chernesky, 1997; Gutierrez & Lewis, 1999; Loden & Rosener, 1991). To maximize the benefits and reduce harmful consequences associated with diversity, it must be recognized that diversity is a fact of life, which cannot and should not be avoided. Agencies must establish constructive mechanisms and forums for managing conflict when it arises. Policies that bar discrimination and encourage difference must be established (Chernesky, 1998). In-service training activities that enhance cultural competence and appreciation for diversity must be implemented. Rituals that bring agency employees, clients, and others together in ways that celebrate diversity can be instituted. Social agencies dealing with diversity should not aim to homogenize themselves. Rather, the goal should be to encourage members to collaborate "to achieve mutual goals while recognizing their diversity . . . and valuing and respecting fundamental differences" (Johnson & Johnson, 2000, p. 473).

As knowledge about formal organizations developed, many scholars became disenchanted with the mechanistic classical definitions, and they crafted new conceptualizations, which highlighted other organizational features. For example, *natural systems paradigms,* similar to the human relations school, emphasized the relevance of noneconomic, social rewards and informal communication and leadership structures for understanding organizational dynamics (Etzioni, 1964). These new conceptualizations drew attention to behavioral and normative patterns that emerged as organizational members attempted to minimize stress and organizations tried to survive and maintain themselves (Scott, 1992). Organizational culture, the shared norms, beliefs, values, symbols, and rituals that give meaning, direction, and guidelines for individual and collective behavior, became a focus of study (Bolman & Deal, 1997; Edwards & Gummer, 1988).

Open-systems frameworks expanded on classical definitions by underscoring organizations' links with their environments. They depicted organizations as loosely coupled sets of interrelated, interacting subsystems (Buckley, 1967; Morgan, 1997). Proponents of these views argued that an organization's form is determined, to a large extent, through environmental exchanges (Lawrence & Lorsch, 1967; Scott, 1992).

Many other definitions of formal organizations, which attempt to integrate earlier perspectives and account for new knowledge, have emerged (see Bolman & Deal, 1997; Hasenfeld, 1992b; Morgan, 1997; Scott, 1992; Shafritz & Ott, 2001). Each definition is a metaphor of sorts that provides an important, albeit incomplete, image of reality. Taken together, they suggest that formal organizations are rationally based social entities, characterized by predictable and habitual interaction patterns (organizational structures) that are explicitly arranged for the accomplishment of stated purposes. They are organic, dynamic, and open systems in which alliances form and reform among organizational members and interest groups as they try to meet organizational goals and their own interests. Typically, organizations develop unique cultures and multiple formal and informal power centers that affect their operations. As open systems they respond not only to internal institutional pressures, but also to external political, economic, and social forces in the environment.

Key Components of Formal Organizations

Organizational theorists (for example, Leavitt, 1965; Scott, 1992) and students of human services agencies (for example, Brager & Holloway, 1978; Hasenfeld, 1983; Weissman, Epstein, & Savage, 1983) suggest that to understand their practice setting, social workers should attend to five key components of organizations. These components are depicted in Table 11-1:

Table 11-1. Key Components of Organizations	
Goals	An agency's officially stated mission, as well as the operating policies that are established to maintain smooth functioning and survival in shifting environments. Typically, agencies have multiple stated and unstated goals, which may compete with and complement each other.
Internal Structures and Culture	Formal and informal habitual interaction patterns. Internal structures provide the framework through which an agency implements its service mission and agency members gain support, validation, and guidance. Informal structural processes in the form of an organization's culture affect an agency's operations by creating a climate that gives primacy to particular values, practices, and goals.
Service Technologies and Programs	The activities, tools, and practices human service agencies use to assist clients. Human service technologies are "intensive," "indeterminate," and sensitive to environmental pressures.
Membership Interests and Characteristics	Organization members are social actors who carry out an agency's work. An organization's members are stakeholders who have an interest in the agency's programs, as well as their own place in the agency. To understand their actions one must examine the positions they hold, the power and resources they control, their reference groups and linkages with other organizational members, and the impact of specific agency processes and changes on their work lives.
Environmental Context	A multidimensional set of interacting external forces that affect an agency's operations and structures. An agency's external environment can be understood as a set of concentric circles that consist of the distal environment, proximal geographic and sociocultural surroundings, and task environment.

(1) goals (stated mission or purpose) and other external and internal demands faced by an agency; (2) internal structures and culture; (3) service technologies and programs; (4) membership interests and characteristics; and (5) environmental context, including physical setting, prevailing mood, and resources.

Goals

An agency's goals represent its efforts to respond to multiple demands: to serve clients, to maintain smooth internal operations, and to adapt to shifting environmental conditions. One would expect an agency's goals to be complementary. However, several factors can lead to displacement and conflict among goals. Consider, for example, the goals of service. An agency's service goals include official goals, as articulated in mission statements and other public pronouncements, and operative goals that outline actual operating policies (Perrow, 1961). Official goals usually are formulated in vague, overly broad terms to maintain maximum support among key constituent groups. Operative goals, in contrast, are more precise and reveal how an agency makes daily program decisions and allocates scarce resources such as money and staff. Operative goals reflect not only an agency's efforts to fulfill its mission, but also its attempts to maintain itself and remain adaptive.

When responding to competing pressures, official service goals may be subverted and other, sometimes covert, goals may emerge. For example, many mental health clinics establish waiting lists to prevent social workers' caseloads from getting too large and to ensure that clients receive adequate clinical services. Although these procedures may facilitate efficient clinic operations and be consistent with professional standards, they can become organizational barriers to service delivery. It is well documented that long waiting lists make service unavailable and inaccessible to many people. Furthermore, long waiting lists and lengthy intake procedures can serve latent purposes by enabling agencies to "cream off" pools of preferred (i.e., "motivated") clients who are most likely to accept the agencies' "brand" of service (Brager & Holloway, 1978; Gitterman & Miller, 1989). In this instance, agency decisions justified by self-maintenance needs may lead to practices that clash with service goals and interfere with the delivery of care to potential clients.

Internal Structures and Culture

Formal Structures. Organizations' internal structures consist of role sets (networks of related role positions) and predictable patterns of interaction that exist among agency members. They are the means through which services are delivered to clients (Rothman, 2001). Specific organizational structures and administrative practices shape the provision of service and, ultimately, affect an agency's ability to attain its goals (Gutierrez, GlenMaye, & DeLois, 1995). Formal organizational structures are most apparent in an agency's rules and regulations, task specializations, and hierarchical authority structures, as depicted in organization charts and administrative manuals.

No particular formal structure is best suited for all agencies. The structure that best suits a particular facility depends on such factors as its mission, the nature of its services, environmental conditions, and the training of its staff (Netting, Kettner, & McMurtry, 1998). Decentralized, collegial structures may work well in smaller agencies such as family services centers with highly professionalized staff working independently of each other. More formalized, professional bureaucratic structures seem better suited to larger organizations such as child protection agencies and multiservice centers that need expert knowledge yet require close coordination and communication among workers (Litwak, 1961). Matrix and project structures

(Miles, 1975; Morgan, 1997), in which professionals work as members of interdisciplinary teams assigned to particular functions or projects (for example, intake, discharge planning, aftercare), are better fits for agencies such as hospitals and addictions treatment centers with many functional specialties requiring input from employees who are drawn from several professional disciplines.

Informal Structures and Culture. In addition to formal structures, all agencies have informal structures and networks, which are more fluid than formal structures and more closely linked with members' personal attributes (Etzioni, 1964). These emergent networks include the unofficial interaction and communication patterns that develop as people adapt to their work settings and do their jobs (Monge & Contractor, 2001). They can be thought of as work-based mutual-aid networks. One discovers them by observing who people talk to, where they go for advice, and how they actually complete their work assignments (Weissman, Epstein, & Savage, 1983).

An agency's organizational culture is an important aspect of its informal structure (Ashkanasy, Wilderom, & Peterson, 2000). Concisely defined, an agency's culture is "the way we do things around here" (Deal & Kennedy, 1982, p. 4). An agency's culture consists of patterns of shared beliefs and assumptions that have evolved over time as an organization's members struggle with the demands of adaptation and integration. An agency's culture tends to be ingrained. Thus, while one may be able to identify an organization's primary culture easily, cultural practices do not change quickly in response to internal or external pressure (Meenaghan & Gibbons, 2000).

Cultural practices indirectly affect organizational behavior by creating a climate that gives primacy to particular values and behaviors. These values and behaviors work sufficiently well that they are taught to new members as the "correct" way to act, think, and feel about their role, their work, and the agency itself (Bolman & Deal, 1997; Schein, 1992). For example, social justice was highly valued in an agency serving an urban homeless population. Veteran case managers told new employees, state auditors, and others that "our job is to make the system work for our clients." Although the agency's mission statement stressed social and vocational rehabilitation and addictions treatment as part of its mandate, new employees learned very quickly that case advocacy was a priority. Although efforts were made to help clients change dysfunctional behaviors that contributed to their homelessness, workers' passion and intensity was most apparent in advocacy efforts when they argued for more resources and persuaded other agencies to "take a chance" with their clients.

An agency's culture reflects the values of the formal system and their reinterpretation in the informal system. Consequently, the organizational culture, as expressed in daily activities of staff, may differ markedly from the agency's purported values as articulated in formal documents. An agency's culture is molded by many factors, including its history, its institutional and physical setting, its staff, its communication networks, and its authority structures (Bolman & Deal, 1997; Katz & Kahn, 1978). The culture evolves over time as workers respond to job pressures, establish social supports, and create comfortable working environments.

Informal, emergent structures and the organizational culture can "oil the wheels" of an agency by providing incentives and explanations in areas in which the formal structure is deficient (Barnard, 1968; Perrow, 1986). They also can undermine the formal structure by furnishing competing arguments and legitimizing people who are disillusioned with agency goals, programs, and procedures. The evolution of informal structures is affected by the exchanges that take place among formally designated authority figures, line workers, and their unofficial peer leaders. Thus, depending on staff members' experiences with members of administration and their interpretation of administrative motives, they may view a particular program initiative as either a potentially useful innovation or more "busy work."

Consider, for example, the following. In response to a mandate from state regulators, the director of an addictions treatment facility ordered all workers to write "interdisciplinary biopsychosocial summaries" for clients. The purpose of these summaries, which were to be included in the clients' clinical records, was to document that staff members from each professional discipline were involved in developing comprehensive intervention plans with clients. The workers in one clinic embraced the new procedure, whereas those in another clinic opposed it, citing increased paperwork and time constraints.

An examination of the two clinics revealed that the staffs' reactions were directly related to each clinic's culture. In the first clinic, there was a history of collaboration between line workers and supervisors about procedural changes. Thus, when the new procedure was proposed, workers' opinions were sought, and the procedure was modified on the basis of their input. The line workers believed that they were treated fairly, and they incorporated the procedure into their routines. In the second clinic, there was a history of many procedural changes in which workers' opinions were not solicited. Thus, when the new procedure was introduced, staff members rallied around each other to oppose the change. Even when the clinic manager offered to meet with staff about their concerns, staff members remained skeptical. No past experience led them to believe that meaningful collaboration would occur. Thus, while the informal structure reinforced collaboration and cooperation in the first clinic, in the second clinic, an emergent, adversarial climate existed that clashed with the formal structure. In both clinics, staff members' access to organizational decision-making affected the organizational culture and contributed to the evolution of informal structures that had a marked effect on agency operations, staff morale, and the care that clients received.

Service Technologies and Programs

Social service technologies are the activities and tools (for example, assessment forms and diagnostic tests and professional knowledge and skills) agencies use to assist clients. Four of their characteristics have particular relevance for organizationally based practice. First, human services technologies are "intensive." They draw on a variety of techniques that are selected, in part, based on feedback from clients (Thompson, 1967). Second, most technologies are indeterminate. Their effects are variable and uncertain, and consensus about desirable outcomes may not exist (Sarri & Hasenfeld, 1978). Third, for many, minimal evidence for effectiveness exists. Fourth, although the technologies are applied within an agency context, they are extremely sensitive to environmental pressures (Brager & Holloway, 1978).

These characteristics can cause dilemmas for social services agencies, which strive for technological predictability and certainty (Savage, 1987). To increase their control over their work, agencies try to seal off their core technologies from environmental and other influences by developing routines and ideological systems that support the use of particular practice theories and service strategies (Hasenfeld, 1992a; Mintzberg, 1979; Thompson, 1967). Although the ideologies and routines fulfill an organizational self-maintenance function by reducing stress and uncertainty, they can become ingrained and resistant to change. Consequently, they may have unintended consequences: Clients seeking assistance may find that they receive what an agency has to offer rather than what they need, and workers who question prevailing practice models may face deep-rooted ideologically based and structurally supported opposition.

To understand how an agency frames its practice, social workers should identify the core technologies that are central to agency operations. Then, they should locate the ideologies and routines that support these technologies. To increase their professional autonomy within an agency, social workers must develop their knowledge of core technologies. In addition, they must identify and understand the organizational processes and culture that support the core technologies. They should appeal to an agency's own quality control mechanisms to evaluate existing practice approaches, and they should emphasize responsiveness to client need as a criterion for validating the helping process (see Lauffer, 1984). To alter existing "rules" governing the way services are delivered, social workers must appeal to an agency's commitment to fair and responsive service delivery. They must show how new technologies and service programs can meet client needs for assistance, as well as an agency's survival and maintenance needs.

Membership Interests and Characteristics

"Social actors" who perform agency tasks for monetary and other reinforcers carry out the work of human service agencies. "Without them, there is no organization, no structure, no situation . . . [They] are the instruments of [organizational] continuity . . . and change" (Scott, 1992, p. 19). Although members may believe in an agency's mission, their views on agency policies and their actions will vary depending on such factors as their personal attributes, job titles and functions, and involvement in other organizations and groups.

Agency members are stakeholders who are interested in both the success of an agency's programs and their place in the agency. Thus, to understand their motives and actions, one should examine an agency's programs and goals and how any changes will affect different personnel. Agency members generally act in their own self-interests, as well as those of an agency and its clients. If a particular programmatic change adds to a worker's power, prestige, and security, he or she is apt to support it; if the same change threatens his or her position, the worker is likely to oppose it. A hospital social worker, for example, may assume responsibility for coordinating discharge planning because she believes she will be able to help clients. Her enthusiasm for the task will increase if she perceives that her new role will add to her status and influence. Another worker, who also believes that the change will aid clients, may be less supportive of it if he suspects that it will harm his organizational position by drawing resources away from other projects with which he is involved.

Clearly, one must examine many variables to understand agency members' actions and motives. Although individuals usually act to protect their self-interests, it often is difficult to define their interests. Thus, to predict how agency members may act in particular situations, one must examine the organizational positions they hold (for example, job title and function), the power and resources they control (for example, access to information, materials, and support [Kanter, 1979]), and the effect of specific organizational changes and processes on their work lives. If these factors are understood, one should be able to predict a worker's actions under different circumstances. If these factors remain unknown, it becomes more difficult to anticipate how agency members will react to different organizational practices (Brager & Holloway, 1978; Gummer, 1990; Mechanic, 1962).

Environmental Context

The environmental context consists of a multidimensional set of interacting politico-legal, economic, technological, ecological, physical, and sociocultural forces that affect an agency's programs and structures. The effect
of these forces can be demonstrated by several examples. First, hospitals
have become more formalized because of directives from regulatory bodies
and concerns about lawsuits. For example, they have developed detailed
and prescriptive written policies and procedures for virtually all organizational practices. Second, the public's changed sentiment, welfare reform
legislation, and the availability of fingerprinting technologies have supported the rise of an "administrative culture" (Bane & Ellwood, 1994) in
some public assistance offices that puts a higher priority on preventing
fraud than on assisting vulnerable people. Third, whether social workers
discuss condom use as a way to reduce the risk of HIV infection with high
school students is contingent on authorization from community residents
such as parents, religious leaders, and politicians.

An agency and its environment can be thought of as a set of concentric
circles with the agency in the middle. The outer circle is the distal environment, that is, the broad political, economic, and social conditions that affect all agencies. The distal environment changes slowly and cannot be
altered by individual agencies. It sets the parameters for the types of services and programs that emerge in society (Hasenfeld, 1983). For example,
the political mood that led to welfare and health care reform changed fundamentally the way health and social services agencies operate and the care
they provide for clients.

The next circle covers the proximal geographic and sociocultural context. The neighborhoods and communities in which agencies are located
have a direct effect on service arrangements. Such agency programs as health
fairs and bicultural counseling services are often based on community needs
assessments. The way they are delivered may be shaped by input from community members and their representatives (Gutierrez, 1992).

The third circle is the agency's task environment, and it has the most
immediate effect on an agency's daily operations. The task environment
includes an agency's beneficiaries (clients and family members), its funders,
providers of nonfiscal resources, competitors, providers of complementary
services, members of its service network, and legitimators (for example,
advocacy groups and governmental bodies) (Lauffer, 1984). The task environment directly affects whom an agency serves and how it serves them.
For example, agencies that exist in unfriendly task environments, characterized by competitiveness and unpredictable funding, must devote more
of their resources to organizational survival, leaving fewer resources for

client services. In contrast, agencies with friendlier task environments can direct more attention and effort toward service innovation.

Several dimensions of an agency's environment help explain the variability in the programs that are delivered in different agencies (Brager & Holloway, 1978; Hahn, 1994; Hasenfeld, 1983; Perrow, 1986). First, the practice ideologies and rules regulating different fields of practice limit the types of programs that are permitted. Second, political trends, economic conditions, and personal values affect the public's support for social services programs. Third, demographic changes, as well as competition for scarce resources (for example, funding and clients), spur agencies to become innovative.

Answers to questions such as the following will help social workers discover how the environment affects an agency and its capacity to adapt to environmental pressures:

- What are the agency's funding sources, and what government bodies regulate its policies and programs?
- What client populations does the agency serve, and how does it attract new clients?
- What mechanisms exist to ensure that the agency is responsive and accountable to clients, funders, and other constituents?
- How does the agency obtain information about the environment?
- What is the quality of the agency's communication (open or closed, friendly or hostile) with different environmental groups (local politicians, other agencies, and the mass media, for example)?

Organizational Practice

Competent organizational practitioners see beyond the boundaries of individual cases. They maintain a flexible focus that allows them to understand how the troubles of individual clients represent larger practice issues in their agencies. They often share a worldview distinguished by "a strong sense of what is just in and for the world" (Mondros & Wilson, 1994, p. 15; see also Minkler, 1997). Similar to community organizers, good organizational practitioners are "conscious contrarians" (Mondros & Wilson, 1994). They are concerned about fairness, as well as personal freedom (Figueira-McDonough, 1993). They are committed to the empowerment of vulnerable and disenfranchised groups. They have chosen careers that embrace social justice and empowerment and that permit them to be the "consciences" of their agencies. They challenge people's thinking and seek different ways of doing things. Whereas other professionals may look for pathology and mental disorders to understand a client's behavior, social workers in their role as "conscious contrarians," while not minimizing pathology, try to identify client strengths and locate community supports that can be drawn on to promote adaptive functioning (Minkler, 1997).

When someone is referred to a social services agency, several things can happen. In an ideal situation, the client's needs fit neatly within the agency's service structure, and he or she receives help. Even in an agency that is carefully designed to be responsive to clients, however, there may occasionally be a poor match between a client's needs and the agency's capacity to meet them. When adequate services exist elsewhere and a social worker assesses that a client can be helped by another facility, he or she may refer him to that agency. In other instances (for example, when the poor fit is an "isolated" case), the social worker may opt to advocate on the client's behalf, creatively interpret policies, and "stretch" existing programs so that they help the client. When the poor fit represents more serious organizational dysfunction that affects a class of clients, social workers have an ethical and professional responsibility to encourage organizational change. How they do this is a function of such factors as the nature and severity of the organizational problem, their assessment of the conditions in their agencies, support from management and other staff, and their own resources.

An extensive body of social work literature addresses strategies for promoting innovation and change "from the ground up" in social agencies (see, for example, Bargal & Schmid, 1992; Brager & Holloway, 1978; Frey, 1990; Kettner, Daley, & Nichols, 1985; McGowan, 1978; Netting, Kettner, & McMurtry, 1998; Resnick & Patti, 1980; Rothman, Erlich, & Teresa, 1981). Although this literature cannot be reviewed in depth in this chapter, seven core practice tasks can be gleaned. To produce changes in social services agencies, social workers must: (1) Define the organizational problems that block service delivery. (2) "Read" the agency. (3) Pinpoint feasible solutions. (4) Develop and select a strategy for organizational change. (5) Prepare the agency and themselves for change. (6) Initiate the change strategy. (7) Monitor, evaluate, and revise the strategy so the change will be institutionalized. The following case example illustrates aspects of these practice tasks.

Case Illustration

Two social workers employed at the Princeshire Clinic, an alcoholism treatment facility affiliated with a large medical school, identified a problem that troubled them:

> Over a three-month period we noticed that 15 applicants were turned away because they were diagnosed with schizophrenia or bipolar disorder, which

the intake workers said made them "inappropriate" for treatment in an alcohol clinic. All had serious drinking problems and would have been admitted if they did not have coexisting mental disorders.

Defining the Problem

Organizational change begins when social workers determine that an organizational element is adversely affecting an agency's responsiveness to clients (Brager & Holloway, 1978; Resnick & Patti, 1980). Problem definitions
focus the change effort and suggest its consequences for the agency, clients, and society. Useful problem definitions have several features:

- They are concrete and operational (make abstract concepts observable).
- They are client-centered (stress the significance of the problem for
  the care of clients).
- They locate a problem in the agency by specifying whether it is struc-
  tural (related to an agency's policies and procedures), technological
  (arising from an agency's practice modalities), or personnel related
  (caused by the characteristics or competence of the agency's staff)
  (Brager & Holloway, 1978).
- They do not confuse a problem with its solution.
- They put a problem in context by suggesting why it exists (its history,
  sources, and adaptive functions).
- They can be partialized (broken down into component parts).
- They suggest possible solutions.

The two social workers at the Princeshire Clinic developed the following
problem definition:

> We discovered that recently a group home for patients discharged from the
> state psychiatric hospital opened up near the clinic. Although residents re-
> ceived medication and therapy, some began to drink heavily. The case man-
> agers referred those people to our clinic. Since we had no policy on applicants
> with mental disorders, the alcoholism counselors who conducted most of
> the intake interviews declined to admit them. We clearly had a structural
> problem in the clinic. We also had a technological problem because we had
> no services for clients with dual diagnoses.
>
> We believed that the problem was an important one because people in
> need of help were being excluded from the clinic. Thus, we believed that
> the services were not being provided equitably.
>
> Because clinic resources were limited and there was resistance to admit-
> ting these applicants, we decided to partialize our plans. Specifically, we
> planned to request that one of us be assigned to intake and that we assess 15

clients with dual diagnoses for admission. We hoped to develop and evaluate one treatment group designed specifically for them.

Reading the Agency

Once an initial problem definition is formulated, social workers must "read" their agency (that is, identify and assess the salient forces affecting its stability). They must ascertain how different constituent groups and individuals perceive the problem and how these groups might react to any proposal for change. They also must identify key individuals who must be involved in a change effort—critical decision makers who can give the go-ahead for change, facilitators who will support a change and who can influence other key actors, and resisters who will actively or passively oppose change (Brager & Holloway, 1978). Several useful tools, such as organizational ecomapping (Mattaini, 1993) and force-field analysis (Brager & Holloway, 1992), can be used to analyze exchanges among subsystems and for locating organizational supports and resistances for different change options.

The social workers at the Princeshire Clinic used these tools when they analyzed their agency:

> We completed an organizational ecomap in which we identified the relevant agencies and personnel that would affect our plans. They included the clinic director (the critical decision maker), our supervisor (facilitator), the alcoholism counselors (resisters), other social workers (most of whom were neutral), the clients, the group home, the medical school, and the state departments of substance abuse and mental health.
>
> We used a force-field analysis to assess the prospects for change by identifying organizational and environmental forces that could be drawn upon to support our ideas. Essentially, by constructing a balance sheet that depicted the countervailing forces that support or oppose systemic changes, we were able to clarify some of the factors that would work for us or against us as we tried to initiate organizational change. A simple force-field analysis is depicted in Figure 11-1. It lists only the major driving and restraining forces that would affect our plans. (See Brager and Holloway, 1992, for a more in-depth discussion of the uses of force-field analysis in planning organizational change.)

As depicted in Figure 11-1, the clinic director was committed to providing good client care, and he encouraged staff to be innovative and take initiative. State and local pressure to assist de-institutionalized patients with serious mental illnesses was growing, and at least two other substance abuse clinics in the city had established small programs for clients with dual

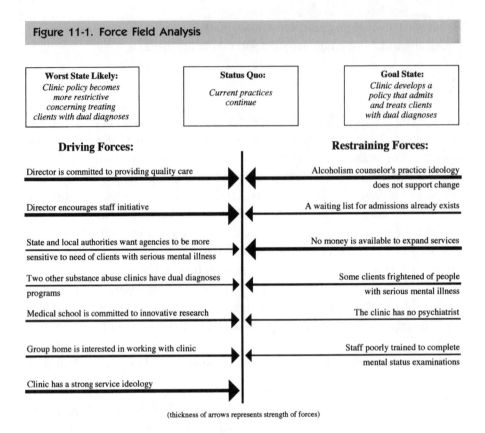

Figure 11-1. Force Field Analysis

Worst State Likely:	Status Quo:	Goal State:
Clinic policy becomes more restrictive concerning treating clients with dual diagnoses	Current practices continue	Clinic develops a policy that admits and treats clients with dual diagnoses

Driving Forces: **Restraining Forces:**

Director is committed to providing quality care

Alcoholism counselor's practice ideology does not support change

Director encourages staff initiative

A waiting list for admissions already exists

State and local authorities want agencies to be more sensitive to need of clients with serious mental illness

No money is available to expand services

Two other substance abuse clinics have dual diagnoses programs

Some clients frightened of people with serious mental illness

Medical school is committed to innovative research

The clinic has no psychiatrist

Group home is interested in working with clinic

Staff poorly trained to complete mental status examinations

Clinic has a strong service ideology

(thickness of arrows represents strength of forces)

diagnoses. The medical school was research oriented and urged the clinic to be innovative. The group home was interested in developing a joint initiative. The clinic had a strong service ideology.

Counteracting these driving forces were restraining forces: The alcoholism counselors' practice ideology did not support a change. They believed strongly that the clinic's purpose was to treat primary alcoholic clients; they were worried about extending existing scarce resources to people who were not "primary alcoholics." The clinic already had a waiting list for other applicants, and there was no money available to expand services. Some clients were frightened by seeing people with obvious mental disorders in the waiting room. The clinic had no psychiatrist to consult on the care of such clients, and staff were poorly trained to complete mental status examinations.

Pinpointing Feasible Solutions

Social workers must develop potential solutions that are acceptable to their constituents and that will maximize an agency's responsiveness to the broadest range of clients based on their preliminary analyses. Because agency members have interests tied to existing practices and because any change requires effort, social services agencies, similar to other social systems, will resist change (Frey, 1990). Practitioners can reduce their agencies' resistances and increase the feasibility of proposed solutions in several ways. For example, partializing and introducing a change incrementally will make it more acceptable (Rothman, Erlich, & Teresa, 1981). Feasibility also increases when potential solutions are directly relevant to the identified problem, are simple, do not depart radically from an agency's ideology, are reversible (can be undone), are operational, and are economic (their potential benefits justify the costs involved).

The two social workers described the next steps they took:

> After we completed our assessment, we obtained our supervisor's permission to visit the two facilities providing services for clients with dual diagnoses; we also searched the professional literature. We decided that by modifying our ideas we might be able to persuade the staff to consider them. We opted to propose that the clinic admit 15 group home residents on a trial basis and that these clients should be assigned to our team (an alcoholism counselor who backed the idea was on our team). To gain support, we suggested that our supervisor assess the applicants' needs to be certain we could handle them. We also proposed that a non-confrontational, skills-focused treatment group should be formed for these clients. (The literature and the other facilities recommended this type of group for adults with dual diagnoses.)

Selecting a Change Strategy

Social workers must make two decisions at this point. First, they must decide whether to intervene alone or with a task group. Because of the risks involved, the feelings evoked, line workers' relative lack of power, and the need to delegate tasks and responsibilities, organizational change from below usually involves group-based strategies. Individual strategies are more viable when social workers are more certain about views of key actors or have direct access to them.

Second, they must decide whether to use collaborative, mediatory, or conflict strategies (Brager & Holloway, 1978; McGowan, 1978). A collaborative strategy, characterized by open communication and joint action, works best when there is little disagreement about a problem and its solution, the participants' relative power is equal, and relationships are close. A mediatory strategy, distinguished by negotiation, persuasion, and political maneuvering, is used when a social worker hopes to reach a compromise despite some disagreement about the situation (see Fisher, Ury, & Patton, 1991; Simons, 1987). A conflict strategy, which is adversarial and coercive, is used only when there is fundamental disagreement between parties and a social worker decides that an agency will not respond to other strategies. Because this strategy is volatile, it is rarely used for internal change. In most situations, social workers use collaboration and mediation to influence their agencies, as did the two social workers at the Princeshire Clinic:

> We decided to recruit our supervisor and the alcoholism counselor on our team and form an ad hoc dual diagnosis study group to gain credibility and influence. Both agreed, and our supervisor informed the director that we were meeting to discuss clinical issues that arose in assisting clients with mental disorders. To avoid arousing undue concern from other staff members, we decided not to invite staff from the group home to join the study group. We planned to meet with them periodically to share our ideas with them and to get their input.
>
> We worked collaboratively to develop our ideas. Our limited experience with a few clients with co-existing substance use and mental disorders, who "slipped through" the intake process, suggested that we could help them. We were concerned about medication, but a case manager from the group home told us that the group home's psychiatrist would provide medication and case consultation.
>
> We decided to use mediation with the director, alcoholism counselors, and clients. We planned to appeal to the director's commitment to client care (a commitment that was a central element in our agency's culture) and point out how a creative program would impress funders and the medical school. To reach the counselors we considered discussing our limited experiences working with clients who were dually diagnosed at two of the weekly all-staff case conferences. We decided to address client concerns by asking the agency to purchase informational pamphlets on alcoholism and mental illness. We also planned to have the alcoholism counselor on our team speak about psychiatric symptoms in his alcohol education groups.

Preparing the Agency and Staff Members for Change

For change to occur, agency staff must become aware of the organizational problem, be dissatisfied with the status quo, and have hope that realistic options exist for correcting the problem. In short, a system that has organized itself around a problem must be destabilized. One can increase awareness and induce stress in several ways. Social workers can raise their concerns at staff meetings and in discussions with individual staff members.

A relatively safe and effective tactic is to ask "informational questions" (Brager & Holloway, 1978). Workers simply ask questions (without suggesting answers) at staff meetings. Social workers can also induce stress if they pick up on any "general" dissatisfaction that exists and use this mood to challenge the myth that "everything is OK" in an agency.

Besides inducing stress, social workers must position themselves personally and structurally to maximize their capacity to promote change (Brager & Holloway, 1978; Mechanic, 1962). They can increase their personal influence by appealing to values and interests they share with other workers and by doing favors for them. They can gain credibility by developing knowledge and expertise on the problem situation and sharing their knowledge with others. Structurally, they can increase their power by aligning themselves with authority figures in an agency, by forming coalitions with informal peer leaders, and by joining committees that allow them to work directly on the problem (Holloway & Brager, 1989), as the two social workers at the Princeshire Clinic did:

> Once we decided that our plan was feasible, we tried to increase our co-workers' awareness of the problem. At staff meetings we asked whether anyone was familiar with state initiatives for treating clients with dual diagnoses. We wondered aloud what happened to "all the clients" that we sent away from the clinic. We also began to speak individually with some alcoholism counselors and offered to help those who were having trouble with some clients. Our supervisor met regularly with the clinic director and gave him written reports summarizing our agency visits and literature search. She also described anecdotal impressions from our clinical work with clients who were dually diagnosed.
>
> As a result of our actions we began to notice a change in staff attitudes. They no longer reacted negatively when we asked about clients who had mental disorders. They also seemed interested in hearing about our experiences.

Initiating the Change Strategy

When agency members have been prepared, social workers can make their proposal public. At this time they must decide to whom to make the proposal and how to make the presentation. They also must divide tasks and prepare a negotiating strategy. They should anticipate that they may be asked to modify their plans, and they should think about how to do so. They must shape their arguments, develop alternatives and trade-offs, and identify any leverage they have (Fisher, Ury, & Patton, 1991). In this regard, the two Princeshire Clinic social workers did the following:

We decided that our supervisor should bring the proposal to the director. He respected her and had accepted her opinions on other matters. The alcoholism counselor, together with us, would float the idea without its specifics among our coworkers. Although we knew that this was risky because one of them might argue against the plan before it was fully outlined for the director, we hoped to prepare them for change and uncover any opposition.

Our supervisor proposed to the director that the clinic admit 15 group home residents and assign them to our team. A social worker and the alcoholism counselor would form and lead a skills-focused group for them with a goal of helping them establish sobriety. The group would meet twice a week for an hour. The group home's psychiatrist would continue to medicate the clients.

Our supervisor suggested that we monitor the group and make any required changes over the next 12 months. At that time we would write an evaluation report, so that the director could decide whether to continue the program.

The director agreed with our plans, but he decided to proceed more cautiously and incrementally. He agreed to admit 10 applicants only, and he reduced the evaluation period to six months. He also directed the supervisor to give him biweekly reports on the clients' progress. He said that he would expand the program if our initial results were promising. He reserved the right to abort the program at any time.

Monitoring, Evaluating, and Revising the Strategy

After a proposal has been accepted, workers implement their plans. Among the challenges they face during this stage are maintaining the commitment of superiors, nurturing members of the task group, and maintaining links with other organizational operations. They also must handle any new opposition that arises, alter agency and program structures if needed, and standardize procedures to facilitate generalization and dissemination of the findings (Brager & Holloway, 1978; Gummer, 1990; Resnick & Patti, 1980).

The two social workers at the Princeshire Clinic described their experiences during this stage as follows:

During the trial period, 15 clients with dual diagnoses were admitted to the clinic. Five were rehospitalized, so there were never more than 10 people attending the clinic. We discovered that we could not manage 10 clients in one group. Therefore, we formed two groups of five people. Some of the clients who were less compliant with medication schedules decompensated (experienced dramatic psychotic symptoms) in the waiting room. This upset other clients and staff, and we had to respond to the fear that was generated.

One activity that was particularly helpful involved having three clients with dual diagnoses and the group home's psychiatrist come to a staff meeting to talk about the problems they faced in recovery.

Our study group continued to meet weekly, and our supervisor gave regular reports to the director. We closely monitored the clients' attendance at group and individual sessions, their drinking status, and their general level of functioning. At three months, we wrote a draft procedure for working with clients with dual diagnoses. At the end of six months, we delivered a final report, which the director presented at a staff meeting. Essentially, the outcomes of our project supported our initial ideas about treating clients with dual diagnoses in the clinic. We confirmed that the presence of clients with coexisting substance abuse and mental disorders did not disrupt clinic operations. Other clients continued to be treated in a timely manner, and clinic resources were not diverted from other areas. Furthermore, clients with dual diagnoses seemed to benefit from our help. They attended regularly, six established between four and five months of sobriety, and their adaptation to community living improved.

The director accepted and revised our draft procedures and authorized us to continue to admit clients with dual diagnoses. He also began working with members of the agency's task environment to prepare a proposal cosponsored by the medical school to get state funding to expand services for these clients.

Conclusion

Social workers are organizational professionals who must decide every day how to help clients humanely and effectively. Inevitably, they will encounter agency arrangements that thwart their efforts and obstruct the fair delivery of care. Thus, it is crucial that they are willing and able to look beyond case work and explore all options for assisting people in need. We have learned a great deal about human service agencies in recent years. "No longer are [they] a backdrop, but rather—for good or ill—they are a significant reality" (Meyer, 1979, p. 12) in professional practice. To challenge dysfunctional organizational processes, social workers must develop a reflective skepticism about their agencies. They must be masterful clinicians who are knowledgeable about and skilled at organizational assessment and intervention. They must become "conscious contrarians" (Mondros & Wilson, 1994) who will question existing service arrangements and prod their agencies and other professionals to think critically about what they do. By starting with an attitude of helping people and a commitment to social justice, they will find the opportunity and courage to use their knowledge and skills to enhance their agency's capacity to serve clients and the common good.

References

Ashkanasy, N. M., Wilderom, C. P. M., & Peterson, M. F. (Eds.). (2000). *Handbook of organizational culture and climate*. Thousand Oaks, CA: Sage.

Bane, M. J., & Ellwood, D. T. (1994). *Welfare realities: From rhetoric to reform*. Cambridge, MA: Harvard University Press.

Bargal, D., & Schmid, H. (Ed.). (1992). Organizational change and development in human service organizations [Special issue]. *Administration in Social Work, 16*(3/4).

Barnard, C. (1968). *The functions of the executive*. Cambridge, MA: Harvard University Press.

Blau, P. M., & Scott, W. R. (1962). *Formal organizations: A comparative approach*. San Francisco: Chandler.

Bolman, L. G., & Deal, T. E. (1997). *Reframing organizations* (2nd ed.). San Francisco: Jossey-Bass.

Brager, G., & Holloway, S. (1978). *Changing human service organizations*. New York: Free Press.

Brager, G., & Holloway, S. (1992). Assessing prospects for organizational change: The uses of force-field analysis. *Administration in Social Work, 16*(3/4), 15–28.

Buckley, W. (1967). *Sociology and modern systems theory*. Englewood Cliffs, NJ: Prentice Hall.

Chernesky, R. H. (1997). Managing agencies for multicultural services. In E. P. Congress (Ed.), *Multicultural perspectives in working with families* (pp. 17–33). New York: Springer.

Chernesky, R. H. (1998). Advancing women in the managerial ranks. In R. L. Edwards, J. A. Yankey, & M. A. Altpeter (Eds.), *Skills for effective management of nonprofit organizations* (pp. 200–218). Washington, DC: NASW Press.

Dane, B. O., & Simon, B. L. (1991). Resident guests: Social workers in host settings. *Social Work, 36*, 208–213.

Deal, T. E., & Kennedy, A. A. (1982). *Corporate cultures*. Reading, MA: Addison-Wesley.

Edwards, R. L., & Gummer, B. (1988). Management of social services: Current perspectives and future trends. In P. R. Keys & L. H. Ginsberg (Eds.), *New management in human services* (pp. 1–29). Silver Spring, MD: National Association of Social Workers.

Etzioni, A. (1964). *Modern organizations*. Englewood Cliffs, NJ: Prentice Hall.

Figueira-McDonough, J. (1993). Policy practice: The neglected side of social work intervention. *Social Work, 38*, 179–188.

Fisher, R., Ury, W., & Patton, B. (1991). *Getting to yes* (2nd ed.). New York: Penguin Books.

Frey, G. A. (1990). A framework for promoting organizational change. *Families in Society, 71*, 142–147.

Gerth, H., & Mills, C. W. (Eds.). (1958). *From Max Weber: Essays in sociology.* New York: Oxford University Press.

Gitterman, A. (1989). Testing professional authority and boundaries. *Social Casework, 70,* 165–171.

Gitterman, A., & Miller, I. (1989). The influence of the organization on clinical practice. *Clinical Social Work Journal, 17,* 151–163.

Gouldner, A. (1963). The secrets of organizations. In *Social welfare forum 1963: Official proceedings,* 90th annual forum, National Conference on Social Welfare, Cleveland, Ohio, May 19–24, 1963 (pp. 161–177). New York: Columbia University Press.

Gummer, B. (1990). *The politics of social administration.* Englewood Cliffs, NJ: Prentice Hall.

Gutierrez, L. M. (1992). Empowering ethnic minorities in the twenty-first century: The role of human service organizations. In Y. Hasenfeld (Ed.), *Human services as complex organizations* (pp. 320–338). Newbury Park, CA: Sage Publications.

Gutierrez, L., GlenMaye, L., & DeLois, K. (1995). The organizational context of empowerment practice: Implications for social work administration. *Social Work, 40,* 249–258.

Gutierrez, L. M., & Lewis, E. A. (1999). *Empowering women of color.* New York: Columbia University Press.

Hage, J., & Aiken, M. (1970). *Social change in complex organizations.* New York: Random House.

Hahn, A. J. (1994). *The politics of caring: Human services at the local level.* Boulder, CO: Westview Press.

Hartman, A. (1993). The professional is political [Editorial]. *Social Work, 38,* 365–366, 504.

Hasenfeld, Y. (1983). *Human service organizations.* Englewood Cliffs, NJ: Prentice Hall.

Hasenfeld, Y. (1987). Power in social work practice. *Social Service Review, 61,* 469–483.

Hasenfeld, Y. (1992a). The nature of human service organizations. In Y. Hasenfeld (Ed.), *Human services as complex organizations* (pp. 3–23). Newbury Park, CA: Sage Publications.

Hasenfeld, Y. (1992b). Theoretical approaches to human service organizations. In Y. Hasenfeld (Ed.), *Human services as complex organizations* (pp. 24–44). Newbury Park, CA: Sage Publications.

Holloway, S., & Brager, G. (1989). *Supervising in the human services: The politics of practice.* New York: Free Press.

Jackson, S. (1992). Team composition in organizational settings: Issues in managing an increasingly diverse workforce. In S. Worchel, W. Woods, & J. Simpson (Eds.), *Group process and productivity* (pp. 138–173). Newbury Park; Sage.

Johnson, D. W., & Johnson, F. P. (2000). *Joining together: Group theory and group skills* (7th ed.). Boston: Allyn & Bacon.

Johnson, D. W., & Johnson, R. (1989). *Cooperation and competition: Theory and research*. Edina, MN: Interaction Book Company.

Kanter, R. M. (1979, July–August). Power failures in management circuits. *Harvard Business Review*, pp. 65–75.

Katz, D., & Kahn, R. L. (1978). *The social psychology of organizations* (rev. ed.). New York: John Wiley & Sons.

Kettner, P., Daley, J. M., & Nichols, A. W. (1985). *Initiating change in organizations and communities*. Monterey, CA: Brooks/Cole.

Kurzman, P. A., & Akabas, S. H. (Eds.). (1993). *Work and well-being: The occupational social work advantage*. Washington, DC: NASW Press.

Lauffer, A. (1984). *Understanding your social agency*. Newbury Park, CA: Sage Publications.

Lawrence, P. R., & Lorsch, J. W. (1967). *Organization and environment: Managing differentiation and integration*. Boston: Harvard University Graduate School of Business Administration.

Leavitt, H. J. (1965). Applied organizational change in industry: Structural, technological, and humanistic approaches. In J. G. March (Ed.), *Handbook of organizations* (pp. 1144-1170). Chicago: Rand McNally.

Lipsky, M. (1984). Bureaucratic disentitlement in social welfare programs. *Social Service Review, 58*, 3–27.

Litwak, E. (1961). Models of bureaucracy which permit conflict. *American Journal of Sociology, 67*, 177–184.

Loden, M., & Rosener, J. B. (1991). *Workforce America! Managing employee diversity as a vital resource*. Homewood, IL: Irwin.

Lubove, R. (1965). *The professional altruist: The emergence of social work as a career, 1880–1930*. New York: Atheneum.

Marriott, A., Sexton, L., & Staley, D. (1994). Components of job satisfaction in psychiatric social workers. *Health & Social Work, 19*, 199–205.

Martin, P. Y. (1987). Multiple constituencies and performance in social welfare organizations: Action strategies for directors. *Administration in Social Work, 11*(3/4), 223–239.

Mattaini, M. A. (1993). *More than a thousand words: Graphics for clinical practice*. Washington, DC: NASW Press.

McGowan, B. G. (1978). Strategies in bureaucracies. In J. S. Mearig (Ed.), *Working for children: Ethical issues beyond professional guidelines* (pp. 155–180). San Francisco: Jossey-Bass.

Mechanic, D. (1962). Sources of power of lower participants in complex organizations. *Administrative Science Quarterly, 7*, 349–364.

Meenaghan, T. M., & Gibbons, W. E. (2000). *Generalist practice in larger settings: Knowledge and skill concepts*. Chicago: Lyceum.

Meyer, C. H. (1979). Introduction. In C. H. Meyer (Ed.), *Making organizations work for people.* Washington, DC: National Association of Social Workers.

Miles, R. E. (1975). *Theories of management.* New York: McGraw-Hill.

Minkler, M. (Ed.). (1997). *Community organizing and community building for health.* New Brunswick, NJ: Rutgers University Press.

Mintzberg, H. (1979). *The structure of organizations.* Englewood Cliffs, NJ: Prentice Hall.

Mondros, J. B., & Wilson, S. M. (1994). *Organizing for power and empowerment.* New York: Columbia University Press.

Monge, P. R., & Contractor, N. S. (2001). Emergence of communication networks. In F. M. Jablin & L. L. Putnam (Eds.), *The new handbook of organizational communication: Advances in theory, research, and methods* (pp. 440–502). Thousand Oaks, CA: Sage.

Morgan, G. (1997). *Images of organization* (2nd ed.). Thousand Oaks, CA: Sage Publications.

Netting, F. E., Kettner, P. M., & McMurtry, S. L. (1998). *Social work macro practice* (2nd ed.). New York: Longman.

O'Reilly, C., Caldwell, D., & Barnett, W. (1989). Work group demography, social integration, and turnover. *Administrative Science Quarterly, 34,* 21–37.

Perrow, C. (1961). The analysis of goals in complex organizations. *American Sociological Review, 26,* 856–866.

Perrow, C. (1978). Demystifying organizations. In R. C. Sarri & Y. Hasenfeld (Eds.), *The management of human services* (pp. 105–120). New York: Columbia University Press.

Perrow, C. (1986). *Complex organizations: A critical essay* (3rd ed.). New York: McGraw-Hill.

Resnick, H., & Patti, R. J. (Eds.). (1980). *Change from within: Humanizing social welfare organizations.* Philadelphia: Temple University Press.

Rhodes, M. L. (1991). *Ethical dilemmas in social work practice.* Milwaukee, WI: Family Service America.

Rothman, J. (2001). Approaches to community intervention. In J. Rothman, J. L. Erlich, & J. E. Tropman (Eds.), *Strategies of community intervention* (6th ed., pp. 27–64). Itasca, IL: F. E. Peacock.

Rothman, J., Erlich, J. L., & Teresa, J. G. (1981). *Changing organizations and community programs.* Newbury Park, CA: Sage Publications.

Sarri, R. C., & Hasenfeld, Y. (Eds.). (1978). *The management of human services.* New York: Columbia University Press.

Savage, A. (1987). Maximizing effectiveness through technological complexity. *Administration in Social Work, 11*(3/4), 127–143.

Schein, E. H. (1992). *Organizational culture and leadership.* San Francisco: Jossey-Bass.

Scott, W. R. (1992). *Organizations: Rational, natural, and open systems* (3rd ed.). Englewood Cliffs, NJ: Prentice Hall.

Shafritz, J. M., & Ott, J. S. (Eds.). (2001). *Classics of organization theory* (5th ed.). Orlando, FL: Harcourt College Publishers.

Simons, R. L. (1987). Generic social work skills in administration: The example of persuasion. *Administration in Social Work, 11*(3/4), 241–254.

Taber, M. A. (1987). A theory of accountability for the human services and implications for social program design. *Administration in Social Work, 11*(3/4), 115–126.

Terborg, J. Castore, C., & DeNinno, J. (1976). A longitudinal field investigation of the impact of group composition on group performance and cohesion. *Journal of Personality and Social Psychology, 34,* 782–790.

Thompson, J. D. (1967). *Organizations in action.* New York: McGraw-Hill.

Toseland, R. W., & Rivas, R. F. (1998). *An introduction to group work practice* (3rd ed.). Boston: Allyn & Bacon.

Vinter, R. D. (1959). The social structure of service. In A. J. Kahn (Ed.), *Issues in American social work* (pp. 242–269). New York: Columbia University Press.

Walsh-Bowers, R., Rossiter, A., Prilleltensky, I. (1996). The personal is the organizational in the ethics of hospital social workers. *Ethics and Behavior, 6,* 321–335.

Weber, M. (1947). *The theory of social and economic organization* (A. H. Henderson & T. Parsons, Trans.). Glencoe, IL: Free Press. (Originally published in 1924).

Weissman, H., Epstein, I., & Savage, A. (1983). *Agency-based social work.* Philadelphia: Temple University Press.

Zald, M. N. (2001). Organizations: Organizations as polities; an analysis of community organization agencies. In J. Rothman, J. L. Erlich, & J. E. Tropman (Eds.), *Strategies of community intervention* (6th ed.) (pp. 133–144). Itasca, IL: F. E. Peacock.

CHAPTER 12

Generalist Practice: People and Programs

Mark A. Mattaini

As is clear from the chapters in this book, social work practice includes work with and for individuals, families, formed and natural groups, neighborhoods and communities, organizations, and even nations. The profession developed, in significant part, from separate professional groups that were working at each level; these groups came together as the National Association of Social Workers only in the 1950s. Until the 1970s, most graduate schools of social work were organized by "method"—casework, group work, community organization, and administration—and most students were trained for practice in only one of these areas. With the work of Bartlett (1970) and others in the late 1960s and early 1970s, the "common base" of social work knowledge and values at all systemic levels was clarified. Generalist practice is an effort to expand the worker's knowledge base so that he or she can choose the most promising interventive strategy at the most appropriate level.

There are four requirements for selecting the most effective and efficient approach to dealing with client problems: (1) an understanding of the needs of the case arrived at collaboratively with the client, (2) the skills of practice at multiple system levels (as reflected in the preceding chapters), (3) knowledge of how to mix and phase these skills effectively, and (4) a clear commitment to shared power. Much of social work practice happens through organizations and "programs" that—at least ideally—emerge and evolve in response to the particulars of the social problems that they address. Therefore, basic program development skills are an important facet of generalist practice. These areas are sketched in this chapter.

Generalist practice is an organic whole, not simply an aggregation of additive roles. Although it may be necessary to learn practice in artificially discrete pieces, ideally, graduate-level practitioners do not so much see themselves as being "group workers," "administrators," and "advocates" at different moments in time as they recognize the coherence and flow among the activities they perform as social workers and see how they work together to address clients' needs.

Different functions require somewhat different skills (although many are useful at multiple levels). Skills for working with smaller systems also often are components of work with larger systems. For example, empathic listening skills learned in work with individuals certainly are also important in work with families and community members. Group work skills are important not only in practice in which the small group is the focal system, but also in organizational and community practice. Ultimately, the goal is to achieve a professional identity as a generalist social worker who does what is necessary to engage the problem, in collaboration with the client, at whatever systemic level provides the best opportunities to achieve the client's vision consistent with collective well-being. Figure 12-1, for example, is an ecomap portraying the situation of a 32-year-old former client of the author, Robert, who was struggling with several issues, including depression, what he defined as a "sexual addiction" for which he participated in a 12-step group (which he indicated had not worked well for him), limited and conflicted interpersonal relationships, and vocational and economic failure.

(Note that all the arrows that represent interpersonal exchanges in the figure are thin, reflecting a high overall level of isolation.)

Even practitioners who define themselves as "clinical social workers" might intervene with a client such as Robert individually, see him and his girlfriend together, have some contact with his parents, encourage him to try different Sex Addicts Anonymous groups, and refer him to other services. Generalist workers might identify additional potential points of intervention as well; they might design a new form of group service to address the needs of lonely and socially isolated individuals (Gambrill, 1996) with ties to singles programs in synagogues, churches, and cultural organizations; or they might lead or participate in efforts to build new systems to improve vocational and educational access in the neighborhood. Any point on the ecomap, therefore, is "fair game" for a generalist practitioner as long as there is reason to believe intervening at that point may help the client address his problems or achieve his goals.

The model of generalist practice presented in this chapter is rooted primarily in ecobehavioral theory. Although the author's experience and a great deal of empirical data suggest that this model is particularly robust, there are other well-accepted ways to conceptualize generalist practice, including working from a psychosocial model, a task-centered model, or an

Figure 12-1. An Ecomap Depicting Central Features of Robert's Case

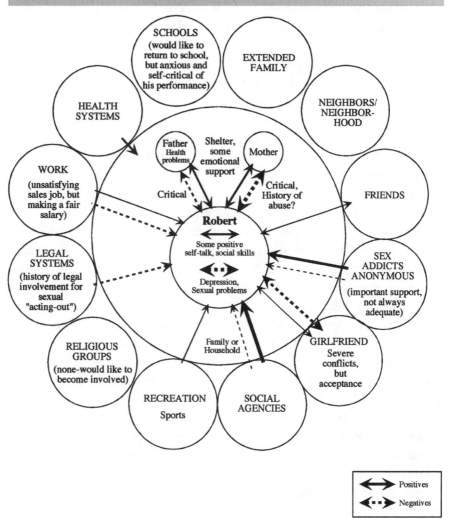

ecological model. Responsible generalist practitioners will expose themselves to multiple options and decide what is best on the basis of experience and available data.

Changing Behavior

All practice is about change, and change always involves action—behavior—of some sort. In some cases, for example with people living with severe mental illness, the treatment goal may be stabilization or sustaining a current level of functioning and avoiding deterioration. Even under these circumstances, if there is a need for social work, it is because someone must do something to help—to provide sufficient support for client action or to change or support actions by others in the environment. The required action may be overt, such as acting more assertively, or covert, such as changing self-talk or learning to manage visceral activity such as that involved in anger (see Chapter 7). The same basic behavioral principles apply whether the goals in a particular case are to affect the actions of an individual client, modify patterns of behavior in a family, or advocate that representatives of a social institution relate differently to clients. Specific practice tasks, however, as well as ways of understanding the multivariate matrix within which behavior occurs, vary considerably in each of these examples, partly because of the increasing complexity of the phenomena of interest, which reductionistic thought cannot capture.

If the service contract developed collaboratively with a client calls for helping him or her to feel better emotionally, the social worker may model, prompt, and reinforce behavioral activation (Jacobson et al., 1996) as well as encouraging more accurate self-talk ("cognitive therapy"). If the client's life situation is highly aversive, however, a further level of complexity may be indicated. Under these circumstances, the social worker can encourage and assist the client to "experiment" in his or her own life space and to begin to take control of the factors that lead to his or her emotional struggles (an empowerment approach). Simply helping the client to adjust to oppression would not be a responsible goal of practice.

In many cases, the client's (overt and covert) behavior is shaped, prompted, and maintained by the actions of others. Depression, for example, can be deeply rooted in family (and other social) processes (Biglan, 1991; Brown & Harris, 1978; Lerner, 1997) as well as in biological factors. Family therapists and those who work with people with severe behavioral problems have long recognized that if the behavior of one member of an interactive system changes, homeostatic forces will tend to return that person and the overall system to the previous state; the problems associated with returning delinquent youths to their previous living situation are a common example (Wolf, Braukmann, & Ramp, 1987). If dramatic enough change occurs, however, the effects may reverberate and be amplified through other parts of the system, resulting in a new configuration. Family intervention often seeks this sort of meaningful and, it is hoped, irreversible, "restructuring" (Minuchin, Simon, & Lee, 1996). Even more complicated patterns are present at higher systemic levels.

How do these abstract notions work in a more operationalized sense? That is, how does one construe them in the behavioral terms used here and determine analytically at what level to intervene? The concept of "interlocking contingencies" is the critical bridge. Individual actions that occur within any "cultural entity"—a transactional group like a family, school, or neighborhood—tend to be shaped by patterns of exchange among the people and forces who constitute the formal or informal group, often in conjunction with events outside the system itself.

Interventions in such transactional webs are best selected by identifying those that are concurrently most powerful and most accessible. For example, family systems tend to maintain repetitive patterns of interaction (Minuchin's 1974 "structure"), which may or may not have positive outcomes for the family as a whole. Such patterns constitute the culture of the family. The transactional behaviors maintained by the group that, in the aggregate, constitute group culture are technically labeled "cultural practices" (Glenn, 1991). Much of social work practice, after one moves beyond the level of work with individuals, involves helping clients change patterns of cultural practices within self-organizing groups.

Multiple Options in Generalist Practice

An examination of the factors that maintain a problem behavior or factors that are missing that may support a behavior to be achieved can suggest possible interventive strategies on multiple levels. Look, for example, at the contingency diagram in Figure 12-2, which traces some of the factors related to instances of overly harsh, aggressive actions by a single parent toward a child (Mattaini, McGowan, & Williams, 1996).

A careful analysis of the figure suggests that one could have an effect on this pattern in a variety of ways, including individual intervention (teaching the mother to respond to the child's provocation more effectively), family treatment (perhaps focused on reducing coercive exchanges and increasing the rate of positive exchanges), group work (for example, for parenting skills or mutual aid), community organizing (to strengthen social networks and reduce specific environmental stresses that affect the class of isolated single parents), or establishing programmatic responses on an organizational basis (broad-based family support programs). The generalist practitioner regards all of these options as possibilities in planning services and often considers combinations that may produce synergistic effects. Within a shared power framework, clients and social workers together can consider and elaborate the multiple options; each of the people involved can contribute to planning and action in the case from their own skills and strengths. Because every combination of clients and social workers is different, the particular approach to intervention that is constructed in each case may also vary. Examples of possible strategic options for preventing child maltreatment at each level are discussed in the following sections.

Figure 12-2. Factors Contributing to a High Rate of Aggressive, Coercive Acts toward a Child by a Single Mother

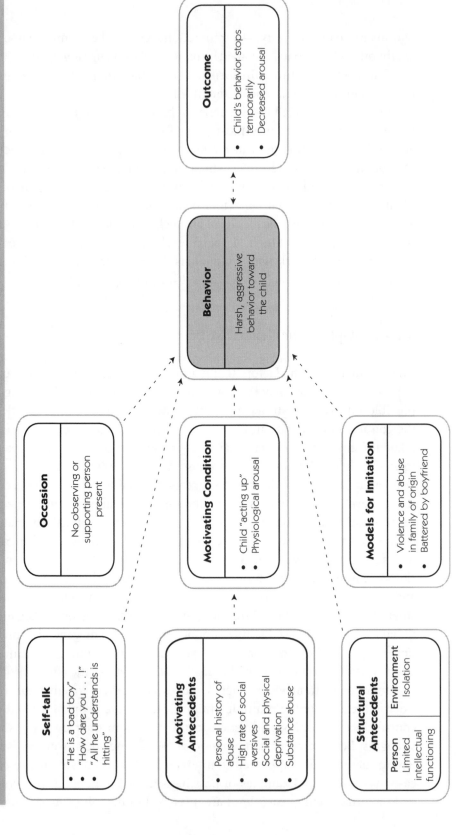

Individual Work with Parents

When a parent is overwhelmed, it may well make sense to begin work with that individual. For example, in one case, a mother was distressed because she believed her three-year-old daughter was disobedient; the mother often became enmeshed in verbal arguments with the child. Observations of the mother and daughter at home, however, indicated that the girl nearly always obeyed her mother and that the primary problem appeared to be that the mother displaced frustrations from other sources onto her child. If the pattern had continued, it is likely that the problems would have escalated because the child had begun to imitate her mother's verbally aggressive modeling, which could lead to an abusive spiral (Patterson, 1976). Interventions in this case focused on resolving those environmental issues that could be effectively addressed, developing new ways to cope with those that could not be changed, and building positive parent–child interactions characterized by positive reinforcement. Although individual intervention (with attention to environmental factors) was an efficient approach in this case, a primary focus on family interaction patterns may be indicated in other situations.

Family Consultation

Family intervention, which includes work on restructuring interactional patterns within the family, as well as on building bridges to external supports and ameliorating stresses from multiple systems, is a demonstrably effective approach in families in which children are maltreated (Brunk, Henggeler, & Whelan, 1987; Mattaini, McGowan, & Williams, 1996). This interventive strategy can be differentially responsive to many of the multiple interacting factors associated with abuse (see Figure 12-2).

In family treatment, not only can parents learn new strategies for building relationships with the child and managing behavior less coercively, but older children in particular can also be coached to deal with parents differently (Serna et al., 1991), and problems with other systems can be directly addressed. If the family members are seen at home, they can work with the practitioner to construct and practice new skills in the setting where they need to be used, which reduces the problem of generalizing what is learned in a training situation to the home. Therefore, family consultation is a powerful and flexible strategy. However, it can be expensive to deliver and does not offer the same potential for expanding social networks as do some group and community approaches, discussed next. This network expansion may be crucial for "insular" parents, a particularly challenging subgroup of maltreating parents (Dumas & Wahler, 1985; Mattaini, 1999; Wahler, 1980).

Group Work

Parenting groups are a particularly common approach, partly because of their cost-efficiency and partly because they sometimes offer unique advantages which other modalities may not. Parents who receive group training, for example, often find that the supportive network of the group can help them to construct new family repertoires and also help them to find ways to address problems with other social systems (Brunk, Henggeler, & Whelan, 1987).

Parent groups can be an effective approach for teaching both coping skills (Whiteman, Fanshel, & Grundy, 1987) and specific parenting techniques. Nevertheless, evidence suggests that skills learned in a group may not generalize well to the home unless in-home coaching is a component of the program (Howing et al., 1989). Goldstein, Keller, and Erné (1985) found that with the addition of four "transfer-enhancing" techniques, generalization can be enhanced: (1) "overlearning" (the parent is given numerous opportunities to learn the skills to a high, almost automatic level of mastery); (2) "stimulus variability" (the parent learns to use the skills under an intentionally wide range of conditions, not simply in one way with one co-actor in a parenting group); (3) identical elements (skills learned in the group are practiced in exactly the same way with parent aides in the home at a later time); and (4) programmed reinforcement (parent aides are specifically trained to note and reinforce use of new skills in the home, which research suggests does not usually occur unless it is explicitly designed into the program). Without such additional elements, many parents do not consistently transfer what they learn in groups to the home.

Recent work has shown the dramatic advantages of working with parents, or working with families, in multifamily groups. Webster-Stratton, for example, found that parenting education in groups became progressively more effective when it moved from a focus on parenting skills alone to one on parenting skills and mutual support, and more effective yet when an emphasis on building bridges to community systems was also incorporated (Webster-Stratton, 1997). The recent movement toward community-centered practice with families (Sviridoff & Ryan, 1997) is consistent with these findings; not surprisingly for a generalist social worker, the boundaries between work with families, group work, and community practice are, and need to be, highly permeable.

Community Practice

There is strong evidence that overall parental stress level is a significant contributor to child maltreatment, both on a broad statistical level (Straus

& Kantor, 1987) and from intensive observations of cases. For example, Wahler (1980) found that a mother's increased number of positive contacts with friends on a particular day was associated with reductions in the number of mother–child problems and suggested that to achieve long-term success it is crucial to address this factor. One effective response to such findings is to work with individual parents to enrich their social experiences (Mattaini, 1999). In many communities, however, there are a large number of at-risk parents in similar circumstances. Community-level intervention then becomes a practical response. For example, Wolfe (1991) and associates incorporated informal activity groups in a community setting as a component of an abuse prevention program that also included individual behavioral training and guidance in parenting and the availability of respite care.

Lightburn and Kemp (1994) described a family support program with which they were associated for some time that not only is deeply rooted in the community, but also emphasizes obtaining feedback from the community, developing community among the participants, and using an educational and mutual-aid approach that builds consciously on historic roots in the settlement house movement. As Lightburn and Kemp reported, clients can make excellent use of "learning collectives" that use resources in the group to develop and test alternative life strategies. This program is, of course, an outstanding example of the use of a shared power perspective on practice, and current data indicate that such programs can have multiple positive effects (Comer & Fraser, 1998).

Even higher-level community interventions, such as those targeting economic development or the reduction of drug-related problems, are also likely to have an effect on the incidence of child maltreatment. Of course, if a family is referred because a child is in imminent danger, the social worker ordinarily would not devote most of his or her professional energies to economic development. Therefore, the need to interweave and phase multilevel strategies is clear (see, for example, Rothman, 1995). One may see a parent in a skills-training group, provide family-based consultation in the home, refer the parent to an ongoing support group, and advocate for the development of additional community-level resources. Of course, the social worker can only do so effectively if he or she understands the problem in depth and has the skills to intervene at these multiple levels. For this reason, training in generalist practice is crucial, even though it is not possible to be equally versed in everything. At the least, the social worker should know when to refer a client to a person with other skills or a program with other resources; ideally, he or she should know how to provide a rich array of services as well.

One way to begin thinking this way is to identify interventions at multiple levels that could benefit clients one is seeing now. Although the reader may find it valuable to complete this exercise individually, groups of students (who are likely to have different strengths and perspectives) may be able to develop a richer array of service options. (See Exercise 12 in Appendix C for details of this procedure.) Ideally, a social worker should be able to identify more than one possible interventive strategy at each systemic level (individual, family, group, community, or organization); further analysis and collaboration with clients should then help him or her to select the most potentially effective and efficient strategies.

An implicit case-to-class (or case-to-cause) phenomenon is present in generalist practice. If the social worker sees or learns from others in the agency that all the staff members are seeing a number of similar cases, it may make sense to step back and think about programmatic approaches that can efficiently respond to the issues that the class of clients is facing. A "planner" may also propose a programmatic response, but practitioners who are intimately and analytically familiar with the issues, in concert with clients (who are even more deeply embedded in the issues and have a different form of knowledge), may be more likely to develop programs that genuinely address the clients' needs. To design and develop excellent programs, practitioners have an organic tie to the realities of the issues, as opposed to an exclusively abstract understanding of them.

Program Planning, Design, and Development

Program planning, design, and development are not the exclusive province of administrators or planners, who often have only limited knowledge of the realities and complexities of clients' lives. Organizations and the programs they offer often do not work well for people (Meyer, 1979). Given the stubbornness of many social problems (and the current state of knowledge), even the best-designed and -implemented programs may produce marginal results in many cases. Effective programs that genuinely meet client needs and respond to social problems are more likely to be designed by or with extensive input from practitioners who have been immersed in the issues for some time in shared power collaborations with clients and other agency staff (see examples in Hanson, 1997). Obviously, in an organization that has a genuine commitment to shared power, clients and community members will also have strong voices in program planning and evaluation.

The following material outlines the program development process in an idealized fashion. Not all programs develop in this way, and the process is usually recursive, circling back on itself. Furthermore, a social worker may be involved only in parts of this process, for example, joining a project after the needs assessment has been completed or being responsible only for developing a new program design if an evaluation indicates that the goals and objectives are not being satisfactorily achieved. A general framework for program development, adapted from Kettner, Moroney, and Martin (1990), is portrayed in Figure 12-3.

Note that although a general direction is portrayed in the figure, it is common for program developers to circle back to earlier stages, particularly if the program appears not to be working as well as it might.

Problem Analysis

Programs emerge to address social problems and common difficulties experienced by a class of people as opposed to unique "private troubles" affecting only one individual. Program design should flow directly from analysis and assessment of the problem. One important thing to remember is that the problem should not be defined as lack of services (Kettner, Moroney, & Martin, 1990). For example, a lack of foster care or of inpatient drug rehabilitation facilities is not a social problem. Those services are responses to social problems. Defining the problem in terms of lack of a particular service profoundly limits the consideration of alternative options (for example, one would not even consider intensive home-based services to prevent and respond to family breakdown if the problem is defined as lack of foster care). Family breakdown should, in that case, be the problem to be analyzed.

Figure 12-3. The Program Development Cycle

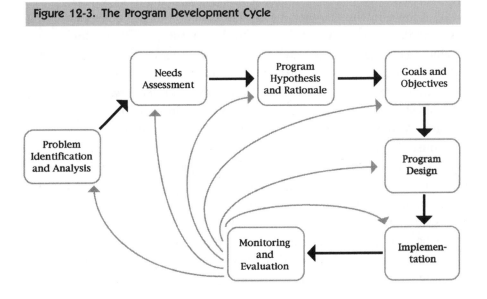

Problem analysis proceeds by examining what is known about the problem, both locally by contact with people who are affected and more globally by searching the literature to explore the etiology and epidemiology and available responses to the problem. There are often obvious or subtle social justice dimensions involved in the social construction of, and the development of responses to, social issues. Those dimensions must be explicitly identified and considered in exploring programmatic options. Investigation of associated factors that may affect program design (such as cultural factors that influence which responses are likely to be most acceptable) and of available conceptual frameworks for understanding the issue is valuable at this stage.

Needs Assessment

As the social worker and the agency learn more about the problem, they usually must learn how many clients or potential clients the problem affects, in what ways, and to what extent. If the agency is responsible for child protective services or preventive services in a large geographic area, with thousands of potential clients who are at high risk for abuse or neglect, its program obviously must be different from one designed to meet the moderate needs of a few families. Needs assessment provides the data required to answer questions about the extent of clients' needs. Although it is possible, and sometimes necessary, to implement complex and expensive needs assessment strategies (Kettner, Moroney, & Martin, 1990), some needs assessment is usually better than none, and often a modest strategy produces adequate data from which to proceed. Neuber and Associates (1980) suggested the three-pronged strategy depicted in Figure 12-4.

As shown in the diagram, needs assessment can begin by examining existing data sources; not only statistical data but also other information, including qualitative data, may be of value. Another major source of data is key informants, including professionals, community leaders, and others who are immersed in the local situation. Through interviews (or occasionally questionnaires) those persons can provide information that captures the unique dimensions of the problem in the service area.

Consumers (clients) or potential consumers can provide rich, grounded data that are essential to understanding the problem and developing responsive programs. Consumer's perceptions may differ dramatically from those of staff or other key informants, sometimes as a result of cultural or class differences and sometimes simply because their experiences of services have been different. Although maximizing consumer involvement in needs assessment involves work, the data consumers provide are different from what can be obtained in any other way and are clearly required in

Figure 12-4. A Comprehensive Needs Assessment Framework

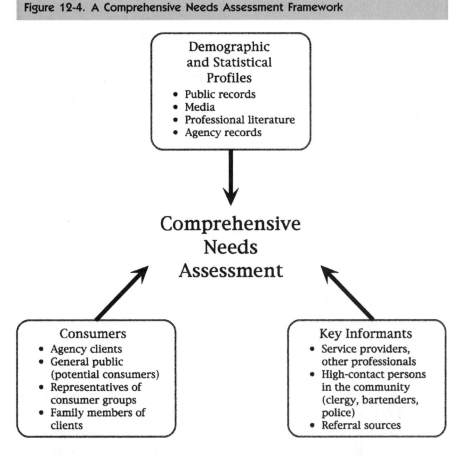

SOURCE: After Neuber, K.A., & Associates (1980). *Needs Assessment: A Model for Community Planning.* Newbury Park, CA: Sage Publications.

organizations that authentically value the sharing of power. There are a range of available approaches to needs assessment that vary along the dimensions of community involvement and empowerment, breadth, and rigor (Marti-Costa & Serrano-Garcia, 1983). It is often valuable to think about multiple options with key stakeholders including community members and consumers before deciding how to proceed.

The social worker may not always have the resources or sanction to complete a full needs assessment. An administrator may define the broad parameters of the program on the basis of long experience, essentially using herself or himself as the only key informant, and instruct the practitioner how to proceed. Even under these circumstances, examining the relevant literature to enrich the work is a low-cost strategy (and often an ethical imperative), and informal contact with other informants and consumers of services can often be incorporated seamlessly into planning.

Establishing the Program Rationale

An effective program intervenes in the multicausal chain that produces and maintains the problem. Program developers who have not thought this chain through explicitly usually produce programs that fail to work well because they rely on doing the right thing essentially by accident. If an organization is charged with preventing child abuse, a worker may decide, based on his or her own interest, that the program should consist of a six-session educational group to teach at-risk parents about child development and what they can realistically expect from their children. There is an implicit causal chain here, which suggests that the lack of knowledge and unrealistic expectations contribute significantly to abuse. As it happens, the available data do not generally support this model (Wolfe, 1991). Other approaches are better supported by theory and research. For example, it is known from the literature that isolation and poverty increase the risk of child maltreatment. Programs that target those factors are much more likely to be effective than the educational model discussed above.

For a more detailed example, see Figure 12-5. Work conducted by the PEACE POWER Working Group (Mattaini, 2001), looking at youth violence prevention, suggests that there are a number of sub-clusters of violent incidents in which youth participate, most of which may need to be addressed in a comprehensive prevention program (Mattaini, Twyman, Chin, & Lee, 1996). One of those clusters involves threatening or violent action to save face, for example when confronted by someone in authority like a teacher. A number of factors, as shown in the figure, are contributing factors to such behavior, including:

- a history in which threats of violence lead people to back down from the confrontation (as they do here again), and in which threats and violence are associated with gaining or maintaining status;
- a life filled with many other aversives that increase the negative valence of confrontation and the positive valence of escaping confrontation;
- models of violent response to confrontation; and
- self-talk suggesting that confrontation is equivalent to intolerable disrespect.

An effective prevention program may address several of these, as well as other factors. The program rationale, in other words, grows from an understanding of the reasons why the problem occurs and what is known about effective prevention. The rationale can be framed as one or more "if-then-because" statements, for example: "If young people are exposed to models who deal with confrontation in assertive but respectful ways, then the rate of threats and violence will decrease, because the young people will learn

Figure 12-5. Factors Shaping and Maintaining Threatening or Violent Responses to Confrontation by a Person in Authority

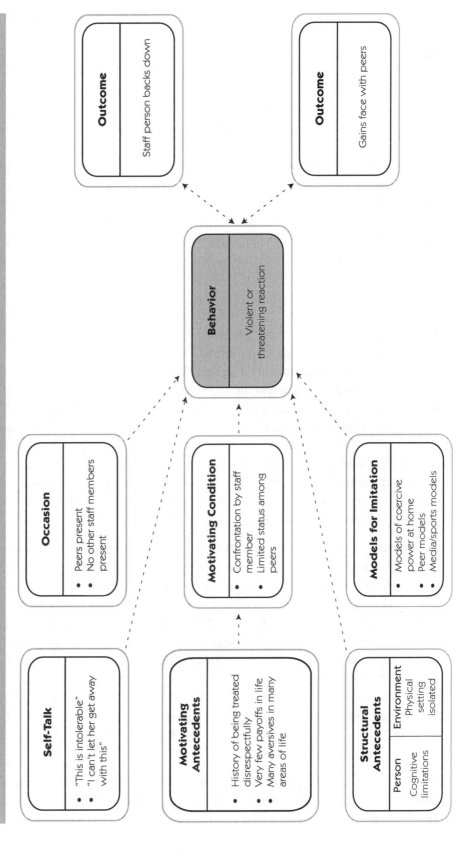

alternative, less costly and more effective behavioral repertoires from those models." The program rationale for a prevention program aimed at youth violence will necessarily involve a number of such statements, since we know that causes and supports for youth violence are multiple. (In fact, the most useful programs probably are those that involve the construction of cultures of nonviolent power in families, organizations and communities; see Mattaini, 2001, for more information.) Also, thinking in generalist terms, there are usually multiple options for having an impact on any particular link in the causal network. For example, models of alternative ways of coping with confrontation could come through individual work, collaboration on developing videotapes, contact with positive mentors, group skills training, or many other approaches.

Goals and Objectives

Once the program rationale is clear, goals and objectives flow directly from the conceptual model. The range of real options is often constrained by contextual and organizational factors and limited resources; sometimes the program may be able to address only a subset of the relevant factors, and in some cases for political reasons, the program may need to include components that the social workers designing it do not believe are central but that other crucial stakeholders do.

Goals are usually defined as general statements about what the program is meant to achieve ("to reduce the incidence of child maltreatment in Columbia County"), whereas objectives are more specific, measurable parts of the goals. Major types of objectives include the following:

- impact objectives, which target changes in the overall rate of a problem among a specific population (for example, "To reduce the rate of repeated reports of child abuse and neglect in the county by 20 percent by July 1, 2002")
- outcome objectives, which target (usually short-term) change among program participants (for instance, "To decrease the use of power-assertive discipline techniques among parents identified by the county child protective services agency by 70 percent after eight sessions, as measured by videotaped observations of parent–child interactions")
- process objectives, which describe program activities or inputs (such as, "To provide 270 home visits during 2001, as reported by the agency's management information system").

These types of objectives are hierarchical; impact objectives, which are not often difficult to evaluate given limited resources, usually have one or more outcome objectives associated with them. Outcome objectives in turn often have one or more process objectives associated with them. Note that each of these objectives, of whatever type, should be clear, specific, measurable, and have clear timelines for completion. After goals and objectives have been determined, the social worker and others involved in program development must determine exactly who will do what to achieve the goals—the process of program design.

Program Design

Established goals and objectives can subsequently be used in at least two ways. They can and should be used as the basis for program evaluation, discussed later. Goals and objectives are also important for planning the activities to be included in the program, although by themselves they provide only partial guidance. Setting an objective related to reducing the rate of depression among a group of young single mothers, for example, is a useful starting point. However, such an objective does not tell one much about how it will be achieved. That decision is made on the basis of the conceptual program rationale that emerged from the needs assessment and problem analysis. If social isolation is hypothesized to be a major causal factor in maintaining the young mothers' depression, for example, program activities that flow from this analysis may include support groups and case management to enhance positive connections with natural networks.

Program activities defined at this abstract level, however, are just overall strategies for addressing the issue; there is tremendous variation among "support groups," for example. Really adequate program design includes clear specification of who will do what when—who will lead the group, who will attend, what the schedule and structure of the group will be, and what activities will occur in the group meetings. Although there should generally be some relatively clear plans in place before the program begins, in most cases these activities will evolve over time, based on ongoing evaluation of how well the program is approaching its objectives.

Program Implementation

Program implementation generally requires the cooperative, coordinated effort of groups of people (line staff, supervisors, administrators, support staff, and clients). These individuals often function as members of task groups (staff groups, committees, and interdisciplinary teams) that must function effectively if the program is to be well implemented. Social workers and others have studied effective task groups and have learned that it is possible for social workers, whether as group leaders or as members of groups, to work toward more effective team functioning (Toseland & Rivas, 1995; Tropman, 1996). Specific techniques for encouraging effective team-work and empowerment are now available, and every social worker in-volved in programming should be familiar with them (Daniels, 2000).

Beyond the specifics of task group work, agency context and culture also have major effects on program implementation. It is possible, but ap-parently uncommon, to construct an explicit "empowerment culture" in an organization (Lowery & Mattaini, 1999). Certain practices are charac-teristic of such an organization across all levels, for example:

- Authentic dialogue in which all participants have strong voices, as opposed to hierarchical arrangements rooted in adversarial power, is common. Foster parents, for example, feel respected and heard in planning.
- Information is freely shared among stakeholders, rather than being used to consolidate competitive positions. Line workers are aware, for example, of the fiscal resources available to the program.
- Evaluation activities are inclusive; all actors are heard in the process. For instance, biological parents review and contribute to evaluation materials that are submitted to courts.
- Case activities are carried out on the basis of shared contribution and responsibility, so that actors such as foster or biological parents par-ticipate from their strengths, and their roles can expand as their ex-pertise grows.

Such organizational practices do not emerge automatically; practices in other parts of the organization, particularly groups with administrative and supervisory responsibilities, must be carefully designed to support shared power.

Staff members who are involved in implementing programs also must be trained and supervised. It is usually a mistake to assume that staff members already have the knowledge and skills required to implement a program and will apply them effectively. Every program is different, and some level of training is almost always required, in part to give staff members oppor-tunities to think through how to apply what they know, and use what they have to contribute, in a new setting. Even highly competent staff members may not apply what they know effectively under new conditions without explicit attention to staff development (Windsor et al., 1984).

Effective supervision does not involve speaking "longer, louder and meaner" (Daniels, 2000, p. 17) to obtain improved performance. Rather, it primarily involves the following steps, which are generally best done collaboratively with the staff involved:

- pinpointing what needs to be done,
- finding ways to track whether it is happening (measuring),
- providing feedback on performance,
- reinforcing performance, and
- evaluating whether staff activity is leading to achievement of objectives.

This model, drawn from Daniels, has broad applicability. By itself, it does not capture every situation, but this general frame can help social workers achieve excellence and resolve problems in most situations. The literature on social work supervision provides additional guidance. One important way to pinpoint what should be done clinically, for example, is to ask questions in supervision such as "What does the client want help with?" and "What are you doing to help the client?" (Harkness & Hensley, 1991). Reinforcing what the person is doing right is much more effective than simply giving orders and criticizing inadequate performance. According to research conducted by Komaki (1998) and others, key features of effective leadership include high levels of monitoring (exploring the performance of the supervisee), followed relatively quickly with consequences, particularly recognition of positive contributions, encouragement, and opportunities to describe how one achieved positive outcomes. The concept of the "emotional bank account" is also useful; supervisees respond better to corrective feedback if there are at least three times as many "deposits" (recognition and appreciation for contributions) as "withdrawals" (instances of corrective feedback) (Latting, 1992).

Most graduate social workers develop programs that require staff development, effective team functioning, and supervision of other staff. These are yet other functions that the generalist social worker should be prepared to take on when the practice situation requires.

Program Evaluation

As seen in previous chapters, monitoring practice is an organic part of all social work practice at all systemic levels. Program evaluation can be thought of as practice monitoring at a programmatic level, and in fact data collected in routine practice monitoring can often be aggregated for program evaluation purposes. Determining what the program is doing and how well it is doing can be a natural part of the process. It may be surprising to realize how little effort it would take to evaluate programs if they were designed from the beginning with a curiosity about and a commitment to finding out how they are doing.

Program evaluation is a professional discipline in itself, and some organizations and individuals specialize exclusively in performing evaluations, which can become complex and expensive (Rossi, Freeman, & Lipsey, 1999). Most programs, however, do not need to expend so much effort to make a credible beginning. Although there are many ways that program evaluation can be subdivided, in general there are two primary types of evaluation: (1) formative, and (2) summative. A formative (or developmental [Berk & Rossi, 1990]) evaluation occurs as the program is initiated and implemented, primarily to address questions such as,

- "Is the program reaching enough of the at-risk population?"
- "How much service is being provided?"
- "How many resources, and of what kinds, are being expended?"

In a summative evaluation, one looks at how the program has fared during a specified period of time and examines performance on process objectives (program activities and inputs), outcomes for clients, and sometimes impact on the target community. These factors can be combined with data about expenditures to perform cost-effectiveness and cost–benefit analyses as well.

Program evaluation is really not about producing reports, of course. It is ultimately meaningless unless what is learned from the evaluation is fed back into the program development process to help sharpen goals and objectives and to improve services to clients. It is a common, but serious, mistake to think that one undertakes a program evaluation primarily to satisfy funders, although such pressures are real and increasing. Rather, evaluations, if thoughtfully done, are primarily important to the program itself. As is true for all steps of the process, evaluation should be planned and conducted in partnership with the community and with clients/consumers. Different groups of stakeholders may value different outcomes, and may also have different takes on the kind of evidence needed to demonstrate usefulness. Challenging as such collaboration is, evaluations that honor multiple perspectives are more likely to be useful and used than those that do not.

Proposal Writing

A good deal of funding for social work practice comes from contracts with governmental entities; grants from private and public sources; and in public agencies, directly from budget allocations. These funds are generally allocated on the basis of written proposals that are submitted in response to requests for proposals or proposals that are submitted as a regular part of the funding cycle. Proposal writing (and locating potential recipients of proposals) is to some extent an art and can be a full-time job, but most graduate social workers will be routinely involved in the preparation of such requests for funding. Excellent books on preparing proposals are available (see, for example, Coley & Scheinberg, 2000), but a few essential points can be summarized here.

Getting funding is not easy. Most proposals (except for regular continuation funding requests) are not funded, so it is essential not to become discouraged if a proposal is not funded. When proposals are not funded, it is important to consider any corrective feedback as nondefensively as possible and to realize that the funding process is often highly political. Frequently, professionals submit proposals more to become known to funders, to become part of the network, and to test the waters for future submissions than to receive immediate funding. Funders tend to support the programs they know, and this tendency is not as unfair as it may seem because funders prefer giving money to those whom they are confident will use it well. A major objective of a proposal, in fact, is to build confidence in an organization and a program.

Although who one knows and the luck of the draw (especially the particular reviewers who read a submission) are important factors in funding decisions, a good deal can be done to enhance the chances that a proposal will be accepted. First, the proposal must be on time—extensions are almost never possible. Therefore, back-up people, back-up computers, back-up copying machines, and so forth are necessary to ensure that a deadline will be met. Second, the proposal must appear professional (with graphs and figures if appropriate) and be neat, grammatically perfect, and pitched to the audience that will read it. Proposals geared to professional peers require a different approach than those to lay advisory boards, for example. Third, enthusiasm and genuine confidence in the suggested approach must be evident. Fourth, most funders have a particular format they require for proposals, and it is essential to follow that format scrupulously. In general, the format is likely to include most of the elements of program design that have been discussed here; this fact suggests that if an organization has an effective program development process in place, much of the necessary material will already be on hand.

All Things to All People?

Generalist practice can be overwhelming. There is so much to know—so many clinical, monitoring, programmatic, supervisory, and other skills to master—that social workers may be tempted simply to narrow their focus and learn one aspect very well. Although there is a place for specialization, method is not it. Graduate social workers must be familiar enough to select intervention strategies that are based on clients' needs rather than on limitations of their knowledge and to apply their skills effectively as part of organizational structures. In short, they need to be "masters of social work."

By this point it should also be clear that some practice processes are common across systemic levels, and that some practice skills are generically useful, but also that one needs special skills and relies on somewhat different strategies at different system levels. At all levels, the social worker must find some way to "engage" or "join" the client system, thus potentiating his or her value as a support (reinforcer) and guide to potentially improved outcomes. One must, with all client systems, gather information (exploration), organize that information analytically in a way that leads to collaborative interventive strategies (assessment), and selectively intervene at points and in ways identified by the assessment. All of this should occur within a shared-power dynamic, in which social worker and clients share contributions, responsibility, and obligations. In work with an individual, data collected may include emotions, levels of support and coercion within the household, and selected personal history, because these data reflect the salient behaviors and the contingencies that shape them. In work with a neighborhood, one may be most interested in determining who the most powerful figures and organizations are and what the employment, economic, and educational levels of community residents are, because these data tell one a great deal about current and potential contingency networks. In either case, one must first obtain the information, organize it, and understand its implications before one moves to interventive planning.

At the same time, social workers cannot be specialists in everything. Most specialization in social work occurs by field of practice; generalist social workers rely on multiple modalities (individual, group, family, community), focused by institutions, social problems, and population groups. They must know about the problems faced by clients that their organizations work with; about service structures, resources, and policies relevant to these problems; and about the variety of ways to intervene to address them. They may also be particularly skilled in some interventive modalities and may sometimes refer clients for specialized services (for example, to groups for those who batter or programs for children with autism). Still, a sense that one never knows enough may remain, and this is true. As long as clients come with problems that social workers are unable to help them resolve, individual practitioners and the field as a whole must remain committed to progressively expand knowledge and deepen skills. Social workers individually and collectively make a special commitment to contribute to the construction of human alternatives, not out of charity, but because they recognize that we are all organically connected. Particularly as long as some among us are denied our basic human rights, whether by societal oppression or in ways as personal as family violence, there is more to learn and more to do.

References

Bartlett, H. M. (1970). *The common base of social work practice*. Silver Spring, MD: National Association of Social Workers.

Berk, R. A., & Rossi, P. H. (1990). *Thinking about program evaluation*. Newbury Park, CA: Sage Publications.

Biglan, A. (1991). Distressed behavior and its context. *Behavior Analyst, 14,* 157–169.

Brown, G. W., & Harris, T. (1978). *Social origins of depression: A study of psychiatric disorder in women*. New York: Free Press.

Brunk, M., Henggeler, S. W., & Whelan, J. P. (1987). Comparison of multisystemic therapy and parent training in the brief treatment of child abuse and neglect. *Journal of Consulting and Clinical Psychology, 55,* 171–178.

Coley, S. M., & Scheinberg, C. A. (2000). *Proposal writing* (2nd ed.) Newbury Park, CA: Sage Publications.

Comer, E. W., & Fraser, M. W. (1998). Evaluation of six family-support projects: Are they effective? *Families in Society, 79,* 134–148.

Daniels, A. C. (2000). *Bringing out the best in people* (2nd ed.). New York: McGraw-Hill.

Dumas, J. E., & Wahler, R. G. (1985). Indiscriminate mothering as a contextual factor in aggressive-oppositional child behavior: "Damned if you do, damned if you don't." *Journal of Abnormal Child Psychology, 13,* 1–17.

Gambrill, E. (1996). Loneliness, social isolation, and social anxiety. In M. A. Mattaini & B. A. Thyer (Eds.), *Finding solutions to social problems: Behavioral strategies for change* (pp. 345–371). Washington, DC: American Psychological Association.

Glenn, S. S. (1991). Contingencies and metacontingencies: Relations among behavioral, cultural, and biological evolution. In P. A. Lamal (Ed.), *Behavioral analysis of societies and cultural practices* (pp. 39–73). New York: Hemisphere.

Goldstein, A. P., Keller, H., & Erné, D. (1985). *Changing the abusive parent*. Champaign, IL: Research.

Hanson, M. (Ed.). (1997). *Maternal and child health program design and development: From the ground up; collaboration and partnership*. New York: Columbia University School of Social Work.

Harkness, D., & Hensley, H. (1991). Changing the focus of social work supervision: Effects on client satisfaction and generalized contentment. *Social Work, 36,* 506–512.

Howing, P. T., Wodarski, J. S., Gaudin, J. M., Jr., & Kurtz, P. D. (1989). Effective interventions to ameliorate the incidence of child maltreatment: The empirical base. *Social Work, 34,* 330–338.

Jacobson, N. S., Dobson, K. S., Truax, P. A., Addis, M. E., Koerner, K., Gollan, J. K., Gortner, E., & Prince, S. E. (1996). A component analysis of cognitive-behavioral treatment for depression. *Journal of Consulting and Clinical Psychology, 64,* 295–304.

Kettner, P. M., Moroney, R. M., & Martin, L. L. (1990). *Designing and managing programs: An effectiveness-based approach.* Newbury Park, CA: Sage Publications.

Komaki, J. L. (1998). *Leadership from an operant perspective.* London: Routledge.

Latting, J. K. (1992). Giving corrective feedback: A decisional analysis. *Social Work, 37,* 424–430.

Lerner, S. (1997). Chemical reaction. *Ms, 8*(1), 56–61.

Lightburn, A., & Kemp, S. P. (1994). Family-support programs: Opportunities for community-based practice. *Families in Society, 75,* 16–26.

Lowery, C. T., & Mattaini, M. A. (1999). The science of sharing power: Native American thought and behavior analysis. *Behavior and Social Issues, 9,* 3–23.

Marti-Costa, S., & Serrano-Garcia, I. (1983, Summer). Needs assessment and community development: An ideological perspective. *Prevention in Human Services,* pp. 75–88.

Mattaini, M. A. (1999). *Clinical intervention with families.* Washington, DC: NASW Press.

Mattaini, M. A., with the PEACE POWER Working Group (2001). *Peace power for adolescents: Strategies for a culture of nonviolence.* Washington, DC: NASW Press.

Mattaini, M. A., McGowan, B. G., & Williams, G. (1996). Child maltreatment. In M. A. Mattaini & B. A. Thyer (Eds.), *Finding solutions to social problems: Behavioral strategies for change* (pp. 223–266). Washington, DC: American Psychological Association.

Mattaini, M. A., Twyman, J. S., Chin, W., & Lee, K. N. (1996). Youth violence. In M. A. Mattaini & B. A. Thyer (Eds.), *Finding solutions to social problems: Behavioral strategies for change* (pp. 75–111). Washington, DC: American Psychological Association.

Meyer, C. H. (1979). Introduction: Making organizations work for people. In C. H. Meyer (Ed.), *Making organizations work for people* (pp. 1–12). Silver Spring, MD: National Association of Social Workers.

Minuchin, S. (1974). *Families and family therapy.* Cambridge, MA: Harvard University Press.

Minuchin, S., Simon, G. M., & Lee, W. (1996). *Mastering family therapy: Journeys of growth and transformation.* New York: John Wiley & Sons.

Neuber, K. A., & Associates. (1980). *Needs assessment: A model for community planning.* Newbury Park, CA: Sage Publications.

Patterson, G. R. (1976). The aggressive child: Victim and architect of a coercive system. In E. J. Mash, L. A. Hamerlynck, & L. C. Handy (Eds.), *Behavior modification and families* (pp. 267–316). New York: Brunner/Mazel.

Rossi, P. H., Freeman, H. E., & Lipsey, M. W. (1999). *Evaluation: A systematic approach* (6th ed.). Thousand Oaks, CA: Sage Publications.

Rothman, J. (1995). Approaches to community intervention. In J. Rothman, J. L. Erlich, & J. E. Tropman (Eds.), *Strategies of community intervention* (5th ed., pp. 26–63). Itasca, IL: F. E. Peacock.

Serna, L. A., Schumaker, J. B., Sherman, J. A., & Sheldon, J. B. (1991). In-home generalization of social interactions in families of adolescents with behavior problems. *Journal of Applied Behavior Analysis, 24,* 733–746.

Straus, M. A., & Kantor, G. K. (1987). Stress and child abuse. In R. E. Helfer & R. S. Kempe (Eds.), *The battered child* (4th ed., pp. 42–59). Chicago: University of Chicago Press.

Sviridoff, M., & Ryan, W. (1997). Community-centered family service. *Families in Society, 78,* 128–139.

Toseland, R. W., & Rivas, R. F. (1995). *An introduction to group work practice* (2nd ed.). Boston: Allyn & Bacon.

Tropman, J. E. (1996). *Effective meetings: Improving group decision making* (2nd ed.). Thousand Oaks, CA: Sage Publications.

Wahler, R. G. (1980). The insular mother: Her problems in parent–child treatment. *Journal of Applied Behavior Analysis, 8,* 27–42.

Webster-Stratton, C. (1997). From parent training to community building. *Families in Society, 78,* 156–171.

Whiteman, M., Fanshel, D., & Grundy, J. F. (1987). Cognitive–behavioral interventions aimed at anger of parents at risk of child abuse. *Social Work, 32,* 469–474.

Windsor, R. A., Baranowski, T., Clark, N., & Cutter, G. (1984). *Evaluation of health promotion and education programs.* Mountain View, CA: Mayfield.

Wolf, M. M., Braukmann, C. J., & Ramp, K. A. (1987). Serious delinquent behavior as part of a significantly handicapping condition: Cures and supportive environments. *Journal of Applied Behavior Analysis, 20,* 347–359.

Wolfe, D. A. (1991). *Preventing physical and emotional abuse of children.* New York: Guilford Press.

The Contexts of Practice

CHAPTER 13

Fields of Practice

Sheila B. Kamerman

What goes around comes around. Graduate social work education began with a focus on specialized fields of practice because there was no holistic concept of social work practice. Over time, the profession developed a comprehensive concept of a shared core of knowledge, values, and skills, beginning with a common core for casework and moving to include other social work methods: group work; community organizing; administration; and, much later, policy practice. So strong was the emphasis on the common core that the context of practice was given limited attention. In the 1970s, social workers recognized that the overall field of social welfare had expanded and diversified greatly and, as a consequence, other professions and disciplines were entering the field and carving out pieces that were relevant to their expertise. Adequate professional social work performance increasingly required some specialization in addition to the core of common knowledge. As a result, social work curricula now increasingly reflect a concentration in a field of practice in addition to a social work method.

In this context, "fields of practice" refers to the distinctive settings, population groups, or social problem areas in which social workers practice and to which social workers adapt their practice. What is meant by fields of practice, how these fields relate to the overall social welfare domain, what the most salient fields are for today's social work professional, how the concept of field of practice relates to social work methods and fits in a social work curriculum, and how different fields can be assessed are the focuses of this chapter. But first, some history.

Background and Context

The debate about the balance between an emphasis on social work methods and fields of practice has been long-standing in social work education

319

and still is not fully resolved. The two major professional organizations, the National Association of Social Workers (NASW) and the Council on Social Work Education (CSWE), have played important roles in advancing the concept of fields of practice, but their ambivalence continues to be reflected in various publications. Thus, a brief review of historical development of the concept also offers some insight into the important role that these organizations have played—and can continue to play—in the development of social work knowledge and skills.

The preface to the 18th edition of the *Encyclopedia of Social Work* (Minahan, 1987) stated that its purpose was "to provide an objective overview of social work in the United States—and its history, its current concerns and interests, the state of its art, and its view of the future" (p. v). However, although the 15th and 16th editions of the *Encyclopedia* (Lurie, 1965; Morris, 1971) contained entries on fields of practice, neither the 17th edition (Turner, 1977) nor the 18th edition did so. Moreover, although there is a Reader's Guide "box" ("Fields of Practice," 1995) in the 19th edition that cross-references a miscellany of topics under the rubric of "Fields of Practice," there is no article on the subject, no reference in the index, and no explanation of the concept. Why there was an almost 25-year hiatus in the coverage of this topic is not clear. Even the concept of specialization received little, if any, attention in the 18th edition. But when entries referred to this concept, fields of practice seemed to be the focus. Thus, for example, Briar (1987) stated that

> The trend toward specialization continues in social work. . . . Specializations continue to be defined according to (1) the population served, as in the cases of child welfare and aging; (2) the focal problem, such as substance abuse; (3) the practice setting as in corrections or health; or (4) some combination of the above. (pp. 396–397)

CSWE Attends to Fields of Practice

Perhaps even more significant than the lack of attention to fields of practice for more than two decades in the definitive sourcebook of social work knowledge was the reverse pattern in social work education, in which there was a dramatic increase in attention to fields of practice in the social work curricula. Thus, for example, CSWE's 1983 *Curriculum Policy for the Master's Degree and Baccalaureate Programs in Social Work Education* (cited in Minahan, 1987) stated that the curriculum for the MSW "is to require a concentration of specialized knowledge and practice skills in one or more areas relevant to social work . . . . Each graduate program will determine which concentrations it will make available to students and the framework it will use to organize them" (p. 963). The four concentrations listed were field of practice, population groups, problem areas, and methods, and a combination of method and one other concentration was urged. The statement offered no explanation of why fields of practice was separated from population groups and problem areas, even though they were all treated as fields of practice in earlier NASW and CSWE publications.

Even more revealing was Vinton's 1989 survey of 98 accredited MSW programs designed to assess trends in social work education concentrations and specializations that reported that between 1974 and 1989 the major trend was a move from specialization by method only to a specialization by method and field of practice (Vinton, 1995). Although Vinton understated this development by following the earlier CSWE conceptualization, separating fields of practice from social problems and population groups, she pointed out that ever since a 1979 survey, specialization by fields of practice had dramatically increased and that health and mental health, family and children's services, and aging were the dominant fields in both 1979 and 1988. Among the other fields represented in the social work curricula in this survey were corrections, school social services, mental retardation and developmental disabilities, substance abuse, industrial social work, and social services for women. Vinton characterized this development as a "boutique" effect, but most social work scholars would label it for what it is—an increase in the number of fields of practice. Whether this growth makes for dysfunctional fragmentation or greater opportunities for needed expertise is addressed later.

First Field, then Common Core

How, then, did the concern with fields of practice emerge, and what are the implications for education in social work today? Kahn (1965) pointed out that social work began to mature as a profession only when several different streams of service interventions and reform came together. The symbol of this unification and the climax of a long process toward "conceptual, methodological, ideological and organizational unity" (Kahn, 1965, p. 750) was the creation of NASW in 1955. In effect, from the establishment of the Conference of Boards of Public Charities in 1874 (which became the National Conference of Charities and Corrections in 1879 and later the National Conference on Social Welfare) to the mid-1940s, when the various streams began to move toward comprehensiveness, coherence, and integration, the social work profession focused its attention on the development of individual fields of practice. The five "major" fields, identified as far back as the 1920s and the Milford Conference of 1923–1928 (*Social Casework*, 1929/1974) were family welfare, child welfare, medical social work, psychiatric social work, and school social work. Later, NASW added the field of corrections to this listing and combined child and family welfare. (In current terms, these fields are child and family welfare, health and mental health, school social work, and corrections.) Little, if any, attempt was made in those years to identify a common core of social work practice.

The key element in social work professional developments after World War II was the recognition of a core of knowledge, values, and skills shared by all social workers. It is this core that permitted interfield mobility and the notion that one's identification with a particular method of intervention (casework, group work, community organization, or administration) was more important than the setting in which one practiced.

Returning to Fields

For the next 15 years, social work responded to the earlier problem of fragmentation and to the dynamics of professionalization by suggesting that there was a generic core of social work practice and that whatever variations existed were linked more to method than to field (insofar as "field" was limited to specific settings). However, with further growth and maturation, the search for greater refinement of practice theory and skills resumed.

CSWE began exploring the field-of-practice concept in 1959, identifying nine fields as salient (Bartlett, 1961): public assistance, family welfare, child welfare, corrections, psychiatric social work, medical social work services and public health, school social work, group services, and community planning. Note that from the outset, population groups, social problems, and settings were all included as the basis for the different fields of practice. Moreover, Bartlett (1961) also stressed the need to distinguish between "the operations of professional social workers and a consistently defined area of practice within which social workers operate" (p. 16).

Even more important than this CSWE initiative was NASW's establishment of its first Commission on Social Work Practice in 1955. This commission, which functioned until 1963, began to explore the definitional issues related to social work practice soon after its establishment. The commission's Subcommittee on Fields of Practice reported its recommendations to NASW in 1962. The subcommittee's members, who represented the intellectual leadership of the profession at that time, rediscovered the value of specialization with regard to settings, problems and tasks, and client or population groups and determined why specialization by fields of practice should be re-established, in addition to specialization by method.

Stressing the value of a two-dimensional model, one based on method and the other based on field of practice, the subcommittee's report confirmed that fields of practice were a "characteristic feature of social work" (Bartlett, 1965, p. 758) and strongly supported the concept as an organizing principle to be applied to social work knowledge, values, and skills and to supplement the existing conceptualization of social work practice by method. It further stressed that within any given field of practice, all methods (casework; group work; community organization; and, in current terms, administration and policy development and analysis) should be represented; that the particular cluster of interventions used might also vary by field of practice; and, perhaps even more important, that the patterns of fields of practice would vary from time to time in response to social change.

Bartlett (1965) also urged the development of criteria for defining emerging fields of practice. Earlier, drawing on the work of the NASW Commission on Social Work Practice, which she chaired, she had presented her framework for analyzing a field of practice (Bartlett, 1961):

- the problem (condition, phenomenon, task) of central concern, which is the starting point
- the system of organized services (policies and programs) established to respond to the problem
- the client population served
- the knowledge, values, and skills (or interventions) used in the field.

Bartlett (1961) concluded:

As analysis proceeds from field to field, these components may well be redefined and new elements may be identified. It should be noted that a field of practice, as defined, has a distinct identity. There are certain problems and activities that run all through social welfare. These are important, but we do not think of them as representing fields. *Those areas that have developed a relatively stable constellation of organized services, theory, methods, and other characteristics . . . can be recognized as fields.* (p. 41, italics added)

Bartlett's Refinements

In the last edition of the *Encyclopedia of Social Work* to have an article on the topic of fields of practice (Morris, 1971), Bartlett reminded the profession that the original concept was based on the different types of practice that emerged in the various settings (programs and social services) and the ways in which these settings shaped social work practice. With the development of the concept of a core of social work knowledge, defining fields of practice in terms of settings, programs, and services alone was not sufficient. The definition should now include practice in relation to different problems and population groups as well.

Bartlett pointed out that fields of practice have been a feature of social work since the profession emerged. She argued that efforts to develop a more coherent and internally consistent definition had not been successful because most fields "developed largely through historical accident and do not lend themselves to logical definition" (Bartlett, 1971, p. 1477). Thus, there was a need to include practice in relation to different social problems and with different population groups, as well as in different settings, all under fields of practice. Bartlett also stated that criteria for determining what is a field of practice must reflect the specific types of practice adaptations that arise in connection with the development of new forms of social services.

"One characteristic of fields that has created difficulty in defining criteria," Bartlett (1971) observed, "is the changing nature of settings, programs, and social services within which social work is practiced. . . . Societal problems and programs come and go, assuming a multiplicity of forms as they emerge, combine, and sometimes fade away" (p. 1478). She noted that some fields will disappear, other fields will be combined (and subsequently recombined), and still other fields will emerge. For example, she suggested that the health and psychiatric fields might combine and that child and family welfare would probably be integrated. In effect, she suggested that over time the profession might find certain fields of practice were no longer relevant or no longer distinctive and that new fields would arise.

Drawing on the work of the subcommittee and the original formulations of the NASW Commission on Social Work Practice, Bartlett (1971) presented specific criteria for identifying a field of practice:

- a major human need or social problem and the services organized to meet the need or problem
- a distinctive social work contribution to the overall program and to the population served (those who have the need or problem)
- social work practice in the field that demonstrates the common and essential elements of all social work practice (knowledge, values, and intervention techniques), including administration, research, and policy
- specialized competence required to practice effectively in the particular field
- criteria for fields that are flexible and not held to a standard of covering practice completely in a logical manner. As social change occurs, new fields will emerge and old ones may disappear or merge with others.

Bartlett concluded by stressing that the notion of social problem should be combined with that of field of practice as an extension of the concept, not as a separate concept.

To round out the picture, the report of the NASW Commission on Social Work Practice (1962) called attention to three other important aspects of fields of practice:

1. Private practice of social work is not a field of practice in the sense under discussion. Theoretically, there might be private practice in any or all fields. Like certain other dimensions (public/voluntary, sectarian/nonsectarian, urban/rural), it is independent of the fields-of-practice notion.
2. Not every social worker is working at a given moment in a professionally recognized field of practice. Some inevitably will be working in newly emerging fields of practice, not yet fully recognized or established. Schools and professional organizations need to take account of this.
3. A large complex agency such as a settlement house or a community center may be identified with more than one field of practice (p. 14).

Fields of Practice Today

Defining the Concept

Drawing on the work of Bartlett, the NASW Commission on Social Work Practice, Kahn, and Briar, this author offers the following definition of social work *fields of practice*: the context for practice that is shaped and developed in response to the *settings* in which social workers practice (for example, public or private social agencies; government or nongovernmental organizations; and distinctive organizations, such as the workplace, hospitals, and military bases), the social *problems* in which social workers intervene (including child, elder, or spouse abuse; substance abuse; homelessness; chronic mental illness; and poverty), and the client *populations* whom social workers help (children, youths, families, older people, racial and ethnic groups, and refugees).

The assumption of the concept of field of practice is that there is a core foundation of social work knowledge, values, and skills that applies to all social work practice but that the arena in which social workers practice is so large and diversified that there are distinctive variations in practice within the fields of social work and social welfare. These variations provide the basis for significant practice specializations that have implications for all social work methods (work with individuals, families, and groups; community organization and development; administration and management; and policy formation and analysis).

Salient Fields

"Social welfare"—a term used interchangeably in the United States with "social sector" and "social policy" and internationally with "social services" and "the social protection system"—is an institution that comprises all the policies and programs by which a government guarantees or affirms a defined minimum level of income, consumption rights, and an overall standard of living. The term "human services," used in the United States, is still another variation on this lexicon. Governments achieve this overall goal through the use of distributive principles and mechanisms based on other than market criteria. For example, financial or social need, vulnerability, social risk, and age may all be criteria for the receipt of government-provided, -funded, or -regulated social benefits and services.

Kahn (1979) conceptualized six components of the social sector following the model developed earlier in Great Britain (Townsend et al., 1970): health care, education, housing, income transfers, employment, and personal social services. (The British did not include employment services, but Kahn did, following the practice of several other countries.) One could add a seventh system: the justice system.

Social workers may—and indeed do—practice in all six (or seven) "social services." However, they are the dominant profession only in delivering the personal social services, whether through a freestanding and independent delivery system (such as child welfare or child and family services or services for older people) or as an adjunctive service. Thus, the various fields of social work practice include those in which social work plays an ancillary role (which may be a major one), as well as those in which it is the host profession.

The fields of practice based in settings in which social work plays an adjunctive role today include:

- health and mental health (earlier termed "medical and psychiatric social services" but excluding public health, which now has its own established professional base)
- education (school-based social services but not the formal educational component, which clearly has its own professional base)
- housing (social services, including services for homeless people)
- employment (social services at or linked to work and the workplace, a relatively new field of practice)
- justice (corrections)
- income transfers (not the delivery of cash assistance, which is no longer an individualized service, but social services linked to welfare and the social insurance programs, which also have largely disappeared in recent years, but may yet re-emerge).

The personal social services—and social work's commitment to these services in the various fields of practice—have expanded and become increasingly diversified since the War on Poverty programs for poor people and the expanded social services programs linked to public assistance in the 1960s, the enactment of Title XX of the Social Security Act of 1974 (P.L. 93-647) and its transformation of the social services field in the 1970s (Gilbert, 1977), and the explosion in the establishment of categorical service programs in the 1970s and 1980s.

In this context, personal social services encompass the totality of publicly subsidized and publicly and privately delivered individualized services that are designed to meet both the ordinary and special needs of individuals and families (Kahn, 1979; Kamerman & Kahn, 1976):

- information, referral, advocacy, and advice
- therapy, counseling, help, and rehabilitation
- life cycle development and socialization
- protection, practical help, and care
- self-help and mutual aid.

Historically, the personal social services emerged as services for people who were poor, troubled, or deviant (for example, juvenile delinquents, vagrants, and people who abuse substances), but they have expanded since the 1970s in response to the demands and needs of broader population groups, including frail older people, people with chronic illness or developmental disabilities, young parents, and working parents.

Although they are not necessarily delivered through any one system (public or private, for-profit or nonprofit, religious or secular, integrated or categorical), these services have been recognized in the United States and many other advanced industrialized countries as sharing common functions, regardless of the setting in which they are provided (residential facility, community center, workplace, school, home, family and children's services agency, senior citizens center), the age group served (children, youths, adults, or older individuals), or the presenting problem (alcoholism, parent-child or marital conflict, social isolation, and so forth). However, here, too, subfields are emerging as separate fields of practice.

It has been the spate of federal legislation on social services enacted since the 1960s that has led to the emergence and growth of new fields of practice within the personal social services. For example, the 1974 passage of Title XX of the Social Security Act (P.L. 93-647; now the Social Services Block Grant [SSBG]) permitted the states to use federal funds flexibly for whichever services they viewed as worthwhile. As a result, in 1994, 29 different services were funded under this law for children, youths, families, and older individuals, with significant variations among the states (U.S. House of Representatives, 1996). In addition to the general social services funding provided by the SSBG, many categorical programs were established by federal legislation, each (or perhaps each cluster) contributing to the development of yet another field of practice. Thus, for example, among the numerous categorical initiatives that were enacted between 1965 and 1997 were the Older Americans Act of 1965 (P.L. 89-73), providing funds for social services and meal services for older people; the various child welfare amendments to the Social Security Act, providing funds for foster care; adoption assistance; preventive, protective, and supportive services for troubled children and their families; support for living arrangements for youths who are too old to be in foster care; the developmental disabilities program; the Americans with Disabilities Act of 1990 (P.L. 101-336); the 1974 Runaway and Homeless Youth Act (P.L. 93-415); family planning services; child care services; and services for homeless people, people who abuse drugs or alcohol, and refugees.

The U.S. House of Representatives' 1992 report *Federal Programs Affecting Children and Families* listed 36 federal social services programs for children and families (along with 15 income transfer programs, 29 education-related programs, 19 health-related programs, nine child nutrition programs, and more than 10 housing-related programs). Certainly, if students are to practice social work with children and their families, they should be familiar with these programs. And knowing something about these programs (and a lot about some of them) clearly has implications for the nature of practice and the kinds of interventions that can be used, as well as for whom help can be provided.

Thus, in addition to the fields of practice that are derived from the major non-social work components of the social sector (health and mental health, school-based social services, corrections, and employment-related social services), within the personal social services domain, one can identify at least two major fields of practice (child and family welfare and services for older people) and several smaller fields (services for adolescents, services for people who abuse alcohol or drugs, military social services, services to refugees and immigrants, services for people with physical disabilities, and services to people who have developmental disabilities). And some would add the emerging field of international social welfare.

There is no way that a social worker can develop expertise in all these fields, let alone in a two-year period. Clearly, just knowing the relevant federal policies and programs and the relevant state and local policies and their various requirements regarding who can be served and what services can be provided points to the need to set some parameters. And the natural parameters are what constitute a field of practice. Moreover, although today emphasis is placed on community-based services in each field, the prevalence of service delivery models varies from field to field, with some stressing home-based services and others stressing neighborhood-based rather than home-based services, and some inherently focused on an authoritative model and others on a voluntary model. Furthermore, there are variations in the use and emphasis on the practice modes that are field-specific. Finally, whether one uses the overarching concept of personal social services to identify the special social work domain, the concept of field of practice has its own internal validity and clearly is a central component of social work education and practice.

No school can support training in all the fields (and all social work methods), but all schools should provide training at least in the major fields. And all should aim to include one or two smaller fields that have particular salience for their own institution or community. For example, graduate schools of social work in large urban communities with high proportions of immigrants and refugees should include courses and practice experience in this field.

Most important, even if schools cannot mount the expertise for in-depth training, all should try to identify and monitor the emergence of new fields so they can respond to new professional practice and educational needs. New fields are likely to emerge as a consequence of new categorical legislation (the 1987 Stewart B. McKinney Homeless Assistance Act [P.L. 100-77] and the development of social services for homeless people, for example). They are also likely to emerge when a new problem arises and efforts are made to cluster relevant interventions (such as social services to people infected with HIV and their families) or when new settings emerge for social work practice, as with the increase in opportunities for social workers in international organizations and arenas. Or, when fields disappear (for instance, public assistance, when the program became an entitlement and social services were separated from the delivery of cash benefits). Curricula must be adapted or modified to take account of these developments. Moreover, all schools should teach students how to conceptualize and identify a field of practice and how to analyze or assess the field in which they are practicing or intend to practice. This framework for assessing a field of practice is presented next.

Assessing a Field of Practice

This framework is applicable whether social work is the host profession or plays an adjunctive role in relation to another profession and whether one uses the overarching concept of personal social services or assesses only the discrete, categorical social services fields (although this author believes that an understanding and use of the former is essential for understanding how the several fields relate to each other). Applying the framework to an emerging field and comparing the results across fields can help clarify whether a new field is emerging or an established one is phasing out. An outline of the generic framework, which can be applied to any field, is presented in Table 13-1. In this section, the major components are described and illustrations from different fields are given.

Major Components of the Framework

There are seven major components of the framework:

1. the target or focal point (population, problem, setting)
2. earlier historical responses
3. relevant legislation and policies
4. program models and the delivery system
5. modes of practice (interventions) and staffing patterns
6. research, evaluation, and outcomes
7. current issues, trends, and debates.

The Target or Focal Point. Fields of practice are organized around specific population groups, such as children (and their families), adolescents, older people, or women; or around specific problems, such as substance abuse, homelessness, AIDS, delinquency, or domestic violence; or around distinctive settings, such as hospitals, schools, military bases, rural or urban communities, the workplace, or international organizations. These targets become the takeoff points for identifying the specific laws, programs, and practice interventions that are designed to respond to the needs of each group, problem, or setting.

Earlier Historical Responses. Although the major fields of practice have existed for a long time, many of the most significant developments date from the 1960s and 1970s—the years when federal social services policy really took shape with the dramatic expansion of federal social protection policies. Thus, although many social programs (for example, orphanages and homes for aged individuals) were originally funded by private philanthropies, they emerged in the 1960s in the form of public services, funded largely by the federal government and attached to public assistance. Counseling services and child care services, for instance, were viewed in these years as ways to help recipients of Aid to Families with Dependent Children (AFDC) to move off the welfare rolls and into employment or to cope better with the difficulties of daily life on their meager incomes. Only in the 1970s, when the delivery of social services was separated from the delivery of cash benefits, did these services develop a distinctive, independent

Table 13-1. A Framework for Assessing a Field of Practice

I.   The target population (such as children, youths, older people, or women), the problem addressed in the field (for example, substance abuse, homelessness, AIDS, or immigrant and refugee status), or the specialized settings (including schools, the workplace, hospitals and clinics, or prisons)

II. Earlier historical responses to the problem, population, or settings

III. Framework for provision
   A. Laws and regulations
   B. Explicit and implicit policies (manifest and latent goals, objectives, and purposes)
   C. Funding
   D. Policy-making agency and distribution of responsibility among the levels of government: federal, state, and local
   E. Criteria for eligibility
   F. Coverage (the proportion of the population with the problem or need that is eligible for the service) and take-up (the proportion of eligible people who receive the service)
   G. Comparative perspectives (optional, as relevant)

IV. Program models and delivery systems
   A. Program function: access, entry, or liaison service, case or treatment service, social utility or developmental service, or a combination (specify which)
   B. Community service (neighborhood- or home-based), residential facility, or both
   C. Formal or informal service (self-help or mutual aid)
   D. Administrative auspices (public or private nonprofit or private for-profit, sectarian or nonsectarian, autonomous freestanding or part of a system other than the personal social services)
   E. Funding
   F. Mission
   G. Access (how clients/consumers find out about and obtain the service)
   H. Channeling (How do clients/consumers get processed through the organization or agency?)
   I. Characteristics of the clientele: criteria for eligibility and the number and types of clients served
   J. Links with other services in the same field or in different fields

V.   Practice modes and staffing patterns
   A. Types of services provided and interventions used
   B. Innovative practice modes
   C. Staffing patterns
      1. Professional and paraprofessional roles
      2. Specialist, generalist, case manager roles
      3. Individual or team roles
      4. Unidisciplinary or multidisciplinary staff

VI. Research, evaluation, outcomes
   A. Theoretical knowledge base used or not
   B. Knowledge of effects, effectiveness, impact, and costs
   C. Program innovations
   D. Critiques

VII. An overview of issues, trends, and debates, including positions taken by interest groups and professional associations, new legislative proposals, quantitative and qualitative adequacy of service provisions

NOTE: This framework builds on an earlier formulation developed during the 1970s by a committee at the Columbia University School of Social Work.

identity, valued for the help they could provide, not just as supplements to financial assistance.

Services in the workplace date from 19th-century employers' paternalistic provision of benefits, but also blossomed in the 1970s and 1980s as the workplace became more diverse and a higher proportion of the population (almost two-thirds of the nonaged adults) were in the workforce. This change, along with the increase of women in the workforce, made the workplace a more accessible point of entry for many types of help.

Identifying how help was provided for a particular population or problem in the past permits those who make assessments to discern whether a specific field of practice is well established, with a long history of attention, such as services to children and their families, or a newly emerging field, such as services to people with HIV or AIDS. It also helps to understand current developments in programs and practice.

Relevant Legislation and Policies. A key component in learning about a field of practice is identifying the relevant legislation. Laws, whether federal or state, define the parameters of practice—what type of help can be offered, how much can be offered, and to whom. Thus, for example, if the target population is older people, it would be essential to know something about Old Age and Survivors Insurance and Medicare, the two most important universal entitlement programs for older people; Supplemental Security Income and Medicaid, the two most important means-tested entitlements for poor older people; and the Older Americans Act of 1965 and the SSBG, the two most important personal social services programs for older people.

The Older Americans Act established the general philosophy in this field of practice, which emphasizes the planning, coordination, and delivery of personal social services for older people. Moreover, it provides funds specifically for senior citizens centers, congregate meal services, home-delivered meals (Meals-on-Wheels), and a variety of services for frail older people. It is not an entitlement program, but it is a universal program; the services may be provided to any older person in need, regardless of income. About $1 billion was appropriated by Congress for these services in 1994.

The SSBG provides funds for a wide range of services for individuals and families with low or moderate incomes. Typically, about half the resources, about $1.4 billion out of a total of $2.8 billion estimated in 1996 (U.S. House of Representatives, 1996), go to older people for such services as home help, foster care, counseling, and information and referral services. In contrast to the programs funded under the Older Americans Act, eligibility for these services is limited to those who qualify on the basis of low income, not just need. Thus, despite the seemingly significant funds that are expended, many needy older people may still not qualify for SSBG social services. Nonetheless, these social services and the Older Americans Act services are essential to the operation of any social services agency that serves older people, and all these benefits and services are central to the knowledge and skills of the social workers who practice with this population. A similar picture emerges with regard to social services for low-income children and their families, paid for through SSBG funds.

If the target population is children and their families, social workers would need to know about those policies shaping the social infrastructure for this group, such as Temporary Assistance to Needy Families (TANF), part of the 1996 law that provides cash assistance to poor families with children (the Personal Responsibility and Work Opportunity Reconciliation Act of 1996, P.L. 104-193) and replaced AFDC and the relevant state variations; Medicaid and Title XXI of the Social Security Act, which provides federal funds for child health insurance; and the basic provisions of the Food Stamp Program. In addition, knowledge of the specific federal (and as relevant, state) child and family legislation would be essential, including the 1980 amendments to the Social Security Act (Titles IV B and IV E) (P.L. 96-272), covering foster care, foster care prevention, adoption and, subsequently, support for living arrangements for youths aging out of foster care; the 1993 amendments to the Omnibus Budget Reconciliation Act of 1986 (P.L. 103-66) regarding family preservation and family support services; the SSBG provisions for children and their families, referred to earlier; and the 1996 TANF-related child care service provisions.

If the field of practice is organized around a problem or setting, the relevant legislation is equally important. For example, if the problem is homelessness, the most important federal legislation is the Stewart B. McKinney Homeless Assistance Act, which provides funds for shelters and soup kitchens, some counseling and referral services, and a miscellany of other services for homeless people. If practice is based in a medical setting, such as a clinic or hospital, Medicare and Medicaid (Titles XVIII and XIX, respectively, of the Social Security Act) would be the key laws for social workers to know, in addition to Title XX.

Although the major focus here has been on federal legislation, it is equally—and perhaps, increasingly—important for social workers to be familiar with relevant state legislation, too, and with state variations on federal laws. Thus, the enactment of the Personal Responsibility and Work Opportunity Reconciliation Act of 1996 introduced great flexibility into how states can use federal funds for child care and child and family social services as well as cash assistance. Moreover, Title XXI of the Social Security Act enacted in 1997 (P.L. 105-33) greatly expanded federal funding for health insurance for children in low- and moderate- income families but permits states wide latitude in the specifics of their programs.

Program Models and the Delivery System. Once the first three components are identified, it is necessary to explore the range of program models
and where a particular agency fits in the larger social services delivery system. Thus, for example, one would want to know whether an agency is
public or private, religious or sectarian, and part of a large organization or
a small and specialized program. All this information has immediate implications for the kinds of help that can be offered, the client population that
can be served, and the skills and knowledge needed to provide help.

Today, most fields of practice emphasize the provision of help to individuals in their own homes or communities. Thus, even though child and
family services agencies may offer a variety of service programs, including
residential care and treatment and foster family care, the emphasis is on
providing treatment and supportive services to children and their families
while they are living at home; this is often the case for emotionally troubled
children, for children who have developmental or physical disabilities, and
for children of parents who have been neglectful or otherwise inadequate.
Similarly, agencies that serve older people also concentrate on providing
services that sustain older people in their own homes.

With regard to alternative program models, social services for adolescents may be used as an illustration. Among the possible service options
for adolescents, in addition to residential treatment facilities and group
homes, are school-based services, both medical clinics and peer support
groups; community-based services for pregnant teenagers and teenage
mothers that offer counseling, family planning services, parenting classes,
child care services, and tutoring; multiservice programs that facilitate adolescents' transition from school to work and provide various other health
and mental health, education, employment, and personal social services;
and programs for delinquent or predelinquent youths. Some of these programs are for teenage girls, others are for teenage boys, still others are for
adolescent parents, and some serve a mixed population of adolescents. Social
workers who practice with adolescents must be familiar with these alternatives, be able to assess which are appropriate for a particular teenager who
requests or needs help, and know how to help an adolescent qualify for the
needed help.

Similarly, programs that deal with substance abuse include residential
treatment programs; outpatient programs; and self-help groups, such as
Alcoholics Anonymous. Knowing what each program provides and what
type of person and problem can be best treated in each can help social
workers achieve more effective practice.

In addition, social workers must know who is eligible for help in different programs. For example, are services limited to those who live in a particular neighborhood? Are they means-tested and thus limited to poor

people, or are they universal and available to all, perhaps with income-related fees? Unfortunately, regardless of the field of practice, the supply of services (except for the entitlement programs) is not adequate to meet even the needs of those who qualify for help. Nevertheless, knowing the criteria for eligibility often enables social workers to find an appropriate "fit" for their clients.

Social workers also must know how people find and gain access to different kinds of help, that is, whether they do so on their own or with the help of professionals. For some groups and some types of problems, there are special services just for this purpose. Thus, for example, for older people, for parents in need of child care, for women, and for people who abuse drugs or alcohol, various types of information and referral services, hotlines, and crisis services provide information about the kinds of help available and where to go for help. Some people are able to take the information provided and proceed on their own, but others require more assistance.

Modes of Practice and Staffing Patterns. In some fields, the core help involves personal social services provided by social workers. Thus, in agencies serving children and their families, the core staff are often those with master's or bachelor's degrees in social work, depending on the knowledge and level of skill that the tasks require. These social workers must be prepared to assess the severity of the problem and the type of help needed; to provide short- or long-term, more intensive or less intensive, individual, group, or family counseling and other practical helping services; to ensure that multiple types of help are provided, if needed; and to establish appropriate links with other agencies.

In other fields, especially in multidisciplinary settings, social work practice may involve teamwork with other professionals, such as physicians and nurses in a hospital or clinic or lawyers in the courts. In some settings, such as schools or large corporations, even if the actual practice is carried out by social workers, effective intervention requires knowledge of the host institution, the constraints that the institution imposes, and other specialized staff.

Sometimes new modes of practice may develop in a particular field, such as the emergence in the 1980s of comprehensive, short-term, intensive, and goal-oriented interventions ("family preservation") in child and family services whose objective is to avoid the placement of neglected or abused children in foster care. Social workers in other fields gradually began to test this mode of intervention, for example, when the objective was to avoid the institutionalization of delinquent or emotionally disturbed adolescents and to help families through particular crises. In short, interventive methods may be specific to a field of practice or may be used or adapted by many fields. In either case, one needs specialized knowledge to choose which modes are appropriate for which clients.

Research, Evaluation, and Outcomes. One question that is frequently raised is "Is social work intervention effective?" Two types of research are especially relevant for answering the question: one for the evaluation of programs and the other for the evaluation of individual practice interventions. Thus, for example, in the innovative practice mode just described, the central issue is whether it is effective in reducing the rate of placement and resolving crises. Studies have found that this mode can be helpful when it is used along with a variety of other services, but that it may not, by itself, achieve all that it was initially thought to. On the one hand, recognizing the limitations of a particular intervention can be important for developing a new program or changing an existing one. On the other hand, it is equally as important to know when a program is successful. For example, good-quality child care services have been shown to have important positive consequences for young children from poor families. Thus, facilitating access to such programs can be beneficial for young children from dysfunctional families (as well as for those from well-functioning families, of course). From another perspective, the knowledge that certain types of self-help groups have proved effective in dealing with certain problems, such as alcoholism and domestic violence, can help social workers recommend particular treatment modes for clients.

Current Issues, Trends, and Debates. Finally, it is important to know what the major current developments are in one's chosen field of practice, which issues are being debated, and who is taking the different stances. Obviously, how the problem is defined has major implications for policy, program, and practice. Thus, for example, in the field of homelessness, a major issue is whether the problem is one of individual dysfunction (mental illness or substance abuse) or the lack of affordable housing, or some combination of the two. Similarly, there is a debate about whether child abuse is a problem of family pathology or inadequate social policy or both. And those who work in the field of services to adolescents differ on how much attention should be given to young fathers compared with young mothers and whether providing free, readily available contraceptives would be more effective in reducing teenage pregnancy than would the use of peer support groups, counseling, or a more punitive approach. Some of these issues can be resolved through research, but others may reflect differences in ideologies or values about the role that the government should play in family matters. Such issues vary not only across fields of practice but within fields and over time.

Conclusion

Graduate social work education began with a focus on specialized fields of practice, and there was no holistic concept of social work method. Over time, it was recognized that there was a core body of social work knowledge that stressed the distinctiveness of social work intervention methods in relation to this core. Since the 1960s, leading practitioners and theoreticians have advocated a two-dimensional model that organizes graduate social work education along two axes: (1) interventive method and (2) field of practice. With the explosion in the size and diversity of the U.S. social sector since the 1960s and the recognition that personal social services has been a distinctive domain within the social sector since the 1970s, the need to organize professional education around both axes, including the different fields of practice, has become more urgent.

The delineation is not meant to suggest that fields of practice is a static concept. These fields are more fluid than the social work methods because they emerge, disappear, combine, and recombine in response to social change, new social problems, changing values, and new legislation. For professional social workers to begin to practice with appropriate expertise, so they are competitive with professionals from other disciplines who work in the same or related fields, they must have expertise in a particular field of practice. Only a practitioner who has been exposed to and become conscious of the field-of-practice dimension can make an optimum contribution to practice.

This chapter has traced the development of the field-of-practice concept, demonstrated its relevance to social work practice today, provided a framework for analyzing the various fields, and illustrated how this framework can be used in several fields. The challenge is for both social work researchers and educators to be vigilant in monitoring the fields as they change and in adapting and refining the relevant knowledge base for students.

References

Adoption Assistance and Child Welfare Act of 1980, P.L. 96-272, 94 Stat. 500.

Americans with Disabilities Act of 1990, P.L. 101-336, 104 Stat. 327.

Bartlett, H. M. (1961). *Analyzing social work practice by fields.* New York: National Association of Social Workers.

Bartlett, H. M. (1965). Social work practice. In H. L. Lurie (Ed.-in-Chief), *Encyclopedia of social work* (15th ed., pp. 755–763). New York: National Association of Social Workers.

Bartlett, H. M. (1971). Social work fields of practice. In R. Morris (Ed.-in-Chief), *Encyclopedia of social work* (16th ed., Vol. 2, pp. 1477–1481). New York: National Association of Social Workers.

Briar, S. (1987). Direct practice: Trends and issues. In A. Minahan (Ed.-in-Chief), *Encyclopedia of social work* (18th ed., Vol. 1, pp. 393–398). Silver Spring, MD: National Association of Social Workers.

Fields of practice: Reader's guide. (1995). In R. L. Edwards (Ed.-in-Chief), *Encyclopedia of social work* (19th ed., Vol. 2, p. 1028). Washington, DC: NASW Press.

Gilbert, N. (1977). The transformation of the social services. *Social Service Review, 51*, 624–641.

Kahn, A. J. (1965). Social work fields of practice. In H. L. Lurie (Ed.-in-Chief), *Encyclopedia of social work* (15th ed., pp. 750–754). New York: National Association of Social Workers.

Kahn, A. J. (1979). *Social policy and social services* (2nd ed.). New York: Random House.

Kamerman, S. B., & Kahn, A. J. (1976). *Social services in the United States.* Philadelphia: Temple University Press.

Lurie, H. L. (Ed.-in-Chief). (1965). *Encyclopedia of social work* (15th ed.). New York: National Association of Social Workers.

Minahan, A. (Ed.-in-Chief). (1987). *Encyclopedia of social work* (18th ed.). Silver Spring, MD: National Association of Social Workers.

Morris, R. (Ed.-in-Chief). (1971). *Encyclopedia of social work* (16th ed.). New York: National Association of Social Workers.

NASW Commission on Social Work Practice, Subcommittee on Fields of Practice. (1962). Identifying fields of practice in social work. *Social Work, 7*(2), 7–14.

Older Americans Act of 1965, P.L. 89-73, 79 Stat. 218.

Omnibus Budget Reconciliation Act of 1986, P.L. 103-66, 107 Stat. 571, 608 (1993 amendments).

Personal Responsibility and Work Opportunity Reconciliation Act of 1996, P.L. 104-193, 110 Stat. 2105.

Runaway and Homeless Youth Act, P.L. 93-415, 88 Stat. 1129 (1974).

Social casework: Generic and specific (Report of the Milford Conference). (1974). Washington, DC: National Association of Social Workers. (Originally published in 1929).

Social Security Act, P.L. 93-647, 88 Stat. 2337 (1974).

Social Security Act, P.L. 96-272 (1980).

Social Security Act, P.L. 105-33, Stat. 4901(a) (1997).

Stewart B. McKinney Homeless Assistance Act, P.L. 100-77, 101 Stat. 482 (1987).

Townsend, P., Sinfield, A., Kahan, B., Mittler, P., Rose, H., Meacher, M., Agate, J., Lynes, T., & Bull, D. (1970). *The fifth social service.* London: Fabian Society.

Turner, J. (Ed.-in-Chief). (1977). *Encyclopedia of social work* (17th ed.). Washington, DC: National Association of Social Workers.

U.S. House of Representatives, Committee on Ways and Means. (1996). *Overview of entitlement programs: The 1996 green book.* Washington, DC: U.S. Government Printing Office.

U.S. House of Representatives, Committee on Ways and Means. (1998). *Overview of entitlement programs: The 1998 green book.* Washington, DC: U.S. Government Printing Office.

U.S. House of Representatives, Subcommittee on Children, Youth and Families. (1992). *Federal programs affecting children and their families, 1992.* Washington, DC: U.S. Government Printing Office.

Vinton, L. (1995). The boutique effect in graduate social work education. *Journal of Teaching in Social Work, 11*(1/2), 3–13.

CHAPTER 14

The Profession in Historical Context

Jerry R. Cates

Introduction: Relevance of History to Social Workers

Social work's history, which cannot be understood apart from the history of social welfare and the broader society, can be an energizing part of one's professional identity. Historical understanding provides role models, teaches lessons to inform new practice and policy, and, at the most fundamental level, fosters critical thinking. A commitment to social justice, and a legacy of debate about its fulfillment, are prominent themes in that history.

Well-known role models for social workers abound in the historical literature (Trattner, 1986) and others await wider appreciation. They include both individuals credentialed as social workers and, especially in the early years, persons without such credentials who self-identified and were accepted as social workers. They also include those whose efforts may not have been labeled as social work at the time, but whose work resonates with contemporary social work concerns, particularly where social justice issues are involved. Two examples will illustrate. Jane Addams, one of the founders of the profession and one of the nation's best known and most admired persons of her time, has achieved near-iconic status in American culture. What she accomplished in the areas of women's issues, labor relations, civic improvement, and international peace work—to give only a partial listing—brought her the Nobel Peace Prize, a remarkable place in history, and such role model influence that a leading biographer titled his book *American Heroine* (Davis, 1973). For a role model not traditionally labeled a social worker but deserving of wider social work attention, consider Nannie Helen Burroughs, early 20th-century African American community activist in Washington, D.C. Against formidable odds, she founded a training institute for young African American women, many of whom moved from the rural South to be prepared by her for life in the urban north. As social worker Artis (1993) documents, Burroughs became a forceful and nationally respected spokesperson for the Black community on social welfare issues, and a fighter for civic betterment in Washington. Her accomplishments in the face of the profound racism and sexism of her time deserve serious study by contemporary social workers (Barnett, 1978; Higginbottom, 1993).

In addition to providing role models, historical study can stimulate new ideas for contemporary practice and policy. These can have enormous impact. For example, political scientist Piven and her social work professor co-author, Cloward, published an historically grounded, social control interpretation of the functions of public welfare that was both pioneering and explosive in its impact in the scholarly realm as well as the world of social activism, community organizing, and the national welfare rights movement (Piven & Cloward, 1971; Specht & Courtney, 1994, p. 166; Trattner, 1983; Weir, Orloff, & Skocpol, 1988, p. 26). For other examples of extremely influential, historically based social welfare analyses central to the concerns of professional social work, see the works of Wilson (1987), and Skocpol (1992).

A serious study of social work's history can cultivate critical thinking. There are vivid examples of once-dominant professional attitudes and concepts that are jarring, if not stunning, to contemporary sensibilities. For example, listen to prominent Progressive Era social worker John Adams Kingsbury who, as Commissioner of Public Charities, led New York City's huge public welfare department from 1914 to 1918. While telling Theodore Roosevelt of his accomplishments, he spotlighted reforms for mentally disabled children. Using language of the time, he told of his pride in taking the children away from their families and putting them in large institutions. These young "mental defectives" were "a burden to their hardworking mothers and a social menace to the community." They needed to be "permanently segregated" behind institutional walls: made comfortable, to be sure, but isolated from the normal world. Children of "normal minds" simply could not be permitted "to mingle with idiots." "Defectives" must not be allowed to reproduce another problematical generation (Kingsbury, n.d.). In so describing his policies, Kingsbury was articulating the "best" and leading progressive thought of his day in which the scientific validity of the eugenics movement's theories was taken for granted. The American "eugenic creed" assumed "the supreme importance of heredity" and believed that "the unfit must be eliminated or at least limited in number and the fit encouraged to increase their numbers, an objective [to] be achieved through . . . scientific knowledge and social application of heredity" (Pickens, 1968, p. 55).

Kingsbury's total career record includes remarkably humanitarian achievements. In fact, he was labeled a dangerous radical in his day for the vigor with which he challenged American centers of power in the interests of social justice, particularly in the area of national health insurance (Fox, 1986; Kingsbury, 1939; Newsholme & Kingsbury, 1933). That he, like his professional contemporaries, could employ eugenics concepts that would be discredited within two decades is a lesson to us all. It sharply reminds us of the historically conditioned nature of our assumptions and practice knowledge, and it underlines the need to cultivate a critical, reflective attitude toward current practice and policy "givens," an attitude that can be nurtured through the serious study of history.

The study of history is dynamic and often highly contested. Interpretations change as research and scholarly debates progress. Many times the best available knowledge of an historical development is to know the competing interpretations found in the literature, including assessments of the adequacy of research strategies employed. For example, see the vigorous, extended scholarly debates about such topics as the role of social control in American public assistance (Piven & Cloward, 1971; Trattner, 1983), the way in which racism has figured in the creation of inner city poverty and how responses to racism should influence poverty policy (Katz, 1989; Orfield, 1991; Wilson, 1987), the treatment of the poor in American social security (Cates, 1983; Derthick, 1979; Schieber, 1999; Skocpol with Ikenberry, 1995), and, as will be discussed in this chapter, the "true" identity and mission of the profession of social work. As social work historian Leighninger (1995) points out, "Historical research relies on elements that are familiar to social scientists: the development of hypotheses, or guiding questions; the systematic gathering and analysis of evidence to understand the relationship among factors being studied; and the discovery of patterns or principles to explain these relationships" (p. 1263).

A Profession Takes Form: 1880 to 1930

In the late 19th and early 20th centuries, a profession recognizable as modern social work emerged. It came about in a period of great change. As the 19th century closed, the rapidly expanding industrial economy experienced severe economic fluctuations, bringing hardship for the working classes clustered in urban centers and jammed into crowded, unhealthy tenements. Labor unrest was met with violent repression. This was a time of enormous immigration: the labor of these new workers was essential to the economy, but native-born Americans were often unsettled by the influx of newcomers.

The new profession descended from the work of a group of reformers collectively known as the Charity Organizations Society (COS) movement that sought to reshape the ways in which American poor had been receiving help. In this fifty-year period, COS currents mingled with those of a very different development, the settlement movement. Adding to the mixture were the efforts of various other urban reformers, some of whom overlapped with the settlement movement; these included the child-saving movement as well as researchers and writers with journalistic and academic connections. All this made for a rich and complex situation, full of options for shaping a new profession. The choices made in this period fundamentally shaped the course of the profession for many years and they still, in large part, frame contemporary debates about the proper mission of social work. Those choices revolved around the themes of individual casework, the place of community, and the role of social reform in the profession.

Charity Organization Society Lineage, 1880s to 1920s

"Scientific charity" was the approach taken by the Charity Organization Society (COS) movement, and it was an attempt to be organized, planful and, above all, controlling in regard to the perceived menace of poverty or "pauperism" as it was usually labeled. Led by upper-class representatives, mostly Protestant women, the movement sought to curb, if not totally eliminate, all publicly financed aid to the poor, and to make relief strictly a private exercise of charity. This was to be done in a business-like fashion, through careful investigation and coordination of casework to determine need, and to distinguish those "worthy" of help from the "unworthy." It marked a break from the past in that religious proselytizing was to be banned from the work of helping the poor and replaced with a bureaucratic approach. Cities were divided into districts; records were maintained to ensure no cases received overlapping help. Salaried staff known as "paid agents" performed necessary administrative and investigative functions. However, the heart of the whole system was the "friendly visitor," the volunteer who went to the homes of the poor to provide help to her social inferiors. "Scientific charity," according to its leading theorist, Josephine Lowell, "must be toward a person in an inferior circumstance to his benefactor. We cannot be charitable to our equals—in the sense of the word with which we are dealing" (Katz, 1996, p. 74). The help to be given was the advice and sterling moral example of a middle- or upper-class visitor who could somehow show them a better way; precisely how this was to be done wasn't very clear. The advice was to be "friendly," yet dispensed without sentiment and— importantly—given without money. Tangible expressions of aid, such as cash, were an absolute threat to the poor, and could be given only in the most extreme situations because they would undermine the work ethic. "Not alms but a friend" was the gentler framing of it, "repressing pauperism" the tougher one.

Poverty was automatically assumed to be the result of personal moral failure; most often the culprits were seen as sheer idleness and drink. If it proved absolutely impossible to avoid provision of publicly financed cash support, then the COS movement insisted such aid be given only behind the walls of a residential institution for the poor—(the poorhouse) and never in the form of "outdoor relief" or cash support given to people in their own homes. Under strict supervision in the poorhouse, proper discipline would impart moral renewal and ensure appropriate deference was shown by the paupers to their benefactors. All this was codified into a "theory of scientific charity" as expressed in the writings of leaders such as Josephine Lowell (1884). Some leaders of the COS movement clung to their theory into the early 1900s, despite the fact that it was never possible to reach their goal of abolishing outdoor relief. The number of needy fluctuated dramatically as the volatile late 19th century economy underwent recessions and depressions that threw large numbers of even the most devoted adherents of the American work ethic into deep poverty (Katz, 1996; Lubove, 1969).

The COS movement was the response of uneasy upper classes to the social and economic dislocations of the time. The social control functions of the efforts were not disguised: helping explicitly went hand-in-hand with self-conscious attempts to keep in their place immigrants, laboring classes, and the impoverished who were seen as posing serious threats to American stability and well-being. Fear that the working class might come to demand help as a right was never far from the minds of COS leaders. Katz tells us one such figure, Humphreys Gurteen, explicitly compared the threat of a rising class of poor demanding their "rights" to a Frankenstein monster accidentally created through too-liberal alms giving (Katz, 1996, p. 77). Friendly visiting was to be a method of calming class relations, a supplement to other forms of control such as the use of armed troops to control strikes—something which first happened in the 1870s (Katz, 1996, p. 69). Ultimately, the COS movement drastically failed to achieve its goals, a fact recognized by some of its most prominent leaders who began to see that scientific charity was impotent in the face of structural causes of mass unemployment. In time, the intense moralizing and resistance to tangible help on the part of COS workers came to be seen as useless and even cruel by some of the movement's own leading theorists. For example, Josephine Lowell, by 1896, had left the COS behind and was working for higher wages for the working classes, union organizing, and economic reform. Another major COS leader, Edward Devine, by the 1920s, would observe that he and others in the COS movement had actually "caused . . . pauperism by our failure to provide for the necessities of life" (Katz, 1996, p. 86).

For all its failures and negative features, it remains the case that modern social work can see in the COS work crude prototypes of some of its cherished features. The movement disengaged helping from religious proselytizing, established a focus on the individual situation, and enunciated the importance of individual investigation of situations. The movement promoted the value of careful administrative coordination of activities, and the necessity of an objective, scientific approach to helping (even if the actual COS implementation of this imperative was anything but scientific or objective). However imperfectly these things were implemented in COS activities, their importance as ideals was passed on to later caseworkers who sought to improve upon them (Leiby, 1984).

Individual Casework Focus and Emergent Professional Identity, 1900s to 1920s

One such COS caseworker who sought to better the COS movement's sorry track record was Mary Richmond. She provided national leadership in moving casework beyond the limits of friendly volunteer visiting, replacing the visitor with a professionally trained and salaried social caseworker. In her book, *Social Diagnosis* (1917), the first major theoretical treatise of professional casework, she presented her schema for analyzing individual need in the context of the dynamic interplay among six sets of "forces": family, personal, neighborhood, civic, private charity, and public relief. As Specht and Courtney (1994) put it, she was groping toward something later generations would term a social systems approach, but doing so before such theoretical formulations were available to her. Her book was of enormous importance to caseworkers as they sought to define themselves as members of a new profession. The book, while short on what to do in terms of actual intervention after the careful social diagnosis was made, still stands out as landmark on the road to professionalization because of its systematic approach, its focus on understanding the client in context of the environment, its theme of learning from the client through careful listening, and the goal of actually helping clients chart their own courses rather than imposing morally superior advice on them. Even before the appearance of her 1917 book, the COS movement had been inspired by Richmond's pleas for professionalization and professional education, leading to the establishment of the first formal training for professional social casework in 1897 at The New York School of Philanthropy (which eventually evolved into the Columbia University School of Social Work), and by 1919 there were 17 such schools. Richmond joined the Russell Sage Foundation and used her position to encourage the development of social work education, publishing, in 1922, another important book, *What Is Social Case Work?*

Community Focus and Emergent Professional Identity, 1900s to 1920s

One leading historian of American social welfare, Katz, (1996) refers to the settings in which social work emerged as "the city wilderness" (p. 163), a reference to the often overwhelming nature of urban centers for the flood of migrants and immigrants, many of whom spoke little, if any English. The turn-of-the-century urban world was a daunting one for those at the lower ends of the social order: crowded, unsanitary housing, an absence of government protections for workers, exploitation of child labor, political corruption, intense poverty—all underscored the need for help.

As 20th-century casework evolved out of the failures of COS, the attention to environment flagged by Richmond meant a considerable focus on community. One way of interpreting this is historian Katz's view of some COS workers as using a "mediation" approach. They stood between individuals and families on the one hand and the complex intense world of the industrial urban centers on the other hand. Katz observes, some of the COS workers drew on common sense and knowledge of the city's workings to help often bewildered clients. Not promoted as part of the formal theory of scientific charity and done almost as an afterthought, Katz portrays this work as one of the most genuinely useful things done for clients. They "interceded with churches, relief agencies, and relatives. They accompanied clients to doctors, hospitals, and courts. They helped them find housing and jobs. In short, they became experts on urban survival" (Katz, 1996, p. 170).

A more detailed examination of this mediation and linking function as provided by Lubove (1969) is revealing. The new, Richmond-style caseworkers became links between large institutional systems (medical hospitals, schools, mental institutions, and justice systems) and the neighborhoods and families from which clients came. He identifies a pattern that was repeated in a variety of institutional settings: institutional administrators, realizing their own professional goals could be enhanced if they had better knowledge of client lives outside the professional setting, turned to caseworkers and their home visits for this information. The emergence of medical social work illustrates the pattern of social workers as the eyes and ears of other professionals. Physician John Cabot, in 1905, instituted social services in the Massachusetts General Hospital in Boston. Influenced by earlier COS work in Baltimore and New York, Cabot's medical social service initiative marked an important development in the emergence of social casework. It established the precedent of social work in a host setting and use of the home visit as a key tool.

The new medical social workers were seen as enhancing three distinct medical purposes: (1) improving medical diagnoses, (2) enhancing patient compliance with prescribed medical interventions, and (3) helping alter the environment itself through public health initiatives. Physicians' diagnoses were aided by caseworker-provided information; for example, one Boston General doctor asked a caseworker to check out the validity of a patient's remarks: "This patient tells us stories of abuse at home by his sons. He is depressed and moody—Can you tell us what the conditions are there?" (Lubove, 1969, p. 28). Caseworkers could improve patient compliance with treatment plans by helping them to understand and accept what must be done. As Lubove (1969) observes: "Immigrants and workers crowding the hospital clinics might comprehend a dispensary physician's diagnosis of tuberculosis but not necessarily the relevance of his prescription—plenty of sunlight, fresh air, ventilation, and high standards of personal hygiene to protect others" (p. 27). Social workers, too, had to struggle to see the relevance of the prescriptions given the misery of the overcrowded, tenement houses and the scarcity of sunlight, fresh air, and hygienic conditions there. Such observations eventually led some social workers to move into the realm of community and policy reform in an attempt to make such prescriptions meaningful. For example, the previously mentioned John Kingsbury became New York's Commissioner of Public Charities by moving up through COS ranks as a caseworker. His casework notebooks contain poignant descriptions of his attempts to implement the "sunshine, ventilation, good food, sanitation" prescriptions of physicians for his poor tubercular clients in New York's tenements. For instance, there are notes of one young woman who regularly wrapped herself as warmly as she could, climbed the stairs of her tenement to the roof and sat next to the chimney in her wooden chair, hoping the fresh air and sunshine would allow her to survive the disease and carry out her marriage plans. Kingsbury was not alone in being propelled in the direction of social reform and policy advocacy by such experiences (Kingsbury, 1912).

The third community aspect of the new casework helped to reduce the incidence of disease. Through such efforts as the crusade against tuberculosis, in which early social workers played leadership roles, it was shown the community itself could organize in the interest of improved health. The net effect of all this was to begin to "socialize" the hospital in the sense of extending the health promotion efforts beyond the walls of the hospital, into the community, and to bring environmental information and resources inside the institutions (Lubove, 1969, p. 28).

The multiple, community-focused functions of the new casework, in hindsight, are impressive and seem eminently logical. Acceptance of them at the time, though, was anything but smooth. Despite Cabot's support, other physicians were often suspicious of the new caseworkers. Some doctors were intolerant of newcomers who might want to infringe on medical prerogatives. This was aggravated as the new caseworkers quickly decided to reject nurses as potential professional mentors (in the sense that nurses were aids to doctors) and sought to emulate the professional standing of doctors themselves. The new social workers wanted to move beyond being the "eyes and ears" of physicians and relate to the doctors as one professional to another. Other physicians simply did not believe in the new environmental perspective, insisting that medicine was about the business of curing diseases, not making social calls. Acceptance of the new caseworkers proceeded by fits and starts, but the role did take hold, and a professional niche was created (though not necessarily always on the "one professional relating to another" model the early social workers wanted). The pattern of "socializing an institution" that Lubove describes for medical social work is found in other professional areas. School social workers emerged as large, urban school systems needed someone to reach out beyond the walls of the school building. Similar developments occurred in mental institutions as new caseworkers helped psychiatrists strengthen their approach by cultivating community and family connections (Lubove, 1969, pp. 22–84).

Settlements, Social Reform, and Emergent Professional Identity, 1880s to 1930s

The Progressive Era, that period extending approximately from 1880 to the outbreak of World War I, contained a remarkable outpouring of urban reform efforts, with the settlement movement being of particular interest to the history of social work. Settlements emerged side-by-side with the Richmond-style, environmentally anchored casework. At times overlapping, at times in tension, and in some ways converging, these two developments were central to the emergence of social work. Other reform impulses of the time were important as well, such as the child-saving movement and the work of journalists and university-affiliated researchers.

"Spearheads for reform" is the apt term used by Davis (1967) to describe the settlement movement. "The settlement house became one of the principal instruments in this first war on poverty. Located in the middle of the worst neighborhoods . . . it provided a center of sympathy, help, and hope to nearby slum dwellers. The settlement house, at its best became a social center, school, homemaking class, kindergarten, play and recreation center, and an informal housing and employment bureau" (Davis, 1967, pp. ii–vii). Neighborhood improvement efforts drew settlement workers quickly into the larger arena of urban reform and politics: "settlement leaders quickly

learned that it would be impossible to transform the neighborhood without also 'reforming' urban society. Nearly all the questions they dealt with—
education, labor standards, housing improvements, the condition of women
and children, parks and playgrounds, sanitation and so on—involved public policy . . . settlement workers, often against their own predilections,
were pulled into the vortex of politics." (p. viii).

The "house" of the settlement house movement was the building in which
residents lived in the midst of their poorer neighbors. Some residents were
volunteers, others had stipends, and others, including famous people of
the day, came for visits. Beginning simply as "good neighbors" to the poor,
they sought to learn from their neighbors, to teach them, and, bit by bit, to
find their paths to ever-increasing usefulness to the neighborhood, city,
and nation. Like their casework sisters, settlement workers were intent on
being systematic and scientific in their work (though they were less concerned about achieving professional status than the caseworkers). They
pioneered neighborhood surveys that documented residential patterns and
community needs. This naturally led to university research connections.
They also formed partnerships with journalists such as Paul Kellogg, who
gained social work fame with his comprehensive survey of community needs
in Pittsburgh and his long tenure as editor of *Survey*, the leading social
work journal of its time.

The American settlement movement was inspired by an English proto-
type, Toynbee Hall, though a distinctively American model quickly emerged.
Katz (1996) summarizes the American characteristics: they were more democratic, less sectarian, more likely to deal with immigrant populations, and
demonstrated more pronounced social reform, social research, and social
activism commitments than their British counterparts. To this list, Skocpol
(1992) adds distinctively American gender dynamics: women were much
more important than in Britain: women outnumbered men and "perhaps
most telling, the United States had many successful mixed-gender settlements in which women were leaders" (p. 346). A new generation of college-
educated American women had found an opportunity to exercise their
talents and they went to it with vigor and success.

The first American settlement house was the Neighborhood Guild on
the Lower East Side of New York (it eventually became the College Settlement). They spread to many urban centers, numbering 400 by 1910 (Katz,
1996). Lillian Wald's Henry Street Settlement gained a national reputation
for social reform successes. By far, the most famous settlement house was
Hull House, established on Chicago's Halsted Street by Jane Addams and
Ellen Gates Starr. Addams became one of the best-known Americans of
the early 20th century. As Katz (1996) puts it, "for people across the
country, she embodied the transcendence of stale political division, the

reconciliation of social divisions, the active service in the public interest central to the ideals of grass-roots progressivism" (p. 167).

In addition to their pioneering work in policy and community advocacy, social research, and civic improvement, settlement house residents originated what has become one of the mainstays of social work practice— group work. As described by Schopler and Galinsky (1995), settlement workers discovered the value of group formats to pursue a wide-ranging agenda including advocacy "to fight for improved housing, better working conditions, and increased recreational opportunities," educational groups for citizenship lessons, and early, experimental efforts "to promote therapeutic groups . . . classes for treating tuberculosis in the homes of the poor in 1907, meetings for youthful drug addicts at Hull House in 1909, and experimental groups for the emotionally disturbed at Chicago State Hospital in 1918. . . ." (p. 1131). These early efforts emphasized the congruence of group work with democratic principles and often stressed contact across cultural and ethnic groups. By the 1940s, a more narrowly defined group treatment approach, heavily influenced by psychoanalytic thought, prevailed. However, during the coming decades a much wider range of group models emerged and the original group work ideals of the settlement movement were not lost.

Another strand of reform mingling with all the above, but having its own distinctive roots is known as the child–saving movement, a term that references a large collection of reform movements focused on rescuing and protecting children. Among the best-known early names associated with this movement is Charles Loring Brace who, through the New York Children's Aid society, pioneered the practice of relocating large numbers of needy and presumably homeless children from the East to new homes in the North Atlantic and Midwest, often with farmers who had need of labor. Between 1853 and 1929 it is estimated that more than 31,000 children were placed in homes through the work of this society. In many a ways the practice was a revival of the colonial practice of indentured servitude and, as Costin (1985) puts it, "there were charges that Brace's program was based on prejudices against immigrants, [and] that many of the children were unnecessarily removed from their parents" (p. 39). By the beginning of the 20th century, greater attention was being placed on how foster placements were being handled and the process of professionalization had begun in child welfare.

The Profession Coalesces: Pivotal Decision in the 1930s and Continuing Debate

A rich mix of elements was available to shape the new profession: Richmond's version of casework with its strong environmental focus; the

settlement movement's emphasis on community development, social reform, and political involvement; and a commitment to systematic, careful procedures, as scientific as possible, to undergird helping efforts. By
1930, a fascinating development had occurred that stands as a landmark
in the profession's history: leadership of the profession had passed firmly
into the hands of casework, but not the environmentally focused casework pioneered by Richmond. Instead, leadership passed to an inner-
directed psychiatric version. What accounts for this turn of events? Most
scholars agree it was shaped in large part by the new profession's intense
drive to be accepted as a "real" profession, with a unique mission, a scientific base for practice and strict control, by way of education, over who
could enter it. That most prestigious of all professions, medicine, was
adopted as a role model.

Lubove (1969) provides the classic accounting of developments. The
early psychiatry-social work link proved important to the emerging field of
casework, and at first it followed the familiar pattern of reaching out beyond the walls of clinics and institutions into patient's homes and communities. However, very quickly psychiatric social workers began to
de-emphasize environment as they emulated their psychiatrist mentors.
Increasingly, inner-directed psychology came to dominate this branch of
casework: "personality" over "environment." Around 1920, as Lubove
observes, it was clear that "a critical decision facing social workers . . . was
whether to continue along the lines of the psycho-social casework expounded by Mary Richmond . . . or to embrace the psychotherapy which
some psychiatric social workers were beginning to view with favor" (p.
83). As it turns out, the psychiatric framework eclipsed the Richmond
model. The psychiatric caseworker emerged as the "queen of the caseworkers" in terms of status, pay, and professional visibility (p. 86). This tri-
umph went hand-in-hand with another development: growing social work
acceptance of Freudian thought. It was the Freudian-psychiatric-caseworker
model that prevailed. While illustrations of psychoanalytic fervor are plen-
tiful in the historical literature, Lubove lets social worker Ethel Ginsberg's
comment stand as representative of them all as she looks back, from the
vantage point of 1940, on the great inroads Freudian thought had made in
American social work by then. "How sterile our work was before Freud
and how fertile it has become through his genius" (Lubove, 1969, p. 88).
By 1930, Freudian-influenced, psychiatric casework was presented in much
of the professional literature as the leading model of social work practice in
virtually all areas of casework: school social work, medical social work,
family guidance, and others.

Freudian thought provided a new "scientific" body of theory for the
profession that would, hopefully, give it a unique niche in the world of
professions. (However, a nagging problem remained—how, exactly did

psychiatric casework differ from psychiatry?) Another way to look at these developments is to consider the famous Abraham Flexner speech of 1915. Flexner, a physician and leading medical educator, fresh on the heels of revolutionizing medical education in the U.S., was asked by the National Conference of Charities and Corrections, the largest organization of social workers, to address them on the question of whether or not social work was a profession. Definitely not was his response, and, further, social work would never be a profession until it met criteria that seemed reasonable to him. His criteria, unsurprisingly, reflected an idealized accounting of medicine's professional contours. A profession, he pronounced, must have: a unique role in society, a scientific basis, a method for translating the knowledge produced by science into practical ends, a specific technique that could be passed on through professional education, and its own professional literature (Austin, 1983).

Chief among Flexner's criteria was the need to develop a unique professional "technique" that could be passed on through formal education. Much of the professional development in the 1920s can be seen as a drive to live up to Flexner's charge by narrowing the profession's focus down to one particular framework: psychiatry. In considering all of this, however, it is important to keep in mind Lubove's observation that when we say psychiatric casework dominated the profession by 1930 and kept its leadership position well into the 1950s, we are speaking primarily in terms of nationally visible spokespersons, leading publications, and dominant influences in schools of social work. These were certainly hugely important matters, but they were not the totality of social work. This leading influence was primarily an urban (Eastern and Midwestern), White, and largely women's phenomenon. Despite this high-profile, very public face of the profession, the actual extent to which psychiatric, particularly Freudian, frameworks, were implemented in day-to-day social work practice in settings all around the country is still very much open to question (Field, 1980). Even with this caveat in mind, though, it remains true that the psychiatric turning point was a profoundly important professional development as it determined the leading public face of the profession.

The decision to embrace a narrow, psychiatric version of casework as the profession's core identity by 1930 remains a flashpoint for debate about the historical legacy and true mission of social work in light of the growth of private practice and popularity of clinical social work in recent decades. Lubove describes the consequences of the 1930 turning point as momentous (1969). It "deflected social work's attention from the social and cultural environment and from relevant insights provided by the social sciences" (p. 117). Ironically, he points out, when the profession turned from Richmond's environmentally anchored casework to the inner-focused, psychotherapeutic model, this actually undermined rather than strengthened the new profession's search for security and a unique identity: "If psychiatric knowledge and technique were fundamental to social work, then what distinguished the social worker from the psychiatrist, and social casework from psychotherapy, except the social worker's inferior training? It was one thing to reject Mary Richmond's formulation, or minimize social work's liaison and resource mobilization function, but quite another to fail in substituting some specific alternative function which really differentiated the social worker from the psychiatrist" (p. 117). Another influential historian, Katz (1996), visits the same point in a trenchant, if not caustic, summing up: social work "chose the wrong alternative. As social workers rejected urban mediation and abandoned social reform, they became second-class therapists, inferior in standing, if not in competence, to psychologists and psychiatrists . . . With some irony social workers did not in fact become either therapists or professionals. Instead, they became badly paid servants of bureaucracies and the state" (p. 172).

To be sure, the intense search for a unique identity, status, prestige, and improved salaries was fundamental to the psychiatric turning point. However, this is not the whole story. The dramatic impact of World War I (1914–1918) on society must be taken into account. As Davis (1967) demonstrates, the war, in the name of patriotism, snuffed out much of the Progressive Era's lively debate about societal reform. Following the war, there was a conservative backlash that produced a national Red Scare (a wave of paranoia about the threat of communist subversion from within accompanied by large scale political repression—a forerunner of a similar phenomenon in the early 1950s). In this period of social and political backlash, social criticism became a risky enterprise, and Jane Addams saw society undergoing a general "political and social sag" (Davis, 1967, p. 229). Jane Addams also saw her own popularity plunge as she was branded a socialist and communist for her peace efforts during World War I and her social reform positions (for example, the Daughters of the American Revolution ejected her from their membership). While her standing as one of the country's most admired figures had recovered by the time of her death in 1935, the drastic fluctuation in her popularity signified the rapid pace of change in society as a whole. Other limitations to the Lubove and Katz analyses must be kept in mind. Lubove's history ends in the early 1930s; thus, it misses the meaningful resurgence of activism and reform in social work circles produced in the 1930s New Deal era (Leighninger, 1987, p. 75). A similar process occurred in the 1960s, spurred by the civil rights movement and the War on Poverty (Jansson, 1997, pp. 232–234).

Katz's assertion that social work has never become a profession is a highly sensitive one, not infrequently heard (Hopps and Collins, 1995), and

extremely controversial. The charge, though, is not a sustainable one, however much the profession's history is marked by a near-obsessive worry
over this very point. Social worker Austin (1983) offers a breath of fresh
air and a wider perspective on this. He visits, yet again, the psychiatric
turning point, this time by means of a systematic analysis of the famous
1915 Abraham Flexner speech that he sees as a leading impetus of the
drive toward medical-psychiatric professionalism. Flexner's pronouncement
that social work was not a profession and could only become one by emu-
lating medicine, Austin concludes, was "probably . . . the most significant
event in the development of the intellectual rationalization for social work
as an organized profession" (p. 357). Social work, Austin argues, too na-
ively took Flexner to heart. In a compelling analysis, he dissects logical
flaws in the Flexner argument and concludes that social work should stop
trying to live up to this physician's long-ago pronouncement: "It is time to
exorcise his ghost and turn our attention to the significant issues that emerge
from the distinctive social responsibilities of professional social work" (p.
375). To exorcise that ghost, it is time for social work to, in effect, relax and
accept that fact that it *already* is an established, major profession, regardless of what some sociologists or historians might say: "When, or if, social
workers themselves believe that social work is an established profession,
and act on that belief, other groups in society are likely to agree" (p. 375).

Basically, Austin argues, an occupation is recognized as a profession when
"it asserts a right to be accorded such recognition by other professional
groups and can make it hold" (p. 374). In seeking too hard to prove to
others that social work is, indeed, a scientifically based profession, Austin
believes, there has been a nonproductive preoccupation with (a) defining a
unitary model of social work practice that would smoothly integrate all the
strikingly wide range of tasks and functions addressed by social work, and
(b) a de-emphasis of such things as case management, social care, and
mediating tasks as being "not professional." Both these preoccupations
should be set aside. The profession should make peace with the fact that it
is a widely diverse, multifaceted enterprise and that a single, intellectually
elegant "unitary model" of practice is not likely to be reached anytime
soon. Acceptance of this, coupled with more self assurance about the
profession's already achieved status as a profession will allow social work
to accept that increased attention to case management, linking-mediating
tasks, and social reform will enhance, not diminish, professional status for
they speak to unique functions not addressed by other professions and are
faithful to original elements in social work's historic mission.

Another contemporary, influential framing of the issues of professional
status, reform, and mediating functions is provided by social work scholars Specht and Courtney (1994) in their passionately argued and highly

provocative book, *Unfaithful Angels: How Social Work Has Abandoned Its Mission*. Taking aim at the modern growth of psychotherapy and private practice in social work, they conclude an excessive number of social workers have been led astray from the profession's historic community-based and social reform mission. Seduced by credentialism, status, and higher salaries, too many, as they see it, had, by the 1990s, become "unfaithful angels," which is a reference to Balzac's quote about "sweetly smiling angels with pensive looks, innocent faces and cash-boxes for hearts" (frontispiece). On the question of whether social work has achieved professional status, their position coincides with Austin's and not Katz's: there is no doubt that social work is a well-established profession. However, Specht and Courtney are concerned with the terms on which professional status has been achieved—its core identity—and they show much less tolerance than Austin for a very wide-ranging diversity in social work approaches, believing that psychotherapy and private practice have grown so large they are distorting the overall shape of the profession.

On the issue of whether environmentalism and social reform ended with the psychiatric turning point, Specht and Courtney dispute Katz's assertion that social work's reform impulse evaporated by 1930. They integrate into their analysis the subsequent New Deal and War on Poverty environmentalism, activism, and reform. This is done with pointed and at times blunt argumentation. During the 1960s: "Community organization, advocacy, and anti-poverty programs became the order of the day. Overwhelmed, the psychiatric social workers who had reigned professionally supreme for many years beat an ignominious retreat; however, though down, they were not out. In the later 1970s they reappeared with a new name, clinical social work, to ride the crest of a new social work wave . . . ." (ix).

The debate about the "true" nature of social work, and the competing claims for leadership that come from the multiple sectors of the profession will undoubtedly continue. As it does, references to history will play an important role as parties to the debate frame their positions, in part, within competing interpretations of the historical record. A part of the historical record that warrants serious attention, and that we now turn to, is the place of the modern welfare state in the development of the profession.

Modern Welfare State Development: Gender, Race, and Inequality

The emergence of the modern welfare state is intimately involved with social work's development. Blurred boundaries between public and private service sectors caused by developments such as contracting, licensing, accreditation, and other regulatory functions have meant that even those social workers not working for a governmental agency are deeply affected by the decisions made by local and federal governments. The welfare state is not simply backdrop for the profession's historical development: social workers have played key roles in shaping the welfare state and the state, in turn, has profoundly shaped the profession.

Maternalist and Paternalist Welfare State Construction: Post Civil War to 1920s

The remarkable outpouring of reform energy shown in the Progressive Era was, in large part, women's energy. This had led one prominent scholar (Skocpol, 1992) to assess these early steps toward an American welfare state as an exercise in maternalist welfare state construction. The "maternalist" framing fits because of the leadership role of women, because women themselves framed their social reform goals in maternal conceptualizations, such as national "social housekeeping" efforts and roles as "mothers of the nation," and, finally, because the substance of the policy reforms targeted women and children (Skocpol, 1992).

Maternalist successes are more fully appreciated when put in the context of American paternalist policy failures. In the late 19th century, when western European countries were developing early, nationally centralized versions of the modern welfare state centered on benefits for working men and their dependents, the United States was conspicuously devoid of such developments—with one exception. The one arena in which the U.S. showed dramatic welfare growth was the rise of a national system of civil war pensions for Union veterans. However, this system was extinguished by the 1920s. Its ending was something of a temporary dead-end in welfare state development.

The civil war pension system story is an important and not widely known one (Skocpol, 1992). While it has been common to argue that the federal government did not involve itself, in a major way, in welfare programs until the 1930s New Deal era, Skocpol (1992) points out the inaccuracy of this view. The federal government actually developed its first large-scale welfare program in the aftermath of the Civil War when Congress passed retirement and disability benefits for Union veterans. Over time, benefits were liberalized and benefits for dependents added. Largely because of Republican and Democratic competition to liberalize benefits to win elections, the civil war pension system evolved into a large, fairly generous for its time, welfare system that was administered without the stigma often associated with welfare. The reach of this early welfare system is summed up by Skocpol: "In 1910, approximately 35% of northern men aged 65 and over were on the pension rolls, whereas less than 10 percent of men residing in the South were federal pensioners (some of these were ex-slave veterans and many others were [W]hite Union veterans who had migrated from the North)" (1992, pp. 135–136).

However, as the civil war generation died away by the 1920s, the generous system of social provision died with it and was not replaced with European style "paternalist welfare state" provisions. "Paternalist" in that the typical pattern in European states was for male-operated state bureaucracies to administer social provisions (various industrial social insurances) to male workers and their dependents. One might have expected that the large-scale federal involvement in welfare represented by the civil war pension movement would have paved the way for a permanent federal welfare role by the early 20th century. However, as has been noted, this did not happen. In fact, the first two decades of the 20th century saw a series of unsuccessful attempts to establish paternalist national policies in the areas of health insurance, unemployment insurance, and old age insurance, with courts and various levels of American government being highly resistant to these proposals. (However, in some policy areas there were modest achievements at individual state levels as in the case of experimentation with state-level unemployment insurance systems and workmen's compensation systems). In part, resistance to institutionalizing a paternalistic national welfare state structure in the 1920s grew out of reformers' fear of the manner in which electoral politics had propelled the growth of the Union pension system. In a manner that showed a direct line of descent from the COS fear of welfare and "outdoor relief," reformers by the 1920s were fearful that institutionalizing social welfare on the generous, dignified terms found in the pension system would be a corrupting step, in effect, buying votes with welfare.

In contrast to the stalled paternalist welfare structure of the 1920s, the same period saw a string of remarkable American successes in establishing social provisions for women and children, in effect creating significant steps in the direction of a potential maternalist welfare state. Creation of the federal Children's Bureau, very-wide-spread adoption of state-level mother's pensions (an early form of welfare for women and dependent children), an array of protections for women in the workplace—all constituted remarkable achievements in an era when most comparable initiatives for male workers were being rejected. The contrast is all the more striking when one considers that before 1920 most American women were not allowed to vote. Women achieved these successes through a massive, highly coordinated national system of women's clubs and social reform movements. A crucial element in their successes was the formulation of an ideology of civic improvement framed in terms of women as caretakers of modern civilization. In the words of Skocpol (1992) there was a "remarkable kind of maternalist political consciousness at a time when U.S. industrial workers were not very politically class-conscious . . . American women used their clubs and federations to engage in 'municipal housekeeping' and to propose new public social policies to help mothers, children, and families" (p. 529). Important leadership elements in this maternalist social welfare policy drive came from women in the newly developing social work profession, though social work was only one among very many sectors involved. However, the incipient national "maternalist" welfare state did not come to be. The important steps taken in the 1920s were not followed by a maternalist wave of development in the next phase of social welfare state development: the 1930s New Deal array of policies and programs, created as a result of the economic devastation and political turmoil following the 1929 crash in the economy and the resulting Great Depression. In the New Deal era, the country took a different direction than that envisioned by the women social welfare leaders of the 1920s; nevertheless, their achievements stand out as a remarkable chapter in the history of social welfare and social work. By putting their stamp on the proto-welfare state developments of the 1920s, women leaders, including social workers, had put in place policies, organizations, and arguments that would have a prominent place in the next phase of welfare state development: the New Deal.

Bifurcated Welfare State: 1930s New Deal to 1960s War on Poverty and Beyond

Central, distinguishing characteristics of the modern American welfare state that emerged from Roosevelt's 1930s New Deal administration are its "bifurcated" and "reluctant" nature (Jansson, 1997; Skocpol, 1988). The term "reluctant" is used because the American version is late in emerging, has less generous benefits, and is incomplete compared to western European systems (for example, no comprehensive national health insurance or national family allowance system). It is bifurcated as, essentially, a two-part, or split-level structure with a fundamental institutional and political division between respectable, politically very strong "social security" level and a stigmatized, politically vulnerable "welfare" level (Skocpol, 1988, p. 295). The top tier has a long history of powerful connotations of being "earned" benefits for the "worthy." The lower level, welfare, exists in what Katz (1996) calls "the shadow of the poorhouse," with ungenerous benefits, and a history of stigmatizing "unworthy" beneficiaries. The differences between the two are not accidental. New Deal architects were careful to distinguish between social insurance and welfare and invested considerable resources and ingenuity in elevating the image of social insurance in the public mind and derogating the image—and reality—of welfare (Cates, 1983). Separation of the two parts of the social welfare system was reinforced by New Deal failure to embrace national full employment policies which, if achieved, would have placed more people under protection of the work-related upper tier (Skocpol, 1988). Former settlement house participants and social workers from the preceding decades played key roles in the creation of the New Deal welfare state and its evolution during the following decades. Illustrative names of such social work figures include Frances Perkins (first Secretary of Labor), Julia Lathrop (first director of the federal Children's Bureau), Grace Abbot (another director of the Children's Bureau), Florence Kelly (leader of the Consumer League), Harry Hopkins (Roosevelt's first director of national relief efforts), and John Collier (New Deal director of the Bureau of Indian Affairs).

Much of social work's efforts have been focused on poorer clients occupying the lower tier of the bifurcated welfare state. This has had important, complex ramifications. At times the profession has had a good track record of advocating for the needy in policy circles, particular during the New Deal and War on Poverty eras (Spano, 1982; Specht and Courtney, 1994). On the other hand, the profession has a history of ambivalence about this association with poverty, welfare, and the stigmatized. One manifestation of this has been the at-times wide gap between professional social work circles and the separate realm of public welfare officials. This gap is an ironic and unfortunate phenomenon for many reasons, not the least being the central role played by social workers in the creation of the federal-state system of public assistance programs. From 1935 until the early 1950s, social worker Jane Hoey directed the federal Bureau of Public Assistance, which had administrative oversight for federal-state public assistance. The energy and commitment shown by Hoey during nearly two decades of leadership were formidable. Leighninger (1987) tells of one governor who telephoned Washington, D.C., to complain about the "red-haired devil" in his office (Hoey) ordering him around on welfare matters (p. 91). She fought for a just implementation of welfare that would provide benefits with respect and dignity. Too often, however, she was overruled and even censored for her efforts by administrative superiors in the Social Security Board/Social Security Administration, who either feared the development of a too-liberal welfare program or simply did not see the programs as worth the effort (Cates, 1983; Cates, 1988).

Given the historically close alignment between economic and racial divisions in this country, the bifurcated, or split-level construction of the welfare state has meant the lines have been "racially charged" (Skocpol, 1988, p. 302). African Americans were overwhelmingly excluded from the top, social insurance, portion of the welfare state at the time of its creation. The original 1935 social security act excluded agricultural labor and small firm labor from both unemployment and old age social insurance. This meant the majority of African Americans were excluded from initial coverage, a situation with deep, long-lasting consequences. Too much New Deal labor and social welfare legislation was "a sieve with holes sized so that the majority of our workers would drop through" observed the National Association for the Advancement of Colored People's (NAACP) Charles Houston (1935). In the lower tier, public assistance features were built into the New Deal public assistance provisions of the social security act that gave the South a free hand to treat African Americans in a severely discriminatory way.

Between World War I and the mid-1950s, African Americans transformed themselves from a predominantly rural to predominantly urban population, and emerged as powerfully concentrated clusters of swing votes in national elections. Then, as a result of victories achieved in the modern civil rights victories of the 1960s, African Americans emerged as fully incorporated into national electoral processes. They were then positioned to press for improved access to all aspects of the modern welfare state, and, in effect, to undo the racial overlay of the welfare state division. Unfortunately, this did not occur. The 1960s War on Poverty, though it achieved many successes (Levitan and Taggert, 1976; Plotnik and Skidmore, 1975), failed utterly to eliminate the deep pockets of northern, inner city, African American poverty that originated in Progressive Era migration and segregation. In fact, many scholars believe the War on Poverty inadvertently escalated racial polarization in the welfare state because of its failure to live up to its promises to abolish poverty and its resulting failure to overcome the New Deal's exclusion of African Americans from full participation in the upper tier of the welfare state. In addition, the proximity of the War on Poverty to both the civil rights movement and the devastating urban riots of the 1960s precipitated a serious White backlash in which perceptions of race, violence, and welfare were blurred in a confused, stereotyped, and powerful fashion (Lieberman, 1998; Quadagno, 1994). Racial divisions in the welfare state have a long history and remain a central concern as will be discussed in the next section.

Racial Duality in the Welfare State and the Profession: Post-Civil War to the 1960s

As Orfield, a leading scholar of segregation and desegregation, observes, "race is the most fundamental cleavage in American history" (1988, p. 314). This is a view that resonates both with legendary African American scholar W. E. B. DuBois's famous declaration that "the problem of the 20th century is the problem of the color-line" (1900) and contemporary social policy

analyst William Julius Wilson's plea on the eve of the 21st century, to overcome the nation's "racial divide" (Wilson, 1999).

Ringer's conceptual framework of racial duality (1983) is a useful way to
view the historical intertwining of racism, social welfare, and social work.
In this formulation, America's history is situated in the total history of "five
centuries of [W]hite European expansion throughout the world" by forceful conquest and domination of nonwhite populations (Ringer & Lawless,
1989, p. xiii). In the emerging American nation-state, White colonists/
colonialists built a two-part social-political structure that was a template
for the nation's future struggles over racial equality. One realm, which Ringer
terms the domain of "we the people" was "rooted in the rights and sovereignty of the people and regulated by the normative code of the American
creed . . ." (Ringer, 1983, p. 8). The American creed enshrined the democratic rights of full citizenship. Entry into this "people's domain" was initially restricted to Whites. The other domain, outside the circle of "we the
people" has been governed by a racial creed legitimating the use of force,
exploitation, and fraud to subordinate non-White groups. In this, the concept of "race" has been a social-political construction, not a biological one.
The term has often been used as shorthand for both race and ethnicity—
a point vividly demonstrated by the fact that definitions of "White" and
"non-White" vary considerably throughout history. The coexistence of
these two domains, "we the people" and "others," is a fundamental structural duality in American history. Much of that history is one of struggles
by the excluded to achieve entry into the full democratic rights of the
"people's domain." Each racial-ethnic group's history has been a series of
unique encounters with this structure of duality, and those encounters
permeate the history of social welfare and social work in ways not yet
fully understood.

African American Struggles with Duality. The size of the African American population, the extent to which Black exclusion and segregation was
written into the legal and political foundations of the country, and the
intensity of the struggles to overcome these obstacles, have in many ways
made the African American the "central non-White figure in a [national]
racial drama" (Ringer, 1983, p. 153). African American duality was enforced through three distinct systems of separation and control as discussed
by Orfield (1988): slavery, Jim Crow segregation, and the modern urban
ghetto. Slavery was overturned only after a long struggle that culminated
in America's bloodiest war. Jim Crow segregation emerged after the Civil
War and produced a rigid system of racial separation and discrimination
backed by the use of lethal force, including lynchings. While the precise
origins of the phrase "Jim Crow" are obscure and uncertain, the label refers

to a system of local and state laws that, peaking in southern and border states, codified a system of racial segregation that touched virtually all aspects of life (Vann, 1966). By 1880, the system of Jim Crow segregation had achieved acceptance at the national level by leading White intellectuals, political leaders, and most of the general White population. It was not overturned until the African American civil rights successes of the 1960s. The third system of separation and control has been the modern urban ghetto: racially segregated pockets of inner-city poverty. This system has its origins in the fierce residential segregation that faced African Americans as they migrated north in the first half of the 20th century. This system has remained little changed since the last major national antipoverty effort in the 1960s, and at the present time it constitutes the central dilemma of the modern welfare state.

The profession of social work emerged in the midst of national White acceptance of Jim Crow segregation. The emergent profession was overwhelmingly White. Systematic denial of African American access to education of all types, coupled with growing insistence on graduate education as the key to professional entry, meant racial duality was deeply imprinted into the structure of the new profession. Every facet was affected: who joined the profession, who was served by it, the nature of its interventions, its knowledge base, the profession's policy and reform priorities, as well as the content of social work education. For the most part, social workers of the Progressive Era functioned within limits set by prevailing White racist norms. This theme is encapsulated in an incident that is often pointed to as one of the high points of Progressive Era social work political influence.

In 1912, Theodore Roosevelt bolted the Republican party, running for president as the candidate of the Progressive party, a campaign many progressive social workers saw as "the climax of their long struggle for social justice" (Davis, 1967, p. 194). Social workers had written the industrial and social planks of the party platform, and the best-known social worker in the country, Jane Addams, was chosen to speak in favor of the nomination of Roosevelt. However, Addams was presented with a dilemma: White southern progressives objected to the seating of African American delegates from their states. Coming on the heels of an earlier, losing fight to have a "Negro equality" plank written into the Progressive Party platform, Addams found this hard to take. Roosevelt, however, decided against challenging the White supremacists, fearing he would lose the national election without southern support. Jane Addams, too, reluctantly acquiesced, and the southern African American delegates were rejected. Addams subsequently tried to explain to the African American community both her own and the Progressive Party's positions on race in an article published in the NAACP's journal, Crisis, arguing that if the Progressives achieved national office, a general era of reform would ensure which would, over the long run, improve race relations (Addams, 1912).

This incident epitomizes the fact that racial justice was seen as too much to add to the progressive reform agenda: it was feared that standing up to racism would undermine their ability to achieve anything else of substance. In addition to this calculation of what appeared politically feasible, the thinking of White settlement leaders and caseworkers was not free of the racist stereotyping of the day. Even Jane Addams, as Iglehart and Becerra point out, was capable of telling 1908 African Americans their progress was, in part, blocked by their own cultural disadvantages in that they lacked "some of the restraints of the traditions which. . . . [Italians, Greeks, and Russians] bring with them" (2000, p. 122).

For the most part, White social workers were indeed, in the words of Allen (1974), "reluctant reformers" when it came to racial justice. Katz's (1996) summary of Chicago settlement leaders' attitudes toward racial justice also captures the tone of most of the national White settlement and caseworker movement: "Jane Addams, Edith Abbott, Sophonisba Breckenridge, and Florence Kelley led the left wing of the settlement movement. They understood how [B]lacks had been exploited. . . . Nonetheless, when it came to practical policies, no differences separated them from their more openly racist colleagues. . . . The more liberal settlement leaders advocated economic and political equality, but not social equality; worked hard to improve Black living conditions within the ghetto; and accepted segregation either as inescapable or desirable. All of them refused to integrate their settlement houses. Even when the racial compositions of their neighborhoods changed, most settlements remained [W]hite islands, and [only a] . . . handful of settlements opened to serve [B]lacks" (p. 183).

Katz (1996) and Kusmar (1976) trace the origins of the modern inner-city pockets of African American poverty to the Progressive Era racial segregation that was imposed on the newly arriving African American migrants. Katz argues that Progressive Era leadership's acceptance of residential segregation thus implicates them in the creation of the modern Black, urban ghetto (p. 181). The experiences of Black urban communities have been fundamentally different from the experiences of immigrants: "the history of Chicago's [B]lacks and of [B]lacks in every other city, did not recapitulate the experiences of European immigrants. No immigrant group ever lived in neighborhoods as segregated as the [B]lack ghetto. With each decade, as they left the center of cities for new homes in the suburbs, European immigrants and their children lived in less segregated surroundings. By contrast, [B]lack segregation, higher from the start, continued to increase. European immigrants were allowed, even encouraged to move out of ethnic enclaves; [B]lacks were prevented from leaving the ghetto" (Katz,

1996, p. 182). White tactics to enforce segregation included a very wide range of devices, including: the use of force against Blacks who tried to move into White neighborhoods, the burning of crosses on lawns, the creation of restrictive covenants (agreements written into home purchase contracts not to resell to African Americans), the formation of White neighborhood organizations ostensibly to promote neighborhood well-being but with the actual purpose of monitoring the racial composition of the neighborhood, agreements among real estate agents to "steer" African American customers away from White neighborhoods, and "redlining," the practice of racial discrimination in the mortgage and insurance industries (Dreier, 1996; Farley, 1996). Another key factor was the de facto underwriting of residential segregation by the federal government itself in its post-1930s Federal Housing Administration home mortgage programs that were operated, for decades, in a manner that was "[W]hites only" (Calmore, 1996). In the words of the Washington, D.C., Citizen's Commission on Civil Rights, "Federal policy makers cooperated with state and local governments, real estate brokers, developers and financial institutions to assure that minorities were excluded from assistance designed to benefit the middle class and that low-income housing was provided only on a segregated basis. . . . For [Blacks], the government's housing policies meant that they were confined to ghettos, lacking choice and access to the jobs and services that would have afforded the opportunity to become part of the mainstream" (Citizens Commission on Civil Rights, 1981, pp. 81–82, quoted in Boger & Wegner, 1996).

While the White face put to professional social work in the Progressive Era dominated until the civil rights movement of the 1950s and 1960s, there were important African American currents of social work practice and education from the turn of the century onward. In the face of exclusion, African Americans created their own settlement houses and other social welfare systems (Gordon, 1991; Iglehart & Becerra, 2000; Ross, 1978), developed their own schools of social work, and created their own approaches to social work practice at the same time they fought against exclusion and oppression. In so doing they not only served their own communities, they made vital contributions to the social work profession as a whole.

One of the earliest professionally trained African American social workers was George Edmund Haynes who, in 1910, graduated from the New York School of Philanthropy. Attending school on a New York Charity Organization Society fellowship, he specialized in the study of social problems of Blacks who had migrated to the urban North. His growing expertise in this area eventually led to his leadership role in the founding of the National League on Urban Conditions Among Negroes, later to become the National Urban League (NUL). This organization grew to national scope and became the first major social welfare agency designed to serve the needs of urban African Americans. As executive director of the of the NUL, he established the country's first formal training program in social services (though not a full-fledged school of social work) for African Americans at Fisk University in Nashville. He was clear about the need for Black social workers and Black-focused professional social work education: "to know people very well one must live with them . . . [and] share with them the life of the Negro world . . . Only Negroes live within that world" (quoted in Carlton, 1982, p. 90).

Except for token representation in some White schools, African Americans, until the midpoint of the 20th century, turned primarily to Atlanta University and Howard University for graduate social work education; before 1920 even those options were not available. Another early African American social worker, Jesse O. Thomas, observed, "In 1919–1920 there was not a colored person who had received training at an accredited school of social work south of Washington or east of St. Louis" (Thomas, 1967, p. 117). Thomas, head of the southern branch of the NUL at the time, was asked to address the 1920 National Conference of Social Workers in New Orleans. In a setting that graphically embodied the intersection of social work and Jim Crow segregation, African American social workers were made to sit in the gallery while White social workers sat on the main floor of the conference hall. Thomas refused to give his speech under these segregated conditions, upon which the Whites moved to the gallery and listened to his appeal for the creation of a Black school of social work at Atlanta University, something that was accomplished within the year (Thomas, 1967, pp. 118-125). When Howard University, in Washington, D.C., began to offer social work training in 1935 (a fully accredited school of social work was developed by 1943), these two universities became the nation's leading sources of professionally educated African American social workers.

Forrester B. Washington, long-time dean of the Atlanta school, was an early leader in the development of Black social work curriculum content because he believed White social work schools simply were not capable of preparing social workers—of any race—to work in Black communities. African Americans, he said in 1929, had "a different social background which has nothing to do with heredity and a great deal to do with environment" (Yabura, 1970, p. 30). He pointed to the long tradition of distinctive helping institutions in Black communities: resources that had been developed in response to White exclusion. Social workers who had learned to work successfully with the problems faced by African Americans had eventually "developed an elaborate technique to meet these difficulties—but it was not learned in school. They had to acquire it by trial and error method and of course during the 'learning period' the clients are the sufferers." He was intent on institutionalizing such knowledge. From 1927 through the early 1940s, the school offered what must have been the largest collection of social work courses in the country on topics such as "The Techniques of Community Work Among Negro People; Industrial Problems of Negro People; The Conduct of Social Surveys in Negro Communities" and others. Such Black content declined by the mid-1940s, the victim, according to Yabura (1970), of the growing clout of White social work accreditation circles, which were not receptive to such courses.

During the 1920s and for decades afterwards, the Atlanta school worked with a remarkable African American community activist, Lugenia Burns Hope. In 1908, Hope, building on her COS experiences in Chicago, had established the Neighborhood Union, which adapted the settlement house movement to the Black communities around Atlanta University. Her work epitomizes the contributions of large numbers of African American community builders, north and south, who labored to develop services for their communities. For thirty years, she led the organization, developing a striking array of services: kindergartens, health facilities, day care centers, playgrounds, neighborhood centers, tuberculosis drives, citizenship schools, as well as providing leadership in the development of low-cost housing for the poor. Her work inspired similar efforts by African American community leaders around the South. As a faculty member at the Atlanta school of social work, she was able integrate her community-based practice with teaching (Gary, 1986; Rouse, 1989).

Forrester B. Washington's focus on a distinctively African American identity for the Atlanta school of social work was different from the approach taken by Inabel Burns Lindsay, African American social worker, and first dean of the Howard University School of Social Work. Deeply committed to fostering social work responsiveness to the African American community, she nevertheless resisted attempts to frame the school as a "Negro school," wanting, instead, one with a reputation as being open to students of all races. She was alert to racism in social work education and practice and was the first to speak out again a long-standing practice in schools of social work around the country of "assigning Black students to field placements in public welfare agencies, but seldom . . . to the much sought after placements in hospitals and mental health agencies." Upon her urging, the accreditation body of the time mandated a stop to the practice (Hawkins & Daniels, 1985, p. 3). Similarly, in the days before the modern civil rights movement, she helped organized a boycott with Johns Hopkins Hospital social workers to protest that institution's refusal to allow African Americans, including her social work field students, to eat in the White-only cafeteria. She monitored field agencies closely and removed students from social work agencies that refused to change their practices of segregating restroom facilities or calling African American clients by first names while addressing Whites with titles (Hawkins & Daniels, 1985, p. 3). By the 1960s, both Atlanta University and Howard transformed their curricula to make Black content increasingly visible as an educational theme. In the case of Howard, this produced a school of social work mission known as the "Black Perspective in Social Work," a distinctive approach to the profession that has structured the social work education of students of all races enrolled there.

The work of African American social workers in the era of Jim Crow segregation constitutes a profound professional heritage. It documents community strength and responsiveness in the face of oppression. The achievements constitute a legacy for all social work. In an era when narrow, psychiatric-oriented casework dominated the profession, African American communities and schools helped keep alive what is now termed community-based practice. The early efforts of leaders such as Washington and Haynes to forge African American curriculum content were forerunners of contemporary Africentric and Afrocentric social work practice models (Everett, Chipungu, & Leashore, 1991; Schiele, 2000), and they prefigured the profession's much later commitment to multiculturalism and cultural competence in practice (Fellin, 2000).

As the welfare state developed in the New Deal era of the 1930s, and in accordance with prevailing Jim Crow segregation, the cluster of White New Deal reformers who helped shaped policies was accompanied by an informal and segregated "Black cabinet" of so-called "race advisors." Confined to an advisory role, these African Americans were given the challenging task, to say the least, of "advising" the Roosevelt administration about how to demonstrate some degree of responsiveness to the severe depression era needs of African Americans. This was a daunting task in an era when Roosevelt, bowing to southern demands, would not even support legislative proposals to make lynching a federal crime (Kirby, 1980). Included in this group, for a brief period, was Forrester B. Washington, who left Atlanta University to become a New Deal race advisor, only to resign after six months and return to his social work deanship, frustrated by the tokenism of the race-advising effort (Kirby, 1980). "Those who think that because these Negro advisors are in Washington they can lay back and be assured of good care" were in for disillusionment he told the *Afro-American* newspaper and pointed to the extent to which the new social security legislation ignored the plight of Blacks (Washington, 1935).

Other Black social workers in the coming decades played nationally important roles in challenging racial duality in the welfare state. Lester

Granger, as head of the NUL, promoted a social casework, employment-preparation approach toward improving the lot of African Americans and also served as an important advisor to the military about integration of the armed forces in the late 1940s (Brown, 1991; Parris & Brooks, 1971; Weiss, 1974). Whitney M. Young, after spending time himself as dean of the Atlanta University School of Social Work, succeeded Granger at NUL and led that organization into the era of the modern civil rights movement. Presidents Johnson and Nixon turned to him for advice on poverty and race issues. He became an important bridge between Black America and U.S. corporate leadership. Young also served as president of the National Association of Social Workers and the National Conference on Social Welfare in the 1960s. In those roles, he helped move both organizations in the direction of social activism (Weiss, 1989). "Social work was born in an atmosphere of righteous indignation, of divine discontent . . . " he told the National Conference on Social Welfare in his 1967 inaugural address, but the drive for professional status had diminished the commitment to social action and social work had "made a fetish of methodology." As paraphrased by Weiss, Young believed "too many social workers looked down their noses at the poor; too many were uncomfortable with issues of race and religion. They had come to be seen not as crusaders but as "'experts in adjustment and accommodation'" (Weiss, 1989, p. 207).

The Struggle of Other Racial and Ethnic Groups with Duality. Each racial-ethnic group in American history has had its own unique encounter with the nation's structure of racial duality, and for those encounters occurring after the birth of the profession, social work has been a part of the experience. The Native American encounter is strikingly different from the African American one in that treaty rights and tribal sovereignty have been important structural features that, especially in recent decades, have helped shape the social welfare and social work roles. One whole sector of the New Deal era is known as the Indian New Deal (Parman, 1976; Philp, 1977; Taylor, 1980) and points to a fundamental shift in national policy from assimilation and destruction of Indian and tribal identity to a new policy of preserving Indian cultural heritage and land. John Collier, former community social worker, led this reformist drive as Bureau of Indian Affairs (BIA) Commissioner from 1933 to 1945 (Kelly, 1983). The intersection of this reform effort with the developing welfare state had decidedly mixed outcomes. On the one hand, Collier backed Indian involvement in New Deal work relief programs such as the Indian Civilian Conservation Corps. On the other hand, he was a key player in an illegal New Deal era agreement to exclude Southwest reservation residents from participation in the new federal-state public assistance programs (Cates, 1988).

The rise of Indian tribal and pan-tribal political activism following World War II (Cornell, 1988) led to increasing levels of Indian self-determination in all aspects of Indian life, including social welfare and social work arenas. This is demonstrated, for example, by the passage of the 1978 Indian Child Welfare Act (ICWA) (Matheson, 1996), which established profound changes in the way Indian children were handled in the child welfare system by building in safeguards to protect tribal involvement in the decision making in an effort to curtail what had been a serious outplacement of foster and adoptive Indian children to non-Indian families (Matheson, 1996; Weaver & White, 1999). The intensity with which American Indian racial duality has been defended by Whites can be seen vividly in the social welfare record. Nevada, for decades, delayed instituting an Aid to Families with Dependent Children program, in part because White legislators did not want to pay state tax dollars for benefits going to Indian children (Leighninger, 1987). The state of Arizona, in the early 1950s, eliminated its federal-state Crippled Children's Services program, throwing disabled White children out of programs, rather than bow to federal pressure to serve Indian children as well (Cates, in progress).

The histories of other racial-ethnic groups are equally distinctive. In the case of Asian Americans, work such as Takaki's (1998) important history of Asian Americans has expanded our knowledge of the experiences of people from a very wide range of backgrounds: Japanese, Chinese, Korean, Filipino, Asian Indians, as well as Vietnamese and other Southeast Asians. The historical record of the intersection of each of these groups with social welfare in general, and social work in particular, is less well developed, though there are some significant bodies of historical research. For example, the specific enactment of racial duality in New Deal Works Progress Administration programs in the then-territory of Hawaii have been analyzed by social worker Heirakuji (1993), showing the precise interplay of social welfare policy with the prevailing racial hegemony in which subordination of a variety of Asian Americans was central. In the realm of Japanese American history, much attention has been given to the World War II tragedy in which the U.S. government forced approximately 120,000 Japanese American citizens and permanent residents into concentration camps solely on the grounds of their race. There was a little-known federal Bureau of Public Assistance program for residents of the camps and fuller knowledge of its operations awaits research in the agency's National Archives holdings. The role of Japanese American community-based services and the general profession of social work in the post-war coerced dispersal of Japanese Americans out of the camps to locations other than their original West Coast homes, though well-described in the general historical literature, is generally not incorporated into the social work history literature

(Drinnon, 1987; Girdner and Loftis, 1969; Hansen and Mitson, 1974; Thomas & Mishimoto, 1946). However, important historical research about the camp experience by or about social workers does exist. For example, social worker Takahashi's research (1980, 1998) analyzes the administration of the camps as well as the effects of racism on Japanese Americans. Building on her internment camp research, she became the Congressional lobbyist for the Japanese American Citizens League, an organization that was a key player in passage of the 1988 Civil Liberties Act. This legislation provided to the camp survivors, approximately forty years after their release, a financial payment and letter of apology from the federal government. Following passage of this legislation, Takahashi then worked with the U.S. Justice Department, helping locate individuals eligible for the payments. For an overview of the lengthy process leading to this national legislation see the federal government report *Personal Justice Denied* (U.S. Commission on Wartime Relocation and Internment of Civilians, 1983).

Incorporating into accounts of the profession's history the varied experiences of Hispanic/Latino Americans in a way that is faithful to all the wide range of groups—Chicanos, Puerto Ricans, Cubans, Central Americans, and others—largely remains an unfulfilled scholarly challenge. A very significant exception to this statement is the work of Iglehart and Becerra (2000) on the history of social services and American ethnic communities in general and Mexican American self-help efforts in particular. Gordon (1999) also has made a valuable contribution in this direction with her recent work of "microhistory" that analyzes the intersection of the early 20th century child-saving movement with powerful currents of Southwestern race hatred and the location-specific nature of racial definitions. She documents the story of fifty-seven "foundlings," Irish American children from New York who in 1904 were placed, legally and appropriately in terms of the procedures of the day, in new homes with Mexican American families in Clifton, Arizona. The children were accompanied on the trip to Arizona by Sisters of Charity nuns who ran the New York Foundling Hospital from which the children came. Gordon documents that when the children boarded the train in the Northeast they were socially defined as "non-White" in that Irish Americans at the turn of the century were not seen as "Whites" in the urban Northeast. When the children exited the train in Arizona, however, Anglos there defined the children as eminently "White." Different locales meant different definitions of "race," and Anglo determination to preserve racial differences and White hegemony in the Southwest was backed up with force. When White citizens saw that "White" children were being placed with Mexican American families, a vigilante group kidnapped them all and distributed them to whichever White family was first to ask for them. In this process, the mob threatened the lives of

the nuns if they did not turn over the children. Subsequent court challenges by the staff of the New York Foundling Hospital were unsuccessful
in their attempts to reclaim the children from the vigilantes. Gordon's work
is a compelling analysis of racial hatred, backed up by violence, as it played
out in a social welfare arena.

Forrest (1989) offers one of the few historical treatments of the "Hispanic New Deal," a dual federal social welfare effort to preserve the cultural
heritage of northern New Mexico's Hispano villages and to provide economic support. Her study traces the unfulfilled promises of both the New
Deal effort and similar efforts in the 1960s War on Poverty. Numerous
other aspects of the Latino and Hispanic encounter with duality in social
welfare and social work arenas await attention. For example, the unique
status of the Commonwealth of Puerto Rico has yet to be carefully interpreted in light of the history of social work and social welfare activities
there (Carr, 1984).

Conclusion: Individual Social Workers, Social Justice, and the Future of Social Work History

For a text addressed to future social work professionals, it is fitting to conclude with illustrations of front-line social workers who grappled with social justice issues emerging in the daily rounds of their work, and who did
so in ways that contributed to historic turning points. Three illustrations
are discussed. These are followed by comments about directions for future
historical research.

Elizabeth Chief. An American Indian social worker in the federal Bureau of Indian Affairs (BIA) in the late 1940s, Elizabeth Chief had first-
hand knowledge of the desperate conditions faced by Native Americans of
the Southwest. Indian disease rates were among the highest and life spans
among the shortest of any group in the U.S. Chief had often "traveled on
horseback over rough trails to assist mothers with malnourished small children and to investigate the condition of Indians who were drinking polluted water from irrigation ditches." She was well acquainted with the link
between this suffering and the long-standing, illegal actions of New Mexico
and Arizona in totally excluding from the public assistance benefits of the
Social Security Act those Indians residing on reservations. This discrimination had been in place since the passage of the act in 1935, and had been
well known to, tolerated by, and even condoned by the federal agencies
responsible for policy oversight: the BIA and the Social Security Board (Cates,
1988). The exclusion of needy aged, blind, and dependent children was
under girded by southwestern denial of the Indian right to vote. Using
photographs, need data, and details of her own observations, she conveyed

the dimensions of the desperate situation, coupled with strong statements about the culpability of the New Mexico State Department of Public Welfare, to the National Conference of Indian Affairs. This information, in turn, became the basis of a remarkable "Starvation without Representation" article by Will Rogers, Jr., in the national publication *Look Magazine* (Rogers, 1947). The BIA, stung by Chief's actions, retaliated by ordering her to relocate away from her New Mexico home to a new assignment on the Pine Ridge Reservation in South Dakota (Philp, p. 59). However, it was too late to prevent her impact: Chief had made a significant contribution to a complex series of political events in 1948–49 that eventually led to Indian voting rights and Indian access to public welfare in the Southwest.

Bennie Parish. In 1962, Bennie Parish was a public welfare caseworker in Oakland, California, when he refused to go on a midnight raid against his welfare clients. For this refusal, he was fired as insubordinate (Piven and Cloward, 1971, p. 166.) California, as did many states, routinely subjected welfare recipients to stark degradation rituals to force them off welfare rolls. These were directed with particular force against African American clients. Among the more notorious of the degradation rituals was the midnight raid (Bell, 1965; Piven & Cloward, 1971). Caseworkers were ordered to visit client homes, unannounced and usually late at night, to look for signs of a male presence. If such signs were found (a shoe, a child's response to the worker's questioning about mother's boyfriends) or if the client refused to open the door to the unannounced visit, the woman and her children would be cut from the welfare roll without a hearing or right of appeal. Midnight raids combined with the so-called man-in-the-house rule to produce the following "logical" sequence. If a woman receiving Aid to Families with Dependent Children (AFDC) benefits were suspected of "seeing a man:" (1) She must be engaging in sexual intercourse outside of marriage which meant she was immoral, which, in turn, meant she was an "unfit" parent to whom welfare payments should not be made and whose children might be removed for this reason alone; and (2) the man she was seeing could be assumed to be the father of her children and should be held responsible for their financial support. Thus, it was justifiable to terminate her immediately from the rolls (Bell, 1965).

These practices had gone on for decades, with federal oversight agencies, the Department of Health, Education, and Welfare (HEW) and its subordinate Bureau of Public Assistance, doing virtually nothing to challenge the states even though the federal agencies carried statutory authority and responsibility for seeing that the federal-state welfare system was administered with equity. When Parish was fired, he protested and filed a lawsuit. As part of his case, the unconstitutionality of midnight raids was highlighted. Eventually, he won his court case and was reinstated. In part as a reaction to national publicity about the case, HEW eventually did what it could have done all along: issued new federal rules prohibiting midnight raids in the AFDC program. The rules, in turn, became part of a substantial series of legal cases and other developments, which, by the late 1960s, had vindicated welfare clients' rights to fair hearings and other aspects of due process.

Peter Buxton. After his experience as a military psychiatric social worker, Peter Buxton became a San Francisco public health caseworker. In the late 1960s, he came across published accounts of the then still ongoing and now infamous Tuskegee syphilis experiment. He was outraged to learn that impoverished African American men in rural Alabama were being subjected to a decades-long, federal-government-sponsored human experiment to study the crippling and lethal effects of syphilis. The men had both treatment and knowledge of their diagnosis withheld from them by federal and local health officials so that medical researchers could study the disease's progression. Upon learning of this, Buxton immediately protested to top levels of the U.S. Public Health Service. Despite initial rebuffs and attempts to intimidate him, he persisted, and, as historian Jones, in his important book, *Bad Blood*, puts it, "in the end it was Peter Buxton (and the press) that stopped Tuskegee" (Jones, 1981, p. 203). Congressional hearings were conducted, national and international outrage ensued, and the human experimentation was brought to an end. In the wake of these events, federal legislation was enacted that permanently altered the national research landscape, establishing federal requirements for informed consent and other procedures to protect humans involved in federally supported research.

The examples of Chief, Parish, and Buxton have been chosen to illustrate several points. The actions of these three little-known social workers demonstrate that one does not have to be among the most famous persons of her time (Jane Addams) or an advisor to presidents (Whitney Young) to make contributions that prove to be historically significant. They demonstrate the historically conditioned "given" nature that injustice often takes. In each situation, the injustice at stake was nothing new, and each was an open secret. Knowledge may not have been widely dispersed among the general public, but in each case knowledge of the oppression's long-standing existence was no secret in professional and policy circles. Doing normal work, each of these social workers was presented with "normal" oppressions that had a dismaying degree of acceptance by those in authority at the time.

The examples illustrate social workers operating in the joint realms of structural bifurcation and racial dualism that mark the 20th century welfare state. Each case carries the theme of populations of color excluded from the "people's domain" of full rights. The exclusion of Indians from welfare and electoral politics were key factors in maintaining a structure of Anglo dominance in the southwest. The AFDC midnight raids, while not applied exclusively to African Americans, were applied to them with selective force and frequency and served as a tool in an overall structure of racial domination. The Tuskegee experiment, as Jones demonstrates, was drenched in racist assumptions in all its aspects. The three situations underscore a fundamental fact of life for the profession: the 20th-century emergence of the massive governmental, bureaucratic social welfare state as the ground on which much of the profession operates. For all its duality, reluctance, and bifurcation, the welfare state has been an institutional power that has accomplished much good. The examples discussed here also illustrate that when turned to the wrong ends, the massive welfare state can inflict numbing degrees of oppression. However, when professionals follow commitments to social justice and resources are mobilized, reform can follow. A final observation: in none of these examples is it accurate to portray the social work role as a single-handed victory against injustice. Such an exaggeration is not necessary to appreciate the magnitude of the contributions made by these front-line workers as they played key parts in larger series of events that promoted justice and that warrant them honorable places in the profession's history.

The interpretive record of that history is very much in flux. Recent decades have seen enormous developments in multiple areas of historical scholarship: accelerated growth in African American history (Meier & Rudwick, 1986), the emergence of feminist, historical interpretations of welfare state development (Abramovitz, 1996; Diamond, 1983; Gordon, 1990; Koven and Michel, 1992; Skocpol, 1992), and what amounts to a groundswell of scholarly attention and new research into social welfare history by some of the nation's leading historians, sociologists, and political scientists (Katz, 1989 and 1996; Skocpol, 1992; Weir, Orloff, & Skocpol, 1988).

Another important development is the emergence of new histories of sexual minority communities (Berube, 1991; D'Emilio, 1983; Duberman, 1986; Duberman, Vicinus, & Chauncey, 1989; Katz, 1976; Lauritsen & Thorstad; 1974; Marcus, 1992). Social worker Poindexter's essay (1997) on the origins of the modern gay civil rights movement and the relevance of that history to social work is, hopefully, the precursor to new research about the profession's relationship with sexual minority communities. As Poindexter observes, "it would . . . be useful for the profession to review the history of its response to the oppression of gay men and lesbians and to acknowledge its marked absence from the early struggles of this population, as well as its more recent support of some aspects of the battle against oppression. Such knowledge is important for the profession's self-understanding and identity and deserves serious attention" (p. 615).

We can also look forward to advances in our understanding of social work's role in the struggles for justice by the full range of racial and ethnic groups in our society as well as the social work responses to diversity and intolerance in all their forms. A major theme in future historical research is bound to be continued attention to the intertwining of helping and controlling, paradoxically joined functions that run throughout the historical record of social work and social welfare (Gaylin et al., 1978). A deeper, more refined and useful understanding of social work's history awaits the integration of all these scholarly developments. Such knowledge will play an important role in social work's continuing drive to define itself, for, as we have seen, passionate contemporary debates about the identity, mission and future of social work are often grounded in interpretations of its history.

References

Abromowitz, M. (1996). *Regulating the lives of women*. Boston: South End Press.

Addams, J. (1912). The progressive party and the Negro. *Crisis, 5*, 30–31.

Allen, R. (1974). *Reluctant reformers: racism and social reform in the United States*. Washington, DC: Howard University Press.

Artis, L. (1993). *Nannie Helen Burroughs: A study of accommodationist and feminist-activist elements in her career*. PhD dissertation, Howard University School of Social Work, Washington, DC.

Austin, M. (1983). The Flexner Myth and the history of social work. *Social Service Review, 57*, 357–377.

Barnett, E. (1978). Nannie H. Burroughs and the education of Black women. In S. Harley and R. Terborg-Penn, (Eds.), *The Afro-American woman: Struggles and images*. Port Washington, NY: Kennikat Press.

Berube, A. (1991). *Coming out under fire: The history of gay men and women in World War Two*. New York: Plume.

Bell, W. (1965). *Aid to dependent children*. New York: Columbia University Press.

Boger, J., & Wegner, J. (1996). *Race, poverty, and American cities*. Chapel Hill, NC: University of North Carolina Press.

Brown, A. (1991). A social work leader in the struggle for racial equality: Lester Blackwell Granger. *Social Service Review, 65*(2), 266–280.

Calmore, J. O. (1996). Spatial equality and the Kerner Commission Report. In J. C. Boger & J. W. Wegner (Eds.), *Race, poverty, and American cities*. Chapel Hill, NC: The University of North Carolina Press.

Carlton, I. (1982). *A pioneer social work educator: George Edmund Haynes*. PhD dissertation, University of Maryland at Baltimore.

Carr, R. (1984). *Puerto Rico: A colonial experiment*. New York: Vintage Books.

Cates, J. (1983). *Insuring inequality: Administrative leadership in Social Security, 1935–1952*. Ann Arbor, MI: The University of Michigan Press.

Cates, J. (1988). Administrative justice, Social Security, and the American Indian. In P. Simbi (Ed.), *Administrative justice in public services: American and African perspectives.* Stevens Point, WI: Worzalla Publishing Company.

Cates, J. (in progress). *The politics of Native American public welfare.*

Cornell, S. (1988). *The return of the native: American Indian political resurgence.* New York: Oxford University Press.

Costin, L. (1985). Historical context of child care. In J. Laird & A. Hartman (Eds.), *A handbook of child welfare.* New York: Free Press.

Davis, A. (1967). *Spearheads for reform: The settlements and the progressive movement, 1890–1914.* New York: Oxford University Press.

Davis, A. (1973). *American heroine: The life and legend of Jane Addams.* New York: Oxford University Press.

D'Emilio, J. (1983). *Sexual politics, sexual communities: The making of a homosexual minority in the United States, 1940–1970.* Chicago: University of Chicago Press.

Derthick, M. (1979). *Policymaking for Social Security.* Washington, DC: The Brookings Institution.

Diamond, I. (Ed.). (1983). *Families, politics, and public policy.* New York: Longman.

Dreier, P. (1996). America's urban crisis. In J. C. Boger & J. W. Wegner (Eds.), *Race, poverty, and American cities.* Chapel Hill, NC: The University of North Carolina Press.

Drinnon, R. (1987). *Keeper of concentration camps: Dillon S. Myer and American racism.* Berkeley, CA: University of California Press.

Duberman, M. (1986). *About time: The gay past.* New York: Sea Horse.

Duberman, M., Vicinus, M., & Chauncey, G. (Eds.). (1989). *Hidden from history: Reclaiming the gay and lesbian past.* New York: Meridian.

DuBois, W. E. B. (1900). To the nations of the world. In A. Meier, E. Rudwick, & F. Broderick (Eds.), *Black protest thought in the 20th century.* Indianapolis, IN: Bobbs-Merrill.

Everett, J., Chipungu, S., & Leashore, B. (1991). *Child welfare: An Africentric perspective.* New Brunswick, NJ: Rutgers University Press.

Farley, R. (1996). Black-White residential segregation: The views of Myrdal in the 1940s and trends of the 1980s. In O. Clayton (Ed.), *An American dilemma revisited: Race relations in a changing world.* New York: Russell Sage Foundation.

Fellin, P. (2000). Multiculturalism revisited. *Journal of Social Work Education, 36*(2), 261–278.

Field, M. (1980). Social casework practice during the psychiatric deluge. *Social Service Review, 54,* 482–507.

Forrest, S. (1989). *The preservation of the village: New Mexico's Hispanic population and the New Deal.* Albuquerque: University of New Mexico Press.

Fox, D. (1986). Kingsbury, John Adams. In W. Trattner (Ed.), *Biographical dictionary of social welfare in America*. New York: Greenwood Press.

Gary, R. (1986). Hope, Lugenia Burns. In W. Trattner (Ed.), *Biographical dictionary of social welfare in America*. New York: Greenwood Press.

Gaylin, W., Glasser, I., Marcus, S., & Rothman, D. (1978). *Doing good: The limits of benevolence*. New York: Pantheon.

Girdner, A., & Loftis, A. (1969). *The great betrayal*. London: Macmillan.

Gordon, L. (Ed.). (1990). *Women, the state, and welfare*. Madison, WI: University of Wisconsin Press.

Gordon, L. (1991). Black and White visions of welfare: Women's welfare activism, 1890–1945. *Journal of American History, September 1991*, 559–590.

Gordon, L. (1999). *The great Arizona orphan abduction*. Cambridge: Harvard University Press.

Hansen, A., & Mitson, B. (Eds.). (1974). *Voices long silent: An oral inquiry into the Japanese American evacuation*. Fullerton, CA: California State University Press.

Hawkins, B., & Daniels, M. (1985). Inabel Burns Lindsay. *Urban Research Review*. 10(2), 1–3.

Heirakuji, L. (1993). *Hawaii and the New Deal: A case study of the works progress administration*. DSW dissertation, Howard University, Washington, DC.

Higginbottom, E. B. (1993). *Righteous discontent: The women's movement in the Black Baptist church, 1880–1920*. Cambridge, MA: Harvard University Press.

Hopps, J., & Collins, P. (1995). Social work profession overview. In *Encyclopedia of social work* (19th ed.). Washington, DC: NASW Press.

Houston, C. (1935, February 6). Houston calls Wagner-Lewis Bill a sieve. *Afro-American*, 1939, p. 4.

Iglehart, A., & Becerra, R. (2000). *Social services and the ethnic community*. Prospect Heights, IL: Waveland Press, Inc.

Jansson, B. (1997). *The reluctant welfare state: American social welfare policies: Past, present and future*. Pacific Grove, CA: Brooks/Cole Publishing.

Jones, J. (1981). *Bad blood: The Tuskegee syphilis experiment*. New York: The Free Press.

Katz, J. (1976). *Gay American history: Lesbians and gay men in the U.S.A.* New York: Crowell.

Katz, M. (1989). *The undeserving poor: From the war on poverty to the war on welfare*. New York: Pantheon.

Katz, M. (1996). *In the shadow of the poorhouse: A social history of welfare in America*. New York: Basic Books.

Kelly, L. (1983). *The assault on assimilation: John Collier and the origins of Indian policy reform*. Albuquerque, NM: University of New Mexico Press.

Kingsbury, J. (1912). Notebooks. Washington, DC: John Adams Kingsbury Papers, Manuscript Division, Library of Congress.

Kingsbury, J. (1939). *Health in handcuffs*. New York: Modern Age Books.

Kingsbury, J. (n.d.). Memorandum for Colonel Roosevelt regarding the welfare work of the Mitchell administration. Washington, DC: John Adams Kingsbury Papers, Manuscript Division, Library of Congress.

Kirby, J. (1980). *Black Americans in the Roosevelt era: Liberalism and race*. Knoxville, TN: The University of Tennessee Press.

Koven, S., & Michel, S. (Eds.). (1992). *Gender and the origins of welfare states in Western Europe and North America*. New York: Routledge.

Kusmar, K. (1976). *A ghetto takes shape: Black Cleveland, 1870–1930*. Urbana: University of Illinois Press.

Lauritsen, J., & Thorstad, D. (1974). *The early homosexual rights movement (1864–1990)*. New York: Times Change Press.

Lieberman, R. C. (1998). *Shifting the color line: Race and the American welfare state*. Cambridge: Harvard University Press.

Leiby, J. (1984). Charity organization reconsidered. *Social Service Review, 58*(4), 522–538.

Leighninger, L. (1987). *Social work: Search for identity*. New York: Greenwood Press.

Leighninger, L. (1995). Historiography. *Encyclopedia of social work* (19th ed.). Washington, DC: NASW Press.

Levitan, S., & Taggert, R. (1976). *The promise of greatness*. Cambridge, MA: Harvard University Press.

Lowell, J. (1884). *Public relief and private charity*. New York: Putnam's.

Lubove, R. (1969). *The professional altruist: The emergence of social work as a career, 1880–1930*. New York: Atheneum.

Marcus, J. E. (1992). *Making history: The struggle for gay and lesbian equal rights, 1945–1990*. New York: HarperCollins.

Meier, A., & Rudwick, E. (1986). *Black history and the historical profession*. Urbana: University of Illinois Press.

Matheson, L. (1996). The politics of the Indian Child Welfare Act. *Social Work, 41*(2), 232–235.

Newsholme, A., & Kingsbury, J. (1933). *Red medicine: Socialized health in Soviet Russia*. New York: Milbank Foundation.

Orfield, G. (1988). Race and the liberal agenda: The loss of the integrationist dream, 1965–1974. In M. Weir, A. Orloff, & T. Skocpol (1988). *The politics of social policy in the United States*. Princeton, NJ: Princeton University Press.

Orfield, G. (1991). *The closing door: Conservative policy and Black opportunity*. Chicago: University of Chicago Press.

Parris, G., & Brooks, L. (1971). *Blacks in the city: A history of the National Urban League*. Boston: Little, Brown.

Parman, D. (1976). *The Navajos and the New Deal*. New Haven, CT: Yale University Press.

Philp, K. (1977). *John Collier's crusade for Indian reform, 1920–1954*. Tucson, AZ: University of Arizona Press.

Pickens, K. (1968). *Eugenics and the progressives*. Nashville, TN: Vanderbilt University Press.

Piven, F. F., & Cloward, R. (1971). *Regulating the poor: The functions of public welfare*. New York: Random House.

Plotnick, R., & Skidmore, F. (1975). *Progress against poverty: A review of the 1964–1974 decade*. New York: Academic Press.

Poindexter, C. (1997). Sociopolitical antecedents to Stonewall: Analysis of the origins of the Gay Rights Movement in the United States. *Social Work, 42*(6), 607–615.

Quadagno, J. (1994). *The color of welfare: How racism undermined the war on poverty*. New York: Oxford University Press.

Richmond, M. (1917). *Social diagnosis*. New York: Russell Sage Foundation.

Richmond, M. (1922). *What is social case work?* New York: Russell Sage Foundation.

Ringer, B. (1983). *"We the People" and others: Duality and America's treatment of its racial minorities*. New York: Tavistock Publications.

Ringer, B., & Lawless, E. (1989). *Race-Ethnicity and society*. New York: Routledge.

Rogers, W. (1947). Starvation without representation. *Look Magazine*, 3 February 1948, 3.

Rouse, J. (1989). *Lugenia Burns Hope, Black Southern reformer*. Athens, GA: University of Georgia Press.

Ross, E. (1978). *Black heritage in social welfare*. Metuchen, NJ: Scarecrow Press.

Schieber, S. (1999). *The real deal: The history and future of Social Security*. New Haven, CT: Yale University Press.

Schiele, J. (2000). *Human services and the Afrocentric paradigm*. New York: Haworth Press.

Schopler, J. H., & Galinsky, M. J. (1995). Group practice overview. In *Encyclopedia of social work* (19ᵗʰ ed.). Washington, DC: NASW Press.

Skocpol, T. (1988). The limits of the New Deal system and the roots of contemporary welfare dilemmas. In M. Weir, A. Orloff, & T. Skocpol (Eds.), *The politics of social policy in the United States*. Princeton, NJ: Princeton University Press.

Skocpol, T. (1992). *Protecting soldiers and mothers: The political origins of social policy in the United States*. Cambridge, MA: Harvard University Press.

Skocpol, T. with Ikenberry, J. (1995). The road to Social Security. In T. Skocpol (Ed.), *Social policy in the United States: Future possibilities in historical perspective*. Princeton, NJ: Princeton University Press.

Spano, R. (1982). *The rank and file movement in social work*. Washington, DC: University Press of America.

Specht, H., & Courtney, M. (1994). *Unfaithful angels: How social work has abandoned its mission*. New York: The Free Press.

Takahashi, R. (1980). *Comparative administration and management of five war re-location authority camps: America's incarceration of persons of Japanese ancestry during World War II.* PhD dissertation, University of Pittsburgh: Pittsburgh.

Takahashi, R. (1998). U.S. concentration camps and exclusion policies: Impact on Japanese American women. In G. Kirk & M. Okazawa-Rey (Eds.), *Women's lives: Multicultural perspectives, 2nd edition.* Mountain View, CA: Mayfield Publishing Company.

Takaki, R. (1998). *Strangers from a different shore.* Boston: Little Brown.

Taylor, G. (1980). *The New Deal and American Indian tribalism.* Lincoln, NE: University of Nebraska Press.

Thomas, D., & Nishimoto, R. (1946). *The spoilage: Japanese-American evacuation and resettlement during World War II.* Berkeley, CA: University of California Press.

Thomas, J. (1967). *My life in white and black.* New York: Exposition Press.

Trattner, W. (Ed.). (1983). *Social welfare or social control? Some historical reflections on regulating the poor.* Knoxville, TN: University of Tennessee Press.

Trattner, W. (Ed.). (1986). *Biographical dictionary of social welfare in America.* New York: Greenwood Press.

U.S. Commission on Wartime Relocation and Internment of Civilians. (1983). *Personal justice denied.* Washington, DC: Government Printing Office.

Washington, F. (1935, March 9). Washington raps, Jones extols New Deal in Atlanta. *Afro-American,* p. 6.

Vann, R. (1966). *The strange career of Jim Crow.* New York: Oxford University Press.

Weaver, H., & White, B. (1999). Protecting the future of indigenous children and nations: An examination of the Indian Child Welfare Act. *Journal of Health and Social Policy, 10*(4), 35–50.

Weir, M., Orloff, A. S., & Skocpol, T. (1988). *The politics of social policy in the United States.* Princeton, NJ: Princeton University Press.

Weiss, N. (1974). *The National Urban League, 1910–1940.* New York: Oxford University Press.

Weiss, N. (1989). *Whitney M. Young, Jr. and the struggle for civil rights.* Princeton, NJ: Princeton University Press.

Wilson, W. J. (1987). *The truly disadvantaged: The inner city, the underclass, and public policy.* Chicago: The University of Chicago Press.

Wilson, W. J. (1999). *The bridge over the racial divide: Rising inequality and coalition politics.* Berkeley, CA: University of California Press.

Yabura, L. (1970). The Legacy of Forrester B. Washington: Black social work educator and nation builder. In *Proceedings of the fiftieth anniversary of the Atlanta University School of Social Work.* Atlanta: Atlanta University School of Social Work.

NASW Code of Ethics

Preamble

The primary mission of the social work profession is to enhance human well-being and help meet the basic human needs of all people, with particular attention to the needs and empowerment of people who are vulnerable, oppressed, and living in poverty. A historic and defining feature of social work is the profession's focus on individual well-being in a social context and the well-being of society. Fundamental to social work is attention to the environmental forces that create, contribute to, and address problems in living.

Social workers promote social justice and social change with and on behalf of clients. "Clients" is used inclusively to refer to individuals, families, groups, organizations, and communities. Social workers are sensitive to cultural and ethnic diversity and strive to end discrimination, oppression, poverty, and other forms of social injustice. These activities may be in the form of direct practice, community organizing, supervision, consultation, administration, advocacy, social and political action, policy development and implementation, education, and research and evaluation. Social workers seek to enhance the capacity of people to address their own needs. Social workers also seek to promote the responsiveness of organizations, communities, and other social institutions to individuals' needs and social problems.

The mission of the social work profession is rooted in a set of core values. These core values, embraced by social workers throughout the profession's history, are the foundation of social work's unique purpose and perspective:

- service
- social justice
- dignity and worth of the person
- importance of human relationships
- integrity
- competence.

This constellation of core values reflects what is unique to the social work profession. Core values, and the principles that flow from them, must be balanced within the context and complexity of the human experience.

Purpose of the NASW Code of Ethics

Professional ethics are at the core of social work. The profession has an obligation to articulate its basic values, ethical principles, and ethical standards. The *NASW Code of Ethics* sets forth these values, principles, and standards to guide social workers' conduct. The *Code* is relevant to all social workers and social work students, regardless of their professional functions, the settings in which they work, or the populations they serve.

The *NASW Code of Ethics* serves six purposes:

1. The *Code* identifies core values on which social work's mission is based.
2. The *Code* summarizes broad ethical principles that reflect the profession's core values and establishes a set of specific ethical standards that should be used to guide social work practice.
3. The *Code* is designed to help social workers identify relevant considerations when professional obligations conflict or ethical uncertainties arise.
4. The *Code* provides ethical standards to which the general public can hold the social work profession accountable.
5. The *Code* socializes practitioners new to the field to social work's mission, values, ethical principles, and ethical standards.
6. The *Code* articulates standards that the social work profession itself can use to assess whether social workers have engaged in unethical conduct. NASW has formal procedures to adjudicate ethics complaints filed against its members.* In subscribing to this *Code,* social workers are required to cooperate in its implementation, participate in NASW adjudication proceedings, and abide by any NASW disciplinary rulings or sanctions based on it.

The *Code* offers a set of values, principles, and standards to guide decision making and conduct when ethical issues arise. It does not provide a set of rules that prescribe how social workers should act in all situations. Specific applications of the *Code* must take into account the context in which it is being considered and the possibility of conflicts among the *Code's* values, principles, and standards. Ethical responsibilities flow from all human relationships, from the personal and familial to the social and professional.

Further, the *NASW Code of Ethics* does not specify which values, principles, and standards are most important and ought to outweigh others in instances when they conflict. Reasonable differences of opinion can and do exist among social workers with respect to the ways in which values, ethical principles, and ethical standards should be rank ordered when they conflict. Ethical decision making in a given situation must apply the informed judgment of the individual social worker and should also consider how the issues would be judged in a peer review process where the ethical standards of the profession would be applied.

Ethical decision making is a process. There are many instances in social work where simple answers are not available to resolve complex ethical issues. Social workers should take into consideration all the values, principles, and standards in this *Code*

---

*For information on NASW adjudication procedures, see *NASW Procedures for the Adjudication of Grievances.*

that are relevant to any situation in which ethical judgment is warranted. Social workers' decisions and actions should be consistent with the spirit as well as the letter of this *Code*.

In addition to this *Code*, there are many other sources of information about ethical thinking that may be useful. Social workers should consider ethical theory and principles generally, social work theory and research, laws, regulations, agency policies, and other relevant codes of ethics, recognizing that among codes of ethics social workers should consider the *NASW Code of Ethics* as their primary source. Social workers also should be aware of the impact on ethical decision making of their clients' and their own personal values and cultural and religious beliefs and practices. They should be aware of any conflicts between personal and professional values and deal with them responsibly. For additional guidance social workers should consult the relevant literature on professional ethics and ethical decision making and seek appropriate consultation when faced with ethical dilemmas. This may involve consultation with an agency-based or social work organization's ethics committee, a regulatory body, knowledgeable colleagues, supervisors, or legal counsel.

Instances may arise when social workers' ethical obligations conflict with agency policies or relevant laws or regulations. When such conflicts occur, social workers must make a responsible effort to resolve the conflict in a manner that is consistent with the values, principles, and standards expressed in this *Code*. If a reasonable resolution of the conflict does not appear possible, social workers should seek proper consultation before making a decision.

The *NASW Code of Ethics* is to be used by NASW and by individuals, agencies, organizations, and bodies (such as licensing and regulatory boards, professional liability insurance providers, courts of law, agency boards of directors, government agencies, and other professional groups) that choose to adopt it or use it as a frame of reference. Violation of standards in this *Code* does not automatically imply legal liability or violation of the law. Such determination can only be made in the context of legal and judicial proceedings. Alleged violations of the *Code* would be subject to a peer review process. Such processes are generally separate from legal or administrative procedures and insulated from legal review or proceedings to allow the profession to counsel and discipline its own members.

A code of ethics cannot guarantee ethical behavior. Moreover, a code of ethics cannot resolve all ethical issues or disputes or capture the richness and complexity involved in striving to make responsible choices within a moral community. Rather, a code of ethics sets forth values, ethical principles, and ethical standards to which professionals aspire and by which their actions can be judged. Social workers' ethical behavior should result from their personal commitment to engage in ethical practice. The *NASW Code of Ethics* reflects the commitment of all social workers to uphold the profession's values and to act ethically. Principles and standards must be applied by individuals of good character who discern moral questions and, in good faith, seek to make reliable ethical judgments.

Ethical Principles

The following broad ethical principles are based on social work's core values of service, social justice, dignity and worth of the person, importance of human relationships, integrity, and competence. These principles set forth ideals to which all social workers should aspire.

Value: *Service*

Ethical Principle: *Social workers' primary goal is to help people in need and to address social problems.*

Social workers elevate service to others above self-interest. Social workers draw on their knowledge, values, and skills to help people in need and to address social problems. Social workers are encouraged to volunteer some portion of their professional skills with no expectation of significant financial return (pro bono service).

Value: *Social Justice*

Ethical Principle: *Social workers challenge social injustice.*

Social workers pursue social change, particularly with and on behalf of vulnerable and oppressed individuals and groups of people. Social workers' social change efforts are focused primarily on issues of poverty, unemployment, discrimination, and other forms of social injustice. These activities seek to promote sensitivity to and knowledge about oppression and cultural and ethnic diversity. Social workers strive to ensure access to needed information, services, and resources; equality of opportunity; and meaningful participation in decision making for all people.

Value: *Dignity and Worth of the Person*

Ethical Principle: *Social workers respect the inherent dignity and worth of the person.*

Social workers treat each person in a caring and respectful fashion, mindful of individual differences and cultural and ethnic diversity. Social workers promote clients' socially responsible self-determination. Social workers seek to enhance clients' capacity and opportunity to change and to address their own needs. Social workers are cognizant of their dual responsibility to clients and to the broader society. They seek to resolve conflicts between clients' interests and the broader society's interests in a socially responsible manner consistent with the values, ethical principles, and ethical standards of the profession.

Value: *Importance of Human Relationships*

Ethical Principle: *Social workers recognize the central importance of human relationships.*

Social workers understand that relationships between and among people are an important vehicle for change. Social workers engage people as partners in the helping process. Social workers seek to strengthen relationships among people in a purposeful effort to promote, restore, maintain, and enhance the well-being of individuals, families, social groups, organizations, and communities.

Value: *Integrity*

Ethical Principle: *Social workers behave in a trustworthy manner.*

Social workers are continually aware of the profession's mission, values, ethical principles, and ethical standards and practice in a manner consistent with them. Social workers act honestly and responsibly and promote ethical practices on the part of the organizations with which they are affiliated.

Value: *Competence*

Ethical Principle: *Social workers practice within their areas of competence and develop and enhance their professional expertise.*

Social workers continually strive to increase their professional knowledge and skills and to apply them in practice. Social workers should aspire to contribute to the knowledge base of the profession.

Ethical Standards

The following ethical standards are relevant to the professional activities of all social workers. These standards concern (1) social workers' ethical responsibilities to clients, (2) social workers' ethical responsibilities to colleagues, (3) social workers' ethical responsibilities in practice settings, (4) social workers' ethical responsibilities as professionals, (5) social workers' ethical responsibilities to the social work profession, and (6) social workers' ethical responsibilities to the broader society.

Some of the standards that follow are enforceable guidelines for professional conduct, and some are aspirational. The extent to which each standard is enforceable is a matter of professional judgment to be exercised by those responsible for reviewing alleged violations of ethical standards.

1.   Social Workers' Ethical Responsibilities to Clients
1.01 Commitment to Clients
Social workers' primary responsibility is to promote the well-being of clients. In general, clients' interests are primary. However, social workers' responsibility to the larger society or specific legal obligations may on limited occasions supersede the loyalty owed clients, and clients should be so advised. (Examples include when a social worker is required by law to report that a client has abused a child or has threatened to harm self or others.)

1.02 Self-Determination
Social workers respect and promote the right of clients to self-determination and assist clients in their efforts to identify and clarify their goals. Social workers may limit clients' right to self-determination when, in the social workers' professional judgment, clients' actions or potential actions pose a serious, foreseeable, and imminent risk to themselves or others.

1.03 Informed Consent
(a)   Social workers should provide services to clients only in the context of a professional relationship based, when appropriate, on valid informed consent. Social workers should use clear and understandable language to inform clients of the purpose of the services, risks related to the services, limits to services because of the requirements of a third-party payer, relevant costs, reasonable alternatives, clients' right to refuse or withdraw consent, and the time frame covered by the consent. Social workers should provide clients with an opportunity to ask questions.

(b)   In instances when clients are not literate or have difficulty understanding the primary language used in the practice setting, social workers should take steps to ensure clients' comprehension. This may include providing clients with a detailed verbal explanation or arranging for a qualified interpreter or translator whenever possible.

(c)   In instances when clients lack the capacity to provide informed consent, social workers should protect clients' interests by seeking permission from an appropriate third party, informing clients consistent with the clients' level of understanding. In such instances social workers should seek to ensure that the third party acts in a manner consistent with clients' wishes and interests. Social workers should take reasonable steps to enhance such clients' ability to give informed consent.

(d)   In instances when clients are receiving services involuntarily, social workers should provide information about the nature and extent of services and about the extent of clients' right to refuse service.

(e)   Social workers who provide services via electronic media (such as computer, telephone, radio, and television) should inform recipients of the limitations and risks associated with such services.

(f)   Social workers should obtain clients' informed consent before audiotaping or videotaping clients or permitting observation of services to clients by a third party.

1.04 Competence

(a)   Social workers should provide services and represent themselves as competent only within the boundaries of their education, training, license, certification, consultation received, supervised experience, or other relevant professional experience.

(b)   Social workers should provide services in substantive areas or use intervention techniques or approaches that are new to them only after engaging in appropriate study, training, consultation, and supervision from people who are competent in those interventions or techniques.

(c)   When generally recognized standards do not exist with respect to an emerging area of practice, social workers should exercise careful judgment and take responsible steps (including appropriate education, research, training, consultation, and supervision) to ensure the competence of their work and to protect clients from harm.

1.05 Cultural Competence and Social Diversity

(a)   Social workers should understand culture and its function in human behavior and society, recognizing the strengths that exist in all cultures.

(b)   Social workers should have a knowledge base of their clients' cultures and be able to demonstrate competence in the provision of services that are sensitive to clients' cultures and to differences among people and cultural groups.

(c)   Social workers should obtain education about and seek to understand the nature of social diversity and oppression with respect to race, ethnicity, national origin, color, sex, sexual orientation, age, marital status, political belief, religion, and mental or physical disability.

1.06 Conflicts of Interest

(a)   Social workers should be alert to and avoid conflicts of interest that interfere with the exercise of professional discretion and impartial judgment. Social workers should inform clients when a real or potential conflict of interest arises and take reasonable steps to resolve the issue in a manner that makes the clients' interests primary and protects clients' interests to the greatest extent possible. In some cases, protecting clients' interests may require termination of the professional relationship with proper referral of the client.

(b)   Social workers should not take unfair advantage of any professional relationship or exploit others to further their personal, religious, political, or business interests.

(c)   Social workers should not engage in dual or multiple relationships with clients or former clients in which there is a risk of exploitation or potential harm to the client. In instances when dual or multiple relationships are unavoidable, social workers should take steps to protect clients and are responsible for setting clear, appropriate, and culturally sensitive boundaries. (Dual or multiple relationships occur when social workers relate to clients in more than one relationship, whether professional, social, or business. Dual or multiple relationships can occur simultaneously or consecutively.)

(d)   When social workers provide services to two or more people who have a relationship with each other (for example, couples, family members), social workers should clarify with all parties which individuals will be considered clients and the nature of social workers' professional obligations to the various individuals who are receiving services. Social workers who anticipate a conflict of interest among the individuals receiving services or who anticipate having to perform in potentially conflicting roles (for example, when a social worker is asked to testify in a child custody dispute or divorce proceedings involving clients) should clarify their role with the parties involved and take appropriate action to minimize any conflict of interest.

1.07 Privacy and Confidentiality

(a)   Social workers should respect clients' right to privacy. Social workers should not solicit private information from clients unless it is essential to providing services or conducting social work evaluation or research. Once private information is shared, standards of confidentiality apply.

(b)   Social workers may disclose confidential information when appropriate with valid consent from a client or a person legally authorized to consent on behalf of a client.

(c)   Social workers should protect the confidentiality of all information obtained in the course of professional service, except for compelling professional reasons. The general expectation that social workers will keep information confidential does not apply when disclosure is necessary to prevent serious, foreseeable, and imminent harm to a client or other identifiable person. In all instances, social workers should disclose the least amount of confidential information necessary to achieve the desired purpose; only information that is directly relevant to the purpose for which the disclosure is made should be revealed.

(d)   Social workers should inform clients, to the extent possible, about the disclosure of confidential information and the potential consequences, when feasible before the disclosure is made. This applies whether social workers disclose confidential information on the basis of a legal requirement or client consent.

(e)   Social workers should discuss with clients and other interested parties the nature of confidentiality and limitations of clients' right to confidentiality. Social workers should review with clients circumstances where confidential information may be requested and where disclosure of confidential information may be legally required. This discussion should occur as soon as possible in the social worker-client relationship and as needed throughout the course of the relationship.

(f)   When social workers provide counseling services to families, couples, or groups, social workers should seek agreement among the parties involved concerning each individual's right to confidentiality and obligation to preserve the confidentiality of information shared by others. Social workers should inform participants in family, couples, or group counseling that social workers cannot guarantee that all participants will honor such agreements.

(g)   Social workers should inform clients involved in family, couples, marital, or group counseling of the social worker's, employer's, and agency's policy concerning the social worker's disclosure of confidential information among the parties involved in the counseling.

(h)   Social workers should not disclose confidential information to third-party payers unless clients have authorized such disclosure.

(i)   Social workers should not discuss confidential information in any setting unless privacy can be ensured. Social workers should not discuss confidential information in public or semipublic areas such as hallways, waiting rooms, elevators, and restaurants.

(j)   Social workers should protect the confidentiality of clients during legal proceedings to the extent permitted by law. When a court of law or other legally authorized body orders social workers to disclose confidential or privileged information without a client's consent and such disclosure could cause harm to the client, social workers should request that the court withdraw the order or limit the order as narrowly as possible or maintain the records under seal, unavailable for public inspection.

(k)   Social workers should protect the confidentiality of clients when responding to requests from members of the media.

(l)   Social workers should protect the confidentiality of clients' written and electronic records and other sensitive information. Social workers should take reasonable steps to ensure that clients' records are stored in a secure location and that clients' records are not available to others who are not authorized to have access.

(m)   Social workers should take precautions to ensure and maintain the confidentiality of information transmitted to other parties through the use of computers, electronic mail, facsimile machines, telephones and telephone answering machines, and other electronic or computer technology. Disclosure of identifying information should be avoided whenever possible.

(n)   Social workers should transfer or dispose of clients' records in a manner that protects clients' confidentiality and is consistent with state statutes governing records and social work licensure.

(o)   Social workers should take reasonable precautions to protect client confidentiality in the event of the social worker's termination of practice, incapacitation, or death.

(p)   Social workers should not disclose identifying information when discussing clients for teaching or training purposes unless the client has consented to disclosure of confidential information.

(q)   Social workers should not disclose identifying information when discussing clients with consultants unless the client has consented to disclosure of confidential information or there is a compelling need for such disclosure.

(r)   Social workers should protect the confidentiality of deceased clients consistent with the preceding standards.

1.08 Access to Records

(a)   Social workers should provide clients with reasonable access to records concerning the clients. Social workers who are concerned that clients' access to their records could cause serious misunderstanding or harm to the client should provide assistance in interpreting the records and consultation with the client regarding the records. Social workers should limit clients' access to their records, or portions of their records, only in exceptional circumstances when there is compelling evidence that such access would cause serious harm to the client. Both clients' requests and the rationale for withholding some or all of the record should be documented in clients' files.

(b)   When providing clients with access to their records, social workers should take steps to protect the confidentiality of other individuals identified or discussed in such records.

1.09 Sexual Relationships

(a)   Social workers should under no circumstances engage in sexual activities or sexual contact with current clients, whether such contact is consensual or forced.

(b)   Social workers should not engage in sexual activities or sexual contact with clients' relatives or other individuals with whom clients maintain a close personal relationship when there is a risk of exploitation or potential harm to the client. Sexual activity or sexual contact with clients' relatives or other individuals with whom clients maintain a personal relationship has the potential to be harmful to the client and may make it difficult for the social worker and client to maintain appropriate professional boundaries. Social workers—not their clients, their clients' relatives, or other individuals with whom the client maintains a personal relationship—assume the full burden for setting clear, appropriate, and culturally sensitive boundaries.

(c)   Social workers should not engage in sexual activities or sexual contact with former clients because of the potential for harm to the client. If social workers engage in conduct contrary to this prohibition or claim that an exception to this prohibition is warranted because of extraordinary circumstances, it is social workers—not their clients—who assume the full burden of demonstrating that the former client has not been exploited, coerced, or manipulated, intentionally or unintentionally.

(d)   Social workers should not provide clinical services to individuals with whom they have had a prior sexual relationship. Providing clinical services to a former sexual partner has the potential to be harmful to the individual and is likely to make it difficult for the social worker and individual to maintain appropriate professional boundaries.

1.10 Physical Contact

Social workers should not engage in physical contact with clients when there is a possibility of psychological harm to the client as a result of the contact (such as cradling or caressing clients). Social workers who engage in appropriate physical contact with clients are responsible for setting clear, appropriate, and culturally sensitive boundaries that govern such physical contact.

1.11 Sexual Harassment

Social workers should not sexually harass clients. Sexual harassment includes sexual advances, sexual solicitation, requests for sexual favors, and other verbal or physical conduct of a sexual nature.

1.12 Derogatory Language

Social workers should not use derogatory language in their written or verbal communications to or about clients. Social workers should use accurate and respectful language in all communications to and about clients.

1.13 Payment for Services

(a)   When setting fees, social workers should ensure that the fees are fair, reasonable, and commensurate with the services performed. Consideration should be given to clients' ability to pay.

(b)   Social workers should avoid accepting goods or services from clients as payment for professional services. Bartering arrangements, particularly involving services, create the potential for conflicts of interest, exploitation, and inappropriate boundaries in social workers' relationships with clients. Social workers should explore and may participate in bartering only in very limited circumstances when it can be demonstrated that such arrangements are an accepted practice among professionals in the local community, considered to be essential for the provision of services, negotiated without coercion, and entered into at the client's initiative and with the client's informed consent. Social workers who accept goods or services from clients as payment for professional services assume the full burden of demonstrating that this arrangement will not be detrimental to the client or the professional relationship.

(c)   Social workers should not solicit a private fee or other remuneration for providing services to clients who are entitled to such available services through the social workers' employer or agency.

1.14 Clients Who Lack Decision-Making Capacity
When social workers act on behalf of clients who lack the capacity to make informed decisions, social workers should take reasonable steps to safeguard the interests and rights of those clients.

1.15 Interruption of Services
Social workers should make reasonable efforts to ensure continuity of services in the event that services are interrupted by factors such as unavailability, relocation, illness, disability, or death.

1.16 Termination of Services

(a)   Social workers should terminate services to clients and professional relationships with them when such services and relationships are no longer required or no longer serve the clients' needs or interests.

(b)   Social workers should take reasonable steps to avoid abandoning clients who are still in need of services. Social workers should withdraw services precipitously only under unusual circumstances, giving careful consideration to all factors in the situation and taking care to minimize possible adverse effects. Social workers should assist in making appropriate arrangements for continuation of services when necessary.

(c)   Social workers in fee-for-service settings may terminate services to clients who are not paying an overdue balance if the financial contractual arrangements have been made clear to the client, if the client does not pose an imminent danger to self or others, and if the clinical and other consequences of the current nonpayment have been addressed and discussed with the client.

(d)   Social workers should not terminate services to pursue a social, financial, or sexual relationship with a client.

(e)   Social workers who anticipate the termination or interruption of services to clients should notify clients promptly and seek the transfer, referral, or continuation of services in relation to the clients' needs and preferences.

(f)   Social workers who are leaving an employment setting should inform clients of appropriate options for the continuation of services and of the benefits and risks of the options.

2.   Social Workers' Ethical Responsibilities to Colleagues
2.01 Respect
(a)   Social workers should treat colleagues with respect and should represent accurately and fairly the qualifications, views, and obligations of colleagues.
(b)   Social workers should avoid unwarranted negative criticism of colleagues in communications with clients or with other professionals. Unwarranted negative criticism may include demeaning comments that refer to colleagues' level of competence or to individuals' attributes such as race, ethnicity, national origin, color, sex, sexual orientation, age, marital status, political belief, religion, and mental or physical disability.
(c)   Social workers should cooperate with social work colleagues and with colleagues of other professions when such cooperation serves the well-being of clients.

2.02 Confidentiality
Social workers should respect confidential information shared by colleagues in the course of their professional relationships and transactions. Social workers should ensure that such colleagues understand social workers' obligation to respect confidentiality and any exceptions related to it.

2.03 Interdisciplinary Collaboration
(a)   Social workers who are members of an interdisciplinary team should participate in and contribute to decisions that affect the well-being of clients by drawing on the perspectives, values, and experiences of the social work profession. Professional and ethical obligations of the interdisciplinary team as a whole and of its individual members should be clearly established.
(b)   Social workers for whom a team decision raises ethical concerns should attempt to resolve the disagreement through appropriate channels. If the disagreement cannot be resolved, social workers should pursue other avenues to address their concerns consistent with client well-being.

2.04 Disputes Involving Colleagues
(a)   Social workers should not take advantage of a dispute between a colleague and an employer to obtain a position or otherwise advance the social workers' own interests.
(b)   Social workers should not exploit clients in disputes with colleagues or engage clients in any inappropriate discussion of conflicts between social workers and their colleagues.

2.05 Consultation
(a)   Social workers should seek the advice and counsel of colleagues whenever such consultation is in the best interests of clients.
(b)   Social workers should keep themselves informed about colleagues' areas of expertise and competencies. Social workers should seek consultation only from colleagues who have demonstrated knowledge, expertise, and competence related to the subject of the consultation.

(c)   When consulting with colleagues about clients, social workers should disclose
      the least amount of information necessary to achieve the purposes of the con-
      sultation.

2.06 Referral for Services
(a)   Social workers should refer clients to other professionals when the other pro-
      fessionals' specialized knowledge or expertise is needed to serve clients fully or
      when social workers believe that they are not being effective or making reason-
      able progress with clients and that additional service is required.
(b)   Social workers who refer clients to other professionals should take appropriate
      steps to facilitate an orderly transfer of responsibility. Social workers who refer
      clients to other professionals should disclose, with clients' consent, all pertinent
      information to the new service providers.
(c)   Social workers are prohibited from giving or receiving payment for a referral
      when no professional service is provided by the referring social worker.

2.07 Sexual Relationships
(a)   Social workers who function as supervisors or educators should not engage in
      sexual activities or contact with supervisees, students, trainees, or other colleagues
      over whom they exercise professional authority.
(b)   Social workers should avoid engaging in sexual relationships with colleagues
      when there is potential for a conflict of interest. Social workers who become
      involved in, or anticipate becoming involved in, a sexual relationship with a
      colleague have a duty to transfer professional responsibilities, when necessary,
      to avoid a conflict of interest.

2.08 Sexual Harassment
Social workers should not sexually harass supervisees, students, trainees, or colleagues.
Sexual harassment includes sexual advances, sexual solicitation, requests for sexual
favors, and other verbal or physical conduct of a sexual nature.

2.09 Impairment of Colleagues
(a)   Social workers who have direct knowledge of a social work colleague's impair-
      ment that is due to personal problems, psychosocial distress, substance abuse,
      or mental health difficulties and that interferes with practice effectiveness should
      consult with that colleague when feasible and assist the colleague in taking re-
      medial action.
(b)   Social workers who believe that a social work colleague's impairment interferes
      with practice effectiveness and that the colleague has not taken adequate steps to
      address the impairment should take action through appropriate channels estab-
      lished by employers, agencies, NASW, licensing and regulatory bodies, and other
      professional organizations.

2.10 Incompetence of Colleagues
(a)   Social workers who have direct knowledge of a social work colleague's incom-
      petence should consult with that colleague when feasible and assist the col-
      league in taking remedial action.
(b)   Social workers who believe that a social work colleague is incompetent and has
      not taken adequate steps to address the incompetence should take action through

appropriate channels established by employers, agencies, NASW, licensing and regulatory bodies, and other professional organizations.

2.11 Unethical Conduct of Colleagues
(a)   Social workers should take adequate measures to discourage, prevent, expose, and correct the unethical conduct of colleagues.
(b)   Social workers should be knowledgeable about established policies and procedures for handling concerns about colleagues' unethical behavior. Social workers should be familiar with national, state, and local procedures for handling ethics complaints. These include policies and procedures created by NASW, licensing and regulatory bodies, employers, agencies, and other professional organizations.
(c)   Social workers who believe that a colleague has acted unethically should seek resolution by discussing their concerns with the colleague when feasible and when such discussion is likely to be productive.
(d)   When necessary, social workers who believe that a colleague has acted unethically should take action through appropriate formal channels (such as contacting a state licensing board or regulatory body, an NASW committee on inquiry, or other professional ethics committees).
(e)   Social workers should defend and assist colleagues who are unjustly charged with unethical conduct.

3.   Social Workers' Ethical Responsibilities in Practice Settings
3.01 Supervision and Consultation
(a)   Social workers who provide supervision or consultation should have the necessary knowledge and skill to supervise or consult appropriately and should do so only within their areas of knowledge and competence.
(b)   Social workers who provide supervision or consultation are responsible for setting clear, appropriate, and culturally sensitive boundaries.
(c)   Social workers should not engage in any dual or multiple relationships with supervisees in which there is a risk of exploitation of or potential harm to the supervisee.
(d)   Social workers who provide supervision should evaluate supervisees' performance in a manner that is fair and respectful.

3.02 Education and Training
(a)   Social workers who function as educators, field instructors for students, or trainers should provide instruction only within their areas of knowledge and competence and should provide instruction based on the most current information and knowledge available in the profession.
(b)   Social workers who function as educators or field instructors for students should evaluate students' performance in a manner that is fair and respectful.
(c)   Social workers who function as educators or field instructors for students should take reasonable steps to ensure that clients are routinely informed when services are being provided by students.
(d)   Social workers who function as educators or field instructors for students should not engage in any dual or multiple relationships with students in which there is a risk of exploitation or potential harm to the student. Social work educators and field instructors are responsible for setting clear, appropriate, and culturally sensitive boundaries.

3.03 Performance Evaluation

Social workers who have responsibility for evaluating the performance of others should fulfill such responsibility in a fair and considerate manner and on the basis of clearly stated criteria.

3.04 Client Records

(a)   Social workers should take reasonable steps to ensure that documentation in records is accurate and reflects the services provided.

(b)   Social workers should include sufficient and timely documentation in records to facilitate the delivery of services and to ensure continuity of services provided to clients in the future.

(c)   Social workers' documentation should protect clients' privacy to the extent that is possible and appropriate and should include only information that is directly relevant to the delivery of services.

(d)   Social workers should store records following the termination of services to ensure reasonable future access. Records should be maintained for the number of years required by state statutes or relevant contracts.

3.05 Billing

Social workers should establish and maintain billing practices that accurately reflect the nature and extent of services provided and that identify who provided the service in the practice setting.

3.06 Client Transfer

(a)   When an individual who is receiving services from another agency or colleague contacts a social worker for services, the social worker should carefully consider the client's needs before agreeing to provide services. To minimize possible confusion and conflict, social workers should discuss with potential clients the nature of the clients' current relationship with other service providers and the implications, including possible benefits or risks, of entering into a relationship with a new service provider.

(b)   If a new client has been served by another agency or colleague, social workers should discuss with the client whether consultation with the previous service provider is in the client's best interest.

3.07 Administration

(a)   Social work administrators should advocate within and outside their agencies for adequate resources to meet clients' needs.

(b)   Social workers should advocate for resource allocation procedures that are open and fair. When not all clients' needs can be met, an allocation procedure should be developed that is nondiscriminatory and based on appropriate and consistently applied principles.

(c)   Social workers who are administrators should take reasonable steps to ensure that adequate agency or organizational resources are available to provide appropriate staff supervision.

(d)   Social work administrators should take reasonable steps to ensure that the working environment for which they are responsible is consistent with and encourages compliance with the NASW Code of Ethics. Social work administrators should take reasonable steps to eliminate any conditions in their organizations that violate, interfere with, or discourage compliance with the Code.

3.08 Continuing Education and Staff Development

Social work administrators and supervisors should take reasonable steps to provide or arrange for continuing education and staff development for all staff for whom they are responsible. Continuing education and staff development should address current knowledge and emerging developments related to social work practice and ethics.

3.09 Commitments to Employers

(a) Social workers generally should adhere to commitments made to employers and employing organizations.

(b) Social workers should work to improve employing agencies' policies and procedures and the efficiency and effectiveness of their services.

(c) Social workers should take reasonable steps to ensure that employers are aware of social workers' ethical obligations as set forth in the NASW Code of Ethics and of the implications of those obligations for social work practice.

(d) Social workers should not allow an employing organization's policies, procedures, regulations, or administrative orders to interfere with their ethical practice of social work. Social workers should take reasonable steps to ensure that their employing organizations' practices are consistent with the NASW Code of Ethics.

(e) Social workers should act to prevent and eliminate discrimination in the employing organization's work assignments and in its employment policies and practices.

(f) Social workers should accept employment or arrange student field placements only in organizations that exercise fair personnel practices.

(g) Social workers should be diligent stewards of the resources of their employing organizations, wisely conserving funds where appropriate and never misappropriating funds or using them for unintended purposes.

3.10 Labor-Management Disputes

(a) Social workers may engage in organized action, including the formation of and participation in labor unions, to improve services to clients and working conditions.

(b) The actions of social workers who are involved in labor-management disputes, job actions, or labor strikes should be guided by the profession's values, ethical principles, and ethical standards. Reasonable differences of opinion exist among social workers concerning their primary obligation as professionals during an actual or threatened labor strike or job action. Social workers should carefully examine relevant issues and their possible impact on clients before deciding on a course of action.

4.   Social Workers' Ethical Responsibilities as Professionals

4.01 Competence

(a) Social workers should accept responsibility or employment only on the basis of existing competence or the intention to acquire the necessary competence.

(b) Social workers should strive to become and remain proficient in professional practice and the performance of professional functions. Social workers should critically examine and keep current with emerging knowledge relevant to social work. Social workers should routinely review the professional literature and participate in continuing education relevant to social work practice and social work ethics.

(c)   Social workers should base practice on recognized knowledge, including em-
      pirically based knowledge, relevant to social work and social work ethics.

4.02 Discrimination
Social workers should not practice, condone, facilitate, or collaborate with any form of
discrimination on the basis of race, ethnicity, national origin, color, sex, sexual orientation, age, marital status, political belief, religion, or mental or physical disability.

4.03 Private Conduct
Social workers should not permit their private conduct to interfere with their ability
to fulfill their professional responsibilities.

4.04 Dishonesty, Fraud, and Deception
Social workers should not participate in, condone, or be associated with dishonesty,
fraud, or deception.

4.05 Impairment
(a)   Social workers should not allow their own personal problems, psychosocial dis-
      tress, legal problems, substance abuse, or mental health difficulties to interfere
      with their professional judgment and performance or to jeopardize the best in-
      terests of people for whom they have a professional responsibility.
(b)   Social workers whose personal problems, psychosocial distress, legal prob-
      lems, substance abuse, or mental health difficulties interfere with their pro-
      fessional judgment and performance should immediately seek consultation
      and take appropriate remedial action by seeking professional help, making
      adjustments in workload, terminating practice, or taking any other steps nec-
      essary to protect clients and others.

4.06 Misrepresentation
(a)   Social workers should make clear distinctions between statements made and
      actions engaged in as a private individual and as a representative of the social
      work profession, a professional social work organization, or the social worker's
      employing agency.
(b)   Social workers who speak on behalf of professional social work organizations should
      accurately represent the official and authorized positions of the organizations.
(c)   Social workers should ensure that their representations to clients, agencies,
      and the public of professional qualifications, credentials, education, compe-
      tence, affiliations, services provided, or results to be achieved are accurate.
      Social workers should claim only those relevant professional credentials they
      actually possess and take steps to correct any inaccuracies or misrepresenta-
      tions of their credentials by others.

4.07 Solicitations
(a)   Social workers should not engage in uninvited solicitation of potential clients
      who, because of their circumstances, are vulnerable to undue influence, ma-
      nipulation, or coercion.
(b)   Social workers should not engage in solicitation of testimonial endorsements
      (including solicitation of consent to use a client's prior statement as a testimo-
      nial endorsement) from current clients or from other people who, because of
      their particular circumstances, are vulnerable to undue influence.

4.08 Acknowledging Credit

(a) Social workers should take responsibility and credit, including authorship credit, only for work they have actually performed and to which they have contributed.

(b) Social workers should honestly acknowledge the work of and the contributions made by others.

5. Social Workers' Ethical Responsibilities to the Social Work Profession

5.01 Integrity of the Profession

(a) Social workers should work toward the maintenance and promotion of high standards of practice.

(b) Social workers should uphold and advance the values, ethics, knowledge, and mission of the profession. Social workers should protect, enhance, and improve the integrity of the profession through appropriate study and research, active discussion, and responsible criticism of the profession.

(c) Social workers should contribute time and professional expertise to activities that promote respect for the value, integrity, and competence of the social work profession. These activities may include teaching, research, consultation, service, legislative testimony, presentations in the community, and participation in their professional organizations.

(d) Social workers should contribute to the knowledge base of social work and share with colleagues their knowledge related to practice, research, and ethics. Social workers should seek to contribute to the profession's literature and to share their knowledge at professional meetings and conferences.

(e) Social workers should act to prevent the unauthorized and unqualified practice of social work.

5.02 Evaluation and Research

(a) Social workers should monitor and evaluate policies, the implementation of programs, and practice interventions.

(b) Social workers should promote and facilitate evaluation and research to contribute to the development of knowledge.

(c) Social workers should critically examine and keep current with emerging knowledge relevant to social work and fully use evaluation and research evidence in their professional practice.

(d) Social workers engaged in evaluation or research should carefully consider possible consequences and should follow guidelines developed for the protection of evaluation and research participants. Appropriate institutional review boards should be consulted.

(e) Social workers engaged in evaluation or research should obtain voluntary and written informed consent from participants, when appropriate, without any implied or actual deprivation or penalty for refusal to participate; without undue inducement to participate; and with due regard for participants' well-being, privacy, and dignity. Informed consent should include information about the nature, extent, and duration of the participation requested and disclosure of the risks and benefits of participation in the research.

(f) When evaluation or research participants are incapable of giving informed consent, social workers should provide an appropriate explanation to the participants, obtain the participants' assent to the extent they are able, and obtain written consent from an appropriate proxy.

(g)   Social workers should never design or conduct evaluation or research that does not use consent procedures, such as certain forms of naturalistic observation and archival research, unless rigorous and responsible review of the research has found it to be justified because of its prospective scientific, educational, or applied value and unless equally effective alternative procedures that do not involve waiver of consent are not feasible.

(h)   Social workers should inform participants of their right to withdraw from evaluation and research at any time without penalty.

(i)   Social workers should take appropriate steps to ensure that participants in evaluation and research have access to appropriate supportive services.

(j)   Social workers engaged in evaluation or research should protect participants from unwarranted physical or mental distress, harm, danger, or deprivation.

(k)   Social workers engaged in the evaluation of services should discuss collected information only for professional purposes and only with people professionally concerned with this information.

(l)   Social workers engaged in evaluation or research should ensure the anonymity or confidentiality of participants and of the data obtained from them. Social workers should inform participants of any limits of confidentiality, the measures that will be taken to ensure confidentiality, and when any records containing research data will be destroyed.

(m)   Social workers who report evaluation and research results should protect participants' confidentiality by omitting identifying information unless proper consent has been obtained authorizing disclosure.

(n)   Social workers should report evaluation and research findings accurately. They should not fabricate or falsify results and should take steps to correct any errors later found in published data using standard publication methods.

(o)   Social workers engaged in evaluation or research should be alert to and avoid conflicts of interest and dual relationships with participants, should inform participants when a real or potential conflict of interest arises, and should take steps to resolve the issue in a manner that makes participants' interests primary.

(p)   Social workers should educate themselves, their students, and their colleagues about responsible research practices.

6.   Social Workers' Ethical Responsibilities to the Broader Society
6.01 Social Welfare
Social workers should promote the general welfare of society, from local to global levels, and the development of people, their communities, and their environments. Social workers should advocate for living conditions conducive to the fulfillment of basic human needs and should promote social, economic, political, and cultural values and institutions that are compatible with the realization of social justice.

6.02 Public Participation
Social workers should facilitate informed participation by the public in shaping social policies and institutions.

6.03 Public Emergencies
Social workers should provide appropriate professional services in public emergencies to the greatest extent possible.

6.04 Social and Political Action

(a)   Social workers should engage in social and political action that seeks to ensure that all people have equal access to the resources, employment, services, and opportunities they require to meet their basic human needs and to develop fully. Social workers should be aware of the impact of the political arena on practice and should advocate for changes in policy and legislation to improve social conditions in order to meet basic human needs and promote social justice.

(b)   Social workers should act to expand choice and opportunity for all people, with special regard for vulnerable, disadvantaged, oppressed, and exploited people and groups.

(c)   Social workers should promote conditions that encourage respect for cultural and social diversity within the United States and globally. Social workers should promote policies and practices that demonstrate respect for difference, support the expansion of cultural knowledge and resources, advocate for programs and institutions that demonstrate cultural competence, and promote policies that safeguard the rights of and confirm equity and social justice for all people.

(d)   Social workers should act to prevent and eliminate domination of, exploitation of, and discrimination against any person, group, or class on the basis of race, ethnicity, national origin, color, sex, sexual orientation, age, marital status, political belief, religion, or mental or physical disability.

Universal Declaration of Human Rights

On December 10, 1948 the General Assembly of the United Nations adopted and proclaimed the Universal Declaration of Human Rights the full text of which appears in the following pages. Following this historic act, the Assembly called upon all Member countries to publicize the text of the Declaration and "to cause it to be disseminated, displayed, read and expounded principally in schools and other educational institutions, without distinction based on the political status of countries or territories."

Preamble

Whereas recognition of the inherent dignity and of the equal and inalienable rights of all members of the human family is the foundation of freedom, justice and peace in the world,

Whereas disregard and contempt for human rights have resulted in barbarous acts which have outraged the conscience of mankind, and the advent of a world in which human beings shall enjoy freedom of speech and belief and freedom from fear and want has been proclaimed as the highest aspiration of the common people,

Whereas it is essential, if man is not to be compelled to have recourse, as a last resort, to rebellion against tyranny and oppression, that human rights should be protected by the rule of law,

Whereas it is essential to promote the development of friendly relations between nations,

Whereas the peoples of the United Nations have in the Charter reaffirmed their faith in fundamental human rights, in the dignity and worth of the human person and in the equal rights of men and women and have determined to promote social progress and better standards of life in larger freedom,

Whereas Member States have pledged themselves to achieve, in co-operation with the United Nations, the promotion of universal respect for and observance of human rights and fundamental freedoms,

Whereas a common understanding of these rights and freedoms is of the greatest importance for the full realization of this pledge,

Now, Therefore THE GENERAL ASSEMBLY proclaims THIS UNIVERSAL DECLA-RATION OF HUMAN RIGHTS as a common standard of achievement for all peoples and all nations, to the end that every individual and every organ of society, keeping this Declaration constantly in mind, shall strive by teaching and education to promote respect for these rights and freedoms and by progressive measures, national and international, to secure their universal and effective recognition and observance, both among the peoples of Member States themselves and among the peoples of territories under their jurisdiction.

Article 1.
All human beings are born free and equal in dignity and rights. They are endowed with reason and conscience and should act towards one another in a spirit of brotherhood.

Article 2.
Everyone is entitled to all the rights and freedoms set forth in this Declaration, without distinction of any kind, such as race, colour, sex, language, religion, political or other opinion, national or social origin, property, birth or other status. Furthermore, no distinction shall be made on the basis of the political, jurisdictional or international status of the country or territory to which a person belongs, whether it be independent, trust, non-self-governing or under any other limitation of sovereignty.

Article 3.
Everyone has the right to life, liberty and security of person.

Article 4.
No one shall be held in slavery or servitude; slavery and the slave trade shall be prohibited in all their forms.

Article 5.
No one shall be subjected to torture or to cruel, inhuman or degrading treatment or punishment.

Article 6.
Everyone has the right to recognition everywhere as a person before the law.

Article 7.
All are equal before the law and are entitled without any discrimination to equal protection of the law. All are entitled to equal protection against any discrimination in violation of this Declaration and against any incitement to such discrimination.

Article 8.
Everyone has the right to an effective remedy by the competent national tribunals for acts violating the fundamental rights granted him by the constitution or by law.

Article 9.
No one shall be subjected to arbitrary arrest, detention or exile.

Article 10.
Everyone is entitled in full equality to a fair and public hearing by an independent and

impartial tribunal, in the determination of his rights and obligations and of any criminal charge against him.

Article 11.

(1)   Everyone charged with a penal offence has the right to be presumed innocent until proved guilty according to law in a public trial at which he has had all the guarantees necessary for his defence.

(2)   No one shall be held guilty of any penal offence on account of any act or omission which did not constitute a penal offence, under national or international law, at the time when it was committed. Nor shall a heavier penalty be imposed than the one that was applicable at the time the penal offence was committed.

Article 12.

No one shall be subjected to arbitrary interference with his privacy, family, home or correspondence, nor to attacks upon his honour and reputation. Everyone has the right to the protection of the law against such interference or attacks.

Article 13.

(1)   Everyone has the right to freedom of movement and residence within the borders of each state.

(2)   Everyone has the right to leave any country, including his own, and to return to his country.

Article 14.

(1)   Everyone has the right to seek and to enjoy in other countries asylum from persecution.

(2)   This right may not be invoked in the case of prosecutions genuinely arising from non-political crimes or from acts contrary to the purposes and principles of the United Nations.

Article 15.

(1)   Everyone has the right to a nationality.

(2)   No one shall be arbitrarily deprived of his nationality nor denied the right to change his nationality.

Article 16.

(1)   Men and women of full age, without any limitation due to race, nationality or religion, have the right to marry and to found a family. They are entitled to equal rights as to marriage, during marriage and at its dissolution.

(2)   Marriage shall be entered into only with the free and full consent of the intending spouses.

(3)   The family is the natural and fundamental group unit of society and is entitled to protection by society and the State.

Article 17.

(1)   Everyone has the right to own property alone as well as in association with others.

(2)   No one shall be arbitrarily deprived of his property.

Article 18.
Everyone has the right to freedom of thought, conscience and religion; this right includes freedom to change his religion or belief, and freedom, either alone or in community with others and in public or private, to manifest his religion or belief in teaching, practice, worship and observance.

Article 19.
Everyone has the right to freedom of opinion and expression; this right includes freedom to hold opinions without interference and to seek, receive and impart information and ideas through any media and regardless of frontiers.

Article 20.
(1)   Everyone has the right to freedom of peaceful assembly and association.
(2)   No one may be compelled to belong to an association.

Article 21.
(1)   Everyone has the right to take part in the government of his country, directly or through freely chosen representatives.
(2)   Everyone has the right of equal access to public service in his country.
(3)   The will of the people shall be the basis of the authority of government; this will shall be expressed in periodic and genuine elections which shall be by universal and equal suffrage and shall be held by secret vote or by equivalent free voting procedures.

Article 22.
Everyone, as a member of society, has the right to social security and is entitled to realization, through national effort and international co-operation and in accordance with the organization and resources of each State, of the economic, social and cultural rights indispensable for his dignity and the free development of his personality.

Article 23.
(1)   Everyone has the right to work, to free choice of employment, to just and favourable conditions of work and to protection against unemployment.
(2)   Everyone, without any discrimination, has the right to equal pay for equal work.
(3)   Everyone who works has the right to just and favourable remuneration ensuring for himself and his family an existence worthy of human dignity, and supplemented, if necessary, by other means of social protection.
(4)   Everyone has the right to form and to join trade unions for the protection of his interests.

Article 24.
Everyone has the right to rest and leisure, including reasonable limitation of working hours and periodic holidays with pay.

Article 25.
(1)   Everyone has the right to a standard of living adequate for the health and well-being of himself and of his family, including food, clothing, housing and medical care and necessary social services, and the right to security in the event of

unemployment, sickness, disability, widowhood, old age or other lack of liveli-
hood in circumstances beyond his control.
(2)   Motherhood and childhood are entitled to special care and assistance. All children, whether born in or out of wedlock, shall enjoy the same social protection.

Article 26.
(1)   Everyone has the right to education. Education shall be free, at least in the elementary and fundamental stages. Elementary education shall be compulsory.
Technical and professional education shall be made generally available and higher
education shall be equally accessible to all on the basis of merit.
(2)   Education shall be directed to the full development of the human personality
and to the strengthening of respect for human rights and fundamental freedoms. It shall promote understanding, tolerance and friendship among all nations, racial or religious groups, and shall further the activities of the United
Nations for the maintenance of peace.
(3)   Parents have a prior right to choose the kind of education that shall be given to
their children.

Article 27.
(1)   Everyone has the right freely to participate in the cultural life of the community,
to enjoy the arts and to share in scientific advancement and its benefits.
(2)   Everyone has the right to the protection of the moral and material interests
resulting from any scientific, literary or artistic production of which he is the
author.

Article 28.
Everyone is entitled to a social and international order in which the rights and freedoms set forth in this Declaration can be fully realized.

Article 29.
(1)   Everyone has duties to the community in which alone the free and full development of his personality is possible.
(2)   In the exercise of his rights and freedoms, everyone shall be subject only to such
limitations as are determined by law solely for the purpose of securing due recognition and respect for the rights and freedoms of others and of meeting the
just requirements of morality, public order and the general welfare in a democratic society.
(3)   These rights and freedoms may in no case be exercised contrary to the purposes
and principles of the United Nations.

Article 30.
Nothing in this Declaration may be interpreted as implying for any State, group or
person any right to engage in any activity or to perform any act aimed at the destruction of any of the rights and freedoms set forth herein.

*(Adopted and proclaimed by General Assembly resolution 217 A (III) of 10 December
1948)*

Sample Classroom Exercises

Following are some examples of exercises that can be used in conjunction with this text, in class sessions, in associated skills laboratories, or in other ways. Because the foundation course covers so much content, it is important that students have an opportunity to "process" what they are learning, to organize the material for themselves, to put their learning into words, and to practice skills. There are many approaches to this kind of experiential learning, and the illustrations here are merely suggestive. Teachers and students likely will find a style that works for a particular class. This may include some mix of role-playing, small-group discussion, and other participatory presentations. What is important is that students act on and express their grasp of course content so that they experience some of the dilemmas, ambiguities, and challenges that are inevitable in practice. Exercises such as these do not lead to "right answers," and thus they help students to become more comfortable in taking risks and living with uncertainty, using their own judgment, and co-constructing new and creative responses to real-world situations.

The material that follows includes an introductory exercise on empathic listening, followed by one exercise for each chapter of the book. (Students and faculty are encouraged to send feedback regarding these exercises to ctlowery@earthlink.net as part of "shaping" the text for the next edition.)

Preliminary Exercise: Empathic Listening

A basic skill for all forms of social work practice is empathic listening, which is a way of expressing respect for others (clients, colleagues, and so forth) and building relationships, as well as for collecting the information needed to develop intervention plans. Crucial aspects of empathic listening include:

- actually hearing what the other person is saying (listening for both content and associated emotions),
- communicating verbally and nonverbally that you are hearing what the other person is saying, and

- listening nonjudgmentally, being careful to avoid even subtle punishment for honest expression (for example, the statement "So you didn't mean to treat your child so abusively?" includes a not so subtle punitive message).

In this exercise, the class should be divided into groups of three (one or two groups of two can be used, if necessary). Each group's members should decide among themselves who is to take each role (roles are rotated after approximately 10 minutes). One person should take the role of a "person with a problem"—which can be a real (but not overwhelming) issue or one "borrowed" from someone else the student knows. Another person should be designated as the "listener," and the third should be designated as the "observer," who will identify what the listener did well, and what the listener might do to listen and communicate empathy even more effectively. (Note that the role is not to criticize what was done wrong!)

For the first two minutes (the instructor may want to announce the times), the listener is to simply listen without saying anything at all but try to communicate interest and empathy only nonverbally. For the next two minutes, the listener can only use one- or two-word "furthering" responses, like "um-hmm" or "I see." Then for the remaining time, the listener can ask brief questions meant to elicit information and can use empathic paraphrasing. (For example, "It sounds like you were feeling very frustrated when she said that.") The listener should completely avoid making suggestions or asking "leading questions" that have suggestions built in. When the role-play is complete, the three partners should discuss the experience briefly. (These stages should be either posted on the board or given in handouts.)

After brief discussion, the roles in the triad should be rotated, with another student taking the role of the listener, and using the same progression; after another 10 minutes, the roles should again be rotated so everyone has taken every role. The class may then want to pursue a general discussion about the experience, why these skills are so important, and why they are so challenging.

Exercise 1: Taking an ecosystemic perspective

Divide the class into groups of 6 to 8, each of which is to draw an ecomap that captures the dynamics of the following case (or another provided by the instructor) on a large sheet of paper.

Case example. An 18-year-old single mother of a two-year-old daughter was referred to child protective services (CPS) by an emergency department physician of a local hospital. The two-year-old was brought in by her mother, Ms. Chin, a second-generation Chinese American woman, because the child was crying in pain from severe burns on her buttocks. The mother's explanation was that the child had backed into the open oven door when the mother was removing cookies she had just baked. The mother was extremely agitated and fearful.

The social worker at CPS learned from the mother that she had somewhat limited social supports—the father of the child visited occasionally and her parents, who were in poor health, lived on another floor in the same building, but she did not work or socialize outside her apartment house. Beyond the family, she had only one real friend, an elderly woman living alone in the apartment next door. Ms. Chin had not finished high school because she had become pregnant; she had no job skills, and although she seemed intelligent and aware of the seriousness of her situation, her affect was flat and she seemed to be quite depressed. The child appeared to be developmentally normal, affectionate with her mother, and outgoing in the social worker's presence.

Ms. Chin was worried that her description of the accident would not be believed and that CPS would remove her daughter from her care. The social worker had the impression that the mother was concerned about her daughter's welfare and that this might have been a true accident, not an instance of child abuse. When the social worker later talked with the neighbor who knew the mother, she learned that the mother often became impatient with the child, but the neighbor had not observed hitting or anything else that she regarded as abusive.

The social worker had to make a decision about the immediate health and welfare of the child: Did this case require immediate placement to protect the child? Was this a woman who would respond to help, and what would the interventions be? The assignment for the small groups, however, is not to make a decision, but rather to organize case data in ways that could be helpful for planning—to "see" the case ecosystemically, including social and cultural factors.

Creating the ecomap. In drawing the ecomaps, consider the interrelatedness of the case variables, what is known and not known about the case, and what limitations and potentials for help are present in the case. Ecomaps drawn by different groups might emphasize different points for intervention, depending on the way they are drawn.

A typical ecomap will include:

- circles depicting the case variables in sectors,
- arrows to depict exchanges among systems and variables, and
- shading or colors to identify the point or points of intervention indicated by the perspective taken on the case.

Groups should share their ecomaps with the class, followed by a discussion focused on understanding the case in its transactional complexity.

Exercise 2: Morality and Social Justice

Working in dyads or triads, discuss the following questions:

- What groups or institutions have provided guidelines or taboos for your moral behavior? What was considered unacceptable (e.g., disloyalty, sexual behavior, drinking), and what was considered important (e.g., success, education, patriotism) in your family of origin, your peer groups, religious organizations, communities, and other groups and institutions that have influenced your values?
- What moral expectations do you have of yourself as a social worker? How consistent are these with the moral expectations you grew up with?
- What moral expectations do you have of your colleagues?
- Recognizing the essential interconnections among all people, institutions, and the natural world, as well as the impact of larger sociocultural and corporate forces, what personal responsibility do you feel for constructing a just world?

After comparing your answers to the questions above, as a class, discuss and record how actualizing your moral perspectives could contribute to a "just" world. Do not attempt to define a just world first, but build a "just" world from the moral standards that are operating in the class.

Exercise 3: Ethical Practice

Part 1

One of the most difficult—but crucial—demands of the NASW *Code of Ethics* is that the social worker intervene with impaired colleagues when issues such as substance abuse or personal problems interfere with their work with clients.

Break the class into dyads (groups of two). In each dyad, have one student take the role of the impaired worker and the other the role of a colleague. (The instructor may wish to model a minute or two of an interaction between the two in front of the class first.) Each dyad should now role-play a serious conversation in which the colleague expresses his or her concern, listens to the impaired colleague, and clarifies the next steps that he or she will take if the impaired colleague does not take appropriate action.

After approximately five minutes, the class should discuss the experience, its emotional effect, and the importance of taking such steps. Then, the members of each dyad should switch roles, this time discussing another issue with serious ethical or values implications, such as a worker who appears to be becoming romantically involved with a student he or she is supervising, a worker who is treating colleagues in the organization disrespectfully, or a worker who is making ethnically offensive comments. Again after approximately five minutes of interaction, the entire class should process their experiences.

Part 2

Case background. Margaret, a social worker at the local counseling center, has been counseling the Patterson family for approximately seven months now. Recently, while Mr. Patterson was temporarily unemployed, Margaret became aware of an incident of harsh parental discipline that she had questions about. Margaret discussed the incident with the family and decided not to file a report with the child protective services (CPS) agency at this time. As a result of recent experiences with CPS, it was Margaret's conclusion that CPS intervention "may do more harm than good." Margaret was convinced that she could reach the family through their already-established relationship, which was reported to be quite strong. It was Margaret's judgment that the incident was an isolated one and that if she reported the family to CPS, they would resent the reporting and would not return for counseling. "Having worked with CPS before in this community," said Margaret, "I am convinced the family would get no help at all there."

Analysis. Using the decision-making strategy presented in Chapter 3, complete a systematic analysis of the ethical dilemma. Determine what action you would take in this case, and justify your choice of action.

Exercise 4: Diversity and Culture

Before beginning this exercise, it is important that everyone in the group recognize the need for mutual respect and curiosity when discussing core personal and cultural values. Start by giving each member of the class the opportunity to answer the question, "How do you self-identify culturally?" For purposes of this exercise, cultural groups can be loosely defined as including any group that mutually supports particular practices, beliefs, and values over time within the group. This broad definition includes, for example, ethnic, religious, and national cultures as well as many smaller social networks. The instructor or group leader usually should go first to act as a model. It is important that each person be allowed to define himself or herself in his or her own way—for many students, race and religion may be the most salient factors, but for others sexual orientation or cohort factors may be most important. (It may be necessary to remind the class of this fact because on occasion, members of the class may interrupt each other to question whether the other is using the "right" categories.)

As each person provides his or her self-identification, list it on large sheets of paper or on the chalkboard. The instructor or group leader then breaks the larger group into smaller groups having one or more central features in common. Those who do not fit into any simple system of grouping can form their own "diversity caucus."

Each small group is then given 20 minutes to discuss the following questions and to prepare a report to give to the larger group. To encourage honesty, it is important to remind those participating that many cultures teach and encourage biases toward those who are not members of the group, and that as a result, we all carry biases that we need to recognize. Point out that the more honest the discussion, the more useful it will be.

- What messages (positive and negative) did you receive in childhood about your own group?
- What messages (positive and negative—honesty is critical here) did you receive in childhood about members of particular other groups, including those of other races and differing sexual orientations?
- Which of your most important values came primarily from the microculture of your family and which from larger cultural entities or groups?
- What do you not understand about one particular culture that is not your own?
- How may your cultural background and values affect your practice—now and in the future?

After 30 minutes, each group sends a reporter to participate in a panel discussion in front of the larger group. After the reporters summarize the group discussion, the instructor and other members of the class are given the opportunity to ask members of the panel questions to clarify and deepen mutual understanding.

Source: Adapted in part from Nakanishi, M., & Rittner, B. (1992). The Inclusionary Cultural Model. *Journal of Social Work Education, 28,* 27–35.

Exercise 5: Self-Knowledge for Practice

Personal life experience is one source of knowledge on which every social worker depends. Your own life experiences mold and influence not only your personal life but your professional practice as well. If you had a strong family background, for example, you will draw a great deal of emotional strength from those experiences, but it may be more difficult for you to deeply understand experiences of clients with very different histories. Or, if you come from a family in which substance abuse was a factor, this will have multiple effects on your practice. It is crucial that you deepen your self-awareness, including knowledge of areas about which you need to be particularly sensitive, as well as strengths you draw from your personal history. This exercise is designed to help you begin such exploration, which you will want to continue throughout your career because you will periodically discover new facets of yourself in your work.

In a small group of four to six people, take a moment to write down answers to these questions individually:

- In what two areas of my practice do I need to be especially sensitive to possible interference from my personal history?
- What are two particular strengths I bring to practice from my personal history?

Do not bring to the surface issues that you do not feel comfortable sharing (although you should process such issues at some point yourself or, preferably, with someone you trust). When everyone has completed this, take turns going around the circle, first discussing your responses to the first question. Use a Native American Talking Circle method: Each person takes his or her turn and speaks without interruption; when that person is done, the next person takes his or her turn. Save general discussion until everyone has taken a turn. Be sure to listen to and support each other in this exercise and to keep your own comments brief; avoid self-absorption! After you have processed the first question, use the same procedure to examine the second question.

Exercise 6: Monitoring

Part 1

Examine the graphs shown in Figure 6-4. In small groups, describe what you see.

- How is the couple doing at various points in the case?
- What variables seem to be interrelated in some way?
- If you were the social worker, how might you use the graphs in practice with the clients?

Part 2

It is important to experience what your clients experience, to the extent possible, to build sensitivity and empathy. For example, if you use tools such as rapid assessment instruments in your practice, you may want to try them out yourself first. This is an exercise in which you prepare sequential ecomaps that reflect changes in your own life. To begin, individually draw an ecomap of your own life six months ago (or one year ago, if the changes over that period are more noticeable) and then one for the present. Next share the ecomaps with another student. Discuss the experience of seeing your own life visually and of sharing it with someone whom you probably do not know intimately.

Exercise 7: Practice with Individuals

(Note: Other sample cases can be substituted using the process outlined here.)

Case example: José is a 28-year-old graphic artist who is seeking help at the community mental health center because he has been experiencing anxiety and depression. Since he recently learned that he tested positive for HIV, he has been unable to concentrate on or to complete his work assignments, to sleep at night, or to eat regularly. Although he is married and has two children, José, a first-generation Mexican American, has also had occasional sexual liaisons with men, and his physician assumes that is how he contracted the virus. Although he is largely asymptomatic, José is concerned about his health, his job status, and his ability to care for his family. However, his most immediate concern is that he does not feel that he can disclose his health status to either his wife or his parents. José's parents now live with his younger brother in a small town in another state. José feels that his diagnosis would be particularly hard for his parents to accept for cultural reasons.

In spite of his good health, José has missed days at work and has received several warnings from his supervisors, who are baffled by the recent deterioration in his work performance. His wife is also concerned about his lack of motivation at work and his "hypochondria." At home, he makes excuses for not being near his children and is avoiding sexual contact with his wife.

Engaging and envisioning. Divide the class into two circles, with two empty chairs in the center of each. Have one student take the role of José and the other that of a social worker in each circle. These students should role-play the first 10 minutes of an initial interview, with a focus on engagement and envisioning an improved situation toward which the worker and client might aim. The student playing the social worker can interrupt the role-play at any point and ask the observing students to make suggestions regarding how to move ahead at difficult points; the other students in the circle should remain quiet except when their help is requested by the social worker. The instructor can move back and forth between the two circles, leading brief mini-discussions of the process thus far and periodically asking other students to take one of the roles.

After completion of one or two 10-minute segments of role-play, the overall group can discuss the following questions:

- What value dilemmas or ethical issues did this scenario raise?
- What did the social workers do that contributed to engaging the client?
- What else might they have done to further engagement?
- To what extent were the worker and client able to move beyond describing the problem situation and toward envisioning a better reality they might work toward?
- To what extent did the role-plays exemplify shared power? How?

Exercise 8: Social Work with Families—the Genogram

Essentially, the genogram is a visual intergenerational family tree. Charting and recording intergenerational patterns can be useful in health histories, including causes of death (Hartman & Laird, 1983); for understanding family immigration patterns and connections in different geographical places; for adoptions; for understanding intergenerational patterns related to substance use; and in other circumstances in which relationships relevant to the work being done need to be clarified.

To understand the patterns in one's own family history, each student begins by drawing a three- or four-generation (grandparents, parents, self and siblings, children) genogram. Each can select one or two patterns they want to explore at this time (types of losses, twin births, alcoholism) and chart these with the usual gender, age,

Figure C-1.

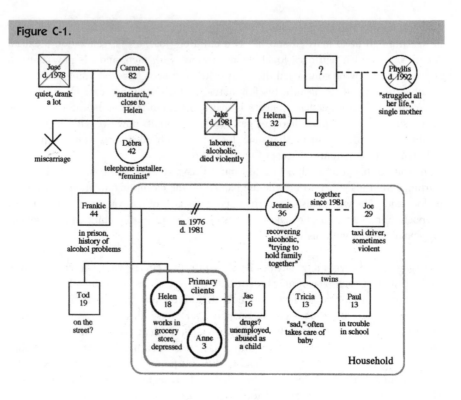

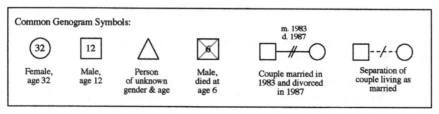

Common Genogram Symbols:

(32)	[12]	△	⊠ 6	□—//—○	□--/--○
Female, age 32	Male, age 12	Person of unknown gender & age	Male, died at age 6	m. 1983 d. 1987 Couple married in 1983 and divorced in 1987	Separation of couple living as married

marriage and divorce, and birth and death categories in the genealogical chart. For example, the model (Figure C-1) includes occupations and alcohol histories for a family in treatment.

Note how the primary client system is "boxed off" and located within a larger household system. Students should share what they have learned from this exercise, as well as their reflections on when constructing genograms may or may not be helpful in work with clients.

REFERENCE: Hartman, A., & Laird, J. (1983). *Family-centered social work practice.* New York: Free Press.

Exercise 9: Practice with Groups

Background. You are the leader of a group of 9th and 10th graders (15- and 16-year-olds) in a school-sponsored group for underachievers (students who do not do homework, talk a lot in class, or do not concentrate on school work). These students do not have many friends in school and have been identified by classroom teachers as those who make trouble for other students. These students hang out together after school and outside the group.

The purpose of this group is to help these students develop skills and attitudes that will lead them to succeed in school. The group was formed three or four months ago and is now in the work, or ongoing, phase (Tuckman's [1965] "performing" stage of group development). For example, in recent sessions, the group members have talked about their families and discussed how to respond when they are angry with other students and teachers.

Several of the group members went dancing at a club on Saturday night, and this is the first group meeting since the dance. While she was dancing with Ellen, Jane said to her, "You look gorgeous. I could really go for you." Ellen left abruptly and did not return to the dance.

At the next meeting Ellen came in a little late. When she arrived, several group members immediately asked her, "Where did you disappear Saturday?" Ellen responded, pointing to Jane, "Ask her!" Jane says, "What are you talking about?" There is some arguing back and forth, but finally Ellen is persuaded to tell her story. Then the group members criticized and "dumped on" Jane.

Instructions for role-plays:

1. Assign the roles of the leader, Ellen, Jane, and two to three other members of the group.
2. There are two ways to begin this role-play:
   • Begin the group where the scenario left off.
   • Have Ellen leave the room and start the role-play with her coming to the group late.
3. The leader and the members (especially the leader) must respond to this inter-personal obstacle. The members should stay in their roles. The role-play should last five to seven minutes. After that time, the leader and one member should switch roles and continue the role-play. However, before the switch, members should give feedback to the leader about what helped and what did not help.
4. Finally, one group member should serve as a recorder who will report back to the class the feedback given to each leader.

Reference: Tuckman, B. W. (1965). Developmental sequence in small groups. *Psychological Bulletin, 63*, 384–399.

SUGGESTED READING: Shulman, L. (1967). Scapegoats, group workers, and preemptive intervention. *Social Work, 12*, 37–43.

NOTE: This exercise was developed by Renée Solomon, associate professor, Columbia University School of Social Work, New York.

Exercise 10: Eliciting Multiple Perspectives in Communities

In any community group, there will be a wide range of perspectives on issues facing the community, even when there seems to be a high level of shared concern. For the social worker, this situation raises the problem of how to ensure that multiple perspectives, particularly those that are typically silenced, get heard and validated. In the following exercise, students use their everyday experiences to learn a strategy for providing all members with a voice in the process. The exercise uses Freire's "pedagogy of the question" to elicit various perspectives and to encourage critical reflection on their meaning.

1. Select a topic that is part of the everyday experience of all students in the class (such as some aspect of their experience in the class or as students in the school). Choose something likely to be substantive.

2. Pose the topic to the class in the form of a series of questions, for example, "How do you experience issues of race (or gender, respect, sexual orientation, or another thematic issue) in your field placement or in this school?" "How could this issue be better addressed?" "What obstacles do you see to addressing this issue honestly and helpfully?" Write these questions on an index card.

3. Use a talking circle format, with everyone seated in a single circle. One student or the instructor, holding the card, reads the first question aloud and answers it in his or her own way. Answers should be relatively brief and as thoughtful as possible. Use newsprint and marker pens (so a record exists) to record the various points of view. The card is then passed to the next person, who answers to same question. Only the person holding the card may speak, and no one else may interrupt. Participants may pass, but then must wait until the card comes around again to speak. The card should go around the circle three times, using a new but related question each time (a single question can also be used for multiple rounds).

4. After the circle has been completed three times, the class can discuss together what they heard in the responses. Ensure that both minority and majority perspectives are captured. Also focus on what people are learning about what other people think. Encourage critical reflection on both content and process. Note any general (or generative) themes that connect the students' experience to wider institutional, social, and political issues. Encourage discussion of these issues from multiple perspectives.

5. Close by exploring with the class ways in which the material might be used as a basis for further discussion and action. How can the multiple voices that emerge from this process be nurtured and encompassed in the longer term? How might this process be useful in other groups? To what extent is it consistent with various cultural norms, and is this an advantage or a disadvantage?

This exercise is useful at three levels: (1) It generates thematic material from the students' experiences that will be similar to content that they will encounter in the community, (2) it models a strategy that students can use in their own practice, and (3) it provides a vehicle for enhancing students' empowerment (if material relevant to the class gets a response). Each of these three levels should be identified by the instructor in the discussion that follows the exercise.

Exercise 11: Practice with Organizations

Divide the class into groups of six to eight people. Each group should prepare a five-minute role-play scenario about a problem in service delivery (a situation in which agency procedures or service arrangements do not "work for people") drawn from one of their fieldwork placements. The scenarios selected should be real and reflect a general organizational issue.

Each small group should present their scenario to the class, then lead a discussion of the following questions:

- How is the client not being well served in this scenario?
- What alternative service arrangements realistically could be constructed that might work better?
- What resources would be required, and what obstacles overcome, to make these changes?
- What could be one small, realistic first step toward the identified goal?
- How is a process of shared power relevant to the arrangements being discussed here?

The same process should be used with each scenario prepared by each of the other small groups.

Exercise 12: Generalist Practice: Practice Possibilities at Multiple System Levels

A social worker can, and sometimes must, respond to a client's needs in many ways and at multiple system levels. The material in Chapter 12 discussed such responses to the problem of child abuse and neglect, but a similar approach is important in working with many social problems. This exercise is designed to encourage creativity and analytic thought in deciding on effective interventive strategies.

In small groups of four to six people, choose one type of case that at least one student in that group is currently working with (if possible, choose something other than child maltreatment). In each small group, do the following:

- On large pieces of paper, draw an hypothesized causal chain involved in maintaining the problem in at least some cases. Do not aim for perfection; spend no more than 10 minutes developing this conceptual model.
- On another large sheet of paper, develop a three-column table. In the first column, list system levels (individual, family, group, neighborhood, community, organization). In the second column, list at least one possible and useful interventive strategy for each system level in the first column. In the third column, note the reasons why you have identified each strategy, based on the conceptual model of the problem you have sketched. Spend no more than 15 minutes on this table.
- Next, a reporter from each group briefly explains the conceptual model and table of interventions outlined to the full group without interruption. When all groups have reported, open the floor for general discussion, with particular emphasis on areas of contrast among the small groups.

Exercise 13: Fields of Practice

Divide the class into three or four groups, depending on field of practice (for example, family and children's services, health services, school social work). Each group should role-play an interview with the following client (or one selected by the class and instructor) for about 10 minutes and then answer the questions listed after the case example below. The groups should then report their conclusions, and the class can contrast the responses as they vary between fields. Note that a client like this may surface in practically any field of practice; the question is how the case would be dealt with in each.

Case example. At your fieldwork agency, your supervisor has asked you to help Gina, a 38-year-old, single European American homeless woman who has two children in foster care. She was recently picked up by the police following a mugging in which she was beaten severely. She had told the police, "I just want to be left alone— by everyone." Until five years ago, when she was hospitalized for six months for what she called a "nervous breakdown," Gina worked as a laboratory technician in a local hospital. For the past four years, she has been in and out of the shelter system, which she entered after her boyfriend battered her. Her two children (ages six and eight) were removed from the home for neglect about six months ago, and she has lived on the streets since shortly thereafter, in the process losing all benefits. Outreach workers have recently observed Gina raving and ranting at pedestrians. She also has a history of drinking heavily (although she is sober at the moment). She reports no extended period of sobriety for the past four years. When asked about her drinking, Gina says, "I drink because I have problems."
Questions:

- What kind of services could Gina receive from your agency? What barriers are present?
- What other services and systems might be relevant to providing assistance in this case?
- What policy dilemmas does this case raise within your field of practice?
- Does this case raise any value dilemmas for you?

Exercise 14: The Profession

Break the class into groups of five to seven people. Ask each group to spend 20 minutes answering the following questions, noting their answers with markers on large sheets of paper that can be hung on the wall:

- Why did you enter a graduate social work program?
- What is your biggest concern about social work as a profession?
- How important is social work's historic commitment to social justice to you? Why?

After these small group discussions, each group should report back to the full class. After these reports, general themes should be extracted in a large group discussion.

Index

Abbot, Grace, 359
Abbott, Edith, 363
Acceptance and commitment therapy
 (ACT), 178–179
Addams, Jane, 208, 340, 349, 353, 362, 363
Advocacy, community-level, 253–254
African Americans
 racial duality and, 361–368, 374
 welfare raids against, 372, 373
 welfare state and, 359–360
Afrikaners, 88–90
Afrocentric models, 122
Agencies. *See* Organizations
Aging, culture of, 82–83
Aid to Families with Dependent Children
 (AFDC), 330, 369, 372, 373
Al-Islam, 80
Alcoholism treatment facility case, 277–285
Alliance for Children and Families, 201
American Association of Social Workers, 50
American Community Survey, 245
American Declaration for Rights of Indig-
 enous Peoples, 32
Americans with Disabilities Act of 1990,
 328
Argueta, Ronalth Ocheaeta, 32
Aristede, Jean-Bertrand, 28–29
Art knowledge, 116–117
Asian Americans, 369–370
Assertiveness training, 180–181
Assessment. *See also* Monitoring
 community, 243–244
 contextual analysis of focal behaviors
  and transactions and, 172–173
 ecosystem scan and, 166–170
 ecosystems perspective and, 19

of ethnocultural factors, 190
in family work, 187–189
function of, 165–166, 192
identification of focus for work and,
 170–171
identification of interventive tasks
 and, 173–175
program, 309–310
Asset-based social welfare, 252–253
Association for Improving the Condition of
 the Poor, 50
Association for the Advancement of Social
 Work with Groups (AASWG), standards
 of practice, 219, 220
Atlanta University School of Social Work,
 366–368

B design, 143
Bad Blood (Buston), 373
Barbie doll, 83
Bartlett, H. M., 323–325
Beck Depression Inventory, 133
Behavioral-cognitive approach, 121, 122
Behavioral science, 102
Behaviorally anchored rating scales, 171,
 172
Bifurcated welfare state, 358–360
Black nationalism, 80
Black Perspective in Social Work, 367
Boundedness, 88–90
Brace, Charles Loring, 350
Brazil, 31, 40
Breckenridge, Sophonisba, 363
Briar, S., 320
Brief therapy, solution-focused, 193
Bunch, C., 38, 41

417

Bureau of Indian Affairs, 368, 371, 372
Bureau of Public Assistance, 359, 369, 372
Burger, Julian, 31
Burroughs, Nannie Helen, 340–341
Buston, Peter, 373

Cabot, John, 346, 347
Caregiving, 190–192
Case Process Chart, 140
Cases
    integrating sources of knowledge in,
        126–127
    knowledge derived from, 107–109
    transactional ecomaps and defining,
        154–157
Categorical ethnicity, 84–86
Center for Women's Global Leadership, 25
Charity Organization Society (COS) move-
    ment, 50, 342–346, 357
Chief, Elizabeth, 371–372
Child maltreatment
    community practice and, 298–300
    factors contributing to, 296
    family consultation and, 297
    family intervention and, 202
    group work and, 298
    individual work with parents and,
        297
Children's Bureau, 357
Citizen's Commission on Civil Rights, 364
Civil Liberties Act of 1988, 370
Civil rights movement, 353, 368
Classroom exercises
    on diversity and culture, 408–409
    on ecosystemic perspective, 406–407
    on eliciting multiple perspectives in
        communities, 413–414
    on empathic listening, 405–406
    on ethical practice, 408
    on fields of practice, 415–416
    on generalist practice, 415
    on monitoring, 410
    on morality and social justice, 407
    on practice with groups, 412–413
    on practice with individuals, 410–411
    on practice with organizations,
        414–415
    on self-knowledge for practice,
        409–410
    on social work profession, 416
    on social work with families,
        411–412
    use of, 405

Clients
    approaches to dealing with, 291
    diversity among, xvii–xviii
    knowledge of, 107–108
Clinical analytic design, 109, 110
Clinical rating scales, 137
Closed-ended groups, 218
Closed systems, 11, 13
Clune, W. H., III, 82
Coalition Against Trafficking in Women
    (CATW), 40
Code of Ethics
    development of, 50–51
    function of, 265
    NASW, 53, 55, 56, 64–65, 381–399
    (See also NASW Code of Ethics)
Cognitive approach, 123
Cohesion, 221
Collaboration, 240
College Settlement, 349
Collier, John, 359, 368
Commission on Social Work Practice (Na-
    tional Association of Social Workers),
    322–325
Communication
    emotions in family, 195
    in individual work, 159–160
    nonverbal, 159–160
Communities Organized for Public Service
    (COPS), 201
Community-centered services, 153
Community/communities
    assessment of, 243–244
    classroom exercises on eliciting
        multiple perspectives in, 413–414
    as collective power relationships,
        234–235
    ecomap of, 14
    effect of agencies of, 275
    explanation of, 232
    mapping neighborhood, 244–248
    meaning of, 231–232
    as place, 232–333
    as shared social ties, 233–234
Community economic development (CED),
    253
Community practice
    asset-based social welfare programs
        and community development
        and, 252–253
    challenging social systems and,
        253–254
    collaboration and, 240

Community practice (*continued*)
community assessment and, 243–244
contextual thinking and, 243
critical consciousness and, 241–242
current models of, 237
dialogue as basis for community
action and, 242
empowerment and, 239, 240–243,
248–250
generalist approach to, 236, 238
with maltreating parents, 298–300
mapping communities and, 244–248
models of, 235–236
monitoring and evaluating, 254–255
overview of, 230–231
participation and, 240–241
small groups and, 250–251
social networks and, 251–252
social programs and, 252
theoretical foundations of, 238–239
Comparison-group studies, 145–146
Conceptual map
case specifics and, xviii
client diversity and, xvii–xviii
contexts of practice and, xxi–xxii
explanation of, xiv–xvi
practice approaches and, xix–xx
practice processes and, xx–xxi
professional purpose, values, and
ethics and, xvi–xvii
social justice and power and, xvi
sources of knowledge and, xix
system levels and, xviii–xix
Concerns Report Method, 246
Confidentiality, 54–55
Connectedness
ecosystems perspective and, 20–21,
154
reciprocity and, 186–187
in supportive family groups, 195
Coons, J. E., 82
Cortès, Ernesto, Jr., 201
Cottrell, L. S., Jr., 249
Coulton, Claudia, 230
Council on Social Work Education
(CSWE)
curriculum policy statement of,
209–210, 320
fields of practice and, 320–322
values and ethics and, 52–53
Coyle, G. L., 223
Crippled Children's Services, 369
Critical consciousness, 240–241

Culture/cultures
of aging, 82–83
classroom exercise of, 408–409
ethnicity and, 82–83
knowledge of, 114–115
nature of, 79
of organizations, 271–272
Current events knowledge, 113–114
*Curriculum Policy for the Master's Degree and
Baccalaureate Programs in Social Work
Education* (CSWE), 320, 321

Dale, James, 75
Decade for Women (United Nations), 35,
36
Decision making
ethical approaches to, 59–61
role of values in, 48–50
Declaration on the Elimination of Violence
against Women (United Nations), 33
Deloria, Vine, 115
Deontologists, 59
Department of Health, Education, and
Welfare (HEW), 372, 373
Depression, 133–134, 294
Designs. *See also* Monitoring
clinical analytic, 109, 110
explanation of, 140, 141, 307
group, 105–106, 142, 145–146
single-case, 106–107, 109, 110,
142–145
Devine, Edward, 344
Dewey, John, 208
Direct observation, 134–135
Disabilities, 189–190
Diversity. *See also* Culture/cultures;
Multiculturalism; *specific groups*
among clients, xvii–xviii
classroom exercise on, 408–409
in organizations, 267
responses to, 74–75
in self-organizing systems, 8
Domestic violence, 41
Draft Declaration on the Rights of Indigenous Peoples, 32
Duality. *See* Racial duality
DuBois, W.E.B., 360
Duty to tell the truth, 55

Ecobehavioral approaches
assessment and, 165–175
engagement and, 158–163
envisioning and, 163–165

Ecobehavioral approaches (*continued*)
    explanation of, 121–123
    focus of, 157
    intervention and, 175–181
    model of, 204–205
Ecological approach
    ecosystems perspective and, 13,
        101–102
    explanation of, 186–187
    use of, 121
Ecology, 6
Ecomaps
    community, 14
    examples of, 5, 11, 12, 293
    function of, 4, 5, 13
    goal, 164
    practice choices and, 15–17
    transactional, 154–157
Economic development, 42–43
Ecosystem scan
    elements of, 166, 168–170
    interview guide to develop, 167–168
Ecosystems perspective
    advances in, 6–9
    assessment and, 19
    benefits and drawbacks of, 17–19
    classroom exercise on, 406–407
    connectedness and, 20–21, 154
    ecological science and, 101–102
    ecomap and choices in practice and,
        15–17
    explanation of, 4–5
    function of, 125–126
    practice approaches and, 120
    roots of, 6
    structure of systems and, 10–15
    systemic thinking vs. linear thinking
        and, 9–10
Educational inequality, 81–82
*Educational Policy and Accreditation
    Standards* (Council on Social Work
    Education), 52–53
Empathic listening exercise, 405–406
Empowerment. *See also* Power
    commitment to, 276
    in community practice, 239, 240–
        243, 248–250
    explanation of, 161
    social justice and, 33–34
Encyclopedia of Social Work (National Asso-
    ciation of Social Workers), 188–189,
    320, 323

Engagement
    envisioning and, 163–164
    in family work, 187–189
    individual work and, 158–163
Entrophy, 11
Environment, of agencies, 275–276
Envisioning, 163–165
Equifinality, 6
Ethical absolutism, 59
Ethical dilemmas
    case example and, 61–62, 66–69
    framework for analyzing, 59–61
    model for analyzing, 62–70
    in social work practice, 55–58
Ethical practice, 408
Ethical relativism, 59
Ethics
    explanation of, 53
    legal responsibilities and, 54–55
    overview of, xvii
    shifts in concerns regarding, 50–51
    in social work education, 52–53
    values vs., 52
Ethnic cleansing, 39
Ethnic groups/ethnicity, 190. *See also* Cul-
    ture/cultures; Diversity;
    Multiculturalism; *specific groups*
    boundedness and, 88–90
    categorical, 84–86
    culture and, 82–83
    social justice and, 79–81
    transactional model of, 86
Etzioni, Amitai, 263
Evaluation, 224–225. *See also* Assessment;
    Monitoring
Evidence-based practice (EBP), 99–100,
    122
Existential approach, 123
Experimental research, 105–107

Family genograms, 203
Family Preservation and Support Services
    Act, 201
Family preservation services, 201–202
Family support programs
    with community involvement, 299
    explanation of, 199–201
Family work
    assessment, planning, and monitor-
        ing and, 192–195
    case example of, 184–185, 189–192
    classroom exercise on, 411–412

Family work (*continued*)
 ecobehavioral model and, 204–205
 ecological perspective and, 186–187
 family preservation and, 201–204
 family support and, 199–201
 health family functioning and,
  195–197
 with maltreating parents, 297
 multiple families, 197–199
 overview of, 185–186
 preparing for engagement and
  assessment in, 188–189
Fawcett, S. B., 248, 249
*Federal Programs Affecting Children and
 Families* (U.S. House of Representatives), 328
Female genital mutilation (FGM), 40
Fiduciary responsibility, 54, 55
Fields of practice
 aspects of, 323–325, 337
 assessment of, 329–336
 background and context of, 319–320
 classroom exercise on, 415–416
 contemporary, 326–329
 Council on Social Work Education
  and, 320–321
 defining concept of, 325
 developments in, 321–323
 explanation of, 319
First International Conference on Human
 Rights in Teheran, Iran (1968), 30
Fisk University, 365
Flexner, Abraham, 352, 354
Food Stamp Program, 333
Force-field analysis, 279, 280
Formal organizations. *See also* Organizations
 environmental context of, 275–276
 explanation of, 266, 268
 goals of, 269–270
 key components of, 268–269
 membership interests and characteristics of, 274
 social service technologies and
  programs of, 273–274
 structures and culture of, 270–273
Formal structures of organizations, 270–
 271
Formative evaluation, 310
Foundation against Trafficking in Women
 in the Netherlands, 39
Freire, P., 77, 92
Friedman, E., 25

GABRIELA, 39–40
Gay and Lesbian Alliance against Defamation (GLAAD), 88
Gay civil rights movement, 374
General systems theory (GST)
 ecosystems perspective and, 11, 13
 explanation of, 6, 10
 function of, xviii
Generalist practice
 behavioral change and, 293–295
 challenges of, 311–312
 classroom exercise on, 415
 community interventions in, 298–300
 ecobehavioral theory and, 292–293
 establishing program rational in,
  304–306
 family consultation in, 297
 goals and objectives of, 306–307
 group work in, 298
 individual work with parents in, 297
 multiple options in, 295
 needs assessment in, 302–303
 overview of, 291–292
 problem analysis in, 301–302
 program design in, 307
 program evaluation in, 309–310
 program implementation in, 307–309
 program planning, design, and
  development in, 300–301
 proposal writing in, 310–311
Generic consistency principle
 ethical dilemma resolution based on,
  60
 explanation of, 59–61
Genetics, 100–102
Genograms, 203
Geographic Information Systems (GIS),
 245
Germain, C. B., 211, 238
Gerontological research, 103
Ginsberg, Ethel, 351
Goal Attainment Follow-Up Guides, 138
Goal attainment scaling, 225
Goal ecomaps, 164
Goodwin, J., 89
Granger, Lester, 367–368
Graphing, 138
Green, J. W., 79, 82
Group designs
 explanation of, 105–106
 requirements for, 142
 use of, 145–146

Group work
    approaches to, 210–211, 292
    efficacy in, 224
    exercise for, 412–413
    historical background of, 208–210
    mainstream model of, 213–214
    with maltreating parents, 298
    monitoring and evaluation of,
        224–225
    multiple-family, 197–199
    reciprocal model of, 212–213
    remedial model of, 213
    social goals model of, 211–212
    time issues in, 217–219
Groups
    composition of, 216–217
    leadership in, 219–220
    orientation of, 217
    participation in, 223–224
    processes in, 220–223
    purpose of, 214–215
    self-help, 214
    structure of, 215–216
Gurteen, Humphreys, 344

Habits of the Heart, 232
Haleem, Asma Abedel, 40
Hall, Helen, 187
Harlow, Illana, 73
Hate groups, 87–88
Hayes, George Edmund, 364
Head Start Family Support Centers, 252
Health & Social Work, 188
Health care
    assessment of issues related to, 190–192
    women's rights in, 41
Heller, K., 232
Henry Street Settlement, 349
Hill, Anita, 90
Hispanic Americans, 370–371
Hispanic New Deal, 371
History knowledge, 113–114
Hmongs, 78
Hoey, Jane, 359
Homer, Elizabeth, 32
Hope, Lugenia Burns, 366
Hopkins, Harry, 359
Houston, Charles, 360
Howard University School of Social Work,
    365, 366
Hull House, 349, 350
Human rights. *See also* Social justice;
    Women's rights
        empowerment and, 33–34

gender-based violence and, 25, 35–42
for indigenous peoples, 31–32
overview of, 26–27
relationships and, 29–30
social justice and, 26–27, 30, 43–44
Web sites on, 46
Human rights legislation, 46–47
Human service agencies, 264–266
Human services, 326

Immigrants, 184–185, 196–197
Indian Child Welfare Act (ICWA), 369
Indian Civilian Conservation Corps, 368
Indian New Deal, 368
Indigenous peoples, 31–32, 43–44
Individual practice
    assessment and, 165–175
    classroom exercise on, 410–411
    core practice processes and skills
        and, 157–158
    defining the case and, 154–157
    engagement and, 158–163
    envisioning and, 163–165
    funding for services and, 153–154
    intervention and, 175–181
    organizational context of services
        and, 152–153
    overview of, 151–152
Informal structures, 271–273
Innoculation, 181
Intensive family intervention programs,
    201–202
Intergenerational patterns, 203
Interlocking contingencies, 294–295
International Bill of Human Rights (United
    Nations), 30–31, 43
International Covenant on Civil and Politi-
    cal Rights (United Nations), 30
International Covenant on Economic,
    Social and Cultural Rights (United
    Nations), 30
International Women's Tribunal Centre
    (IWTC), 25
Interpersonal learning, 222
Intervention
    exposure to different transactions
        and experiences and, 176–177
    function of, 175–176
    identification of tasks for, 173–175
    skills training as, 179–181
    working with verbal and private
        events, 177–179
Irish Americans, 370
Islam, 42, 80, 81

Jain, Devaki, 42–43
Japanese American Citizens League, 370
Japanese Americans, 369–370
Judaism, 84

Kelley, Florence, 359, 363
Kenya, 41
Kingsbury, John Adams, 341–342, 347
Knowledge
    of art and literature, 116–117
    of biology, behavior, and culture,
        100–102, 172–173
    from the case, 107–110
    cultural perspectives and, 114–116
    definitions of, 95
    of history and current events,
        113–114
    integrated in case, 126–127
    nature of, 96–97
    personal experience and, 109, 111–113
    practice-relevant research and,
        102–107
    practice wisdom and, 97–100
    relevant sources of, xix
    theoretical and conceptual frame-
        works and, 117–126
Kozol, J., 81, 82
Kunstler, J. H., 43

Lathrop, Julia, 359
Latinos, 370–371
Leadership
    in communities, 250
    in groups, 219–220
Legal issues, 53–55
Legal rights, 29–30
Legislation
    fields of practice and, 332–333
    human rights, 46–47
Leighninger, L., 342, 359
Liberal arts knowledge, 116–117
Lindsay, Inabel Burns, 366
Linear thinking, 9–10
Listening skills, 159, 405–406
Literature knowledge, 116–117
Loktev, Julia, 184
Lowell, Josephine, 343, 344
Loyalty, 55

Mainstream model, 213–214
Mairs, Nancy, 87
Managed care, 152, 154
Marital Happiness Scale, 138, 139
Martìnez, Demetria, 73

Maternalist welfare state, 356–358
Mayer, C. H., 151
Measurement. See also Monitoring
    approaches to, 134
    Case Process Chart for, 140
    observation used as, 134–135
    qualitative matrix and, 140, 141
    rapid assessment instruments as,
        138–140
    rating scales for, 135–138
Medicaid, 333
Medical social workers, 346–348
Medicare, 333
Medium Term Philippine Development
    Plan, 39
Mexican Americans, 370
Midnight raids, 372–373
Minnesota Gay Homicide Study, 40
Moment of Impact, 184
Monitoring. See also Assessment
    challenges regarding, 146
    classroom exercise on, 410
    community practice, 254–255
    design and, 134, 140, 142–146
    in group work, 225
    of group work, 224–225
    measurement and, 134–141
    overview of, 132–133
    principles of, 133–134, 171
Moral rights, 29–30
Morality exercise, 407
Multiculturalism, 74–75
Multiple-family therapy
    background of, 197–198
    use of, 198–199
Muslims, 42, 80–81
Mutual aid model, 212–213

Nairobi Forward-Looking Strategies for the
    Advancement of Women, 39
NASW Code of Ethics
    application of, 56–58, 64–65
    ethical principles of, 383–384
    ethical standards of, 385–399
    function of, 53, 55, 56
    preamble of, 381
    purpose of, 382–383
NASW Policy Statements, 188–189
National Association for the Advancement
    of Colored People (NAACP), 360
National Association of Social Workers
    (NASW)
    Code of Ethics, 53, 55, 56, 64–65,
        381–399

National Association of Social Workers
    (NASW) (*continued*)
        Commission on Social Work
            Practice, 322–325
        fields of practice and, 320–322
        Policy Statements, 188–189
        Standards of Practice, 219
National Conference of Charities and Cor-
    rections, 352
National Conference of Indian Affairs, 372
National Conference on Social Welfare, 368
National League on Urban Conditions
    Among Negros, 364
National Urban League (NUL), 365, 368
Native Americans
        Elizabeth Chief and, 371–372
        family-in-tribal environment
            example, 192–195
        racial duality and, 368–369, 373–374
Natural systems paradigms, 268
Naturalistic research, 103–104
Needs assessment, 302–303
Negative entropy, 11
Neighborhood Guild, 349
Neighborhood Union, 366
New Deal era, 358–360, 367, 368
New York Children's Aid Society, 350
Nonjudgmentalism, 74–75
Nonverbal communication, 159–160

Observation, 134–135
Okin, S. M., 25
Oklahoma City bombing, 80, 81
Older Americans Act of 1965, 328, 332
Olea, Maria, 41
Omnibus Budget Reconciliation Act of
    1986, 333
Open-ended groups, 218
Open-systems frameworks, 268
Organizational practice
        analysis of agency and, 279–280
        case illustration of, 277–285
        classroom exercise on, 414–415
        defining problem in, 278–279
        developing feasible solutions and,
            280–281
        initiating change strategy and,
            283–284
        monitoring, evaluating and revising
            strategy and, 284–285
        overview of, 276–277
        preparing agency and staff members
            for change and, 282–283
        selecting change strategy and, 281–282

Organizations
        case illustration of, 277–285
        diversity in, 267
        environmental context of, 275–276
        focus of, 276–277
        formal, 266, 268–269
        goals of, 269–270, 285
        membership interests and character-
            istics of, 274
        overview of, 263–264
        service technologies used by, 273–274
        social and human service, 264–266
        structures of, 270–273

Palleja, J., 151
Panel on Understanding and Control of
    Violent Behavior (National Academy of
    Sciences), 33
Parents
        community-level intervention for,
            298–300
        factors contributing to child
            maltreatment by, 296
        family consultation with, 297
        group work with, 298
        individual work with, 297
Parish, Bennie, 372–373
PEACE POWER Working Group, 304, 305
Perkins, Frances, 359
Permanent Forum for Indigenous Peoples
    (United Nations), 32
Person-in-environment practice, 3–4, 121
Personal experience, 109, 111–113
Personal Justice Denied (U.S. Commission
    on Wartime Relocation and Internment
    of Civilians), 370
Personal Responsibility and Work Opportu-
    nity Reconciliation Act of 1996, 333
Personal social services, 327
Poetry, 116–117
Power. *See also* Empowerment
        in everyday life, 248
        as influence, 247
        shared, xvi, 21, 161–163, 172, 196
        social, 34–35
        social justice and, xvi
Power-mapping, 248
Practice approaches
        application of, 125
        ecosystems perspective and, 120
        explanation of, 120–124
Practice wisdom
        application of, 99–100
        types of, 97–99

Princeshire Clinic case, 277–285
Private practice, 152
Problem analysis, 301–302
Program design, 307
Program development cycle, 301
Program evaluation, 309–310
Progressive Era, 348, 353, 356, 362–364
Project 12-Ways, 204
Proposal writing, 310–311
Prostitution trafficking, 39–40
Psychiatric social workers, 351–353
Psychodynamic theories, 119
Psychosocial approach
    explanation of, 121
    focus of, 157
    use of, 119

Qualitative matrix, 140, 141
Qualitative research, 104–105
Quantitative research, 104, 105

Race, 86–90
Racial duality
    African Americans and, 361–368
    Asian Americans and, 369–370
    explanation of, 360–361
    Hispanic Americans and, 370–371
    Native Americans and, 368–369
Racial reasoning, 90–91
Radical constructionism, 96–97
Rao, A., 34
Rapid assessment instruments (RAIs)
    explanation of, 138–140
    use of, 143, 145
Rappaport, J., 239
Rating scales
    application of, 135–136
    behaviorally anchored, 171, 172
    clinician, 137
    graphing, 138, 171
    reliability and validity of, 137
    self-anchored, 136–138
Reciprocal model
    explanation of, 212–213
    group processes in, 222
Reilly, N., 38, 41
Relationships, 7
Religious practices, 115–116
Remedial model, 213, 222
Research
    experimental, 105–107
    function of, 134
    naturalistic, 103–104
    practice-relevant, 102–103

    qualitative, 104–105
    quantitative, 104, 105
Reynolds, Bertha Capen, 152
Richmond, Mary, 345, 346, 350, 351, 353
Rivas, R. F., 209
Rogers, Will, Jr., 372
Roosevelt, Theodore, 341, 362
Runaway and Homeless Youth Act, 328

Sackett, D. L., 100
Sandoval, Petrona, 41
Scapegoating, 223–224
Schiff, B., 89
Schwartz, W., 219
Scientific charity, 343
Scientific method, 96
Segregation, 361–362, 365, 367
Self-anchored scales
    explanation of, 136–137
    graphing, 138
    use of, 143
Self-determination, 111
Self-disclosure
    benefits of, 221–222
    group participation and, 223
    use of, 111–112
Self-help groups, 214, 225
Self-knowledge exercise, 409–410
Self-monitoring
    explanation of, 179–180
    graphing and, 138
    steps in, 174
Self-organizing networks, 7–8
Self-talk, 178
Settlement house movement, 50, 187,
    348–350
Sevilla, Rebeca, 40
Sexual minority communities, 374
Shared power
    connectedness principle and, 21
    in direct practice, 161–163
    explanation of, xvi
    family groups and, 196
    in individual practice, 161–163, 172
    social justice and, 161
Single-case designs
    clinical analytic, 109, 110
    explanation of, 106–107, 109
    use of, 142–145
Single parents. *See* Parents
Siyiankoi, Agnes, 41
Skills training, 179–181
Small groups, 250–251. *See also* Groups
Smith, D. M., 29–30

Social and human service agencies, 264–
    266. *See also* Organizations
Social Diagnosis (Richmond), 345
Social empowerment, 33–34
Social goals model, 211–212
Social justice. *See also* Human rights
    autonomy and public-private sphere
        and, 28–29
    classroom exercise on, 407
    Declaration of Human Rights for
        Indigenous Peoples and, 31–32
    economic development and, 42–43
    ethnicity and, 79–81
    explanation of, xvi
    family functioning and, 197
    force, wealth, and knowledge and,
        34–35
    human rights abuses against women
        and, 35–43
    human rights and, 26–27, 30, 43–44
    International Bill of Human Rights
        and, 30–31
    mapping, 247–248
    philosophical base of, 27–28
    rights and relationships and, 29–30
    settlement houses and, 187
    shared power and, 161
    violence and, 33–34
Social Network Map, 251–252
Social networks, 251–252
Social policy, 30–31
Social power, 34–35
Social science knowledge, 102
Social Security Act Amendments of 1980,
    333
Social Security Act of 1974
    Native Americans and, 371
    Title XX, 327
    Title XXI, 333
Social service technologies, 273–274
Social Services Block Grant (SSBG), 327–
    328, 332–333
Social skills training, 180
Social welfare, 326
Social work education
    African American, 364–366
    role of values and ethics in, 52–53
    trends in, 321, 337
    undergraduate vs. graduate, x
Social work practice
    approaches to, xix–xx
    classroom exercise on, 416
    complexities of, xi–xiv

conceptual map of, xiv–xxii
contexts of, xxi–xxii
development of, 291
functions of, xi
funding issues and, 153–154
nature of, ix
processes of, xx–xxi
purpose of, x–xi, xvi–xvii
Social work profession
    bifurcated welfare state and,
        358–360
    Charity Organization Society
        movement and, 343–345
    community focus and, 346–348
    history of, 340–342, 371–375
    individual casework focus and,
        345–346
    maternalist and paternalist welfare
        state and, 356–358
    during 1930s, 350–355
    racial duality in welfare state and,
        360–371
    settlement house movement, social
        reform and, 348–350
Social workers
    cultural understanding in, 76–79
    medical, 346–348
    as nonpunitive audience, 159
    psychiatric, 351–353
    relationship between agencies and,
        285
    role models for, 340–341
    self-awareness in, 112–113
Solution-focused brief therapy, 193
South Africa, 88–90
Spiritual practices, 115–116
Starr, Ellen Gates, 349
Stewart B. McKinney Homeless Assistance
    Act, 333
Strengths perspective
    explanation of, 15–16, 123
    value of, 18
Sugarman, S. D., 82
Summative evaluation, 310
System levels, xviii–xix
Systemic thinking, 9–10
Systems
    boundaries of, 11
    closed, 11, 13
    openness of, 11–12
    reciprocal elements of, 12–13
    structure of, 10–11, 13–15
    transactional patterns and, 12

Tack-centered approach, 122
Takahashi, R., 370
Tamouth, Fatima Zahra, 42
Task Attainment Scaling, 135–136
Task environment, 275–276
Task groups, 307–308
Temporary Assistance to Needy Families
    (TANF), 333
Terrorism, 77–78
Terrorist Attack of September 11, 2001, 77,
    80–81
Theories
        function of, 118–120
        overview of, 117
        selection of, 117–118
Thomas, Clarence, 90
Thomas, Jesse O., 365
Thompson, Gayla, 41
Toseland, R. W., 209
Toubia, Nahid, 40
Toynbee Hall, 349
Transactional ecomaps, 154–157
Transactional ethnicity, 86–90
Transactional webs, 295
Trautmann, Elna, 89
Truth, 55
Tuskegee syphilis experiment, 373, 374

Unfaithful Angels: How Social Work Has
    Abandoned Its Mission (Specht &
    Courtney), 355
United Nations, 30–31, 46
Universal Declaration of Human Rights
    (United Nations)
        articles of, 31, 401–404
        explanation of, 25, 30
        preamble of, 400–401
Utilitarian approach, 59

Values
        in decision making, 48–50
        dilemmas related to conflicting,
            55–58
        ethics vs., 52
        explanation of, xvii
        legal responsibilities and, 54–55
        in social work education, 52–53
Vinton, L., 321

Violence
        gender-based, 35–42
        social justice and, 33–34
        social power and, 34–35

War crimes, 38–39
War on Poverty, 353, 359, 360
Washington, Forrester B., 365–367
Web teaching, x
Welfare state
        bifurcated, 358–360
        emergence of modern, 355–356
        maternalist and paternalist, 356–358
        racial duality in, 360–371
West, Cornel, 90–91
What Is Social Case Work? (Richmond), 346
Whitman, Walt, 116–117
Wiggin, Andrew, 32
Wilson, E. O., 101
Wilson, William Julius, 361
Women
        changing role of, 28
        violence against, 25–26
        welfare state and, 356–358
Women's rights
        abuse within family and, 41–42
        Global Campaign and Vienna
            Tribunal for Women's Human
            Rights and, 38
        grassroots efforts and, 37–38
        as human rights, 25, 35
        mainstreaming agendas and, 37
        sexuality and, 40–41
        trafficking in prostitution and, 39–40
        violations of the body and, 40
        to vote, 357
        war crimes and, 38–39
        worldwide conferences and agendas
            and, 35–36
Works Progress Administration programs, 369
World Conference on Human Rights, Vienna
    (1993) (United Nations), 25–26, 30, 38
World War I, 353
World War II, 369

Young, I. M., 29
Young, Whitney M., 368
Youth violence prevention, 304, 305

About the Editors

Christine T. Lowery, PhD, is associate professor, School of Social Welfare, University of Wisconsin-Milwaukee. She is from the Laguna (New Mexico) and Hopi (Arizona) tribes and has 12 years of social work experience with American Indians in both urban and reservation settings. Her research has focused on substance abuse, addiction and recovery processes with American Indian women and sociocultural change among Indian Elders on the reservation.

Mark A. Mattaini, DSW, ACSW, is Director of the Ph.D. in Social Work Program, Jane Addams College of Social Work, University of Illinois at Chicago. His writing, research, and current practice focus on youth violence prevention, practice theory, and analysis of cultural systems. He is editor of the journal *Behavior and Social Issues*, and author or co-editor of eight books on social work practice and social issues. His experience is in family services, residential care, substance abuse, and mental health settings.

Carol H. Meyer, DSW, was Norman Professor of Family and Child Welfare, Columbia University School of Social Work, New York. She was long interested in social work practice theory and wrote extensively on ecosystems theory and assessment. Her practice experience was in public and voluntary family and child welfare agencies. Professor Meyer passed away on December 2, 1996.

About the Contributors

Jerry R. Cates, PhD, is associate dean of the Jane Addams College of Social Work, University of Illinois at Chicago. He is writing a book on the politics of American Indian participation in public assistance and has published on the historical development of social security and public assistance.

Meredith Hanson, DSW, is associate professor, Graduate School of Social Service, Fordham University, New York, where he teaches courses in clinical practice, generalist practice, and social work with alcohol- and drug-involved individuals, families, and groups. His teaching, practice, and scholarly interests include agency-based practice, program design and development, addictions treatment, international social work, and social work practice with adults with co-existing substance use and mental disorders.

Sheila B. Kamerman, DSW, is Compton Foundation Centennial Professor for the Prevention of Children and Youth Problems, Columbia University School of Social Work, New York, where she also codirects the Cross-National Studies Research Program. She teaches social policy and international social welfare and has published widely on U.S. and comparative child and family policies and programs.

Susan P. Kemp, PhD, is associate professor, School of Social Work, University of Washington, Seattle. She was formerly a member of the practice faculty, School of Social Work, Columbia University, New York. Dr. Kemp's research interests include community-based and environmental social work practice and social work history.

Randy H. Magen, PhD, is associate professor, Department of Social Work, University of Alaska, Anchorage. His research interests include group work and domestic violence. He has recently published book chapters and articles on parent training, support groups for cancer survivors, and the connection between child maltreatment and woman abuse.

Marian Mattison, DSW, ACSW, is chair, Social Work Department, Providence College, Providence, Rhode Island. Dr. Mattison has presented numerous workshops and training seminars on ethical decision making for the NASW Rhode Island Chapter, local hospitals, and human services agencies throughout Rhode Island.

Brenda G. McGowan, DSW, is Ruth Harris Ottman Professor of Family and Child Welfare, Columbia University School of Social Work, New York, where her primary teaching responsibilities are in the areas of clinical practice, program development, and family and children's services. Author or co-author of four books and a number of articles on delivery of family services, she is a former member of the NASW National Committee on Inquiry.

Edward Scanlon, PhD, is assistant professor, University of Kansas, School of Social Welfare. His current areas of interest include housing and well-being and the relationship between social work and the labor movement.

MORE RESOURCES FROM NASW PRESS!

The Foundations of Social Work Practice: *A Graduate Text, 3rd Edition, Mark A. Mattaini, Christine T. Lowery, and Carol H. Meyer, Editors.* In the context of a professional evolution in which potent forces are driving advances in social work knowledge and practice, the third edition of the best-selling textbook *Foundations of Social Work Practice* builds on and, in some cases, wrestles with these developments. Individual chapters may be used in any order consistent with an instructor's syllabus. Group and skills-building class exercises are useful teaching tools for different modalities and learning styles.

ISBN: 0-87101-349-5. July 2002. Item #3495. $49.99.

Resiliency: *An Integrated Approach to Practice, Policy, and Research, Roberta R. Greene, Editor.* Social workers require both the understanding of how people successfully meet life challenges and the knowledge to build client strengths, adaptation, healing, and self-efficacy. This comprehensive volume integrates social work theory, policy, research, and method to promote and improve resilience-based practice. Faculty across curriculum, students, and practitioners will find this timely book an invaluable text.

ISBN: 0-87101-350-9. January 2002. Item #3509. $44.99.

African American Leadership: *An Empowerment Tradition in Social Welfare History, Iris B. Carlton-LaNey, Editor.* For far too long, the huge contribution of African Americans to the social work profession has been relegated to little more than a footnote. Sixteen painstakingly researched chapters discuss the birth of social welfare activities, both informal and formal, and introduce founding members of organizations such as the National Urban League and the National Association of Colored Women. Written from a social work perspective and framed within a historical context, these profiles and their accompanying lessons help today's practitioner make the connection to current issues.

ISBN: 0-87101-317-7. April 2001. Item #3177. $43.99.

The Social Work Dictionary, *4th Edition, Robert L. Barker.* With nearly 8,000 terms, the fourth edition of *The Social Work Dictionary* is a fundamental tool for understanding the language of social work and related disciplines. This user-friendly resource provides all the terms, concepts, organizations, historical figures, and values that define the profession. No practitioner or student should be without the definitive lexicon of social work!

ISBN: 0-87101-298-7. 1999. Item #2987. $44.99.

Multicultural Issues in Social Work, *Patricia L. Ewalt, Edith M. Freeman, Stuart A. Kirk, and Dennis L. Poole, Editors.* A collective vision of multiculturalism. *Multicultural Issues in Social Work* calls for research and practice based on the knowledge that individuals cannot be readily identified by single cultural categories. Faculty will find the book superb for teaching courses that meet curriculum policy requirements for content about diversity, and researchers, policy makers, and practitioners will find it a helpful resource in their work with diverse populations.

ISBN: 0-87101-266-9. 1996. Item #2669. $39.99.

(Order form and information on reverse side)

ORDER FORM

Qty.	Title	Item #	Price	Total
__	The Foundations of Social Work Practice	3495	$49.99	_____
__	Resiliency	3509	$44.99	_____
__	African American Leadership	3177	$43.99	_____
__	The Social Work Dictionary	2987	$44.99	_____
__	Multicultural Issues in Social Work	2669	$39.99	_____

POSTAGE AND HANDLING
Minimum postage and handling fee is $4.95. Orders that do not include appropriate postage and handling will be returned.

Subtotal	_____
Postage and Handling	_____
DC residents add 6% sales tax	_____
MD residents add 5% sales tax	_____
Total	_____

DOMESTIC: Please add 12% to orders under $100 for postage and handling. For orders over $100 add 7% of order.

CANADA: Please add 17% postage and handling.

OTHER INTERNATIONAL: Please add 22% postage and handling.

❑ **Check** or **money order** (payable to NASW Press) for $ _____.

❑ **Credit card**
   ❑ NASW Visa* I ❑ Visa I ❑ NASW MasterCard* I ❑ MasterCard I ❑ Amex

_____   _____
Credit Card Number   Expiration Date

Signature _____

            Use of these cards generates funds in support of the social work profession.

Name _____

Address _____

City _____ State/Province _____

Country _____ Zip _____

Phone _____ E-mail _____

NASW Member # (if applicable) _____

(Please make checks payable to NASW Press. Prices are subject to change.)

NASW PRESS
P. O. Box 431
Annapolis JCT, MD 20701
USA

Credit card orders call
1-800-227-3590
(In the Metro Wash., DC, area, call 301-317-8688)
Or fax your order to 301-206-7989
Or order online at http://www.naswpress.org

Visit our Web site at http://www.naswpress.org.   CPFN02